CIMA

Paper E2

Enterprise Management

Study Text

WORKING TOGETHER FOR YOU

CIMA Publishing is an imprint of Elsevier
The Boulevard, Langford Lane, Kidlington, Oxford, OX5 1GB, UK
225 Wyman Street, Waltham, MA 02451, USA
Kaplan Publishing UK, Unit 2 The Business Centre, Molly Millars Lane, Wokingham, Berkshire
RG41 2QZ

Copyright © 2012 Elsevier Limited and Kaplan Publishing Limited. All rights reserved.

No part of this publication may be reproduced, stored in a retrieval system or transmitted in any form or by any means electronic, mechanical, photocopying, recording or otherwise without the prior written permission of the publisher.

Permissions may be sought directly from Elsevier's Science and Technology Rights Department in Oxford, UK: phone: (+44) (0) 1865 843830; fax: (+44) (0) 1865 853333; email: permissions@elsevier.com. You may also complete your request online via the Elsevier homepage (http://elsevier.com), by selecting Support & Contact then Copyright and Permission and then Obtaining Permissions.

Notice
No responsibility is assumed by the publisher for any injury and/or damage to persons or property as a matter of products liability, negligence or otherwise, or from any use or operation of any methods, products, instructions or ideas contained in the material herein.

British Library Cataloguing in Publication Data
A catalogue record for this book is available from the British Library

ISBN: 978-0-85732-569-3

Printed and bound in Great Britain

12 13 14   10 9 8 7 6 5 4 3 2 1

Contents

		Page
Chapter 1	CIMA verb hierarchy	1
Chapter 2	Introduction to strategy formulation	9
Chapter 3	Strategic analysis	47
Chapter 4	Competitive environments	103
Chapter 5	Alternative approaches to strategy formulation	123
Chapter 6	Developments in strategic management	149
Chapter 7	Organisational culture	177
Chapter 8	Management and leadership	213
Chapter 9	Relationships in the working environment	275
Chapter 10	Management control	335
Chapter 11	Corporate governance, ethics and social responsibility	377
Chapter 12	Principles of project management	433
Chapter 13	Project Stages – Initiation	451
Chapter 14	Project Stages – Planning	479
Chapter 15	Project Stages – Execution, control and completion	537
Chapter 16	Project management methodologies	575
Chapter 17	People and projects	601

chapter
Intro

Paper Introduction

How to Use the Materials

These Official CIMA learning materials brought to you by Elsevier/CIMA Publishing and Kaplan Publishing have been carefully designed to make your learning experience as easy as possible and to give you the best chances of success in your *'Enterprise Management'* computer based assessments.

The product range contains a number of features to help you in the study process. They include:

- a detailed explanation of all syllabus areas;
- extensive 'practical' materials;
- generous question practice, together with full solutions;
- an exam preparation section, including a suggested approach on how to tackle the pre-seen information, both before and during the exam

This Study Text has been designed with the needs of home-study and distance-learning candidates in mind. Such students require very full coverage of the syllabus topics, and also the facility to undertake extensive question practice. However, the Study Text is also ideal for fully taught courses.

This main body of the text is divided into a number of chapters, each of which is organised on the following pattern:

- *Detailed learning outcomes* expected after your studies of the chapter are complete. You should assimilate these before beginning detailed work on the chapter, so that you can appreciate where your studies are leading.
- *Step-by-step topic coverage*. This is the heart of each chapter, containing detailed explanatory text supported where appropriate by worked examples and exercises. You should work carefully through this section, ensuring that you understand the material being explained and can tackle the examples and exercises successfully. Remember that in many cases knowledge is cumulative: if you fail to digest earlier material thoroughly, you may struggle to understand later chapters.

- *Activities*. Some chapters are illustrated by more practical elements, such as comments and questions designed to stimulate discussion.

- *Question practice*. The test of how well you have learned the material is your ability to tackle exam-style questions. Make a serious attempt at producing your own answers, but at this stage do not be too concerned about attempting the questions in exam conditions. In particular, it is more important to absorb the material thoroughly by completing a full solution than to observe the time limits that would apply in the actual exam.

- *Solutions*. Avoid the temptation merely to 'audit' the solutions provided. It is an illusion to think that this provides the same benefits as you would gain from a serious attempt of your own. However, if you are struggling to get started on a question you should read the introductory guidance provided at the beginning of the solution, where provided, and then make your own attempt before referring back to the full solution.

The final two chapters of this Study Text provide you with the guidance you need. They include the following features:

- A brief guide to revision technique.
- A note on the format of the exam. You should know what to expect when you tackle the real exam, and in particular the number of questions to attempt.
- Guidance on how to tackle the exam itself.
- A table mapping revision questions to the syllabus learning outcomes allowing you to quickly identify questions by subject area.
- Revision questions. These are of exam standard and should be tackled in exam conditions, especially as regards the time allocation.
- Solutions to the revision questions.
- Two mock exam.

You should plan to attempt the sample paper just before the date of the real exam. By this stage your revision should be complete and you should be able to attempt the sample paper within the time constraints of the real exam.

If you work conscientiously through the official CIMA Study Text according to the guidelines above you will be giving yourself an excellent chance of success in your exam. Good luck with your studies!

Icon Explanations

 Definition – these sections explain important areas of knowledge which must be understood and reproduced in an exam environment.

 Key Point – identifies topics which are key to success and are often examined.

 Supplementary reading – indentifies a more detailed explanation of key terms, these sections will help to provide a deeper understanding of core areas. Reference to this text is vital when self studying.

 Test Your Understanding – following key points and definitions are exercises which give the opportunity to assess the understanding of these core areas.

 Illustration – to help develop an understanding of particular topics. The illustrative exercises are useful in preparing for the Test your understanding exercises.

 Exclamation Mark – this symbol signifies a topic which can be more difficult to understand, when reviewing these areas care should be taken.

Study technique

Passing exams is partly a matter of intellectual ability, but however accomplished you are in that respect you can improve your chances significantly by the use of appropriate study and revision techniques. In this section we briefly outline some tips for effective study during the earlier stages of your approach to the exam. Later in the text we mention some techniques that you will find useful at the revision stage.

Planning

To begin with, formal planning is essential to get the best return from the time you spend studying. Estimate how much time in total you are going to need for each subject you are studying for the Certificate in Business Accounting. Remember that you need to allow time for revision as well as for initial study of the material. You may find it helpful to read "Pass First Time!" second edition by David R. Harris ISBN 978-1-85617-798-6. This book will provide you with proven study techniques. Chapter by chapter it covers the building blocks of successful learning and examination techniques. This is the ultimate guide to passing your CIMA exams, written by a past CIMA examiner and shows you how to earn all the marks you deserve, and explains how to avoid the most common pitfalls. You may also find "The E Word: Kaplan's Guide to Passing Exams" by Stuart Pedley-Smith ISBN: 978-0-85732-205-0 helpful. Stuart Pedley-Smith is a senior lecturer at Kaplan Financial and a qualified accountant specialising in financial management. His natural curiosity and wider interests have led him to look beyond the technical content of financial management to the processes and journey that we call education. He has become fascinated by the whole process of learning and the exam skills and techniques that contribute towards success in the classroom. This book is for anyone who has to sit an exam and wants to give themselves a better chance of passing. It is easy to read, written in a common sense style and full of anecdotes, facts, and practical tips. It also contains synopses of interviews with people involved in the learning and examining process.

With your study material before you, decide which chapters you are going to study in each week, and which weeks you will devote to revision and final question practice.

Prepare a written schedule summarising the above and stick to it!

It is essential to know your syllabus. As your studies progress you will become more familiar with how long it takes to cover topics in sufficient depth. Your timetable may need to be adapted to allocate enough time for the whole syllabus.

Students are advised to refer to the notice of examinable legislation published regularly in CIMA's magazine (Financial Management), the students e-newsletter (Velocity) and on the CIMA website, to ensure they are up-to-date.

The amount of space allocated to a topic in the Study Text is not a very good guide as to how long it will take you. For example, the material relating to Section A 'Basic Mathematics' and Section C 'Summarising and Analysing Data' each account for 15% of the syllabus, but the latter has more pages because there are more illustrations, which take up more space. The syllabus weighting is the better guide as to how long you should spend on a syllabus topic.

Tips for effective studying

(1) Aim to find a quiet and undisturbed location for your study, and plan as far as possible to use the same period of time each day. Getting into a routine helps to avoid wasting time. Make sure that you have all the materials you need before you begin so as to minimise interruptions.

(2) Store all your materials in one place, so that you do not waste time searching for items around your accommodation. If you have to pack everything away after each study period, keep them in a box, or even a suitcase, which will not be disturbed until the next time.

(3) Limit distractions. To make the most effective use of your study periods you should be able to apply total concentration, so turn off all entertainment equipment, set your phones to message mode, and put up your 'do not disturb' sign.

(4) Your timetable will tell you which topic to study. However, before diving in and becoming engrossed in the finer points, make sure you have an overall picture of all the areas that need to be covered by the end of that session. After an hour, allow yourself a short break and move away from your Study Text. With experience, you will learn to assess the pace you need to work at.

(5) Work carefully through a chapter, making notes as you go. When you have covered a suitable amount of material, vary the pattern by attempting a practice question. When you have finished your attempt, make notes of any mistakes you made, or any areas that you failed to cover or covered more briefly.

(6) Make notes as you study, and discover the techniques that work best for you. Your notes may be in the form of lists, bullet points, diagrams, summaries, 'mind maps', or the written word, but remember that you will need to refer back to them at a later date, so they must be intelligible. If you are on a taught course, make sure you highlight any issues you would like to follow up with your lecturer.

(7) Organise your notes. Make sure that all your notes, calculations etc can be effectively filed and easily retrieved later.

Structure of subjects and learning outcomes

Each subject within the syllabus is divided into a number of broad syllabus topics. The topics contain one or more lead learning outcomes, related component learning outcomes and indicative knowledge content.

A learning outcome has two main purposes:

(a) To define the skill or ability that a well prepared candidate should be able to exhibit in the examination

(b) To demonstrate the approach likely to be taken in examination questions

The learning outcomes are part of a hierarchy of learning objectives. The verbs used at the beginning of each learning outcome relate to a specific learning objective e.g.

"Evaluate the proposed strategy to expand into the North American market."

The verb **'evaluate'** indicates a level five learning objective.

These verbs are outlined in the first chapter of the text.

PAPER E2
ENTERPRISE MANAGEMENT

Syllabus overview

Paper E2 moves away from the emphasis on functional knowledge within Paper E1 Enterprise Operations, towards an holistic, integrated view of management across the organisation. Building on important concepts in strategic management, this paper develops tools and techniques for identifying the key types of competitive environment. The skills and tools of project management are also addressed. Finally, the paper introduces the skills and tools needed to work with, manage and develop teams. This includes both the legal aspects of managing individuals, as well as the softer elements of negotiation and leadership skills.

Syllabus structure

The syllabus comprises the following topics and study weightings:

A	Strategic Management and Assessing the Competitive Environment	30%
B	Project Management	40%
C	Management of Relationships	30%

Assessment strategy

There will be a written examination paper of three hours, plus 20 minutes of pre-examination question paper reading time. The examination paper will have the following sections:

Section A – 50 marks
Five compulsory medium answer questions, each worth ten marks. Short scenarios may be given, to which some or all questions relate.

Section B – 50 marks
One or two compulsory questions. Short scenarios may be given, to which questions relate.

E2 – A. STRATEGIC MANAGEMENT AND ASSESSING THE COMPETITIVE ENVIRONMENT (30%)

Learning outcomes
On completion of their studies students should be able to:

Lead	Component	Indicative syllabus content
1. discuss different competitive environments and key external characteristics of these environments.	(a) discuss the nature of competitive environments; (b) distinguish between different types of competitive environments.	• PEST analysis and its derivatives. [3] • The use of stakeholder mapping. [3] • Qualitative approaches to competitive analysis. [4] • Competitor analysis and competitive strategies (both qualitative and quantitative tools of competitor analysis will be used). [4] • Sources, availability and quality of data for environmental analysis. [3], [4] • Porter's Five Forces model and its use for assessing the external environment. [3] • Porter's Diamond and its use for assessing the competitive advantage of nations. [6]
2. discuss developments in strategic management.	(a) discuss concepts in established and emergent thinking in strategic management; (b) compare and contrast approaches to strategy formulation; (c) explain the relationships between different levels of strategy in organisations.	• Perspectives on the strategic management of the firm (including transaction cost, resource-based view and ecological perspective). [5], [6], [11] • Approaches to strategy (e.g. rational, adaptive, emergent, evolutionary or system based views. [5] • Levels of strategy (e.g. Corporate, business-level, functional) (*Note:* Candidates are not expected to identify or evaluate options). [2]

E2 – B. PROJECT MANAGEMENT (40%)

Learning outcomes
On completion of their studies students should be able to:

Lead	Component	Indicative syllabus content
1. discuss tools and techniques of project management.	(a) identify a project, a programme and their attributes; (b) apply suitable structures and frameworks to projects to identify common project management issues; (c) construct an outline of the process of project management; (d) identify the characteristics of each phase in the project process; (e) apply key tools and techniques, including the evaluation of proposals; (f) produce a basic project plan incorporating strategies for dealing with uncertainty, in the context of a simple project; (g) identify structural and leadership issues that will be faced in managing a project team; (h) compare and contrast project control systems; (i) discuss the value of post-completion audit; (j) apply a process of continuous improvement to projects.	• The definition of a programme, a project, project management, and the contrast with repetitive operations and line management. [12] • 4-D and 7-S models to provide an overview of the project process, and the nine key process areas (PMI) to show what happens during each part of the process.[12], [16] • The benefits and limitations of having a single process for managing projects. [16] • Key tools for project managers (e.g. Work Breakdown Structure, network diagrams (Critical Path Analysis), Gantt charts, resource histograms, gates and milestones). [14] • Earned Value Management. [15] • Evaluation of plans for projects. [14] • The key processes of PRINCE2 and their implications for project staff. [16] • Managing scope at the outset of a project and providing systems for configuration management/change control. [15] • The production of basic plans for time, cost and quality. [13], [14] • Scenario planning and buffering to make provision for uncertainty in projects, as part of the risk and opportunities management process. [14] • Organisational structures, including the role of the project and matrix organisations, and their impact on project achievement. [17] • Teamwork, including recognising the life-cycle of teams, team/group behaviour and selection. [17] • Control of time, cost and quality through performance and conformance management systems. [15] • Project completion, documentation, completion reports and system close-down. [15] • The use of post-completion audit and review activities and the justification of their costs. [15]

Learning outcomes
On completion of their studies students should be able to:

Lead	Component	Indicative syllabus content
2. evaluate the relationship of the project manager to the external environment.	(a) produce a strategy for a project; (b) recommend strategies for the management of stakeholder perceptions and expectations; (c) explain the roles of key players in a project organisation.	• Determining and managing trade-offs between key project objectives of time, cost and quality. [12] • Stakeholders (both process and outcome), their power and interest, and their needs and expectations, marketing and communications to enhance perceptions. [17] • Roles of support structures, including project management offices, as well as project sponsors (SROs), boards, champions, managers and clients. [17]

E2 – C. MANAGEMENT OF RELATIONSHIPS (30%)

Learning outcomes
On completion of their studies students should be able to:

Lead	Component	Indicative syllabus content
1. discuss concepts associated with the effective operation of an organisation.	(a) discuss the concepts of power, bureaucracy, authority, responsibility, leadership and delegation; (b) demonstrate the importance of organisational culture; (c) identify the nature and causes of conflict; (d) discuss alternative approaches to the management of conflict.	• The concepts of power, authority, bureaucracy, leadership, responsibility and delegation and their application to relationships within an organisation and outside it. [8] • Organisational culture: definition, classification, importance. [7] • The sources of conflict in organisations and the ways in which conflict can be managed to ensure that working relationships are productive and effective. [9]
2. discuss the activities associated with managing people and their associated techniques.	(a) analyse the relationship between managers and their subordinates, including legal aspects affecting work and employment; (b) discuss the roles of negotiation and communication in the management process, both within an organisation and with external bodies; (c) discuss the effectiveness of relationships between the finance function and other parts of the organisation and with external stakeholders; (d) Identify tools for managing and controlling individuals, teams and networks, and for managing group conflict; (e) compare and contrast ways to deal effectively with discipline problems; (f) explain the process and importance of mentoring junior colleagues; (g) analyse issues of business ethics and corporate governance.	• Disciplinary procedures and their operation, including the form and process of formal disciplinary action and dismissal (e.g. industrial tribunals, arbitration and conciliation). [10] • The nature and effect of legal issues affecting work and employment, including the application of relevant employment law (i.e. relating to health, safety, discrimination, fair treatment, childcare, contracts of employment and working time). [10] • Communication skills (i.e. types of communication tools and their use, as well as the utility and conduct of meetings) and ways of managing communication problems. [9] • Negotiation skills. [9] • Managing the finance function to maximise its value to the organisation through lean operation (e.g. business process outsourcing, shared service centres) and contribution to other functions (e.g. embedding finance personnel in business and strategic decision processes). [9] • Management of relationships with professional advisors (accounting, tax and legal), auditors and financial stakeholders (investors and financiers) to meet organisational objectives. [9] • The principles of corporate governance and the CIMA Code of Ethics for Professional Accountants, and their relevance to the role, obligations and expectations of a manager. [11] • How to lead and manage a team. [9] • The role of a mentor, and the process of mentoring. [9] • Motivating team members. [9] • The use of systems of control within the organisation (e.g. employment contracts, performance appraisal, reporting structures). [10]

Chapter 1

CIMA verb hierarchy

Chapter learning objectives

CIMA VERB HIERARCHY

CIMA place great importance on the choice of verbs in exam question requirements. It is therefore critical that you answer the question according to the definition of the verb used.

CIMA verb hierarchy

1 Managerial level verbs

In managerial level exams you will mainly meet verbs from levels 2, 3 and 4. Occasionally you will also see level 1 and level 5 verbs.

Level 2 – COMPREHENSION

What you are expected to understand

VERBS USED	DEFINITION
Describe	Communicate the key features of.
Distinguish	Highlight the differences between.
Explain	Make clear or intelligible/state the meaning or purpose of.
Identify	Recognise, establish or select after consideration.
Illustrate	Use an example to describe or explain something.

Level 3 – APPLICATION

How you are expected to apply your knowledge

VERBS USED	DEFINITION
Apply	Put to practical use.
Calculate	Ascertain or reckon mathematically.
Demonstrate	Prove with certainty or exhibit by practical means.
Prepare	Make or get ready for use.
Reconcile	Make or prove consistent/compatible.
Solve	Find an answer to.
Tabulate	Arrange in a table.

Level 4 – ANALYSIS

How you are expected to analyse the detail of what you have learned.

VERBS USED	DEFINITION
Analyse	Examine in detail the structure of.
Categorise	Place into a defined class or division.
Compare and contrast	Show the similarities and/or differences between.
Construct	Build up or compile.
Discuss	Examine in detail by argument.
Interpret	Translate into intelligible or familiar terms.
Prioritise	Place in order of priority or sequence for action.
Produce	Create or bring into existence.

Level 5 – EVALUATION

How you are expected to use your learning to evaluate, make decisions or recommendations..

VERBS USED	DEFINITION
Advise	Council, inform or notify.
Evaluate	Appraise or assess the value of.
Recommend	Propose a course of action.

2 Further guidance on managerial level verbs that cause confusion

Verbs that cause students confusion at this level are as follows:

Level 2 verbs

- **The difference between "describe" and "explain"**

    An explanation is a set of statements constructed to describe a set of facts which clarifies the **causes**, **context**, and **consequences** of those facts.

For example, if asked to **describe** the features of activity based costing (ABC) you could talk, among other things, about how costs are grouped into cost pools (e.g. quality control), cost drivers identified (e.g. number of inspections) and an absorption rate calculated based on this cost driver (e.g. cost per inspection). This tells us what ABC looks like.

However if asked to **explain** ABC, then you would have to talk about why firms were dissatisfied with previous traditional costing methods and switched to ABC (causes), what types of firms it is more suitable for (context) and the implications for firms (consequences) in terms of the usefulness of such costs per unit for pricing and costing.

More simply, to describe something is to answer "what" type questions whereas to explain looks at "what" and "why" aspects.

- **The verb "to illustrate"**

The key thing about illustrating something is that you may have to decide on a relevant example to use. This could involve drawing a diagram, performing supporting calculations or highlighting a feature or person in the scenario given. Most of the time the question will be structured so calculations performed in part (a) can be used to illustrate a concept in part (b).

For example, you could be asked to explain and illustrate what is meant by an "adverse variance".

Level 3 verbs

- **The verb "to apply"**

Given that all level 3 verbs involve application, the verb "apply" is rare in the real exam. Instead one of the other more specific verbs is used instead.

- **The verb "to reconcile"**

This is a numerical requirement and usually involves starting with one of the figures, adjusting it and ending up with the other.

For example, in a bank reconciliation you start with the recorded cash at bank figure, adjust it for unpresented cheques, etc, and (hopefully!) end up with the stated balance in the cash "T account".

- **The verb "to demonstrate"**

    The verb "to demonstrate" can be used in two main ways.

    Firstly it could mean to prove that a given statement is true or consistent with circumstances given. For example, the Finance Director may have stated in the question that the company will not exceed its overdraft limit in the next six months. The requirement then asks you to demonstrate that the Director is wrong. You could do this by preparing a cash flow forecast for the next six months.

    Secondly you could be asked to demonstrate how a stated model, framework, technique or theory could be used in the particular scenario to achieve a specific result – for example, how a probability matrix could be used to make a production decision. Ensure in such questions that you do not merely describe the model but use it to generate the desired outcome.

Level 4 verbs

- **The verb "to analyse"**

    To analyse something is to examine it in detail in order to discover its meaning or essential features. This will usually involve breaking the scenario down and looking at the fine detail, possibly with additional calculations, and then stepping back to see the bigger picture to identify any themes to support conclusions.

    For example, if asked to analyse a set of financial statements, then the end result will be a set of statements about the performance of the business with supporting evidence. This could involve the following:

    (1) You could break down your analysis into areas of profitability, liquidity, gearing and so on.

    (2) Under each heading look at key figures in the financial statements, identifying trends (e.g. sales growth) and calculating supporting ratios (e.g. margins).

    (3) Try to explain what the figures mean and why they have occurred (e.g. why has the operating margin fallen?).

    (4) Start considering the bigger picture – are the ratios presenting a consistent message or do they contradict each other? Can you identify common causes?

    (5) Finally you would then seek to pull all this information together and interpret it to make some higher level comments about overall performance.

The main error students make is that they fail to draw out any themes and conclusions and simply present the marker with a collection of uninterpreted, unexplained facts and figures.

- **The verb "to discuss"**

    To discuss something is very similar to analysing it, except that discussion usually involves two or more different viewpoints or arguments as the context, rather than a set of figures, say. To discuss viewpoints will involve looking at their underlying arguments, examining them critically, trying to assess whether one argument is more persuasive than the other and then seeking to reach a conclusion.

    For example, if asked to discuss whether a particular technique could be used by a company, you would examine the arguments for and against, making reference to the specific circumstances in the question, and seek to conclude.

- **The verb "to prioritise"**

    To prioritise is to place objects in an order. The key issue here is to decide upon the criteria to use to perform the ordering. For example, prioritising the external threats facing a firm could be done by considering the scale of financial consequences, immediacy, implications for the underlying business model and so on.

    The main mistake students make is that they fail to justify their prioritisation – why is this the most important issue?

Level 5 verbs

- **The verb "to evaluate"**

    To evaluate something is to assess it with a view to placing a value on it, in many respects "evaluate" should be seen as a higher level version of "analyse" and "discuss" and could include qualitative and quantitative factors within your criteria. Your resulting arguments will need to be prioritised and weighed against each other to form a conclusion.

    For example, suppose you are asked to evaluate a proposed strategy in paper E3. At its simplest your answer could contain a series of arguments for and against the strategy. Each argument should be discussed to assess its importance. The arguments can then be weighed up against each other to form a conclusion. You are thus evaluating the factors within each argument and then evaluating the arguments against each other.

With such questions many students struggle to generate enough points or arguments. Part of the solution is to produce mental checklists when studying the paper concerned. These give criteria to use for valuing the matter at hand. With the above example on strategy evaluation, criteria could include any of the following:

- Are there any useful calculations – e.g. NPV, impact on profit?
- Does the strategy resolve any major threats faced by the firm?
- Does the strategy capitalise on the firm's strengths or do weaknesses need resolving first?
- Does the strategy enhance the firm's competitive strategy?
- Does the strategy lead to a better "fit" with the environment?
- What are the risks and are they acceptable?
- What are the implication for different stakeholders and would it be acceptable to them?
- What are the resource implications- how feasible is the strategy?

Use of such a checklist will ensure you have enough points to pass.

In some questions you may have to do more preliminary work before you can evaluate. For example, if asked to evaluate a firm's approach to change management you would start by identifying what type of approach they are taking (referencing to different models of change management) before you can evaluate it.

- **The difference between the verbs "to evaluate", "to advise" and "to recommend"**

All three level 5 verbs involve a mixture of identifying relevant issues, analysing them, evaluating them and then finishing with some form of conclusion. Some writers see this as a three step approach:

(1) **What?** Identify relevant issues
(2) **So What?** Why are the issues relevant? How significant are they?
(3) **What now?** What response is required by the firm being considered?

The difference between the level 5 verbs lies in where the main emphasis is in these three steps. With "advise" and "recommend" the examiner will be looking for more detail in step 3. Recommendations in particular could involve formulating a plan of action that includes both short and long term aspects.

CIMA verb hierarchy

chapter 2

Introduction to strategy formulation

Chapter learning objectives

- Compare and contrast approaches to strategy formulation.
- Explain the relationships between different levels of strategy in organisations.

Introduction to strategy formulation

1 Session content diagram

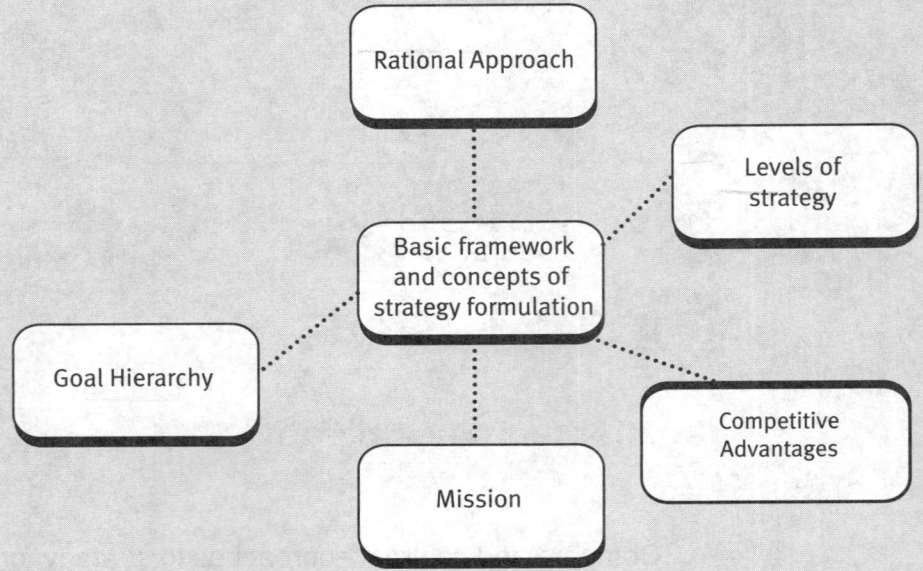

2 What is strategy?

Strategy is about:

 CIMA defines **strategy** as *a course of action, including specification of resources required, to achieve a specific objective* and a **strategic plan** as *a statement of long-term goals along with a definition of the strategies and policies which will ensure achievement of these goals*.

Common themes in strategy

- purpose and long-term direction
- scope of the organisation's activities
- meeting the challenges from the firm's external environment
- using the organisation's internal resources and competencies effectively
- delivering value to the people who depend on the firm – various stakeholders.

Whatever interpretation is put on strategy, the strategic actions of an organisation will have widespread and long-term consequences for the position of the organisation in the marketplace, its relationship with different stakeholders, and overall performance.

Mintzberg's five Ps of strategy

Henry Mintzberg suggests various definitions of strategy covering the five Ps.

- Strategy as a **plan** – a direction, a guide or course of action into the future, a path to get from here to there.
- Strategy as a **pattern** of consistent behaviour over time, giving the impression of a logically thought out strategy. A company that perpetually markets the most expensive products in its industry pursues what is commonly called a high-end strategy, just as a person who always accepts the most challenging of jobs may be described as pursuing a high-risk strategy.
- Strategy as a **ploy,** which can be seen as a manoeuvre in a competitive business game. For example a firm might add unnecessary plant capacity. The intention is not to produce the goods but to discourage a competitor from entering the market. The strategy is not the activity but the deterrence.
- Strategy as a **position** is a means of identifying where an organisation places itself in an environment or market.
- Strategy as a **perspective** consists not just of a chosen position but also of a unique way of perceiving the world, of interpreting information from it and judging its opportunities and choices. As such, it can refer to organisation culture. Different organisations with different strategic perspectives might respond to the same environmental stimulus in different ways. In this respect Mintzberg is suggesting that the organisation's strategy is similar to the individual's personality.

3 Strategic management

The strategic management process is essentially concerned with the decisions organisations make about their future direction and the development and implementation of strategies which will enhance the competitiveness of organisations. There are many different approaches to strategic management but they all have the aim of establishing the purpose of the organisation and guiding managers on how to implement strategies to achieve organisational goals.

There are many questions that you could ask about the organisations that surround us:

- How did they reach the situation they are in today?
- Why are they producing particular products or services?
- How did they come to be located where they are?
- Why are they serving a certain part of the marketplace?
- How did they end up with their particular set of senior managers?
- Why are they organised in the way they are?

All of these questions address different but interrelated aspects of an organisation and all these aspects come together to influence how effective the organisation will be in achieving its objectives. How these major – or strategic – decisions are made and how they are implemented is the process of strategic management.

This is something that is applicable to all organisations whether large or small, public or private, profit or non-profit making.

Illustration 1 – The strategy of Tesco plc

Many companies publish the details of their strategy on their websites. Tesco plc has published a clear seven part strategy which aims to broaden the scope of the business to enable it to deliver strong sustainable long-term growth. Their seven key areas are:

- To grow the UK core
- To be an outstanding international retailer in stores and online
- To be as strong in everything we sell as we are in food
- To grow retail services in all our markets
- To put our responsibilities to the communities we serve at the heart of what we do
- To be a creator of highly valued brands
- To build our team so that we create more value

'In 1997, Tesco set out a strategy to grow the core business and diversify with new products and services in existing and new markets. This strategy enabled us to deliver strong, sustained growth over the past 14 years. We've followed customers into large expanding markets in the UK – such as financial services, general merchandise and telecoms – and new markets abroad, initially in Europe and Asia and more recently in the United States.

In order to reflect changing consumer needs and the increasingly global nature of our business we've evolved our strategy. The strategy now has seven parts and applies to our five business segments – the UK, Asia, Europe, the United States and Tesco Bank.'

Taken from Tesco plc website, April 2012

Test your understanding 1

Required:

(a) What skills does Tesco need to keep ahead of its competitors such as other supermarkets?

(5 marks)

(b) What sorts of opportunities exist for Tesco?

(5 marks)

(c) What threats does Tesco face in its environment?

(5 marks)

(d) What resources does Tesco deploy to grasp the opportunities and face the threats?

(5 marks)

Further examples of company strategies

It is a useful exercise for students to look at the websites of some well known organisations, or the organisations they work for, and read their strategies. The following extracts have been taken from the websites of Nokia and the Coca-Cola Company.

Nokia

Key elements of Nokia's strategy:

- build a new winning mobile ecosystem in partnership with Microsoft
- bring the next billion online in developing growth markets
- invest in next-generation disruptive technologies
- increase our focus on speed, results and accountability

Nokia's strategy is about investing in and ensuring their future. Their new strategy is supported by changes in leadership, operational structure and approach.

'I have incredible optimism,' said Stephen Elop, Nokia President and CEO, 'because I can see fresh opportunity for us to innovate, to differentiate, to build great mobile products, like never before, and at a speed that will surpass what we have accomplished in the past.'

An important part of this strategy has been the forming of a strategic partnership with Microsoft. Nokia hope that this will help them to regain lost ground in the smartphone market. Together, they intend to build a global ecosystem that surpasses anything currently in existence. The Nokia-Microsoft ecosystem will deliver differentiated and innovative products with unrivalled scale in terms of product breadth, geographical reach and brand identity.

Taken from the Nokia website, April 2012

Coca-Cola Corporation

What will drive our success in the future? Not just growth, but sustainable growth – meeting our short-term commitments while investing to meet our long-term goals. And we have a vision and clear goals to guide our journey to achieve long-term growth – the kind of long-term growth that allows careers to flourish.

> We are building on our fundamental strengths in marketing and innovation, driving increased efficiency and effectiveness in interactions with our system and generating new energy through core brands that focus on health and wellness. We are poised to capture the opportunity in so many ways. Here are just a few:
>
> With the world's most recognised family of brands, we deliver more than 3,500 beverages to over 200 countries around the world – not just soft drinks, but juice and juice drinks, sports drinks, water, even coffee and milk. And every day we explore new ways to create and share beverages to energise, relax, nourish, hydrate and enjoy.
>
> As the world's largest distributor of non-alcoholic beverages, we maintain a trusted local presence in every community we serve. We are constantly looking ahead to anticipate what our communities may need and gathering resources to support them.
>
> We've increased our annual marketing budget substantially, launched many new products, and developed a model to help our retail customers maximise their sales while we continue to plan for the next one, five and ten years in business.
>
> *Taken from the CocaCola Corporation website, April 2012*

4 Levels of strategy

Strategy occurs at different levels in the organisation. For large organisations, the top of the hierarchy is where **corporate strategy** is made. This provides the framework for the development of **business strategy**, which looks at the strategy for each Strategic Business Unit (SBU). The business strategy in turn provides the framework for **functional or operational strategies**. The different levels of strategy formulation are therefore interdependent in that strategy at one level should be consistent with the strategies at the next level.

Smaller organisations may not have all three levels.

Introduction to strategy formulation

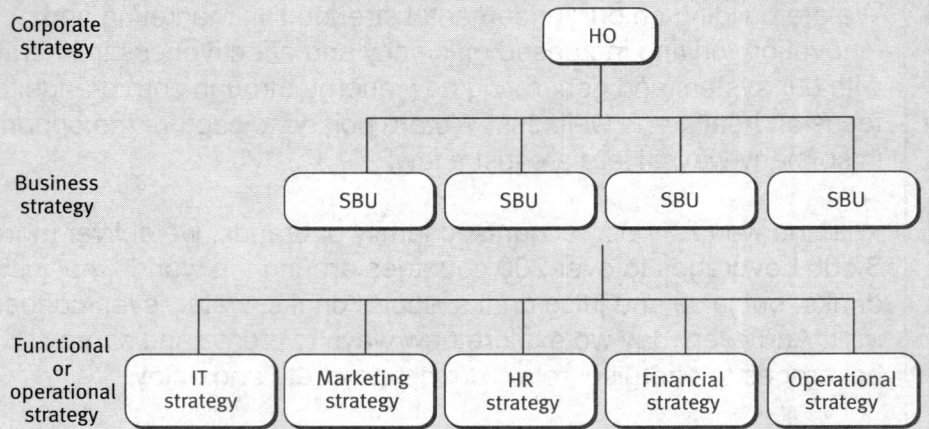

- **Corporate strategy (balanced portfolio of strategic business units)**

    What businesses is the firm in? What businesses should it be in?

    These activities need to be matched to the firm's environment, its resource capabilities and the values and expectations of stakeholders.

    How integrated should these businesses be?

- **Business strategy (balanced portfolio of products)**

    Looks at how each business (SBU) attempts to achieve its mission within its chosen area of activity.

    Which products should be developed?

    What approach should be taken to gain a competitive advantage?

> A strategic business unit (SBU) is defined by CIMA as: *a section, usually a division, within a larger organisation, that has a significant degree of autonomy, typically being responsible for developing and marketing its own products or services.*

- **Functional or operational strategy (balanced portfolio of resources)**

    Looks at how the different functions of the business support the corporate and business strategies.

More detail on the levels of strategy

Corporate strategy

The corporate centre is at the apex of the organisation. It is the head office of the firm and will contain the corporate board. Corporate strategy is typically concerned with determining the overall purpose and scope of the organisation, in other words what type of business or businesses should the organisation be in. Common issues at this level include:

- decisions on acquisitions, mergers and sell-offs or closure of business units;
- relations with key external stakeholders such as investors, the government and regulatory bodies;
- decisions to enter new markets or embrace new technologies (sometimes termed diversification strategies);
- development of corporate policies on issues such as public image, employment practices or information systems.

Decisions at this level tend to be complex and non routine in nature because they often involve a high degree of uncertainty based on what might happen in the future.

Business strategy

This level of strategy is concerned with how an operating or strategic business unit approaches a particular market. Management of the SBU will be responsible for winning customers and beating rivals in its particular market. Consequently, it is at this level that competitive strategy is usually formulated. The considerations at this level will include:

- marketing issues such as product development, pricing, promotion and distribution.
- how should it segment the market – should it specialise in particular profitable segments?

Business strategy should be formulated within the broad framework of the overall objectives laid down by the corporate centre to ensure that each SBU plays its part. The extent to which the management of the SBU is free to make competitive strategy decisions varies from organisation to organisation and reflects the degree of centralisation versus decentralisation in the management structure of the firm.

Functional strategies

The functional (sometimes called operational) level of the organisation refers to main business functions such as sales, production, purchasing, human resources and finance. Functional strategies are the long-term management policies of these functional areas. They are intended to ensure that the functional area plays its part in helping the SBU achieve the goals of its corporate strategy.

Test your understanding 2

V plc operates in the leisure and entertainment industry. It has a range of different ventures worldwide including fitness centres, casinos, cinemas and sports bars, each of which operates as a separate business.

Required:

Distinguish between the different levels at which strategy should exist in V plc and explain what would be involved at each level.

(10 marks)

Elements of strategy

There are three main elements of strategy; Financial, Competitive and Investment and resource.

- Financial strategy is concerned with the organisation's relationship with the providers of capital.
- Competitive strategy is concerned with how and where the organisation should compete.
- Investment and resource strategy is concerned with how management uses the finance it has available.

These three are interrelated.

```
         Competitive
          strategy
       How and where
        to compete?
       ↗            ↘
Investment and        Financial strategy
resource strategy  ← Relations with providers
How management        of capital
uses the finance
```

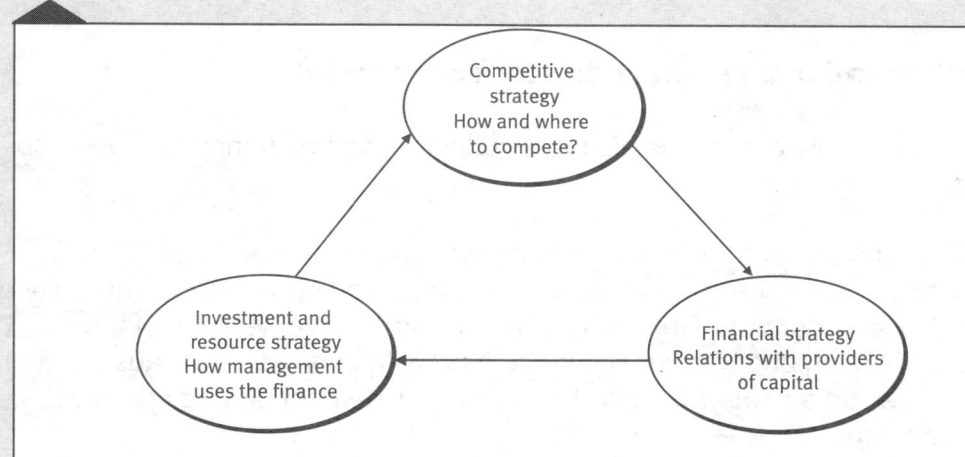

Successful competitive strategy generates earnings and cash flows that provide the finance for resources.

They are also related to the three levels of strategy, with financial strategy taking place at the corporate level, competitive strategy taking place at the business level and investment and resource strategy taking place at the functional level.

Example:

The items below are interrelated, but the dominant strategy has been highlighted.

Tick which element strategy is dominant	Competitive strategy	Financial Strategy	Investment & resource strategy
Expenditure on brand support and advertising			✓
How to attract customers	✓		
Obtaining funds at the optimum cost		✓	
Delivering an adequate return to the shareholders		✓	
Which markets to enter and exit	✓		
Which products to market	✓		
R & D expenditure on new techniques and products			✓
How to outperform rivals	✓		
Managing stock and other working capital areas			✓
Capital expenditure			✓

5 The rational approach to strategy formulation

The rational approach is also referred to as the traditional, formal or top-down approach.

The rational strategic planning process model is based on rational behaviour, whereby planners, management and organisations are expected to behave logically. First defining the mission and objectives of the organisation and then selecting the means to achieve this. Cause and effect are viewed as naturally linked and a strong element of predictability is expected.

The rational approach is seen as having four main steps:

(1) Analysis of current position
(2) Formulation of strategic options
(3) Implementation of strategies
(4) Monitor, review and evaluation

The model below shows a framework of the rational approach and clearly shows the various stages which management may take to develop a strategy for their organisation.

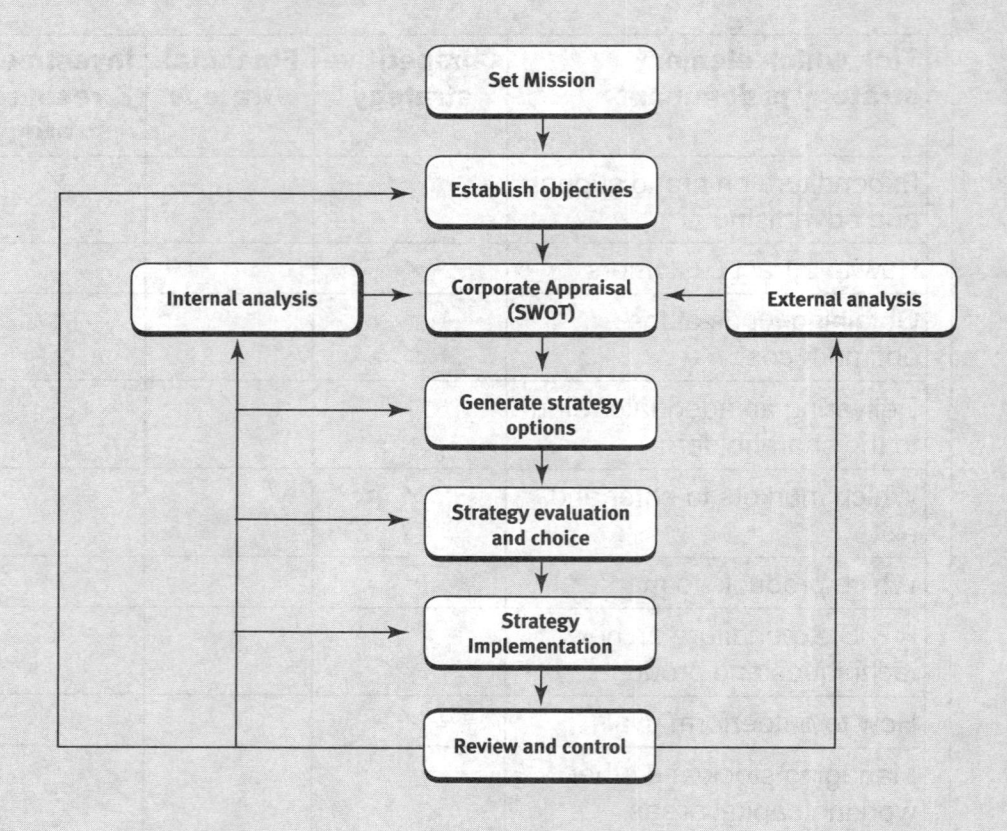

```
                    Set Mission
                         ↓
              → Establish objectives
              │          ↓
Internal analysis → Corporate Appraisal ← External analysis
              │       (SWOT)
              │          ↓
              → Generate strategy
              │     options
              │          ↓
              → Strategy evaluation
              │     and choice
              │          ↓
              → Strategy
              │   Implementation
              │          ↓
              → Review and control
```

The rational approach follows a logical step-by-step approach:

- Determine the mission of the organisation.
- Set corporate objectives.
- Carry out corporate appraisal – involving analysis of internal and external environments.
- Identifying and evaluating strategic options – select strategies to achieve competitive advantage by exploiting strengths and opportunities or minimising threats and weaknesses.
- Evaluate each option in detail for its fit with the mission and circumstances of the business and choose the most appropriate option.
- Implementing the chosen strategy.
- Review and control – reviewing the performance of the organisation to determine whether goals have been achieved. This is a continuous process and involves taking corrective action if changes occur internally or externally.

Each of the different stages in the model above will be looked at in more detail in this, and the following chapter.

Ensure you are comfortable with this model as you will refer back to it throughout this syllabus area.

A formal top-down strategy process within a large organisation

Large organisations will often formalise the process of strategy formulation. The following are typical features of the process:

(1) *A designated team responsible for strategy development.* There are several groups involved in this process:

   (a) A permanent strategic planning unit reporting to top management and consisting of expert staff collecting business intelligence, advising divisions on formulating strategy and monitoring results.

   (b) Groups of managers, often the management teams of the SBUs, meeting periodically to monitor the success of the present strategies and to develop new ones. These are sometimes referred to as strategy away days because they often take place away from the office to avoid interruptions.

(c) Business consultants acting as advisers and facilitators to the process by suggesting models and techniques to assist managers in understanding their business environments and the strategic possibilities open to them. You will be reading about many of these models and techniques later.

(2) *Formal collection of information for strategy purposes*. The management team will call upon data from within and outside the firm to understand the challenges they face and the resources at their disposal. This information can include:

(a) Environmental scanning reports compiled by the business intelligence functions within the firm, including such matters as competitor behaviour, market trends and potential changes to laws.

(b) Specially commissioned reports on particular markets, products or competitors.

(c) Management accounting information on operating costs and performance, together with financial forecasts.

(d) Research reports from external consultancies on market opportunities and threats.

(3) *Collective decision-taking by the senior management team*. This involves the senior management team working together to develop and agree business strategies. Techniques such as brainstorming ideas on flip charts and using visual graphical models to summarise complex ideas will assist this process. Also, arriving at a decision will involve considerable conflict as particular managers are reluctant to see their favoured proposal rejected and a different strategy adopted.

(4) *A process of communicating and implementing the business strategy.* This can be accomplished using a combination of the following methods:

(a) Writing a formal document summarising the main elements of the plan. This will be distributed on a confidential basis to other managers and key investors, and also perhaps to other key stakeholders such as labour representatives, regulatory bodies, major customers and key suppliers.

(b) Briefing meetings and presentations to the stakeholders mentioned above. Frequently, reporters from the business press will be invited to ensure that the information reaches a broader public. Naturally, the fine detail will remain confidential.

(c) The development of detailed policies, programmes and budgets based on achieving the goals laid out in the business strategy.

(d) The development of performance targets for managers and staff. These ensure that everyone plays their part in the strategy (and perhaps receive financial rewards for doing so).

(5) *Regular review and control of the strategy*. Management will monitor the success of the strategy by receiving regular reports on performance and on environmental changes. Today, the sophisticated competitive strategies of many firms have necessitated the development of more complex performance measurement systems to supplement traditional budgetary control information. These are variously termed enterprise resource management systems and balanced scorecards. There has also been an increased emphasis on competitor and other environmental information to assist managers in steering their businesses.

6 Mission, goals and objectives

From the diagram of the rational model, the first step of the model is setting the mission for the organisation.

Mission

A mission is a broad statement of the overall purpose of the business and should reflect the core values of the business. It will set out the overriding purpose of the business in line with the values and expectations of stakeholders. (*Johnson and Scholes*)

There are a number of fundamental questions that an organisation will need to address in its search for purpose (*Drucker*).

These are:

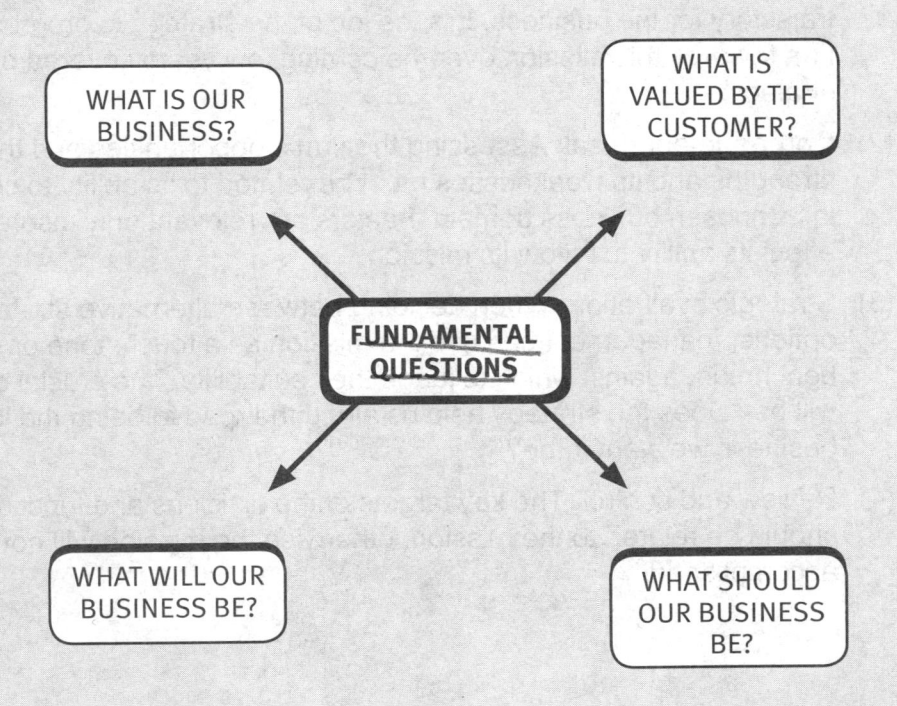

- WHAT IS OUR BUSINESS?
- WHAT IS VALUED BY THE CUSTOMER?
- WHAT WILL OUR BUSINESS BE?
- WHAT SHOULD OUR BUSINESS BE?

(FUNDAMENTAL QUESTIONS)

Mission statement

The mission statement is a statement in writing that describes the basic purpose of an organisation, that is, what it is trying to accomplish. It is possible to have a strong sense of purpose or mission without a formal mission statement.

There is no one best mission statement for an organisation as the contents of mission statements will vary in terms of length, format and level of detail from one organisation to another.

Mission statements are normally brief and address **three main questions**:

- Why do we exist?
- What are we providing?
- For whom do we exist?

For example:

- British Airways seeks to be 'the worlds favourite airline'
- Starbucks mission is to 'inspire and nurture the human spirit – one person, one cup and one neighbourhood at a time.'

Roles of mission statements

Mission statements help at four places in the rational model of strategy:

(1) Mission and objectives. The mission sets the long-term framework and trajectory for the business. It is the job of the strategy to progress the firm towards this mission over the coming few years covered by the strategy.

(2) Corporate appraisal. Assessing the firm's opportunities and threats, its strengths and its weaknesses must be related to its ability to compete in its chosen business domain. Factors are relevant only insofar as they affect its ability to follow its mission.

(3) Strategic evaluation. When deciding between alternative strategic options, management can use the mission as a touchstone or benchmark against which to judge their suitability. The crucial question will be, 'Does the strategy help us along the road to being the kind of business we want to be?'

(4) Review and control. The key targets of the divisions and functions should be related to the mission, otherwise the mission will not be accomplished.

Purposes of mission statements (Hooley et al.):

(1) To provide a basis for consistent planning decisions.

(2) To assist in translating purposes and direction into objectives suitable for assessment and control.

(3) To provide a consistent purpose between different interest groups connected to the organisation.

(4) To establish organisational goals and ethics.

(5) To improve understanding and support from key groups outside the organisation.

> **Examples of reasons for existence**
>
> Companies within the same industry may have different reasons for existing.
>
> **Manufacturing**
>
> - Rolls Royce exists to make a small number of high quality luxury cars with a distinctive image.
> - Ford exists to sell a large volume of different types of car to a global market.
>
> **Travel**
>
> - Ryanair and EasyJet exist to provide low-cost, no frills flights from the UK to destinations in Europe.
> - British Airways exists to provide a quality service to economy, business and first class passengers to destinations around the world.
>
> **Financial services**
>
> - Coutts and Co exists to provide an individualised banking service to a particular group of customers.
> - First Direct exists to provide low-cost telephone-based financial services to a wide range of customers.

Content of a mission statement – David

David provides a useful list of what areas should be included in a mission statement:

- *Customers*. A statement making reference to who the organisation's customers are.
- *Markets.* A statement of where the firm competes.
- *Products or services*. A description of the firm's major products or services.
- *Concern for survival, growth and profitability*. The broad economic objectives of the firm.
- *Philosophy*. A statement of the organisation's basic values and standards of behaviour.
- *Concern for employees.* A statement of the firm's attitude to its employees.
- *Concern for public image*. A statement as to how much concern the organisation has of its public image and all its stakeholders.
- *Self-concept*. A statement of the organisation's strength and distinction relative to competitors.

Vision

While a mission statement gives the overall purpose of the organisation, a vision statement describes a picture of the "preferred future."

A vision statement describes how the future will look if the organisation achieves its mission.

Illustration 2 – Mission and vision of the BBC

British Broadcasting Corporation (BBC) has a clear mission and vision.

Mission – to enrich people's lives with programmes and services that inform, educate and entertain.

Vision – to be the most creative organisation in the world.

It is also becoming popular for companies to state their values.

> *Values*:
>
> - Trust is the foundation of the BBC: we are independent, impartial and honest.
> - Audiences are at the heart of everything we do.
> - We take pride in delivering quality and value for money.
> - Creativity is the lifeblood of our organisation.
> - We respect each other and celebrate our diversity so that everyone can give their best.
> - We are one BBC: great things happen when we work together.

Once the mission has been established, the rational model moves on to establishing objectives. Often organisations set high level goals first, which feed into more measurable objectives.

Goals

Mintzberg defines goals as the intention behind an organisation's decisions or actions. He argues that goals will frequently never be achieved and may be incapable of being measured. Thus for example 'the highest possible standard of living to our employees' is a goal that will be difficult to measure and realise. Although goals are more specific than mission statements and have a shorter number of years in their timescale, they are not precise measures of performance.

Objectives

Mintzberg goes on to define objectives as goals expressed in a form in which they can be measured. Thus an objective of 'profit before interest and tax to be not less than 20% of capital employed' is capable of being measured.

The link between mission, goals and objectives

The mission is normally an open-ended statement of the organisation's purpose and strategies, goals and objectives translate the mission into strategic milestones for the organisation's strategy to reach.

Introduction to strategy formulation

Objectives generally possess four characteristics which set it apart from a mission statement:

(1) a precise formulation of the attribute sought
(2) an index or measure for progress towards the attribute
(3) a target to be achieved
(4) a time-frame in which it is to be achieved.

> **Objectives**
>
> The acronym often used when setting objectives is **SMART:**
>
> - **S**pecific means 'clearly expressed', e.g. 'improve performance' is too vague; 'improve operating profit' is better.
> - **M**easurable means quantifiable, e.g. 'improve image' v 'increase operating profit to 20% of turnover'.
> - **A**chievable means perceived as achievable by those being held responsible for achieving them, e.g. 'improve operating profit to 80% of turnover' probably will be impossible to achieve. Unachievable objectives demotivate those held responsible for them.
> - **R**elevant means explicitly linked to the overall goals of the business, e.g. 'increase customer retention by 5%' is relevant to the overall goal of 'delight our customers'.
> - **T**imely. Timescales have to be set if the objective is ever to be achieved, e.g. 'by 31 December 20X2'.
>
> Objectives perform a number of functions:
>
> - **Planning.** Objectives provide the framework for planning. They are the targets which the plan is supposed to reach.
> - **Responsibility.** Objectives are given to the managers of divisions, departments and operations. This communicates to them:
>   – the activities, projects or areas they are responsible for
>   – the sorts of output required
>   – the level of outputs required.
> - **Integration.** Objectives are how senior management coordinate the firm. Provided that the objectives handed down are internally consistent, this should ensure goal congruence between managers of the various divisions of the business.

- **Motivation.** Management will be motivated to reach their objectives in order to impress their superiors, and perhaps receive bonuses. This means that the objectives set must cover all areas of the mission. For example, if the objectives emphasise purely financial outcomes, then managers will not pay much heed to issues such as social responsibility or innovation.

- **Evaluation.** Senior management control the business by evaluating the performance of the managers responsible for each of its divisions.

You may be familiar with these five functions (often recalled using the acronym **PRIME**).

The goal structure:

- Be clear of the mission & vision
- Set the goals
- Each goal should be broken down into a number of factors that affect the goal, these are the *Critical Success Factors* (CSF's)
- For each CSF there must be one measurement, this is a *Key Performance Indicator* (KPI)
- For each CSF there should also be a *performance target* for the forthcoming budget exercise

CSF + KPI + Target = Objective

The hierarchy is shown below:

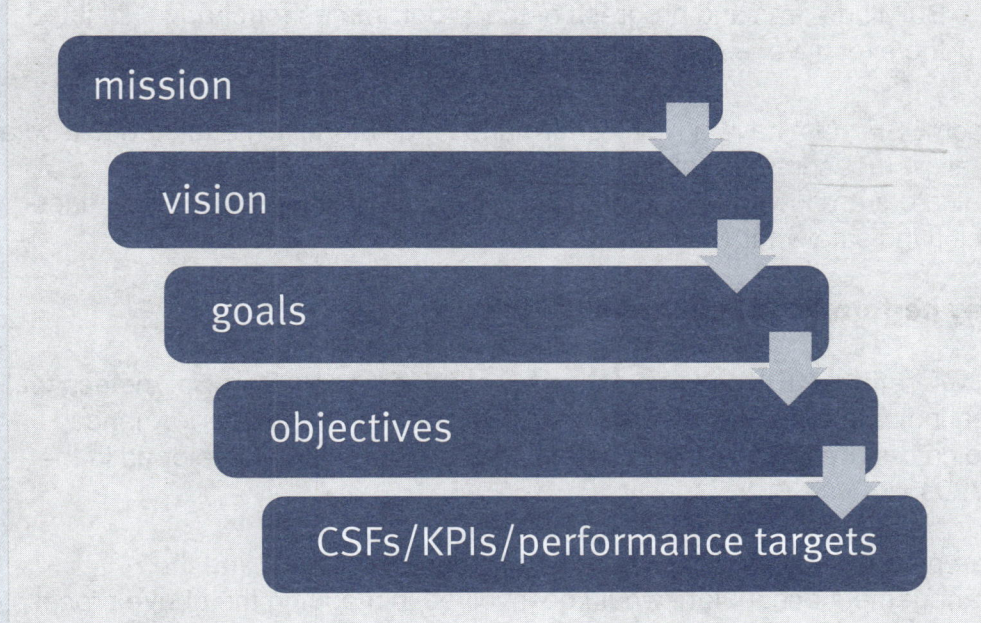

mission → vision → goals → objectives → CSFs/KPIs/performance targets

You can see from this that the company's mission is translated into goals and then objectives:

Strategic objectives reached by following strategies communicated to management as numerous......

Tactical objectives which in turn are implemented and reviewed through setting a large number of......

Operational objectives which may be communicated to managers and staff responsible through their......

Critical Success Factors, Key Performance Indicators and individual performance targets. Whilst the mission is normally an open-ended statement of the firm's purposes and strategies, strategic objectives and goals translate the mission into strategic milestones for the business strategy to reach. In other words the outcomes that the organisation wants to achieve.

Critical success factors

These can be defined as 'those things that must go right if the objectives and goals are to be achieved'.

Critical success factors may be financial or non-financial, but they must be high-level.

There are two types of CSF:

- Monitoring – keeping abreast of ongoing operations, e.g. expand foreign sales.
- Building – tracking progress of the 'programmes for change' initiated by the executive, e.g. decentralise the organisation.

Each CSF must have a Key Performance Indicator (KPI) attached to it so as to allow measurement of progress towards the CSF. Performance indicators are low-level and detailed. They are measures of performance which indicate whether the CSFs have been achieved or not.

Key performance indicators (KPIs)

CIMA defines KPIs as quantitative but not necessarily financial metrics that can indicate progress towards a strategic objective. Key performance indicators are integral to the balanced scorecard ideas developed in the 1990s.

The process is a participative one at management level and the management accountant would be involved in mapping the above process, developing the KPIs and monitoring them.

Individual performance targets

In is important to note that **target setting** motivates staff and enables the entity to control its performance and that the objectives set will apply to the entity as a whole, to each business unit, and also to each individual manager or employee.

If the goals of the individual are derived from the goals of the business unit, and these are in turn derived from the goals of the entity, 'goal congruence' is said to exist. Attainment by individuals or units of their objectives will directly contribute towards the fulfilment of corporate objectives.

> ### Illustration 3 – Tesco's objectives and KPIs
>
> Tesco's core purpose is to **create value** for customers to earn their lifetime loyalty.
>
> Their success depends on people: the people who shop with them and the people who work with them.
>
> Tesco has a well-established and consistent strategy for growth, which has allowed them to strengthen their core UK business and drive expansion into new markets.
>
> As we saw in illustration 1, part of Tesco's strategy is:
>
> - To put our responsibilities to the communities we serve at the heart of what we do
>
> **Under this objective, Tesco use Key Performance Indicators (KPIs) to measure progress:**
>
> - Reduce CO_2 emissions from existing stores and distribution centres by at least 50% by 2020 against a baseline of 2006. Annual target reported as percentage reduction against previous year
> - Reduce CO_2 emissions from new stores by 50% by 2020 against a baseline of 2006
> - Reduce by 50% the amount of CO_2 used in our distribution network to deliver a case of goods by 2012 against a baseline of 2006. Annual target reported as percentage reduction against previous year
> - Percentage of store waste recycled
> - Staff and customer fund-raising (£)
> - Donate at least 1% of pre-tax profits to charities and good causes

- Helping customers live healthy lives – staff and customers active (millions of people)
- Helping customers choose healthy food (number of promotions)
- Increase the number of eligible own-brand lines with nutritional or front-of-pack GDA labelling (% of total number of eligible brands)
- Supplier Viewpoint – average score (% of scores that are favourable)
- Response rate of suppliers (%)
- Staff being trained for their next job.

Critical success factors

'Critical success factors (CSFs) are those things that must go right for the organisation to achieve its mission.'

The advantages of identifying CSFs are that they are simple to understand; they help focus attention on major concerns; they are easy to communicate to co-workers; they are easy to monitor; and they can be used in concert with strategic planning methodologies.

Using critical success factors as an isolated event does not represent critical strategic thinking, but when used in conjunction with a planning process, identifying CSFs is extremely important because it keeps people focused. Clarifying the priority order of CSFs, measuring results, and rewarding superior performance will improve the odds for long-term success as well.

There are four basic types of CSFs according to **Rockart**. They are:

- Industry CSFs resulting from specific industry characteristics.
- Strategy CSFs resulting from the chosen competitive strategy of the business.
- Environmental CSFs resulting from economic or technological changes.
- Temporal CSFs resulting from internal organisational needs and changes.

Critical success factor	Source of CSF	Primary measures and targets
(1) Increase number of customers.	Industry	95% customer retention rate; 15% new customers per yr.
(2) Install PC-based customer service hotline.	Strategy	90% of customer queries answered in 1 hour.
(3) Increase number of customer service reps	Strategy	3 reps per 100 customers.
(4) Restructure capital structure.	Environmental	Lower cost of capital by 2%.
(5) Raise employee morale and productivity.	Temporal	Increase employee retention rate to 95%/yr.

Things that are measured get done more often than things that are not measured. Each CSF should be measurable and associated with a target goal. You don't need exact measures to manage. Primary measures that should be listed include critical success levels (such as number of transactions per month) or, in cases where specific measurements are more difficult, general goals should be specified (such as moving up in an industry customer service survey).

When setting standards, raising standards often raises results (and the reverse is also true).

Test your understanding 3

The directors of The Nice Sandwich Group (NSG) have recently employed a new management team via a recruitment consultancy which specialises in food sector appointments. Padmay has very high unemployment and the vast majority of its workforce has no experience in a food manufacturing environment.

NSG has agreed to make and supply sandwiches to agreed recipes for the Superior Food Group (SFG) which owns a chain of supermarkets in all towns and cities within Padmay. SFG insists that it selects the suppliers of the ingredients that are used in making the sandwiches it sells and therefore NSG would be unable to reduce the costs of the ingredients used in the sandwiches. NSG will be the sole supplier for SFG.

The number of sandwiches sold per year in Padmay is 625 million. SFG has a market share of 4%.

The average selling price of all sandwiches sold by SFG is $2.40. 90% of all sandwiches sold by SFG are sold before 2 pm each day. The majority of the remaining 10% are sold after 8 pm. It is the intention that all sandwiches are sold on the day that they are delivered into SFG's supermarkets.

The finance director of NSG has stated that he believes a target sales margin of 32% can be achieved, although he is concerned about the effect that an increase in the cost of all ingredients would have on the forecast profits.

Required:

Explain FIVE critical success factors to the performance of NSG on which the directors must focus if NSG is to achieve success in its marketplace.

(10 marks)

Objectives in a not-for-profit organisation

Public sector organisations and charities often have difficulty in using traditional private sector based approaches to objective setting since they do not make a profit by which their success or failure can be measured. One way to address this problem is to use the following approach:

The 'three Es approach' of the Audit Commission:

- **Effectiveness** looks at the outputs (the goal approach); the 'goal approach' looks at the ultimate objectives of the organisation, i.e. it looks at output measures. For example, for an NHS hospital, have the waiting lists been reduced? Have mortality rates gone down? How many patients have been treated?

- **Efficiency** looks at the link between outputs and inputs (the internal processes approach); The 'internal processes approach' looks at how well inputs have been used to achieve outputs – it is a measure of efficiency. For example, what was the average cost per patient treated? What was the average spend per bed over the period, and what was the bed occupancy rate that this achieved?

- **Economy** looks solely at the level of inputs, e.g. did the hospital spend more or less on drugs this year, or on nurses' wages?

> The best picture of the success of an organisation is obtained by using all of the above approaches and by examining both financial and non-financial issues. Think about effectiveness meaning 'doing the right things' and efficiency 'about doing things right'.
>
> Most of the organisations in exam questions will be profit-seeking companies. However some may involve charities, councils, schools, hospitals and other organisations where profit is not the main objective. With such an 'NFP' a discussion of objectives is likely to be problematic for the following reasons:
>
> - It is more likely to have multiple objectives. A large teaching hospital may want to give the best quality care and treat as many patients as possible and train new doctors and research new techniques. Conflict is inevitable.
>
> - It will be more difficult to measure objectives. How can one measure whether a school is educating pupils well? Performance in exams? Percentage going on to university? Percentage getting jobs? Percentage staying out of prison once they leave?
>
> - There may be a more equal balance of power between stakeholders. In a company, the shareholders hold ultimate power. If they do not use it, the directors generally get their way. In a school, the balance of power may be more even (or even undefined) between parents, governors, the headmaster and the local education authority.
>
> - The people receiving the service are not necessarily those paying for it. The government and local NHS trusts determine a hospital's funding, not the patients. Consequently, there may be pressure to perform well in national league tables at the expense of other objectives.

7 Corporate appraisal, options, choice and implementation

Corporate appraisal

Look back at the diagram of the rational model, you can see that once the mission and objectives have been set, the next stage is to carry out a corporate appraisal (SWOT). Corporate appraisal and analysis are key parts of strategy formulation. This will be covered in chapter 3.

Generate strategic options, evaluation and choice

After the analysis has been carried out, the next steps in the rational model are to generate strategic options and make strategic choices.

Strategic choice is the process of choosing the alternative strategic options generated by the SWOT analysis. Management need to seek to identify and evaluate alternative courses of action to ensure that the business reaches the objectives they have set. This will be largely a creative process of generating alternatives, building on the strengths of the business and allowing it to tackle new products or markets to improve its competitive position.

The strategic choice process involves making decisions on:

- On what basis should the organisation compete?
- What are the alternative directions available and which products/markets should the organisation enter or leave?
- What alternative methods are available to achieve the chosen direction?

Achieving competitive advantage

When developing a corporate strategy, the organisation must decide upon which basis it is going to compete in its markets. This involves decisions on whether to compete across the whole marketplace or only in certain segments.

Competitiveness is essentially the ability of a firm, sector or economy to compete against other firms, sectors or economies.

Why is competitive structure important?

The number of competing firms in an industry, their strength and the ease of entry for new firms have an impact on:

- the level of choice for consumers
- the degree of competition in terms of price, promotion, new product developments
- the profitability of firms in the industry
- the likelihood of illegal collusive agreements.

A further consideration is the way in which the organisation can gain **competitive advantage**, that is anything that gives on organisation an edge over its rivals and which can be sustained over time. To be sustainable, organisations must seek to identify the activities that competitors cannot easily copy and imitate (We will return to this in a later chapter when the resource-based view to strategy is introduced).

According to Porter, there are three generic strategies' through which an organisation can generate superior competitive performance (known as generic because they are widely applicable to firms of all sizes and in all industries):

(1) Cost leadership – same quality but low price
(2) Differentiation – innovative, enabling differentiation
(3) Focus – concentrating on a small part of the market

The adoption of one or other of these strategies by a business unit is made on the basis of:

- an analysis of the threats and opportunities posed by forces operating in the specific industry of which the business is a part;
- the general environment in which the business operates;
- an assessment of the unit's strengths and weaknesses relative to competitors.

The general idea is that the strategy to be adopted by the organisation is one which best positions the company relative to its rivals and other threats from suppliers, buyers, new entrants, substitutes and the macro-environment, and to take opportunities offered by the market and general environment.

Decisions on the above questions will determine the generic strategy options for achieving competitive advantage.

Strategic direction

The organisation also has to decide how it might develop in the future to exploit strengths and opportunities or minimise threats and weaknesses. There are various options that could be followed, including:

- Market penetration. This is where the organisation seeks to maintain or increase its share of existing markets with existing products.

- Product development. Strategies are based on launching new products or making product enhancement which are offered to its existing markets.

- Market development. Strategies are based on finding new markets for existing products. This could involve identifying new markets geographically or new market segments.

- Diversification. Strategies are based on launching new products into new markets and is the most risky strategic option.

Strategic methods

Not only must the organisation consider on what basis to compete and the direction of strategic development, it must also decide what methods it could use. The options are:

- Internal development. This is where the organisation uses it own internal resources to pursue its chosen strategy. It may involve the building up a business from scratch.

- Takeovers/acquisitions or mergers. An alternative would be to acquire resources by taking over or merging with another organisation, in order to acquire knowledge of a particular product/market area. This might be to obtain a new product range or market presence or as a means of eliminating competition.

- Strategic alliances. This route often has the aim of increasing exposure to potential customers or gaining access to technology. There are a variety of arrangements for strategic alliances, some of which are very formalised and some which are much looser arrangements. We will return to the topic of strategic alliances in a later chapter.

Evaluation of strategic options

The evaluation stage considers each strategic option in detail for its feasibility and fit with the mission and circumstances of the business. By the end of this process, management will have decided on a shortlist of options that will be carried forward to the strategy implementation stage. The various options must be evaluated against each other with respect to their ability to achieve the overall goals. Management will have a number of ideas to improve the competitive position of the business.

Strategy implementation

The strategy sets the broad direction and methods for the business to reach its objectives. However, none of it will happen without more detailed implementation. The strategy implementation stage involves drawing up the detailed plans, policies and programmes necessary to make the strategy happen. It will also involve obtaining the necessary resources and committing them to the strategy. These are commonly called tactical and operational decisions:

- Tactical programmes and decisions are medium-term policies designed to implement some of the key elements of the strategy such as developing new products, recruitment or downsizing of staff or investing in new production capacity. Project appraisal and project management techniques are valuable at this level.
- Operational programmes and decisions cover routine day-to-day matters such as meeting particular production, cost and revenue targets. Conventional budgetary control is an important factor in controlling these matters.

8 Review and control

The last step in the rational model is review and control. From the model you can clearly see the review and control process. Where issues are discovered, parts of the model will have to be re-visited.

This is a continuous process of reviewing both the implementation and the overall continuing suitability of the strategy. It will consider two aspects:

(1) Does performance of the strategy still put the business on course for reaching its strategic objectives?
(2) Are the forecasts of the environment on which the strategy was based still accurate, or have unforeseen threats or opportunities arisen subsequently that might necessitate a reconsideration of the strategy?

Johnson, Scholes and Whittington

The Johnson, Scholes and Whittington (JSW) model of strategic planning is a modern development of the rational planning model. It consists of three elements (analysis, choice, implementation) but instead of presenting these linearly, it recognises interdependencies. For example, it might only be at the strategy into action (implementation) stage that an organisation discovers something that sheds light on its strategic position. The other key difference is that Johnson, Scholes and Whittington argue that strategic planning can begin at any point. For example, firms might decide that they will launch an internet sales division without first carrying out any strategic analysis or choosing how the new strategy might compete.

Introduction to strategy formulation

Strategic analysis
- External analysis to identify opportunities and threats
- Internal analysis to identify strengths and weaknesses
- Stakeholder analysis to identify key objectives and to assess power and interest of different groups
- Gap analysis to identify the difference between desired and expected performance.

Strategic choice
- Strategies are required to 'close the gap'
- Competitive strategy – for each business unit
- Directions for growth – which markets/products should be invested in
- Whether expansion should be achieved by organic growth, acquisition or some form of joint arrangement.

Strategic implementation
- Formulation of detailed plans and budgets
- Target setting for KPIs
- Monitoring and control.

9 Chapter summary

Objectives
- Specific
- Measurable
- Achievable
- Relevant
- Timely

Rational approach
- Mission
- Objectives
- Analysis
- Options
- Choice
- Implementation
- Review and control

Levels of strategy
- Corporate
- Business
- Functional

Goal Hierarchy
- Mission
- Goals
- Objectives
- Critical Success Factors (CSFs)
- Key Performance Indicators (KPIs)
- Target

Basic framework and concepts of strategy formulation

Competitive advantage
- Cost leadership
- Differentiation
- Focus

Mission
- What is our business?
- What is valued by our customer?
- What will our business be?
- What should our business be?

Test your understanding answers

Test your understanding 1

(a) Examples of the skills Tesco needs are:

- Innovation.
- Purchasing.
- Marketing.
- Efficiency.
- Customer focus.
- Flexible approach.

(b) The sort of opportunities that may arise are:
- new markets. Tesco now operate in 13 markets outside the UK, the most recent international development is in India.
- growth of on line shopping.
- closure/takeover of smaller supermarkets.
- growth of the personal finance market.

(c) The main threat is competition. Tesco is the largest UK supermarket, with a 30% market share. Asda and Sainsburys are second and third respectively with around 17% each, and Morrisons are fourth with around 11%. There have been many takeovers in this industry and competition is fierce. In the international markets, the threat is that they cannot establish the brand in the overseas markets or they are unable to operate in the international markets as they would like.

(d) Tesco is likely to deploy, for example, strategic management and marketing skills, financial resources, innovation skills, design skills, and its brand image.

Test your understanding 2

As there will be various different levels within V plc, each will have its own strategies. They are usually classified into:

Corporate – the purpose and scope of V plc

This will encompass V Plc's mission statement leading to its goals and objectives that feed down to lower levels of strategy. Decisions will be made about the longer term direction of V plc.

The corporate strategy involves the scope of V plc's activities and the matching of these to its environment, its resource capabilities and values and the expectations of different stakeholders, e.g. Should V plc expand into operating theme parks?

Business – how each of V plc's strategic business units (SBU) attempts to achieve its mission.

Within V plc the fitness centres, casinos, cinemas and sports bars operate as a separate business units.

The business level strategy of each SBU will relate to the strategic decisions such as being customer focused, the choice of products, exploring new opportunities and gaining competitive advantage, etc, e.g. Should fitness centres compete on the basis of low cost, value for money or high quality? Which new fitness products/services will be developed and how they will be released to the markets.

Functional – how the various functions within the organisation contribute to the achievement of V plc's overall objectives.

This strategy focuses on the issues such as resources, processes and people.

The activities of the functions within V plc such as finance, marketing and human resources need to focus on assisting in the achievement of V plc's overall strategies, e.g. How should V plc seek to recruit, train and retain croupiers for its casinos?

Test your understanding 3

Critical success factors are as follows:

Product quality

The fact that the production staff have no previous experience in a food production environment is likely to prove problematic.

It is vital that a comprehensive training programme is put in place at the earliest opportunity. NSG need to reach and maintain the highest level of product quality as soon as possible.

Supply quality

The quality of delivery into SFG supermarkets assumes critical significance. Time literally will be of the essence since 90% of all sandwiches are sold in SFG's supermarkets before 2 pm each day. Hence supply chain management must be extremely robust as there is very little scope for error.

Technical quality

Compliance with existing regulations regarding food production including all relevant factory health and safety requirements is vital in order to establish and maintain the reputation of NSG as a supplier of quality products. The ability to store products at the correct temperature is critical because sandwiches are produced for human consumption and in extreme circumstance could cause fatalities.

External credibility

Accreditation by relevant trade associations/regulators will be essential if nationwide acceptance of NSG as a major producer of sandwiches is to be established.

New product development

Whilst NSG have developed a range of healthy eating sandwiches it must be recognised that consumer tastes change and that in the face of competition there will always be a need for a continuous focus on new product development.

Margin

Whilst NSG need to recognise all other critical success factors they should always be mindful that the need to obtain the desired levels of gross and net margin remain of the utmost importance.

Notes:

(i) Only five critical success factors were required.

(ii) Alternative relevant discussion and examples would be acceptable.

Introduction to strategy formulation

chapter 3

Strategic analysis

Chapter learning objectives

- Discuss the nature of competitive environments.
- Compare and contrast approaches to strategy formulation.

Strategic analysis

1 Session content diagram

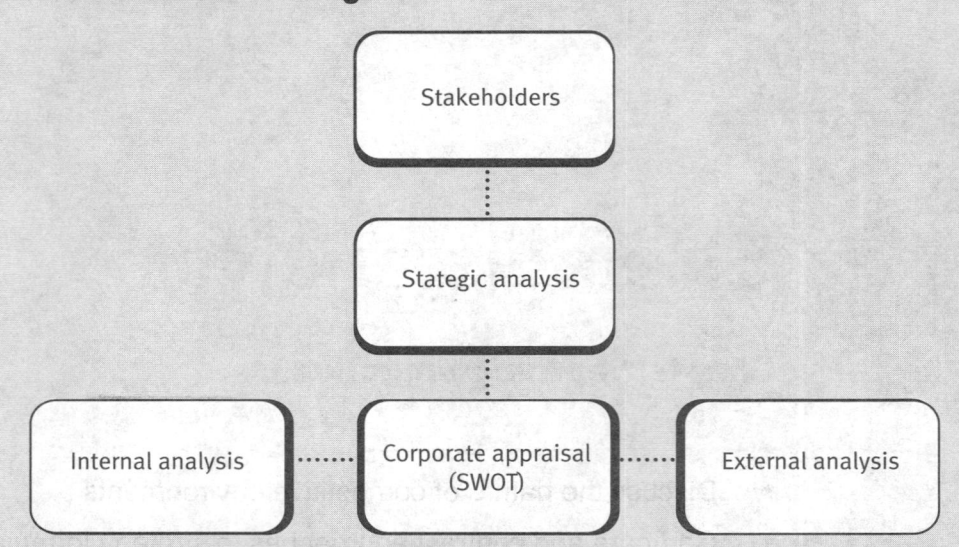

```
            Stakeholders
                 |
          Stategic analysis
                 |
   ┌─────────────┼─────────────┐
Internal      Corporate       External
analysis      appraisal       analysis
              (SWOT)
```

2 Stakeholder analysis

There are a number of different individual and interest groups both inside and outside the organisation who will have views of the strategic development of the organisation and who can affect or be affected by the performance of the organisation, These groups or individuals are referred to as stakeholders.

Strategic decision-making requires managers to consider stakeholders when setting the mission and objectives of the firm. This is for two broad groups of reasons:

- Issues of stakeholder power. This view observes that, like it or not, management must recognise that stakeholders can affect the success of a strategy, depending on whether they support or oppose it. For example, customers refusing to buy products, shareholders selling their shares or staff striking would disrupt any strategy. The view concludes that management should consider stakeholders before setting strategic objectives.

- Issues of organisational legitimacy. This more radical view suggests that firms are required to be good citizens because they are only permitted to exist by society on sufferance of not abusing their power. Consequently, although working primarily for the shareholders, management must ensure that its decisions do not ignore the interests of other stakeholders.

Stakeholders may include any or all of the following groups:

- Shareholders
- Directors

- Employees
- Trade unions
- Customers
- Suppliers
- Government
- Pressure groups
- General public and local people

There are different classifications of the above stakeholders, for example **internal** stakeholders (employees and management); **connected** stakeholders (shareholders, customer and suppliers); and **external** stakeholders (governments, community, pressure groups). **Primary** stakeholders have a formal contractual relationship in a strategy or a project. **Secondary** stakeholders have no formal relationship.

Illustration 1 – McDonald's

McDonald's has felt the brunt of its external stakeholders in recent years. It misjudged the public surge of sympathy for a local French sheep farmer, who damaged one of their restaurants in Millau as a anti globalisation protest. This case was widely reported by the media and compounded to a 40% fall in sales of McDonald's as consumer confidence in French beef had all but collapsed following a spate of BSE.

McDonald's also had to confront a religious group in Italy where it was seeking to double its chain of outlets. A Catholic newspaper attacked fast food as targeting the holiness of food. Such coverage reflects the hostility of those who view McDonald's as the unacceptable face of American-dominated global capitalism.

Some pressure groups believe the US fast food giant has usurped local historic cuisine and helped homogenise town centres.

On a more positive note the British Hedgehog Preservation Society persuaded the company, after six years of lobbying, to redesign the McFlurry dessert pots to make them safer for these prickly creatures.

After seven years of testing McDonald's has finally selected new trans-fat-free oil for cooking its famous French fries. McDonald's had been under pressure for moving more slowly than smaller rivals to rid its oil of the artery-clogging trans-fats.

Managing stakeholders – the Mendelow matrix

It is important that companies recognise the objectives of each group of stakeholders. These vary and can conflict with each other making the task of managing stakeholders more difficult.

A process for managing stakeholders is:

- Identify stakeholders and determine each group's objectives
- Analyse the level of interest and power each group possesses
- Place each stakeholder group in the appropriate quadrant of the Mendelow matrix
- Use the matrix to assess how to manage each stakeholder group.

Mendelow's Matrix

	Level of Interest Low	Level of Interest High
Level of Power Low	**A** Lack of interest and power means they are likely to accept what they are told. **MINIMAL EFFORT** [DIRECTION]	**B** Present strategy as rational then may stop them joining forces with powerful dissenters. **KEEP INFORMED** [EDUCATION/ COMMUNICATION]
Level of Power High	**C** Keep them satisfied. Assure them of the likely outcomes of the strategy well in advance. **KEEP SATISFIED** [INTERVENTION]	**D** Can be major drivers or major opponents of change. Need to assure them that the change is necessary. **KEY PLAYERS** [PARTICIPATION]

Some stakeholder groups wield greater power than others. The government's legislative power is comprehensive, and rulings of the Competition Commission have a direct effect upon the objectives and strategies of companies affected. Examples are:

- in 2004, UK based supermarket chain, Morrisons bought over rival chain Safeway for £3bn ($5.2bn), making them the fourth largest supermarket chain in the UK. The takeover was only cleared on condition that both groups sold one of its existing stores in towns where both were present;
- in newspaper publishing, Rupert Murdoch was blocked from taking over other newspapers on the grounds of safeguarding freedom of opinion across a range of views.

Assessing the power and interest of stakeholders

Assessing power of stakeholders

Factors that may be associated with a particular group having high power are:

- Status of the stakeholders, for example:
    - their place in the organisational hierarchy
    - their relative pay
    - their reputation in the firm
    - their social standing (e.g. ministers of religion may carry considerable power due to their social status).

- Claim on resources, for example:
    - size of their budget
    - number and level of staff employed
    - volume of business transacted with them (e.g. suppliers and customers)
    - percentage of workers they speak for (e.g. a trade union).

- Formal representation in decision-making processes:
    - level of management where they are represented
    - committees they have representation on
    - legal rights (e.g. shareholders, planning authorities).

Assessing interest of stakeholders

This will be more complex because it involves two factors:

- Where their interests rest. We assume that powerful stakeholders will pursue their self-interest. It is important to consider what they wish to achieve. It is possible to make some generalisations, for example:
    - managers – want to further the interests of their departments and functions as well as their own pay and careers;
    - employees – require higher pay, job security, good working conditions and some consultation;
    - customers – want fair prices, reliable supply and reassurance about their purchases;
    - suppliers – want fair prices, reliable orders, prompt payment and advance notification of changes;
    - local government – wants jobs, contribution to local community life, consultation on expansions and so on.

    In practice, we would need to interview the powerful stakeholders to find out precisely what they wanted.

- How interested they are. Not all stakeholders have the time or inclination to follow management's decisions closely. Again, some generalisations are possible about what will lead to interest, for example:
    - high personal financial or career investment in what the business does;
    - absence of alternative (e.g. alternative job, customer, supplier or employer);
    - potential to be called to account for failing to monitor (e.g. local councils or government bodies, such as regulators);
    - high social impact of firm (e.g. well-known, visible product, association with particular issues).

Strategies to deal with stakeholders

Scholes suggests the following strategies to deal with stakeholders depending on their level of power and interest.

Low Interest – Low power: Direction

Their lack of interest and power makes them open to influence. They are more likely than others to accept what they are told and follow instructions.

High Interest – Low power: Education/communication

These stakeholders are interested in the strategy but lack the power to do anything. Management need to convince opponents to the strategy that the plans are justified; otherwise they will try to gain power by joining with parties in boxes C and D.

Low Interest – High power: Intervention

The key here is to keep these stakeholders satisfied to avoid them gaining interest and moving to box D. This could involve reassuring them of the outcomes of the strategy well in advance.

High Interest – High power: Participation

These stakeholders are the major drivers of change and could stop management plans if not satisfied. Management therefore need to communicate plans to them and then discuss implementation issues.

Stakeholder analysis table

The following table looks at the main stakeholder groupings and assesses the general concerns and objectives of each group.

Stakeholder group	General concerns/objectives	Example
Shareholders	<ul><li>A steady flow of income (dividends)</li><li>Possible capital growth</li><li>Continuation of business</li></ul>	If an organisation wishes to follow a strategy that will involve a large capital injection, the shareholders will be unhappy if the injection has an adverse effect on their income stream.
Directors/Managers	<ul><li>Pay and status</li><li>Job security</li><li>Individual performance measures</li></ul>	If an organisation wishes to follow a strategy that results in a particular department being reduced in size or abolished, the manager of that department is likely to be hostile to the plans.

Employees	• Job security • Pay and conditions • Job satisfaction	If an organisation wishes to follow a strategy that results in workers being given more responsibility for monitoring quality, the employees may be unhappy unless this increased role is supported by an increase in wages.
Trade unions	• The problems of the employees • Taking an active part in the decision-making process	If an organisation wishes to follow a strategy that results in a manufacturing plant being closed, the union will be unhappy if it has not been consulted and if there is no scheme for helping the employees find alternative employment.
Customers	• Receiving goods and services of a reasonable quality • Paying a reasonable price for those goods and services	If an organisation wishes to follow a strategy that increases the quality of a product at the same time as increasing the price, *existing* customers may not be willing to pay more for the product, while *new* customers are not attracted to a product that they will view as being of low quality.

Suppliers	• Being paid promptly for goods and services delivered • Receiving regular repayments of any capital provided (e.g. banks)	If an organisation wishes to follow a strategy that improves the working capital management by paying suppliers late, existing suppliers may decide to stop supplying the organisation, leading to the increased cost of finding new suppliers.
Government / pressure groups / the general public and local people	• The organisation is meeting relevant legal requirements • The organisation does not harm the outside environment	If an organisation wishes to follow a strategy that relies on increased use of shops based in out-of-town retail centres, this will be affected by government attitudes towards increased road building and society's attitude towards this method of shopping.

Test your understanding 1

Chatman Theatre is a charitable trust with the objective of making multicultural films and stage productions available to a regional audience. The organisation is not for profit. The aim to bring diversity of films, plays and dance that would otherwise be inaccessible to a regional audience.

The theatre needs to have strict budget focus, since a charity can become bankrupt. In order to achieve the required income, relationships must be built with a range of stakeholders.

Required:

Identify a few key stakeholders and ideas that would assist in building relationships.

(10 marks)

Strategic analysis

> **Managing stakeholders in different organisations**
>
> Consider three different types of organisation that are investigating the same strategy of bringing down costs by reducing wages and making employees work more flexible shifts.
>
> The first step is to identify the main stakeholders affected by the decision, and assess their level of power and interest. From this analysis, the Mendelow matrix can be used to guide management on how to manage the stakeholders.
>
> ### Organisation 1 – Contract cleaning company
>
> - The main employees affected will be the cleaners themselves.
> - Since unskilled workers are easy to replace, they have high interest in the decision but low power.
> - From the Mendelow matrix, the strategy here should be **'keep informed'**.
> - The organisation will therefore keep the cleaners informed of the decision but will probably impose the decision on the workforce.
> - This imposition is likely to be enacted quickly, i.e. the strategy will take place almost immediately.
>
> ### Organisation 2 – Accountancy training company
>
> - The main employees affected will be the lecturers.
> - Since these lecturers are very difficult to replace, they have high interest in the decision and high power.
> - From the Mendelow matrix, the strategy here should be **'key players'**.
> - The organisation may not be able to enforce their strategy without the cooperation of the lecturers. It may decide that this strategy will not succeed.

> **Organisation 3 – Local public library service**
>
> - The main employees affected will be the library staff.
> - They will have high interest in the decision.
> - Although these employees may be easy to replace, they are likely to be highly unionised. The power of the union will affect the decision-making process.
> - From the Mendelow matrix, the strategy here will be **'keep informed'** if the union power is deemed to be low and **'key players'** if the union power is deemed to be high.
> - The organisation may decide to consult with the union before any final decisions are made.
> - Owing to the lengthy procedures that often exist within the public sector, it is likely that any change in working conditions will be subject to a number of reviews, and implementation will not be rapid.

3 Managing stakeholder conflict

The objectives of the stakeholder groups will inevitably be different and may be in direct conflict. For example, the staff's desire for better pay and work conditions may conflict with the shareholders' desire for higher profits and the customers' desire for lower prices. The job of management is to develop and implement strategy with these differences in mind. This can be further complicated in organisations where the employees are also shareholders.

The techniques available to resolve conflict are:

- *Prioritisation*. Management can specify that any strategy considered must at a minimum satisfy one or more specific objectives before they are prepared to consider it.

- *Weighting and scoring* objectives in terms of importance. Each objective is weighted according to its relative importance to the organisation. Each strategic option is scored according to how well it satisfies the objective. A ranking is calculated for each option by multiplying its weighting by its score, and the strategic option with the highest overall ranking is accepted.

- Creation of a wider *balanced scorecard* set of performance measures.

Cyert and March suggest the following rational techniques that are not so obvious:

- *Satisficing* usually by negotiation to keep most and not necessarily all powerful stakeholders happy. It usually emerges as a result of negotiation between the competing stakeholders.

- *Sequential attention* by giving stakeholders turns to realise their objectives. Therefore, staff may get a large pay rise every 3 years but, in between, pay remains static while dividends are paid.

- *Side payments* where compensation is given to make up for not addressing particular stakeholders' objectives. For example, a local community may have a new leisure centre built by a company whose new superstore will inevitably increase noise and traffic congestion in the area.

- *Exercise of power* where deadlock is overcome by powerful figures forcing through their preferred strategic option.

Stakeholders' competing objectives

Traditionally, the shareholders' objectives have been translated into financial objectives such as profit or profitability (e.g. return on capital employed or earnings per share).

These accounting measures have several drawbacks when used as strategic targets:

- They are not useful for start-up businesses. During their first few years, many firms do not make a profit or return a positive cash flow due to the high costs of set-up and getting established in the market. Profitability measures are better suited to mature businesses.

- They are inherently short-termist. Because profit is an annual measure, it encourages management to focus on short-term returns at the expense of the long-term development of the business. Hence, managers may decide to cut product development, promotion or staff development to improve profit performance at the expense of the long term.

- They provide no control over strategic behaviour. The profit figure is a financial summary of the effects of a year's economic activity. The competitive strategy of the firm will seek to do business in particular ways in order to make this profit. This strategy should also feature in the goal structure.

- They can be manipulated by creative accounting. Consequently, the strategic targets of firms usually contain a mixture of financial and non-financial measures of performance. These ensure that:
  - managers follow courses of action consistent with the competitive strategy;
  - shareholders and others can form an opinion of the success of the firm's strategy even when financial results are low; the strategic objectives can be more easily translated into tactical and operational;
  - objectives for divisions and processes without an immediately discernible impact on profits (e.g. human resources, marketing, etc.).

The debate on the primacy of financial targets widens when we recognise the impact of other stakeholders and the issues of corporate social responsibility.

Maximisation of shareholder wealth as an objective

Traditional economic theory specifies that the objective of the firm is to maximise profit. However, this assumption does not accurately reflect the goals of the shareholder for a number of reasons:

- It is a **single-period measure** (typically annual). The shareholder wants financial returns across many years.
- It **ignores risk.** Shareholders will require higher returns if risks are higher but will be satisfied with lower returns if risks are low.
- It **confuses profit with cash flows to the investor**. The investor wants cash flows, not a figure for profit on the income statement.

A more appropriate version of rational shareholder objectives is either **maximisation of the present value of the free cash flows** of the business, or **maximisation of the share price**.

Competing objectives

It has been shown that profit-seeking, not-for-profit and public sector organisations may have competing objectives arising from:

- conflict between profit and social responsibilities
- differences in the goals of particular managers
- conflicts between the goals of influential stakeholder groups.

This has important implications in the following areas:

- *Development of consistent strategies.* If the organisation does not have clear objectives, or if its objectives are in conflict with one another, then it will not be able to follow consistent courses of action. For example, a firm that seeks to satisfy objectives for short-term dividends while also pursuing long-term growth will eventually be forced to sacrifice one or the other due to lack of funds.

- Deciding between strategic options. Options are evaluated against the objectives of the business before management agree to devote resources. However, if one option provides a good financial return while another provides jobs in an area of high unemployment, a firm with both financial and social responsibility objectives will not be able to choose.

- Development of appropriate performance measures. The more objectives an organisation has, the more control measures it will need to monitor performance towards them. If the objectives are competing, there is a danger of conflicting signals or, worse, excessive focus on one at the expense of the rest. For example, a school will have many objectives such as producing good citizens, ensuring emotional development, catering for special needs, and so on. However, parents and government prefer to have a single measure to decide whether a school is performing well or badly and tend to focus on examination results. This immediately distorts behaviour in the school towards exam results at the expense of other equally worthy objectives.

Test your understanding 2

Required:

(a) Prepare a list of what you think the organisational and management objectives of a town's public swimming pool funded by a local authority might be.

(5 marks)

(b) Explain how the 'three Es approach' of the Audit Commission may be applied by the swimming pool management.

(5 marks)

(c) Identify and analyse the stakeholders of the swimming pool.

(10 marks)

4 Corporate Appraisal (SWOT)

Look back to the diagram of the rational model in the previous chapter, you can see that once the mission and objectives have been set, the next stage is analysis. Analysis is made up of internal and external analysis which feed into corporate appraisal.

Corporate appraisal (SWOT) provides the framework to summarise the key outputs from the external and internal analysis. Corporate appraisals are useful for organisations in a number of ways:

- they provide a critical appraisal of the strengths, weaknesses, opportunities and threats affecting the organisation.
- they can be used to view the internal and external situation facing an organisation at a particular point in time to assist in the determination of the current situation.
- they can assist in long-term strategic planning of the organisation.
- they help to provide a review of an organisation as a whole or a project.
- they can be used to identify sources of competitive advantage.

How to carry out a good SWOT analysis

- Identify key strengths, weaknesses, opportunities and threats. It can be useful to show them as follows:

Resource Based (Internal)

S	W
• The things we are doing well • The things we are doing that the competition are not • Major successes	• The things we are doing badly (need to correct or improve) • The things we are not doing but should be • Major failures
O	**T**
• Events or changes in the external environment that can be exploited • Things likely to go well in the future	• Events or changes in the external environment we need to protect ourselves from or defend ourselves against • Things likely to go badly in the future

Position Based (External)

Strategic analysis

- Try to suggest how to convert weaknesses to strengths, threats to opportunities
- Advise on how to remove weaknesses that leave the organisation exposed to threats
- Match strengths to opportunities
- Remember, if something is a threat to us, it is likely to be a threat to our rivals. Can we exploit this?

The strengths and weaknesses normally result from the organisation's internal factors, and the opportunities and threats relate to the external environment. The strengths and weaknesses come from internal position analysis, using tools such as resources audits and Porter's value chain, and the opportunities and threats come from external position analysis using tools such as PEST(EL) and Porter's five forces model.

The analysis tools used in corporate appraisal can be summarised as shown below: These tools will be looked at in more detail in this chapter.

Elements of SWOT	Environment	Analytical tools
Strengths and Weaknesses	Internal	- Resources audit - Porter's value chain
Opportunities and Threats	External	- PEST(EL) - Porter's five forces

Test your understanding 3

Envie Co owns a chain of retail clothing stores specialising in ladies' designer fashion and accessories. Jane Smith, the original founder, has been pleasantly surprised by the continuing growth in the fashion industry during the last decade.

The company was established 12 years ago, originally with one store in the capital city. Jane's design skills and entrepreneurial skills have been the driving force behind the expansion. Due to unique designs and good quality control, the business now has ten stores in various cities.

Each store has a shop manger that is completely responsible for managing the staff and stock levels within each store. They produce monthly reports on sales. Some stores are continually late in supplying their monthly figures.

> Envie runs several analysis programmes to enable management information to be collated. The information typically provides statistical data on sales trends between categories of items and stores. The analysis and preparation of these reports are conducted in the marketing department. In some cases the information is out of date in terms of trends and variations.
>
> As the business has developed Jane has used the service of a local IT company to implement and develop their systems. She now wants to invest in website development with the view of reaching global markets.
>
> **Required:**
>
> (a) Construct a SWOT analysis with reference to the proposal of website development.
>
> **(8 marks)**
>
> (b) Explain how the use of SWOT analysis may be of assistance to Envie Co.
>
> **(5 marks)**

5 Internal analysis

The first element which is required to feed into the corporate appraisal is internal analysis. Internal analysis is needed in order to determine the possible future strategic options by appraising the organisations internal resources and capabilities. This involves identifying those things that the organisation is particularly good at in comparison to that of its competitors.

Two key techniques that can be used for internal analysis are

- an audit of resources and competences
- Porter's value chain model.

Resources audit

The resources audit identifies the resources that are available to an organisation and seeks to start the process of identifying competencies.

Resources are usually grouped under four headings:

- Physical or operational resources (e.g. land, machinery, IT systems).
- Human resources (e.g. labour, organisational knowledge).
- Financial resources (e.g. cash, positive cash flows, access to debt or equity finance).
- Intangibles (e.g. patents, goodwill).

Resources can be identified as either basic or unique:

- **Basic resources** are similar to those of competitors and will be easy to obtain or copy.
- **Unique resources** will be different from competitors and difficult to attain. The more unique resources an organisation has, the stronger its competitive position will be.

The key is to know what you have available to you and how this will help you in any strategic initiative. At the same time the organisation needs to know what it is lacking and how things may change in the future.

Competences can also be classified into two types:

- **Threshold competences** – attainment avoids competitive disadvantage. It represents those processes, procedures and product characteristics that are necessary to enter a particular market.
- **Core competences** – attainment gives the basis for competitive advantage over others within that market, or to change the competitive forces in that market to our advantage.

Over time core competences can become threshold as customer expectations develop and organisations battle for competitive advantage.

A competence audit analyses how resources are being deployed to create competences and the processes through which these competences may be linked. The key to success is usually found at this level.

Source of distinctive capabilities

Kay (1997) writes of distinctive capabilities arising from four sources:

(1) *Competitive architecture.* These are the relationships that make up the organisation. These can be divided into:
   - internal architecture: relations with employees;
   - external architecture: relations with suppliers and customers;
   - network architecture: relations between a group of collaborating firms.

   These deliver distinctive capabilities that are greater than the sum of the parts.

(2) *Reputation.* This is the high esteem that the public have for the firm. Among customers, it is a reason to buy the product and to remain loyal, while for investors, suppliers and potential employees, it is a reason to become involved and give exceptional levels of support to the firm. Kay argues that reputation must be built and maintained over time and requires detailed attention to all aspects of the firm's products, procedures and processes.

(3) *Innovative ability.* This is the ability to develop new products, services or solutions. These stave off competitors and enable the firm to enjoy the high margins of early lifecycle markets. Innovation frequently demands collaboration among staff and with suppliers and customers. Consequently, it builds on the architectures of the firm.

(4) *Ownership of strategic assets.* This is close to the barriers to entry discussed earlier. The firm may have a unique source of materials or possess exclusive legal rights to a market or invention.

Stalk et al. (1992) suggest four principles of capabilities-based competition:

(1) The building blocks of corporate strategy are business processes, not products and markets.

(2) Competitive success depends on the ability to transform these processes into strategic capabilities able to provide superior value to the customer.

(3) Creating these capabilities requires group-wide investments that transcend traditional functional or business unit boundaries.

(4) Therefore, the champion of capabilities-based strategy is the chief executive officer (CEO).

Superior competitive performance will result from the firm using these competences to outperform rivals on five dimensions:

- Speed. More able to incorporate new ideas and technologies into its products.
- Consistency. All its innovations satisfy the customer.
- Acuity. Ability to see its environment clearly and forecast changing needs.
- Agility. Ability to adapt on many fronts simultaneously.
- Innovativeness. Ability to generate and combine business ideas in novel ways.

Test your understanding 4

"Over time core competencies become threshold."

Required:

Discuss the above statement in relation to the mobile phone industry.

(10 marks)

Porter's Value Chain

The second model used for internal analysis is Porter's value chain. Michael Porter suggested that the internal position of an organisation can be analysed by looking at how the various activities performed by the organisation added or did not add value, in the view of the customer. This can be established by using **'the value chain model'**.

This is a model of value activities, those activities that procure inputs, process the inputs, and add value to them in some way to generate outputs for customers, and the relationships between those activities.

Value activity

This is a physically and technologically distinct activity that a firm performs. They are value activities because they should add value to a product or service.

How is it used?

The value chain can be used to design a competitive strategy, by utilising the activities in a strategic manner, it helps identify areas to reduce costs and increase margins. By exploiting linkages in the value chain and improving activities an organisation can obtain a competitive advantage.

Porter views the individual firm as a sequence of value creating activities instead of as an organisation chart detailing business functions. He suggests the business unit of the organisation can be visualised as a business system:

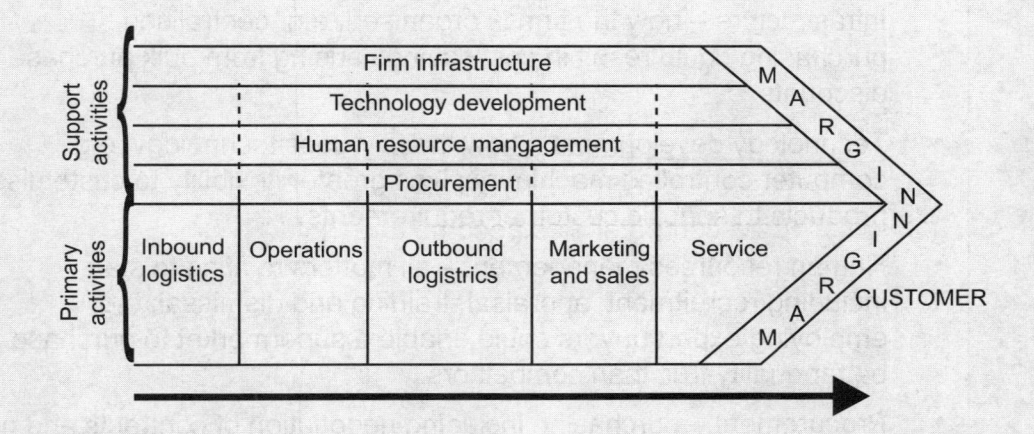

	Firm infrastructure				
Support activities	Technology development				
	Human resource management				
	Procurement				
Primary activities	Inbound logistics	Operations	Outbound logistics	Marketing and sales	Service

→ CUSTOMER (MARGIN)

Value chain detail for a manufacturing company

Primary activities

Those activities involved in the physical creation of the product and its sale and distribution to the buyer as well as after sales service. They add value to the product or service.

- Inbound logistics – receiving, storing and handling raw material inputs; e.g. a just in time system could give a cost advantage.

- Operations – transformation of raw materials into finished goods services; e.g. using skilled craftsmen could give a quality advantage.

- Outbound logistics – storing, distributing and delivering finished goods to customers; e.g. outsourcing delivery could give a cost advantage.

- **Sales and marketing** – making the customer aware of the product or service and providing them with opportunities to buy; e.g. sponsorship a sports celebrity could enhance the image of the product.
- **Service** – activities that occur after the point of sale, such as installation, training and repair; e.g. Marks and Spencer's approach to returns gives it a perceived quality advantage.

Support activities

Those activities that help the primary activities go more smoothly.

- **Infrastructure** – how the firm is organised; e.g. centralised purchasing could result in cost savings arising from bulk purchase discounts.
- **Technology development** – how the firm uses technology; e.g. computer controlled machinery gives greater flexibility to customise products to specific customer requirements.
- **Human resources management** – all matters relating to staff, including recruitment, appraisal, training and dismissal; e.g. employing expert buyers could enable a supermarket to purchase better quality fruit than competitors.
- **Procurement** – purchasing including negotiation of contracts and not restricted to raw materials; e.g. buying a building out of a town centre could give a cost advantage over high street competitors.

Linkages

Value activities are interdependent and connected by linkages.

Linkages exist when the way in which one activity is performed affects the cost and effectiveness of other activities – for example, IS/IT can identify where better information and systems are needed to improve or integrate the linkages; better quality production reduces the need for after sales service, which is the link between improving the operations to provide lower costs in the service area of the value chain.

Linkages require co-ordination, which can often be provided by information technology.

Competitors can often imitate the separate activities of a successful organisation, but it is more difficult to copy the linkages with and between the value chain activities.

An example of the value chain applied to the NHS

Primary activities

- Patients, who would either be transported by their own methods or by ambulances in order to receive the treatment.
- Drugs, dressings and other pharmaceutical supplies.
- Staff who may travel to and from hospitals, to and from other medical establishments and from either of the former to a patients home/destination and so on.
- Medical equipment, such as surgical instruments and monitors.
- Non medical equipment such as beds, linen, catering requirements, cleaning equipment and stationery.
- Warehousing of goods.

A wide range of **logistical activities** take place which are managed by different departments and others which are outsourced such as catering and cleaning. Where control of activities is outsourced there is a chance of a weak link. Think of the importance of cleanliness and nutrition to patient's health.

The **operations** transform the various inputs into the level of service. It is therefore a key link in the chain to ensure the correct level of service delivery.

The **marketing and sales** activities are responsible for raising awareness of the services provided by the NHS and the perception of the quality of service it supplies to the public. The NHS is split into multiple trusts with different specialisms. Inter trust relationships are key to the treatment of certain patients, which creates more linkages in the chain and thus more marketing relationships are required.

Secondary activities are sometimes called support activities as they support the primary activities mentioned above.

Procurement is 'the processes for acquiring the various resource inputs to the primary activities occurs in many parts of the organisation' (Johnson and Scholes). Within a complex organisation, such as a trust, there are many ways to procure goods and services from both the physical approach to the electronic methods.

Technology development ranges from the hospital Consultant's know-how, to computer systems used for medical records, to pharmacy systems linked to drugs. All of these will be managed by human resources some directly employed by the trust, some contracted to the trust and some working for contract companies contracted to the trust.

This is all held together by the **firm's infrastructure**, 'the systems of planning, finance, quality control, information management' (Johnson and Scholes).

Test your understanding 5

Angel Fabrics (AF) is a medium-sized manufacturer of clothing fabrics. Historically, AF has built-up a strong reputation as a quality fabric manufacturer with appealing designs, and has concentrated mainly on the women's market, producing fabrics to be made up into dresses and suits. The designs of the fabrics are mainly of a traditional nature but the fabrics, almost all woven from synthetic yarns, include all the novel features which the large yarn producers are developing.

Three years ago, AF decided that more profit and improved control could be obtained by diversifying through forward integration into designing and manufacturing the end products (i.e. clothes) in-house rather than by selling its fabrics directly to clothing manufacturing companies.

AF's intention had been to complement its fabric design skills with the skills of both dress design and production. This had been achieved by buying a small, but well-known, dress design and manufacturing company, specialising in traditional products, targeted mainly at the middle-aged and middle-income markets. This acquisition appears to have been successful, with combined sales turnover during the first two years increasing to $100 million (+34%) with a pre-tax profit of $14 million (+42%). This increased turnover and profit could be attributed to two main factors: firstly the added value generated by designing and manufacturing end-products, and secondly the increased demand for fabrics as AF was more able to influence their end-users more directly.

> In the last financial year, however, AF had experienced a slow down in its level of growth and profitability. AF's penetration of its chosen retail segment – the independent stores specialising in sales to the middle-class market – may well have reached saturation point. The business had also attempted to continue expansion by targeting the large multiple stores which currently dominate the retail fashion sector. Unfortunately, the buying power of such stores has forced AF to accept significantly lower, and potentially unacceptable, profit margins. The management team at AF believes that the solution is to integrate even further forward by moving into retailing itself. AF is now considering the purchase of a chain of small, but geographically dispersed, retail fashion stores. At the selling price of $35 million, AF would have to borrow substantially to finance the acquisition.
>
> **Required:**
>
> Consider how the AF strategy of forward integration into dress manufacturing has affected its ability to compete. Use Porter's value chain analysis.
>
> **(10 marks)**

6 External analysis

The second element to feed into the corporate appraisal is external analysis.

When establishing its strategy, an organisation should look at the various factors within its environment that may represent threats or opportunities and the competition it faces. This area will be developed further in the next chapter.

The analysis requires an external appraisal to be undertaken by scanning the business external environment for factors relevant to the organisations current and future activities.

External analysis can be carried out at different levels, as seen below. There are a number of strategic management tools that can assist in this process. These included the PEST(EL) framework which helps in the analysis of the macro or general environment and Porter's five forces model which can be used to analyse the industry or competitive environment.

Strategic analysis

Diagram: Two concentric circles. Outer: "The macro-environment (PEST(EL))". Inner: "Industry level (Porter's 5 forces)".

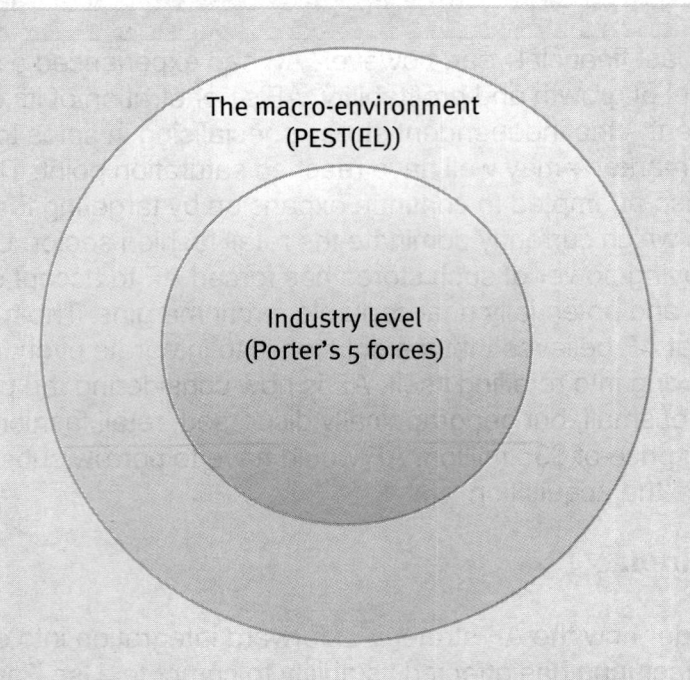

PEST(EL) analysis

The external environment consists of factors that cannot be directly influenced by the organisation itself. These include social, legal, economic, political and technological changes that the firm must try to respond to, rather than control. An important aspect of strategy is the way the organisation adapts to its environment. PEST(EL) analysis divides the business environment into four main systems – political, economic, social (and cultural), and technical. Other variants include legal and ecological/environmental.

PEST(EL) analysis is an approach to analysing an organisation's environment:

- **political influences and events** – legislation, government policies, changes to competition policy or import duties, etc.

- **economic influences** – a multinational company will be concerned about the international situation, while an organisation trading exclusively in one country might be more concerned with the level and timing of domestic development. Items of information relevant to marketing plans might include: changes in the gross domestic product, changes in consumers' income and expenditure, and population growth.

- **social influences** – includes social, cultural or demographic factors (i.e. population shifts, age profiles, etc.) and refers to attitudes, value and beliefs held by people; also changes in lifestyles, education and health and so on.

- **technological influences** – changes in material supply, processing methods and new product development.
- **ecological/environmental influences** – includes the impact the organisation has on its external environment in terms of pollution etc.
- **legal influences** – changes in laws and regulations affecting, for example, competition, patents, sale of goods, pollution, working regulations and industrial standards.

Once completed, the output from the PEST(EL) analysis will help to form the opportunities and threats part of the corporate appraisal.

Other frameworks

There are other examples of frameworks using acronyms for example:

DEEPLIST: demographic, economic, environment, political, legal, informational, social and technological.

Another variation is **LoNGPEST**, which adds a second dimension to the external environment which is the levels at which influences occur. For example local, national and global:

- Lo refers to the local level in which the organisation operates, for example the immediate city or region.
- N is concerned with the home country in which an organisation has its headquarters.
- G represents the global level, which becomes anything outside the local and national environments.
- The practical point for any organisation is that it is irrelevant which acronym is used as long as the process is practised within the company and that they remain aware of the business environment and the changes that are occurring within it.

Once completed, the output from the PEST(EL) analysis will help to form the opportunities and threats part of the corporate appraisal.

Illustration 2 – Applying the PEST(EL) model

In the United Kingdom, railways are facing major challenges. Customers are complaining about poor services. The government is reluctant to spend vast amounts of public money on developing the decaying infrastructure. The inflated costs of commuting by car, such as fuel and congestion charges, are increasing the number of people wanting to use the railways.

Required:

Construct an outline PESTLE analysis for the UK railway industry.

Solution:

Political

The balance of public – private involvement in the running costs and capital investments for rail development is a major issue.

Economic

The growth of commuter travel on the rail system means it is working at close to full capacity. This trend is likely to continue with the rising costs of fuel, making car travel expensive.

There is a need for investment in infrastructure in areas such as longer platforms and new signal systems.

Financing this investment may be difficult.

Social/cultural

Increasing concerns about reliability, particularly in rural areas.

Concerns about the effect that railway construction and travel has on the environment.

Safety issues on trains and at railway stations.

Technological

The development of new train technologies such as the tilting train.

Also following the trends set by air travel by introducing ways to improve the customer experience. For example, offering internet access and on-train entertainment.

Legal

The legal framework for the regulation and power of the railways is a major issue for operators.

Environmental

Environmental impact of major infrastructure developments is a key issue.

Overall, the switch to rail travel is seen to have a positive environmental impact, reducing the congestion and pollution associated with car based travel.

Note: it does not matter under which category an influence has been listed. Some influences may be listed under several categories, for example, government regulation has both legal and political dimensions. All that matters is that regulation has been considered in the analysis.

Test your understanding 6

DM is the world's largest and best-known food service retailing group with more than 30,000 'fast-food' outlets in over 120 countries. Currently half of its restaurants are in the USA, where it first began 50 years ago, but up to 1,000 new restaurants are opened every year worldwide. Restaurants are wholly owned by the group (it has previously considered, but rejected, the idea of a franchising of operations and collaborative partnerships).

As market leader in a fiercely competitive industry, DM has strategic strengths of instant global brand recognition, experienced management, site development expertise and advanced technological systems. DM's basic approach works well in all countries and although the products sold in each restaurant are broadly similar, menus are modified to reflect local tastes. Analysts agree that it continues to be profitable because it is both efficient and innovative.

Strategic analysis

DM's future plans are to maximise global opportunities and continue to expand markets. DM has long recognised that the external environment can be very uncertain and consequently does not move into new locations or countries without first undertaking a full investigation.

You are part of a strategy steering team responsible for investigating the key factors concerning DM's entry for the first time into the restaurant industry in the Republic of Borderland.

Required:

(a) Justify the use of a PEST framework to assist your team's environmental analysis for the Republic of Borderland.

(5 marks)

(a) Discuss one main issues arising from each aspect of the framework.

(10 marks)

Porter's five forces

As well as the macro environmental factors, part of external analysis also requires an understanding of the industry level, or competitive, environment and what are likely to be the major competitive forces in the future. A well-established framework for analysing and understanding the nature of the competitive environment is Porter's five forces model

Porter emphasises that some industries and some positions within an industry are more attractive than others. Therefore central to business strategy is an analysis of industry attractiveness. Porter's five forces model identifies five competitive forces that help determine the level of profitability for an industry or for a firm within an industry.

BARRIERS TO ENTRY
- Which barriers exist?
- To what extent do they limit entry?
- Are we trying to get in or keep others out?

- Economies of scale
- Other cost advantages
- Capital requirements
- Access to distribution
- Patents, government policy
- Reactions of existing firms

GREATEST WHERE
- Competitors are of similar size
- Slow growth in market
- High fixed costs price wars to maintain turnover
- Lack of differentiation

POWER GREATEST WHERE
- Concentration of buyers
- Alternative sources of supply exist
- Cost of purchase is high proportion of total cost
- Threat of backward integration
- Low switching costs
- Buyers have low profits
- Buyers have full information

NEW ENTRANTS

POWER OF BUYERS

RIVALRY AMONGST COMPETITORS

POWER OF SUPPLIERS

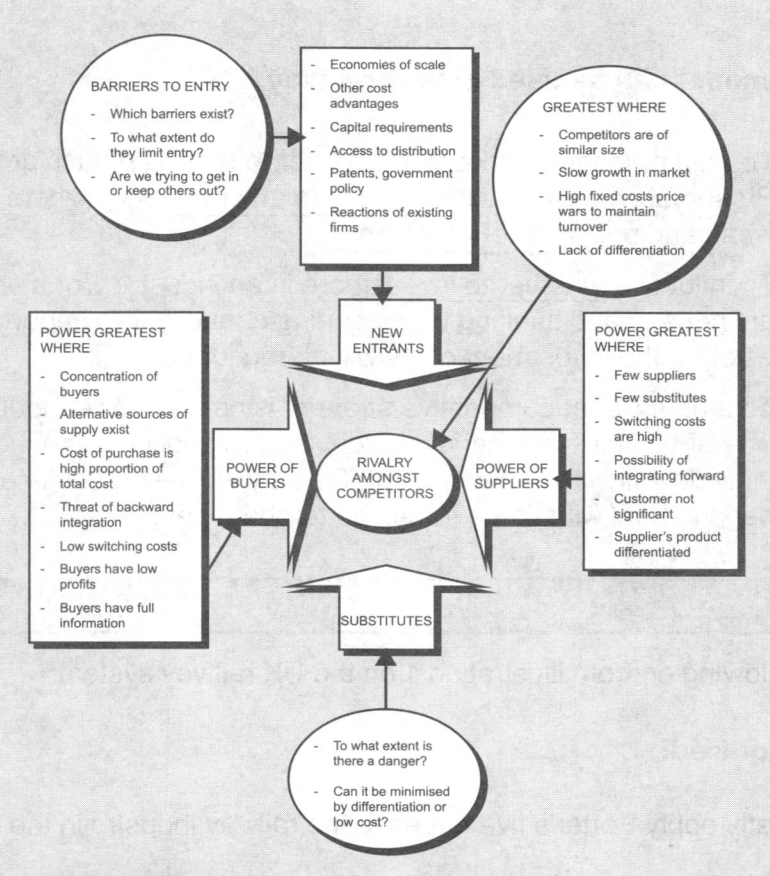

POWER GREATEST WHERE
- Few suppliers
- Few substitutes
- Switching costs are high
- Possibility of integrating forward
- Customer not significant
- Supplier's product differentiated

SUBSTITUTES
- To what extent is there a danger?
- Can it be minimised by differentiation or low cost?

Porter's five forces analysis

Just because a market is growing, it does not follow that it is possible to make money in it. Porter's five forces approach looks in detail at the firm's competitive environment by analysing five forces. These forces determine the profit potential of the industry.

(1) Threat of entry – new entrants into a market will bring extra capacity and intensify competition.

(2) Competition – existing competition & its intensity.

(3) Substitutes – This threat is across industries (e.g. rail travel v bus travel v private car).

(4) Bargaining power of buyers – powerful buyers can force price cuts and/or quality improvements.

(5) Bargaining power of suppliers – to charge higher prices.

Strategic analysis

The model can be used in several ways:

- To help management decide whether to enter a particular industry. Presumably, they would only wish to enter the ones where the forces are weak and potential returns high.

- To influence whether to invest more in an industry. For a firm already in an industry and thinking of expanding capacity, it is important to know whether the investment costs will be recouped.

- To identify what competitive strategy is needed. The model provides a way of establishing the factors driving profitability in the industry. For an individual firm to improve its profitability above that of its peers, it will need to deal with these forces better than they.

Illustration 3 – Applying Porter's five forces model

Following on from illustration 1 on the UK railway system:

Required:

Briefly apply Porter's five forces to the railway industry in the UK.

Solution:

Competitive rivalry

This is largely down to the way the industry operates. Passenger rail services in the UK are divided into regional franchises and run by various operating companies. These companies bid for seven to eight year contracts to run individual franchises. Some firms, including First Group, National Express Group and Stagecoach Group, run multiple franchises.

Some routes will allow more than one operating company, this is particularly the case on longer distance routes, for example journeys from Scotland to London. On these routes, rail operators may be directly competing with other operators and there can be strong rivalry. For other routes, generally the shorter, local rotes, the franchise will only be granted to a single operator who will face no competition from other rail operators.

Substitutes

There are other forms of transport available such as travel by road (e.g. cars and buses) and travel by air.

Buyers

Severe competition over price with low-cost airlines on longer city routes.

Online price comparisons make it easy for customers to select lowest cost option.

New entrants

New companies may enter the market when rail franchises become available for re-tender, although the high capital cost is a barrier to new entrants, as is the need to successfully tender for an available franchise.

Virgin entered the market in the mid 1990, and initially won two rail franchises, although one of these was lost in 2007.

In 1997 Virgin placed the largest rolling-stock order (£1bn) in British history, for new electric tilting trains. By December 2004 Virgin Trains had replaced all the rolling stock it had inherited from British Rail.

Suppliers

With an increasing number of discrete rail and train operators, the allocation of capacity becomes an issue. This is similar to landing slots at airports.

Further detail on Porter's five forces

Barriers to entry

- *Economies of scale*, where the industry is one where unit costs decline significantly as volume increases, such that a new entrant will be unable to start on a comparable cost basis.

- *Product differentiation*, where established firms have good brand image and customer loyalty. The costs of overcoming this can be prohibitive.

- *Capital requirements*, where the industry requires a heavy initial investment (e.g. steel industry, rail transport).

- *Switching costs*, i.e. one-off costs in moving from one supplier to another (e.g. a garage chain switching car dealership).

- *Restricted access to distribution channels* (e.g. for some major toiletry brands 90% of sales go through 12 buying points, i.e. chemist multiples and major retailers). Therefore it is difficult for a new toiletry product to gain shelf space.
- *Cost advantages of existing producers*, independent of economies of scale, e.g. patents, special knowledge, favourable access to suppliers, government subsidies.
- *Government policy;* the government can limit or even foreclose entry to industries with such controls as licence requirements and limits on access to raw materials.

Competition

Intensity of existing competition will depend on the following factors:

- Number and relative strength of competitors – where an industry is dominated by a few large companies rivalry is less intense (e.g. petrol industry, CD manufacture).
- Rate of growth – where the market is expanding, competition is low key.
- Where high fixed costs are involved, companies will cut prices to marginal cost levels to protect volume, and drive weaker competitors out of the market.
- If buyers can switch easily between suppliers the competition is keen.
- If the exit barrier (i.e. the cost incurred in leaving the market) is high, companies will hang on until forced out, thereby increasing competition and depressing profit.
- An organisation will be highly competitive if its presence in the market is the result of a strategic need.

Threat of substitute products

Porter explains that, 'substitutes limit the potential returns … by placing a ceiling on the price which firms in the industry can profitably charge'. The better the price-performance alternative offered by substitutes, the more readily customers will switch.

Bargaining power of buyers

Such factors could include the following:

- Where a buyer's purchases are a high proportion of the supplier's total business or represent a high proportion of total trade in that market.
- Where a buyer makes low profit.
- Where the quality of purchases is unimportant or delivery timing is irrelevant, prices will be forced down.
- Where products have been strongly differentiated with good brand image, a retailer would have to stock the range to meet customer demands.

Bargaining power of suppliers

Such factors could include the following:

- The degree to which switching costs apply and substitutes are available.
- The presence of one or two dominant suppliers controlling prices.
- The extent to which products offered have a uniqueness of brand, technical performance or design not available elsewhere.

Test your understanding 7

Porter suggested that a firm must assess the industry's market attractiveness by considering:

- the extent of the rivalry between existing competitors;
- the bargaining power of suppliers;
- the bargaining power of buyers;
- the threat of substitutes;
- the threat of new entrants.

Required:

(a) If a firm wishes to monitor the bargaining power of buyers, recommend the factors that should be included in the monitoring system implemented by the firm.

(10 marks)

(b) Explain four different methods whereby a firm can reduce the threat of new entrants to an industry.

(8 marks)

(c) Explain the reasons why firms often continue to operate in an industry which is generating below normal returns in the short run.

(7 marks)

Test your understanding 8

The directors of Johnson Packaging Co (JPC), a well-established manufacturer of cardboard boxes, are currently considering whether to enter the cardboard tube market. Cardboard tubes are purchased by customers whose products are wound around tubes of various sizes ranging from large tubes on which carpets are wound, to small tubes around which films and paper products are wound. The cardboard tubes are usually purchased in very large quantities by customers. On average, the cardboard tubes comprise between 1% and 2% of the total cost of the customers' finished product.

The directors have gathered the following information

- The cardboard tubes are manufactured on machines which vary in size and speed. The lowest cost machine is priced at $30,000 and requires only one operative for its operation. A one-day training course is required in order that an unskilled person can then operate such a machine in an efficient and effective manner.

- The cardboard tubes are made from specially formulated paper which, at times during recent years, has been in short supply.

- At present, four major manufacturers of cardboard tubes have an aggregate market share of 80%. The current market leader has a 26% market share. The market shares of the other three major manufacturers, one of which is JOL Co, are equal in size. The product ranges offered by the four major manufacturers are similar in terms of size and quality. The market has grown by 2% per annum during recent years.

- A recent report on the activities of a foreign-based multinational company revealed that consideration was being given to expanding operations in their packaging division overseas. The division possesses large-scale automated machinery for the manufacture of cardboard tubes of any size.

- Another company, Plastic Tubes Co (PTC) produces a narrow, but increasing, range of plastic tubes which are capable of housing small products such as film and paper-based products. At present, these tubes are on average 30% more expensive than the equivalent sized cardboard tubes sold in the marketplace.

Required:

Using Porter's five forces model, assess the attractiveness of the option to enter the market for cardboard tubes as an improved strategy for JPC.

(10 marks)

Evaluation of environmental models

The benefits from using recognised models, such as PEST(EL) and Porter's five forces, for external analysis:

- They ensure that management consider a wide range of potential impacts when devising strategy
- They allow the division of the work in environmental analysis – one team deal with buyers another team with suppliers
- They provide a common language between managers – Porter's five forces and PEST(EL)
- They provide insight into key strategic issues.

However, there are limitations in their use:

- They can distort reality – real business environments do not fit into neat segments

- They present the environment as external – distribution channels as separate and external
- They may cause management to overlook networks – joint ventures & strategic alliances
- They can overload management with analysis.

Data for environmental analysis

In carrying out their external analysis, organisations are faced with vast amounts of information that they must scan to understand their environment.

Responsibility for scanning for environmental data rests at three levels:

- Line management
- Strategic planning team
- Specialist units – business intelligence units.

The main types of information required in making an environmental analysis will cover the following areas.

The economic situation – a multinational company will be concerned about the international situation, while an organisation trading exclusively in one country might be more concerned with the level and timing of domestic development. Items of information relevant to marketing plans might include: changes in the gross domestic product, changes in consumers' income and expenditure, and population growth.

Government action – changes in taxation and subsidies, changes in government spending, import duties, etc.

Legal factors changes – in laws and regulations affecting, for example, competition, patents, sale of goods, pollution, working regulations and industrial standards.

Technological factors – changes in material supply, processing methods and new product development.

The importance of information as a resource cannot be over stressed. As pointed out by Diebold: 'Information, which is in essence the analysis and synthesis of data, will unquestionably be one of the most vital of corporate resources. It will be structured into models for planning and decision-making. It will be integrated into product design and marketing methods. In other words, information will be recognised and treated as an asset.'

Sources of information for environmental analysis

There are many sources of environmental information including:

Economic information from government statistics, trade and banking reports, market information from specialist libraries, etc.

Market information is information about a company's present or possible future markets. Such information will be both commercial and technical.

The **Internet** provides corporate planners with a powerful tool for environmental appraisal. The possibilities are almost without limit: Relations with trading partners – The use of web-based procurement systems has been exploited by a variety of enterprises who found greater freedom and greater effectiveness over more traditional methods such as electronic data interchange systems.

Commercial intelligence – Government agencies now all have websites and information is readily available from a variety of bodies such as Companies House, the Bank of England and internationally recognised credit intelligence agencies such as Dun and Bradstreet.

Specialist on-line databases – Access is possible to specialist on-line databases.

This area will be developed further in the next chapter.

7 Chapter summary

Mendelow Matrix
- Minimal effeort
- Keep informed
- Keep satisfied
- Key player

Stakeholders
- Identify
- Objectives
- Conflicts
- Interest & Power

PEST(EL)
- Political
- Economic
- Social
- Technological
- Environmental
- Legal

Strategic Analysis

Porter's value chain
- Primary activities
- Secondary activities

Corporate Appraisal (SWOT)
- Strengths
- Weaknesses
- Opportunities
- Threats

Internal Analysis

External Analysis

Resources audit
- Basic resources
- Unique resources
- Threshold competencies
- Core competencies

Porter's five forces
- Barriers to entry
- Power of buyers
- Power of suppliers
- Substitutes
- Rivalry

Test your understanding answers

Test your understanding 1

Loyal customers

Chatman Theatre, which is a charity, can use a database to profile the interests and wants of customers. A tailored communication can then be sent.

Given the need to contain costs, this might be by getting customers to sign up to e-list to get up-to-date news and information on future performances.

They could set up a website with booking facilities and send confirmation by email rather than post.

Develop a friend of the theatre group, giving discounts to regular loyal customers.

First time customers

The website could be linked to other relevant websites, such as local attractions and tourist boards, to attract new customers.

The theatre could produce an information pack to attract new mailing list subscribers.

These could be made available in local churches and shops.

Local arts groups

A partnership agreement could be established with arts groups, to co-sponsor events of special interests to given groups of customers.

Local organisations

Try to obtain commercial sponsorship from local companies. Acknowledgement could be given in the monthly programme mailings and preferential facilities offered for corporate hospitality.

Media

Personal invitations could be issued to opening nights, to interview the performers and give an overview of the show.

The above is just a selection of potential relationships with stakeholders.

Test your understanding 2

(a) The objectives of the facility will be derived in a hierarchy from the goals, which in turn would be drawn from the mission. The stakeholders' requirements would be taken into account in formulating the objectives.

The mission would briefly state why the pool exists, what is being provided and for whom it exists – basically what it is striving to achieve, e.g. 'to satisfy the swimming, recreation and entertainment needs of the people of ….'

Although goals are more specific than mission statements and have a shorter time-scale, they would be the ultimate, long-run, open-ended attributes the pool organisation seeks. They would cover the expectations of stakeholders in terms of improving the image, increasing the usage, operating a surplus for self-sustenance, or improving safety, etc.

A 'SMART' (specific, measurable, achievable, relevant and set to a time-scale) objective established by the management may be, for example, 'increasing the number of admissions by 5% by the end of the first quarter of 20X0'.

(b) The three Es are the elements of the phrase 'value for money' and relate to economy, effectiveness and efficiency.

Economy looks at the level of inputs, e.g. did the pool facility spend less on chemicals this year?

Effectiveness looks at the outputs to see if the goals are being achieved.

Efficiency looks at the link between outputs and inputs to ensure that the maximum output is obtained from the resources input.

(c) The pool facility's stakeholders, their general concerns, their level of interest and aspirations, and their level of power and influence have been identified in the table below.

Stakeholder	General concerns	Level of interest/ aspirations	Level of power/ influence	Response by management
Local Authority	Mission fulfilled. Good reputation and image. Funding utilised well. Facilities used by wide cross-section of public in the town.	Low	High	Keep satisfied in meeting expectations of: Financial soundness. Good image and reputation. Varied users.
Pool Committee	Mission fulfilled. Good reputation and image. Funding utilised well. Facilities used by wide cross-section of public in the town.	High	High	Key players. Ensure that they are fully informed at all times and proactively ensure that their expectations are met at all times.
Management	Receive adequate funding. Extensive usage. Implementing mission.	High	High	Committee will need to ensure that management are adequately resourced and motivated to fulfilling the mission.

Strategic analysis

Public	Value for money. Open at convenient times.	Low	Low	Minimal effort in terms of active management of public relations if the mission, goals and objectives are being achieved.
Employees	Job security. Pleasant environment. Job enrichment.	High	High	Key players who will require their needs to be met and satisfied in terms of motivation to achieve objectives.
Swimming Clubs and Associations	Value for money. Priority in usage. Specialised facilities.	High	High	Key players as special interest groups whose specific needs will have to be adequately fulfilled.

Test your understanding 3

SWOT Question – Envie Co

(a) **Strengths:**
Successful company
Steady increase in market share
Experience in the market
Founder's entrepreneurial skills
Good designs
Good quality control
Keen to exploit to technology
Strong IT

Weakness:
Management of information is often out of date
No in-house IT expertise
No web experience
Not sure if the new system will generate new sales
Lack of control over store managers
Out of date reporting from some stores
Over reliance on IT provider

Opportunities:
E-trading can provide a new sales channel and revenue stream
Identification and recording of customer details to enhance customer relationships
Extension of customer base
Global market potential
Cut costs in many areas
Create a vision of a modern company
Develop product range further
Look at employing an IT specialist

Threats:
Customer resistance to on-line shopping
Loss of unique identity; may become just another website trader
Resistance within the company
Effects on existing personnel and working conditions
Costs of developing the website may outweigh the benefits
Security issues
Loss of competitive edge

The above are suggested answers.

(b) The use of SWOT analysis will focus management attention on current strengths and weaknesses of the organisation which will be of assistance in formulating the business strategy. It will also enable management to monitor trends and developments in the changing business environment. Each trend or development may be classified as an opportunity or a threat that will provide a stimulus for an appropriate management response.

Management can make an assessment of the feasibility of required actions in order that the company may capitalise upon opportunities whilst considering how best to negate or minimise the effect of any threats.

Strategic analysis

Test your understanding 4

The mobile phone industry is a dynamic industry where products develop quickly and where customer expectations are continually rising.

Core competencies are those elements which make a company or a product stand out from its competitors. It gives the company competitive advantage.

Over time competitors catch up and develop these competencies for themselves which reduces the original advantage. What was originally an innovative or superior feature becomes the norm. To maintain competitive advantage companies must continually strive to develop their core competencies.

In the mobile phone industry we can see many examples of this.

In the early days of mobile phones, phones were large and clumsy and only enabled telephone calls. Over time phones became smaller and manufacturers competed to produce smaller and smaller units.

Then in 1993, Nokia developed the technology to incorporate the sending of text messages. This was innovative and generated huge interest from customers. Over time, all phones incorporated this technology and the advantage Nokia enjoyed disappeared. Now all mobiles have this technology as a minimum requirement.

Another development was the inclusion of a camera on a mobile. This was first developed by Sharp in 2000. Again over time this has become a basic function on a phone.

There have been many recent developments such as music players, smart phones, Internet access and GPS technology. Almost as soon as a new development is unveiled, the competitors quickly incorporate these features and they become threshold.

Mobile manufacturers need to constantly update their technology to keep ahead of the competitors.

Test your understanding 5

Angel Fabrics (AF) has chosen to use vertical integration to improve its profit and sales performances. This has, until now, been a successful strategy. By ensuring its customer base, increasingly controlled through ownership, it has been able to guarantee sales and utilisation of its fabrics.

The success has been brought about by the ability of the company to increase demand for its fabrics from its internal customers – the now integrated clothing manufacturer. In addition, AF has been able to increase the profit margins on its sales. Research has shown that the further a company moves 'downstream' in the manufacturing and distribution processes (that is, the nearer it is to the final consumer), the higher are the profit margins. This is because it becomes increasingly possible to differentiate and brand the product rather than operate in the commodity style environment as typified by normal fabric production – unless of course the fabric itself has a powerful brand identity, such as being Lycra-enhanced.

Michael Porter's value chain is provides a structure to show the benefits of vertical integration. It evaluates each step of the operations where value-added activities are provided. 'These value-added activities are the physically and technologically distinctive activities which the firm performs' (Porter). The inbound logistics enable the dress-manufacturing unit to have quality fabrics, delivered at the appropriate times, in the right quantity, from within the group. Problems associated with stockholding are minimised. Prices can be transferred between the relevant units to maximise their competitive position.

By creating a larger demand for yarns, the group is now able to counter-balance the power of the large yarn producers, ensuring supply and at competitive prices. So far, the firm has no control over the sale of its finished garments – the outbound logistics. This could occur if the decision to integrate further forward is agreed upon.

It is important to understand that each part of the operation has an impact upon other activities. A failure in one area because of the lack of control or influence can damage the overall performance. The value chain illustrates how marketing and service functions are critical in supporting the manufacturing and distribution activities. It also is important to ensure that each component part of the organisation from purchasing, design, operations (including the technology used), and quality control are integrated and mutually supportive.

Although vertical integration enables AF to exert increased control over its value chain, there is a danger in the loss of flexibility. In particular, the garment-manufacturing part of the group is obliged to buy from the fabric-producing part. This could prevent the purchase of cheaper materials from foreign suppliers, or the use of more attractively designed fabrics. Both of these constraints could reduce the competitiveness of the company. The benefits of the inter-company transfer pricing could lead to inefficiencies within the system – dulled incentives. The fabric-producing part of the organisation may become less competitive because it believes that it has a captive market with the garment-producing unit obliged to buy from it. This complacency could be reduced by insisting upon 'arm's length' trading between the constituent parts of the organisation.

Diversification through vertical integration could harm AF's core competences. By not 'sticking to the knitting', the company could reduce its competitive edge. It needs to concentrate on what it does best, and not become side-tracked into non-core activities. Furthermore, as AF vertically expands, it may become less responsive to environmental and technical change. This lack of flexibility could result in the company being out-manoeuvred by smaller but more focused firms. In addition, by being totally self-contained, the firm may be deprived of technical and marketing insights that might otherwise be available from outsiders.

The increase in fixed costs usually associated with vertical integration will mean a higher breakeven point for sales, and this will result in the company becoming more vulnerable to cyclical variations.

Test your understanding 6

(a) PEST analysis examines the broad environment in which the organisation is operating. PEST is a mnemonic which stands for Political/legal, Economic, Social and Technological factors. These are simply four key areas in which to consider how current and future changes affect the business. Strategies can then be developed which address any potential opportunities and threats identified.

In entering a new overseas market, an environmental analysis is important to help the organisation understand the factors specific to that market so that the specific opportunities and threats posed can be assessed and appropriate action taken.

It is a useful tool for the following reasons:

– It ensures completeness. The majority of issues relevant to an organisation will be covered under one of the four areas of PEST analysis. By reviewing all four areas, DM can be sure that it has done a full and complete analysis of the broad environment.

- All four elements are relevant to examining new markets:
  - *Political/legal*: Each new country entered will have different political systems and laws. DM will need to understand these differences to ensure that they operate within the law in Borderland. They will also want to ensure that there is political stability within the country which will ensure long-term viability of the new operations.
  - *Economic:* Economies are different in different parts of the world. Understanding the local economy in Borderland and how it is expected to develop enables DM to assess the potential within that market as well as any economic issues which they need to consider.
  - *Social*: Each country will have its own cultural differences, and DM can change how they operate depending on Borderland's culture. DM has already shown its willingness to change for each country's different tastes and will want to do so in Borderland too.
  - *Technological*: Each country has a different level of technological expertise and experience. DM might need to change processes to accommodate local systems, or implement training programmes for staff unfamiliar with their technology.
- It is a well-known tool which is easy to understand and use. PEST analysis is a very simple tool that does not require detailed understanding. This means that it is easy to use by the team and simple for Directors to analyse and understand.

(b) Note: The answer has provided a more complete solution than would be required.

Political/legal factors:

- Government grants: Some countries may have grants available for investment in the country. Considering the requirements to gain such grants may enable DM to make use of these.
- Political stability: Given DM's worldwide penetration (over 120 countries) it is likely that Borderland is in a developing region which may be more politically unstable than many countries in which they currently operate. This may affect the long-term potential in the market.
- Regulation on overseas companies: There may be regulation on how overseas companies can operate in the market. In China, for instance, it is common for joint ventures with local companies to be a prerequisite for western companies entering the market.

- Employment legislation: Each country will have different employment legislation e.g. health and safety, minimum wages, employment rights. DM may have to change internal processes from the US model to stay within this legislation within Borderland. Being a good employer is also one of DM's specific strategies.

- Tax legislation: Tax laws will impact the profits available for distribution to the group. High tax levels may discourage DM from entering the market.

- Tariffs and other barriers to trade. Tariffs may be imposed on imports into Borderland. This may put DM at a significant disadvantage compared with local competitors if they aim to import a significant number of items (unlikely on food items, more likely on clothing, fittings etc).

Economic factors

- Economic prosperity: The more prosperous the nation the more money people will have to invest in 'fast-food'. Examining the current and likely future prosperity enables the organisation to understand the potential of this market and the likely future investment required.

- Interest rates: This affects the cost of borrowing within Borderland. If high it may mean overseas funding is necessary. A big differential between interest rates in Borderland and the US is also likely to cause instability in the exchange rate (see below). Interest rates also affect the availability of money for the people of the country. Low interest rates mean more disposable income to spend increasing the potential for DM.

- Exchange rates: DM will be affected by exchange rates for items they export to Borderland (clothing, fittings). An unfavourable movement in exchange rates could make exporting to Borderland expensive and reduce profitability. It can also affect the value of profits when converted back to US dollars.

- Position in economic cycle: Different countries are often at different positions in the economic cycle of growth and recession. The current position of Borderland will affect the current prosperity of the nation and the potential for business development for DM.

- Inflation rates: High inflation rates create instability in the economy which can affect future growth prospects. They also mean that prices for supplies and prices charged will regularly change and this difficulty would need to be considered and processes implemented to account for this.

Social factors

- Brand reputation/anti-Americanism: As a global brand, the reputation of DM might be expected to have reached Borderland. If not, more marketing will be required. If it has, the reputation will need to be understood and the marketing campaign set up accordingly.

  This is particularly relevant given the anti-Americanism which is prevalent currently in some countries. DM may have a significant hurdle to climb to convince people to eat there if this is the case in Borderland.

- Cultural differences: Each country has its own values, beliefs, attitudes and norms of behaviours which means that people of that country may like different foods, architecture, music and so on, in comparison with US restaurants. By adapting to local needs DM can ensure it wins local custom and improve its reputation. Different cultures also need to be considered when employing people, especially given the importance to DM of employee relations. People might have different religious needs to be met or may dislike being given autonomy so the management style needs changing.

- Language problems: Different local languages can create problems, firstly in communication with staff. Secondly, product names need to be considered to ensure they are acceptable in the local language. General Motor's Nova suggested that 'it won't go' in Spanish, for example.

Technological factors

DM may need to train people in the use of their technologies if the local population are unfamiliar with them e.g. accounting systems or tills. In addition, technology might have to be adapted to work in local environments, such as different electrical systems.

Test your understanding 7

(a) The bargaining power of buyers represents a major factor in establishing the attractiveness of an industry. It is therefore important that the power of buyers is monitored in order that organisations are aware of the forces which are important in the development of a strategic plan. Factors which will influence the relative bargaining strength of the buyers include:
- the number of different buyers and sellers in the market;
- the relative size of both the buying and selling organisations;
- the buyer's purchases are large in relation to the total sales of each seller, as a major customer can often dictate terms and conditions, especially if the cost structure of the seller includes a high level of fixed costs;
- the level of profit earned by the buyers is low;
- the product is undifferentiated;
- the 'switching costs' are low;
- the quality of the component purchased is not particularly important in the final product;
- the extent to which buyers can undertake backward integration.

There will be a number of different sources of information that could be obtained to enable a firm to monitor the bargaining strength of buyers. These include:

- Details can be obtained from the financial reports of companies buying the product. The gross margins they report give an indication of the potential for their suppliers to raise prices if the buyer power could be reduced.
- The uniqueness of the technical specification of the product could be considered to reveal whether it is unique or whether several suppliers are capable of making it.
- A survey of the structure of the supply industry will reveal the number and location of alternative suppliers. Estimates can be made of their ability to supply and the costs of transport that might be involved.
- Information may be published by specialist organisations such as industry groups, and ad hoc reports could be commissioned.

(b) There are a number of different barriers to entry that are likely to reduce the number of potential entrants to the industry. Potential competitors can be deterred and competitive advantage retained by any of the following:

- Patents, licences and government/legal constraints. It is possible for a firm to use any of these as a form of protection and to prevent new entrants to the industry. Once this type of legal barrier has been obtained by a firm, it can be of great value in retaining competitive advantage.

- Branding or customer loyalty (differentiation). Often at considerable expense, an organisation will try to establish customer loyalty which will ensure that people will buy the product in preference to other brands and substitutes that are available.

- Economies of scale including the learning curve. In some industries, large-scale operations can produce the products at a lower cost than the smaller producers. This provides an example of 'overall cost leadership' which can be very significant in planning for competitive advantage.

- Access to cheaper factors of production. Some firms are able to produce products at a lower cost, as they have been able to obtain materials, labour, finance or other expenses at a lower rate than their competitors.

- Switching costs. The ability to change to another supplier without many costs being incurred. Incumbent firms can increase these by offering volume discounts, special delivery facilities or electronic ordering systems.

- Control of unique distribution channels. If a firm can exclude other producers from distributing their products through the most effective distribution channels, then this can represent a significant entry barrier.

- The scale of investment needed to establish the operation. If the amount of investment is so large that most competitors are unable to consider entering the industry, this represents a way in which potential competitors can be excluded and the existing firms have competitive advantage and possibly even a monopoly.

- Technological advantages that result in cost leadership. Successful research and development often results in a firm having a process that reduces the cost of production so that competitors are unable to compete on a level playing field. This gives the firm that has invested in the R&D an important advantage over their competitors and will exclude potential entrants to the industry.

(c) There are exit barriers that result in firms remaining in an industry, even though the returns are below the normal level. When a firm realises that the probability of success is low or acknowledges that there is excess capacity in the industry, a decision to close may be appropriate. However, decisions of this kind are often postponed. This is likely to occur if the closure will result in substantial costs being incurred by the firm. These are termed exit costs. In general terms, the costs of closure are estimated to be higher than continuing the operation.

Particular costs are redundancy payments to staff or long-term supply contracts that will result in damages being due as a result of breaking the contract. In these situations, the closing may be delayed until a more appropriate time. The ownership of assets with no resale value or assets shared with other processes could be another factor that delays the decision to close an operation. Similarly, common costs that are absorbed by a particular process may influence the decision to close down a portion or the whole of an operation. Apart from the exit costs, a firm may decide to stay in an industry because the market has a strategic importance to the firm. For example, a commercial bank may continue to provide current (checking) accounts despite their low profitability because they are the cornerstone of a client relationship from which more valuable products can be sold.

Test your understanding 8

In order to assess the attractiveness of the option to enter the market for spirally-wound paper tubes, the directors of JPC could make use of Michael Porter's five forces model.

In applying this model to the given scenario one might conclude that the relatively low cost of the machine together with the fact that an unskilled person would only require one day's training in order to be able to operate a machine, constitute relatively low costs of entry to the market. Therefore one might reasonably conclude that the threat of new entrants might be high. This is especially the case where the market is highly fragmented.

The fact that products are usually purchased in very large quantities by customers together with the fact that there is little real difference between the products of alternative suppliers suggests that customer (buyer) power might well be very high. The fact that the paper tubes on average only comprise between 1% and 2% of the total cost of the purchaser's finished product also suggests that buyer power may well be very high.

The threat from suppliers could be high due to the fact that the specially formulated paper from which the tubes are made is sometimes in short supply. Hence suppliers might increase their prices with consequential diminution in gross margin of the firms in the marketplace.

The threat from competitive rivals will be strong as the four major players in the market are of similar size and that the market is a slow growing market. The market leader currently has 26% of the market and the three nearest competitors hold approximately 18% of the market.

The fact that Plastic Tubes Co (PTC) produces a narrow range of plastic tubes constitutes a threat from a substitute product. This threat will increase if the product range of PTC is extended and the price of plastic tubes is reduced.

The fact that a foreign-based multinational company is considering entering this market represents a significant threat from a potential new entrant as it would appear that the multinational company might well be able to derive economies of scale from large scale automated machinery and has manufacturing flexibility.

Low capital barriers to entry might appeal to JPC but they would also appeal to other potential entrants. The low growth market, the ease of entry, the existence of established competitors, a credible threat of backward vertical integration by suppliers, the imminent entry by a multi-national, a struggling established competitor and the difficulty of differentiating an industrial commodity should call into question the potential of JPC to achieve any sort of competitive advantage. If JPC can achieve the position of lowest cost producer within the industry then entry into the market might be a good move. In order to assess whether this is possible JPC must consider any potential synergies that would exist between its cardboard business and that of the tubes operation.

From the information available, the option to enter the market for cardboard tubes appears to be unattractive. The directors of JPC should seek alternative performance improvement strategies.

Strategic analysis

chapter 4

Competitive environments

Chapter learning objectives

- Distinguish between different types of competitive environments.

Competitive environments

1 Session content diagram

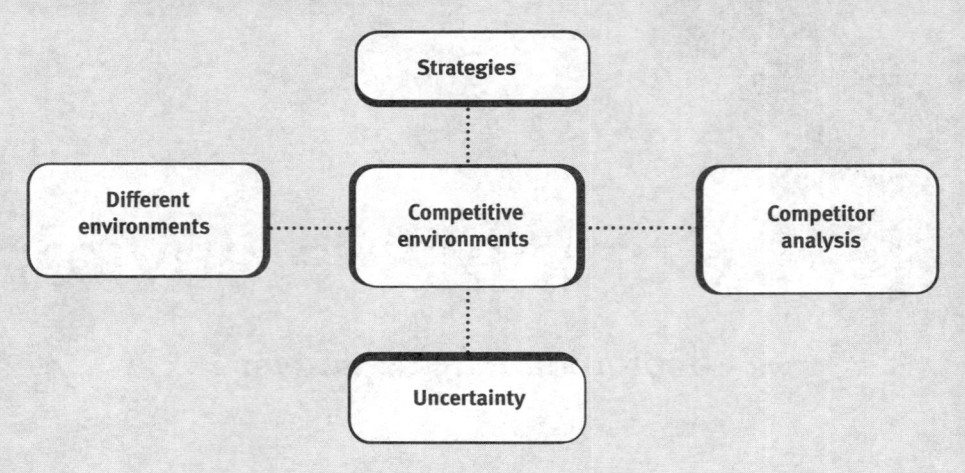

```
                    Strategies
                        |
Different  ········  Competitive  ········  Competitor
environments         environments            analysis
                        |
                    Uncertainty
```

2 Different environments

The environment exerts three basic forms of influence upon the organisation:

- It offers **threats** (to the well-being of the organisation, such as government legislation, or, say, national action by trade unions) and **opportunities** (for exploitation, such as growth in market demand, or new technological possibilities).
- It is the source of organisational **resources** (human resources come from outside the organisation, as do funds and supplies generally).
- It contains interest or '**pressure groups**' that have some kind of direct interest in organisational activities (these range from the general public and government bodies to 'action' groups such as Greenpeace and Animal Rights).

Strategy is concerned with the ability of the organisation to fit with, or cope with, its environment. Since an organisation does not operate in a vacuum it is important that it continually scans its external environment in order that it can develop appropriate responses to take advantage of opportunities, or to minimise threats. An understanding of the external environment is, therefore, a critical element in the development of strategy and can help in determining how to achieve a sustainable competitive advantage.

In chapter 3 external analysis was examined in detail. In that chapter, you looked at the various analytical tools which were used to undertake the external analysis at different levels, namely the PEST(EL) framework which helps in the analysis of the macro or general environment and Porter's five forces model which can be used to analyse the industry or competitive environment.

An organisation can react to its environmental situation (or opportunities and threats) in several ways. It may do nothing if it is convinced that the problem is insignificant or short-term. It may decide to monitor the environment carefully but not to respond just yet. It may increase its flexibility through contingency planning and product-market development. It may decide that the situation is important and urgent and want to plan major strategic change.

> **Strategic implication of different environments**
>
> Environments can exhibit different characteristics, which will affect the strategy of organisations operating within that environment:
>
> - **Stable and unchanging** – In this case the organisation can focus its attention on its past decisions and results, and on attempting to correct its past mistakes. Tactical planning is more important than strategic planning. (For example, British Telecom until recent years operated in a stable marketing environment and could safely invest large amounts of resources in the pursuit of achieving a maximally efficient telephone service.)
>
> - **Stable with minor fluctuations** – This describes an environment characterised by cyclical and/or seasonal fluctuations within a fairly stable structure. (For example, a local government education service will adopt a set of procedures for educating children, only having to adjust its scale of activity to accommodate the changing numbers of children in education.)
>
> - **Gradually changing in a predictable fashion** – This is where an organisation recognises that its environment is slowly being changed into something new and predictable. With this recognition it can begin to make the necessary adjustments to its goals, strategic direction, organisation structure, and systems so that it can proceed in a meaningful way for the future. (Thus with the predictable changing values of women the Girl Guide movement shifted its programmes toward developing the 'new woman' rather than the 'future wife and mother' though some evidence of reversion to the older ideals is evident in the movement's recent (April 2002) re-branding.)

Competitive environments

- **Rapidly changing in an unpredictable fashion** – Within this environment an organisation operates in highly turbulent and unpredictable businesses. Strategic planning is much more important than tactical planning, and effectiveness (doing the right things) is just as essential as achieving efficiency (doing things the best way). (Thus National Health Service hospitals in recent years have endured a succession of shocks and surprises. Private medical care, rapidly changing medical technology, in-depth appraisal of their activities by the National Audit Office (and Audit Commission), new government policies and constraints, rising costs and consumerism have led to hospitals closing, 'opting out', and finding creative ways of adapting to their environment in order to survive.)

Illustration 1 – Strategies adopted in response to environmental

Consider the airline industry

The industry has changed dramatically in the last ten years, with increased competition. Different airlines have chosen different strategies to deal with their changing environment.

- Integration: for example, Air France and KLM, and Lufthansa and Swissair.
- New routes and new services: 'flat beds', showers and massage facilities in first class.
- Cost cutting: for example, BA has outsourced its ticketing administration to India.
- Better branding: focusing on the service differences with the low-cost carriers.

Consider the retail outlet industry

In the competitive multiple retail outlet industry, Marks & Spencer and Sainsbury are constantly struggling to make the right decisions. They regularly change their direction to grasp the opportunities presented by changing patterns of consumer behaviour (new fashion trends, new health issues relating to food) and increasing pressure from competitors (Waitrose, Tesco, Asda, Next, Gap). Marks & Spencer have changed their top management, marketing and design structure to bring in new skills whenever they have found themselves under-performing. Sainsbury have become market leaders in organic foods.

3 Competitor analysis

> CIMA defines competitor analysis as: 'Identification and quantification of the relative strengths and weaknesses (compared with competitors or potential competitors), which could be of significance in the development of a successful competitive strategy.'

The role of competitor analysis

According to Wilson and Gilligan (1997) competitor analysis has three roles:

- to help management understand their competitive advantages and disadvantages relative to competitors;
- to generate insights into competitors' past, present and potential strategies;
- to give an informed basis for developing future strategies to sustain or establish advantages over competitors;

To these we may add a fourth:

- to assist with the forecasting of the returns on strategic investments for deciding between alternative strategies.

Why is competitor analysis important?

The actions of competitors will impact on the profits of a business. This may include:

- price cuts
- launching of a rival product
- aggressive expansion of production which reduces the firm's market sales
- inclusion of costly modifications to the product which the firm must also undertake.

This will have implications for management's choice of strategy. A suitable strategy is one which yields satisfactory financial returns after taking into account the potential responses of competitors.

Grant's four-stage framework for competitor analysis:

(1) **Identifying the current strategy.** This can be identified from what a company says and does. More often than not what they do will be more important than what they say.

(2) **Identifying competitor's objectives.** Knowledge of competitors' goals is an essential component of any analysis. Whether they are driven by short-term cash or profit goals or whether they have the reserves to focus on long-term objectives will result in them exhibiting significantly differing behaviours.

(3) **Identifying a competitors' assumptions about the industry.** A competitors' decisions are governed by their perceptions and assumptions about industry structure and the players with whom they compete. These perceptions will often be driven by the value systems of the senior management.

(4) **Identify the competitors' resources and capabilities.** Without a rigorous analysis of the resources that a competitor possesses there can be no realistic prediction of the seriousness of a possible challenge. It is easy to determine what they are doing but the emphasis here should be on what they are capable of doing. Ideally a company should know as much about its competitors as it knows about itself, this is, of course, unlikely to be achieved but is something for which a company should strive.

The information must be gathered and analysed and presented in the most accessible format to those who will make the decisions on a timely basis. Competitors should be continuously monitored for signs of activity and the industry scanned for the emergence of potential rivals.

Key concepts in competitor analysis

There are some key concepts which are helpful when undertaking competitor analysis. These are **market size**, **market growth** and **market share**.

- A useful starting point to competitor is to gain an understanding of market size. This is usually based on the annual sales of competitors. A challenge in doing this is in actually defining the 'market' (e.g. if undertaking an analysis of Easyjet, is the market the airline market, or the budget airline market – which is most helpful?)

- A second step involves estimating how much the market has grown, for example, over the last year. The importance of growth is relevant to strategy development, since if an organisation has a strategy which involves quick growth, then it would be more attracted to a market which is growing rapidly.

- A third step involves gaining an understanding of market share. This relates to the specific share an organisation has of a particular market. A larger share is usually regarded as being strategically beneficial since it may make it possible to influence prices and reduce costs through economies of scale. The outcome is increased profitability.

The Boston Consulting Group (BCG) model

Boston Consulting Group (BCG)

A model which can be used in competitor analysis when considering market share and market growth is the Boston Consulting Group Model (BCG). This model can look at the position of individual SBUs in relation to the market sector they compete in. Each SBU is assessed in terms of its market share, relative to that of the market leader in their sector. This is mapped against the growth rate of the sector.

By plotting each of its SBUs on the grid (shown below), the organisation is able to assess whether it has a balanced portfolio in terms of products and market sectors. It can also help in the development of strategic options for each SBU, depending on the potential growth in the market sector and the relative strength of the SBU compared to its competitors in that sector.

Boston Consulting Group Growth / Share Matrix

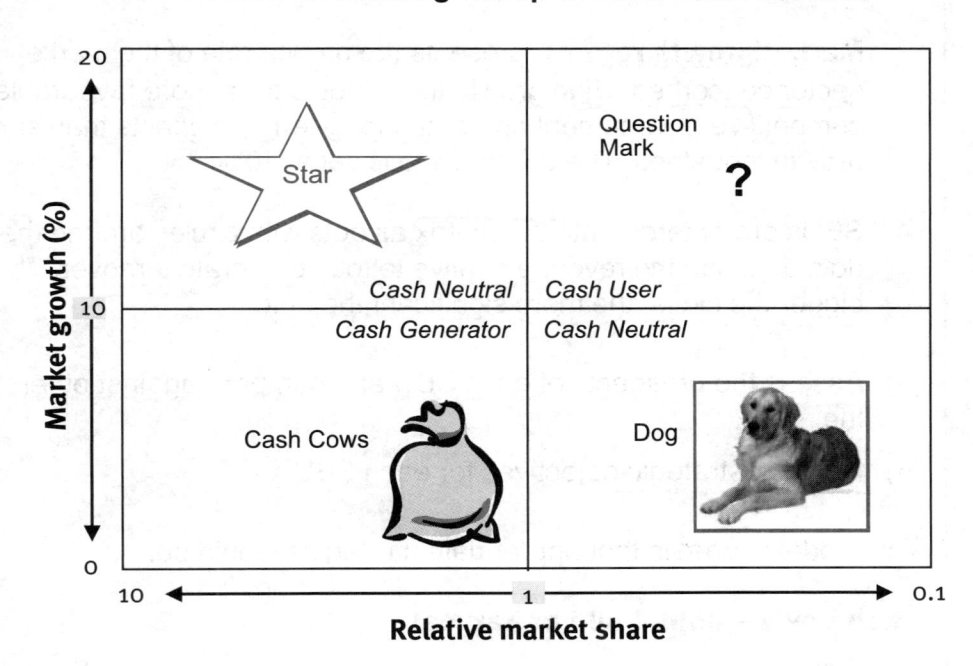

	Cash Neutral	Cash User
Market growth (%) 20 — 10 — 0	Star	Question Mark ?
	Cash Generator	Cash Neutral
	Cash Cows	Dog

Relative market share: 10 ← 1 → 0.1

Strategies recommended by the BCG model:

- Cash cow cash flows to be used to support stars and develop question marks;
- Cash cows to be defended;
- Weak uncertain question marks should be divested to reduce demands on cash;
- Dogs should be divested, harvested or niched;
- If portfolio is unbalanced, consider acquisitions and divestments;

- Harvesting reduces damage of sudden divestment but reduces the value at eventual disposal. A quick sale now may produce larger proceeds;
- SBUs to have different growth targets and objectives and not be subject to the same strategic control systems.

Four main steps:

(1) Divide the company into SBUs.

(2) Allocate each SBU into the matrix depending on the analysis of relative market share and market growth:

Relative market share – the ratio of SBU market share to that of largest rival in the market sector. BCG suggests that market share gives a company cost advantages from economies of scale and learning effects. The dividing line is set at 1. A figure of 4 suggests that SBU share is four times greater than the nearest rival. 0.1 suggests that the SBU is 10% of the sector leader.

Market growth rate – represents the growth rate of the market sector concerned. High growth industries offer a more favourable competitive environment and better long-term prospects than slow-growth industries. The dividing line is set at 10%.

SBUs are entered onto the matrix as dots with circles around the dots denoting the revenue relative to total corporate turnover. The bigger the circle, the more significant the unit.

(3) Assess the prospects of each SBU and compare against others in the matrix;

(4) Develop strategic objectives for each SBU.

The model suggests that appropriate strategies would be:

Cash cows – hold, build or harvest

- High market share in a low-growth market.
- Usually a cash generator and profitable.
- Often cost leaders as possess economies of scale. May be a declining star.
- Low market growth implies a lack of opportunity and therefore the capital requirements are low.
- Profits from this area can be used to support other products in their development stage.
- Defensive strategy often adopted to protect the position.

Star – hold, divest or build

- High market share in high growth areas – usually market leader.
- Offer attractive long-term prospects – may one day become a cash cow.
- Requires large investment in non-current assets and to defend against competitor attacks.

Question marks – build, harvest or divest

- Low market share in high growth industries.
- Opportunity exists, but uncertainty.
- May need to invest heavily to secure market share.
- Could potentially become a star.
- May require substantial management time and may not develop successfully.

Dogs – build, harvest or divest

- Low market share in low growth market.
- To cultivate would require substantial investment and would be risky.
- Could turn into a 'niche' product.
- Often divested or carried as a loss leader.

Limitations of the BCG model:

- Simplistic – only considers two variables;
- Connection between market share and cost savings is not strong – low market share companies use low-share technology and can have lower production costs – e.g. Morgan Cars;
- Cash cows do not always generate cash – Vauxhall motors would be a classic cash cow yet it requires substantial cash investment just to remain competitive – to defend itself!;
- Fail to consider value creation – the management of a diverse portfolio can create value by sharing competencies across SBUs, sharing resources to reap economies of scale or by achieving superior governance. BCG would divert investment away from the cash cows and dogs and fails to consider the benefit of offering the full range and the concept of 'loss leaders'.

Levels of competitors

Kotler (2008) identifies four levels of competitors:

- **Brand competitors**. Firms who offer similar products to the same customers we serve and who have a similar size and structure of organisation as ourselves, for example Pepsi and Coca-Cola.
- **Industry competitors**. Suppliers who produce similar goods but who are not necessarily the same size or structure as ourselves, or who compete in a more limited area or product range, for example British Airways and Singapore Airlines.
- **Form competitors**. Suppliers whose products satisfy the same needs as ours, although they are technically quite different, for example speedboats and sports cars.
- **Generic competitors**. Competitors who compete for the same income as the company, for example home improvements and golf clubs.

Understanding the level of competitors will help organisations to understand the basis on which they must try to compete their market place. It will assist them in defining their competitive strategy.

The extent to which these pose a threat to the firm depends on factors such as:

- *Number of rivals and the extent of differentiation in the market.* Greater numbers of rivals increases the complexity of the industry, but because they are smaller it reduces the danger of one competitor breaking from the rest in an attempt to deliver a knockout blow. Instead each will try to carve a niche and hence increase differentiation. This makes it less likely that one can invade the market of another.
- *Entry and mobility barriers*. These are costs that the firm must pay to get admission to the industry or to the firm's particular segment of it. For example, the Levi Strauss brand has a strong presence in the market for casual clothing. It proved an insuperable impediment when the firm tried to make tailored suits.
- *Cost structure*. If the rival has a high-cost structure this effectively denies entry to a market that contains a cost leader. For example, the high-cost structure of an exclusive department store would effectively deny it access to lower market segments.
- *Degree of vertical integration*. Highly vertically integrated firms have considerable strength in a market. However, they are also inflexible because they are committed to buying from their own upstream supply divisions. International oil firms have repeatedly lost out to discounting petroleum retailers able to buy supplies on the world's spot markets.

As a rule of thumb it is likely that the most significant present or potential competitors are the ones who conform most strongly to one or more of the following descriptions:

- they presently serve the same or similar customers to ourselves;
- they have a similar or cheaper distribution network;
- they are at the same stage of production as ourselves;
- they utilise a similar technology in providing their goods and services;
- they utilise similar types of management and staff skills;
- they have a similar geographical spread.

> Competitor analysis must, therefore, focus on two main issues; acquiring as much relevant information about competitors and subsequently predicting their behaviour.

4 Competitor information

You need to understand what competitors are offering so you can offer at least as much to customers.

In collecting competitor information, organisations must firstly identify who their main competitors are. There may be a number of organisations operating in the market sector, it is important to identify those which pose the largest threat. This may be the market leader, or other organisations of around the same scale, offering similar products or services. It is however also important to continue to monitor the market for new entrants.

Types of information to collect:

- *Competitor's strategy.* Once the main competitors have been identified, information should be collected on their current strategies. Some of this may be established from looking at the products offered, the markets in which they operate and how they are operating within those markets.

- *Competitor's goals and objectives.* This may be established by looking at activities being undertaken by the competitor, for example moving into new markets, or developing new products.

- *Competitor's products and services.* It is important to know how competitor's products and services compare with those offered by the organisation. From this, information can be gathered on the segment of the market the competitor operates in, their pricing and quality strategy, their branding and image.

- *Competitor's resources and capabilities.* It is important to gauge the strength of the competitor in terms of financial, human, intellectual, technological and physical resources. This will help the organisation judge the threat posed by that competitor.

Sources of information

There are a range of different sources available to organisations undertaking competitor analysis, for example:

- Website of competitor. This may contain information about strategy and objectives, as well as details of past performance. It should also provide information about where they operate, in what sectors and what types of products they offer.

- Annual report and accounts of competitors. This is publically available for larger companies and contains information about financial performance as well as details on governance issues and other general information about the company,

- Newspaper articles and on-line data sources on company. An internet search can highlight any articles relating to the company.

- Magazines and journals including trade media, business management and technical journals.

- On-line data services such as FAME to collect financial and statistical information.

- Directories and yearbooks covering particular industries.

- Becoming a customer of the competitor. This can be a good way to obtain information about the products and services offered by the competitor and the level of service offered by them.

- Market research reports and reviews produced by specialist firms such as Mintel, Economist Intelligence Unit, which might provide information on market share and marketing activity.

- Customer market research could be independently commissioned to establish consumer attitudes. This is the most costly of the data sources, but it will be the most specific in meeting the needs of the competitor analysis.

Information sources

Tudor (1992) provides the following categorisation of information sources (some of it is a little dated now, but it is still a very useful listing):

(1) **Primary sources:**
   - Annual reports and statements of competitors or firms in the target market or industry and those of their suppliers.
   - Transcript services from newspapers, analysts and on-line data sources such as proprietary company information services.
   - Statistical sources such as government censuses and surveys of household expenditure, production and demographics.
   - Newspapers and newsletters such as the business press or industry bulletins.
   - Magazines and journals including the trade media, business and management journals, technical journals.
   - Analysis services such as FAME.
   - Patents registered with the national patents office.

(2) **Secondary sources:**
   - Directories and yearbooks covering particular industries (who's who) and ownership patterns (who owns what).
   - Market research reviews and reports produced by specialist research firms including Mintel, Economist Intelligence Unit, etc.
   - Abstracts, index journals and current awareness services. These are specialist databases which index technical articles under codes and keywords. The firm can set up a profile of keywords relevant to its industry and source the material written on it.
   - Government publications such as special reports of select committees on particular industries, economic forecasts and reports.
   - Grey literature. A generic phrase covering theses, conference reports, special research papers, maps and photographs.

(3) **Computer-based information services:**
   - CD-Rom-based abstracts and journals.
   - On-line databases of professional and academic journals, newspapers and business information.
   - Internet resources.

The internet as a source of competitor information

Some competitor intelligence is freely available from the Internet. This information can provide a valuable starting point for developing detailed competitor profiles. Be cautious about acting on competitor intelligence until you have as much complete, accurate, up-to-date information as possible. Published sources can provide only a partial picture, and more strategic information is likely to be confidential.

The Internet has become part of everyday business and personal life and traffic increases worldwide every day. It provides an unsurpassed opportunity for businesses to access new markets and grow their existing markets locally, nationally and globally. There are many challenges to be addressed in ensuring a website is visible and effective. Key amongst these is ensuring that your organisation can measure the effectiveness of its site both in comparison to how it performed last month and last year and how it is performing against its competitors.

An organisations Internet presence is more than just a website and needs to react and evolve to meet competitive and market changes. An organisation needs as much market intelligence and possible to plan and adapt its campaigns and respond to the actions of its competitors.

5 Types of research

Qualitative research

Qualitative research involves the collection on non-numerical data. It investigates more the *why decisions* rather than the *what, where* and *when* decisions which are more associated with quantitative analysis. It is used to gain insight into people's attitudes and behaviours.

In terms of competitor analysis, qualitative research would attempt to discover why customers prefer one product or brand over another. It is largely subjective and can be difficult and expensive to undertake, but can provide valuable information for decision making.

One aspect of competitor analysis which could be addressed by qualitative research is brand perception. This is an attempt to find out what customers feel about certain brands. A company may attempt to get customers to assess one of their products compared to a competitor's product.

With this type of research, customers may be asked for the word they would use to describe these products, for example do they perceive quality, fun, reliability, value for money etc. The main thing to note about this type of research is that it is subjective. Customers' views may not be in line with the company's view about the product, but the customers' views should be listened to as they know what they like and they are the ones buying the product.

This type of research can provide in depth understanding about customer preferences which can aid product development and marketing strategy. However this can be expensive as it often involves employing a specialist agency to undertake the research.

How to undertake qualitative research

There are a number of ways in which this type of research is undertaken:

- *Observation.* Customers or competitors can be observed in how they buy/sell or use the product. The observation can be with or without the knowledge of the customer or competitor.
- *Interviews*. Directly interviewing customers can give a more detailed insight into their views and specific questions about products can be posed. It may even be possible to interview ex-employees of competitors, although care must be taken that no confidentiality rules are breached.
- *Focus groups*. These involve selecting a group of individuals who are representative of a target market and questioning them on their preferences. This type of research can also be useful in testing out new product ideas.
- *Analysis*: This involves the interpreting of the data gathered from the research into meaningful information which the company can use in developing products and setting strategy.

It is worth noting that much of the information required for successful competitor analysis will be qualitative.

Fleisher and Bensoussan (2002) give a full listing of the information that an organisation should gather about their competitors. The broad headings are as follows:

- Products and services
- Marketing
- Human resources
- Operations
- Management profiles
- Sociopolitical

- Technology
- Organisational structure
- Competitive intelligence capacity
- Strategy
- Customer value analysis
- Financial.

Quantitative research

Quantitative research tries to answer the *what, where* and *when* questions. The answers to these questions will be factual and numerical, for example the number of units of a particular product sold or the value of sales in a period. Statistical methods such as ratios or trend analysis can then be used to analyse this data.

When carrying out quantitative analysis, select and discuss only those ratios that have an impact on the company problems. Then compare these ratios with industry averages to discover if the company is out of line with others in the industry.

A typical financial analysis of a firm would include a study of the operating statements for three or five years, including a trend analysis of sales, profit margins, earnings per share, return on investment, liquidity ratios plus a comparison of the firm under study with industry standards.

Non-financial quantitative analysis

Another important aspect of quantitative analysis is the gathering of non-financial data, such as number of customers, customer complaints etc.

The financial indexes are useful, but they cannot show some competitive advantages characteristics such as the product differentiation or the quick responsiveness to customer questions.

This non-financial data is often more useful in terms of competitor analysis. For example a company may want to assess their customer service against the service given by a competitor. They may gather information on the time between order and delivery. This would allow them to ensure that they provide the same, or better service to customers.

Rankings and ratings

Once the quantitative data has been gathered, it can be useful to rank and rate competitors. Competitors can be assigned a score for each product/service area measured. Companies may weight some of these areas if they are viewed as more important. This approach results in an aggregate measure for each competitor which can be compared to the company's own measures for comparison purposes.

Benchmarking:

Once you have assembled detailed information about your competitors, you can **benchmark** your performance against theirs.

Strategic benchmarks

- market share
- return on assets
- gross profit margin on sales.

Functional benchmarks

- % deliveries on time
- order costs per order
- order turnaround time
- average stockholding per order.

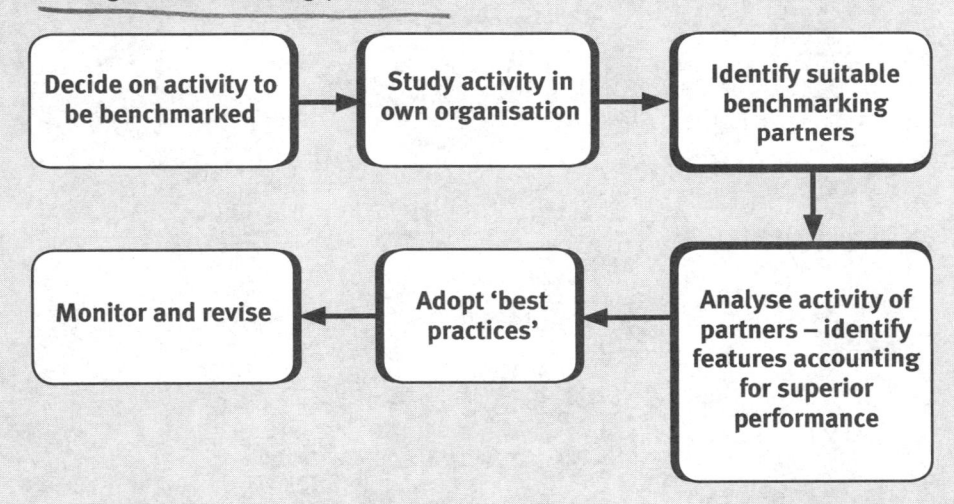

```
Decide on activity to  →  Study activity in  →  Identify suitable
be benchmarked            own organisation       benchmarking partners
                                                        ↓
Monitor and revise  ←  Adopt 'best practices'  ←  Analyse activity of
                                                   partners – identify
                                                   features accounting
                                                   for superior
                                                   performance
```

Test your understanding 1

V, the new CEO of D Company was surprised to find out that the company do not undertake competitor analysis. He was told that as D Company operates in a very dynamic market, things change too quickly to make analysis worthwhile.

Required:

Discuss why competitor analysis is so important and explain the main sources D Company could use to gather information on competitors.

(10 marks)

6 Chapter summary

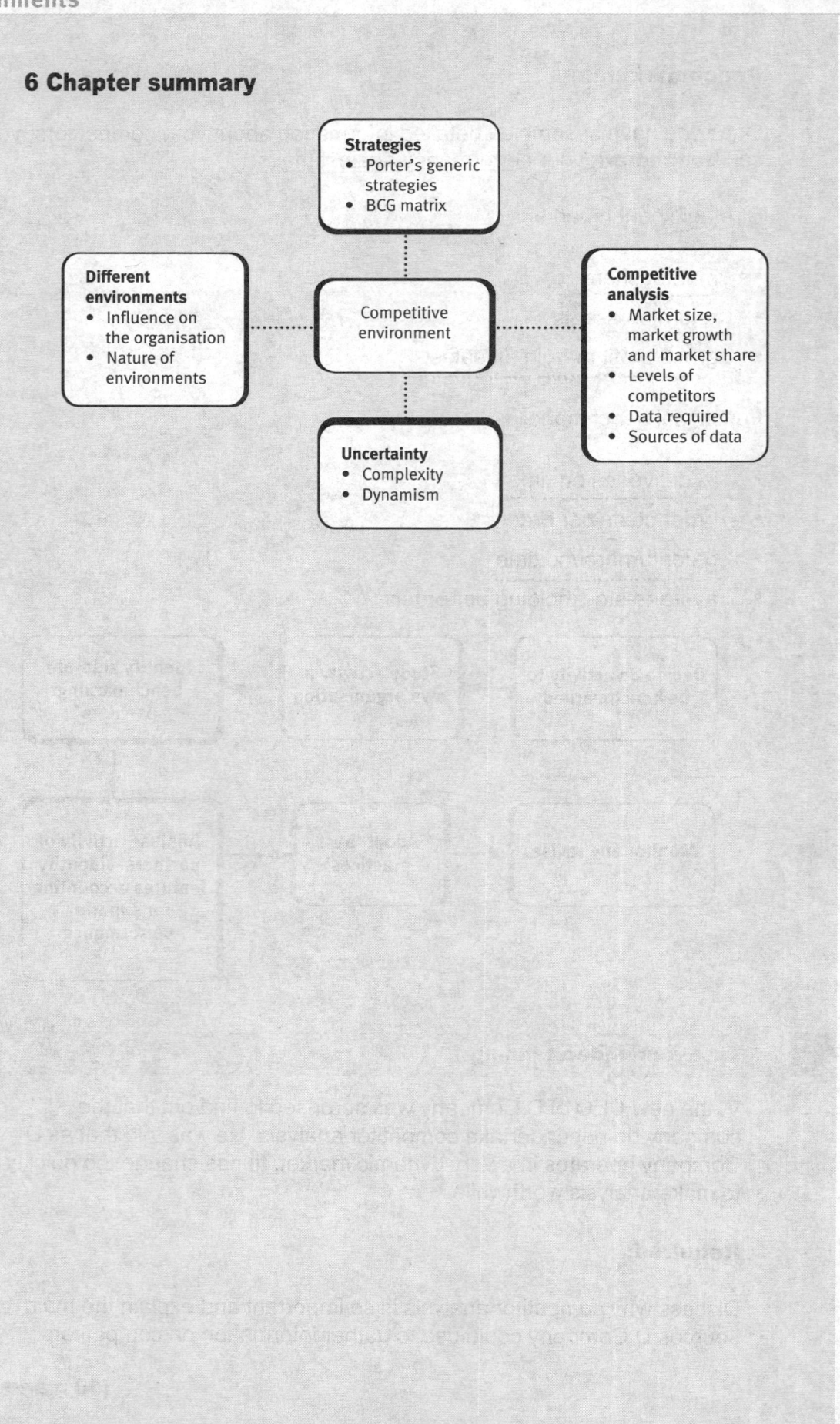

Competitive environment

- **Strategies**
  - Porter's generic strategies
  - BCG matrix

- **Different environments**
  - Influence on the organisation
  - Nature of environments

- **Competitive analysis**
  - Market size, market growth and market share
  - Levels of competitors
  - Data required
  - Sources of data

- **Uncertainty**
  - Complexity
  - Dynamism

Test your understanding answers

Test your understanding 1

For any company it is important to know about the markets they compete in so that they can gain an understanding of which other companies are competing in the same market and how they are going to compete against them. Competitor analysis will help the company recognise their own strengths and weaknesses relative to those of their competitors. This will allow them to assess their competitive advantage and how they can use this to drive their business forward. Competitor analysis is therefore an important stage in the formulation of strategy.

In order to maintain growth, companies must be aware of changes in their marketplace. If new competitors have entered the market this will change the dynamics of the market and could affect the company's profitability. Companies must not only undertake competitor analysis but should continually update it to ensure that they are not left behind in terms of market development. If D Company does not undertake adequate competitor analysis, a new company may have entered the market and this could adversely affect their sales, or competitors may be offering a new range of products, or better services than D Company and this could reduce D Company's customer base.

Competitor analysis will:

- Avoid company's sales lagging behind competitors
- Help a company to maintain profitability
- Assist company to increase profitability
- Aid strategic planning
- Allow companies to analyse the goods and services offered by competitors and help them develop their products and services to compete in the way customers want

Competitor information can be gathered from a variety of sources. Some information which is more readily accessible may be less useful, however very specific information which would be most useful may be difficult or costly to obtain.

There are a range of different sources available to D Company which could be accessed to gain information about its potential competitors, for example:

- *Websites of competitors* – this is readily available information, but will only include the information which the competitor wants to share with the public and will be designed to show the company in the most positive way.

- *Annual report and accounts of the competitor*. Again this is information which is available in the public domain for listed companies.

- *Newspaper articles* and *on-line data sources* on company information.

- *Industry publications*, *trade media*, business management and technical *journals*

- *Government reports and statistics* on industrial sectors may be available.

- *Becoming a customer* of the competitor is a good way of sampling the products and service provided by them.

- *Market research reports* and reviews produced by specialist firms might provide information on market share and marketing activity within the chosen industry.

- *Customer market research* could be independently commissioned to establish consumer attitudes and awareness towards D Company's potential competitors in the various regions. This would potentially be the most useful information as the questions could be specific, but this is a costly way to gather information.

chapter

5

Alternative approaches to strategy formulation

Chapter learning objectives

- Compare and contrast approaches to strategy formulation.

Alternative approaches to strategy formulation

1 Session content diagram

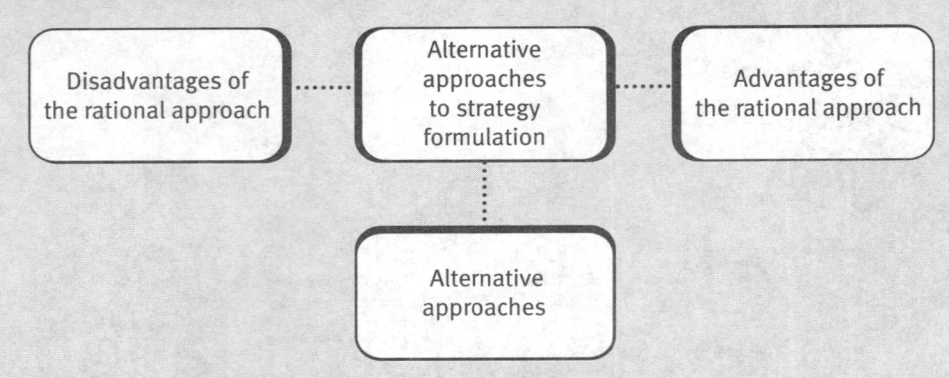

```
[Disadvantages of        [Alternative          [Advantages of
 the rational approach]   approaches            the rational approach]
                          to strategy
                          formulation]
                              |
                         [Alternative
                          approaches]
```

2 Advantages and disadvantages of the rational approach

In chapter 2 the various stages of the rational approach to strategic management were examined, however, a structured step-by-step approach to strategy formulation as suggested by the rational approach can take a significant amount of time and requires a lot of organisational resources. It is important that organisations can see the benefits from the effort required with this approach:

The benefits of the rational approach to strategy formulation

- Long term view – it avoids organisations focusing on short term results.
- Identifies key strategic issues – it makes management more proactive.
- Goal congruence – it ensures that the whole of the organisation is working towards the same goals.
- Communicates responsibility – everyone within the organisation can be made aware of what is required from them.
- Co-ordinates SBU's – it helps business units to work together.
- Security for stakeholders – it demonstrates to stakeholders that the organisation has a clear idea of where it is going.
- Basis for strategic control – clear targets and reports enabling success of the strategy to be reviewed.

However, some writers are critical of the rational approach. In addition to the time required to undertake the rational approach and the cost of the process, there are other areas of criticism.

The problems of the rational approach to strategy formulation

- Inappropriate in dynamic environments – a new strategy may only be established say every five years, which may quickly become inappropriate if the environment changes.
- Bureaucratic and inflexible – radical ideas are often rejected and new opportunities which present themselves may not be able to be taken.

- **Difficulty getting the necessary participation to implement the strategy** – successful implementation requires the support of middle and junior management and the nature of the rational approach may alienate these levels of management.
- **Impossible in uncertain environments** – it is impossible to carry out the required analysis in uncertain business environments.
- **Stifles innovation and creativity** – the rational approach encourages conformity among managers.
- **Complex and costly for small businesses with informal structures** and systems.

> **Further detail on the benefits and drawbacks of the rational model**
>
> ### Benefits of the formal top-down approach to strategy
>
> Business strategy formulation obviously uses a lot of organisational resource. What are the benefits?
>
> - **Avoids short-termist behaviour.** It ensures that management considers the long-term development of the business rather than focusing solely on short-term results and operational results.
> - **Helps identify strategic issues.** By encouraging management to consider the business environment in their plans and decisions, it will help them keep ahead of change and to be more proactive.
> - **Goal congruence.** There are many aspects to this:
>   - It will help coordinate the different business units, divisions and departments and ensure that they work together to realise the full potential of the corporation.
>   - Asset investment decisions will be taken with the long-term needs of the business in mind. This could include design or acquisition of buildings and capital equipment, information systems or acquisitions of other businesses.
>   - Tactical programmes will be congruent with the strategy. This might affect the types of staff recruited and developed, the location of production and distribution facilities or the sorts of products and brands created.

Alternative approaches to strategy formulation

- **Improves stakeholder perceptions of the business.** If the firm demonstrates that it has a clear idea of where it is going, it enables others to make plans based on its future. This may lead to:
  - higher share price because investors are confident of higher future returns;
  - attraction and retention of staff and higher morale because employees can see that their career aspirations may be met within the firm;
  - improved relations with suppliers who feel they can rely on orders in the future.

- **Provides a basis for strategic control.** By having a process of formulation and implementation, this ensures that:
  - There is someone looking after the development of strategy.
  - There are clear programmes and policies being developed to implement it.
  - There are targets and reports enabling review of the success of the strategy.

- **Develops future management potential and ensures continuity.** This relates to the fact that formal strategy formulation is a collective process. This means that:
  - Different functional managers (e.g. finance or marketing) gain an appreciation of the other disciplines of business and so develop into general managers.
  - Providers of information to the strategy process become more deeply involved in the business and develop as a pool of expertise from which the next generation of managers may be recruited.
  - Avoids succession problems when members of senior management retire or move on. The strategy of the firm is understood by all and will outlast the loss of key members of the management team.

Drawbacks of the formal top-down approach to strategy

Some writers are critical of the formal process discussed above, because:

- It is too infrequent to allow the business to be dynamic. This view emphasises the infrequency of the 'strategy round', say every five years, and the time it takes to achieve any change to the strategy. If the environment changes unexpectedly, the firm's performance may deteriorate as it continues to follow a business strategy which has now become inappropriate to its business environment, for example by continuing to make a product no one wants.

- It forbids the development of radical or innovative strategies. The need to retain consensus among the management team means that radical ideas are too often rejected. Writers who advance this argument remind us of the inherent conservatism of committees and of the fact that some of the success stories of the past few decades, such as Microsoft, Intel, Virgin and (at points) Apple and Body Shop, have also been that of firms whose names are associated with radical and visionary entrepreneurs. These business leaders tend to follow the emergent strategy approach.

- It suffers from difficulties of implementation. The formal process is management-led and seeks to pursue the goals of the business. Successful implementation requires the participation, or at least acquiescence, of middle and junior management, together with operative staff. There is a danger that the formal process will not build the support of these people and hence will be misunderstood or resisted. The result will be that the goals of the strategy are not realised.

- There is loss of entrepreneurial spirit. Entrepreneurs are persons who break rules and make changes to conventional ways of doing business. On the other hand, a middle manager in a strategically managed firm will be rewarded for carrying out their allotted part in the strategy and for not breaking the rules. The effect will be to encourage conformity among managers. This will lose the firm potentially successful ventures and perhaps also the services of gifted entrepreneurial managers who may leave in frustration.

- It is impossible in uncertain business environments. Formal business strategy requires that the strategists are able to make reliable assumptions about the future and particularly about the opportunities and threats facing them. Critics argue that the business environment is now more uncertain than ever before. Because in their view, the future cannot be forecast. Some writers argue that management efforts should be diverted from trying to plan strategies and instead should focus on improving the ability of their businesses to respond and adapt to change.

- It is too expensive and complicated for small businesses. The manager of a small business is unlikely to be skilled in the techniques needed for developing the kinds of business strategy described above. Moreover, the opportunity cost in terms of the time away from direct management of the operational parts of the business are likely to be too great.

3 Strategy formulation and small businesses

According to Birley (1982), the formal top-down process may be unsuitable for small businesses for four reasons:

Differences in goals. In a small firm, the goals of the business are often inseparable from the goals of the owner-manager and immediate family group. Small businesses often do not exhibit the economic rationality and single-minded pursuit of dividends and growth often associated with businesses governed by external shareholders. In many small, family run businesses, goals may be a satisfactory income and lifestyle, or passing the business to family members when they retire. Growth may not be a primary consideration

Limited scope of product/market choices. Small-business managers typically consider a much narrower range of strategic options than do their large-business counterparts. The business will often have a narrow scope, based on the skills and knowledge of the proprietor. Management may be reluctant to move too far away from their core business.

Limited resources. Smaller firms lack the resources to invest in new strategic ventures and rapid growth. Therefore, they do not exhibit the sudden strategic leaps envisaged by the rational model. Given their smaller income streams, an unsuccessful strategic investment could destroy the firm.

Organisational structure. Strategic implementation demands the setting up of an appropriate structure and selection of an appropriate team to carry it out. Small firms may not have the personnel available, or the proprietor may be unwilling to lose their absolute control.

4 Environmental uncertainty

Earlier in the chapter we mentioned that the rational model is not appropriate in dynamic or uncertain environments.

> CIMA defines uncertainty as: 'The inability to predict the outcome from an activity due to a lack of information about the required input/output relationships or about the environment within which the activity takes place.'

Uncertainty can also be defined as 'the difficulty in making reliable assumptions about the future'.

Managers' perception of uncertainty will be increased by two factors – complexity and dynamism.

- **Complexity.** This is the number of variables which can impact on the firm and how difficult they are to predict or understand. Also if the relationships between the variables is complex, this will also increase uncertainty.
- **Dynamism.** This is the rate of change of the business environment. Increased dynamism means that management's models of 'how things work' will become out of date much quicker. It also suggests that competitors will be able to respond more quickly to a firm's initiatives.

    Examples of the factors which have increased dynamism include:

    - Swifter information communications. These mean that something happening on one side of the world will have global impacts very quickly.
    - Accelerated product life cycles. Modern competitive strategy leads most firms to invest heavily in research and development to render rivals' products obsolete.

Impact of uncertainty

High uncertainty affects business strategy in several ways:

- Reduces the planning horizon. If a firm operates in an uncertain environment its management are unlikely to develop plans for more than a few years ahead because they accept that they will be subject to large margins of error.
- Encourages emergent strategies. Some writers believe that high uncertainty brings into question the idea of planning a strategy at all.
- Increases information needs of the organisation. Where the environment is no longer predictable, management will require more regular information and on a greater range of factors to make it more certain. This will increase further still if the organisation elects to adopt emergent strategy formulation because the number of recipients of such information will increase.
- May lead to conservative strategies. Managers will tend to stay closer to the 'strategic recipes' that have worked in the past because they fear trying anything new due to not being able to forecast its effects. This approach is flawed because under conditions of high uncertainty there is no reason to believe that old 'recipes' will still work.

Has uncertainty really increased?

The modern assumption is that the business environment has become more uncertain and that more information is needed by management in order to restore certainty. Hatch (1997) observes that 'Environments do not feel uncertain, people do', and the only thing which has demonstrably increased is the amount of environmental information available to management. She ventures that perhaps the world has always been dynamic and complex but that we never fully appreciated it before.

Hatch's suggestion is deliberately far-fetched to make a point. The more environmental data we provide to managers, the more uncertain and stressed-out they may become. This gives weight to the argument, noted before, that in strategy formulation management should focus on only a few key success variables and ignore the rest.

5 Other approaches to strategy formulation

You can see from the above that the rational approach has a number of drawbacks and is not suitable in all situations. There are other recognised approaches to strategic planning, including:

- Emergent approach
- Incremental approaches
- Freewheeling opportunism

Emergent approach

Mintzberg argues that successful strategies can emerge in an organisation without formal, deliberate prior planning. The 'pattern' is often made up of the intended (planned) strategies that are actually realised and any emergent (unplanned) strategies.

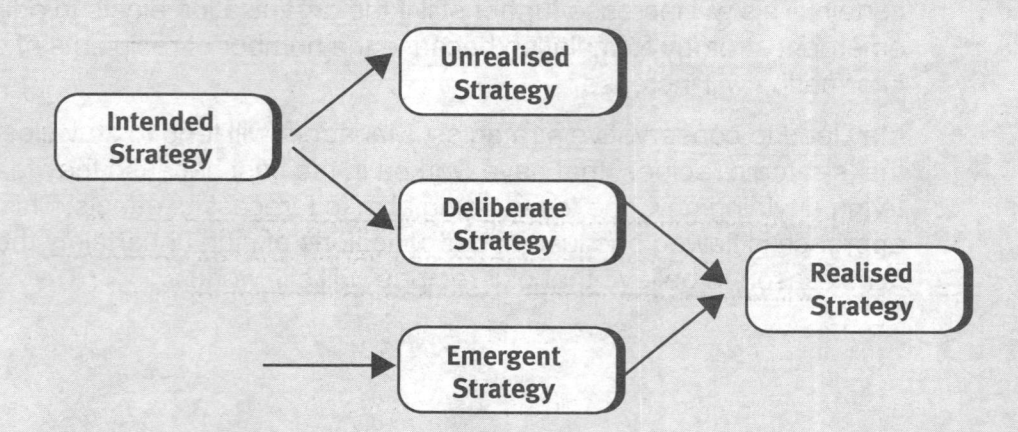

Under the emergent approach a strategy may be tried and developed as it is implemented. If it fails a different approach will be taken. This is likely to result in a more short-term emphasis than with the rational model. To successfully use the emergent approach, the organisation needs to have a culture of innovation.

Mintzberg was not surprised at the failure of intended strategies to be fully realised as deliberate strategies. He regarded it as unlikely that a firm's environment could be as totally predictable as it would need to be for all intended strategies to work out. The emergent strategy is often a response to unexpected contingencies and the resulting realised strategy may, in the circumstances, be superior to the intended strategy.

Some strategies may be deliberately emergent, in that managers may create the conditions for new ideas to flourish and strategies to emerge. This has the effect of focusing attention on the role of the manager as at the heart of the strategy and reduces the importance of the rational process. To do this, Minzberg suggested that a manager must exhibit the following skills:

- *Manage stability*. Managers should be able to master the details of running their business and not feel compelled to constantly rethink the business's strategic future.

- *Detect discontinuity*. This is the ability to detect the subtle environmental changes that may affect the business and be able to assess their potential impact on its future performance. The key to this is that managers must 'know the business'. Formal strategy systems can distance managers from their business and they can subsequently lack the knowledge they need to run it.

- *Manage patterns.* Management should encourage strategic initiatives to grow throughout the business and watch to see how they develop and intervene once this is clear.

- *Reconcile change and continuity*. Managers must realise that radical changes and new patterns of strategy will create resistance and instability in the firm. They must keep radical departures in check, while preparing the ground for their introduction.

Illustration 1 – Honda's emergent strategy

When Honda executives arrived in Los Angeles, they did so with the intention of setting up a subsidiary to sell 250cc and 350cc machines to existing motorcycle enthusiasts. They had no intention of trying to sell smaller bikes such as the 50cc machines that were so popular in Japan because they could not envisage a market for these in a country where everything was bigger and better than back home.

Alternative approaches to strategy formulation

> As things turned out, the sales of the 250cc and 350cc bikes were disappointing. One of the reasons was to do with the mechanical failure of some of their machines. The intended strategy looked to be failing. In the course of their work, however, the Honda executives were using the 50cc machines to run errands around Los Angeles and their presence attracted a lot of attention.
>
> One day the Honda team received a call from a Sears' buyer who proposed selling the 50cc machines through the department chain outlets. For their part the Honda team was reluctant to sell the small bikes because they feared it would alienate serious bikers who might associate the Honda company with 'wimp' machines. Eventually, however, their failure to sell the expected quota of larger machines pushed them into selling the small 50cc machines and to sell them not through specialist motor cycle distributors but through general retailers. Sales took off and a new strategy was born.

Incremental approaches

Lindblom – 'Muddling through'

Lindblom described how government administrators 'muddle through' from year to year rather than carry out bold strategic initiatives. He criticised the rational model as follows:

- In practice, managers confuse the goals and the strategy of the company.
- It is unrealistic to imagine a strategic planner carefully sifting through every possible option to achieve predetermined goals.
- At best, formulation of strategy is a process of evaluating a few slight extensions to existing policies.

Lindblom argued that strategic choice takes place by comparing possible options against each other and considering which would give the best outcome. This approach does not try to identify and review all the potential strategies available to the organisation. Rather it provides a way of monitoring the progress and the direction the organisation is moving in, and allows a change in 'course' if required.

Lindblom did not advocate this approach, he simply recorded its existence. He agreed with critics that in an environment of turbulence and rapid change, minor adjustments to current policies will not allow organisations to adapt sufficiently. The same could be said in circumstances where organisations face threats to their survival, a more radical approach may be required.

Quinn – Logical incrementalism

Quinn takes a more positive view of incrementalism than Lindblom. For Quinn, a manager must map where he or she wants the organisation to go and then proceed towards it in **small steps**, being prepared to adapt if the environment changes or if support is not forthcoming. Quinn's logical incrementalism falls somewhere between the rational approach and the 'muddling through' approach.

He identified that:

- *Managers generally know where they want their organisations to go.* Effective strategists initially work out only a few integrating concepts, principles, or philosophies that can help rationalise and guide the company's overall actions.

- *Strategy is an incremental, step-by-step, learning process.* They proceed step-by-step from early generalities toward later specifics, clarifying the strategy as events both permit and dictate.

- *Managers consciously keep their decisions small and flexible.* In early stages, they consciously avoid over-precise statements that might impair the flexibility or imagination needed to exploit new information or opportunities.

The outcome of this approach is a deliberate policy of small strategic changes within the framework provided by a general sense of strategic direction.

In this approach, the manager's skill is crucial. The main managerial functions are:

- The manager sits at the centre of a network of **formal and informal communications** with staff, customers and others. They will be attuned to the problems and issues confronting the organisation. They may use formal strategy models and techniques to understand these.

- Once they sense that a **need for change** has arisen and that events are pushing the firm in a particular direction, they will start to develop a general strategic vision for the organisation.

- Rather than present the strategy full-blown, and risk opposition, the manager will **build political support** for the ideas by revealing them to key committees or on management retreats.

- Commitment will be gained to an **initial trial of the strategy**. This will build further commitment among those charged with making the project a success and erode the consensus in favour of the old way of doing business.

- This consensus will build and **press the strategic change forward incrementally**.

The use of formal strategic frameworks is valuable in developing and communicating the changed strategy. This is the logical element in Quinn's methodology because it ensures that the process leads somewhere. The incrementalism comes from the need to subordinate rapid change to the process of gaining consensus and avoiding resistance.

As we can see, Mintzberg and Quinn are essentially making the same point: that strategies are not always planned or revealed in advance and that management skill is crucial. Unlike Lindblom, they do not see this as unacceptably conservative, but see it as realistic.

Freewheeling opportunism

The alternative to having a long-term strategic plan is not having a plan or having a series of short-term plans as a replacement.

Freewheeling opportunism is a term used to describe the essentially reactive process of management as an alternative to strategic planning.

This suggests:

- clarity of purpose and direction
- mechanism for coordination, communication and control
- develops creativity and commitment of management
- ensures continuity and contingency exists
- increased flexibility to respond to real problems
- decentralisation of decision making and increased autonomy for managers
- more scope for creativity
- increased ability to respond to unexpected opportunities
- perceived by managers to be dynamic, exciting and innovative.

Some criticisms of this approach are that it:

- may encourage managers to pursue their own agenda, which may conflict with the company's aims
- may restrict the ability of the whole organisation to respond to major environmental changes
- may result in pursuit of short-term profit rather than long-term strategy.

6 The positioning and resource-based views

The positioning view and the resource-based view, look at strategy formulation from the point of view of how the organisation attempts to gain competitive advantage.

The positioning view

The **positioning view** sees competitive advantage stemming from the firm's position in relation to its competitors, customers and stakeholders. It is sometimes called an **'outside-in'** view because it is concerned with adapting the organisation to fit its environment.

The positioning approach to strategy takes the view that supernormal profits result from:

- high market share relative to rivals
- differentiated product
- low costs.

Criticisms of the positioning view:

- The competitive advantages are not sustainable. These advantages are too easily copied in the long run by rivals. Supporters of the resource-based view believe that, sustainable profitability depends on the firm's possession of unique resources or abilities that cannot easily be duplicated by rivals.
- Environments are too dynamic to enable positioning to be effective. Markets are continually changing due to faster product life cycles, the impact of IT, global competition and rapidly changing technologies.
- It is easier to change the environment than it is to change the firm. Supporters of the positioning view seem to suggest that organisations can have its size and shape changed at will to fit the environment.

The resource-based view of strategy

The **resource-based view** sees competitive advantage stemming from some unique asset or competence possessed by the firm. This is called an **'inside-out'** view because the firm must go in search of environments that enable it to harness its internal competencies.

Until the 1990s, most writers took a positioning view; however, more recently, the resource-based perspective has become popular.

Principles of resource-based theory

Barney (1991) argues that superior profitability depends on the firm's possession of **unique resources**. He identifies four criteria for such resources:

- *Valuable*. They must be able to exploit opportunities or neutralise threats in the firm's environment.
- *Rare*. Competitors must not have them too, otherwise they cannot be a source of relative advantage.
- *Imperfectly imitable*. Competitors must not be able to obtain them.
- *Substitutability*. It must not be possible for a rival to find a substitute for this resource.

Resources are combined together to achieve a competence. **A core competence** is something that you are able to do that is very difficult for your competitors to emulate. Threshold competencies are those actions and processes that you must be good at just to be considered as a potential supplier to a customer. If these are not satisfied, you will not even get a chance to be considered by the buyer.

Organisations need to ensure that they are continually monitoring their marketplace to ensure that their core competencies are still valid and that all thresholds are duly satisfied.

Prahalad and Hamel coined the term core competence, which has three characteristics:

- it provides potential access to a wide variety of markets (extendability);
- it increases perceived customer benefits; and
- it is hard for competitors to imitate.

Prahalad and Hamel's work on core competencies focuses on the strategic intent of an organisation to leverage its internal capabilities and core competencies to confront competition. This is sometimes referred to as strategic stretch.

Examples are Honda's core competence in small engines; Apple and technology; Sony and electronic miniaturisation; Volvo and safety; Amazon.com's IT/IS interface with customers. They extend them to a wide variety of products.

They argue that core competences can be destroyed by failure to invest in them. Prahalad and Hamel's formulation carries profound implications for the management accounting function. Management accounting is traditionally built on a responsibility centre model, whereas the view of the authors (and of several of the other resource-based view writers) is that the object of control should be competences and processes rather than business units and divisions.

The implications of the resource-based view for strategy development

- The notion of core competences spreads beyond the ability of the firm to compete just in particular markets and industries. By using techniques that focus on products and markets individually, we may develop strategies which deplete the firm's wider core competences.

- The resource-based view seems to suggest that strategy involves deciding what makes the firm unique and building strategy on that, extending into any products or markets where it will work. In the resource-based view strategy starts with the corporate appraisal, not with the mission of the business.

- The resource-based view can lead to different conclusions. The basis of the resource-based view is the suggestion that the firm should retain any unique strategic assets it has, outsource the remainder, and focus on building up relationships with internal and external stakeholders to develop its internal knowledge so as to improve performance and innovation.

> **Further detail on the resource-based view**
>
> **The implications of the resource-based view for strategy development**
>
> - Conflict with conventional product/market-based views of strategy. The notion of core competences spreads beyond the ability of the firm to compete just in particular markets and industries. Yet many of the models we have used, such as the Porter models and the product life cycle, tend to discuss particular products and markets and develop strategic prescriptions for them. This leads to two possibilities:
>
> - By using techniques that focus on products and markets individually, we may develop strategies which deplete the firm's wider core competences (e.g. by deciding to withdraw from a market or to cut costs by outsourcing a crucial source of organisational learning).

- Even where a firm is involved in a range of industries and has a unique core competence across them all, it is no guarantee of competitive advantage against more focused players in each market (e.g. in the 1980s, IBM had a unique global architecture, reputation and ownership of proprietary technology. This did not stop it from being beaten into second or third place by focused rivals in each of its sub-industries of software development, consulting, PCs and mainframe systems).

- Challenges the rational model of strategy. The RBT view seems to argue that strategy should not be a process of deciding a product/market mission and competing in markets by establishing what the customer wants and exploiting the weaknesses of rivals. Instead, it suggests that strategy involves deciding what makes the firm unique and building strategy on that, extending into any products or markets where it will work. The impacts of this are:
    - RBT strategy starts with the corporate appraisal, not with the mission of the business. Indeed, the mission must adapt to fit the most recent extension of core competence.
    - There is a much higher emphasis on finding an environment to match the firm rather than vice versa (management seems to be saying 'all we have is a hammer so our markets are anything that involves hitting things'). This reasoning could lead to very diverse strategies or perhaps a complete drying-up of strategic avenues (as they run out of things to hit).
    - Investors cannot be clear what industry they are investing in. This may increase perceived risk and hence destroy shareholder value by reducing the share price.

- RBT can lead to different conclusions. The basis of RBT is the suggestion that the firm should retain any unique strategic assets it has, outsource the remainder, and focus on building up relationships with internal and external stakeholders to develop its internal knowledge so as to improve performance and innovation. Consequently, it fits well with modern concepts in network organisation management such as:
    - teamworking
    - collaboration with suppliers and customers
    - flexible working practices
    - creation of participative culture.

However, an alternative conclusion might be that unique knowledge is too valuable to risk losing in networks that could easily be 'burgled' by rivals, through enticing contract staff and suppliers/customers to defect. This might encourage management to deliberately keep knowledge under close control by bringing production in-house, putting staff on restrictive long-term contracts and segmenting trade secrets on a 'need-to-know' basis.

Companies which have adopted the resource-based view

Amazon

Amazon.com turned the stable, mature industry of book retailing upside-down. Using its skills by developing a user-friendly IT interface, it grasped the opportunity of meeting the customers' needs for convenience whilst paying a low price. Customers enjoy an on-line buying experience that allows them with a few clicks of their mice to browse book covers, search from over two million titles, view expert and general reader reviews, choose a basket of books and pay for them including delivery within 24 hours for most titles. They can subsequently track their order.

Amazon.com has achieved success in the way it has focused on its skills (developing one of the best IT interfaces for e-commerce) whilst networking to resource the rest of the business – a network of publishers and book warehouses (for the product), couriers (for handling delivery), credit card operators (for handling payment). To ensure satisfaction to its main customers and keep the well-established book retailers at bay, it does maintain some warehouses which stock the best selling titles. Its prices, including delivery costs, are quite competitive.

Marks & Spencer, recognising their core skills, have asked Amazon.com to manage their on-line shopping infrastructure. Meanwhile Amazon.com have extended the on-line shopping experience to other products including music.

Saga

Saga established a strong leadership in supplying financial services (e.g. insurance) *and* holidays to the 'wrinklies and crinklies' or WOOFs (well-off older folks). The Core Competencies that enable Saga to enter apparently different markets:

- Clear distinctive brand proposition that focuses solely on a closely-defined customer group.
- Leading direct marketing skills – database management; direct-mailing campaigns; call centre sales conversion.
- Skills in customer relationship management.

Black and Decker

Black and Decker's core technology of small motors allowed them to succeed in three markets – home workshop; home cleaning; home maintenance appliance.

Approaches to strategy formulation

Resource-based view versus positioning view

The positioning view focuses on an analysis of competitors and markets before objectives are set and strategies developed. It is an outside-in view.

The essence of this view is ensuring that the organisation has a good "fit" with its environment. The idea is to look ahead at the market and predict changes to enable the organisation to control change rather than having to react to it.

The main problem with the positioning view is that it relies on predicting the future of the market. Some markets are volatile and make estimating future changes impossible in the longer term.

The resource-based view focuses on looking at what the organisation is good at. It is an inside-out view.

The essence of this view is for the organisation to identify its core competencies and build strategies around what they do best, and what competitors find hard to copy.

In practice, more organisations are tending towards the resource-based view for the following reasons:

- Strategic management should focus on developing core competencies.
- Greater likelihood of implementation. Basing a strategy on present resources will reduce the disruption and expenditure involved in implementation.
- It will avoid the firm losing sight of what it is good at.

Test your understanding 1

Your 18 year old neighbour, Josh, has recently left school and has decided that he wants to pursue an entrepreneurial career. He has inherited a sum of money from his grandmother that he aims to invest in his first business venture. In order to be better prepared for the business world he enrolled in a Business Studies course at a local college. After only 6 weeks of the course, Josh decided that he had gained enough knowledge and decided not to continue with the course. He was impatient to launch his career and wanted to focus his energy on his first business venture.

The key element that Josh picked up on the college course was that the key to business success was planning. The lecturer explained that there are different levels of planning (from strategic down to operational) and different types of planning. Josh didn't pay attention to all the detail, but he came away with a clear understanding that planning was important.

For his first business venture Josh intends to set up a computer games development company. He has always had a keen interest in computer games and is skilled in computer technology. He believes he knows the types of games which would sell. He has developed a plan for his business:

(1) Buy a top level gaming computer

(2) Set aside one month to create the game

(3) Approach local games stores directly and convince them to sell the game

(4) Also use word of mouth and the internet to promote the game

Josh has a lot of belief in himself and his ability but asks you for a second opinion to ensure he's not missed anything vital.

Required:

(a) Explain the different levels of planning and comment on whether Josh has fully considered each level.

(6 marks)

(b) Explain the different approaches to strategic planning and consider which might be most appropriate to Josh.

(10 marks)

Test your understanding 2

The F Company consists of automobile engine, marine engine and aerospace engine businesses. It has built its global reputation for engine design and quality on its engineering capability. Though the marine engine business has not been performing well for some time, the F Company has dominated the supply of engines for the luxury end of the automobile market for years. Unfortunately for the F Company, however, the market in luxury automobiles is changing. Exchange rate movements and increased production costs have made the F Company less competitive and its rivals are rapidly catching up in terms of engine quality and design. As a result, the latest annual report shows turnover down, margins reduced and the company barely breaking even.

You have just attended a strategy meeting at the F Company in which:

- Manager A argued that the automobile engine business strategy was wrong.

- Manager B claimed that the major problem had been the failure to properly implement functional strategies.
- Manager C said that more attention should be paid to the threats and opportunities of the external environment so that the F Company could position itself more realistically.
- Manager D claimed that the company should really be seeking to develop further its core engineering competence if it were going to regain its competitiveness in the market place.

After the meeting, a junior manager who had been in attendance asks you to explain what his senior colleagues had been talking about.

Required:

(a) Explain the differences between corporate level strategy, business level strategy and functional level strategy in the F Company.

(6 marks)

(b) Identify the theoretical perspective on strategy formation adopted by Manager C and Manager D.

(12 marks)

(c) Explain the concept of 'core competences' and their relevance to the F Company.

(7 marks)

7 Chapter summary

Disadvantages of the rational approach
- Costly
- Time consuming
- Inappropriate in dynamic environments
- Stifles innovation
- Inappropriate for small businesses

Advantage of the rational approach
- Long term view
- Goal congruence
- Co-ordination
- Stakeholder security
- Incorporates control

Alternative approaches to strategy formulation

Positioning view
- 'Outside-in'

Alternative approaches
- Emergent
- Muddling through
- Logical incrementalism
- Free wheeling opportunism

Resource-based view
- 'Inside-out'

Alternative approaches to strategy formulation

Test your understanding answers

Test your understanding 1

(a) **Levels of planning**

There are three levels of planning: corporate, business and operational.

Corporate planning aims to give a business a long term direction that allows it to cope with its environment and use its resources and competencies in a way that best achieves competitive advantage. It aims to satisfy the business' goals and choose actions that can be implemented to the best effect.

Business planning concerns making decisions for each business unit that will let it compete in particular markets. It is about ensuring strategic plan are achieved and focuses on the medium term success of the business.

Operational planning is concerned with managing resources, processes and people in the short term. It is performed to ensure that business plans are achievable.

The strategies at all levels should be consistent and one should flow from the other.

Josh's plan seems very operational. He has not considered his environment (such as buyer needs, economic climate, barriers to entry etc.) or set definite goals for his business. There appears to be little corporate planning.

There is a small element of tactical planning in terms of approaching shops and using the internet to promote the game(s) but this needs to be expanded further. He has also considered some elements of operational planning (in terms of buying a top level computer) but he needs to extend this into other key resources such as staff, premises, distribution etc.

(b) Approaches to corporate planning

There are a number of ways in which a business might choose to carry out its strategic planning process:

The rational approach

This breaks the process into three distinct steps: strategic analysis (examining the businesses external and internal environment), strategic choice (choosing how best to succeed within this environment) and strategic implementation (putting strategic choices into action). It is a very logical process with clearly defined steps and aims to make a business proactive towards its environment.

Johnson, Scholes and Whittington suggested that each step was interdependent and that each step should be reviewed and possible re-performed after each other step. They also suggested that any step could be the starting step in the process.

The emergent approach

This suggests that strategies emerge over time rather than being developed from an in-depth analysis of the business environment. It aims to recognise the difficulties that some businesses have with strategic analysis. Businesses often start with a planned strategy, but some of this will not be able to be realised due to changes in the market or due to internal factors. Businesses also take advantage of new opportunities which have presented themselves even if these were not in the original plan. The result can be a different outcome than was originally planned.

Logical Incrementalism

Quinn suggested that businesses will have a view as to where they want to be in the future but they will proceed in small steps. With this approach strategy is a step by step learning process. This allows decisions to be small and flexible and allows new opportunities to be exploited

Resource-based view

With the resource-based approach, the business looks at the resources and competences they have and use these to drive the business forward. It is referred to as an inside-out view. The strategy is built up around what the business does best and what others find hard to copy.

Alternative approaches to strategy formulation

From the above, it is unlikely that the rational approach would suit Josh as he is not really at the stage of long term planning. Logical Incrementalism may work for him as he would be able to take his plans step by step and let the longer term plan develop from this. Probably the most suitable approach for Josh at this stage would be the resource-based approach. He has knowledge of the market and has good technical skills. He can use these key skills to create the new game and see where it takes him. It is best for him to get the business up and running, create a viable product and survive for the first six months or a year. After that time he can be more rational and focused and expand his plans over the longer term.

Test your understanding 2

(a) Levels of strategy

Corporate strategy is concerned with the overall running of the business, in particular what industries it will operate in. The F Company appears to have diversified into a number of different industries, notably the production of engines for automobiles, marine vessels and aircraft. Although each of these industries has its own special needs the requirements may be similar, in which case the diversification can be viewed as being concentric.

Business strategy is concerned with how the company aims to be successful within each market. The F Company has gone for a strategy of differentiating its product from its rivals through building a reputation for high quality design and production. This will only be successful if customers are prepared to pay more for these superior products and if rivals cannot duplicate these specialities (Manager A seems to doubt whether this is still true).

Functional strategy refers to how the various functions of the organisation are put together to meet the business strategy outlined above. For example, if the company aims for good quality design then the Human Resource function will need to recruit and retain designers who can provide this. Similarly the purchasing function will need to purchase high-quality raw materials in order to build quality engines.

If the functional strategy is not implemented properly, then the business and corporate level strategies cannot be met (this appears to be the argument of Manager B).

(b) Manager C is arguing that the most important consideration for The F Company in setting its strategy is consideration of the external environment.

This entails looking at the immediate environment in which The F Company operates, for example looking at:

- rivals to see what products they are offering (this appears to be a serious problem to The F Company).
- suppliers of raw material to see if any reduction in price might be obtained (to increase margins).
- customer needs to see if any new products might have a market (for example, what kind of engines will be required in the next generation of passenger aircraft).

The F Company should also look at the general environment that affects the entire industry. The company should look at:

- political pressures (in case of any relevant legislation, particularly over engine emissions).
- technology that might alter the way engines are made.
- economic issues such as future exchange rates since these obviously affect The F Company.
- the overall economic situation that will affect the demand for sea and air travel which will have a knock-on effect for The F Company.
- social issues, such as the demand for cleaner car engines (or engines capable of running on alternative fuel sources).

All of the above can be combined to identify the major threats to The F Company as well as any opportunities that can be exploited to expand sales and/or margins.

Manager D, on the other hand, is arguing that the most important consideration for setting strategy is to look inside the company. In other words this entails looking at what sets the company apart from its rivals by making sure that this advantage is not lost due to the functional strategy being adopted. This means that if The F Company has a reputation for manufacturing high-quality products this must be maintained. This may cause difficulties given the current situation since the temptation may be to cut costs in response to external pressures..

(c) Core competences are features of the organisation that differentiate it attractively in the eyes of the market. They should be identified as 'strengths' in a strategic SWOT analysis of the firm.

An organisation should aim to develop two kinds of competences:

- Distinguishing competences can give the organisation some kind of competitive advantage, or allow it to exploit new opportunities: they should be difficult to imitate, in order to sustain the advantage in the face of competitor response.

- Threshold competences refer to areas in which an organisation must do well in order to keep up with its competitors. Since we are told that The F Company has built its global reputation for engine design and quality on its engineering capability, this has previously been its distinguishing competency

However, competitors are now catching up in terms of engine quality and design. Manager D may therefore be correct to argue that engineering has now become a threshold competency: one which The F Company must protect in order to regain its competitiveness.

Exchange rate movements and increased production costs do not affect this core engineering competency – but they do make it less easy to exploit profitably. While Manager A argues that The F Company should divest itself of its less profitable product line, and Manager C recommends identifying external threats and opportunities (repositioning to a lower end of the automobile market, perhaps, or identifying new markets), The F Company will need to maintain and exploit its core competency. It would be difficult for it to diversify into non-engineering areas, for example, without losing this competitive edge, but it might use its engineering competency to develop new products or markets and extend its brand.

chapter 6

Developments in strategic management

Chapter learning objectives

- Distinguish between different types of competitive environments.
- Discuss concepts in established and emergent thinking in strategic management.

Developments in strategic management

1 Session content diagram

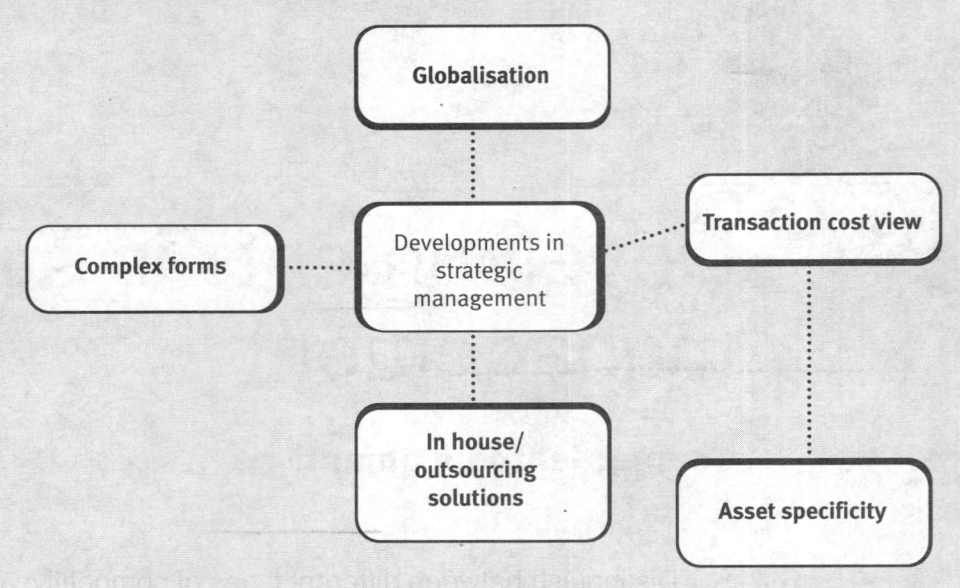

[Diagram: Central node "Developments in strategic management" connected to: Globalisation, Complex forms, Transaction cost view, In house/outsourcing solutions, Asset specificity]

2 Globalisation

Most commentaries on developments in strategic management start with observations about the changes in the business environment. These changes are seen as the result of a number of developments including the drive by multinational companies to seek new markets as domestic markets become saturated. In addition, the liberalisation of trade and the deregulation and privatisation of industries, and developments in the technology of communication and transportation have helped the move towards globalisation.

Presented with opportunities for greater and cheaper access to foreign markets on the one hand, and with the threat of increasing competition on the other, companies have been forced to change the way they manage and operate their businesses.

Business environments are changing as the result of a number of developments. These include:

- The drive by multinational companies to seek new markets as domestic markets become saturated.
- The deregulation and privatisation of industries.
- Consolidation and development of trading blocks.
- Liberalisation of trade.
- Free trade opening up new opportunities in emerging markets.
- Potential cost & market share advantages.
- Lower production costs in developed countries.

- Development in communications network.
- Development in transportation technologies and networks.
- Global financing.
- Developments in the technology of communication and transportation.

All of these factors have helped to produce a global market and mean that companies are able to compete more easily anywhere in the world, with the effect that competition has become even fiercer. Companies have been forced to change the way they manage and operate their businesses.

The impact of globalisation on strategy

A major challenge for business growth will be the ability to deal effectively with the demands of a global economy. As global competition becomes increasingly evident, organisations must choose the geographical boundaries in which they are going to operate, for example retain a strong domestic force, or at the other extreme, become a global player. In most industries organisations can no longer afford to formulate and implement strategies in response to just local conditions; they must be willing to adapt to the conditions of a 'borderless world'.

A number of factors will influence an organisation's ability to operate effectively as a global player, for example in terms of organisational structure, cultural issues and the need for a set of specific leadership skills. All these factors have implications for global effectiveness and development and implementation of strategies.

Although on the one hand, markets are becoming global, there is also a trend towards customisation – with the product/service adapted to some extent for local conditions, hence the need to 'think global, act local'; this is sometimes termed 'glocalisation'.

Porter states that any organisation structure competing in a global market has to balance two dimensions:

- global dimension for world-wide coordination to achieve economies of scale;
- local dimension that enables country managers to respond to local customer needs.

How organisations organise themselves to become global players raises some key challenges. Conventionally, this has been done by establishing or acquiring subsidiaries in other countries, but more recently, alliance and networks are becoming a vital aspect to achieve success within a global marketplace.

3 National competitive advantage – Porter's Diamond

The internationalisation and globalisation of markets raises issues concerning the national sources of competitive advantages that can be substantial and difficult to imitate. **Porter** (1992) in his book, *The Competitive Advantage of Nations*, explored why some nations tend to produces firms with sustained competitive advantage in some industry more than others.

He tried to answer the following questions:

- Why does a nation become the home base for successful international competitors in an industry? Germany is renowned for car manufacture; Japan is prominent in consumer electronics.
- Why are firms based in a particular nation able to create and sustain competitive advantage against the world's best competitors in a particular field?
- Why is one country often the home of so many of an industry's world leaders?

Porter called the answers to these questions the determinants of national competitive advantage. He suggested that there are four main factors which determine national competitive advantage and expressed them in the form of a diamond.

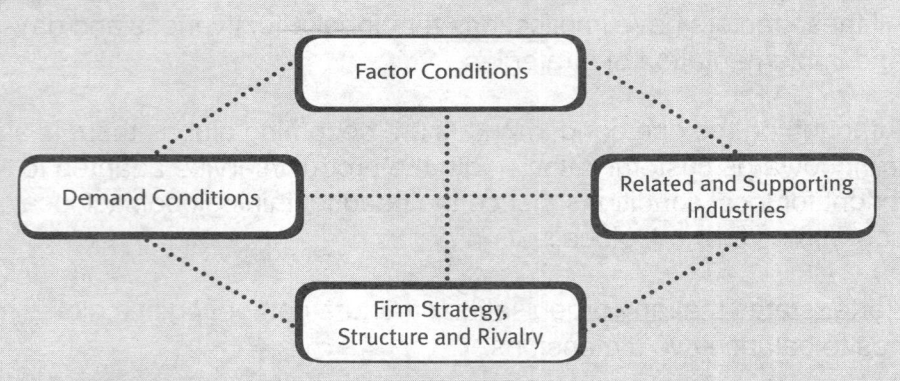

- **Factor conditions.** Factor conditions include the availability of raw materials and suitable infrastructure.
- **Demand conditions.** The goods or services have to be demanded at home: this starts international success.
- **Related and supporting industries.** These allow easy access to components and knowledge sharing.
- **Firm strategy, structure and rivalry.** If the home market is very competitive, a company is more likely to become world class.

Porter concludes that entire nations do not have particular competitive advantages. Rather, he argues, it is specific industries or firms within them that seem able to use their national backgrounds to lever world-class competitive advantages.

Further detail on Porter's Diamond

Demand conditions

The demand conditions in the home market are important for three reasons:

(1) If the demand is substantial it enables the firm to obtain the economies of scale and experience effects it will need to compete globally.

(2) The experience the firm gets from supplying domestic consumers will give it an information advantage in global markets, provided that:

   (a) its customers are varied enough to permit segmentation into groups similar to those found in the global market as a whole;

   (b) its customers are critical and demanding enough to force the firm to produce at world-class levels of quality in its chosen products;

   (c) its customers are innovative in their purchasing behaviour and hence encourage the firm to develop new and sophisticated products.

(3) If the maturity stage of the product lifecycle is reached quickly (say, due to rapid adoption), this will give the firm the incentive to enter export markets before others do.

Related and supporting industries

The internationally competitive firm must have, initially at least, enjoyed the support of world-class producers of components and related products. Moreover success in a related industry may be due to expertise accumulated elsewhere (e.g. the development of the Swiss precision engineering tools industry owes much to the requirements and growth of the country's watch industry).

Factor conditions

These are the basic factor endowments referred to in economic theory as the source of so-called comparative advantage. Factors may be of two sorts:

(1) **Basic factors** such as raw materials, semi-skilled or unskilled labour and initial capital availability. These are largely 'natural' and not created as a matter of policy or strategy.

(2) **Advanced factors** such as infrastructure (particularly digital telecommunications), levels of training and skill, R&D experience, etc.

Porter argues that only the advanced factors are the roots of sustainable competitive success. Developing these becomes a matter for government policy.

Firm structure, strategy and rivalry

National cultures and competitive conditions do create distinctive business focuses. These can be influenced by:

- ownership structure
- the attitudes and investment horizons of capital markets
- the extent of competitive rivalry
- the openness of the market to outside competition.

Other events

Porter points out that countries can produce world-class firms due to two further factors:

(1) *The role of government*. Subsidies, legislation and education can impact on the other four elements of the diamond to the benefit of the industrial base of the country.

(2) *The role of chance events*. Wars, civil unrest, chance factor discoveries, etc. can also change the four elements of the diamond unpredictably.

Illustration 1 – Porter's diamond illustration

Porter's diamond applied to the scotch whisky industry

Factor conditions:

Natural factor conditions: Scotland has ready availability of the raw materials required for whisky production. This includes a plentiful water supply and a climate suited to growing the crops required in the production process.

Advanced factor conditions: Over the years, knowledge and a skilled workforce has developed in Scotland. In addition the name 'Scotch' can only be applied to whisky which has been produced in Scotland and 'Scotch' is known throughout the world and recognised for its quality.

Demand conditions:

A strong home demand is the starting point for international competitive advantage. The domestic consumers become more sophisticated and demanding, which drives up the quality of all products. This is true in the case of Scotch whisky, there is a strong home demand (around 15% of all Scotch is sold in Scotland).

Related and supporting industries:

There are over 100 working distilleries in Scotland, all requiring the support of other industries. As a result there are strong bottling, cooperage and distribution industries which support the whisky producers.

Firm strategy, industry structure and rivalry:

There are over 100 working distilleries throughout Scotland, many of these are small and only produce one or two specialist malt whiskies. This has generated competition between the distillers to produce the best quality whisky and this in turn increases the quality of all products in the industry.

Test your understanding 1

Required:

Apply Porter's Diamond to the US personal computer (PC) industry.

(10 marks)

Difficulties with Porter's Diamond

Although not as popular as his models of five forces, value chain and generic strategies, this model has still achieved a lot of recognition for Porter. It is not, however, without its difficulties:

- *Companies not countries*. The industries that must succeed globally have their own management and strategies. By focusing on their country of origin Porter does not explain why a given country produces both stars and duds in the same industry. For example, Toyota and Honda are both Japanese car makers which are a success. Nissan and Mazda are less successful and have been rescued by Renault and Ford, respectively.

- *Ignore multinational or global corporations*. The idea that Microsoft is an American company seems outdated when we consider that their staff, shareholders and customers are from all over the world. Porter's model seems to apply better to firms that are exporting and less well to ones who are actually setting up outside of their home country.

- *Ignores the target country*. Commercial success or failure will depend more on the environment in the target country than it will on the environment in the home country. Therefore it is necessary to analyse the target country too.

- *Less applicable to services*. Porter's examples are restricted to manufacturing and closely allied industries such as banks and management consultancies. It is hard to see how his model would apply to say Starbucks where so much of the product and staffing depends on the local economy.

4 More complex forms of organisations

Globalisation has changed the competitive strategies of organisations. In addition, there have been changes in terms of the growth and diversification strategies pursued. While some organisations still pursue organic growth, there has been a move away from this strategy towards growth via different structural forms, such as mergers, takeovers, alliances and outsourcing. This has resulted in more complex forms of organisational structure.

Growth and diversification strategies pursued include:

- **New ventures** – organic development by using the resources of the existing entity or by acquiring additional resources.
- **Mergers & Acquisitions** – when an organisation may pursue growth by taking over or merging with an established business in the field of its interest.

- **Strategic alliance** – a formal relationship in which two or more companies legally contract to co-operate in defined ways to achieve specific commercial objectives, e.g. joint ventures, consortia, franchising and licensing.

- **Subcontracting or Outsourcing** – one organisation delegates some of its activities under contract to external companies. (Outsourcing will be discussed in more detail later in this chapter).

- **Network organisations** – virtual organisations, which have been described as a series of strategic alliances that an organisation creates with suppliers, manufacturers and distributors to produce and market a product. (Network organisations will be discussed in more detail later in this chapter).

Further detail on strategic alliances

A strategic alliance can be defined as where two or more organisations share resources and activities to pursue strategies. There are different forms of alliance, some which depend on formalised inter-organisational relationships and others which are much looser arrangements and informal networks between organisations. For example:

Joint ventures which involve two or more organisations setting up a newly created organisation, which is jointly owned and managed as a third separate entity. This form of alliance is often used where organisations want to enter new markets.

Consortia are short-term legal entities and will usually be focused on a particular project, with sunk costs from each of the partners and which terminate at the end of the project.

Franchising, allows the franchisee to undertake specific activities, such as manufacturing, distribution or selling, whilst the franchiser is responsible for managing the brand and marketing (e.g. Coca-Cola, The Body Shop, McDonald's).

Licensing gives the right to manufacture a patented product, for a fee.

Johnson, Scholes and Whittington (2008) suggest the ingredients of successful alliances include:

- a clear strategic purpose for all parties in the alliance;
- compatibility between parties;
- defining and meeting performance expectations – having clear goals, governance, and organisational arrangements;
- trust and integrity between the partners to the alliance.

5 Network organisations

The current business world is increasingly using practices such as subcontracting labour or outsourcing production that gives rise to the network organisation. This type of organisation depends on others to carry out its activities through a complex network of contracts and relations with external specialised organisations.

Lysons & Farrington define a network as 'a series of strategic alliances that an organisation creates with suppliers, manufacturers and distributors to produce and market a product'.

Network organisations can choose to **'buy-in'** a range of value-creating activities through:

- *Contract staffing* – network organisations often only retain a small cohort of core staff, the rest would be contract or temporary staff
- *Use of specific capital assets* – the network organisation frequently leases its IT facilities.
- *Outsourcing elements* of service or production – ancillary services such as cleaning have often been outsourced, the network organisation takes this further by outsourcing the production of its products and distribution of its products.
- *Reliance on outside organisations for referral of business* – many network organisations have mutual customer-sharing arrangements and will cross-sell their products.

There are a number of issues posed by the development of network organisations:

- How do firms decide which activities and assets to 'buy-in'?
- Why have network organisations become so important in recent years?
- How can management develop systems to control operations in a network organisation?

Illustration 2 – An example of a network organisation – Amazon

To illustrate the notion of a network organisation, a good example to use is the online retailer Amazon.com. Amazon provides a customer website interface that enables the visitor to search and browse the catalogue of products. The customer can order the product online and expect to receive it by courier within a few days.

Amazon sits in the middle of a network of other organisations. It has contract arrangements with book warehouses throughout the world to process and dispatch its orders so that it need keep only the 80,000 top-selling titles in stock. These warehouses keep Amazon notified of their stock position (which is automatically transferred to the customer web pages as approximate delivery times). The same is the case for the other product ranges that they offer.

Amazon also has arrangements with couriers, credit card operators and publishers to provide it with the information and services it will need. From the customer's point of view, it 'feels' like one organisation: the products arrive in Amazon packaging and they have their own account with the company. The company also keeps them informed about new products in areas similar to ones they have bought before.

Yet in fact, Amazon owns relatively few physical assets and staff to back up its service.

A network organisation can be viewed as extreme outsourcing, whereby the organisation identifies their core activities and focuses on these activities alone, outsourcing all others. The view is that they gain no competitive advantage from carrying out the non-core activities. They select a third party to undertake these activities, allowing them to focus on their core business.

In the case of Amazon, the core competence (the activity they do better than others, that others find hard to copy) is their website design.

Developments in strategic management

> ### Organisations which 'buy-in' activities and assets
>
> Customers are not always aware which activities are being provided by the organisation they are contracting with and which activities are being supplied by other parties. Some examples are given below:
>
> **Airways**
>
> A customer of an airline has the impression that everything is supplied by the airline itself. In fact it is likely that telephone booking, aircraft maintenance, on-board catering and luggage handling are provided under a contract from other firms.
>
> **UK Hospitals**
>
> A patient in hospital will receive medical treatment, food and accommodation services. However, the hospital may use private contractors for cleaning, laundry and catering while at the same time relying on other hospitals for the use of specialist equipment, e.g. scanning. Many staff may also be employed on a contract basis.
>
> **UK Railways**
>
> A passenger will buy their ticket from a train-operating company and travel according to the timetable the company has laid down. The train itself may be owned by a separate leasing company, depart from a station and along lines operated by a third company, yet maintained by a fourth. The on-board catering will be provided by a fifth firm and the train cleaned by a sixth firm.

6 Transaction costs view of the firm

From network organisations above, you can see that organisations make decisions about what activities to undertake in-house, and which to outsource to a third party. This is an important decision for organisation to make. Outsourcing requires careful consideration and monitoring, can be costly to set up and it can be problematic to reverse outsourcing decisions in the short term.

Transaction cost theory (TCT) (**Coase and Williamson**) provides a means for making the decision about which activities to outsource and which to perform in-house.

Transaction cost theory suggests that organisations choose between two approaches to control resources and carry out their operations:

- **Hierarchy solutions** – direct ownership of assets and staff, controlled through internal organisation policies and procedures;
- **Market solutions** – assets and staff are 'bought in' from outside under the terms of a contract (for example, an outsourcing agreement).

It may be helpful to think of this theory as a more complex version of the familiar 'make-or-buy' decision. Management will make in-house the things that cost them more to buy from the market and will adopt the market when transaction costs are lower than the costs of ownership. However, Williamson looks beyond just the unit costs of the product or service under consideration. He is specifically interested in the costs of control that (together with the unit costs) make up transactions costs.

Examples of market solutions

The following forms of market solutions are networks:

- *Contract staffing* – this may include both low-level operative staff, and also highly-skilled specialists with scarce intellectual capital, such as IT analysts and designers, project managers and engineers.
- *Outsourcing parts of the IT department of an organisation* – multiple outsourcing agreements with many IT providers so as to provide cutting-edge IT platforms at the lowest possible cost.
- *Mutual customer sharing* – networks of organisations relying upon referral business from outside firms.
- *Leasing assets* – specifically leased assets such as machinery, customised office accommodation or exhibition equipment.

Hierarchy solutions – costs will include:

- staff recruitment and training;
- provision of managerial supervision;
- production planning;
- payments and incentive schemes to motivate performance;
- the development of budgetary control systems to coordinate activity;
- divisional performance measurement and evaluation;
- provision and maintenance of fixed assets, such as premises and capital equipment.

Developments in strategic management

Market solutions – costs:

> **Transaction costs = 'buy-in' costs + external control cost**

External control costs will include:

- negotiating and drafting a legal contract with the supplier;
- monitoring the supplier's compliance with the contract (quality, quantity, reliability, invoicing, etc.);
- pursuing legal actions for redress due to non-performance by the supplier;
- penalty payments and cancellation payments if the firm later finds it needs to change its side of the bargain and draft a new contract with the supplier.

External control costs arise because of the following risk factors:

- **Bounded rationality:** the limits on the capacity of individuals to process information, deal with complexity and pursue rational aims.
- **Difficulties in specifying/measuring performance**, e.g. terms such as 'normal wear and tear' may have different interpretations.
- **Asymmetric information:** one party may be better informed than another, who cannot acquire the same information without incurring substantial costs.
- **Uncertainty and complexity.**
- **Opportunistic behaviour:** each agent is seeking to pursue their own economic self-interest. This means they will take advantages of any loopholes in the contract to improve their position.

Asset specificity

The degree of *asset specificity*, is the most important determinant of transaction cost. Asset specificity is the extent to which particular assets are of use only in one specific range of operations.

The more specific the assets are, the greater the transaction costs would be were the asset to be shared and hence the more likely the transaction will be internalised into the hierarchy. On the other hand, when assets are non-specific the process of market contracting is more efficient because transaction costs will be low.

There are **six main types of asset specificity:**

(1) **Site specificity** – the assets may be immobile, or are attached to a particular geographical location, for example:
  – locating a components plant near the customer's assembly plant;
  – building hotels near a certain theme park or tourist attraction;
  – building of pipelines and harbours to service an oilfield.

(2) **Physical asset specificity** – this is a physical asset with unique properties, for example:
  – reserves of high-quality ores;
  – a unique work of art or building.

(3) **Human asset specificity** – where workers have particular skills or knowledge, for example:
  – specific technical skills relevant to only one product;
  – knowledge of systems and procedures peculiar to one organisation.

(4) **Dedicated asset specificity** – a man-made asset which has been made to an exact specification for a customer and only has one application, for example:
  – Eurotunnel; military defence equipment; Sydney Harbour Bridge.

(5) **Brand name capital specificity** – a brand and associations that belong to one family of:
  – products and would lose value if spread wider, for example:
  – Coca-Cola; McDonald's.

(6) **Temporal specificity** – the unique ability to provide service at a certain time, for example:
  – the right to conduct radio broadcasts at an allotted time;
  – rights to exploit an asset for only a limited number of years.

Asset specificity examples

There are six main types of asset specificity:

- *Site specificity* suggesting that once sited the assets may be immobile – Amazon has no site specificity since its 'selling space' is in webspace, meaning it can share its website with second-hand bookshops all over the world.

- *Physical asset specificity* when parties make investments in machinery or equipment that are specific to a certain transaction; these will have lower values in alternative uses. For example, DHL delivery vans have low physical asset specificity in that they can be used to deliver a wide variety of products making it easy for DHL to network with other organisations; Blue Circle Cement has trucks that deliver wet cement, these are highly physically specific (to cement) and therefore cannot easily be shared in a network.

- *Human asset specificity* occurs when workers have knowledge or skills that are highly suited to one particular task, for example Direct Line Insurance call-centre staff have highly flexible skills and are sub-contracted to other companies, whereas your Kaplan lecturer has highly specific knowledge and skills that make it difficult to sub-contract them for other activities than training accountants.

- *Brand name specificity* – Amazon has low brand name specificity which allows it to sell different types of goods, for instance books, CDs, white goods etc.

- *Dedicated asset specificity* where the assets are made by a supplier to an exact specification of a customer, and would be useless for any other company to use, for example, a machine designed specifically to manufacture Apple iPod players would be useful to Apple only since they control exclusive rights to iPod patents; whereas a machine designed to manufacture ordinary MP3 players could be used by many different manufacturers and therefore could be shared within a network.

- *Temporal specificity* arises when the timing of performance is critical, such as with perishable agricultural commodities – for instance, Tesco Home Shopping service utilises its own refrigerated delivery vans to deliver to customers due to the perishable nature of the food they deliver.

Eurotunnel plc

Consider the example of Eurotunnel plc. This company has a single asset, a tunnel under the English Channel linking the British Isles to the main European continent, which opened in 1994 having cost nearly £5bn to build. Apart from some telecommunications potential, this extremely expensive asset has no conceivable alternative use other than as a rail tunnel. In addition to operating its own shuttle services for passengers and freight, over 30 % of the company's revenues come from other railway companies which pay Eurotunnel to use the tunnel. This includes the Eurostar consortium that operates specially built trains between London and various destinations in France and Belgium.

This is a situation of high asset specificity. High asset specificity arises where a supplier must invest in expensive assets with no alternative use in order to supply a client. This poses a substantial risk to the supplier because if the contract is withdrawn, it will not be able to recoup its investment. Few will take this risk without a guarantee of orders in the long term. Eurotunnel plc is locked into the train operators. At the same time, the train operators are locked into Eurotunnel because their investment in rolling stock and stations would be useless without the tunnel.

Williamson examines the effect of such high 'asset specificity' on transaction costs. Williamson predicts that such high asset specificity will therefore result in bilateral (or quasi-bilateral) contracts between the firm and its supplier. High asset specificity results in the buyer being denied the opportunity to periodically choose between rival producers on an external market, instead being forced to enter a long-term contract with the sole supplier. Eurotunnel has the exclusive right to operate the tunnel until 2086, and the rail operators signed agreements which committed them to certain minimum financial payments to Eurotunnel. In return, they have the right to use up to 50% of the tunnel capacity. It can be seen that the high asset specificity of Eurotunnel has led to high transactions costs in the form of the contracts and franchise agreements around it.

Williamson's conclusion is that high asset specificity will lead firms to bring supply in-house rather than bear the high transactions costs of the market. Indeed, he suggests that extremely high asset specificity may result in no suppliers coming forward on the market. In this connection, it is significant to note that Eurotunnel began life as a political creation of the British and French governments rather than as a private business initiative.

Eurotunnel combines a number of the asset specificity types: temporal (limited franchise till 2086), dedicated asset and site specificity.

Developments in strategic management

Transaction cost theory approaches are being used in strategic considerations for a number of reasons:

(1) *Identification of distinctive competencies* – according to transaction cost theory this will be an operation or an asset that cannot be provided by another organisation without increasing the transaction costs or risks to the firm.

(2) *To support organisational restructuring* – organisations should sell off upstream or downstream divisions that can be provided at lower transaction costs by the market.

(3) *To predict the impacts of developments in information technology* – it is believed that the cost of searching for a supplier, maintaining the supplier/buyer relationship have been reduced by developments in Information Technology (IT). These are often put under the umbrella of ecommerce.

A critique of transaction cost theory

Consider the following decisions made by leading organisations in relation to transaction cost theory:

- Does Disney Corporation operate visitor and cast accommodation at its theme parks because it is cheaper than offering the financial safeguards necessary to encourage hotel operators to invest in such specific assets?

- Is the reason that Procter & Gamble develops its own brands for foods and detergents that the uncertainties about brand values and strategy make it very expensive to draft contracts to lease brands from brand owners?

- Did the same consideration lie behind Grand Metropolitan's decision to buy Pillsbury rather than simply license the Burger King brand from it?

- Do large firms undertake in-house staff and management development programmes because colleges and potential recruits are unwilling to bear the costs of training themselves in such specific skills?

- Are some staff paid far more than they could otherwise get on the job market because they possess specific skills which the firm cannot buy from the labour market?

The growth of the network organisation, however, seems to challenge Williamson's theory because it represents a breakdown in hierarchies and features a much greater use of the market to provide inputs and customers. Several explanations may be offered for this phenomenon:

- Organisations may have underestimated the costs of internal control. Firms undertake activities internally when the transactions costs of external provision are too great. However, this assumes that management can accurately quantify the costs of controlling the internal operation.

- Transaction costs may have been reduced by the impact of information technology, e.g. common computer assisted design (CAD) systems allow collaboration in research and development with geographically remote suppliers.

- Communications technology such as teleconferencing, e-mail and intranets permit much lower cost and timely maintenance of supplier relationships than was possible using face-to-face methods. Firms now have access to global partners because the cost of searching for suitable suppliers or buyers is reduced by IT.

- Globalisation has made firms less reliant on a single customer, similarly, buyers will have a choice of suppliers rather than a single monopoly supplier. Firms may be more prepared to undertake asset specific investment in this global market place. Malone et al. suggest a significant shift to increased outsourcing will occur as firms become able to network in an 'unbiased market' rather than being faced with the choice between internal production or reliance on a monopoly partner.

Transaction cost analysis may explain the trend to network organisations if it can be shown that external pressures are forcing firms to reduce costs. For example, it may be that increased shareholder pressure or market competition is forcing managers to break down their empires in order to gain the lower transaction costs available from external partnerships.

Developments in strategic management

Test your understanding 2

'Asset specificity' is a term used within Transactions Cost Theory. It has been defined as the extent to which particular assets are only of use in one specific range of operations. It has further been suggested that asset specificity falls into six categories: site specificity, physical asset specificity, human asset specificity, dedicated asset specificity, brand name capital specificity and temporal specificity.

Supporters of resource-based views of strategy contend that a firm's sustainable competitive advantage is generated from its possession of unique assets that cannot be easily irritated by other firms. These unique assets have been called core competencies or distinctive capabilities.

Network organisations have been defined as those which are reliant on relationships with other organisations to carry out their work.

Required:

(a) Briefly explain what transaction costs are and how resource-based views of strategy can be used for competitive advantage.

(6 marks)

(b) Interpret the six categories of asset specificity by explaining what they mean.

(12 marks)

(c) Discuss whether analysis of transactions cost has any influence on the increase in numbers of network organisations.

(7 marks)

Test your understanding 3

Red Sky Fashions ("Red Sky") is a clothing manufacturer, which sells its designs exclusively via its website. The online fashion industry is becoming more competitive and Red Sky's CEO is looking at how savings can be made in the company to make it more competitive. She is focusing her attention for saving on the customer services department as she sees this department as simply a cost to the business. She feels that savings could be made if she were to outsource the department.

The customer service department currently employs 25 members of staff. The department is responsible for; setting up new customer accounts, processing customer orders (online and telephone) and responding to customer queries.

Required:

Using transaction cost theory explain to the CEO what she has to consider in making the decision to outsource the customer services department. Include a discussion on asset specificity.

(10 marks)

7 Chapter summary

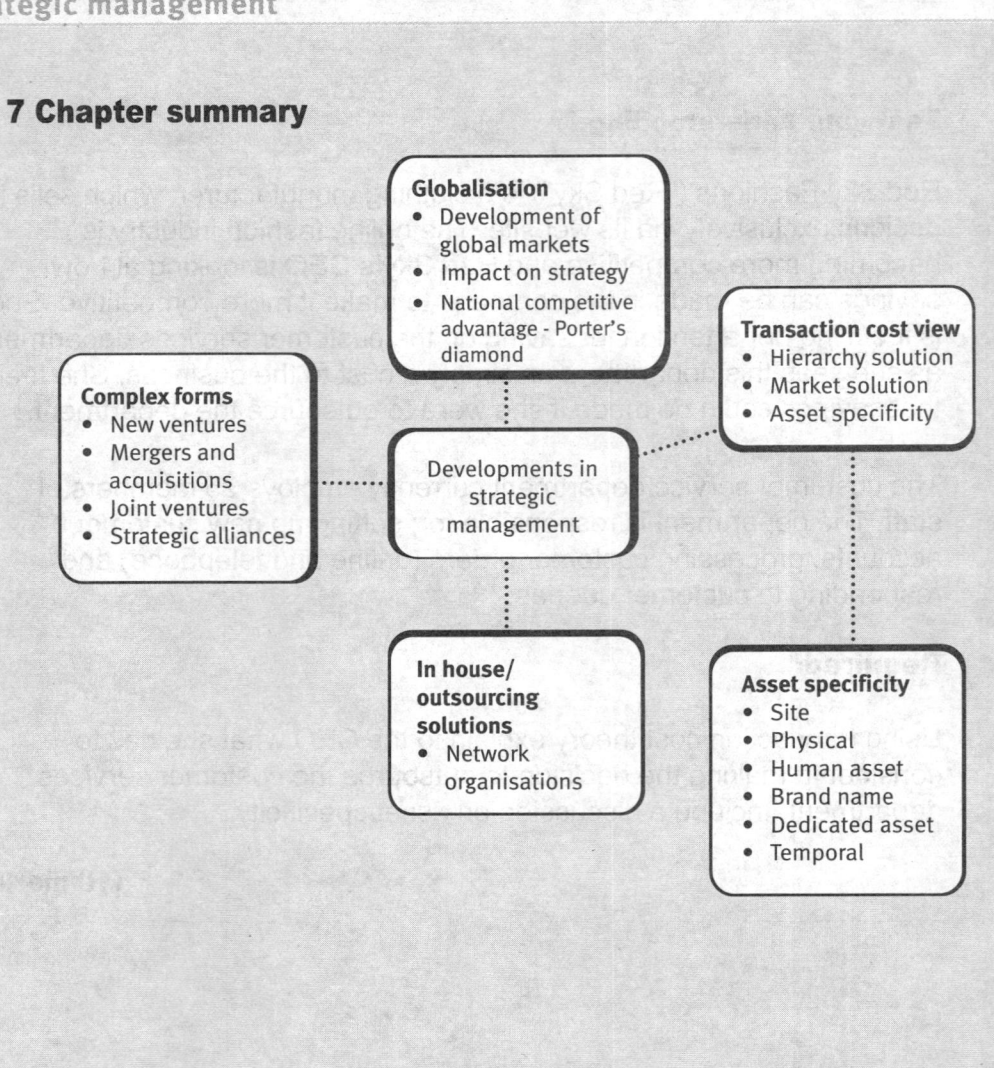

Globalisation
- Development of global markets
- Impact on strategy
- National competitive advantage - Porter's diamond

Complex forms
- New ventures
- Mergers and acquisitions
- Joint ventures
- Strategic alliances

Transaction cost view
- Hierarchy solution
- Market solution
- Asset specificity

Developments in strategic management

In house/outsourcing solutions
- Network organisations

Asset specificity
- Site
- Physical
- Human asset
- Brand name
- Dedicated asset
- Temporal

Test your understanding answers

Test your understanding 1

Factor conditions: large population of well-trained engineers.

Demand conditions: large population of individuals and businesses who need or want PCs.

Related and supporting industries: many component manufacturers close by; large and well-endowed universities.

Firm strategy, structure and rivalry: an entrepreneurial economy allowed many startups and the best survive the intense rivalry.

Test your understanding 2

(a) Transactions cost analysis is concerned with more than just unit costs of products or services. It is also concerned with the costs of control specifically relating to the delivery of a product or provision of a service. Transactions costs come about between stages in a production or supply process and it may be both internal to, and external from, the firm itself. In respect of an external supply, such costs may include drafting legal contracts and monitoring supply and quality. Similarly, internal costs of quality control and human resource management may be included as transactions costs. Such costs exist because all parties want to have protection against loss, and contractual arrangements may be used by each to protect their position.

Resource-based views of strategy take the view that unique assets which cannot be easily replicated by other firms can act as a defence. They may be viewed in Porter's terms as a defence barrier allowing the firm to reduce threats and exploit opportunities within a highly competitive environment. Such unique assets may enable a firm to achieve supernormal profits, that is those which cover more than the normal opportunity cost of capital.

(b) The six categories of asset specificity may be interpreted as follows:

(1) Site specificity relates to the assets which are connected to a particular geographical position, for example, locating a goods distribution organisation close to a motorway network.

(2) Physical asset specificity is concerned with identifying particular physical assets or possessions with particular attributes such as valuable mineral deposits or natural ingredients with particular healing qualities.

(3) Human asset specificity is associated with very specialist knowledge or skills such as that possessed by surgeons or an employee who has particular knowledge of a specialist process.

(4) Dedicated asset specificity relates to an asset which was built for a single purpose or application, such as bridges or dedicated buildings.

(5) Brand name capital specificity concentrates a brand name to one family of products or services such as might be employed by a food manufacturer, type of engine or air travel service provider.

(6) Temporal specificity is concerned with providing a specialist product or service at a specific time, as might be employed by a television broadcaster.

Some of these categories may be employed together by the same provider; for example, a broadcaster might employ human asset specificity in terms of a presenter delivering the broadcast at a specific time (temporal specificity) from a purpose-built studio (dedicated asset specificity).

(c) Network organisations establish relationships with other organisations to supply goods and services. They are concerned with more than just outsourcing as they look to other organisations to supply core products as well as ancillary services. There are many examples of such organisations, particularly in respect of leisure services and supply of produce such as flowers being delivered to domestic households through a worldwide network.

Oliver Williamson stated that the reduction of transaction costs occurs by vertical integration resulting in organisations becoming more divisionalised and complex. Many organisations do carry out their own branding, training, ancillary service provision and often pay more than the going market rate in order to retain key staff. This approach seems to be at odds with the theory of networking as described above. Networking is reliant on market forces to provide goods and services in order to meet customer demands. The principle is quite straightforward: if the market can supply the product or service at an appropriate level of quality more cheaply than the firm itself, then let it do so.

This aims to increase shareholder value by reducing organisational costs.

The reasons for the diversity existing may be as a result of:

- Firms underestimating the cost of internal control to provide goods and services in-house. This is a constant concern of organisations which may have been exacerbated by the traditional form of absorption costing. Essentially, many firms believe that the provision of a good or service by an outside contractor may be 'more expensive', but this may be based on false assumptions regarding in-house costs because of arbitrary and sometimes absurd apportionments of fixed overheads. Activity-based costing has done much to identify true overhead costs associated with specific products and services.

- Advances in information technology have led to a reduction in transaction costs. The perception of the need to rely on a single source of supply, possibly a monopoly supplier is no longer as prominent as it once was. Electronic developments have in themselves led to greater awareness of choice and outsourcing.

- The development of trust between contracting partners have also led to greater outsourcing. Many organisations have entered long-term relationships with suppliers and customers, resulting in much higher degrees of trust and collaboration for mutual benefit.

- The traditional economic theory of a hierarchical organisation as provided by classical organisational theorists has become outdated. Although such organisations have been able, in general, to provide management with high degrees of control, they have not necessarily operated in the best interests of shareholders. In fact, large hierarchical organisations have often developed as a result of agency theory and managers building their own empires, securing their own positions and creating power domains. These have not necessarily had increasing shareholder value as the main driver. Such organisations may have, in fact, been operating inefficiently, but they survive because of their sheer size and market power.

Transactions Cost Analysis has forced firms to look more seriously at their own supply costs. It has caused them to look in more detail at how well they meet their shareholder requirements. This, in turn, has led them to take note of market forces in delivering their product or service in a cheaper manner. Thus, it can be argued that Transactions Cost Analysis has to some extent influenced the increase in the number of network organisations.

Transactions Cost Analysis firmly embraces the concept of continual improvement. This, in itself, may be facilitated by networks of contracts, both internal and external. All employees within an organisation have customers, whether they are internal or external. The increasing development of network organisations is clear, but firms must be wary of losing their core competencies by other network firms recruiting key staff. Some staff, for example, are placed on restrictive long-term contracts to protect the firm. This, in turn, may lead to reduced overall efficiency, but it is a natural response by a firm to protect its position.

Test your understanding 3

Transaction cost theory suggests that two solutions must be compared when making an outsourcing decision:

- The in-house or hierarchy solution.
- The outsourced or market solution.

As cost saving is the driver in this scenario, both solutions should be costed to ascertain if the market (outsourced) solution would be cheaper.

When considering the hierarchy solution, all internal costs associated with the running of the customer services department must be considered. This will include the direct cost of employing the 25 members of staff plus the overheads associated with employees, such as office space, benefits and human resources. It will also include the cost of the assets needed for the department to function, such as desks, chairs, computer and telephone equipment. Other internal costs would be training, supervision, maintenance of equipment and IT support.

The market solution will principally be the transaction cost for the service provided by the outside company, plus the external control costs.

The level of transaction costs will be influenced by the specificity of the assets required for the contract.

- In this case the assets would have fairly low specificity as regards physical specificity as the assets needed would be fairly general and could be used for many different companies and industries.
- There would also be low site specificity as the outsourcer could be located anywhere in the world.

- Likewise brand name and dedicated asset specificity would also be low.

- Human asset specificity would be higher in that the outsourcer would have to build up the skills and knowledge relating to the product and designs of Red Sky, but this would reduce over time.

- Temporal specificity could also be high in that the customer services department would have to be available to answer calls from customers without delay. If customers are encouraged to correspond by email rather than telephone, then this could also reduce.

Overall the transaction costs for a fairly general customer services department is likely to be fairly low.

However the external control costs can be significant and must be carefully considered. They include:

- Negotiating the contract, including tendering an legal costs in drafting the contract.

- Enforcing costs which will include setting up service level agreements, quality assurance testing and managing the relationship with the outsourcer.

Red Sky would also have to consider the potential reputation risk it could face by outsourcing its customer services department. Customers may be lost as a result of this decision and that has to be taken account of as part of the consideration.

chapter 7

Organisational culture

Chapter learning objectives

- Demonstrate the importance of organisational culture.

1 Session content diagram

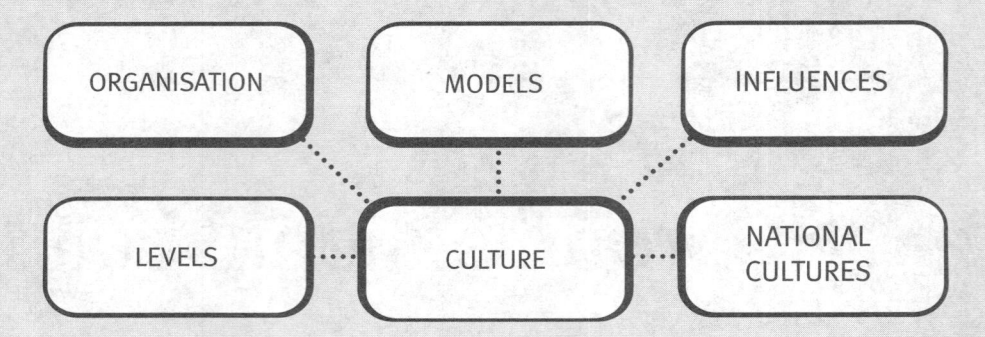

```
ORGANISATION ···· MODELS ···· INFLUENCES
     │             │             │
   LEVELS ···· CULTURE ···· NATIONAL CULTURES
```

2 Organisational culture

Organisations are social arrangements for achieving controlled performance in pursuit of collective goals. (Buchanan & Huczynski 1997).

Organisational culture is an important concept since it has a widespread influence on the behaviours and actions of employees. It represents a powerful force on an organisation's strategies, structures and systems, the way it responds to change and ultimately, how well the organisation performs.

What is culture?

Culture may be defined as:

'the way we do things around here' – by **Handy**

By this Handy means the sum total of the *belief, knowledge, attitudes, norms* and *customs* that prevail in an organisation.

'the collective programming of the mind which distinguishes the members of one category of people from another' – by **Hofstede**

'the collection of traditions, values, policies, beliefs and attitudes that constitute a pervasive context for everything we do and think in an organisation' – by **Mullins**

3 The McKinsey 7-S Model

McKinsey, a US management consultancy, also produced a framework for understanding organisations (the McKinsey 7-S framework). This model highlights the 'hard' and 'soft' aspects of organisations which can influence the culture. Similar to the cultural web framework, it also recognises the inter-relationships between the elements. In the cultural web, you saw that all the elements overlapped, in the 7-S model, lines are drawn between each of the element to show that each element will have an impact on every other element. If one element is changed, then changes in all the other elements will have to be considered.

The seven factors referred to are:

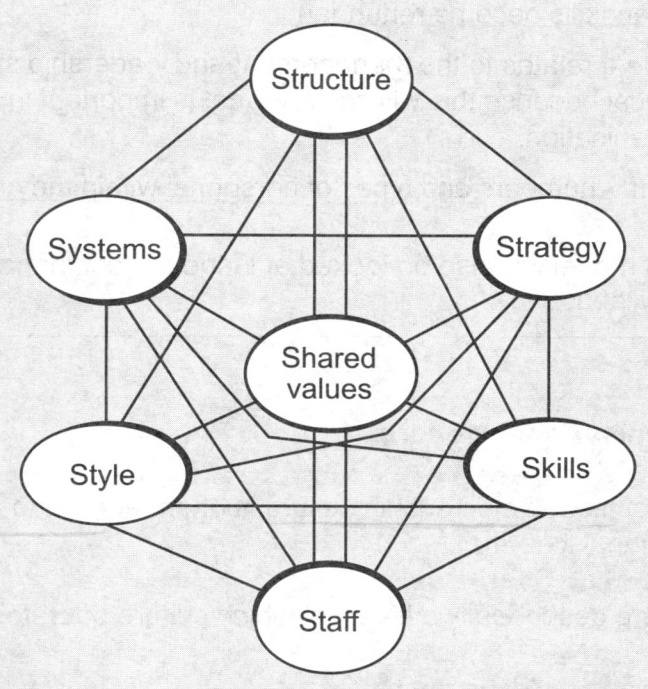

```
              Structure
         /   /   |   \   \
    Systems ─────────── Strategy
       │  \    Shared    /  │
       │    \  values  /    │
      Style ─────────── Skills
         \   \   |   /   /
               Staff
```

- The hard elements are: strategy, structure and systems
- The soft elements are: shared values, skills, style and staff

The hard elements are more visible from outside the organisation, while the soft elements are usually only completely understood from within the organisation.

More detail on the McKinsey 7-S model

The 7-S's - an overview of the seven elements:

- Strategy – The actions that are planned in response to environmental change in order that the organisation achieves its long term goals.

- Structure – how people and tasks are organised. This will consider the way the organisation's departments and divisions relate to each other.

- Systems – the information flows and processes of an organisation. This includes formal and informal procedures that ensure the organisation operates. For example, accounting systems, budgetary systems information technology systems and so on.

- Shared values – also known as super-ordinate goals. These identify what the organisation believes in and stands for, they are the guiding concepts, values and aspirations of the organisation.

- Skills – distinctive capabilities and competencies. A change in strategic focus may mean that new skills need to be acquired as other skills become redundant
- Style – relates to the management and leadership style which will be critical because this will convey what is important in the organisation.
- Staff – numbers and types of personnel within the organisation.

The 7-S model will also be looked at in the project management section of the syllabus.

The organisational iceberg

The idea of hidden elements in culture is often referred to as the organisational iceberg.

The iceberg describes two levels at which culture operates:

- Formal aspects (visible) above the water
- Behavioural aspects (hidden) below the water

The elements of culture above the surface would include:

- goals
- technology
- procedures
- structure
- skills

The hidden elements represent the larger part of the iceberg which is below the water, and that would include:

- attitudes
- style
- communication patterns
- values
- feelings
- beliefs

```
                              Goals
                           Technology
   Visible elements          Structure
                      Procedures    Skills
   ─────────────────────────────────────────────

   Hidden elements
                        Style
                                          Attitudes
                        Communication patterns
                                          Feelings
                        Values
                                          Beliefs
```

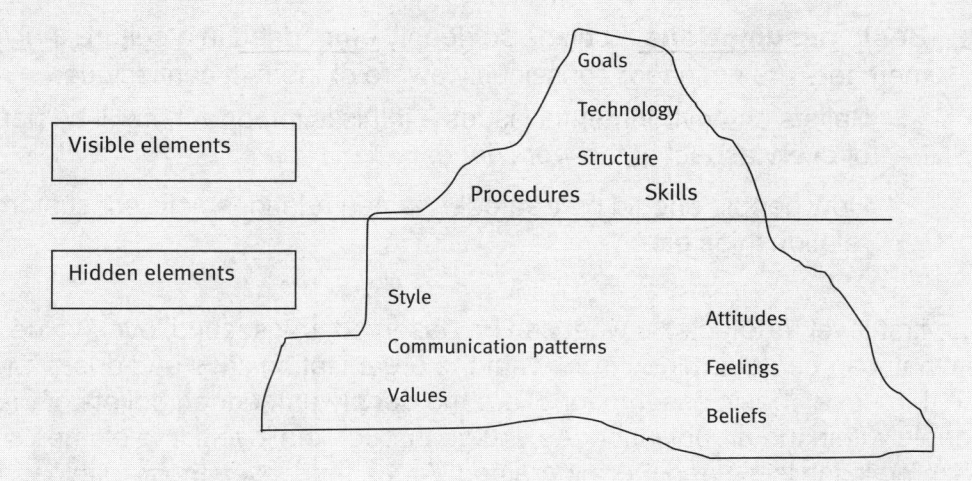

The diagram shows that what the public, customers, suppliers and others outside of an organisation see is only a small part of the picture. Much of what makes the organisation what it is, is intangible or hidden from view. It suggests that it is really only possible to fully understand the workings and culture of an organisation from within.

4 Levels of culture

According to Edgar Schein (1992)

Culture exists at a three of different levels:

(1) **Artefacts and creations** – the things that can be seen, heard and observed. This is largely the view of the organisation that the public experience. It can include items such as:
   – Dress codes – formal or informal, are uniforms worn.
   – Patterns of behaviour – the way people within the organisation as seen as acting.
   – Physical symbols – could include logos and branding.
   – Office layout – including the facilities and furnishings.

(2) **Values** – these can be identified from stories and the opinions of those within the organisation. It can include items such as:
   – Language – the way people communicate both within and outside the organisation.
   – Behaviour – shows what the people in the organisation feel is important.
   – How people justify what they do – values can be deep rooted, many will take for granted that their behaviour is acceptable without questioning it.

(3) **Basic assumptions** – beliefs so deeply embedded in a culture that members are no longer consciously aware of them. It can include:
- Beliefs on environmental issues – if this is important, it will be part of every aspect of the work done.
- How people should be treated – human relations policies, customer relationships etc.

The first level (artefacts) is what can be observed, the second level (values) is what can be determined from what the organisation says and does, and the third level (basic assumptions) are the deeply embedded beliefs of the people within the organisation. As you go through the levels, the elements become less visible and more ingrained. At the third level, those within the organisation may not even be aware of their beliefs, they have become so fundamentally part of their way of being.

For an organisation, understanding this helps them to anticipate problems with their culture and allows them to see how difficult it may be to change. Changing level one items, such as dress codes or office layouts, is relatively easy, but changing values and beliefs can be very difficult. This may also lead to differences between the levels, for example what the organisation says and does may be different to the how is perceived by the outside world. The public may view certain acts as superficial and often do not believe that the underlying beliefs of the organisation have really changed.

5 Influences on culture

The structure and culture of an organisation will develop over time and will be determined by a complex set of variables, including:

Size	How large is the organisation – in terms of turnover, physical size and employee numbers?
Technology	How technologically advanced is the organisation – either in terms of its product, or its productive processes?
Diversity	How diverse is the company – either in terms of product range, geographical spread or cultural make-up of its stakeholders?
Age	How old is the business or the managers of the business – do its strategic level decision makers have experience to draw upon?
History	What worked in the past? Do decision makers have past successes to draw upon; are they willing to learn from their mistakes?

Ownership Is the organisation owned by a sole trader? Are there a small number of institutional shareholders or are there large numbers of small shareholders?

When analysing an organisation, look for clues given as to the culture of the organisation using these main areas, although there are many other influences.

Other influences on culture

As well as the main influences on culture listed above, there are other, more subtle influences:

- The degree of individual initiative – is it encouraged or are decisions always referred upwards?
- The degree of risk tolerance – are managers only allowed to follow low-risk strategies?
- Clarity of direction – is there a clear focus; are these clear objectives and performance expectations?
- The degree of integration between groups – are different units encouraged to work together? Are management aloof or approachable; is communication clear to lower level staff?
- The reward system – are individuals rewarded for succeeding, i.e. are rewards based on performance criteria?
- Conflict tolerance – are employees encouraged to air grievances?
- Communication patterns – is there a formal hierarchy or an informal network?
- Formalisation of clothing and office layout – are there strict rules over this?
- The kind of people employed (graduates, young, old, etc.).

Other writers have suggested influences on culture:

- the national culture (Hofstede, 1991).
- the vision, management style and personality of the founder or other significant dominant managers (Schein, 1985).
- the nature of the business, the type of products and the environment within which the organisation operates (Gordon, 1991).
- the extent of risk connected with the activities of the organisation and the speed of feedback (Deal and Kennedy 1982/1988).

6 Why is culture important?

Culture is that invisible bond, which ties the people of a community together. It refers to the pattern of human activity. The importance of culture lies in its close association with the way of living of the people. The different cultures of the world have brought in diversity in the ways of life of the people inhabiting different parts of the world.

Culture is related to the development of one's attitude. The cultural values of an individual have a deep impact on his/her attitude towards life. They shape an individual's thinking and influence his/her mindset.

Why is culture important?

- It gives an individual a unique identity.
- The culture of a community gives its people a character of their own.
- Culture shapes the personality of a community – the language that a community speaks, the art forms it hosts, its staple food, its customs, traditions and festivities comprise the community's culture.

Within an organisation a good culture:

- is a talent-attractor.
- is talent-retainer.
- engages people.
- changes the view of 'work'.
- creates greater synergy.
- makes everyone more successful.

Advantages of having a strong culture

An organisation's culture has a significant bearing on the way it relates to its stakeholders (especially customers and staff), the development of its strategy and its structure. A strong culture will:

- facilitate good communication and co-ordination within the organisation.
- provide a framework of social identity and a sense of belonging.
- reduce differences amongst the members of the organisation.
- strengthen the dominant values and attitudes.
- regulate behaviour and norms among members of the organisation.

- minimise some of the perceptual differences among people within the organisation.
- reflect the philosophy and values of the organisation's founder or dominant group.
- affect the organisation's strategy and ability to respond to change.

Disadvantages of having a strong culture

A strong culture that does not have positive attributes in relation to stakeholders and change is a hindrance to effectiveness. Other disadvantages of a strong culture are:

- Strong cultures are difficult to change, beliefs which underpin culture can be deep rooted.
- Strong cultures may have a blinkered view which could affects the organisation's ability or desire to learn new skills.
- Strong cultures may stress inappropriate values. A strong culture which is positive can enhance the performance of the organisation, but a strong culture which is negative can have the opposite effect.
- Where two strong cultures come into contact e.g., in a merger, then conflicts can arise.
- A strong culture may not be attuned to the environment e.g., a strong innovative culture is only appropriate in a dynamic, shifting environment.

Illustration 1 – Organisations' views on culture

The following are various examples of the views of organisations on culture, taken from their internet sites:

Tesco plc:

We never take anyone for granted.

Our customers don't have to shop at Tesco. We know that. We have to do absolutely everything we can to make shopping with us the best experience possible, so they keep coming back.

What are Tesco looking for in their employees?

There are people. And then there are Tesco people.
Tesco people are easy to spot because they're always:

- *Passionate* about retail.
- *Focusing* on the customer and striving to understand them better than anyone.

- *Driven* to achieve results through determination and commitment.
- *Committed* to treating people in a fair and consistent way.
- *Willing* to roll their sleeves up to get things done.
- *Determined* to respond energetically to customer feedback.
- *Motivated* to work in partnership with others to achieve individual and team objectives.
- *Adaptable* and *flexible* to thrive in a 24/7 business.
- *Devoted* to seeking feedback on their performance and investing time in their own development.

ASDA:

Working at ASDA is completely different from working anywhere else. Why? It's because there are so many ways our culture is unique. For example we all wear a name badge, we all have daily huddles to keep up to date on how we're performing and sometimes we even all join together for the ASDA chant.

We're one team of over 170,000 colleagues working across the business. Fundamental to this is the "way we do things around here", that's our culture and the way we work.

Our three values are:

- respect for the individual
- strive for excellence
- service to our customers

T mobile:

Our culture:

We're all on a journey here – to be the best. Along the way, we've developed a way of working with each other, and for our customers. This company culture – and hence everything we do here – is based around six guiding principles:

(1) **Value simplicity**
Keep communications and actions precise, always.

(2) **Delight our customers**
Whatever we do, we must be friendly and deliver on what we have promised.

(3) **Think of the team**
Place company goals on a par with personal ambitions.

(4) **Grow our people**
Ensure our most prized asset has the tools, time and encouragement to take advantage of opportunities to learn more.

(5) **Use the whole truth**
If mistakes are made, be honest about them so we can all learn from them.

(6) **Count on me**
Rely on each other, commit ourselves to our customers, colleagues and the company.

Strategy and culture

Culture, strategy and structure

Managers who operate within an existing structure and culture make strategic decisions. Stakeholders who are powerful can influence strategy formulation as their attitudes, beliefs, perceptions and assumptions influence the organisation's objectives.

When public sector monopolies such as British Telecom and the utility companies were privatised, the resulting shift to profit orientation created a dramatic change in their cultures and in management attitudes. This also necessitated the recruitment of new management. The change of strategy required a new culture and structure.

7 Models for categorising culture

Whilst every organisation will have its own unique culture, there are a number of different ways of classifying organisation culture. The following section will consider some of the ways that culture can be classified and the main models used.

Handy's cultural types

Introduction

Handy popularised four cultural types identified by **Harrison**:

(1) Power
(2) Role
(3) Task
(4) Person.

- *Power culture* – **Here, the ego of a 'key person' comes first.**

    Power culture is based on one or a few powerful central individual(s), often dynamic entrepreneurs, who keep control of all activities and make all the decisions. The structure is perhaps best depicted as a web whereby power resides at the centre and all authority and power emanates from one individual. The organisation is not rigidly structured and has few rules and procedures. This type of culture can react well to change because it is adaptable and informal and decision-making is quick.

    This is likely to be the dominant type of culture in small entrepreneurial organisations and family-managed businesses.

- *Role culture* – **Here, the job description of the actor comes first.**

    Role culture tends to be impersonal and rely on formalised rules and procedures to guide decision-making in a standardised, bureaucratic way (e.g. civil service and traditional, mechanistic mass-production organisations). Everything is based on a logical order and rationality. There is a clear hierarchical structure with each stage having clearly visible status symbols attached to it. Each job is clearly defined and the power of individuals is based on their position in the hierarchy. The formal rules and procedures, which must be followed, should ensure an efficient operation.

    Decisions tend to be controlled at the centre, this means that whilst suitable for a stable and predictable environment, this type of culture is slow to respond and react to change.

- *Task culture* – Here, getting the job done right and on time comes first.

    Task culture is typified by teamwork, flexibility and commitment to achieving objectives, rather than an emphasis on a formal hierarchy of authority (perhaps typical of some advertising agencies and software development organisations, and the desired culture in large organisations seeking total quality management). It can be depicted as a net with the culture drawing on resources from various parts of the organisational system and power resides at the intersections of the net. The power and influence tends to be based on specialist knowledge and expert power rather than on positions in the hierarchy. Creativity is encouraged and job satisfaction tends to be high because of the degree of individual participation and group identity.

    A task culture can quickly respond to change and is appropriate where flexibility, adaptability and problem solving is needed.

- *Person culture* – Here, actors fulfil personal goals and objectives whether or not they are congruent with those of the organisation.

    People culture can be divided into two types. The first type is a collection of individuals working under the same umbrella, such as that found in architects' and solicitors' practices, IT and management consultants, where individuals are largely trying to satisfy private ambition. The organisation is based on the technical expertise of the individual employees.

    Other types of organisation with people cultures exist for the benefit of the members rather than external stakeholders, and are based on friendship, belonging and consensus (e.g. some social clubs, informal aspects of many organisations).

Each of the different types of culture described has advantages and disadvantages and in reality, organisations often need a mix of cultures for their different activities and processes.

Handy also matched appropriate cultural models to the levels of managerial activity:

Strategic management	Concerned with direction setting, policy making and crisis handling	Power culture
Tactical management	Concerned with establishing means to the corporate ends & resources	Task culture
Operational management	Concerned with routine activities	Role Culture

Deal and Kennedy 1982/1988 – Strong culture theory

Another categorisation of culture is presented by **Deal and Kennedy**. They suggest that culture can be determined according to two factors:

- Extent of risk connected with the activities of the organisation
- Speed of feedback on the outcome of employees' decisions

Four generic profiles result from these factors:

- **Tough-guy macho** – High risk, quick feedback

    This reflects tough individualistic and high risk-taking organisations. This profile is likely to be an entrepreneurial firm run by the owner. The organisation is made up of people working as individuals who take high risks and receive quick feedback on whether their actions were right. Financial stakes are high and the focus is on speed, resulting in a high pressure environment.

- **Work-hard-play-hard** – Few risk taken, quick feedback

    This culture is where the team is all important and quick feedback from the customer is the key to success.

- **Bet-your-company** – High risk, slow feedback

    This culture is characterised by slow feedback with decision cycles taking years, for example in pharmaceutical research. However, decisions are large scale and risks are

- **Process** – Low risk, low feedback

    This type of culture is where technical performance is of critical importance and there is a need for order and predictability, this is often seen in a bureaucratic organisation.

Test your understanding 1

Up until two years ago, E Company enjoyed a monopoly position in the energy industry. However, a change in government policy has meant that new competition has been encouraged to move into the industry with E Company losing its monopoly. The company now finds itself facing severe difficulties.

E Company has developed a strong culture over the years which can be typified as a role culture. This is now acting as a barrier to the organisation's ability to change, to become more flexible and to be able to respond more quickly to changes in the environment and initiatives by its competitors.

E Company is falling behind its competitors when it comes to innovations in energy services. Developments in new services require staff to work together across functional boundaries. However, this is unheard of in E Company where people fiercely protect their functional specialism and will only work on the tasks specified in their job descriptions.

Required:

(a) Discuss why the characteristics of a role culture may no longer be appropriate for E Company.

(6 marks)

(b) Recommend, with reasons, the type of culture to which the company now needs to move to.

(4 marks)

Test your understanding 2

Required:

Comment on the possible drawbacks of a strong organisational culture.

(10 marks)

Ouchi theories J, A and Z

There are different views on the relationship between culture and organisational performance. A number of researchers believe that culture plays a major role in determining an organisation's ability to implement strategies and contributes to organisational effectiveness and excellence and ultimately, to overall competitive advantage.

Ouchi suggested that there were a number of characteristics that differentiated American organisations from Japanese firms. He compared the American organisation culture (Theory A) with the Japanese approach (Theory J). By modifying their culture, he proposed, American firms could compete more effectively against Japanese organisations. The modified characteristics he called Theory Z.

The features of both American and Japanese firms' culture are compared below.

Function	Japan	USA
Planning	Long term.	Mainly short term.
	Collective decision making.	Individual decision making.
	Decisions start at bottom and considered higher up.	Decisions taken at top and flow downward.
	Slow evolution of decision making.	Fast decisions but slow implementation.
Organisation	Collective responsibility.	Individual responsibility.
	No clear decision responsibility.	Clear, specific decision responsibility.
Staffing	School-leavers recruited, limited staff turnover, lifetime employment.	Recruitment at all stages, high staff turnover and job insecurity.
	Promotion is slow, after transfer between functions.	Promotion is rapid within specialisation.
	Appraisal based on loyalty, with training viewed as long-term investment.	Appraisal based on current performance with reluctant training.
Leading	Leader acts as group member and avoids 'status' trappings.	Leader acts as head of group and displays status differences.
	Overall paternalistic style, avoidance of confrontation.	Domineering style, with face-to-face confrontation.
	Bottom-up communication.	Top-down communication.

Controlling	Control by fellow members through group performance.	Control by superior with focus on individual performance.
	Extensive use of groups.	Limited use of groups.

Ouchi proposed Theory Z as being a compromise. Its main characteristics are as follows:

- Employment – fairly long term to develop a loyal, semi-permanent workforce.
- Evaluation and promotion of personnel – slower, more emphasis is given to training and evaluation than to promotion.
- Career paths – more general with an emphasis on job rotation and more broadly-based training in order to give a person a better feel for the organisation.
- Decision making – carried out with more emphasis on group participation and consensus.
- Control – more attention to internal control procedures coupled with explicit performance measures.
- Responsibility – assigned on an individual basis.
- Concern for staff – expanded to include more aspects of the worker's whole life.

8 The cultural web framework

G. Johnson described a cultural web, identifying a number of elements that can be used to describe or influence organisational culture:

- *The Paradigm*: What the organisation is about; what it does; its mission; its values. The paradigm is influenced by the following six elements:
- *Control Systems*: The processes in place to monitor what is going on. These include internal control systems, performance measurement and reward structures.
- *Organisational Structures*: Reporting lines, hierarchies, and the way that work flows through the business. This includes both the formal structure defined by the organisation chart, and the informal lines of power and influence that indicate whose contributions are most valued.

- *Power Structures*: Who makes the decisions, how widely spread is power, and on what is power based? The real power in the company may involve one or two key senior executives, a whole group of executives, or even a department. The key is that these people have the greatest influence on decisions, operations, and strategic direction.

- *Symbols*: These include organisational logos and designs, and the formal or informal dress codes. This also extends to symbols of power such as parking spaces, or corner offices.

- *Rituals and Routines*: The daily behaviour and actions of people that signal acceptable behaviour. This determines what is expected to happen in given situations, and what is valued by management. This could include routines such as an executive visiting the factory floor to speak to employees each week, or rituals, such as buying a cake when it's your birthday.

- *Stories and Myths*: The past events and people talked about inside and outside the company. Who and what the company chooses to immortalise conveys a message about what is valued within the organisation.

This can be shown in the diagram below:

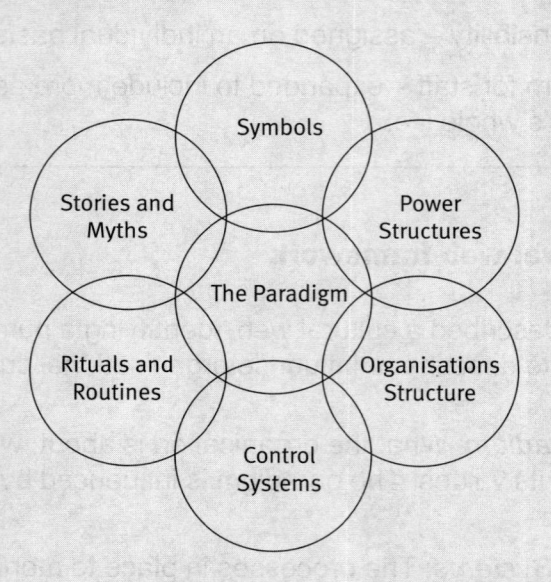

This model can be used to analyse the current organisational culture and to identify changes that could be made to improve it.

More detail on the cultural web framework

To analyse the current culture using the cultural web framework, the following are examples of questions which could be asked under each of the headings. Once all areas have been considered, it should give a good understanding of the culture of the organisation. From this any necessary changes can be made to improve the culture of the organsiation.

Stories and Myths

- What do people say about our organisation?
- What is the reputation of the organisation?
- What do current staff tell new staff about the organisation?
- What do employees talk about when asked about the company?

Rituals and routines

- What do customers expect when they use our services or buy or products?
- What do our employees expect when they come to work?
- What core beliefs are suggested by these behaviours?

Symbols

- Is there a dress code within the organisation?
- Is jargon used which people outside the organisation would not understand?
- Do all branches, offices look the same no matter where they are located?
- Does the organisation have a recognisable corporate image?

Structure

- Is there a formal organisational structure?
- What type of structure is in place – a tall or flat structure?
- Are there any informal reporting lines?

Control systems

- Are there obvious controls in place within the organisation?
- Is the organisation well controlled?
- Are all employees aware of the controls, and of any implication of non compliance?

Power structure

- Who has the power to make decisions within the organisation?
- Is power concentrated at the top of the organisation?
- Is the power used appropriately?

9 Managing in different cultures

As many organisations operate at a global level and face international competition, an understanding of national culture has become increasingly important. Cultural practices vary between different countries and will impact on how organisations operate.

The features of a country's culture have important implications for managing cross border mergers, where problems can arise because of the different ways companies are run as a result of cultural differences. This point is very relevant to organisations who seek to grow through mergers and acquisitions with foreign companies. However, it is important to remember that cultures in society are not permanent and as mentioned earlier, all cultures have sub-cultures and a range of complex and interrelated factors influence organisational culture. The national culture is just of one of these influences.

Hofstede (1990) developed a model to explain national differences by identifying five 'key dimensions' along which national culture seems to vary:

(1) **Power Distance**

This dimension covered how much society accepts the unequal distribution of power, for instance the extent to which supervisors see themselves as being above their subordinates. In countries with high power distance, managers tend to make autocratic decisions and subordinates do what they are told rather than being involved in decision-making. This kind of culture was found, by Hofstede, to be particularly strong in Malaysia, China, Philippines, and Russia. Low power distance means people expect equality in power, such as in Denmark, Austria and Israel.

- High Power Distance means people accept inequality in power.
- Low Power Distance means people except equality in power.

(2) **Uncertainty Avoidance**

Uncertainty avoidance is the degree to which members of society feel uncomfortable with risk, uncertainty and ambiguity, and feel threatened by unusual situations. High uncertainty avoidance will mean risk taking is discouraged and organisations will tend to rely heavily on rules and regulations so that people know what they are doing. This type of attitude is found in Greece, Japan, and Russia. Low uncertainty avoidance means people have high tolerance for the unstructured and unpredictable, this was found in Singapore, Taiwan and Thailand.

- High Uncertainty Avoidance means people are uncomfortable with uncertainty and ambiguity.
- Low Uncertainty Avoidance means people have high tolerance for the unstructured and unpredictable.

(3) Individualism and Collectivism

Individualism is the extent to which people are supposed to take care of themselves and be emotionally independent from others and reflects the values for a loosely knit social framework. This tends to be true for the United States, Canada, Britain and Australia. Collectivism is a preference for a tightly knit social framework in which individuals look after one another and organisations protect their members' interests. This was found to be particularly the case in China, Mexico, Chile, and Peru.

- Individualism means that individuals are expected to take care of themselves.
- Collectivism means that individuals look after one another and organisations protect their members' interests.

(4) Masculinity/Femininity

Masculinity relates to the degree to which masculine values predominate. For example, a focus on power, achievement, assertiveness, and material success as opposed to the stereotypical feminine values of relationships, modesty, sensitivity and concern for others. Masculine values are strong in Japan, Austria, Italy and Germany. Feminine cultural values were found in Sweden, Norway, Finland and Denmark. Both men and women subscribe to the dominant value in masculine and feminine cultures.

- Masculine orientation values achievement, heroism, assertiveness and material success important.
- Feminine orientation values relationships, caring for the weak and quality of life.

(5) Time Orientation

Time orientation is also known as *Confucian v Dynamism*. In this instance Hofstede examined how much society values long standing rather than short term values and traditions. Short term orientation means that people expect fairly rapid feedback from decisions, expect quick profits, frequent job evaluations and promotions, and so on.

- Long Term Orientation means valuing tradition, loyalty, education and training.
- Short Term Orientation means valuing fast promotions and quick profits.

It is important to see that Hofstede was attempting to model aspects of culture that might influence business behaviour, rather than produce national stereotypes or explain the differences he found in historical or socio-geographic terms.

Hofstede also looked at **cultural differences in work-related attitudes**. These include:

- **Leadership** – in some countries, such as those in Latin America, leaders are expected to take a strong personal interest in employees and appear at private social functions such as weddings. In other countries such as Germany such social contact is discouraged. In yet other countries, notably in Asia and Africa, public criticism is intolerable as the loss of self-respect brings dishonour to the employee and his family.
- **Motivation** – the incentives for effective performance must match the culture. It is pointless offering individual bonuses to workers where there are strong group and company loyalties, as in Japan, or where loyalty to an individual's superior is paramount as in Turkey and the Near East.
- **Structure** – research showed that French firms are bureaucratic with orders and procedures set from above, whereas German firms rely more on the professional expertise from the trained knowledge and skill of the more junior employees.

Managing in a multi-cultural environment

In any situation, where you are required to manage in a cross-cultural or multi-cultural environment, there are a number of guidelines that you should follow:

- Always show respect and listen, do not be in a hurry.
- Try to gain an appreciation for the differences between Hofstede's 'masculine' and 'feminine' cultures.
- Do not feel your way is the best way.
- Emphasise points of agreement.
- Discern the perceived definitions of words.
- Do not embarrass anyone in front of others.
- Know or take someone who knows the culture.
- Understand that leadership may mean different things to different countries.
- Do not lose your temper.

Organisational culture

- Avoid clique-building.
- Leave your own 'domestic' management style at home.
- Eliminate stereotypes.
- Learn to tolerate a high degree of unpredictability.

Managers may also have to modify their approach to take account of the following:

- Language
- Religion
- Attitudes
- Social organisation
- Education
- Ethnocentrism (a tendency to regard one's own culture as superior to others).

Test your understanding 3

Required:

If a worker from another country were to come to work or conduct business in the UK what areas may they find different?

(10 marks)

Test your understanding 4

X Company is a manufacturer of non-alcoholic soft drinks and has a well-established position and brand recognition in country Z. The potential for future growth in country Z is however limited, with the market reaching saturation. One option for expansion is to move into new markets in other countries offering their existing product range.

The business development team are evaluating this option and are currently working on proposals to sell their range of drinks in country Y. One possible method of achieving market entry development that the team is investigating is through a joint venture with a company that is already established in country Y and is in the drinks distribution business.

The board of X Company has given the business development team the task of undertaking a feasibility study to explore the viability of the proposed strategy. As part of the feasibility study there needs to be some assessment of industry competition and the attractiveness of the market in country Y. The feasibility study also needs to assess the cultural compatibility of the ways of doing business in country Y compared to how X Company currently operates in country Z.

Required:

Discuss how Hofstede's research on national cultures could be used to assess the cultural compatibility of X Company's market development strategy to form a joint venture with a company in country Y.

(10 marks)

Test your understanding 5

The Globe Hotels (GH) operates hotels in most of the developed countries throughout the world. The directors of GH are committed to a policy of achieving 'growth' in terms of geographical coverage and are now considering building and operating another hotel in Portland. Portland is a developing country which is situated 3,000 kilometres from the country in which GH's nearest hotel is located.

The managing director of GH recently attended a seminar on 'the use of strategic and economic information in planning organisational performance'. He has called a board meeting to discuss the strategic and economic factors which should be considered before a decision is made to build the hotel in Portland.

GH has always used local labour to build and subsequently operate hotels. The directors of GH are again considering employing a local workforce not only to build the hotel but also to operate it on a daily basis.

Required:

(a) Discuss the strategic and economic factors which should be considered before a decision is made to build the hotel.

(10 marks)

(b) Explain TWO ways in which the possibility of cultural differences might impact on the performance of a local workforce in building and operating a hotel in Portland.

(6 marks)

Are culture and conflict connected?

Culture is always a factor in conflict, whether it plays a central role or influences it subtly and gently.

Conflicts between teenagers and parents are shaped by generational culture, and conflicts between spouses or partners can be influenced by gender culture.

In organisations, conflicts arising from different disciplinary cultures escalate tensions between co-workers, creating strained or inaccurate communication and stressed relationships.

Though culture is intertwined with conflict, some approaches to conflict resolution minimise cultural issues and influences. Since culture is like an iceberg – largely submerged – it is important to include it in our analyses and interventions. Icebergs unacknowledged can be dangerous, and it is impossible to make choices about them if we don't know their size or place.

It is important to recognise that there is no one-size-fits-all approach to conflict resolution, since culture is always a factor. Cultural fluency is therefore a core competency for those who intervene in conflicts or simply want to function more effectively in their own lives and situations.

This involves:

- understanding that roles vary across cultures
- acting respectfully
- communicating well
- trying to tame the conflict

10 Summary diagram

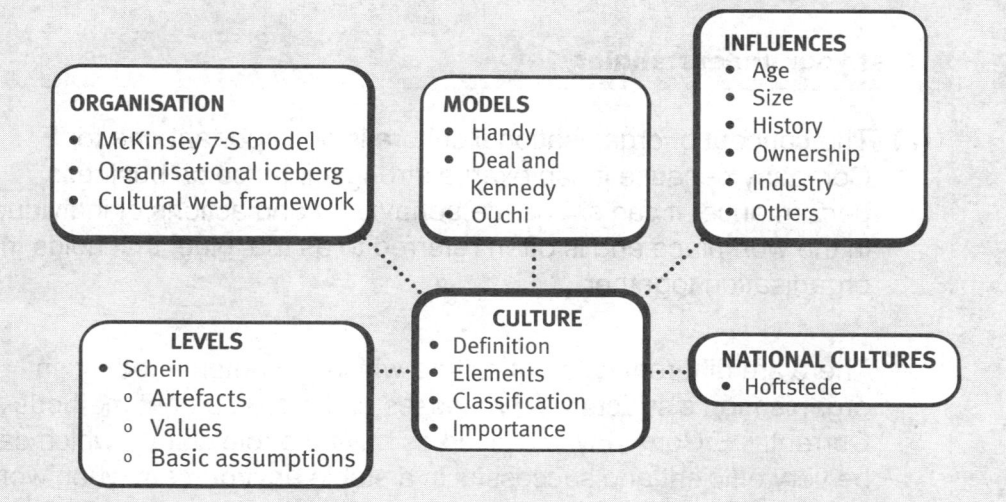

ORGANISATION
- McKinsey 7-S model
- Organisational iceberg
- Cultural web framework

MODELS
- Handy
- Deal and Kennedy
- Ouchi

INFLUENCES
- Age
- Size
- History
- Ownership
- Industry
- Others

LEVELS
- Schein
  - Artefacts
  - Values
  - Basic assumptions

CULTURE
- Definition
- Elements
- Classification
- Importance

NATIONAL CULTURES
- Hofstede

Organisational culture

Test your understanding answers

Test your understanding 1

(a) The concept of organisational culture is an important one for E Company because it can exert a strong influence on business performance. It can shape the behaviours and actions of individuals in the workplace and is often referred to as the 'glue' that holds the organisation together.

There are different types of culture which are determined by an organisation's structures, processes and management methods. Currently, E Company is typified as having a role culture which can be very efficient and successful in a stable environment when work is predictable and the organisation can control its own environment, often by maintaining a monopoly position. However, this type of culture now appears to be having an adverse effect on E Company's performance as the company now faces very different operating conditions since losing its monopoly position. The reasons for this can be explained by examining the characteristics of a role culture.

Role culture works by rationality and logic, and is usually associated with a formal structure with well established rules and procedures. Job descriptions are clearly defined, tightly describing the tasks of an individual's job. This leads to a strict division of labour with people often reluctant to take on wider responsibilities. Rather, they are obsessed by fulfilling narrow job duties, with a preoccupation on day-to-day administration rather than longer term issues. These characteristics would make it difficult for the organisation to be flexible and adapt to the more competitive operating environment, acting as a barrier to the developments needed in E Company.

Within a role culture the organisation is dependent upon various functions, each of which has their own areas of strength and influence, with an emphasis on internal processes. This type of culture is also impersonal, relying on formalised rules and procedures for work routines and communication and to guide decision making in a standardised and bureaucratic way. Relations between staff are dominated by hierarchy and authority with formal and rigid control systems. Individuals are selected for particular roles on the basis of their ability to complete a particular task to the required level: over achievement is not actively pursued. However, these characteristics of a role culture can mean that it is more resistant or very slow to adapt to change and getting people to work together across boundaries is difficult.

Innovation can be stifled, since the culture is one which insists people go through layers in the hierarchy to gain approval. Decisions are made at senior level with little involvement from other members of the organisation. In fact new ideas from below may be regarded with suspicion from above. Individuals are required to perform their job and not to overstep the boundaries of authority. This is occurring in the case of E Company, and would seem to be partly responsible for the lack of flexibility, responsiveness and problem solving capability.

(b) It is apparent that the culture of E Company needs to change and it is recommended that a task culture would be more appropriate given the changes in business conditions.

This type of culture is typified by teamwork, flexibility and commitment to achieving objectives rather than emphasising a formal hierarchy of authority. The task culture is often reflected in a matrix structure or project teams, where the focus is on completing a job or project.

Staff become loyal towards the work rather than towards formal rules. The principal concern is to get the job done, breaking down rigid hierarchies and functions. Therefore, the individuals who are important are those with the skills and ability to accomplish a particular task. Skill and expertise are more important than length of service and position in the organisation, as is currently the case in E Company. People are not hindered in terms of their contribution by tight job descriptions associated with the role culture. Hence, a task culture tends to encourage greater flexibility, with people working together across functional boundaries to achieve organisational objectives.

Team work is fundamental to a task culture, rather than the achievement of individuals. The result is that influence is spread throughout the organisation. By nature a task culture fosters creativity and is adaptable, responsive and able to change very quickly.

Organisational culture

Test your understanding 2

Though there are some benefits of having a strong organisational culture there are also potential drawbacks:

- Strong cultures are difficult to change.
- Strong cultures may stress inappropriate values.
- Where two strong cultures come into contact e.g., in a merger, then conflicts can arise.
- A strong culture may not be attuned to the environment e.g., a strong innovative culture is only appropriate in a dynamic, shifting environment.

Despite these problems it is still possible to agree with Lord Sugar, 'It is essential to retain a strong corporate culture and philosophy, otherwise the business can drift and become confused and lost in direction'.

Test your understanding 3

Let us consider punctuality. Most North American and European countries are 'clock conscious'. Time is money, being late for an appointment is the height of bad etiquette and coming in late to work is unprofessional. However, in many other countries this is not so. Being late for work or an appointment is acceptable and would not have harmful repercussions.

Compared with other countries, the UK office can be a reasonably relaxed and informal environment. Conversations can become personal, humour is seen as a positive and relationships frequently switch between that of friends and colleagues depending on the situation. A new German or Japanese colleague may at first find this unprofessional and lacking in professionalism.

Discussion, gaining consensus and objective criticism are all part of the British business meeting. However, in hierarchical cultures none of the above would take place. Meetings are usually the forum for decisions to be conveyed rather than made, criticising or challenging the ideas of colleagues and seniors would be completely unacceptable and would result in the loss of honour and face.

These brief examples are but three of numerous illustrations of business culture that a foreigner may need to understand before working with the British. If a person came to the UK and was unaware of such issues they may very well be misunderstood if they were constantly late, never contributed in meetings or did not join in with office banter.

Test your understanding 4

Just as an organisation develops its own corporate culture which will influence its strategy and its way of doing business, countries show international differences in how they view the world and develop their own cultures in terms of values and basic assumptions. This is an important concept since it will impact on the ways in which people behave at work and the way things are done in organisations. The effect of different environments is a key factor in determining the cultural compatibility of organisations moving into new territories. A mutual understanding of the different cultures will influence the effectiveness of working relationships and the management styles adopted.

Hofstede's research was developed to explain national culture by mapping different cultural characteristics. The outcomes from the research suggest that countries can be classified according to the four dimensions in which national culture varies and that might influence business behaviour. The dimensions are power distance; uncertainty avoidance; individualism; and masculinity. A country can be classified on these dimensions on a continuum from high to low.

Power distance is the extent to which a society accepts that power in organisations is distributed unequally. In countries with high power distance, managers tend to make autocratic decisions and subordinates do what they are told rather than being involved in decision making.

Uncertainty avoidance is the degree to which members of a society feel uncomfortable with risk, uncertainty and ambiguity and feel threatened by unusual situations. High uncertainty avoidance will mean risk taking is discouraged and organisations will tend to rely heavily on rules and regulations so that people know what they are doing.

Individualism versus collectivism is the extent to which people are supposed to take care of themselves and be emotionally independent from others (individualism), to one where people prefer a tight-knit social framework based on involvement (collectivism).

Masculinity relates to the degree to which masculine values predominate. For example, focus on power, achievement, assertiveness, and material success as opposed to the stereo-typical feminine values of relationships, modesty, sensitivity and concern for others.

Organisational culture

These factors need to be considered when developing strategies in a cross cultural context since Hofstede argues that countries differ significantly in their 'score' on these dimensions. For instance, on the basis of Hofstede's work it has been argued that the Japanese are more collective, cautious, and authoritarian than Anglo Saxon countries. The implication of this is that Japanese methods of management may not work well in these countries and vice versa.

X Company could use Hofstede's work to help in the appraisal of cultural compatibility of the proposed strategy to enter country Y through joint venture. The comparison should not only take account of the two organisations but also the cultural differences between consumers in Company X's existing markets and the consumers in Country Y. If the two countries have significant cultural differences along all four dimensions, the joint venture might not be an attractive proposition.

Market development strategies often fail because whilst financial assessments are sound, insufficient attention has been placed on cultural factors.

Test your understanding 5

(a) Of vital importance is the need for reliable information on which to base the decision regarding the potential investment within Portland, since the lack of such information will only serve to increase the risk profile of GH.

The **strategic factors** that ought to be considered prior to a decision being made to build and operate a hotel in Portland are as follows:

The competition

The key notion here is that of the position of GH relative to its competitors who may have a presence or intend to have a presence in Portland. The strategic management accounting system should be capable of coping with changes that can and will inevitably occur in a dynamic business environment. Hence it is crucial that changes such as, the emergence of a new competitor, are detected and reflected within strategic plans at the earliest opportunity.

The government

The attitude of the government of Portland towards foreign organisations requires careful consideration as inevitably the government will be the country's largest supplier, employer, customer and investor. The directors need to recognise that the political environment of Portland could change dramatically with a change in the national government.

Planning and control of operations within Portland

Planning and control of operations within Portland will inevitably be more difficult as GH might not possess sufficient knowledge of the business environment within Portland. Indeed their nearest hotel is at least 3,000 kilometres away. It is vital the GH gain such knowledge prior to commencing operations within Portland in order to avoid undue risks.

The sociological–cultural constraints

While it is generally recognised that there is a growing acceptability of international brands this might not be the case with regard to Portland. In this respect it is vital that consideration is given to recognition of the relationships in economic life including demand, price, wages, training, and rates of labour turnover and absenteeism.

Resource utilisation

The attitude towards work, managers (especially foreign nationals) and capitalist organisations could severely impact on the degree of success achieved within Portland.

A primary consideration relates to whether or not to use local labour in the construction of the hotel. The perceived 'remoteness' of Portland might make it an unattractive proposition for current employees of GH, thereby presenting the directors of GH with a significant problem.

Communication

Consideration needs to be given to the communication problems that arise between different countries and in this respect Portland is probably no exception. Language barriers will inevitably exist and this needs to be addressed at the earliest opportunity to minimise any risks to GH.

The **economic factors** that ought to be considered prior to a decision being made to build and operate a hotel in Portland are as follows:

Resource availability

The hotel should be designed having given due consideration to the prevailing climatic conditions within Portland which might necessitate the use of specific types of building materials. It might well be the case that such building materials are not available locally, or are in such scarce supply in which case local supply would prove to be uneconomic.

Another consideration relates to local labour being available and reliable in terms of its quality.

Currency stability/restrictions

The stability of the currency within Portland assumes critical significance because profit repatriation is problematic in situations where those profits are made in an unstable currency or one that is likely to depreciate against the home currency, thereby precipitating sizeable losses on exchange. Any currency restrictions need to be given careful consideration. For example, it might be the case that hotel guests would be prohibited from paying accommodation bills in a foreign currency which would be problematic if the local currency was weak.

Legislation

All local and International legislation should be given careful consideration. It might be the case that local legislation via various licences or legal requirements favour local hotels.

Demand

The potential demand within Portland will be linked to the local economy. It is a developing economy and this may bode well for GH. However, again the need for reliable information about the size of the market, the extent of competition, likely future trends etc is of fundamental importance.

Financing

An important decision lies in the availability and associated costs of financing in Portland which might not have mature enough capital markets due to its developmental state. Hence GH might need to finance using alternative currencies.

Note: Other relevant comments would be acceptable.

(b) The directors of GH should be mindful that the effectiveness of a locally employed workforce within Portland will be influenced by a number of factors including the following:

The availability of local skills

If Portland is a lower wage economy it is quite conceivable that a sufficient number of employees possessing the requisite skills to undertake the construction of a large hotel cannot be found. If there are insufficient local resources then this would necessitate the training of employees in all aspects of building construction. This will incur significant costs and time and needs to be reflected in any proposed timetable for construction of the hotel. As far as the operation of the hotel is concerned then staff will have to be recruited and trained which will again give rise to significant start-up costs. However, this should not present the directors of GH with such a major problem as that of training construction staff. Indeed, it is highly probable that GH would use its own staff in order to train new recruits.

Attitudes to work

The prevailing culture within Portland will have a profound impact on attitudes to work of its population. Attitudes to hours of work, timekeeping and absenteeism vary from culture to culture. For example, as regards hours of work in the construction industry in countries which experience very hot climates, work is often suspended during the hottest part of each day and recommenced several hours later when temperatures are much cooler. The directors of GH need to recognise that climatic conditions not only affect the design of a building but also its construction.

A potentially sensitive issue within regarding the use of local labour in the construction of the hotel lies in the fact that national holidays and especially religious holidays need to be observed and taken into consideration in any proposed timetable for construction of the hotel. As regards the operation of a hotel then consideration needs to be given to the different cultures from which the guests come. For example, this will require a detailed consideration of menus to be offered. However, it might well be the case that the local population might be unwilling to prepare dishes comprising ingredients which are unacceptable to their culture due to, for example, religious beliefs.

chapter 8

Management and leadership

Chapter learning objectives

- Discuss the concepts of power, bureaucracy, authority, responsibility, leadership and delegation.

1 Session content diagram

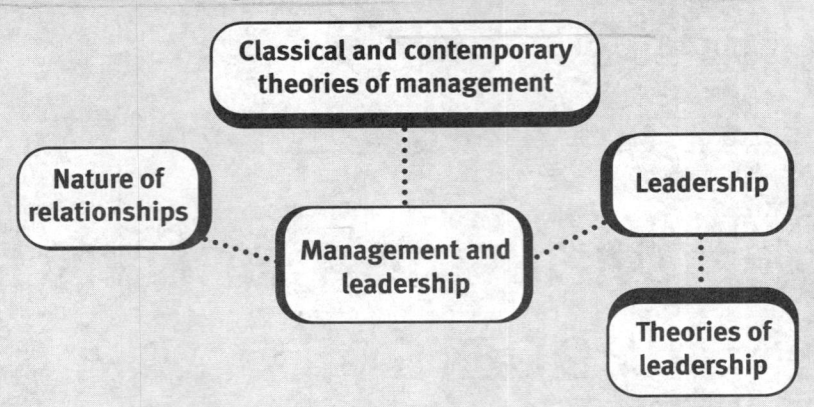

- Classical and contemporary theories of management
- Nature of relationships
- Management and leadership
- Leadership
- Theories of leadership

2 Power, authority, responsibility, and delegation

Individuals within the workplace have different relationships with each other. To be able to analyse the nature of management relationships it is necessary to understand the concepts of power, authority, responsibility and delegation.

Power

Power is the capacity to exert influence, to make someone act according to your own preferences.

Types of power

French and Raven identified five possible bases of a leader's power:

- **Reward power** – a person has power over another because they can give rewards, such as promotions or financial rewards.

- **Coercive power** – enables a person to give punishments to others: for example, to dismiss, suspend, reprimand them, or make them carry out unpleasant tasks.

    Reward power and coercive power are similar but limited in application because they are limited to the size of the reward or punishment that can be given. For example, there isn't much I could get my subordinate to do for a $5 reward (or fine), but there are many, many things they might do for a $50,000 reward (or fine).

- **Referent power** – based upon the identification with the person who has charisma, or the desire to be like that person. It could be regarded as 'imitative' power which is often seen in the way children imitate their parents. Think of the best boss you've ever had – what did you like about them, did it encourage you to act in a similar way?

Psychologists believe that referent power is perhaps the most extensive since it can be exercised when the holder is not present or has no intention of exercising influence.

- **Expert power** – based upon doing what the expert says since they are the expert. You will have a measure of expert power when you join CIMA – people will do as you suggest because you have studied and have qualified. Note – expert power only extends to the expert's field of expertise.
- **Legitimate power** – based on agreement and commonly-held values which allow one person to have power over another person: for example, an older person, or one who has longer service. In some societies it is customary for a man to be the 'head of the family', or in other societies elders make decisions due to their age and experience.

Test your understanding 1

G, the senior partner of L, a medium sized accountancy firm, has worked for L for over twenty years and has a sound knowledge and understanding of the different activities of the firm's business. Over the years, G has become known for his fairness in how he manages staff. He is also well liked and respected for his enthusiastic approach. He always has time to encourage and mentor younger members of staff.

The firm has recently invested in new technology which will improve the effectiveness of its office systems, but will mean the roles and responsibilities of the support staff will change. G, has taken on the unenviable role of leading the project to introduce the technology and new working practices. He knows that the project will be met with resistance from some members of staff and he will need to draw on various sources of power to ensure the changes are successfully implemented.

Required:

Describe the different sources of power that G has and which will help him in introducing the changes.

(10 marks)

Authority

Authority is the right to exercise power such as hiring and firing or buying and selling on behalf of the organisation; the right that an individual has to require certain actions of others; the right to do or act.

Max Weber proposed that authority legitimises the exercise of power within the structure and rules of the organisation. Hence, it allows individuals within an organisation to issue instructions for others to follow. Weber defined three bases for such authority as follows:

Charismatic authority – Here the individual has some special quality of personality which sets the leader apart. Because the charismatic power in the organisation is so dependent on the leader, difficulties arise when he or she has to be replaced. Unless someone else is available, who also possesses the necessary charisma, the organisation either decays or survives in one of the other two forms.

Traditional authority – This authority is based upon custom and practice. The personality of the leader is irrelevant: he or she inherits the status of leader because of the long-standing belief in the natural right to 'rule' which is sometimes handed down.

Rational-legal authority – This is Weber's classic bureaucracy. Power comes from the individual's position in the organisation chart. The ability to perform particular functions and their operations is based on following a set of written rules. This authority is not personal but is vested, impersonally, in the position held.

Link types of authority with power bases

Weber's three types of authority (charismatic, traditional and rational-legal) can be linked to the French and Raven power bases as follows:

Power base	Authority base
Coercive and Legitimate	Traditional
Reward and Referent	Charismatic
Expert	Rational-legal

Test your understanding 2

Until October 2009, Sheila was the Chief Executive Officer (CEO) of X Ltd, a manufacturer of washing machines and similar products. As Marketing Manager in the late 1990s, Sheila had been responsible for adding new products to the company range that boosted company profits, a success that had been largely responsible for Sheila's promotion to CEO.

In 2006, however, the company suffered a number of setbacks, and Sheila, in order to boost sales by bringing products to the market sooner, ordered that all testing of new products should stop.

The consequences were disastrous; X Ltd was overwhelmed with returned merchandise.

In an effort to keep the share price high, Sheila ordered the Finance Director, Bob, to omit the recording of returned products. Bob initially protested that this would be unethical accounting, but eventually complied with Sheila's order. Under further pressure, Bob was also persuaded by Sheila to show an increase in sales and respectable earnings per share figures. Bob managed to do this by adjusting the way the company reported sales, by understating expenses and by generating several hundred false invoices.

A year-end audit exposed the misconduct of the two executives. Sheila was sent to prison for 2 years. Bob was imprisoned for 1 year and was struck off from membership of his professional body.

Required:

Describe the sources of power and authority that would enable someone in Sheila's position to persuade Bob to behave as he did in the above scenario.

(10 marks)

Responsibility

Responsibility involves the obligation of an individual who occupies a particular position in the organisation to perform certain duties, tasks or make certain decisions.

Responsibility means the right to hold subordinates accountable for personal performance and achievement of the targets specified by the organisation's plans. It is the obligation to use authority to see duties are performed.

The scope of responsibility must correspond to the scope of authority given.

If a manager is given responsibility without the necessary authority, he is in the position of being powerless to achieve the levels upon which his performance is being judged.

A person given authority without clear responsibility for achieving specified targets or without having to report to a more senior manager will not know how to use this authority wisely.

Accountability

Accountability describes the need for individuals to explain and justify any failure to fulfil their responsibilities to their superiors in the hierarchy. It refers to being called to account for one's actions and results.

Test your understanding 3

Required:

Briefly describe the concepts of accountability, authority and responsibility.

(10 marks)

Delegation

Delegation is one of the main functions of effective management. Delegation is the process whereby a manager assigns part of his authority to a subordinate to fulfil his duties. However, delegation can only occur if the manager initially possesses the authority to delegate.

Effective delegation

Koontz and O'Donnell state that to delegate effectively a manager must:

- define the limits of authority delegated to their subordinate.
- satisfy themselves that the subordinate is competent to exercise that authority.
- discipline themselves to permit the subordinate the full use of that authority without constant checks and interference.

In planning delegation therefore, a manager must ensure that:

- Too much is not delegated to totally overload a subordinate.
- The subordinate has reasonable skill and experience in the area concerned.
- Appropriate authority is delegated.
- Monitoring and control are possible.
- There is not a feeling of 'passing the buck' or 'opting out'.
- All concerned know that the task has been delegated.
- Time is set aside for coaching and guiding.

Many managers are reluctant to delegate, preferring to deal with routine matters themselves in addition to the more major aspects of their duties. There are several reasons for this:

- Managers often believe that their subordinates are not able or experienced enough to perform the tasks.

- Managers believe that doing routine tasks enables them to keep in touch with what is happening in the other areas of their department.
- Where a manager feels insecure they will invariably be reluctant to pass any authority to a subordinate.
- An insecure manager may fear that the subordinate will do a better job that they can.
- Some managers do not know how or what to delegate.
- Managers fear losing control.
- Initially delegation can take a lot of a manager's time and a common reason for not delegating is that the managers feel they could complete the job quicker if they did it themselves.

Methods of delegation

There are different methods of delegation, which vary in effectiveness:

- *Abdication* – leave issues without any formal delegation, which is very crude and usually an ineffective method.
- *Custom and practice* – an age-old system, the most junior member of staff opens the mail, gets the coffee and so on.
- *Explanation* – manager's brief subordinates along the lines of how the task should be done. (not too little and not too much – a fine balance that requires judgement).
- *Consultation* – Prior consultation is considered to be important and very effective. People, if organised, are immensely powerful; by contributing or withholding their cooperation they make the task a success or failure. Managers admit that sometimes good ideas come from below. In fact the point of view of the person nearest the scene of action is more likely to be relevant.

Benefits of delegation

There are many practical reasons why managers should overcome this reluctance to delegate:

- Without it the chief executive would be responsible for everything – individuals have physical and mental limitations.
- Allows for career planning and development, aids continuity and cover for absence.
- Allows for better decision making; those closer to the problem make the decision, allowing higher-level managers to spend more time on strategic issues.

Management and leadership

- Allowing the individual with the appropriate skills to make the decision improves time management.
- Gives people more interesting work, increases job satisfaction for subordinates; increased motivation encourages better work.

Remember: responsibility can never be delegated. A superior is always responsible for the actions of his subordinates and cannot evade this responsibility by delegation.

Test your understanding 4

Henry has for some time been in charge of a department which was producing satisfactory results before he took over. However, recently, several of his staff have asked whether jobs in other similar departments are available. There have also been a number of unexpected mistakes, and information has not been transmitted properly.

You are Henry's manager. As a result of your concern you have been keeping an eye on the situation. You have found that Henry comes in early every day, stays late, takes large amounts of work home with him, and is showing definite signs of strain. In the meantime his staff appear bored and disinterested.

Required:

(a) Describe the possible causes of this situation.

(6 marks)

(b) Explain the principles for effective delegation.

(6 marks)

(c) Comment on the advantages to both manager and subordinate of effective delegation.

(6 marks)

(d) A common criticism of many managers appear to be 'He/she does not know how to delegate!' Illustrating your answer with appropriate examples, discuss the probable reasons for this statement.

(6 marks)

(e) What determines the amount of power and authority Henry possesses?

(6 marks)

Test your understanding 5

Flavours Fine Foods is a leading producer for the food industry, supplying many of Europe's leading restaurants. Started just five years ago by brothers Lee and Alan Jones, the organisation has grown from a small company employing five people to a multi-divisional organisation employing 120 people.

The organisation's production facility is divided into three separate departments. Each department has a single manager with supervisors assisting on the production lines. The managers and supervisors, all of whom are aware of their roles, work well together. However, although the organisation has grown, the owners continue to involve themselves in day-to-day activities and this has led to friction between the owners, managers and supervisors.

As a result a problem arose last week. Alan Jones instructed a supervisor to repair a machine on the shop floor, which he refused to do without confirmation and instruction from his departmental manager. The supervisor's manager, Dean Watkins, became involved and was annoyed at what he saw as interference in his department's activities. Dean told Alan Jones that he "should have come to me first" because although the responsibility for the overall organisation was a matter for the brothers, action taken in the factory was his through powers that had been delegated to him and through his authority, as manager. In the argument that followed, Alan Jones was accused of failing to understand the way that the hierarchy in such a large organisation operates and that interference with operational decisions by senior management was not helpful.

As a consequence of this, Alan Jones has asked you to explain to him and his brother the issues behind the dispute to clarify the roles of managers and supervisors and to indicate how and why successful delegation might be achieved.

Required:

(a) Explain to Alan Jones the main differences between the work of a manager and that of a supervisor.

(6 marks)

Management and leadership

(b) To correct the problems at Flavours Fine Foods, explain to Alan Jones:

   (i) the need for delegation;

   (ii) how effective delegation might be achieved;

   (iii) problems with delegation;

   (iv) how these problems might be overcome.

(14 marks)

3 Classical and contemporary theories of management

The study of management theory and development of ideas on effective management practice helps in providing an understanding of the principles underlying the process of management and which in turn influences management behaviour in organisations. The main schools of management thinking can be grouped according to their broad approaches as shown below:

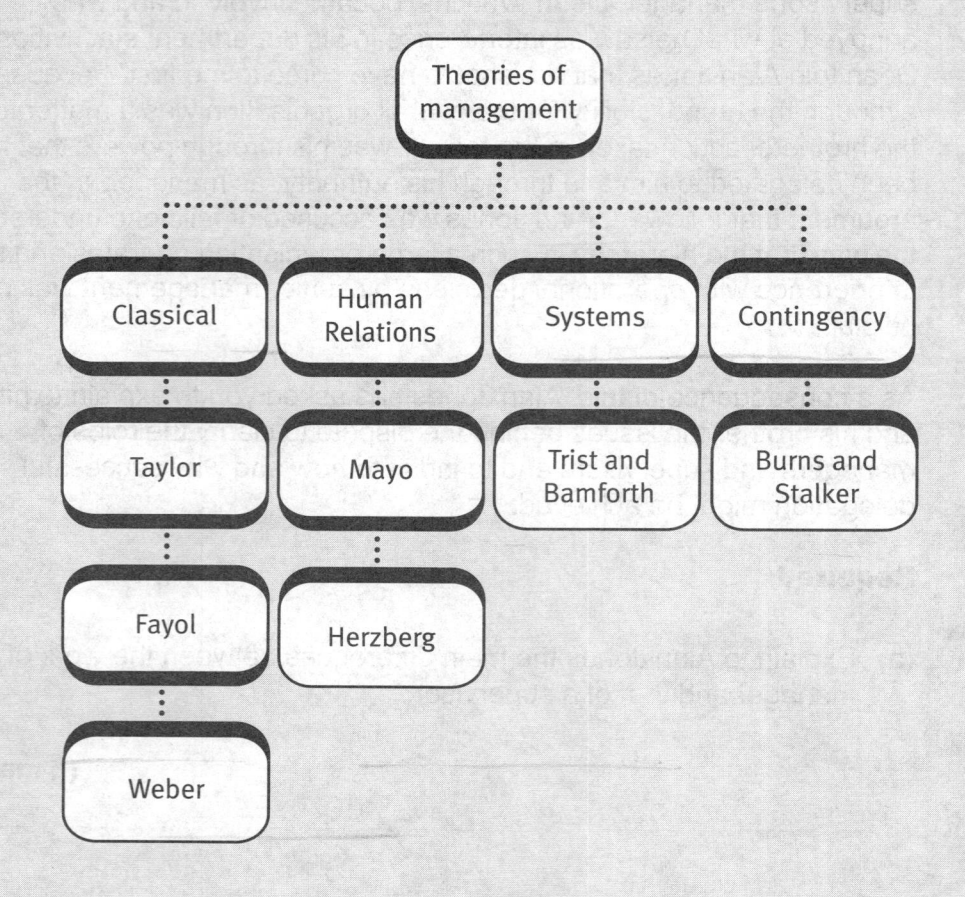

```
                    Theories of
                    management
         ┌─────────────┼──────────────┬──────────────┐
      Classical     Human         Systems       Contingency
                   Relations
         │             │              │              │
       Taylor         Mayo        Trist and      Burns and
                                  Bamforth        Stalker
         │             │
       Fayol        Herzberg
         │
       Weber
```

Classical theories

The classical approach to management emphasises the technical and economic aspects of organisations. It assumes that behaviour in organisations is rational and logical. There are different approaches within the Classical School which can be identified as Scientific Management (Taylor), Administrative Management (Fayol) and Bureaucracy (Weber).

The foundation on which the various theories developed was that management could be learnt and codified. These ideas were developed in an era when mass production and economies of scale were viewed as central to business success. Although some of these theories were developed over a century ago they do continue to inform management practice today.

There are some common interests that all these different perspectives focus on:

- The purpose and structure of organisations and planning of work.
- The technical requirements of each job.
- The principles of management.

Scientific management (Taylor)

Objective of management is to secure the maximum prosperity for both employer and employee:

- One best approach to the job, using work study methods;
- Once employees were trained in the best approach then payment should be based on piece-rate (believed money to be a motivator);
- Well-trained employees delivered high productivity;
- Win:win for both employee and organisation.

Taylor recognised that if specialised knowledge and skills were concentrated in the hands of well-trained and able employees, there would be an improvement in productivity. He therefore broke jobs down into separate functions and then gave each function to an individual. Taylor believed that it was only through the effective use of control by specialists that best use would be made of the resources available to increase the size of the incentive surplus to be shared between efficient staff.

Administrative management (Fayol)

Fayol's approach was to view problems from the managerial aspects and to specifically analyse the work of management, stressing that most management features had universal application

He identified the common features of management as:

- *Forecasting and planning* objectives.
- *Organising* resources to achieve organisational objectives.
- *Co-ordination* company and individual objectives.
- *Commanding* – giving orders and instructions.
- *Controlling* – *comparing* actual performance with expected or budgeted performance.

These features effectively define the role of a manger as we still understand it today.

To enable these Fayol suggested **14 principles of management** for adoption.

(1) *Division of work* and specialisation should be encouraged since it leads to greater productivity.

(2) *Authority* to issue commands should be accompanied by responsibility.

(3) *Leadership*, good leadership should be provided.

(4) *Unity of command*. There should be one person responsible to one boss. Wherever possible, a subordinate should be responsible to one superior. Divided authority and responsibility complicates delegation of duties, responsibilities and authority.

(5) *Unity of direction*. A single plan should be laid down for all employees engaged in the same work activities. In other words, one head and one plan for a group of activities with the same objective.

(6) *Remuneration*. The system of reward should be related where possible to the individual's wants and needs. Pay should be fair to both the employee and the firm.

(7) *Centralisation*. This is always present to a greater or lesser degree. The degree of centralisation or decentralisation should vary according to the circumstances of the organisation.

(8) *Scalar chain*. A clear line of authority is necessary to ensure that managers know who can delegate to them, who they can delegate to, and to whom they are accountable. It should be possible to trace the line of authority from top to bottom of an organisation and it is essential to have vertical and lateral communications.

(9) *Order*. There should be a place for everything and everything in its place. In order to minimise lost time and unnecessary handling of materials, it is essential to have material order and social order in an organisation.

(10) *Equity*. A combination of kindness and justice is required in dealing with employees.

(11) *Subordination of individual interests to the general interest*. The interests and goals of individual members of the organisation should be subservient to the overall organisational goals. The interest of one individual should not prevail over the general good.

(12) *Stability of tenure of personnel*. Successful businesses require stability of tenure. People need to be given time to settle into their jobs and management should avoid a 'hire and fire' mentality.

(13) *Initiative*. All employees should be given the opportunity to use their initiative. All staff need to be encouraged to show initiative within their limits of authority.

(14) *Esprit de corps*. It is the task of management to foster *esprit de corps*, that is, to encourage harmony and teamwork.

Bureaucratic management (Weber)

Max Weber developed his model of the 'ideal type' of bureaucracy, in which he explored the characteristics of a rational form of organisation. Today, the term bureaucracy tends to have many negative connotations, but Weber used it to describe what he believed to be potentially the most efficient form of organisation.

A culture based on formalisation and standardisation.

- Based on hierarchy of authority;
- Strict rules and regulations govern decision making;
- Specialisation in duties, segregated 'offices' and levels.

Weber listed the main characteristics of bureaucracy:

- *Specialisation*. Clear division of labour, so that each member has well-defined roles and responsibilities.
- *Hierarchy*. A hierarchy of authority, in which offices are linked through a clear chain of command.
- *Rules*. Strict rules and procedures govern decision-making and conduct.
- *Impersonality*. Objective and rational decisions rather than personal preferences.

- *Appointed officials.* Managers are selected by their qualifications, education or training.
- *Career officials.* Managers pursue their career within the bureaucracy and work within a defined salary structure.
- *Full-time officials.* Professionalism requires commitment.
- *Public/private division.* Money is used in a limited liability framework to prevent family money being used, as this creates conservatism because of personal risk.

Nowadays, most large organisations, will be bureaucratic. Many others, though smaller, will also have to have a rational structure because they need to conform to regulatory bodies of one sort or another and to legislation.

Because of the formal nature of this type of organisation, the main disadvantages are:

- slow response to change, as many rules have to be changed;
- lack of speedy communication owing to the segregated 'offices' and levels;
- little need for involving staff in decision-making;
- rules stifle initiative and innovative ideas, preventing development;
- no recognition of very important informal relationships.

This type of organisational culture is **not suitable if the firm operates in a dynamic changing environment.**

> ### Test your understanding 6
>
> **Required:**
>
> Comment on the contribution of the scientific school of management to the development of classical organisational and managerial theory and practice.
>
> **(10 marks)**

4 The human relations school

Mayo

Elton Mayo, together with several colleagues, carried out the famous Hawthorne investigations for the Western Electric Company at its Hawthorne works in Chicago during the 1920s and 1930s.

Over the course of five years, Mayo's team altered the worker's working conditions and then monitored how the working conditions affected the workers morale and productivity. The changes in working conditions included changes in working hours, rest breaks, lighting, humidity, and temperature. The changes were explained to the workers prior to implementation.

At the end of the five year period, the working conditions reverted back to the conditions before the experiment began. Unexpectedly the workers morale and productivity rose to levels higher than before and during the experiments. This led to the conclusion that the need for recognition, security and sense of belonging is more important in determining workers' morale and productivity than the physical conditions under which he/she works.

He also concluded that workers were motivated by more than self interest and instead the following applied:

- There is an unwritten understanding between the worker and employer regarding what is expected from them; Mayo called this the psychological contract.
- A worker's motivation can be increased by showing an interest in them.
- Work is a group activity, team work can increase a worker's motivation as it allows people to form strong working relationships and increases trust between the workers.
- Workers are motivated by the social aspect of work, as demonstrated by the workers socialising during and outside work and the subsequent increase in motivation.
- The communication between workers and management influences workers' morale and productivity. Workers are motivated through a good working relationship with management.

Mayo's findings have contributed to organisational development in terms of human relations and motivation theory.

Herzberg

Frederick Herzberg carried forward Mayo's emphasis on the identification of the motivational needs of individuals. His two factor theory of motivation describes motivational and hygiene factors.

- Hygiene factors – are based on a need to avoid unpleasantness. They do not provide any long-term motivating power. A lack of satisfaction of hygiene factors will demotivate staff.
- Motivator factors – satisfy a need for personal growth. Satisfaction of motivator factors can encourage staff to work harder.

Hertzberg believed that only motivators can move employees to action: the hygiene factors cannot. They can only prevent dissatisfaction.

In order to motivate the workforce management must avoid dissatisfaction and put in place motivators to encourage the staff.

Hygiene factors

To avoid dissatisfaction there should be:

- Policies and procedures for staff treatment.
- Suitable level and quality of supervision.
- Pleasant physical and working conditions.
- Appropriate level of salary and status for the job.
- Team working.

Motivational factors

In order to motivate staff managers should provide:

- Sense of accomplishment (achievement) through setting targets.
- Recognition of good work.
- Increasing levels of responsibility.
- Career advancement.
- Attraction of the job.

Herzberg felt that 'you can't motivate dissatisfied people'. Satisfiers or motivators will only generate job satisfaction if the hygiene factors are present.

Herzberg's theory of motivation

C&G Local Authority employs around 8,000 members of staff. It operates as a traditional, formal governmental type of organisation. Over the last few years it has recognised a problem regarding its junior management level in that many of them are failing to meet the expected level of performance.

A team has been set up to investigate the problem and they have decided to hold a series of meetings with all levels of management. Initially they found that the junior managers were reluctant to participate in the meetings, saying that they could see no real value in them. 'We have seen it all before' was a typical response. After the meetings, the team produced a report which identified three main problem areas.

Firstly, it became apparent that the level of morale for all staff was low. Lack of facilities and pressure of work appeared to be the main grievance. There appeared however to be a deeper problem, that of mistrust between the staff as a whole and senior management. The reason for this was unclear.

The second problem appeared to be that junior managers were regarded by staff as poor at managing their sections. In response, the junior managers said that their positions in general were unclear; there were no clear lines of authority, command or responsibility which allowed them to make decisions for their departments. In addition many quoted their roles as being menial and highlighted funding shortages, unrealistic targets, little recognition of their position, no job descriptions and lack of training as problems.

Job security was the third issue. Financial cutbacks and changes in service levels had led to rumours of substantial cutbacks in staff. Rumours were especially strong amongst the junior management. It was felt that new, younger staff would be better trained and would be likely to replace them.

In all, the problems had shown themselves in high labour turnover, which in addition to the problems already outlined, were blamed on low salaries, little opportunity for personal advancement and poor working conditions.

Required:

Using Herzberg's theory of motivation, explain the attitude of the junior managers.

(10 marks)

Solution:

The case illustrates Herzberg's motivation theory, which attempts to explain those factors which motivate the individual by identifying and satisfying the individual's needs, desires and the goals pursued to satisfy these desires.

This theory is based upon the idea that motivation factors can be separated into hygiene factors and motivation factors and is therefore often referred to as a 'two need system.' These two separate 'needs' are the need to avoid unpleasantness and discomfort and, at the other end of the motivational scale, the need for personal development.

A shortage of those factors which positively encourage employees (motivating factors) will cause those employees to focus on other, non job related factors, the so called 'hygiene' factors. These are illustrated in the case with the attitude of the junior management to senior management and their concerns for example with shortages, targets, recognition and training and 'we've seen it all before'.

The most important part of this theory of motivation is that the main motivating factors are not in the environment but in the intrinsic value and satisfaction gained from the job itself. It follows therefore that the job itself must have challenge, scope for enrichment and be of interest to the job holder. This is not the case in the scenario; there appears to be little or no intrinsic satisfaction from the junior manager's work, illustrated by them regarding themselves and their role as menial and their lack of responsibility and decision making powers within their own departments.

Motivators (or 'satisfiers') are those factors directly concerned with the satisfaction gained from the job itself, the sense of achievement, level of recognition, the intrinsic value felt of the job itself, level of responsibility, opportunities for advancement and the status provided by the job. Motivators lead to satisfaction because of the need for growth and a sense of self achievement. Clearly, none of this applies to the junior managers of C&G Local Authority.

A lack of motivators leads to over concentration on hygiene factors; that is those negative factors which can be seen and therefore form the basis of complaint and concern.

Hygiene (or maintenance) factors lead to job dissatisfaction because of the need to avoid unpleasantness. They are so called because they can in turn be avoided by the use of 'hygienic' methods i.e. they can be prevented. Attention to these hygiene factors prevents dissatisfaction but does not on its own provide motivation. Hygiene factors (or 'dissatisfiers') are concerned with those factors associated with, but not directly a part of, the job itself. These can be detected in the scenario; salary and the perceived differences with others, job security, working conditions, the quality of management, organisational policy and administration and interpersonal relations.

Understanding Herzberg's theory identifies the nature of intrinsic satisfaction that can be obtained from the work itself, draws attention to job design and makes managers aware that problems of motivation may not necessarily be directly associated with the work.

> **Maslow's hierarchy of needs**
>
> Maslow developed a hierarchy of needs, shown below.
>
> | Maslow's hierarchy of needs | Related aspects at work |
> |---|---|
> | Self-fulfilment | – Challenging job
– Creative task demands
– Advancement opportunities
– Achievement in work |
> | Ego | – Merit pay increase
– High status job title |
> | Social | – Compatible work group
– Friendships at work |
> | Safety/Security | – Job security
– Fringe benefits |
> | Basic/Physiological | – Basic salary
– Safe working conditions |
>
> According to the model, each individual has a set of needs which can be arranged in a hierarchy. The above diagram has shown the hierarchy in a business context. The largest and most fundamental needs, such as basic pay and safe working conditions are shown at the bottom, and the need for self-fulfilment is at the top, moving through aspects such as job security, friendships at work and status.
>
> The lowest needs must be satisfied first, only then can an individual move to the next level. This can be used as a motivational tool, if the management can determine where individuals are on the hierarchy, they will know that the next level can be used in motivating staff.

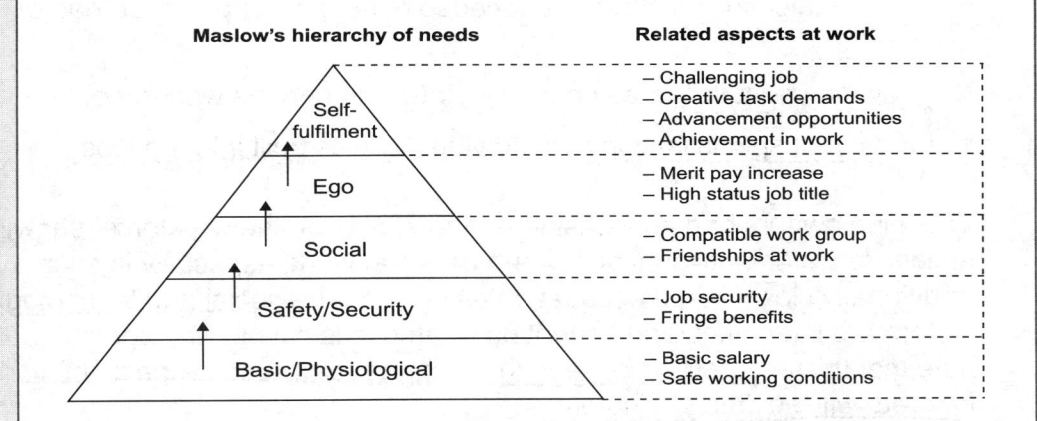

5 Systems theory

Trist and Bamforth

Trist and Bamforth developed a socio-technical systems theory. While he was working at the Tavistock Institute, Trist's most famous research was into the structure and operation of the 'longwall' method of mining in County Durham in the 1940s as it highlighted the interaction between social needs and technological activities. The 'longwall' method introduced new cutting equipment which widened the narrow coal 'face' into a 'longwall'. But very soon the low morale, high absenteeism and deteriorating relationships were so serious that the Tavistock Institute was invited to investigate causes and possible solutions to the problems.

Trist and Bamforth diagnosed that although the new methods had been introduced 'scientifically':

- close-knit groups had been broken up;
- communication was difficult because of the geographical spread of workers;
- new payment schemes caused jealousy among the workforce;
- too much specialisation and individuality was built into the jobs.

The mine owners had not considered the effects on the workforce, showing an ignorance of individual and group needs at work, especially in such a traditionally close-linked occupation as mining. The social and technological factors are interlinked and cannot be treated in isolation. Managers should note that this interaction between the technical and social aspects of work, if ignored, will inevitably bring problems.

6 Contingency theory

Managers, researchers and consultants often found that the methods suggested by the classical management schools did not always work. The idea of one approach being right, whether it be the school of scientific management, classical, human relations or systems, is rejected in favour of contingency. The contingency view suggests that the effectiveness of various managerial practices, styles and techniques will vary according to the particular circumstances of the situation. The problems arise when two such contingencies are in conflict, the theory does not describe how such conflicts can be resolved.

Mechanistic versus Organic Organisations (Burns and Stalker)

Burns and Stalker (1961) distinguished between mechanistic and organic organisations. Burns is quoted as saying: 'The beginning of administrative wisdom is the awareness that there is no one best way of designing a management system.' Burns and Stalker studied the way in which high-technology industries were being introduced into Scotland. The difficulties experienced by low-technology companies in the conversion process to high technology highlighted many organisation structural problems.

Burns and Stalker's studies led them to distinguish between two major types of organisations – **mechanistic** and **organic**. However, they considered these two systems to be located at opposite ends of a continuum, with various combinations in between.

Features of a mechanistic organisation:

- High degree of task specialisation.
- Responsibilities and authority clearly defined.
- Coordination and communication – a responsibility of each management level.
- Selectivity in the release of top level information to subordinates.
- Great emphasis on the organisational hierarchy's ability to develop loyalty and obedience.
- Employees are often locally recruited.
- The mechanistic system was seen to be appropriate in fairly stable conditions where the management of change was not seen to be an important factor. The relationship with Weber's bureaucracy is obvious.

Features of an organic organisation

- Skills, experience and specialist knowledge recognised as valuable resources.
- Integration of efforts via lateral, vertical and diagonal communication channels.
- Leadership based on consultation and involvement in problem-solving.
- Commitment to task achievement, survival and growth more important than loyalty and obedience.
- Employees are recruited from a variety of sources.
- The organic system is seen to be more responsive to change, and is therefore recommended for organisations moving into periods of rapid changes in technology, market orientation, or tasks.

The appropriateness of organisational structure to its environment is a cornerstone of contingency theory.

Contingency theory – Joan Woodward's Essex Studies

Joan Woodward found that by knowing an organisation's primary system of production, you could predict their structure. This view states that all companies should be organised differently according to the underlying production process and product, with the external environment also being considered.

In her analysis of the 100 companies (which ranged in size from 100 to 1000 employees), she identified ten types of technology which were condensed into three main groups.

These are:

- *unit and small batch production* – typical of 'craft' industries;
- *large batch and mass production* – for example, cars;
- *process production* – for example, cement, oil, and food processing.

Differences in production type accounted for many of the differences in organisation structure:

- In *heavily mechanised process technologies* taller hierarchies were found to exist, but with levels of committee rather than straight-line instruction. Since technical expertise is important, people were highly skilled, often graduates, with most of the organisation headcount being involved in administration. Control was far easier in these organisations. They involved groups of more highly skilled workers and job satisfaction was highest.

- *Large batch and mass production companies* have shorter lines of command and thus fewer managers and clerks. There were a traditionally larger number of direct operatives. The large number of semi-skilled workers required for mass production means that the span of control of supervisors is very wide, and this may create an environment where human and industrial relations are strained. Job satisfaction was lowest.

- *Unit and small batch production companies* were found to have short hierarchies, with no manager very far from production work, and a limited number of administrative controls. They tended to involve much smaller groups of more highly skilled workers and job satisfaction was higher. Job satisfaction was middling.

Large batch and mass production systems, because of the high numbers of specialists involved, create more paperwork and demand clearer cut definitions of duties.

Woodward's studies indicated how four major factors in any company (task; technology; people; and structure) were interrelated, and that management needed to be aware that when one of these factors changed, it was vital to recognise the effects this change would have on the other factors. These studies contributed to the debate as to whether technology forced organisations to change their structure and culture.

Contemporary perspectives

The more recent literature on organisations and management is vast and difficult to categorise in the simple ways used for early contributions to organisation theory.

Gareth Morgan has argued that we can view organisations in different ways as we try to understand them. We are rarely aware of the image of organisations we take for granted but, just like the photographs of the Parthenon from different perspectives, they fundamentally influence what we see and the explanations we put forward to make sense of it. However, the Parthenon can be approached from different directions, though not all are equally easy. Different angles will give different perspectives, and by arriving very early in the morning you could get a photograph with unusual lighting and fewer people in it.

The same is true of the way we look at organisations and the process of management.

From one perspective it is helpful to think of organisations as machines, in which the various jobs and departments are carefully designed to work smoothly together to perform certain functions effectively. This is certainly the view implicit in early theories such as classical and scientific management.

Exercise:

What are likely to be the limitations of viewing organisations as machines? Can you think of any other ways of looking at organisations that might be useful?

Solution:

The view of organisations as machines provides some useful insights, but also imposes limitations, which in some circumstances can be severe. For example, the use of basic costing techniques in large multi-product firms may result in misleading information for decision-making. In this type of situation, more sophisticated models which recognise the more complicated nature of the organisation, may be more appropriate.

The limitations of mechanistic perspectives on organisations are as follows:

- They can create organisational forms that have great difficulty adapting to changed circumstances.
- They can result in mindless and unquestioning bureaucracy.
- They can have unanticipated and undesirable consequences as the interests of those working in the organisation take precedence over the goals the organisation was designed to achieve.
- They can have dehumanising effects upon employees, especially those at the lower levels of the organisational hierarchy (Morgan, 1986).

Morgan goes on to argue that there are other ways of viewing organisations that lead to different insights. It is not possible to go into all of those here, but two other perspectives he identifies are the view of organisations as organisms and organisations as cultures. It is important for managers to be able to examine organisational problems from more than one perspective in their search for effectiveness.

7 Leadership

There are many different views on whether managers and leaders are the same. While the job of the manager will normally require some leadership competence, not all leaders are managers. Individuals are often given the title of 'manager' based on their position in the organisation hierarchy, which gives them power and authority (as outlined in the previous section). Leadership, on the other hand, can be viewed as providing direction, creating a vision, and then influencing others to share that vision and work towards the achievement of organisational goals. Leadership can be seen as 'getting other people to do things willingly'.

Leadership comes about in a number of different ways:

- Some leaders are elected – in politics and trade unions.
- Other leaders emerge by popular choice and through their personal drive and qualities.
- Within an organisation a manager is appointed to a position of authority. Leadership is a function of the position.

Various **types of leader** have been identified. The most important ones are:

- the *charismatic* leader – whose influence springs mainly from personality.
- the *traditional* leader – whose influence stems from social prejudice, such as the man at the head of the family.
- the *situational* leader – whose influence can only be effective by being in the right place at the right time.
- the *appointed* leader – whose influence arises directly from a position/status, e.g. most managers and supervisors. This is the bureaucratic type of leadership, where legitimate power springs from the nature and scope of the position within the hierarchy.
- the *functional* leader – who secures the position by doing what he or she does well.

Leadership and management

Sometimes management and leadership are seen as synonymous. There is, however, a difference between the two and it does not follow that every leader is a manager, or that every manager is a leader.

Management is the process of getting things done through the efforts of other people. It focuses on procedures and results. Managers tend to react to specific situations and be more concerned with solving short-term problems. Management suggests more formality and the term 'manager' refers to a position within a structured organisation and with prescribed roles.

Leadership is influencing others to do what he or she wants them to do; it involves human interaction and is often associated with the willing and enthusiastic behaviour of followers – the ability to influence needs the permission of those to be influenced. Leadership is related to motivation, interpersonal behaviour and the process of communication.

Leadership is a dynamic process and is very important at all levels within the organisation, from the board to the shop floor. It does not necessarily take place within the hierarchical structure of the organisation. A leader may have no formal title at all and may rely on personal traits and style to influence followers.

Leaders envision the future; they inspire organisation members and chart the course of the organisation. Every group of people that performs near its total capacity has some person at its head who is skilled in the art of leadership.

Differences in attitudes

There are other differences in attitudes towards goals, conceptions of work, relations with others, self-perception and development between leadership and management.

- Managers tend to adopt impersonal or passive attitudes towards goals, needing to co-ordinate and balance in order to compromise conflicting values. Leaders adopt a more personal and active attitude towards them, creating excitement in work and developing choices that give substance to images that excite people.
- In their relationships with other people, managers maintain a low level of emotional involvement. Leaders have empathy with other people and give attention to what events and actions mean.
- Managers perceive themselves as regulators of the existing order of affairs within the organisation. A leader's sense of identity does not depend upon membership or work roles. Leaders tend to search out opportunities for change.
- Management may be seen more in terms of planning, organising, directing and controlling the activities of subordinates. Leadership, however, is concerned more with attention to communicating with, motivating, encouraging and involving people.
- Management reacts. Leadership transforms – making a difference.

The benefits of leadership

There are many benefits from good leadership, including the following:

- Reducing employee dissatisfaction.
- Encouraging effective delegation.
- Creating team spirit.
- Helping to develop skills and confidence in the group.
- Helping to enlist support and co-operation from people outside the group or organisation.

The skills of a leader

The skill of leadership seems to be a compound of at least four major ingredients:

- The ability to use power effectively and in a responsible manner.

- The ability to comprehend that human beings have different motivation forces at different times and situations.
- The ability to inspire.
- The ability to act in a manner that will develop a climate conducive to responding to and arousing motivations.

Theories of leadership

In the search to explain why some leaders are more effective than others, the following perspectives can be identified:

- Personality, trait or qualities theories.
- Style theories.
- Contingency or situational theories.

8 Personality, trait or qualities theories

Early studies focused on the qualities required by effective leaders. Lists were compiled of required leadership qualities including:

- physical traits, such as drive, energy, appearance and height;
- personality traits, such as adaptability, enthusiasm and self-confidence; and
- social traits, such as co-operation, tact, courtesy and administrative ability.

Certain other writers selected other personal qualities which were thought to be desirable in leaders, who are '**born and not made**' Many great leaders were considered to have:

- above-average intelligence;
- initiative – independence and inventiveness, the capacity to perceive a need for action;
- motivation – the urge to do it;
- self-assurance – self-confidence;
- the 'helicopter factor' – the ability to rise above the particulars of a situation and perceive it in relation to the surrounding context.
- Other 'essential' qualities included enthusiasm, sociability, integrity, courage, imagination, determination, energy, faith, even virility.

The problem with personality or trait theories is that there are always counter-examples that can be given – for instance, when one theorist suggested a good leader must be tall, a short yet effective leader was identified; when one theorist suggested a leader must be tactful and courteous, a rude yet effective leader was found. Clearly good leadership is more than simply possession of a particular physical or psychological attribute.

9 Style theories

The essence of leadership style theories is that a successful leader will exhibit a pattern of behaviour (i.e. 'style') in gaining the confidence of those they wish to lead. Style is a difficult factor to measure or define. The style of a manager is essentially how he or she operates, but it is a function of many different factors.

It is useful to start by looking at the three main styles of leadership:

Autocratic or authoritarian style. '*Do this*'

With this style the leader takes complete control, imposes all decisions on the group and neither asks for or listens to the opinions of others. Autocratic leaders tend to distrust the members of the group and as a result closely supervise and control the actions of the group.

While in many circumstances this style can cause resentment, in other situations it can be necessary. For example in the military, or where safety and security is paramount.

Democratic or participative style. '*Let's work together to solve this*'

With this style there is open discussion between the leader and the group. Ideas from the group are encouraged and while the leader will still ultimately make the decisions, the reasons for the decisions will be explained to the group.

This style is more likely to encourage innovation and creativity and group members are normally more motivated under a democratic leader.

Free reign or delegative style. '*You go and sort out the problem*'

With this style, the leader provides little or no leadership and expects the group to make decisions and solve problems on their own.

Like the autocratic style, this style of leadership can also lead to resentment within the group.

There are a number of theories dealing with style approaches to leadership:

- McGregor – Theory X and Theory Y
- Lewin
- Likert – four systems of management
- Tannenbaum and Schmidt – continuum of leadership styles
- Blake and Mouton – the managerial grid

As we go through these models, consider the similarities in each of the models and identify if the positions in each model fit under the three main styles of leadership discussed above.

Model	Autocratic style	Democratic style	Free reign style
McGregor			
Lewin			
Likert			
Tannenbaum and Schmidt			
Blake and Mouton			

Douglas McGregor – Theory X and Theory Y

Independently of any leadership ability, managers have been studied and differing styles emerge. The style chosen by a manager will depend very much upon the assumptions the manager makes about their subordinates, what they think they want and what they consider their attitude towards their work to be. McGregor came up with two contrasting theories:

- **Theory X** – managers believe:
    - employees are basically lazy, have an inherent dislike of work and will avoid it if possible
    - employees prefer to be directed and wish to avoid responsibility
    - employees need constant supervision and direction
    - employees have relatively little ambition and wants security above everything else
    - employees are indifferent to organisational needs.

Because of this, most people must be coerced, controlled, directed and threatened with punishment to get them to put in adequate effort towards the achievement of organisational objectives. This results in a managerial style which is **authoritarian** – this is indicted by a tough, uncompromising style which includes tight controls with punishment/reward systems.

- **Theory Y** – managers believe:
    - employees enjoy their work, they are self-motivated and willing to work hard to meet both personal and organisational goals
    - employees will exercise self direction and self control
    - commitment to objectives is a function of rewards and the satisfaction of ego
    - personal achievement needs are perhaps the most significant of these rewards, and can direct effort towards organisational objectives
    - the average employee learns, under proper conditions, not only to accept, but to seek responsibility
    - employees have the capacity to exercise a relatively high degree of imagination, ingenuity and creativity in the solution of organisational problems.

This theory results in a managerial style which is **democratic** – this will be indicted by a manager who is benevolent, participative and a believer of self-controls.

Of course, reality is somewhere in between these two extremes.

Most managers, of course, do not give much conscious thought to these things, but tend to act upon a set of assumptions that are largely implicit.

Kurt Lewin

The first significant studies into leadership style were carried out in the 1930s by a psychologist called Kurt Lewin. His studies focused attention on the different effects created by three different leadership styles.

- *Authoritarian* – A style where the leader just tells the group what to do.
- *Democratic* – A participative style where all the decisions are made by the leader in consultation and participation with the group.
- *Laissez-faire* – A style where the leader does not really do anything but leaves the group alone and lets them get on with it.

Lewin and his researchers were using experimental groups in these studies and the criteria they used were measures of productivity and task satisfaction.

- In terms of productivity and satisfaction, it was the democratic style that was the most productive and satisfying.
- The *laissez-faire* style was next in productivity but not in satisfaction – group members were not at all satisfied with it.
- The authoritarian style was the least productive of all and carried with it lots of frustration and instances of aggression among group members.

Likert's four systems of management

An alternative model was put forward by Likert. Likert examined different departments in an attempt to explain good or bad performance by identifying conditions for motivation.

He found that poor performing departments tended to be under the command of 'job-centred' managers. These tended to concentrate on keeping their subordinates busily engaged in going through a specific work cycle in a prescribed way and at a satisfactory rate. (an approach similar to Taylor's scientific management).

Best performance was under 'employee-centred' managers who tended to focus their attention on the human aspects of their subordinates' problems, and on building effective work groups which were set demanding goals. This finding appears to comply with Elton Mayo's findings that one of the components of success was the creation of an elite team with good communications, irrespective of pay and conditions. Such management regards its job as dealing with human beings rather than work, with the function of enabling them to work efficiently.

Likert concluded that the key to high performance is an employee-centred environment with general supervision, emphasis on targets, high performance goals rather than methods, and scope for input from the employee and a capacity to participate in the decision-making processes.

He summarised his findings into four basic leadership styles. He calls them 'systems of leadership':

System 1	System 2	System 3	System 4
Exploitative authoritative	Benevolent authoritative	Consultative	Participative
Decisions Imposed →	Increasing trust in subordinates' ability		Complete trust and discussion
Motivated by threats →	More participative motivational style		Motivated by rewards– goals agreed
Centralised decision making →	Increasing delegation		High degree of delegation
Rare supervisor/subordinate communication →	Increasing communication		Frequent communication
Superior and subordinates act as individuals →	Increasing teamwork		Superior and subordinates act as a team

- *Exploitive authoritative* – which relies on fear and threats. Communication is downward only and superiors and subordinates are psychologically far apart, with the decision-making process concentrated at the top of the organisation. There are certain organisations that have no choice other than to exert exploitative authoritative leadership, such as the Church, Civil Service and armed forces, where there must be little room for questioning commands, for procedural, doctrinal or strategic reasons.

- *Benevolent authoritative type* – a step beyond System 1. There is a limited element of reward, but communication is restricted. Policy is made at the top but there is some restricted delegation within rigidly-defined procedures. Here, the leader believes that they are acting in the interest of the followers in giving them instructions to obey since they are incapable of deciding for themselves the right way to act.

- *Consultative* – Here rewards are used along with occasional punishment, and some involvement is sought. Communication is both up and down, but upward communication remains rather limited. The leader asks followers for their opinions and shows some regard to their views, but does not feel obliged to act upon them.

- *Participative* – Management give economic rewards, rather than mere 'pats on the head', utilise full group participation, and involve teams in goal setting, improving work methods, and communication flows up and down. Decision making is permitted at all levels of the organisation. Leaders are often expected to justify their decisions to followers.

Likert recognised that each style is relevant in some situations; for example, in a crisis, a System 1 approach is usually required. Alternatively when introducing a new system of work, System 4 would be most effective.

His findings suggest that effective managers are those that adopt a System 3 or a System 4 style of leadership. Both are seen as being based on trust and paying attention to the needs of both the organisation and employees.

Tannenbaum and Schmidt

Tannenbaum and Schmidt came up with a continuum of leadership behaviours along which various styles were placed, ranging from 'boss centred' to 'employee centred'. Boss-centred is associated with an authoritarian approach and employee-centred suggests a democratic or participative approach.

The continuum is based on the degree of authority used by a manager and the degree of freedom for the subordinates, as shown below:

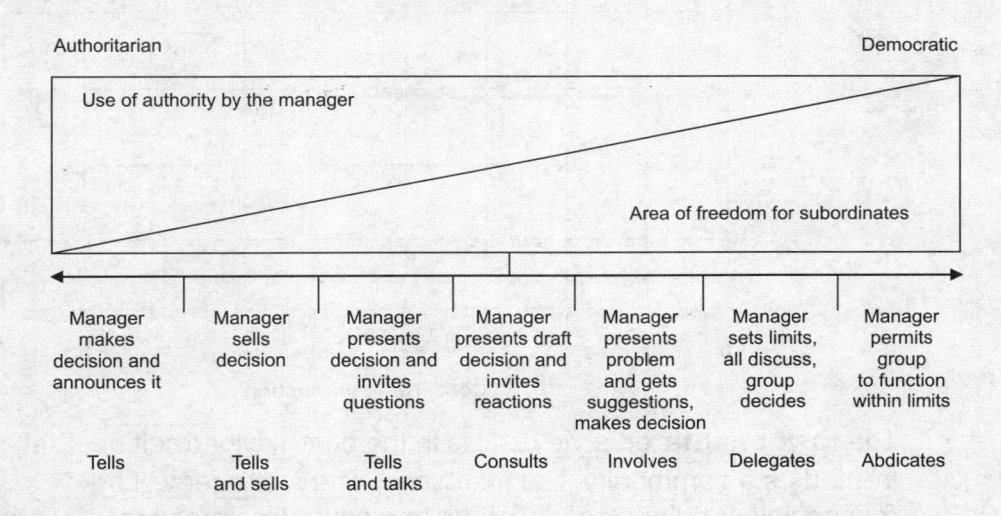

Authoritarian						Democratic
Use of authority by the manager						Area of freedom for subordinates
Manager makes decision and announces it	Manager sells decision	Manager presents decision and invites questions	Manager presents draft decision and invites reactions	Manager presents problem and gets suggestions, makes decision	Manager sets limits, all discuss, group decides	Manager permits group to function within limits
Tells	Tells and sells	Tells and talks	Consults	Involves	Delegates	Abdicates

Blake and Mouton – The Managerial Grid

Effective leaders will have concern both for the goals ('tasks') of their department and for the individual.

Robert Blake and Jane Mouton designed the managerial grid, which charts people-orientated *versus* task-oriented styles. The two extremes can be described as follows:

- **Task-centred leadership** – where the main concern of the leader is getting the job done, achieving objectives and seeing the group they lead as simply a means to the end of achieving that task.

- **Group-centred leadership** – where the prime interest of the leader is to maintain the group, stressing factors such as mutual trust, friendship, support, respect and warmth of relationships.

The grid derived its origin from the assumption that management is concerned with both production and people. Individual managers can be given a score from 1 to 9 for each orientation and then plotted on the grid.

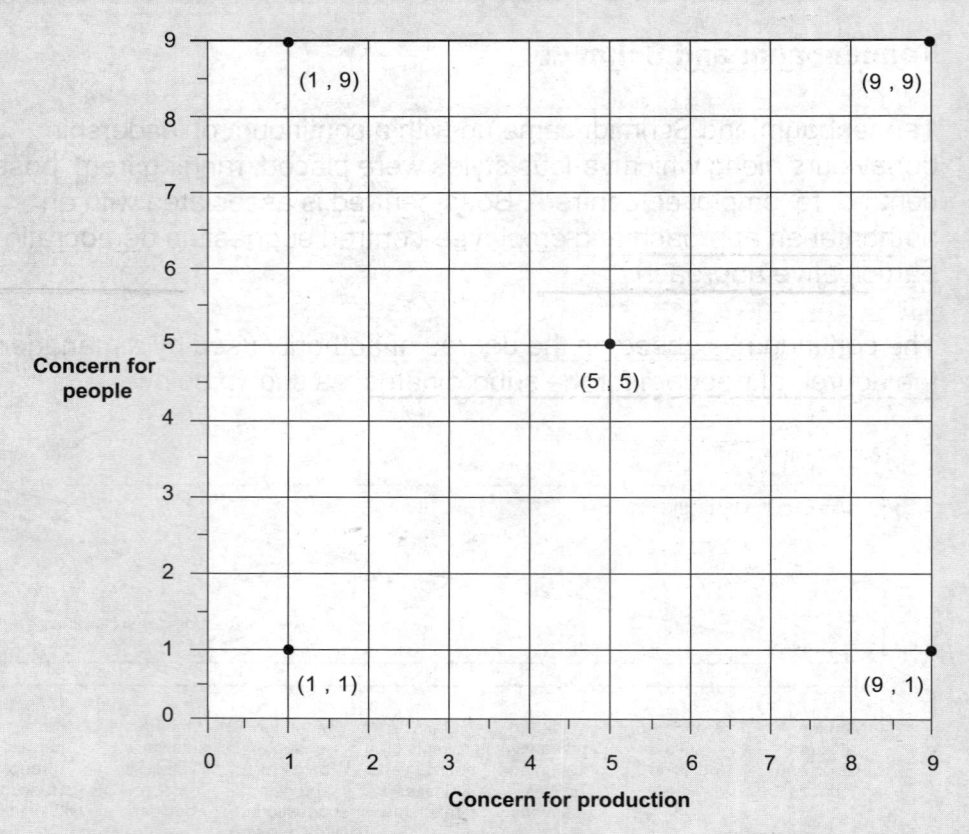

- The **task-orientated** style (9,1) is in the best Taylor tradition. Staff are treated as a commodity, like machines. The manager will be responsible for planning, directing, and controlling the work of their subordinates. It is a Theory X approach, and subordinates of this manager can become indifferent and apathetic, or even rebellious.

- The **country-club** style (1,9) emphasises people. People are encouraged and supported and any inadequacies overlooked, on the basis that people are doing their best and coercion may not improve things substantially. The 'country club', as Blake calls it, has certain drawbacks. It is an easy option for the manager but many problems can arise from this style of management in the longer term.

- The **impoverished** style (1,1) is almost impossible to imagine occurring on an organisational scale but can happen to individuals e.g. the supervisor who abdicates responsibility and leaves others to work as they see fit. A failure, for whatever reason, is always blamed down the line. Typically, the (1,1) supervisor or manager is a frustrated individual, passed over for promotion, shunted sideways, or has been in a routine job for years, possibly because of a lack of personal maturity.

- The **middle road** (5,5) is a happy medium. This viewpoint pushes for productivity and considers people, but does not go 'over the top' either way. It is a style of 'give and take', neither too lenient nor too coercive, arising probably from a feeling that any improvement is idealistic and unachievable.

- The **team** style (9,9) may be idealistic; it advocates a high degree of concern for production which generates wealth, and for people who in turn generate production. It recognises the fact that happy workers often are motivated to do their best in achieving organisational goals.

Style theories – is there one best style?

The difficulty with style theories, even when they attempt to reflect the multidimensional nature of leadership, is that they ignore the important influence of the **context** in which the leader is operating. From the discussions on the leadership styles theories, it should be apparent that there is no one best style of leadership that is equally effective for all circumstances. The best leadership style is the one that fulfils the needs of the group the most, while at the same time satisfying the needs of the organisation.

Management and leadership

Test your understanding 7

Management development

Six supervisors from accountancy departments are on a management development course. One of them, A, has reported his proposals about a case, which they have been studying. The other five have rated A by placing crosses on Blake and Mouton's managerial grid. The results are as shown.

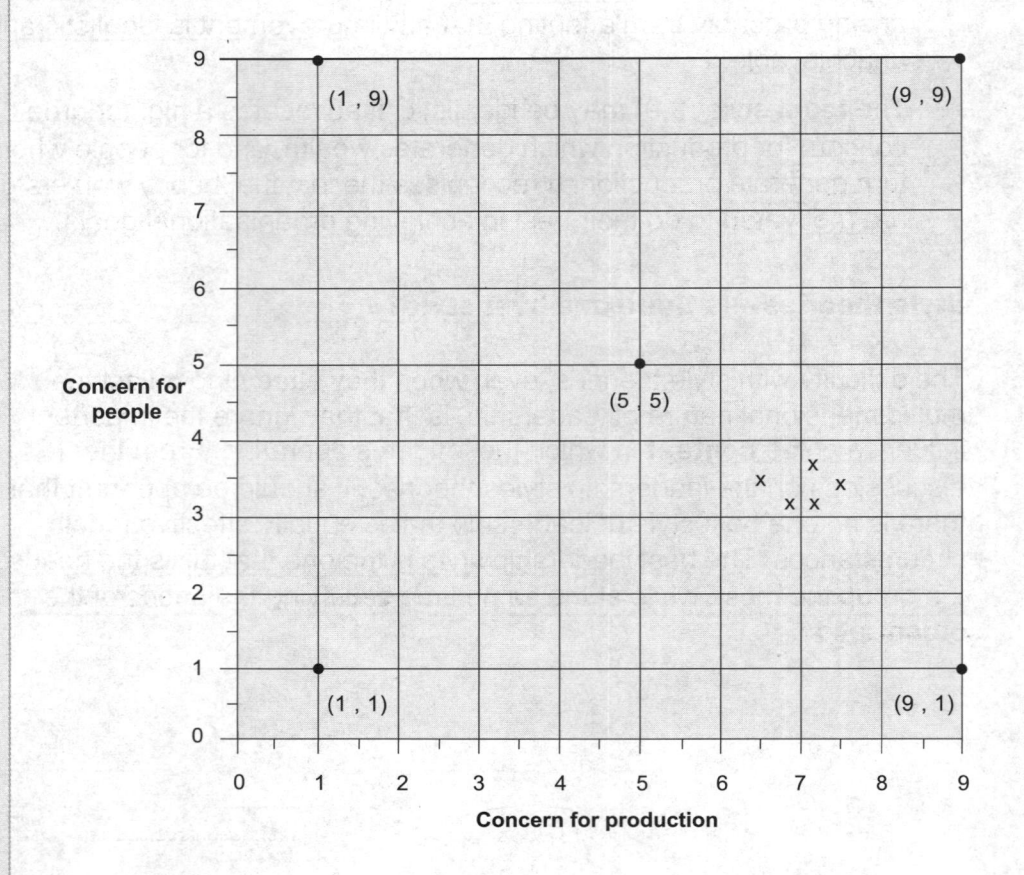

[Blake and Mouton's managerial grid: Concern for people (y-axis, 0–9) vs Concern for production (x-axis, 0–9). Reference points shown at (1,9), (9,9), (5,5), (1,1), (9,1). Five crosses clustered around (6.5, 3.5), (7, 4), (7, 3), (7.5, 3), (7.5, 3.5).]

Required:

(a) Explain what the consultant in charge of the exercise should tell the group about the significance of the result.

(5 marks)

(b) Suggest how A could improve his management style.

(5 marks)

10 Contingency or situational theories

Contingency theory suggests that here is that there is no one best approach to leadership, either in terms of trait or style. A good leader will change their style to suit the situation. The best leadership style is the one that fulfils the needs of the individual, the group, and the organisation.

A more advanced version of simple trait theories is **situational leadership**. The theory here is that leaders are products of particular situations, e.g. Hitler in Germany of the 1930s, Churchill in England of the early 1940s and Mao in China after 1946. A given set of factors exists in certain situations, e.g. economic depression, weak government, high unemployment and a disenchantment with traditional politics. The theory suggests the emergence of a leader, who recognises the problems and has characteristics or traits that fit the needs of the situation.

Theories dealing with contingency or situational approaches to leadership:

- Adair – action centred leadership
- Fielder – contingency model
- Hersey and Blanchard – situational leadership

Adair – Action-centred leadership

Adair's action-centred leadership takes **Blake and Mouton's** ideas one step further, by suggesting that effective leadership regards not only task and group needs as important, but also those of the individual subordinates making up the group:

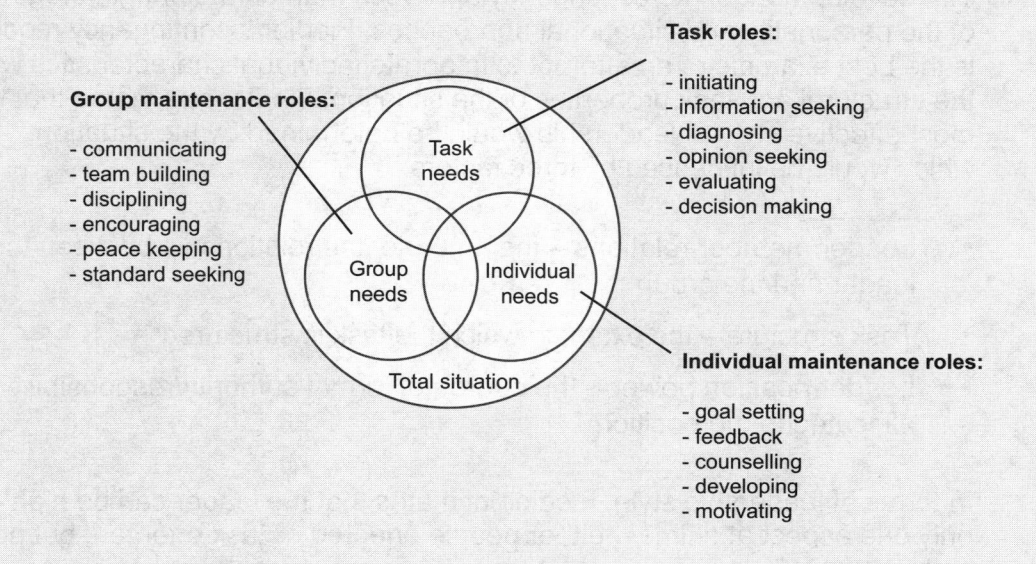

Group maintenance roles:
- communicating
- team building
- disciplining
- encouraging
- peace keeping
- standard seeking

Task roles:
- initiating
- information seeking
- diagnosing
- opinion seeking
- evaluating
- decision making

Individual maintenance roles:
- goal setting
- feedback
- counselling
- developing
- motivating

Task needs / Group needs / Individual needs / Total situation

Adair's model stresses that effective leadership lies in what the leader does to meet the needs of task, group and individuals.

- Task achievement is obviously important for efficiency and effectiveness, but it also can be valuable for motivating people by creating a sense of achievement.
- Teams, almost by definition generate synergy out of the different skills and knowledge of individuals.
- Where individuals feel they have opportunities to satisfy their needs and develop, they are more likely to contribute to creativity and effectiveness.

The key task for the action-centred leader is to understand these processes and bond them together because otherwise there will be a tendency for the organisation to remain static.

However, the three elements can conflict with each other, for example, pressure on time and resources often increases pressure on a group to concentrate on the task, to the possible detriment of the people involved. But if group and individual needs are forgotten, much of the effort spent may be misdirected. In another example, taking time creating a good team spirit without applying effort to the task is likely to mean that the team will lose its focus through lack of achievement.

It is important that the manager balance all three requirements.

Fiedler – Contingency model

The development of the contingency approach marked the bringing together of the personality and situational approaches. Fiedler's contingency model is the best example of an attempt to integrate individual characteristics with the structural and task properties of the situation. Fiedler suggested that the most effective style of leadership would be determined by the situation, which would be influenced by three factors:

- Leader/member relations – the nature of the relationship between the leader and the group
- Task structure – the extent to which the task is structured
- Leader position power – the degree of formal authority/responsibility allocated to the position

In terms of leadership style, Fiedler intimates that the leader can be high on only one aspect at a time – either people oriented or task oriented, but not both.

Fiedler was also talking in terms of effectiveness, that is group effectiveness, but he ignored the question of leader effectiveness which is also an important moderating variable on performance. The personality dimensions are taken in terms of the leader's view of the characteristics of his or her group. He fails to treat the characteristics of the leader as they are viewed by the group. Nor does Fiedler define the situation adequately, either in terms of the situation itself or in terms of the subordinates' definition of the situation. He also overlooks a lot of other moderating variables, including subordinates' expectations of leader behaviour.

Hersey and Blanchard – Situational leadership

Hersey and Blanchard's theory is based on three factors:

- Task behaviour – the extent to which the leader directs what has to be done, and how it should be done.

- Relationship behaviour – the extent to which the leader engages in two way communications.

- Level of maturity – the willingness of the follower to take responsibility for directing their own behaviour.

The leadership style is dependent on the maturity level of the follower. Maturity is not defined as age or psychological stability. The maturity level of the followers is defined as:

M1 – They generally lack the specific skills required for the job in hand and are unable and unwilling to do or to take responsibility for this job or task.

M2 – They are still unable to take on responsibility for the task being done; however, they are willing to work at the task.

M3 – They are experienced and able to do the task but lack the confidence to take on responsibility.

M4 – They are experienced at the task, and comfortable with their own ability to do it well. They able and willing to not only do the task, but to take responsibility for the task.

As the maturity of the follower increases, the leader should reduce the task behaviour and increase the relationship behaviour. They identified four levels of maturity and therefore four leadership styles:

Leadership style	Relationship behaviour	Task behaviour	Maturity
Delegating style	low	low	M4
Participating style	high	low	M3
Selling style	high	high	M2
Telling style	low	high	M1

Of these, no one style is considered optimal for all leaders to use all the time. Effective leaders need to be flexible, and must adapt themselves according to the situation.

11 Transformational leaders

The dynamic nature of the environment facing many organisations today means that there is a constant need to innovate and change. It is suggested that to cope with this type of environment, leaders need to have vision and be creative, innovative and capable of inspiring others. The approach to leadership is re-ferred to as 'transformational leadership' whose distinguishing feature is the ability to bring about significant change. Leaders do this by motivating followers, not just to follow them personally but also to believe in a vision of organisational or political transformation.

The new kind of transformational leader needs a different range of skills from those suggested by traditional management theories.

These new skills according to Boyd encompass:

- anticipatory skills providing foresight in a constantly changing environment;
- visioning skills whereby persuasion and example can be used to induce the group to act in accordance with the leader's purpose or the shared purpose of a larger group;
- value-congruence skills which enable the leader to be in touch with individuals' economic, psychological, physical and other important needs, in order to be able to engage them on the basis of shared understanding;
- empowerment skills involving the willingness to share power and to do so effectively;
- self-understanding so that the leader understands his or her own needs and goals as well as those of the followers.

Boyd believes that there is a need to develop such skills in organisations and to create the conditions in which this type of leadership can emerge.

> In exam questions, you may be asked to "use a model or theory you are familiar with" to explain your analysis of the scenario given. You should therefore be familiar with as many of these models as possible.

Test your understanding 8

As part of your training, you have been sent on a leadership development course. Your manager Peter has worked for BL for over twenty years as the accounts partner. He has a sound knowledge and understanding of the different activities of the firm's business.

Over the years he has demonstrated fairness in how he manages staff and is well liked for his enthusiastic approach. Peter has decided that he needs to dedicate more time and energy managing the business and asked you to take over some of his leadership responsibility especially encouraging and leading the younger members of staff.

He has asked you to think about the different types of leader at BL whilst on the course.

During your time so far you have noted the following leadership styles from three of the partners:

Alan Jones – Alan treats his staff like computerised machines and doesn't consider his employees views, feelings or ambitions.

John Claxton – John barely vacates his office and leaves his employees to get on with the workloads themselves.

Alison Jacobs – Alison gives and takes. She is neither lenient nor too coercive.

Upon your return, Peter has asked for a report on certain matters.

Required:

(a) Provide a definition of leadership.

(4 marks)

Management and leadership

(b) Describe the managerial grid and the five extreme scores identified by Blake and Mouton. Relating what you have learnt to the BL leadership styles.

(10 marks)

(c) Briefly explain Adair's action centred leadership theory.

(6 marks)

(d) Explain whether you feel one style of leadership is effective in all circumstances.

(5 marks)

Test your understanding 9

Before taking up her position as Head of the Finance department of the SOFT Corporation, Joan Timmins had enjoyed a career in the Army where she had attained the rank of major. The military style of command had suited Joan's personality. She is by nature an assertive kind of individual, so giving orders is something that comes naturally to her.

The start of her new post as Head of Finance has not been easy. She has found that her previous style of management has not been well received by her new staff. Her enthusiasm for improving the way things are done in the department is not matched by that of her staff. In fact, if anything, an air of resentment seems to exist in the department. More generally, Joan is finding it difficult to adjust to the whole way of operating in the SOFT Corporation. In her view, so much time seems to be spent in meetings and in consultation generally that she wonders how the organisation manages to compete in the market place as successfully as it does.

Required:

Using any appropriate theory of management style, explain why Joan Timmins is experiencing the difficulties described in her new post, and recommend the kind of management style that might be more appropriate.

(10 marks)

12 Summary diagram

Classical and contemporary theories of management
- Classical
- Human relations school
- Systems theory
- Contingency theory
- Contemporary view

Nature of relationships
- Power
- Authority
- Responsibility
- Delegation

Management and leadership

Leadership
- Transformation leaders
- Leaders and managers

Theories of leadership
- Personality, trait or quality theories
- Style theories
- Contingency and situational theories

Test your understanding answers

Test your understanding 1

A useful framework that can be used to discuss the different sources of power is that proposed by French and Raven and includes referent, reward, coercive, expert and legitimate power.

Referent power is sometimes termed charismatic power and is derived from one's admiration or respect for an individual that can inspire followers. This is gained by the personal qualities of the individual and when followers believe that the leader has desirable characteristics that should be copied, or has inspiration charisma. The scenario mentions that G is known for his fairness and is well liked and respected for his enthusiastic approach. It is therefore likely that he will have referent power which will help him in implementing the changes to working practices.

Reward power is where the leader is able to directly influence the intrinsic or extrinsic rewards available to followers. For example, the ability to provide incentives for individuals to behave in a particular manner and has control over the organisation's resources such as salary, bonuses or promotion. This type of power is usually used in a positive manner, although it can be used in a negative way through the threat of removal of rewards. As senior partner, G will have reward power that he could use to encourage people to adopt the new working practices. As well as financial rewards, G could use intrinsic rewards such as verbal praise and recommendation for promotion.

Coercive power, as the term implies, is the ability to punish or deprive people of things that they value and where the leader uses penalties or sometimes physical punishments to enforce compliance. It is based on fears and the use of the 'stick' or sanction, making life unpleasant for people. The receiver is unlikely to respond to this type of power. Whilst the immediate response might be compliance, it is unlikely to result in long term commitment. It is doubtful that G would want to resort to using this type of power, unless there is strong resistance to the changes, in which case he may have no choice.

Expert power is based on the followers' belief that the leader has certain expertise and knowledge relevant to a particular problem or issue. It will only work if others acknowledge that expertise. G will probably have this power given the time he has worked for the organisation and his sound knowledge and understanding of the firm's different business activities. This experience will be of great help in the drive to introduce new technology and working practices into the organisation and should encourage respect from staff.

Legitimate power, sometimes referred to as position power, is the power which is associated with a particular job. It is when followers accept that the leader has the right to influence them in certain areas or aspects of behaviour. This is often based on the individual's formal position in the organisation. Since G is a senior partner and leader of the project he will be deemed to have legitimate power in managing the changes and hence the right to issue instructions to staff.

The list proposed by French and Raven is not exhaustive and there are other sources of power, such as re-source power, physical power and negative power. Informational power is derived from the ability to control access to information.

Test your understanding 2

Taking the sources of power first, it is useful to make use of a typology such as that by French and Raven, as this helps us to consider the different sources of power in a systematic manner. The authors identify five major sources of power. These are coercive, reward, referent, expert and legitimate power.

Taking each of these sources in turn:

Coercive power is defined as that dependent on fear. In its extreme form, it is the fear that one is likely to feel if threatened by a gun or knife. In the case of organisations, power of this extreme kind is rarely used, but Sheila can be said to have access to coercive power because as the senior manager in the organisation she is in a position to dismiss personnel from their job. Even when this power is not exercised, the potential for its use is still there and subordinates can feel threatened by this potential.

Reward power derives from the capacity of the CEO to reward subordinates for their contribution to the performance of the organisation. These rewards may take many forms from simple praise in recognition for a job well done, through to more material rewards like promotion, salary increases, more interesting work, additional holidays and so on.

Referent power arises out of the admiration which people have for certain individuals. This admiration often includes a desire to be like that individual because he or she has qualities that mark them out from the mass of people. In the organisational context, some managers are able to persuade subordinates to make extraordinary efforts because subordinates wish to please the manager. In the particular case of Sheila, it is difficult to know from the scenario whether or not she possessed the charisma that would persuade subordinates to act to please her. What we do know is that she exhibited qualities in a crises situation that would be unlikely to enhance her referent power in the world of legitimate business.

Expert power is something that Sheila does possess. She demonstrated her marketing and management skills in her previous role as marketing manager. It may be however, that she does not possess the general management skills to perform effectively as CEO. We do not know how competent she was in the role. We do know that X Ltd suffered market setbacks, but these can affect any company irrespective of the skills of the CEO.

Legitimate power represents the power a person receives as a result of his or her position in the formal hierarchy of an organisation. It is the power accorded in the constitution of the organisation to anyone who fills a particular position. So, a policeman is accorded certain powers to arrest people if they break the law, and managers generally may be granted powers to hire and fire personnel, to give instructions, to reward personnel and so on. In the case of CEO, they are given wide-ranging powers such as that of strategy formulation and the power to implement it.

The concept of legitimate power in fact is very similar to the concept of authority to which we now turn.

Power is not, however, the same as authority. Power may be exercised without legitimacy. For example, when any one individual forces another individual to do something which he or she would not otherwise do by a threat of physical violence, then this is not legitimate, unless we are in a war situation. By contrast, the exercise of authority implies the right to influence the actions of others through agreed legitimate means.

In the case under review, it is evident that Sheila, in pressurising Bob to change the figures, was exercising her power of position illegitimately.

> **Test your understanding 3**
>
> The concept of accountability relates to one person having to report to another for actions and results in the former's area of activity.
>
> Authority refers to the scope and amount of discretion given to a person to make decisions. Usually, this is by virtue of that person's position or standing in an organisation. Authority may also be divided into expert and legal authority. As the names imply, expert authority derives from a person's position as an expert on certain matters or doctrines, whereas legal authority is conferred by statute or common law. Thus, a parent will have legal authority over a child under 16 years of age, and an employer will have legal authority over employees as defined by the Health and Safety at Work laws. Authority may also be implied as opposed to being directly stated.
>
> Responsibility relates to the liability a person has when called to account. A person's responsibilities refer to the functions that that person is under a duty to perform on behalf of his/her organisation. Usually, if a person is responsible for a certain area of work, for example management accounts, then he/she is also accountable for its actions. The management accountant would be responsible for management accounts staff and accountable to the finance director, or his/her immediate superior.

Test your understanding 4

(a) **Causes of the situation**

The main reason for the situation in Henry's department is his inability or unwillingness to delegate work.

As a departmental manager, he exercises line authority in respect of his subordinates. Such authority should be used by managers to allocate work, delegate authority, exercise control and direct effort.

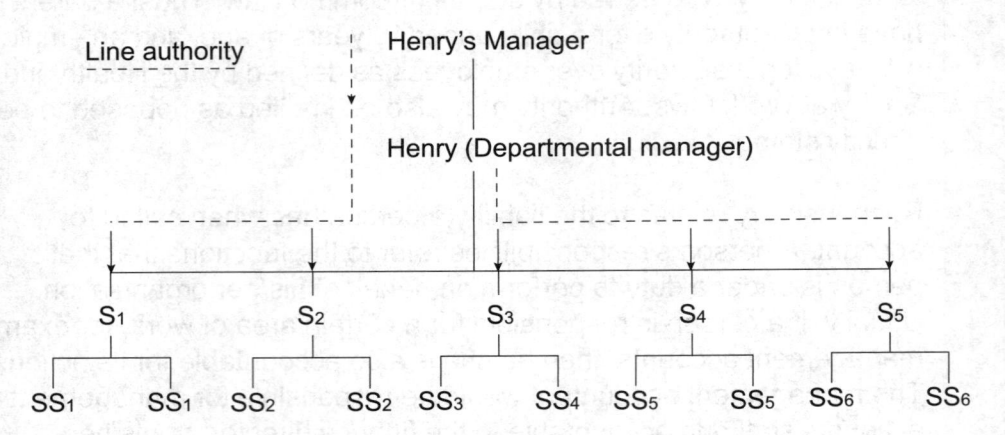

```
Line authority            Henry's Manager
                                |
                                |
                       Henry (Departmental manager)
                                |
    ┌───────────┬───────────┬───┴───────┬───────────┐
    $S_1$       $S_2$       $S_3$       $S_4$       $S_5$
   ┌─┴─┐       ┌─┴─┐       ┌─┴─┐       ┌─┴─┐       ┌─┴─┐
 $SS_1$ $SS_1$ $SS_2$ $SS_2$ $SS_3$ $SS_4$ $SS_5$ $SS_5$ $SS_6$ $SS_6$
```

The organisation chart shows the possible relationship between Henry and his subordinates. He should delegate work to the first level and they in turn should delegate an amount to their subordinates.

There are three levels of management:

- Strategic/Top level management – long-term planning.
- Tactical/Middle level management – implementation of strategic plans.
- Operational/Lower level management – day-to-day activities.

We can place Henry in the tactical or middle management bracket.

He should delegate the day-to-day operational activities to his staff, instead of doing it himself. This leaves his time free for organising and planning the medium-term activities of the department – putting the strategic decisions made by his superiors into place.

Whether he does not delegate because he does not trust his staff to do the work properly or he does not know how to, is a matter only Henry can clarify. As staff are trying to leave, Henry may even feel more pressure to carry most of the work load instead of having to pass it on to inexperienced staff in the future. There may have been changes or reorganisations in the department resulting in a higher workload for Henry, and thus inadequate time for managing his subordinates.

The problems seem to have started recently, therefore, it must be established whether or not Henry is experiencing any external problems, domestic for instance, that are affecting his performance at work.

(b) **Principles of delegation**

Delegation is the passing on to someone else of the freedom and authority to carry out a job for which the delegator is accountable.

Ideally, the process should include a careful and thorough briefing of the subordinate by the senior covering the following points:

(i) the required performance levels
(ii) agreement of the actual tasks assigned
(iii) agreement of the resources allocated
(iv) delegation of authority to do the job
(v) recognition of the responsibility by the senior.

Although there is no single approach to delegation, it should be well planned and ensure that the content is appropriate and understood.

The following principles are essential for delegation to be effective:

- The range of the authority delegated must be clearly understood by both parties and must be within the scope of the delegator's authority.
- It is the manager's responsibility to ensure that the subordinate has sufficient ability and experience to carry out the task. If necessary, training and an initial period of close supervision must be given.

- The manager must have the authority to delegate before he or she does so and must delegate sufficient resources to complete the task.
- The subordinate should have only one immediate superior, so that there is no confusion concerning his or her (space) accountability and responsibility.

(c) **Advantages of effective delegation**

In any large complex organisation, management must delegate some authority and tasks simply because of the limitation (physical and mental) of the workload on any individual and the need for specialisation of certain tasks.

Benefits

(i) Workloads of managers and supervisors are relieved with the subsequent reduction in stress.

(ii) Managers are left free to carry out non-routine tasks while passing on more routine activities to subordinates.

(iii) Specialists are able to develop their specialisms.

(iv) Training of subordinates is assisted by the delegation of tasks. The right opportunity to do a job is a very effective method of training.

(v) Management succession is aided, as subordinates are able to gain experience and become accustomed to working at the higher level of management.

(vi) Decisions can be made sooner by managers with delegated authority on the spot that can respond to changing events.

(vii) The subordinate's work experience is enriched with subsequent increase in job satisfaction leading on to better work.

(viii) The opportunity exists to evaluate the performance of a subordinate before being permanently promoted.

Disadvantages

(i) Decisions taken at a lower level may not be to overall advantage of the organisation.

(ii) The organisation must be able to meet the aspirations through eventual promotion of subordinates who accept delegated duties.

(iii) There may be an increase in costs due to additional payments to the extra member of staff with delegated authority.

(d) **Reasons for statement**

Despite the benefits noted above, in many cases, managers are reluctant to delegate. This may be for a variety of reasons, ranging from lack of confidence in the abilities of subordinates to fear of releasing so many duties to a subordinate that eventually the manager becomes redundant.

There may well also be an organisational culture that does not encourage effective delegation (e.g. delegation is seen as avoiding one's own duty). Additionally, the control and communication systems within the organisation might be so poor that the manager feels that he has to do everything if he is to know what is going on and to retain control. In such circumstances, it is likely that the manager will feel inhibited in developing delegation.

Even in more supportive conditions, however, there may be examples of delegation not carried out effectively:

- unwillingness to delegate.
- delegation only of mundane tasks without satisfaction to the subordinate.
- no proper planning of how delegation is to be carried out.
- delegation of tasks to unsuitable staff either through custom and practice to the next in line no matter what their abilities, or to a favoured member of staff.
- no clear guidance to the subordinate on how tasks are to be performed. In some cases, a manager abdicates responsibility and simply leaves everything to the junior.
- pseudo-delegation where the manager appears to give authority to the subordinate but then makes the final decisions alone.

(e) Power and authority

Authority is the right to use power. It refers to the relationship between people in an enterprise and the discretion that a person has to make decisions. Power can be defined as the ability to coerce individuals or groups into behaving in a predetermined manner.

In an organisation the main sources of power are:

(1) legitimate power the power derived from being in a position of authority;

(2) expert power the power derived from having expert knowledge;

(3) reward power the power derived from having the ability to reward or punish certain behaviour;

(4) referent power the power derived from the ability to charm and gain admiration from individuals and groups;

(5) identity power the power derived from individuals and groups sharing the same values as the power-holder.

One of the major sources of power that Henry possesses is legitimate power. He has been placed in charge of a department and this position will carry with it the authority and responsibility to command subordinates.

Another definition of power is 'the ability to get things done', and the amount of power an individual possesses depends on factors such as:

- the personal charisma and established influence within his or her work groups;
- the level of credibility which is normally based on his or her skills, experience and track record for results;
- the specialist function that he or she is capable of providing and the supply and demand for this specialist advice; and
- the vested power from the position in the organisation structure.

Test your understanding 5

(a) All organisations of whatever size need to understand and address the issues of the relationship between various levels of management, especially the nature, source and limitations of authority, responsibility and delegation. Understanding responsibility, delegation and authority is fundamental to the practice of management. Professional accountants should be able to show an understanding of the problems and challenges associated with these concepts of management. Students are not expected to remember definitions verbatim, but they are expected to show an understanding of the inherent logic contained in these concepts, and to demonstrate a clear distinction between the two main concepts of authority and responsibility.

There are many explanations of what managers do. The most widely understood approach is that of Henri Fayol, who said that managers perform five duties, to forecast and plan, to organise, to command, co-ordinate and control. Managers are ultimately responsible for the efficient use of the organisation's resources and are accountable to the organisation's owners.

At Flavours Fine Foods, the owners (the Jones brothers) must recognise this reality and allow the managers to manage.

It used to be said that a manager did his or her job by getting others to do theirs. In many ways this sums up the role of the supervisor. However, management must ensure that supervisors understand organisational objectives and must make clear the powers and limits of the supervisors' authority. Supervision is an important and integral part of the task and process of management.

(b) The role of the supervisor is critical because of direct contact with and responsibility directly for the work of others. The supervisor is unique; he or she is the interface between management and the workforce and is the direct link between the two, being in direct physical contact with non-managers on a frequent basis. Supervisors are in the front line of management and see that others fulfil their duties, resolve problems first hand and often quickly, direct the work of others and enforce discipline. In addition, they often must have direct knowledge of health, safety and employment legislation and have authority for negotiation and industrial relations within the department.

(i) Without delegation, formal organisations could not exist. Without allocation of authority, responsibility and delegation, a formal organisation cannot be effective. They are critical aspects. Managers must delegate because of the size and complexity of the organisation (certainly an issue for Flavours Fine Foods). Delegation can help overcome the physical and mental limitations of staff, managers and supervisors and it allows management to attend to other matters since routine tasks and decision making can be passed down. However, superiors must call subordinates to account and coordinate their activities.

(ii) Effective delegation can be achieved by assigning agreed tasks to the subordinate, ensuring that resources are allocated and by specifying expected performance levels and ensuring that they are understood. In addition, it is necessary to ensure that the subordinate has the ability and experience to undertake the tasks by maintaining frequent contact and ensuring that the subordinate has authority to do the job. Sufficient authority must be delegated to fulfil the task. This authority in turn may be specific or general; the scenario suggests that the authority of the managers and supervisors is specific. The subordinate should not refer decisions upwards, and the superior should not expect this. In addition there should be no doubts over boundaries; they must be clearly defined as to who holds what authority and who accounts to whom. Therefore there must be clarity as to departmental functions and individual authority, which is at the root of the problem at Flavours Fine Foods.

(iii) Problems with delegation are threefold. Firstly, reluctance from managers who are afraid of losing control, who fear that subordinates may carry out the work badly and who are resentful of subordinate development. Secondly, there is the problem of lack of confidence, lack of self confidence in the manager and often a lack of confidence in the subordinates. Thirdly, there are problems of trust; that is the amount of trust the superior has in the subordinate and the trust that the subordinate feels the superior has in him or her.

(iv) Problems with delegation can be overcome by careful selection and training, an open communication system, the establishment of an appropriate control system and a system that rewards effective delegation.

Test your understanding 6

F W Taylor established what came to be known as the 'scientific' school of management thought.

Scientific management provided a major input into a set of theories jointly known as the 'classical' approach to management. These emphasise formal rules, the specialisation of functions, clear division of responsibilities and the application of common principles to all management duties.

Despite their differing approaches and backgrounds, a common characteristic to their work was a 'formal' approach to organisation and management. The following common basic principles are viewed as the main contributions to the development of organisational and managerial theory and practice.

Formal organisation – Henri Fayol, Taylor and Max Weber all envisaged specialisation of labour, formal organisation, unity of command and a hierarchical order. This perhaps had the disadvantage that, while the skills were developed to maximise efficiency, there was ultimately a risk of over-manning and job demarcation.

Functions of management – This developed from a formal organisation. Fayol developed the idea of formal functions in an organisation; identifying technical, commercial, finance, accounting and security. Within these functions, he defined what a manager had to do (i.e., plan, organise, direct, co-ordinate and control).

Operational efficiency – Fayol created the organisational foundation. It was left to others, such as Taylor to emphasise control and performance. Taylor was a pioneer in time study and operational efficiency.

Motivation and supervision – The traditional view of the scientific approach is that it is coercive, exploitative and even demeaning. Such an interpretation ignores what the scientific managers were endeavouring to do. Taylor was committed to raising the standard of the employee's efforts, making him productive, highly motivated and proud of his job. To that end, he was prepared to reward him well, creating the opportunity to generate corporate wealth as well as improve his own living standards. Many entrepreneurs who have since attempted to emulate Taylor have not taken his ideas and precepts to their ultimate conclusion. This has resulted in the establishing of coercive and exploitative working conditions in the name of 'Taylorism'.

Training – Taylor originally advocated the concept of the 'right man for the job', and was prepared in particular to train employees to do the job to the standard required where necessary.

Management and leadership

Test your understanding 7

(a) The consultant could tell the group the following:

- That supervisor A is perceived to have a high 'concern for production'. In this context that could refer to the case they have been studying. It could also refer to insights others have gained into how A does their job. Either way this high concern for the job would be seen as a positive attribute of A.

- However, A is perceived to have a low 'concern for people'. Again this could refer to how the other supervisors felt they were treated on the course or how they feel A supervises his staff at work.

- This would be viewed as a potential problem with A being too task-orientated.

- These findings are reinforced by the fact that that everybody saw supervisor A in a similar light.

(b) A could improve his management style by any of the following:

- Attending a further training course.
- Delegating more work to subordinates.
- Within this, using more trust rather than explicit control.
- Involving staff in more discussions.
- Asking staff for more feedback concerning his management approach.
- Treating staff more as adults.
- Using more group discussions to make decisions.
- Adopting an 'open door' policy.
- Adopting more 'management by walkabout'.
- Give staff more feedback on the quality of work done.

Test your understanding 8

(a) **Definition of leadership**

Leadership is a conscious activity and in business is about setting goals and inspiring people to give a commitment to achieve the organisation's goals. It is a relationship through which one person influences the behaviour or actions of others.

Leadership is seen as 'a social process in which one individual influences the behaviour of others without the use or threat of violence'.

Leadership can be viewed from three standpoints:

- an attribute of a position e.g. your role at BL as Finance Director
- a characteristic of a person e.g. you are a natural leader, well liked by all
- a category of behaviour e.g. your enthusiastic approach to everything.

From the position of leadership at work, the latter standpoint is most applicable and can be considered as something one person does to influence the behaviour of others. It is all about moving people and things on, getting them from 'a' to 'b' by improving performance, changing the way things are done, making a new product or creating a new or better service.

There are different levels of leadership from the top down to small team leaders, but they will still share the same function — to get people to do the job. How they do that will depend on their attitudes, their perceptions of what motivates people and the prevailing culture of the organisation. If the designated leader cannot communicate the why, how and when of moving from 'a' to 'b' then he or she will neither behave like a leader, nor succeed in the task.

(b) **Blake and Mouton's Managerial Grid**

Blake and Mouton, observed two basic ingredients of managerial behaviour, namely: concern for production and concern for people. Concern for production includes the manager's attitude towards procedures, processes, work efficiency, and volume of output. Concern for people includes personal commitment, sustaining the esteem and trust of the group, maintaining interpersonal relationships and ensuring good working conditions.

Management and leadership

They recognised that it was possible for concern for production to be independent of concern for people. It was therefore possible for a leader to be strong on one and weak on the other, strong on both, weak on both or any variation in between. They devised a series of questions, the answers to which enabled them to plot these two basic leadership dimensions as the axes on the following grid structure:

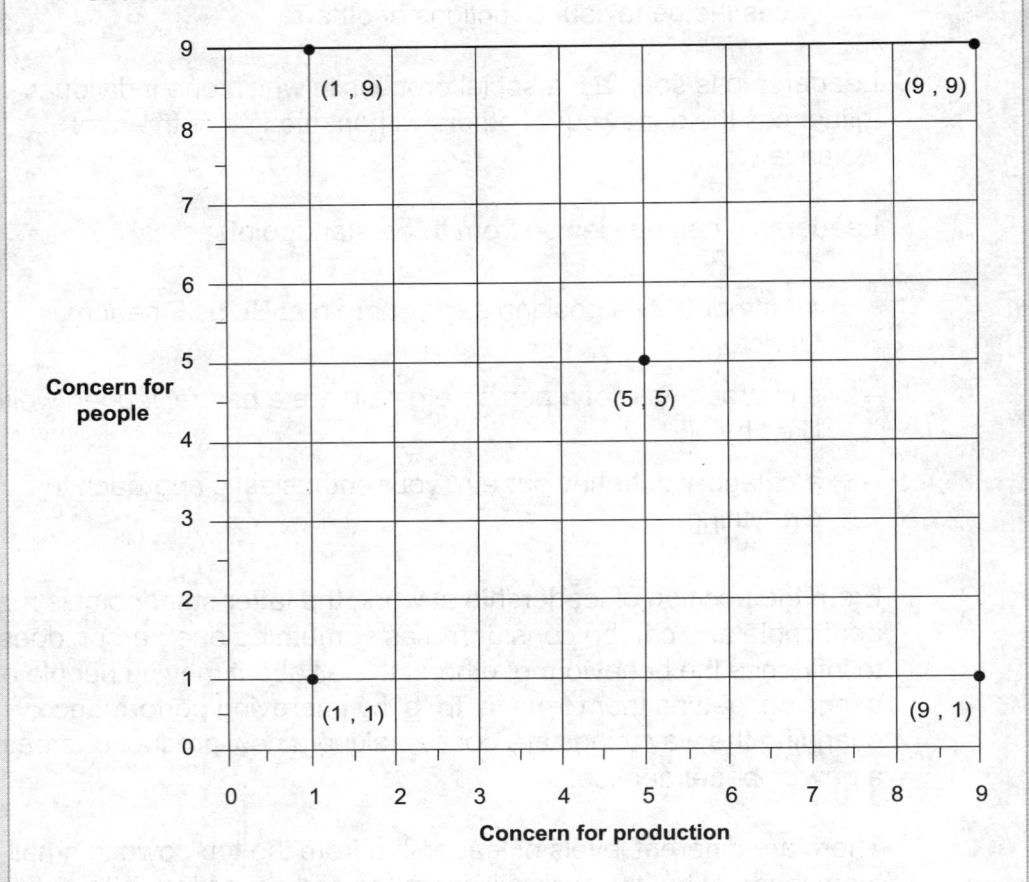

Concern for people (y-axis, 0–9) vs **Concern for production** (x-axis, 0–9)

Plotted points: (1, 9), (9, 9), (5, 5), (1, 1), (9, 1)

A high concern for production will score 9 and a high concern for people will also score 9, the two co-ordinates on the grid indicating the proportion of each concern present. Blake and Mouton picked out these two elements of a manager's job as characterising the leadership role. The implication is that managers should aim for the 9.9 combination; a goal-centred team approach that seeks to gain optimum results through participation, involvement, commitment and conflict solving where everyone can contribute. According to Blake and Mouton, individuals can adapt their style to become more effective personally and, working in a team, can build the synergy needed to raise output above the level that could be achieved individually.

Although there are 81 points of reference in the managerial grid, only five positions are precisely identified and described.

The task-orientated style (9,1) is almost totally concerned with production and has a low concern for people. Subordinates are treated as a commodity, like machines. Their needs are virtually ignored and conditions of work are arranged so that people cannot interfere to any significant extent. This is very similar to Alan Jones who treats his staff like computerised machines and fails to consider their views.

The country club style (1,9) emphasises people and pays little attention to achieving results. The manager is attentive to staff needs and has developed satisfying relationships. People are encouraged and supported, and any inadequacies are overlooked, on the basis that people are doing their best and coercion may not improve things substantially.

The impoverished style (1,1) is almost impossible to imagine, with a lazy manager showing little concern for production and low concern for staff or work targets. This type of manager only makes the minimum effort in either area and will make the smallest possible effort required to get the job done. John Claxton who very rarely leaves his office and makes no effort with his team is an example of this style of leader.

The middle road (5,5) is a happy medium. This viewpoint pushes for productivity and considers people, but does not go 'over the top' either way. It is a style of 'give and take', neither too lenient nor too coercive, arising probably from a feeling that any improvement is idealistic and unachievable. This manager is able to balance the task in hand and motivate the people to achieve these tasks. Alison Jacobs is a good example of this type of leader. She gives and takes and likes to be neither lenient nor coercive to her staff.

The team style (9,9) may be idealistic as it advocates a high degree of concern for production and for people. This manager integrates the two areas to foster working together and high production to produce true team leadership. Peter is the only manager that matches this description. He is the one to follow.

(c) **John Adair (1983)**

Adair put forward a model of action centred leadership, which is based on the premise that effective leadership requires a bringing together of task, team and individual needs. Adair's action-centred leadership takes Blake and Mouton's ideas one step further, by suggesting that effective leadership regards not only task and group needs as important, but also those of the individual subordinates making up the group.

Group maintenance roles:

- communicating
- team building
- disciplining
- encouraging
- peace keeping
- standard seeking

Task roles:

- initiating
- information seeking
- diagnosing
- opinion seeking
- evaluating
- decision making

(Diagram: three overlapping circles labelled "Task needs", "Group needs", "Individual needs", within a larger circle labelled "Total situation")

Individual maintenance roles:

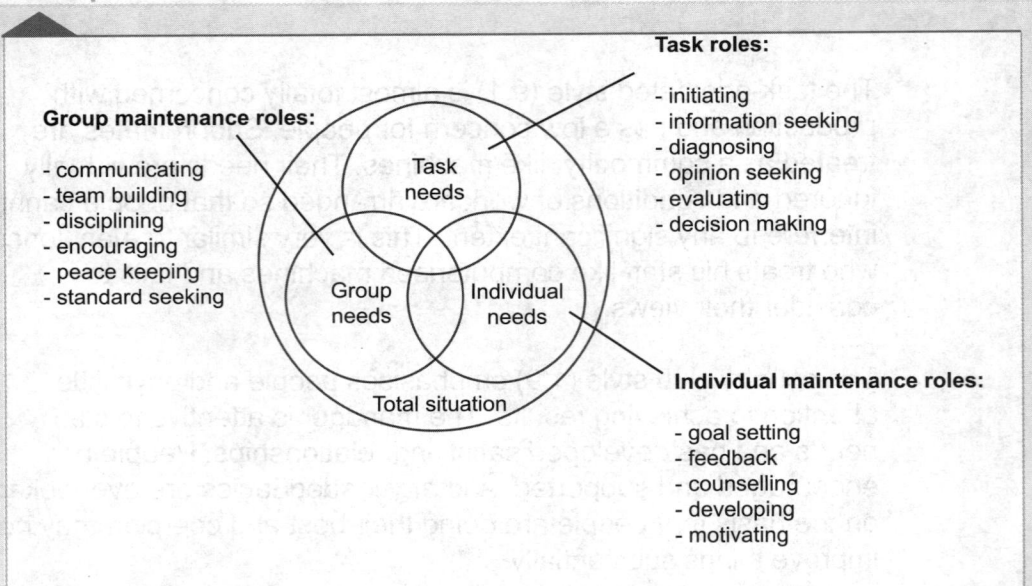

- goal setting
- feedback
- counselling
- developing
- motivating

Adair's model stresses that effective leadership lies in what the leader does to meet the needs of task, group and individuals.

Task achievement is obviously important for efficiency and effectiveness, but it can also be valuable for motivating people by creating a sense of achievement. Effective teams generate synergy out of the different skills and knowledge of individuals. Where individuals feel that they have opportunities to satisfy their needs and develop, they are more likely to contribute to efficiency and effectiveness.

The key is for us to understand these processes and bond them together because otherwise there will be a tendency for the organisation to remain static.

(d) **One best style**

From discussions of leadership it is clear that there is no one style that is equally effective in all circumstances and no one style has proved to be universally superior to the others. The best leadership style is the one that fulfils the needs of the group the most, whilst at the same time satisfying the needs of the organisation.

The variables that define the successful style include:

— The personality of the leader

— The situation of the group – calm or crisis

— The situation within the group – cooperative or militant

— The people within the group – intelligence and interest

Test your understanding 9

Management style is concerned with how a manager deals with subordinates. There are a number of different models but one that is commonly used is that of Lewin.

Using Lewin, Joan could be described as adopting an autocratic style of management. This means that she is telling the subordinates what to do. This style of management probably comes naturally to Joan since it is the style adopted in the armed forces where subordinates are trained to not question their orders. Since Joan has spent a long time in this environment it is the style she is used to.

The workers that Joan is supervising in the Finance department may well be professionally qualified people used to carrying out tasks in their own way without a great deal of supervision.

With these kind of workers an autocratic style is unlikely to be successful, since the workers will resent the reduction in the amount of decision-making they are allowed. Joan will find it more useful to adopt a more democratic management style in which decisions are discussed with the employees rather than being imposed. This should lead to greater worker contentment with resulting gains in productivity and morale.

There will probably be a number of difficulties with persuading Joan to change her management style. The internal factors are that she is used to doing things in 'the army way' (which she did successfully having risen to the rank of major) and she is an assertive person to whom an autocratic style of management is probably most comfortable.

A major external factor that will cause problems is the potential for Joan to 'lose face' by changing to suit her subordinates. She might question the effect this will have on her authority both now and in the future, for example, what happens if they dislike something else, will she be expected to adapt to them again?

Although there are many practical difficulties surrounding this change in style they are not insurmountable. Joan might be encouraged to gradually change her style over time, perhaps by getting key subordinates more involved now and gradually extending this.
An alternative solution would be to involve another senior manager from a different department to help mentor Joan. This would involve working with Joan to discuss practical ways in which her style can evolve.

The above measures are likely to be unsuccessful unless Joan can be persuaded that it is in her interests as well as that of the sub-ordinates and the company to change her style.

chapter 9

Relationships in the working environment

Chapter learning objectives

- Identify the nature and causes of conflict.
- Discuss alternative approaches to the management of conflict.
- Discuss the roles of negotiation and communication in the management process, both within an organisation and with external bodies.
- Discuss the effectiveness of relationships between the finance function and other parts of the organisation and with external stakeholders.
- Identify tools for managing and controlling individuals, teams and networks, and for managing group conflict.
- Explain the process and importance of mentoring to junior colleagues.

Relationships in the working environment

1 Session content diagram

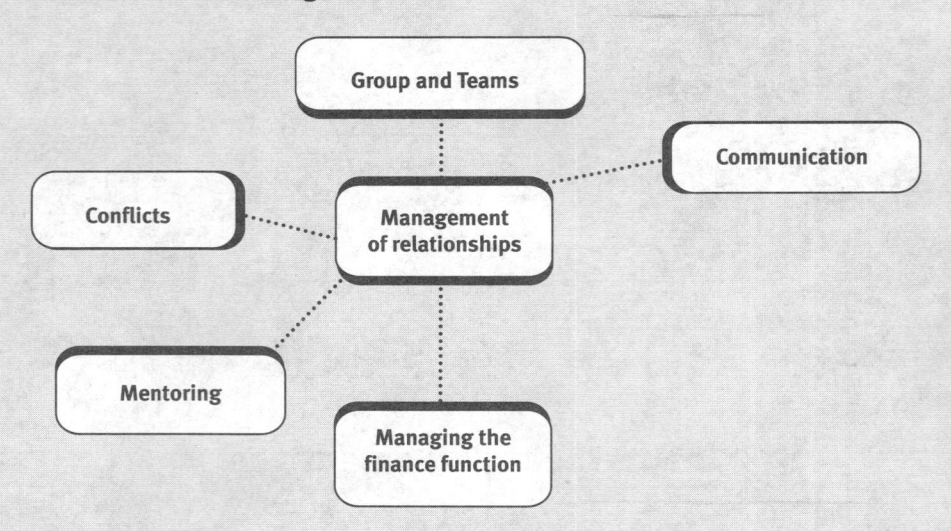

- Group and Teams
- Communication
- Management of relationships
- Conflicts
- Mentoring
- Managing the finance function

2 Groups and teams

Success within organisations is to a large extent dependent on the way in which people, as both individuals and in groups, are managed. People rarely work in isolation at work, since most activities need some coordination through groups of people.

Groups provide security and social satisfaction for their members. They support individual needs and promote communication, formally or informally.

There are many different definitions available to explain what constitutes a group. **Schein** suggests that a group is any number of people who:

- interact with one another;
- are psychologically aware of one another; and
- perceive themselves to be a group.

Whereas teams are a kind of group, all groups are not teams.

Types of groups

- *Informal groups* – individuals join groups to meet their social and security or safety needs. Membership is normally voluntary and informal. Individual members are dependent on each other, influence each other's behaviour and contribute to each other's needs.

- *Formal groups* – organisations use groups to carry out tasks, communicate and solve problems. Membership is normally formal, often determined or constrained by the organisation into departments or divisions.

- *Reference groups* – is a group the individual does not currently belong to but wants to join. (e.g. shop stewards group).
- *Self directed & autonomous groups* – have evolved from autonomous working groups and group technology by Volvo. Based on the theory that the interaction of the task with the individual is best served by groups.

Groups have power structures, leadership structures, role structures, communication structures and sociometric structures. They develop norms, ideologies, characteristic atmospheres, degrees of cohesiveness and morale.

What is a team?

A team is a **formal group**. It has a leader and a distinctive culture and is geared towards a final result.

An effective team can be described as 'any group of people who must significantly relate with each other in order to accomplish shared objectives'.

In order to ensure that the group is truly an effective team, team members must have a reason for working together. They must need each other's skills, talent and experience in order to achieve their mutual goals.

Multiskilled teams bring together individuals who can perform any of the group's tasks. These can be shared out in a flexible way according to availability and inclination.

Multidisciplinary teams bring together individuals with different specialisms so that their skills, knowledge and experience can be pooled or exchanged.

Benefits and problems with groups

Benefits of groups

Within organisations there has been an implicit belief that people working as members of a group or team perform more effectively than if they are organised as individuals. There are a number of benefits from team working:

- **Increased productivity** – working as part of a group can result in a better overall result that could be achieved if each person worked independently. By breaking a task up into its component parts, different members of the group, with different skills, can be working on different aspects of the task at the same time.

- **Synergy** – One person cannot do or be everything, but a team can combine all the main areas of skill and knowledge that are needed for a particular job. Synergy describes the phenomenon in which the combined activity of separate entities has a greater effect than the sum of the activities of each entity working alone – often described as a way of making **2 + 2 = 5**.

- **Improved focus and responsibility** – each member can be given the responsibility for specific tasks, avoiding overloading one person with too much responsibility which may result in a loss of focus.

- **Improved problem solving** – having a group made up of members with different abilities will mean a higher likelihood of having the appropriate knowledge and skills to solve problems.

- **Greater creativity** – the idea that two (or more) heads are better than one. Group discussions can generate and evaluate ideas better that individuals working alone.

- **Increased satisfaction** – working as part of a group can bring social benefits and a sense of belonging to its members. In addition the group will offer support to its members and provide a facility for individual training and development needs.

- **Increased motivation** – members will work hard for the other members of the group. They will feel a collective responsibility and will not want to let the other members down.

- **Improved information flows** – there will be more effective communication through participation in group discussions.

Problems with groups

Unfortunately groups can also have negative as well as positive effects. Subsequent research has identified a number of these negative effects, some of which are discussed below:

- **Conformity.** Individuals can be persuaded by group pressures to agree with decisions which are obviously wrong, and which the person must know to be wrong.

- **The Abilene paradox.** This is a famous case, which demonstrates that the group can end up with an outcome that none of the members wanted. The story was written up as a case by a sociologist whose family all ended up in Abilene, Texas, driving 100 miles through desert heat, though none of them actually wanted to go. They all thought each other wanted to go, and no one wanted to disturb the 'consensus'.

- **Groupthink.** This is a word coined by Irving Janis to describe a common situation which he observed to have occurred within tightly-knit political groups. It occurs within deeply cohesive groups where the members try to minimise conflict and reach consensus without critically testing, analysing, and evaluating ideas.

Some symptoms of groupthink are:

- the raising of protective barriers and the illusion of impregnability.
- a negative attitude towards competing projects.
- an unwavering belief in the group and its decisions.
- a sectarian emphasis on agreement.

It can lead to disastrous results. After the initial 'Bay of Pigs' disaster, when the United States encouraged an abortive 'invasion' of Cuba via the Bay of Pigs, John F Kennedy saw clearly how to try to avoid 'groupthink' and planned his leadership accordingly by insisting on:

- critical evaluation of alternatives;
- independent sub-groups to work on solutions;
- external testing of proposed solutions;
- the leader to avoid domination of the group (which can be unconscious);
- the avoidance of stereotypes of the opposition.

- **'Risky shift' or group polarisation.** This is the tendency for groups to take decisions which are riskier than any that the individual members would take on their own. It now appears that there is also a tendency, under certain circumstances, for groups to take excessively cautious decisions.

Clearly, managers must attempt to minimise these potential problems while harnessing the benefits of groups and teams. This is not easy but recent approaches, such as TQM and the concept of a learning organisation, mean that effective groups are even more critical for organisational effectiveness. Managers need to pay attention to the formation of, and support for, formal groups and also realise that they cannot ignore or suppress informal groups. In relation to informal groups, it is important:

- to let employees know that managers understand and accept them while discouraging dysfunctional behaviour in such groups;
- to try to anticipate how decisions will influence informal groups; and
- to keep formal decisions from unnecessarily threatening informal groups.

Note: many of the ideas of teams in this section will also be applicable to the management of project teams in the project management section of the syllabus.

Group cohesiveness

There are a number of factors which affect the integration of organisational and individual objectives in groups, and hence the cohesiveness of the group. They include:

Membership factors

- *Homogeneity*. Similarity of members is preferred for simple tasks; it leads to easier working but less creative problem-solving. A variety of skills and knowledge is more effective for complex tasks. Homogeneity of status, both internally and externally, leads to a more cohesive group.
- *Alternatives*. If the individual has alternatives, that is he or she can leave the group easily, his or her dependence on the group is reduced. Similarly, if turnover of membership is high, the group will tend to lack cohesion. Management may, of course, deliberately keep changing the membership of awkward groups.
- *Size of group*. The importance of this factor depends on the nature of the particular task. Groups solve problems more quickly and effectively than individuals, but one should also consider cost-effectiveness. As the size of the group goes up, the average productivity of the members goes down; there is less opportunity to participate; individuals' contributions are less discernible; cliques or factions may form; less work is done; and 'social loafing' or 'social noise' may increase.
- *Membership in other groups*. This may detract from cohesion and effectiveness.

Environmental factors

- *Task*: the nature of the task and its organisation must be compatible.
- *Isolation of the group*: external threat and incentives.
- *The climate of management and leadership*: a Theory X type of organisation tends to lead to anti-management groups forming, even if only informally. Leadership style should be appropriate to the task, as we have seen before.

Dynamic factors

- Groups are continually changing, not just in membership but also in understanding each other and of the task.
- Success and failure, there is a tendency to persist in failure.

> **Test your understanding 1**
>
> **Required:**
>
> Explain the advantages and disadvantages of cohesive work groups.
>
> **(10 marks)**

3 Team development

The level of group performance is affected by the manner in which teams come together. According to **Tuckman**, teams typically pass through four stages of development: The stages are:

- **Forming** – at this initial stage, the team members are no more than a collection of individuals who are unsure of their roles and responsibilities until the project manager clearly defines the initial processes and procedures for team activities, including documentation, communication channels and the general project procedures. The project manager must then provide clear direction and structure to the team by communicating the project objectives, constraints, scope, schedules and budget.

- **Storming** – most teams go through this conflict stage. As tasks get underway, team members may try to test the project manager's authority, preconceptions are challenged, and conflict and tension may become evident. The conflict resolution skills and the leadership skills of the project manager are vital at this stage and he or she needs to be more flexible to allow team members to question and test their roles and responsibilities and to get involved in decision-making.

- **Norming** – this stage establishes the norms under which the team will operate and team relationships become settled. Project procedures are refined and the project manager will begin to pass control and decision-making authority to the team members. They will be operating as a cohesive team, with each person recognising and appreciating the roles of the other team members.

- **Performing** – once this final stage has been reached the team is capable of operating to full potential. Progress is made towards the project objectives and the team feels confident and empowered. The project manager will concentrate on the performance of the project, in particular the scope, timescales and budget, and will implement corrective action where necessary.

Not all teams automatically follow these four stages in this sequence. Not all teams pass through all the stages – some get stuck in the middle and remain inefficient and ineffective.

A fifth stage was added to Tuckman's original four:

- **Dorming** – If a team remains for a long time in the performing phase, there is a danger that it will be operating on automatic pilot. 'Groupthink' occurs to the extent that the group may be unaware of changing circumstances. Instead, maintaining the team becomes one of its prime objectives.

In this situation it may be necessary for the group to 'dorm', i.e. to be adjourned or suspended.

4 Team performance

In a group, there is a high level of mutual interaction and awareness which are responsible for powerful forces, which cause the individual to behave, sometimes, rather differently from the way they would behave on their own. It is important to the organisation that these forces work for the organisation and not against it.

There are a number of models/theories which suggest different factors affecting group dynamics and team performance:

- **Belbin** – team roles
- **Role Theory**
- **Steiner** – group dynamics
- **Vaill** – high performance teams
- **DEC** – high performance teams

Belbin – team roles

Belbin suggests that the success of a group can depend significantly upon the balance of individual skills and personality types within the group. A well-balanced group should contain the following eight main character types:

- The **leader** – co-ordinating (not imposing) and operating through others. Tends to be a stable, dominant extrovert.
- The **shaper** – committed to the task, may be aggressive and challenging, will also always promote activity. Tends to be an anxious, dominant extrovert.
- The **plant** – thoughtful and thought-provoking. Tends to be a dominant introvert with a very high IQ.
- The **monitor-evaluator** – analytically criticises others' ideas, brings group down to earth. Tends to be a stable, introverted type of individual with a high IQ.

- The **resource-investigator** – not a new ideas person, but tends to pick up others' ideas and adds to them; is usually a social type of person who often acts as a bridge to the outside world. Tends to be a dominant, stable extrovert.

- The **company worker** – turns general ideas into specifics; practical and efficient, tends to be an administrator handling the scheduling aspects. Tends to be a stable, controlled individual.

- The **team worker** – concerned with the relationships within the group, is supportive and tends to defuse potential conflict situations. Tends to be a stable extrovert who is low in dominance.

- The **finisher** – unpopular, but a necessary individual; the progress chaser who ensures that timetables are met. Tends to be an anxious introvert.

Another role was later added to Belbin's original work:

- The **expert** or **specialist** – a technical person, if needed, to solve technically-based problems.

The description of Belbin's basic eight roles does not mean that a team cannot be effective with fewer than eight members. Members can adopt two or more roles if necessary. However, the absence of one of these functions can mean a reduction in effectiveness of the team.

> **Role theory**
>
> Role theory is concerned with the roles that individuals adopt. Developing a group means identifying distinct roles for each of its members. Any individual can have several roles, varying between different groups and activities. The role adopted will affect the individual's attitude towards other people.
>
> There are several terms associated with role theory.
>
> - **Role ambiguity** arises when individuals are unsure what role they are to play, or others are unclear of that person's role and so hold back co-operation. For example this can arise when a new member joins an established group.
>
> - **Role conflict** arises when individuals find a clash between differing roles that they have adopted. A company finance officer who uncovers fraud by senior management may feel a conflict between the roles of professional confidentiality and honest citizenship.
>
> - **Role incompatibility** occurs when individuals experience expectations from outside groups about their role that are different from their own role expectations.

Relationships in the working environment

- **Role signs** are visible indications of the role. Style of dress and uniform are clear examples of role signs. These may be voluntary (a male accountant wearing a grey or blue suit and a tie) or mandatory (in military, police and hospital occupations).

- **Role set** describes the people who support a lead person in a major role, e.g. the clerk and junior barristers would form part of a senior barrister's role set.

- **Role behaviour** where certain types of behaviour can be associated with a role in an office or works. For instance, the 'crown prince' behaving as if they are heir apparent to a senior position.

Test your understanding 2

Neville is in charge of a group of twelve people involved in complex work. This work is of an ongoing nature. The group has been working together amicably and successfully for a considerable time. Its members value Neville's leadership and the back-up given him by Olivia. She often elaborates on Neville's instructions and deals on his behalf with group members' queries, especially when he is absent on the group's business.

Much of the success of the group has been due to Peter, who is very creative at problem solving, and Rosalinde who has an encyclopaedic knowledge of sources of supply and information. Quentin is an expert on charting and records, and Sheila is invaluable at sorting out disagreements and keeping everyone cheerful. The remaining members of the group also have roles which are acceptable to themselves and to the others.

Recently Olivia resigned for family reasons. Because the workload has been increasing, Neville recruited four new people to the group. Neville now finds that various members of the group complain to him about what they are expected to do, and about other people's failings. Peter and Rosalinde have been unusually helpful to Neville but have had several serious arguments between themselves and with others.

Required:

(a) Analyse the situation before and after the changes.

(7 marks)

(b) Recommend how Neville should ensure that the group reverts to its former cohesiveness.

(8 marks)

Relate your answers to the theories of Belbin and Tuckman.

Steiner – How group dynamics can affect performance

Steiner identified four basic models of group functioning.

- **Additive Model** – every member is able to make a contribution but there is no dependency on other members. The model suggests that the performance of the group will equate to the average skill or ability of its members. In practice performance falls short of the average and the loss of efficiency increases with the size of the group.
- **Conjunctive Model** – high degree of dependency required (assembly line). The model suggests that performance will now be affected by the weakest member. The smaller and more homogeneous the team, the more efficient the team performance.
- **Disjunctive Model** – requirement for the output of the group to be close to that of the most competent member. This model is best applied to things like problem-solving. All the necessary skills required should be available within the group (Belbin) but the group should be kept small. Groups should be heterogeneous to provide these skills and to reduce any tendency towards unproductive group norms. A well-established or homogeneous group may tend to work towards agreement rather than towards an optimum solution.
- **Complementary Model** – used where the task can be divided into separate parts and different skills are needed for each part.

Variations and combinations of the above may be appropriate to meet different circumstances and different structures may be appropriate at different stages. A large committee of many diverse skills may be appropriate to solving a problem (disjunctive), but a small homogeneous subgroup more appropriate for actioning the solution.

This theory considers the size of a group in relation to the number of tasks it needs to carry out, rather than the absolute size of the group. Some degree of 'under-manning' is found to be desirable and beneficial, both for the individuals and for the organisation.

Vaill: high-performance teams

Vaill said that high-performing systems may be defined as human systems that are doing dramatically better than other systems. He claimed that they have a number of common characteristics:

- Clarification of broad purposes and near-term objectives.

- Commitment to purposes.
- Teamwork focused on the task at hand.
- Strong and clear leadership.
- Generation of inventions and new methods.

> **Case study of high performance teams – DEC**
>
> Digital Equipment Corporation (DEC), a computer manufacturer in the 1980s, developed high-performance work systems around empowered teams. This approach was found to improve productivity, reduce the time to introduce new products and improve problem solving and decision making.
>
> Their teams had the following features:
>
> - Autonomous teams – six to twelve members, self managing and self organising.
> - Full "front to back" responsibility – team responsible for a whole section of production.
> - Production targets negotiated between teams and managers.
> - Multi skilled teams – members expected to share skills, no job titles within teams.
> - Members paid according to skill level.
> - Members of teams appraised each other, and involved in recruitment of new team members.
> - Factory layout designed to facilitate communication.
>
> This approach to work design improved productivity, reduced the time required to introduce new products, and led to more effective problem-solving and decision-making. Shop-floor personnel developed a range of analytic, problem-solving, interpersonal, process design and group management skills through this approach, leading in many instances to significant career opportunities and development.

5 Conflict

Conflict is a disagreement, and is when one party is perceived as preventing or interfering with the goals or actions of another. Conflict can occur in a variety of forms and at different levels, for example organisational, group or individual level, arising because of differences between the objectives of different groups within organisations.

Symptoms of conflict

Certain behaviours and attitudes can manifest themselves when conflict exists. Sometimes these behaviours are overt, as when it emerges in the form of a strike, or individuals refusing to communicate with each other at all. However, the management of conflict is likely to be easier and more effective if these symptoms of conflict can be recognised and dealt with at an earlier stage. Such symptoms would probably include some of the following:

- Problems, even trivial ones, being passed up the hierarchy because no one wants to take responsibility for them.
- Hostility and jealousy between groups.
- Poor communications up and down the hierarchy, and between departments.
- Widespread frustration and dissatisfaction because it is difficult to get even simple things done efficiently.
- Problems constantly being polarised around people, usually in different groups, and personalities rather than issues.

Causes of conflict

Mainwaring, in *Management and Strategy* (1999) points out that the difference between causes, characteristics and symptoms is often blurred, but generally the causes include:

- *History*. Conflicts have a tendency for being self-perpetuating.
- *Differences*. Mainly of interests, objectives, priorities and ideologies.
- *Limited resources*. Where there are limited resources, there may be a scramble for what is available.
- *Win/lose situations*. Success for one group often involves failure for others.
- *Interdependencies*. Where relationships, responsibilities or boundaries are not clearly defined, and/or where they are perceived to be unfair.
- *Misunderstandings*. These include communication failures and are common where there already exists some sort of conflict or threat.
- *Conviction beliefs*. If one group is convinced of their essential rightness or goodness, then there may be tendencies to 'enlighten' others, causing resistance.
- *Stress and failure*. If an individual, a group, or an organisation feels unable to cope with pressures and problems, then this is likely to generate fault finding, reality denial and seemingly irrational acts.
- *Change*. Individual, group, organisational and societal change creates new relationships, objectives, perceptions, problems and possibilities.

Types and sources of conflict

Horizontal conflict

The first type of conflict is horizontal. Horizontal conflict occurs between groups and departments at the same level in the hierarchy. The potential for horizontal conflict exists in any situation in which separate departments are created, members have an opportunity to compare themselves with other groups, and the goals and values of respective groups appear mutually exclusive. The main sources of horizontal conflict are:

- *Environment* – each department is geared to fit its external dynamic environment. As the uncertainty and complexity of the environment increase, greater differences in skills, attitudes, power, and operative goals develop among departments. Each department becomes tailored to 'fit' its environmental domain and, thus, is differentiated from other organisational groups. Moreover, increased competition, both domestically and internationally, have led to demands for lower prices, improved quality, and better service. These demands exert more intense goal pressures within an organisation and, hence, greater conflict among departments.

- *Size* – as organisations increase in size, subdivision into a larger number of departments takes place. Members of departments begin to think of themselves as separate, and they erect walls between themselves and other departments. Employees feel isolated from other people in the organisation. The lengthening hierarchy also heightens power and resource differences among departments.

- *Technology* – interdependency creates opportunity for conflict as technology determines task allocation. Groups that have interdependent tasks interact more often and must share resources. Interdependence creates frequent situations that lead to conflict.

- *Goals* – the accomplishment of operative goals by one department may block goal accomplishment by other departments and hence cause conflict, for example operative goals pursued by marketing, finance, legal and production departments often seem mutually exclusive

- *Structure* – divisionalisation and departmentalisation create competition. Pay incentives may be based on competition among divisions. Organisation structure defines departmental groupings and, hence, employee loyalty to the defined groups.

- *Operative goal incompatibility* – each department's operative goals interfere with each other. Goal incompatibility is probably the greatest cause of intergroup conflict in organisations. A typical example of goal conflict may arise between marketing and manufacturing departments. Marketing strives to increase the breadth of the product line to meet customer tastes for variety. A broad product line means short production runs, so manufacturing has to bear higher costs.

- *Task interdependence* – dependence on each other for materials, resources and information. Generally, as interdependence increases, the potential for conflict increases.

- *Uncertainty* – when departments do not know where they stand because activities are unpredictable. When factors in the environment are rapidly changing, or when problems arise that are poorly understood, departments may have to renegotiate their respective tasks. Managers have to sort out how new problems should be handled. The boundaries of a department's territory or jurisdiction become indistinct. Members may reach out to take on more responsibility, only to find that other groups feel invaded.

- *Reward system* – the reward system governs the degree to which subgroups cooperate or conflict with one another. When departmental managers are rewarded for achieving overall organisation goals rather than departmental goals, cooperation among departments is greater. If departments are rewarded only for departmental performance, managers are motivated to excel at the expense of the rest of the organisation.

- *Differentiation* – functional specialisation causes differences in cognitive and emotional orientations. Functional specialisation requires people with specific education, skills, attitudes, and time horizons. The underlying values and traits of personnel differ across departments, and these differences lead to horizontal conflicts.

Vertical conflict

A second type of conflict is vertical. Vertical conflict occurs among individuals and groups at different levels in the hierarchy. Individual employees may have conflicts with their bosses. Managers of international divisions often experience conflict with senior executives located at domestic headquarters. Many of the sources of horizontal conflict above may apply here as well. The other primary sources of vertical conflict are often about power and powerlessness and differences in status and power. Some example are:

- *Power and status* – at the bottom of the hierarchy, workers often feel alienated.

- *Ideology* – different values, e.g. free enterprise *versus* the right to industrial action.

- *Psychological distance* – workers feel isolated from the organisation.

- *Scarce resources* – financial resources affecting remuneration and working conditions, and costs.

6 Destructive and constructive conflict

Conflict can be viewed as an inevitable feature of organisational life, and can result in both positive and negative outcomes. Whilst conflict can have negative consequences leading to dysfunctional behaviours, it can also have positive outcomes. The terms destructive and constructive conflict are used to differentiate between negative or positive outcomes.

Constructive conflict

Constructive conflict is considered useful, positive and beneficial to the organisation as it does not revolve around personality and:

- creates an environment of innovation and change;
- facilitates bringing problems to the surface so that they can be dealt with;
- settles and defines boundaries of authority and responsibility.

Destructive conflict

Destructive conflict tends to be *ad hoc* and personal:

- harmful for the organisation and its involved members;
- causes alienation between groups, within groups and between individuals;
- can be demoralising for those involved.

Daft (1989) noted that several **negative consequences** for organisations that may arise from conflict are as follows:

- diversion of energy – time and effort wasted
- altered judgement – judgement becomes less accurate
- loser effects – the loser may deny or distort the reality and may seek scapegoats
- poor coordination – under intense conflict co-ordination does not happen. Co-operation across groups decreases and groups may actively attempt to jeopardise the goals of other groups.

Management thinking and writing has generally viewed conflict as negative, unhelpful and undesirable. However it is accepted that not all conflict is harmful and a certain degree of conflict is positive, beneficial, desirable and often inevitable.

Some companies have sought to promote team spirit by creating competition between work teams. In some instances this has been successful in reducing absenteeism and bad timekeeping but, when extended to include poor productivity, working relationships have tended to deteriorate. It was found that work teams concentrate on rivalry instead of the tasks to be achieved. A group would take greater interest in impeding the progress of the competing group than in achieving a better result.

Unitary and pluralist perspectives on conflict

The beliefs and attitudes of individuals regarding conflict will profoundly affect how they perceive it, react to it and seek to resolve it. **Fox** has distinguished between 'unitary' ('happy family view' where conflict is regarded as exceptional and destructive) and 'pluralist' (where conflict is seen as natural and can be constructive) perspectives on conflict summarised as follows:

Unitary	Pluralist
• The organisation should be like a family or team with high levels of common purpose.	• The organisation is composed of different groups with different interests.
• Conflict is undesirable, unhealthy and ideally should be avoided.	• Conflict can be indicative of diversity, experimentation, flexibility and change.
• Outbreaks of conflict are attributable to management failures, poor communication, personality clashes, and agitators.	• Conflict is built into the very nature of complex organisations, and indeed of society generally.
• The role of management is to remove and resolve conflict.	• The role of management is to manage conflict productively.
• Those who are responsible for conflict are defined as troublemakers.	• The role of management is to manage conflict productively.

Test your understanding 3

L Ltd is a firm which undertakes road reconstruction and maintenance. The work is carried out by teams which operate independently of each other. The team members have worked together for years and are well integrated. Each team includes a salesman who is responsible for getting additional work, ideally in the area where the team is already working. The teams draw their materials and road-surfacing and other machinery from the company pool, and obtain information on potential customers from a central sales office.

Although the firm's performance has been satisfactory, a new operations manager has decided to try to improve productivity by introducing competition between the teams. This will be done by drawing half of the wages of each team member from a single bonus pool for which all the teams compete.

Required:

Explain how such a policy is likely to affect the behaviour of these groups.

(10 marks)

7 Managing conflict

A useful framework for classifying different ways of handling conflict is the **Thomas-Kilmann Conflict Mode Instrument (TKI).** It is based on two conflict-management dimensions. These are the degree of assertiveness in pursuit of one's interests and the level of co-operation in attempting to satisfy others' interests. The strength of each of these in a particular situation can suggest the ways the conflict may be resolved, as shown:

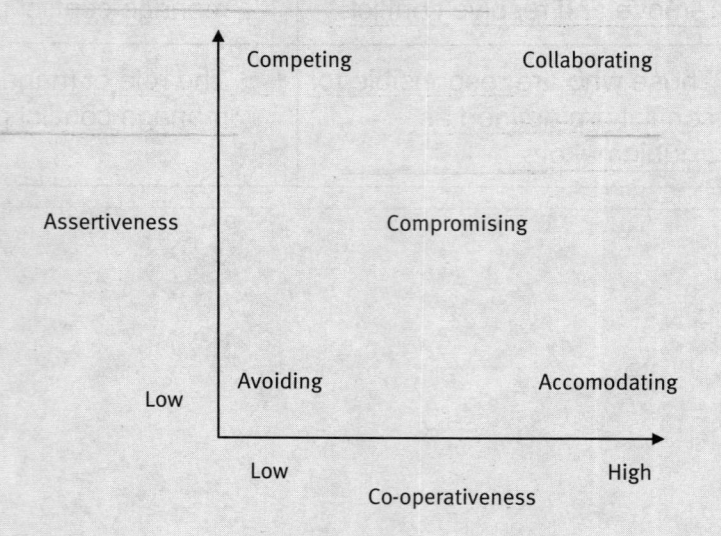

	Low Co-operativeness	High
Assertiveness High	Competing	Collaborating
	Compromising	
Low	Avoiding	Accomodating

This results in five conflict-handling strategies:

- **Competing:** High assertiveness and low co-operativeness – the goal is to 'win'. All or both parties seek to maximise their own interest and goals. They do not co-operate, creating winners and losers as well as causing damage to the organisation and one of the parties.

- **Avoiding:** Low assertiveness and low co-operativeness – the goal is to 'delay'. One or more of the parties seeks to ignore or suppress the conflict.

- **Collaborating:** High assertiveness and high co-operativeness – the goal is to 'find a win-win solution'. A 'win-win' situation is achieved through joint confrontation of the problem and using problem-solving techniques with creative solutions.

- **Accommodating:** Low assertiveness and high co-operativeness – the goal is to 'yield'. One party puts the other party's interests first.

- **Compromising:** Moderate assertiveness and moderate co-operativeness – the goal is to 'find a middle ground'. Negotiation results in each party giving up something and 'meeting half way'. The problem is each party may lose something when there may be a better alternative.

8 Intergroup conflict

Intergroup conflict within organisations can be defined as the behaviour that occurs between organisational groups when participants identify with one group and perceive that other groups may block their groups' goal achievement. It requires three ingredients.

(1) **Group identification.** Employees have to perceive themselves as part of an identifiable group or department.

(2) There has to be an **observable group difference** of some form. The ability to identify oneself as a part of one group and to observe differences in comparison with other groups is necessary for conflict.

(3) **Frustration.** Frustration means that if one group achieves its goal the other will not; it will be blocked. Frustration need not be severe and only needs to be anticipated to set off intergroup conflict. Intergroup conflict will appear when one group tries to advance its position in relation to other groups.

> **Illustration 1 – Rivalry generated by inter-group competition**
>
> The intensity generated by this rivalry can be very severe. In a well-known case, Sherif and Sherif divided boys at a summer school camp into two teams and established clear identities for each with a rivalry between the two. The immediate result was that inter-group competition increased group cohesion. Each group regarded the other as the enemy, and fraternisation and communication between the groups ceased.
>
> Within each group it was found that:
>
> - conformity was demanded, and group requirements outweighed individual needs;
> - group members encouraged a move from informal to formal and from a leadership approach of participation to an autocratic one;
> - the group became better organised.
>
> At the end of the exercise a winning team and losing team resulted. The friction existing between the teams resisted concentrated efforts to remove it. Attempts to run joint teams and act against an outside team were of limited success. It was noted that the winning team retained its spirit and cohesion but became complacent and sought to satisfy the needs of individuals. On the other hand, the losing team sought to allocate blame both inside and outside the group. Its cohesion fell and it ignored the needs of individual members.
>
> In summary, some degree of competition may prove beneficial but the long-term result of excessive competition is likely to be a reduction in efficiency.

Managing intergroup conflict

- **Confrontation.** Occurs when parties in conflict directly engage one another and try to work out their differences. Negotiation is the bargaining process that often occurs during confrontation and that enables the parties to systematically reach a solution. Confrontation is not always successful as there is no guarantee that discussions will focus on a conflict or that emotions will not get out of hand.
- **Third-party consultants.** When conflict is intense and enduring, and department members are suspicious and uncooperative, an expert third-party consultant can be brought in from outside the organisation to meet with representatives from both departments.

- **Member rotation.** It means that individuals from one department can be asked to work in another department on a temporary or permanent basis. The advantage is that individuals become submerged in the values, attitudes, problems and goals of the other department. In addition, individuals can explain the problems and goals of their original departments to their new colleagues. This enables a frank, accurate exchange of views and information.
- **Superordinate goals.** Another strategy is for top management to establish superordinate goals that require cooperation between departments. Conflicting departments then share the same goal and must depend upon one another to achieve it.
- **Intergroup training.** A strong intervention to reduce conflict is intergroup training. This technique has been developed by psychologists such as Robert Blake, Jane Mouton and Richard Walton. When other techniques fail to reduce conflict to an appropriate level, or when other techniques do not fit the organisation in question, special training of group members may be required.

Faced with intergroup conflict, the purpose of any managerial strategy will be to turn the conflict into fruitful competition or, if this is not possible, to control the conflict.

> **Managing Intergroup conflict – training**
>
> Training is a method for managing intergroup conflict.
>
> This training requires that department members attend an outside workshop away from day-to-day work problems. The training workshop may last several days, and various activities take place. This technique is expensive, but it has the potential for developing a company-wide cooperative attitude. The steps typically associated with an intergroup training session are as follows:
>
> - The conflicting groups are both brought into a training setting with the stated goal of exploring mutual perceptions and relationships.
> - The conflicting groups are then separated and each group is invited to discuss and make a list of its perceptions of itself and the other group.
> - In the presence of both groups, group representatives publicly share the perceptions of self and other that the groups have generated, while the groups are obligated to remain silent. The objective is simply to report to the other group as accurately as possible the images that each group has developed in private.

- Before any exchange takes place, the groups return to <u>private sessions to digest and analyse what they have heard</u>; there is great likelihood that the representatives' reports have revealed to each group discrepancies between its self-image and the image the other group holds of it.

- In public session, again working through representatives, each group shares with the other what <u>discrepancies it has uncovered and the possible reasons for them</u>, focusing on <u>actual, observable behaviour</u>.

- Following this mutual exposure, a <u>more open exploration is permitted between the two groups on the now-shared goal of identifying further reasons for perceptual distortions</u>.

- A <u>joint exploration is then conducted of how to manage future relations in such a way as to encourage coop-eration between groups</u>.

After this training experience, department employees <u>understand each other much better</u>. The improved attitudes lead to <u>better working relationships</u> for a long time.

Handy – conditions for successful conflict resolution

<u>Handy</u> identified conditions to be satisfied for the success of argument in resolving differences:

- <u>Constructive argument based on effective group dynamics</u> such as trust, confidence, shared leadership and challenging tasks for the parties involved.
- <u>Free and open expression of feelings and emotion.</u>
- <u>Adequate information and argument by everyone is based on the same thing.</u>

Handy suggested that these conditions can only be met in organisations which are:

- <u>diversified,</u>
- <u>low technology,</u> and
- <u>task orientated.</u>

Mainwaring – strategies for managing conflict

These are the broad strategies for managing conflict in organisations as explained by **Mainwaring** in *Management and Strategy* (1991):

- *Conflict stimulation and orchestration*. This approach actively encourages conflict as a means of generating new ideas and new approaches or of stimulating change. It is a characteristic of matrix structures that deliberately build role conflicts into organisational relationships. There are obvious dangers in generating conflict, not least that they will escalate and perpetuate in a destructive way. However some conflict is necessary to prevent organisational ossification. This approach involves the maintenance and management of constructive conflict as a means of continuous renewal.

- *Conflict suppression*. This involves the use or threatened use of authority or force, or the avoidance of recognition that a conflict situation exists, or smoothing over the conflict by de-emphasising the seriousness of the situation. Such strategies are essentially short-term, and are likely to be perceived as such by those involved.

- *Conflict reduction*. This involves building on areas of agreement and on common objectives, and changing attitudes and perceptions of the parties involved. Techniques that can be used include compromises and concessions. These can be facilitated by independent third party interventions, such as conciliation and arbitration.

- *Conflict resolution*. This seeks to eliminate the root causes of conflict by establishing a consensus. Attitude change is a key element, particularly regarding the possibility of 'win-win' situations where the parties involved are aware of the mutual gains to be derived from co-operation and collaboration.

The mix of strategies used will depend not only on the situation, but also on the assumptions that managers make about conflict.

> Important methods to apply when dealing with organisational conflict are *altering*:
>
> - The context, e.g. new procedures, reducing interdependency, changing work allocation.
> - The issue in dispute by separating into smaller issues, separating people- and task- related issues.
> - Proximity, i.e. physically separating the persons or groups involved.
> - The individuals involved including relocation and dismissal, or changing behaviour through training or organisational development techniques.

9 Dealing with industrial relations conflict

Although vertical conflict can take place without the presence of unions, Trade unions highlight vertical conflict as they try to equalise power differences between workers and management where the ground rules for conflict are formalised by laws and regulations. The sources of vertical conflict reflect the reasons why workers join unions.

The first priority for representatives is loyalty to their group. These can create strategies for avoidance or individualistic approaches:

- *Union avoidance strategies* including 'double-breasting' (setting up new plants in areas of high unemployment, or low union activity), devolving collective bargaining to factory level, removing unions from annual pay rounds whilst giving the right of the union members to be consulted and represented.

- *Individualistic approaches* away from third party involvement using appraisal systems, training and development schemes, performance-related pay systems, share schemes and the same pension and health schemes for all.

- *Collective bargaining* using procedural methods (a prescribed format) ultimately leading to the substantive agreement (defining each party's rewards and responsibilities for the next two to three years) in collective negotiations between workers and management.

New approaches tend to be more co-operative including:

- *Partnership agreements*.
- *Gain sharing* based on bonuses and profit rather than fixed-rate increases.

- *Labour-management teams* based on Japanese quality circles at shop-floor levels, middle management and union leader teams, and at top management, long-term policies to avoid layoffs.
- *Employment security* rather than job security where workers are reassigned to different positions and jobs are dependent on the firm's success.

Test your understanding 4

Conflict is an inevitable feature of organisations but is rarely recognised or understood.

Required:

Describe the causes of conflict and the symptoms of conflict in the workplace.

(10 marks)

Test your understanding 5

The T Textile Company is in a troubled state. The trade union representing the weavers has just negotiated a pay increase for its members, and this has led to a claim by the mechanics, who maintain the machinery, for a similar percentage pay increase so that the traditional differential with the weavers is maintained. The T Textile Company is seeking to resist the mechanics' claim on the grounds that the weavers' extra payment can be justified by increases in productivity, while the maintenance work carried out by the mechanics has not changed. The response of the mechanics has been to threaten industrial action.

The problems for the T Textile Company have been made worse by a dispute between the Weaving Department and the Cloth Inspection Department. All members of the Weaving Department, including the weaving shed managers and its supervisors, receive a bonus based on the productivity of the whole department. Employees in the Cloth Inspection Department are paid a fixed salary based on proven competence and experience.

> The conflict between the departments developed following the appointment of a new manager in the Cloth Inspection Department. The Works Manager has warned the new manager that the quality of output has to improve if the company is to remain competitive. This has resulted in a general tightening up of the standards enforced in the inspection process so that weaving machines are standing idle more frequently than in the past while faults detected during cloth inspection are investigated.
>
> The sight of idle machines has resulted in intense frustration among management and employees in the Weaving Department as every idle machine means a reduction in their bonus payments. The weavers' frustration is now being taken out on the Cloth Inspection Department by adopting a policy of not cooperating.
>
> **Required:**
>
> (a) Explain the causes of the horizontal and vertical conflicts within the T Textile Company.
>
> **(6 marks)**
>
> (b) Discuss how each type of conflict within the T Textile Company might be resolved. Explain what factors might influence the likelihood of a successful outcome for each type of conflict.
>
> **(8 marks)**

10 Communication

An important aspect in the relationship between managers and subordinates is communication. Most organisations will depend to some extent on the speed and accuracy of communication to maintain their competitive edge, and the management function involves both direct and indirect communication. Good communication skills are often included as an essential management competence, since people with good communication skills have been found to make better decisions and tend to be promoted more frequently.

Effective and regular personal communications are vital to ensure coordination and to identify problems quickly.

The process of communication

The communication process can be defined as a process that is used to impart a message or information from a sender to a receiver by using a medium of communication.

The message goes through several stages when it is sent by the sender to the receiver. These stages are as follows:

(1) _Sender._ The sender is the entity that conveys or sends the message.
(2) _Message_. Is what is being transmitted from sender to receiver (words, numbers, gestures on non verbal cues such as body language).
(3) _Encoding_. Encoding is a process through which the message is symbolised.
(4) _Channel._ Channel is the medium through which message is being sent. (email, conversations, meetings, memos etc).
(5) _Receiver._ Is the entity that receives the message.
(6) _Decoding_. Decoding is the process in which the message is translated and meaning is generated out of it. (problems can occur here due to interpretation).
(7) _Feedback_. Is the process through which receiver sends his response.

Barriers to communication

Sender:

- not being clear as to what has to be communicated;
- omitting information;
- choosing words in coding the message that do not accurately reflect the idea/concept, and or choosing words that the intended receipts cannot understand;
- choosing words that provoke an emotional response;
- using technical jargon;
- choosing an inappropriate medium;
- sending too much information;
- sending mixed messages.

Receiver:

- not in an appropriate state to receive the message;
- not wishing to receive the message;
- filtering out elements that he or she does not wish to deal with;
- information overload;
- mindset that does not admit the substance of the message.

Noise may also interfere with communication:

- Physically impairing the receiver's ability to receive or the sender's capacity to receive feedback;
- Physical failure of the medium of transmission;
- Limiting the encoding/decoding capabilities of the sender and receiver;
- Obscuring the message within a mass of communications.

Ways to overcome the barriers

the **sender** should:

- have a definite, clear objective;
- plan the communication;
- ensure that all elements of the communication fit;
- think about the receiver and their situation;
- anticipate reactions to the message and cater for these;
- practise;
- seek and work with the feedback.

the **receiver** should:

- consider their contribution;
- listen attentively;
- check out anything that is vague;
- give feedback.

Non verbal communication

During face to face communication, the following non verbal actions can help to ensure the message is communicated correctly:

- maintain eye contact;
- smile;
- occasionally nod;
- speak at a moderate rate, using an assuring tone.

Non verbal actions can vary across countries and cultures.

Test your understanding 6

Daniel is a young management accountant who, after completing his Institute's examinations recently, was put in charge of a small established accounts department at a subsidiary.

At his first progress review with his superior, he was very confident and enthusiastic about numerous initiatives which he had already taken, or was about to take. Daniel expressed disappointment that his staff were so reactionary and uncooperative.

Enquiries by Daniel's superior among the staff uncovered general dissatisfaction about Daniel's leadership. The younger ones are frightened of him, and feel he has no interest in them. They say he is always in a hurry, and they have no idea of whether their work is up to his requirements or not.

The older ones, who have worked in the department for years, are very worried about his apparently arbitrary and risky decisions. Others are resentful and frustrated that Daniel never bothers to listen to their ideas. Daniel has been informed of these comments.

Required:

Recommend the behaviour which Daniel should adopt to improve the situation.

(10 marks)

11 Meetings

Meetings can be an effective communication method for the manager. In order to ensure that the meeting is effective and useful it is important to adopt the following steps:

- determine the purpose of the meeting
- establish who needs to attend
- determine the agenda in advance
- make suitable arrangements for location and time
- facilitate discussion
- manage the plan of action
- summarise
- publish results/minutes

A rule of thumb of facilitation is that successful meetings are 80% preparation and 20% execution. Part of that preparation is focusing on what needs to happen to have a successful meeting.

Roles of team members in meetings:

- The manager should act as a **facilitator** in the meeting process, setting the agenda and ensuring the meeting achieves its objectives.
- One person needs to act as a **chairperson**, to ensure the agenda is followed.
- The meeting will require a **secretary or administrator** to take minutes.
- Team members will play various roles:
    - protagonists – positive supporter.
    - antagonist – disruptive to the team meetings.

All meeting members must be listened to with respect, but it is the responsibility of the manager to make the whole team aware of the overall project objective, and the role that each team member plays in its achievement.

If the meeting is designed to solve problems, individual team members will be called upon to offer their own expertise and advice on the situation. Other team members will take a more passive role, but will be important in providing an objective perspective on the solutions generated. It is important that a variety of skills are represented at a meeting so that those present can provide varying expert opinions upon the same problem.

Problems with meetings and their solutions

Problems with meetings	Actions to avoid problem
Poor preparation: inappropriate chairperson.	Selection should be based on someone with the requisite range of communication skills.
Poor preparation: the objectives of the meeting are undefined and so unclear.	Ensure that an agenda is produced and circulated prior to the meeting. During the meeting, the chairperson should state the objective(s) and must return the focus of the meeting to the points on the agenda.
There is hostility between some of the attendees.	The chairperson will again need to exercise negotiation skills. Careful use of a seating plan may help to reduce the possibility of conflict. As a last resort, one or both of the parties involved may be asked to leave the meeting.

Lack of enthusiasm or interest in the meeting.	For future meetings, ensure that only those with an interest in the meeting, or whose view is required, are actually invited to the meeting. For the current meeting, suggest a short break or stress the need to reach a conclusion.
Attendees talk too much without regard to the chairperson's requests.	The chairperson must impose some order on the meeting. Possible solutions include asking the participants to speak in accordance with meeting protocols such as a time constraint if necessary, or (worst case) asking them to leave the meeting altogether.
Attendees cannot reach an agreement concerning issues on the agenda.	The chairperson will need to exercise negotiation skills to try to bring the meeting to some agreement. If this is not possible, then attendees may have to agree to differ. However, some action points may be required to ensure that more information is obtained so agreement can be achieved at the next meeting.
There is hostility between some of the attendees.	The chairperson will again need to exercise negotiation skills. Careful use of a seating plan may help to reduce the possibility of conflict. As a last resort, one or both of the parties involved may be asked to leave the meeting.
Action points from previous meetings have not been carried out.	Assuming that minutes were issued correctly, in the current meeting, the chairperson should obtain reasons for actions not being completed. For future action points, ensure that each has a person identified as responsible for completing it. Check the minutes of the meeting to ensure that all action points are included.
Minutes are either too long (information overload) or too brief (do not include appropriate points).	Ensure that the minutes are either minutes of resolution (which contain agreed outcomes) or, if minutes of narration, that they are sufficiently edited to provide the flavour of the discussions, but not small detail.

12 Negotiation

Negotiation is another important skill for managers in their relationship with not only subordinates but with other stakeholders such as suppliers and customers and is defined by three characteristics:

(1) Conflict of interest between two or more parties. What one wants is not necessarily what the others want.

(2) No established set of rules for resolving conflict, or the parties prefer to work outside of an established set of rules to develop their own solution.

(3) Parties prefer to search for an agreement rather than to fight openly, to have one side capitulate, to break off contact permanently, or to take their dispute to a higher authority.

Negotiating is an activity that seeks to reach agreement between two or more starting positions.

The aim of negotiation

There are two types of negotiation process that differ fundamentally in their approach and in their relative prospects for the stability of the agreement that is reached.

The first is called the '**win-win**' approach. In these negotiations, the prospects for both sides' gains are encouraging. Both sides attempt to reconcile their positions so that the end result is an agreement under which both will benefit – therefore the resultant agreement tends to be stable.

The second is called the '**win-lose**' approach. In these negotiations, each of the parties seeks maximum gains and therefore usually seeks to impose maximum losses on the other side.

It is clear that a win/win solution is more likely to lead to a stable solution and a successful business relationship. In real life negotiations, both of these processes tend to be at work together. Therefore, rather than two negotiators adopting one or other of the approaches, negotiations tend to involve a tension between the two.

Examples of negotiations managers might need to undertake:

- on *his/her own behalf* when securing a pay rise, for instance, or an improvement in the terms and conditions of employment.

- on *behalf of a department or functional area,* e.g. securing an acceptable departmental budget.

- with the *external environment* on behalf of the organisation, e.g. obtaining planning permission for an extension to the warehouse.

For the managers involved, the aim in any negotiation is to achieve a settlement that is acceptable to the other parties but which also comes as close as possible to their desired outcome. Negotiation attempts to resolve and accommodate differing interests by moving towards an end point which is acceptable to both sides – a mutually beneficial or **'win-win'** situation.

A **'win-lose'** situation culminates where one group has achieved its objectives at the clear expense of the other. This solution tends to cause dissatisfaction and the situation could deteriorate into a **'lose-lose'** position where the benefits originally gained by the winner are continuously eroded by resistance and a lack of commitment.

The skills of a negotiator

These can be summarised under three main headings:

- **Interpersonal skills** – the use of good communicating techniques, the use of power and influence, and the ability to impress a personal style on the tactics of negotiation.

- **Analytical skills** – the ability to analyse information, diagnose problems, to plan and set objectives, and the exercise of good judgement in interpreting results.

- **Technical skills** – attention to detail and thorough case preparation.

The process of negotiation

The negotiating techniques adopted will depend on the type of bargaining situation. **Walton and McKersie** identify two main types of negotiation: distributive and integrative bargaining.

Distributive bargaining is that which is aimed at resolving pure conflicts of interest on substantive issues e.g. hours of work and rates of pay.

In most bargaining situations it is usual to find that there are some topics that are best discussed on the basis of an **integrative, or joint, approach** aimed at finding a solution from which both sides will benefit substantially.

The negotiation process can be divided into four distinct stages.

- *Preparation* – information gathering – knowing the background to the problem, and the likely constraints acting on each participant.

- *Opening* – both sides present their starting positions, good opportunity to influence the other party.

- *Bargaining* – purpose is to narrow the gap between the two initial positions, persuade other party of the strength of your case. In order to do this, you should use clearly thought out, planned and logical debate.
- *Closing* – agreement is reached, looking for a mutually beneficial outcome.

Guidance for successful negotiation

- Focus initially on each side's primary objective – minor negotiating points can become a distraction in the early stages.
- Be prepared to settle for what is fair – if an agreement is not seen to be fair it is unlikely to be stable. Maintain flexibility in your own position, this makes it easier for the other side to be flexible as well.
- Listen to what the other side wants and make efforts to compromise on the main issues, so that both sides can begin to attain their goals.
- Seek to trade-off wins and losses, so each side gets something in return for everything they give up.

13 Mentoring

What is mentoring?

Since the time of the Ancient Greeks, mentoring has been recognised as a great way of helping people to develop. In Greek mythology, Mentor was an old friend of Odysseus. The Goddess Athena assumed the form of Mentor several times to provide wise and faithful counsel to Odysseus' son. Since then, wise and trusted advisers have been called 'mentors'.

Mentoring is quite simply a relationship where one person helps another to improve their knowledge, work or thinking. It is a very valuable development tool for both the person seeking support (the mentee) and the person giving the support (the mentor).

Who is a mentor?

A mentor should be someone who:

- Can give practical study support and advice.
- Can give technical, ethical and general business guidance.
- Can help with development of interpersonal and work skills.
- Is an impartial sounding board – no direct reporting responsibility.
- Is a good guide, counsellor.
- Is a role model who can help improve career goals.

Quite often a mentor is from the same function (i.e. finance), it is unusual for them to be a direct or indirect line manager. The mentor is normally a role model, having already achieved a status (and possibly qualification) to which the subordinate aspires.

Mentoring works alongside more formal control mechanisms, such as appraisal, and is intended to provide the employee with a forum to discuss development issues which is relaxed and supportive. Mentors often discuss such issues as training, the choice of qualification, interpersonal problems and career goals.

The role of a mentor is to encourage and assist junior members of staff to analyse their performance in order to identify their strengths and weaknesses. The mentor should give honest but supportive feedback and guidance on how weaknesses can be eliminated or neutralised. The mentor could also act as a sounding board for ideas. The process should help junior staff to question and reflect on their experiences.

A mentoring system has both career-enhancing and psychological functions. The career function is concerned primarily with enhancing career advancement through exposure, visibility and sponsorship. The psychological function is more concerned with aspects of the relationship that primarily enhance competence and effectiveness in management roles. A mentoring system should help junior staff in expanding their network of contacts and gain greater exposure in the organisation.

For a mentoring system to be successful, relationships should not be based on authority but rather a genuine wish by the mentors to share knowledge, advice and experience and should be one of mutual trust.

The benefits of mentoring include:

- Faster career progress.
- Excellent value for money for the organisation as the financial cost is relatively small.
- Company image – company does not want to be associated with a poor turnover record – encouraging learning helps staff to achieve their full potential and not look for new employment.
- To preserve the well-being of employees and others, improves employee morale, trust and motivation – employees often feel that real improvements in competences are delivered from the process.

Examples of the benefits of mentoring

Mentoring has many benefits for those involved:

Mentees will find a safe environment where they can admit gaps in knowledge and skills, raise queries and consider their strengths. Below you can see how some of our mentees felt they have gained from their mentoring relationships.

'I gained a better vision of what I want to do in the future, and what steps I must take in order to achieve my goals.'

'I gained a great deal. It was good to talk with someone who was independent of my work, college and home circumstances. I gained an alternative and dispassionate view and I have been able to make a more rational assessment of my priorities.'

'I learned about self belief, having respect for others, becoming more assertive, when to listen and when to ask questions, planning and decision making.'

'I gained a great insight into the practice of running your own business, which is what I would like to achieve myself.'

'My mentor gave a good sounding board and plenty of encouragement towards my impending exams.'

Mentors get a unique opportunity to put something back into their profession while enjoying a fresh challenge and personal and professional development of their own. Richard Garnett MAAT explains why he volunteered as a mentor:

'I felt it was time to give something back to the AAT. I think I have experience I can usefully share with those newer to the AAT. I really hope I helped my mentee to develop. I also think the scheme had some great learning for me too.'

Article by the AAT (Association of Accounting Technicians)

Test your understanding 7

Required:

(a) Briefly explain what is meant by mentoring?

(4 marks)

(b) What are the benefits of mentoring?

(6 marks)

14 Managing the finance function

The importance of the finance function

Historically, the role of the finance function was cost control, variance analysis and reporting on past performance. This role has steadily developed over the years into a more proactive, value adding role. You could say the role has changed from reporting performance to enhancing performance.

The recent financial crisis and recession has highlighted the need for organisations to get the most value from their finance functions. It is important for organisations to ensure that they have properly staffed and trained finance functions to help add value and drive their organisation through the uncertain times ahead.

There is a focus on efficiency for organisations today. They are striving to ensure that all expenditure incurred can be seen to add value, this is known as lean operations. With lean operations, all unnecessary activities, expenditure or waste is eliminated. The finance function is expected to play an important role in this business transformation. Finance is expected to contribute to the strategic decision-making process to help drive the business forward.

Many organisations are now focusing on a more sustainable long-term approach to profitability and value creation. Finance functions are set to play a critical role in promoting this more balanced approach to risk and reward. This includes:

- strengthening the management and understanding of the risks and funding costs associated with particular products and strategies.
- dealing with increasing product complexity, unprecedented market instability and ever more exacting regulatory expectations.

- **coming under pressure from senior management to cut costs**, while providing more effective advice.
- the need to develop a deeper business knowledge and being able to recognise potential weaknesses.
- appreciating what business teams need and expect from them.
- turning data into a genuinely valuable source of information.
- having clear reporting lines, both within the function and into the board and business.

When deciding on their structure, organisations need to decide where to position the finance function to allow them to play the fullest role in driving the business forward. There are several options available:

- The finance function is carried out by an external party – **business process outsourcing (BPO)**.
- The finance function is consolidated as part of a **shared service centre (SSC)**.
- The finance function is **embedded within the business area** as a business partnering role.

Business process outsourcing

An option in the positioning of the finance function is business process outsourcing (BPO). Outsourcing is the act of giving a third-party the responsibility of what would otherwise be an internal system or service. BPO is contracting with a third party (external supplier) to provide part or all of a business process or function.

Many of these involve offshoring, when the outsourced function is in another country.

Benefits of outsourcing:

- Cost reduction through economies of scale. Suppliers can perform the finance function far more cheaply and efficiently than companies working on their own. For example a reduction in working capital or improvements in tax efficiency.
- Access to capabilities. A specialist provider can bring best practice expertise and new investment in resources.
- Release of capacity. Allows the retained finance function to concentrate on their role as business partners, in order to improve decision making.

Drawbacks of outsourcing:

- Loss of control. Business areas may not be able to dictate what information they need and when they need it.

- Over reliance on external providers. The outsourcing partner may dictate what information is to be provided and how it is to be provided. This may not tie in exactly with business needs. It can be difficult and expensive to bring the function back in house.

- Confidentiality and a risk to intellectual property. The outsourcing partner will have access to confidential information, and they may also process information for competitors.

- Risk of unsatisfactory quality. The quality of the information provided may not be as required for decision making purposes.

Shared service centres (SSC)

The finance function across the organisation may be consolidated and run as a central unit, or a shared services centre (SSC).

A SSC refers to the provision of a service by one part of an organisation or group where that service has previously been found in more than one part of the organisation or group. An example would be a large multinational organisation with financial processing centres in several countries in which it operates, chooses to consolidate these activities at one site or shared service centre (SSC).

It is sometimes referred to as 'internal outsourcing'. It allows an organisation to investigate the potential benefits of consolidation of activities, whilst maintaining full internal control and thus minimising control risks.

The advantages of SSC:

- Headcount reductions. Economies of scale can be realised if all the finance personnel are gathered together to form one centre of excellence, rather than being spread across the business areas.

- Reduction in premises and associated costs. Linked with the headcount reduction, there would be associated savings in premises and other overhead costs.

- Potential favourable labour rates in the chosen geographical location. The location of the SSC can be carefully selected to ensure the lowest cost provision.

- Quality of service provision. Learning and sharing of knowledge will occur within the SSC which should lead to improved quality.
- Consistent management of business data. Standard approaches can be developed across the organisation, rather than each individual area developing their own methods.

Drawbacks of SSC:

- Loss of business knowledge. The finance function may not have a detailed knowledge of each part of the business.
- Further from the everyday decision making. The SSC will be unlikely to have day-to-day contact with the business areas which it supports, it may therefore lack the required knowledge to provide up to date information for decision making.
- Business relationships are not as strong. The SSC may not be able to build strong business relationships with the business areas, which may result in them not performing for the business area as well as they could.

The finance function is embedded within the business area as a business partnering role

A dedicated finance function may be set up within each business area. This brings many benefits to both the accountants and the management of the area.

The finance function plays a critical role in providing information for decision-making. In the new business environment where competition is global and fierce, companies need better information than ever before in order to remain competitive. Organisations and their chief executive officers now expect finance directors and financial controllers to become more involved in matters of production, distribution and sales to play a fuller role at a strategic management level, in particular helping to decide which markets to serve with which products.

The advantages of this approach are:

- The finance function is part of the business area it serves. Information can be provided as and when required for business decision making. As a dedicated resources the accountant will be able to play a stronger role within the business.

- Increased knowledge of the business area and its needs. The accountant will be involved in all decisions being made within the business and will build up detailed local knowledge and understanding of the business and its information needs.

- Strong relationships can be built up between the accountants and the management of the business area. Trust is required within this relationship. Accountants that are dedicated resources are expected to act as full business partners.

The disadvantages are:

- Duplication of effort across the organisation. Similar work will be carried out across various business areas.

- Lack of knowledge. There is no sharing of knowledge which can happen within a larger, more diverse team. Best practice may not be being employed and practices within some business areas may become outdated.

- The accountants can feel isolated within the business and may develop their own ways of working which may not constitute best practice. Within the business there may only be one or two dedicated accounting resources, leaving them to work more or less alone. Without a larger team around them, they may not be able to develop the required skills or knowledge.

Companies are never too big or too small to begin strategising the finance function, particularly important when the business is considering major changes in the organisation (a life cycle event) intended to make the company stronger. A few examples of life cycle events that are dependent on a strong finance function include going public, acquiring a business loan and seeking growth through acquisition. These activities rely on thorough knowledge of the core of the business and relate to the longer-term strategic success of the company. Accordingly a company should consider whether the responsibility for these aspects of financial service operations remain in-house.

Decision-making is becoming the basis of competitive advantage and value creation. If markets give all organisations access to similar resources globally and competition causes many routine business processes to converge on world-class standards, the quality of information could become a key differentiator. Enhancing the value of accounting in financial management processes requires a shift in focus away from transaction processing and reporting to a role which is fully integrated into the strategic and daily business activities of the organisation.

Relationships in the working environment

Test your understanding 8

The finance function is continually evolving in line with the demands of the organisations they support. Finance functions are now expected to contribute to decision making at all levels of the organisation, including strategic decision making. Organisations are therefore under pressure to develop finance functions which meet their ever growing demands, but which are also cost-effective.

The finance function must be managed in a way which maximises its value to the organisation.

Required:

Discuss the advantages and disadvantages for the organisation of embedding finance in the business, setting up a shared services centre or outsourcing the finance function (business process outsourcing).

(10 marks)

15 Relationships with professional advisors and external stakeholders

Relationships with professional advisors

In order to meet organisational objectives, all organisation, regardless of size, will require expertise and support of a team or people with a variety of skills. Some of these will be internal to the organisation, while others may be external. Management must therefore build relationships with a variety of professional advisors who will be able to provide knowledge and advice to the organisation to aid decision making.

Here are examples of professional advisors which may be used by an organisation:

- Solicitors
- Accountants
- Tax Consultants
- Insurance Brokers
- IT specialists
- Environmental Advisors.

Why use professional advisors?

There are at least two reasons why it's important to have professional advisors:

(1) They're looking at your business with a dispassionate and unbiased perspective.

(2) As professionals, they can take what they see and help you turn problems into opportunities.

An organisation should always be open to reaching out to others for advice.

Dealing with professional advisors

Often an experienced solicitor for example can also recommend other advisors such as Accountancy and Insurance professionals. Some of them will become important components in your ongoing business, even if you only need to consult them occasionally. It is extremely important to have most of them in place before you make important strategic decisions.

When dealing with professional advisors, it is very important to:

- Have a good working relationship with all of them. Organisations may need to call on them at short notice, and will require the advisor to give full commitment to their issues or concerns.

- Allow them to get to know your business. Advisors are unable to provide correct and worthwhile advice if they do not know all the facts about the situation.

- Keep them up to date with new developments and potential future projects. They may be able to give advice which will set the business on the right track going forward.

When do you seek professional advice?

Advice from experts should be sought when:

- Sales are low – the economy and your competitors are doing well but you're not, it's time to turn to experts for advice.

- Profits are low – often, sales can be good while profits may still be down. You may need to consult with an expert to find out what's eating up your money and causing low profit margins.

- Profits are high – don't lose an opportunity. Contact experts who can help you make the most of this precious time.

- Entering into important contracts/projects – an experienced solicitor will read every important contract you sign and get involved during the negotiation period and the creation of any contracts.

- Your company is being sued – at the first sign of a potential lawsuit, consult legal advice.

- You're considering bringing in new finance – anytime you are considering changing the ownership structure of your company. Always consult with your business adviser, accountant and solicitor when borrowing.

- Initial environmental reviews show the need to improve performance, identify immediate cost savings and improve resource efficiency.

Professional advisors can be very helpful to organisations and can assist them in making strong strategic decisions. It is important that management foster good relationships with a range of professional advisors.

Relationships with auditors

The finance function can support organisations in delivering results and meeting externally imposed rules. Both are important in order to stay in business. External audit's work relates to the financial statements, they are concerned with the financial records that underpin these. The external auditors will review the system of internal control in order to determine the extent of the substantive work required on the year-end accounts. The auditors will identify the areas of weakness and recommendations for improvement. It is important that the management of the finance function know that they are properly managing the risk of any internal control failures. (The growing recognition by management of the benefits of good internal control, and the complexities of an adequate system of internal control have led to the development of internal auditing being recognised as an important form of control.) The finance function should implement any recommendations from the audit to enhance the efficiency and effectiveness of the information sent to management. It is important therefore that the finance function as decision makers fully understand the benefits of a good audit and should be extracting the maximum benefit from the company's audit service.

Relationships with financial stakeholders

We have seen the importance of the finance function in terms of its contribution to internal decision making. Another of its primary purposes is to provide transparency and usefulness to external stakeholders. Stakeholders such as lenders, shareholders and the government are external to the company but still take an interest in the company's performance.

Investors and financiers:

In spite of their absence on a day to day basis, investors and financiers (those lending money to the company) often rely exclusively on the legally mandated reporting requirements of the organisation to gain an understanding of company performance. They rely on the accuracy and predictability of the data coming from the companies in which they invest. They hold the company to performance predictions or forecasts and typically punish those companies that do not meet their expectations by selling their shares. This shows the importance of good data for external reporting and the important role the finance function can play in maintaining credibility with the external community.

Small and emerging businesses:

Financing the company's operations may be the single most important aspect of the finance function for the small and emerging business owner. Approaching banks is often a popular solution; the finance function will provide data on the health of the company and/or forecast its performance. Assembling sketchy documentation may mean that the business does not receive the finance it requires to start or stay in business.

Taxing and statutory authorities:

The finance function must be prepared to gather the necessary information and documentation to support remit-tances to taxing and statutory authorities. Finance need to be familiar with legal and statutory requirements pre-vailing in their respective locations and promote compliance throughout the organisation and then reporting to and filing returns with relevant authorities on a timely basis.

Contribution of finance to other functions:

- Finance people need to be trained not just to furnish and assemble information but to draw insights and communicate these effectively to support decision-making.

- Finance people will be expected to use their understanding of the numbers and metrics to evaluate opportunities and support decision making about investment opportunities and resource allocation.

- The role may need to emerge as a challenging sparring partner, able to challenge in a positive way and will require broader business understanding.

- The finance function is under pressure to enhance its value contribution to the business, deliver information and maintain effective controls in line with ever changing governance needs.

Relationships in the working environment

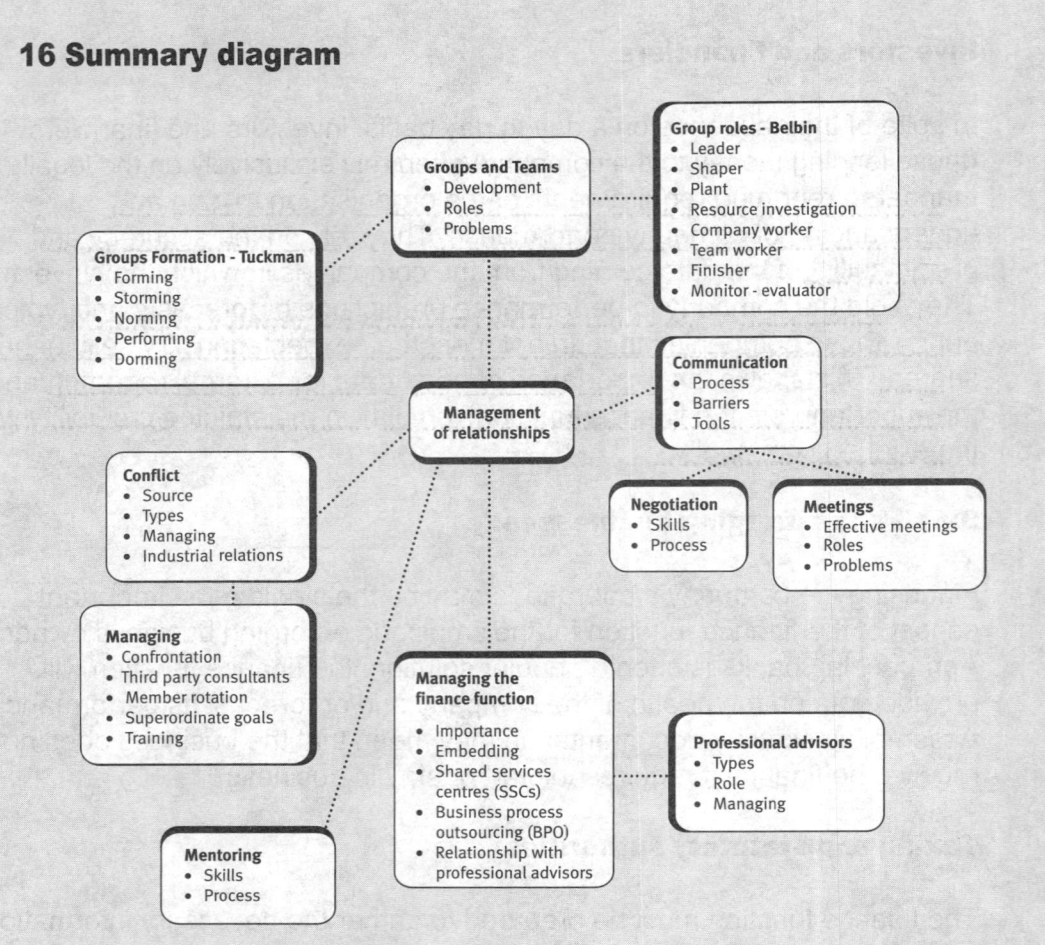

16 Summary diagram

Management of relationships

- **Groups and Teams**
  - Development
  - Roles
  - Problems

- **Group roles - Belbin**
  - Leader
  - Shaper
  - Plant
  - Resource investigation
  - Company worker
  - Team worker
  - Finisher
  - Monitor - evaluator

- **Groups Formation - Tuckman**
  - Forming
  - Storming
  - Norming
  - Performing
  - Dorming

- **Communication**
  - Process
  - Barriers
  - Tools

- **Conflict**
  - Source
  - Types
  - Managing
  - Industrial relations

- **Negotiation**
  - Skills
  - Process

- **Meetings**
  - Effective meetings
  - Roles
  - Problems

- **Managing**
  - Confrontation
  - Third party consultants
  - Member rotation
  - Superordinate goals
  - Training

- **Managing the finance function**
  - Importance
  - Embedding
  - Shared services centres (SSCs)
  - Business process outsourcing (BPO)
  - Relationship with professional advisors

- **Professional advisors**
  - Types
  - Role
  - Managing

- **Mentoring**
  - Skills
  - Process

Test your understanding answers

Test your understanding 1

A group is any number of people who interact with one another, are psychologically aware of each other and perceive themselves to be a group. In a cohesive group, members are more likely to talk in terms of 'we' rather than 'I'. It is also a group in which everyone is friendly or where loyalty to fellow members is high. A cohesive group is also one in which all the members work together for a common goal and where everyone is ready to take responsibility for group chores. Such a group is also one in which its members will defend against external criticism or attack. The norms formed by a cohesive group are likely to be particularly strong and exert considerable influence on the behaviour of its members. Cohesive groups tend to have the following advantages over less cohesive ones:

- more productive in quantity;
- produce higher quality;
  I have a stronger push to complete the task;
- have a greater division of labour and better coordination;
- experience fewer difficulties in communication.

On the other hand, the result of the Bank Wiring Room experiments in the Hawthorne studies showed that cohesive work groups can have disadvantages for any organisation. The norms of a cohesive work group may develop in a way which undermines the goals of the company. In the Bank Wiring Room, persons who turned out too much work were considered 'rate busters' and were subjected to considerable pressure to reduce their output, while 'chisellers' were also pressurised to fall into line.

The effectiveness of a well-integrated work group, in other words, can be used against the company in which it exists as well as for it. This is most clearly seen when a group of employees takes industrial action to pressurise management in a dispute over an issue such as working conditions or a pay claim.

Relationships in the working environment

Test your understanding 2

(a) Neville's group of twelve people is a long established and successful group. It would therefore be operating in Tuckman's fourth and final stage, which he terms 'performing'. In this stage the group is mature and individuals have evolved the roles that each will discharge and the norms of behaviour for group sessions. Such a settled group will be comfortable and familiar with each other, encouraging each individual to fulfil his/her role.

Belbin, a Canadian Professor, has devised a series of questionnaires whereby a person's natural role within a group can be defined. His theory further explains that a successful group has a balance of types.

Neville is fulfilling the 'chairman' role; Peter is the 'plant', capable of innovative solutions but may be low on practical follow through. Rosalinde would be the 'Resource Investigator', Quentin would be a 'company worker', but may also function as a 'Monitor Evaluator', providing an organising, dutiful, unemotional aspect to the group's work. Sheila is the 'Team Worker', defined by Belbin as important in promoting team spirit. Olivia seems to be the 'Completer/Finisher', ensuring that matters are followed through; also during Neville's absence she may act as 'Shaper' in providing the drive and momentum for completion of the work. This analysis suggests that this group is well balanced in having all major team roles present.

The resignation of Olivia could cause an imbalance within the group unless another individual develops into the 'Completer/Finisher' and 'Shaper' roles. Belbin explains that people can adopt different roles in different groups and amend their behaviour to fill a vacant role. However, there will be a temporary imbalance. Furthermore, the resignation of Olivia and her replacement by four new people means that the group reverts to the earlier stages of Tuckman's group formation i.e., forming, storming and norming.

As the group seeks to absorb new unknown people and strange roles are adopted it is inevitable that some people conflict will emerge. This could be aggravated by the increased size of the group. When the group had twelve members, a degree of cohesiveness is possible; however, this is less likely in a group of fifteen, especially when four members are new.

Since Peter and Rosalinde have been unusually helpful to Neville, they are probably aware of this difficulty and are trying to cover Olivia's role gap. However, the friction between them and with others highlights the need for Neville to take action.

(b) To recapture group cohesiveness and efficiency Neville could:

- let the group evolve over time through the four stages until the performing stage is reached when group cohesiveness would be restored. This would incur the intermediate stages when the group members get to know each other, when roles develop and are accepted by others, when disagreements arise. Neville may feel this is a safe option since eleven of the fifteen members are long standing and extra support is coming from Peter and Rosalinde. However, Neville needs to remember that the personality of the new group will be different from the old team – there are new people and roles involved. Also, the size of the group is significantly larger and could not operate in the same way.

- break the group into smaller teams, which may progress through the four stages of formation more quickly. A smaller team can be managed in a more personal manner and this may suit Neville.

- become directly involved in structuring the progression of the group through each stage of formation. He could, for example, influence the development of roles and behaviour norms through his own behaviour in recognising a particular person as the 'Shaper' in the team.

- change the group structure through delegation, assigning individual responsibilities, making some tasks team based instead of personal based. Since the tasks are complex, this may be a current practice.

- emphasise the change and need for a new approach by altering the physical layout of the office. A revised desk seating plan could create its own team influences and separate potential conflict staff.

- introduce a series of team building training sessions in which the group could analyse its own behaviour. This could involve understanding the value that each person brings to the team as well as ensuring that everyone understands the group tasks that must be completed. In the final resort this could lead to the payment of team bonuses based on team, rather than individual, performance.

- whilst introducing any of these recommendations, Neville should consider whether there is a need to change his management style. Likert emphasises that the effective manager can adapt his/her management style in response to changes in staff, tasks and situation. Neville may find it necessary to be less participative in the early stages of group formation. Or even adopt two different styles if he chooses to split the group into two smaller teams.

In summary, it is difficult to make concrete recommendations since a major factor is Neville's own attitudes, strengths, weaknesses etc. As Charles Handy explains, it is necessary to understand the nature of the task, the situation that exists, the attitudes and behaviour of staff and fourthly, the manger's own attitudes, experiences etc.

Test your understanding 3

Road reconstruction and maintenance work will consist of contracts where each contract is different in nature, size and location. The techniques and materials used may be common but the application will be variable. Under this pattern of work there is considerable initiative available to the work team while central control cannot be detailed.

The present teams are cohesive, successful and operate independently of each other. The introduction of competition between groups will heighten the cohesive aspect and reduce the co-operation overall, this can be concluded by the Boys Camp experiments of Sherif and Sherif. This will be accentuated in this example because the change in wage system means that teams are competing for a share of a single bonus pool. The operations manager's introduction of competition will change the attitude and behaviour of the teams. Some of these changes will be beneficial while others will be negative.

The positive changes in behaviour are likely to be:

- An improvement in productivity within the teams. Each team will endeavour to safeguard or increase its share of the bonus pool. The team will concentrate its attention on improving its own productivity through streamlining working practices, ignoring trade demarcation boundaries and working outside normal hours to complete the job.

- The bonus element of the wages can be calculated on a basis of contract profitability as contract time targets. If profitability is the measure then the team will be cost conscious and material wastage, equipment abuse etc will be minimised. However, if the measure is time targets then wastage and machinery abuse will be irrelevant to the team's bonus and management will need a central system to check team behaviour and operations.

- An improvement in timekeeping and attendance should occur. Mayo, in the Hawthorne Experiment, was the first researcher to point out the strong pressure of group colleagues upon the behaviour of any individual within a group. The more cohesive the group, the stronger its peer pressure. Group names will be clearly evident covering areas of attendance, timekeeping, 'breaktimes' and individuals will be pressurised to fulfil their role within the team. As Mayo discovered, if the behaviour of an individual usurps a team name then team members exact a penalty and the offender is subjected to ostracisation, sneering comments and similar social pressure.

- Local sales effort is likely to be increased. If potential customers are logged with a central sales office then once a team has commenced work with a customer, they are likely to 'sell' extra services and develop sales to a maximum. There could be a situation where this is damaging to the organisation. For instance a major customer operating several sites could employ more than one team from the road reconstruction company. If one team disparages the work of another team or causes it to miss a deadline, in order to gain the next slice of work, then the overall company reputation is damaged. This is the potential danger in all situations of local rivalry.

- There will be a change in internal working relationships as group members become less social in behaviour and more task centred. This will increase pressure on newcomers or poor-performers, as time spent in coaching or supporting by other team members becomes resented.

Some of the negative behaviour aspects likely to be experienced could be damaging to ongoing working relationships:

- Firstly, competition will breed selfishness and the bonus shareout will create winners and losers encouraging envy and recriminations between teams and their members.

- Secondly, teams will be selective in the jobs that they undertake. A difficult or potentially low bonus job is likely to be avoided. An additional temptation would arise when a team developed a major customer and was unable to handle all the work generated in the timescale required by the customers. The team may seek to postpone the work and so safeguard future bonuses but would damage customer services in doing so.

- Thirdly, fluctuating wages and internal group pressure to perform could have harmful consequences for individuals and reduce loyalty.

Relationships in the working environment

- Fourthly, there will be severe pressure on the sales person to put the interests of his team first and the company second. Sub-optimising of performance is likely as each team seeks to direct its sales person's efforts for the team's benefit. This selfishness of behaviour could extend to other areas such as machines being drawn from the company pool and not returned promptly for other teams to use. A further example could arise where one team learns of a contract which is in the immediate vicinity of a rival team's current working. The overall benefit of the company dictates that disruption and travelling costs would be minimised by the team in that locality fulfilling that work. But selfish team behaviour may block this.

In summary competition between teams will deeply affect the behaviour of individuals within groups and inter group behaviour.

Test your understanding 4

Conflict can be caused by behaviour intended to obstruct the achievement of the goals of another person. It is any personal divergence of interests between groups or individuals. A certain amount of conflict in an organisation is not only inevitable it is often beneficial, for conflict is both a cause and an effect of change.

The causes of conflict are often difficult to determine accurately, as individuals may themselves be unsure of their motivation and behaviour.

They can be summarised as follows:

- misunderstandings
- perceived inequitable allocation of resources
- interpersonal friction
- insensitive and non-supportive relationships
- differences in status, prestige and power
- failure to communicate openly and honestly
- clashing objectives
- differing sets of values and beliefs
- functional authority being exercised incorrectly
- a climate of distrust, unreasonable pressure, or competition.

The **symptoms of conflict in the workplace** include the following:

- rigid application of, and adherence to, rules and procedures
- frustration and low morale
- encouragement and use of the grapevine
- concealed objectives where an individual or department may feel undervalued and follow other, self-serving objectives
- poor communication, remembering that communication may be vertical and horizontal
- departmental, team and individual rivalries and jealousies
- inter-personal and inter-departmental disputes and arguments
- widespread arbitration and personnel department involvement
- inflexibility to change
- individual's unwillingness to share information
- distorted information
- territorial defence.

Test your understanding 5

(a) The conflict in the T Textile Company encompasses both vertical and horizontal conflict.

Horizontal conflict happens between groups of staff or between departments at the same level in the hierarchy. The conflict between the Weaving Department and the Cloth Inspection Department could be classified as horizontal conflict. The cause of the conflict is due to the fact that the tightening of standards in the inspection process has had the knock-on effect of machines standing idle. This has affected the productivity of weavers and reduced their bonus payments. At a more fundamental level, there is a conflict in the goals of the Departments, the weavers are focused on producing cloth to maximise output and hence receive bonuses. On the other hand, the key objective of the Cloth Inspection Department is the quality standard of the material. The two groups are rewarded in different ways.

Vertical conflict occurs between individuals or groups who are at different levels in the hierarchy, and often arises because of status and power differences amongst groups. In the case of the T Textile Company, conflict has arisen between mechanics and management over status and pay. Mechanics want the same percentage pay increase as weavers but management argues that weavers can justify the increase by increasing productivity, whereas the work carried out by mechanics has not changed. This has led to industrial unrest.

(b) The best approach to managing horizontal conflict in the T Textile Company would be **collaboration** where differences are confronted and jointly resolved. The desired outcome is a win:win for both groups. This could be achieved by holding meetings between the two Departments, including the managers, weavers and inspection staff. Solutions to how quality standards could be maintained while minimising the down time of machines could be discussed. Communications between the different Departments, sharing an understanding of each other's goals and objectives should assist the process. Perhaps, the organisation could look at some of the techniques associated with total quality management in resolving the problems.

The vertical conflict in the T Textile Company is an example of industrial relations conflict over pay claims. This type of conflict may be resolved through negotiation between management and representatives of the mechanics through collective bargaining. The representatives of the mechanics could present a proposal for consideration by management, followed by counter-proposals and concessions.

The outcome will depend on the relative power held by the mechanics (for example, withdraw labour, gain support from other workers and willingness to take industrial action) and the power of management (ability to replace mechanics, ability to switch production to other factories). A win/win situation is desirable but often industrial relations conflict is resolved through compromise.

A useful framework for classifying different ways of handling conflict is known as the TKI. It is based on two conflict-management dimensions. These consist of the degree of assertiveness in pursuit of one's interests and the level of cooperation in attempting to satisfy others' interests. The relative strength of each of these produces five conflict-handling strategies.

It is difficult to determine the degree of assertiveness and the level of cooperation that exist in the case of T Textile Company, so we cannot come to a conclusion here and now but the framework does provide a useful means of considering alternatives if we can gather the necessary information.

The five conflict-handling strategies are:

Avoidance – one or more parties in conflict may seek to avoid, to suppress or to ignore the conflict. This is not recommended as it does not resolve the conflict and may break out again when the parties meet in the future.

Accommodation – this involves one party putting the other's interests first and suppressing their own interest in order to preserve some form of stability and to suppress the conflict. Again, if the causes of conflict are endemic or lasting, the accommodation strategy may not resolve the differences. Also, the accommodating party may well lose out as a result.

Compromise – often seen as the optimum solution. Each party gives something up, and a deal somewhere between the two is accepted after negotiation and debate. However, in compromise, both parties lose something and there may be a better alternative. This approach could be used to resolve the conflict between mechanics and management.

Competition – this is a state where both or all parties do not cooperate, instead they seek to maximise their own interests and goals. It creates winners and losers. The resultant conflict can prove damaging to the organisation as well as to at least one of the parties. So it is not recommended.

Collaboration – from the perspective of all parties, this is likely to be the optimum solution. Differences are confronted and jointly resolved, novel solutions are sought, and a win/win outcome is achieved. This is the proposed strategy to deal with the conflict between weavers and the cloth inspection staff.

For grievances, the informal solutions are also creating havoc, and there should be a formal set of HR policies and a separate formal grievance procedure set out in writing and made available to all staff. This would mean cases being taken higher in the hierarchy and so becoming more impersonal and free from the influence of the line manager who often seems to have recruited the employee without a proper procedure.

Relationships in the working environment

> **Test your understanding 6**
>
> Clearly Daniel must take hold of his situation and the present problems he is faced with. He needs to create contact time with his staff on an individual basis, and should aim to observe such aspects as behaviour, and working patterns in more detail than has been exercised in the past. In relation to the previous aspects his main aim should be to determine the culture of this old-established department. From this he should be able to analyse and establish the cause of the problems experienced.
>
> Once he has put into operation a careful analysis of the existing problems, Daniel must take on a more appropriate and productive style of leadership. The style he uses will be determined by several points. These include his choice of style, the style operated by his predecessor, the nature of the task, the qualifications gained and status enjoyed by those lower than himself. Also the problems of resentment, fear, poor co-operation, and the accusations of arbitrary decision-making must be tackled.
>
> Based upon the information presently available, Daniel should attempt to adopt a participative team management style of leadership. His staff clearly would welcome regular consultation on matters related to their work. The older members of the department who possess valuable experience should be utilised and acknowledged by Daniel.
>
> They are a means of resource to help him run the department. If he communicates with them he will reduce their feelings of resentment towards him, and the level of criticism he is presently experiencing. He should also aim to involve them in the process of decision-making, thus avoiding criticism in connection with arbitrary or risky decisions.
>
> Daniel should aim to improve communication in terms of staff briefing and should be prepared to offer some explanation behind his decisions. A system of departmental briefing should perhaps be established on a weekly basis adopting a semi-formal approach. Younger members of the department require regular communication regarding appraisal, and a system of feedback should be established for their benefit. They will then know their current position and progress. Finally, in terms of Daniel's communication skills he must aim to keep in touch with his team at all times, ensuring that group behavioural patterns, attitudes and work practices are beneficial to the whole department.
>
> Daniel should also aim to attend a management training course, as this can only serve to improve his understanding and approach.

Test your understanding 7

(a) Mentoring is the use of an especially trained individual, or one with particular skills to provide guidance and direction to the trainee, who is often a new recruit possibly at a management level. A mentor would be appointed from within the organisation, not necessarily from the same department as the mentee. If the mentor is from the same department, they would not usually be a direct manager. Where, for example a member of staff is a CIMA student, the mentor may be a qualified member of CIMA from another department. The mentor will usually be a more senior member of staff with knowledge and experience that they are willing share with newer, less experienced member of staff.

Mentoring is a relationship where one person helps another to improve their knowledge, work or thinking. It is a very valuable development tool for both the person seeking support (the mentee) and the person giving the support (the mentor).

(b) There are many benefits from mentoring. There are career-enhancing benefits and personal developmental benefits. From a career-enhancing perspective, the mentor can provide technical help and study support. The mentee is able to discuss openly areas of weakness within their role and the mentor would be able to provide practical advice as to how to overcome these weaknesses. Mentors can help in advising on routes for career development.

Mentoring can also help new members of staff settle in to the organisation, but helping them understand the culture and what is expected of them. This would build the new member of staff's confidence and help them to feel part of the organisation, this will improve their motivation as they feel more able to contribute.

Mentoring can also help improve performance. Where staff come across new challenges or issues that they have never dealt with before, they could discuss these with their mentor rather than their line manager and the mentor may be able to give advice as to how to handle these new issues.

Test your understanding 8

Embedding finance personnel in the business

The finance function plays a critical role in providing information for decision-making.

In the new business environment where competition is global and fierce, companies need better information than ever before in order to remain competitive. Organisations and their chief executive officers now expect finance directors and financial controllers to become more involved in matters of production, distribution and sales to play a fuller role at a strategic management level, in particular helping to decide which markets to serve with which products.

Decisions are only as good as the information on which they are based. Providing this information as and when required relies on thorough knowledge of the core of the business. It can therefore be argued that a company should consider retaining the finance function in-house and positioning it within the business units which it serves.

In this way, finance becomes a part of the business process in a role which is fully integrated into the strategic and daily business activities of the organisation.

An alternative to the embedded finance function is the **shared service centre (SSC)**. This refers to the provision of a service by one part of an organisation or group where that service had previously been found in more than one part of the organisation or group. An example would be a large multinational organisation with financial processing centres in all or several of the countries in which it operates, chooses to consolidate these activities at one site.

Benefits of SSC:

- Headcount reductions
- Cost savings through economies of scale, and reduced labour costs by locating the centre in an area with favourable labour rates
- Maintain internal control
- Best practice can be identified
- Consistency of approach throughout the organisation.

Disadvantages of SSC:

- Loss of business knowledge
- Further from the everyday decision making
- Business relationships are not as strong.

Business Process Outsourcing (BPO)

Business Process Outsourcing (BPO) is contracting with a third party (external supplier) to provide part or all of a business process or function. Many of these BPO efforts involve offshoring.

Offshoring is a type of outsourcing and simply means having the outsourced business function done in another country.

Benefits of outsourcing:

- Cost reduction through economies of scale by using standardised procedures and leading edge technology. Suppliers can perform finance and administration functions far more cheaply and efficiently than companies working on their own.
- Access to capabilities and expertise of the provider. The outsourcing partner will be a specialist provider and so can bring best practice expertise and new investment in resources.
- Outsourcing financial operations can encourage business to be more innovative and focused on value creation. It can free up the time of the remaining finance personnel to focus on value adding activities.

Drawbacks of outsourcing:

- Loss of control. External providers are now relied upon to input the right level of resource and skill required to meet the organisational needs.
- Risk to innovation. Over-reliance on external providers can lead to an erosion of internal knowledge and skills.
- Risk to competitive advantage. Confidentiality and risk to intellectual property are often cited as key reasons why companies choose not to outsource to an external provider.
- Unsatisfactory quality and service or even failure of supplier.

chapter 10

Management control

Chapter learning objectives

- Analyse the relationship between managers and their subordinates, including legal aspects affecting work and employment.

- Compare and contrast ways to deal effectively with discipline problems.

Management control

1 Session content diagram

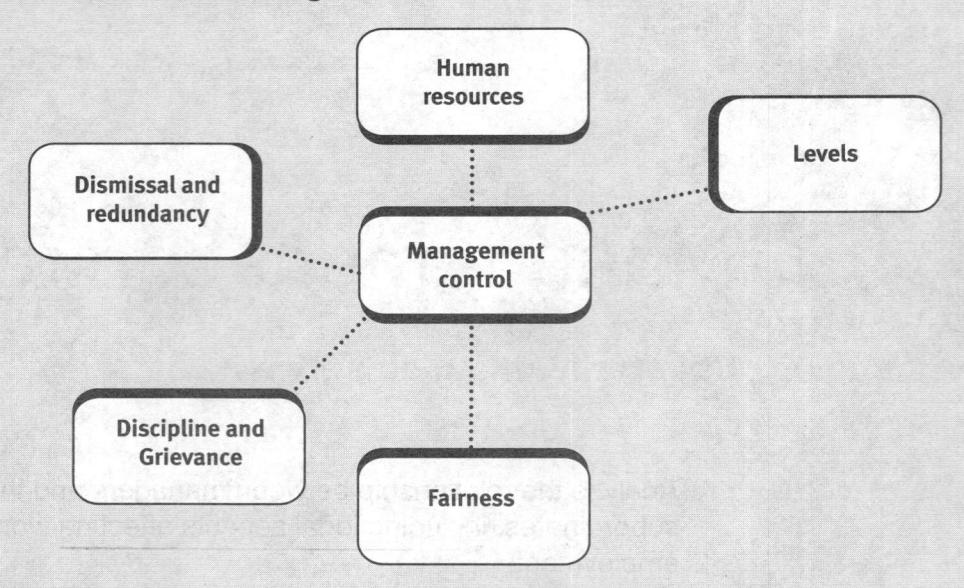

[Diagram: Management control connected to Human resources, Levels, Fairness, Discipline and Grievance, and Dismissal and redundancy]

2 What is control?

An underlying feature of the relationship between managers and their subordinates is management control. Most definitions of management include control or controlling as a function, it is essentially a means of ensuring that the objectives of the organisations are met. One definition of control is:

Control is a primary task and is the process of ensuring the operations proceed according to plan.

The classical approach to management views control as an essential feature of the formal organisation and hierarchical structure of authority. This approach is based on routine procedures, rules and regulations to achieve consistent and predictable behaviour.

A key feature of the scientific management school is the use of job, process analysis and time study to establish the optimum production methods and rates. The worker is not left any discretion to make mistakes. The principles of scientific management make the workplace much simpler for managers to control. It is easier to measure inputs and outputs and compare the performance of workers. A control system to result from this management theory was standard costing, inputs could be planned, costs could be established and variations highlighted. By adding budgeting to include overheads, a powerful control mechanism is available.

The problem with this type of approach to management control, like the problem with the classical management theories, is that it fails to take account of the human element.

A focus on this type of control could lead to:

- Motivation problems. Lack of morale; little worker commitment; no interchangeable skills (people were only trained to do one small part of the job); high staff turnover.
- Quality problems. No overall responsibility; no intrinsic satisfaction from work.
- Little understanding of people. People at work are not necessarily rational, for example they do not always work harder to earn more money and they are sometimes less inclined to work well if closely supervised; budgets sometimes cause problems, for example people might be inclined to purchase poor quality raw materials to stay within budget, thus causing production problems.

The human relations approach emphasises the social organisation and the importance of informal relationships. Elton Mayo's studies on how to improve productivity revealed that work groups impose their own controls on members, such as the rate of work, the vision of work, the members' interaction with managers. This control was imposed through a series of 'punishments', for example ostracising members who were persuaded to comply with the objectives of management rather than the norms set by the group.

Control is, therefore, a feature of interpersonal influences rather than close and constant supervision, recognising that people do not behave as unfeeling robots. This has an impact on control systems, so for example effective budgetary control systems need to recognise the need to involve operational staff in setting budgets so that the staff feel ownership of the budget, and to help avoid demotivating staff with unachievable budget targets.

The contingency approach to management views organisational control as a variable and the nature of effective control will depend on the particular situation. Hence, when considering control in organisations, a control system needs to be unique to that organisation and tailored to meet the needs of a particular organisation, or part of the organisation.

Basic control model

Management accountants should be familiar with the basic (TARA) control system, such as a budgetary control system. In this model:

- T – a standard or **target** is set

- A – the **actual** result is measured
- R – the actual **result** is compared to the standard
- A – **action** (feedback and feedforward) can be used depending on the results

Here we are looking at control in the context of management of relationships, but the same basic structure can be used. Choice of the specific controls to use depends on the reason a system is likely to be out of control, that is the risks to the achievement of the objectives of the system being controlled.

Within the context of human relations management, control will require to be exercised over the recruitment of staff, their performance and legal requirements connected with employment.

When answering questions on management control, two approaches can be used:

- The TARA framework: Go through the stages of the TARA framework, considering the targets which should be set, how the actual results will be measured and compared to the target, and what action should be taken as a result.
- Common sense: in many of the areas of control within an organisation, a common sense approach can be taken. With this approach, consider what needs to be controlled and the best way to control it effectively.

Types of organisational control

- *Personal centralised control.* This approach is likely to be found in small owner-managed organisations where there is centralised decision-making by the owner. Reward and punishment will reinforce conformity to personal authority. Control is carried out by the owner through personal supervision. The authority is based on rights of ownership, charisma or technical expertise. However, as the organisation grows in size and complexity, owners may find increasing external demands on their time and will need to employ others to undertake supervision of day-to-day tasks. In this phase of growth, control moves away from personal centralised control to more bureaucratic control or output control.

- *Bureaucratic control.* Controls will be based on formalised rules, procedures, standardisation and hierarchy. This is achieved through specifications of how employees should behave and carry out their work using formal job descriptions and specification of standard methods for performance of tasks. Reward and punishment systems can be used to reinforce this control strategy. Managers will typically use budgets and standard cost accounting systems.

- *Output control.* This approach is a form of control that is based on the measurement of outputs and the results achieved. It is most appropriate where there is a need for quantifiable and simple measures of organisational performance since it requires a specification of output standards and targets to be achieved. This approach facilitates delegation without the need for bureaucratic controls, because once output standards have been agreed, employees can work semi-autonomously to carry out tasks.

- *Clan or Cultural control.* This form of control requires the development of employees' strong identification with management goals, for example through professional identification and acceptance of the values and beliefs of the organisation. If employees have the necessary skills, experience and ability, they can be given freedom in deciding how to undertake their tasks. This leads to semi-autonomous working with few formal controls. This approach depends on the common agreement of objectives and shared cultural values. It will require careful selection, socialisation and development of employees.

Internal control

Internal control systems exist to enhance the achievement of organisational objectives. They promote the orderly and efficient conduct of business, help keep the business on course, and help it change safely.

In CIMA's framework of control, the control system is seen as consisting of:

- The control environment – management philosophy, operating style and management policies;
- Control procedures – control mechanisms such as segregation of duties, authorisation, reconciliation and so on.

For control over relationships, some of the controls, such as those over contracts and dismissal may be formal (or legal) in nature, whereas others, such as staff appraisal may be informal (or managerial).

Committee of Sponsoring Organisations (COSO)

The COSO model recommends that effective control systems should contain the following elements:

- *The control environment*, which includes the company's strategy for dealing with risk, its culture, codes of conduct, human resource policies and performance reward systems, all of which should support the business objectives.

- *An assessment of risk* to the achievement of the company's objectives, including its compliance with legislation, and an analysis of the objectives of control.
- *Control activities*, for example segregation of duties, authorisation, reconciliations.
- *Communication* and information to ensure that all levels of management in the organisation, but particularly the board, receive timely, relevant and reliable reports on progress against objectives.
- *Monitoring and corrective action* processes embedded in the organisational systems to ensure the effective application of policies and other control mechanisms.

The COSO model places a emphasis on risk assessment and risk management. Risk assessment and risk management are now seen as fundamental to an effective control system. An understanding of the risks specific to an organisation means that the control system can be tailored exactly to the needs of that organisation. This increases its effectiveness by ensuring that significant risks are addressed and reduced costs by ensuring that only the minimum control necessary is in place.

Levels of control

Strategic

This is the level of control operating at board level. It will largely consist of the **setting of the control environment**:

- Strategic planning – determining course to be taken.
- Board procedures – appointment of directors, segregation of duties and so on.
- Setting and reviewing organisational structure.
- Policies on the conduct of the business, financial and other performance measures, risk assessments, environmental and ethical issues and so on.
- Monitoring achievement of and compliance with plans and policies set.

At this level policies on recruitment, selection, appraisal, discipline, training and reward of employees will be set.

Tactical

This is control at the middle management level of the organisation. As an example, strategic control is the responsibility of the production director, tactical control is the responsibility of the production manager, the purchasing manager, and so on who report to the production director. At this level, controls should be in place to **implement the decisions and policies of the board**. Controls at this level include:

- Tactical planning, determining the production requirements and production schedule.
- Production budget.
- Procedures governing recruitment, training, and risk management to name but a few.
- Monitoring the achievement to plans and policies set.

At this level procedures for control the recruitment, selection, appraisal, discipline, training and reward of employees will be established and monitored.

Operational

This occurs at the lower levels of the organisation. Operational controls are designed to **control structured repetitive activities** according to preset rules. For example computerised stock control systems, production scheduling and order processing systems.

The six As of an effective control system

To be effective, a control system should have the following characteristics:

- Acceptable – to the people using it
- Appropriate – for the people using it
- Accessible – simple as possible, and only as technical as necessary
- Action-oriented – timely corrective action should be taken
- Adaptable – flexible to suit changing conditions
- Affordable – cost beneficial

Practical difficulties with control

- many systems are based on forecasting the future, the information is not available or too expensive or time consuming to collect.
- it is not always easy to set the standard to be achieved.
- it is not easy to persuade the people of the need for action.
- control systems often bridge two or more areas of activity and it is difficult to provide everyone with the information they need.
- the accurate, timely internal information that many controls rely on is difficult enough to obtain.
- external information is even harder to obtain for benchmarking.
- it is not always easy to distinguish between controllable and uncontrollable aspects of the operations.

3 Reporting structures

Reporting structures must be in place to ensure that control is effective.

Strategic management must cascade information down through the organisation on the policies they have set. It is essential that all members of the organisation are aware of the policies. The tactical management must then cascade the details of the procedures to the operational levels of the organisation.

At the operational level, the controls set by the procedures should be enforced and any issues must be reported back up through the organisation for corrective action. For example any breaches of health and safety will be discovered at the operational level. These issues must be recorded and reported to management. Depending on the seriousness of the breach, the procedures set by the tactical level may have to be updated, or if deemed very serious, these would be reported to senior management and policies may have to be changed to avoid further breaches.

Human resources departments will have responsibility for much of the reporting in this area. In terms of discipline and grievance for example, all issues must be carefully documented and reported to ensure that the legal requirements have been met and so that senior management are aware of any ongoing issues within the organisation.

chapter 10

Test your understanding 1

S Company develops accountancy software for small-to medium-sized businesses. S Company was established 15 years ago by a graduate in accounting. Despite an increasingly competitive environment, it has grown and diversified to become a global provider of specialised accountancy software.

In order to cope with the increasing size and diversity of the business, additional levels of management and control systems have been introduced, including additional policies, rules and procedures. Unfortunately, the increase in bureaucracy is having the effect of slowing down decision-making processes and limiting ideas for new software development.

The Chief Executive Officer is aware of the conflict between the structural changes and the need for continuous creativity and innovation that are critical to new software development and the future success of the business, but is not sure how to overcome the problem.

Required:

Explain why formal control systems are increasingly necessary as an organisation grows and diversifies and why the use of bureaucratic forms of control in S Company might limit creativity and innovation.

(10 marks)

Control systems in practice

In today's organisations, one of the most important systems of control is the human resources system. The quality of an organisation's employees is fundamental to its success. It is essential for the organisation to get its people system right.

Human Resources are largely responsible for ensuring a number of employment practices are in place in the organisation. These should all contribute to the effectiveness of the organisation.

Some of these, such as appraisal systems, are management controls, while others are legal requirements.

All of the following control systems will be discussed further in this chapter:

- Appraisal system
- Health and Safety

- Discipline and Grievance
- Dismissal and Redundancy
- Fairness in the workplace – Diversity and Equal Opportunities
- Contracts of employment
- Working time and childcare

Note: all legal requirements referred to in this chapter are based on UK legislation, unless otherwise stated.

4 Performance appraisal

A performance appraisal system involves the regular and systematic review of performance and assessment of potential, with the aim of producing action programmes to develop both work and individuals.

Performance appraisal can help improve the efficiency and effectiveness of an organisation. The appraisal system is used by organisations to review, change, inform, monitor, examine and evaluate employees. Through evaluation, it plays a key role in organisational control. It also serves to develop and motivate employees.

Effective appraisal

To be effective, the system must:

- Be applied fairly and consistently
- Have the commitment and support from senior managers
- Be carried out with serious intent
- Relate to the main objectives of organisation
- Be clearly understood by all parties
- Be cost effective to operate

Benefits to organisation

- Provides a system for assessing competence of employees and identifies areas for improvement
- Provides a fair process for reward decisions
- Identifies candidates for promotion, early retirement etc

- Helps identify and formulate training needs
- Improves communication between managers and subordinates
- Provides clear targets linked to corporate objectives
- Provides a basis for HR planning
- Monitors recruitment and induction process against results

Benefits to employees

- Feedback about performance at work and an assessment of competence through comparison of performance against established standards and agreed targets
- Identifies work of particular merit done during review period
- Provides a basis for remuneration
- May be used as an opportunity to discuss future prospects and ambitions
- Identifies training and development needs

Barriers to effective performance appraisal

One aspect of this typical performance appraisal system that can reduce its effectiveness is the appraisal interview. Poor performance appraisal interviews can be confrontational, judgemental, just a chat, a paper exercise, a substitute for the management process that should be undertaken during the year and/or out of date and irrelevant because it is annual, that is things have changed in the year.

Barriers to effective appraisal may be overcome if:

- There is commitment from all parties involved
- There is a system of follow up and feedback
- Recorded agreement between manager and employee about future training and development. Training should be arranged within an agreed time period.
- Alternative methods of appraisal could be used:
  - Self-assessment, which offers the advantage of increasing the employee's responsibility as well as saving the manager's time. However, people are often not the best judge of their own performance and this reduces the effectiveness of the control it offers.

- A combination of self-assessment and assessment by the manager, which offers the advantages of self-assessment but takes more time and means there is a negotiation to reconcile the two opinions.
- 360-degree appraisal, where the reporting process is informed by subordinates of the person reported on, their peers, their customers (internal and external as appropriate) as well as their line manager. This provides a fuller view of performance but is time-consuming and, again, leaves different views to be reconciled.

Evaluating the effectiveness of an appraisal system

Evaluating the effectiveness of the appraisal system

Evaluating the appraisal scheme can involve the following:

- Cost and benefit analysis.
- Investigating if there have been improvements in performance of individuals and the organisation.
- Asking appraisers and appraisees their opinions on the process.
- Monitor performance results.
- Monitoring take up of training and development opportunities.
- Monitoring succession and promotion processes and results.
- Reviewing staff turnover to identify cause of staff leaving.

Drucker – management by objectives

A model which can expand on the setting of targets within the appraisal system is **Drucker's Management by objectives**. Management by objectives can be defined as a type of control strategy which focuses on controlling outputs. Within this model Drucker emphasised that if corporate objectives are to be effective, they must be stated in behavioural or measurable terms, so that any deviation can be highlighted at an early enough stage to permit corrections to be made

This is a process whereby individual goals are integrated with the corporate plan, as part of an ongoing programme of goal setting and performance review involving all levels of management.

Many people have responsibility in an organisation, but managers are held accountable for the work of others as well as their own. Managers, when setting objectives, have a responsibility to:

- agree their own departmental targets with their superiors;
- discuss and agree targets for their staff that are achievable;
- ensure that all targets set are measurable and possible, and that resources are made available together with some setting of priorities;
- ensure that there is a balance between the goals and needs of departments and individuals;
- apply the control system and discuss progress with staff at regular intervals. Where staff jointly set objectives with their manager they achieve valuable feedback on performance, a motivating factor acknowledged by Herzberg.
- ensure continual review and appraisal of results.

Drucker's key objectives

Drucker argues that the nature of the business organisation requires multiple objectives to cover every area where performance and results affect the business.

Drucker suggested the following eight key objectives:

(1) *Profitability* – Growth in earnings per share. At some stage in the planning procedure, probably at the time of developing the strategic plan, this objective will need to be translated into targets for control linking sales, profit and capital employed.

(2) *Innovation* – The board must determine whether it intends to lead in developing technology and products, to follow other companies or to design to meet customer needs.

(3) *Market standing* – Overall marketing policies and objectives such as which products to sell and in which markets.

(4) *Productivity* – Productivity targets will be set in terms of output in relation to manpower, plant, material yields and costs.

(5) *Financial and physical resources* – Financing both working and long-term capital requirements through debt and shares. Physical resource objectives will include the location and acquisition of physical resources over the planning period, whether to lease or buy the assets, etc.

> (6) *Managerial performance and development* – Policies and objectives will cover matters such as organisation and development; measures of performance; training and development; reward systems and organisational culture.
>
> (7) *Worker performance and attitude* – Policies and objectives will cover the development of management and worker relationships.
>
> (8) *Public responsibility* – There may well be objectives relating to social responsibility and business ethics.
>
> Not all of these will apply to all organisations, and emphasis could change in response to environmental changes. The need for balancing objectives is obvious. There has to be a balance between profit and the demands of the future (short-, medium-, and long-term).

5 Health and Safety

A legal requirement which management must adhere to is health and safety legislation. Management have a responsibility to manage the health and safety risks in their workplace. They must think about what, in their organisation, might cause harm to people and ensure that they are doing enough to prevent that harm.

Management must identify the health and safety risks within their organisations and decide how to control them and put the appropriate measures in place.

The Health and Safety at Work Act (HASAWA)

In the UK, the Health and Safety at Work Act 1974 (HASAWA) requires every organisation employing five or more persons to prepare and regularly revise a health and safety policy statement of:

- their policy for health and safety
- the organisation to enforce it
- the arrangements to implement it

and bring it to the attention of the employees.

The following are key areas:

- Provision and maintenance of risk-free plant and systems of work.
- Ensuring the safety in use, handling, storage and transport of articles and substances.

- Provision of information, training, instruction and supervision.
- Maintenance of a safe workplace.
- Provision of means of entry and exit.
- Provision of a safe working environment.
- Adequate facilities.

A *senior member* of the organisation should be responsible for implementing the policy and may be supported by safety officers.

Employees also have basic responsibilities in this regard.

Most companies have a *safety committee and representatives* who have some experience, are entitled to training and are consulted about arrangements to ensure the effectiveness of the health and safety policy implementation.

The Health & Safety Executive (HSE)

The Health & Safety Executive is an independent regulator with the duty to make adequate provision for the enforcement of the HASAWA. The main function of the HSE is providing workplace inspections to ensure compliance with the law and enforce the legal requirements, if necessary. The HSE also provides an advisory service to employers and unions.

Safety committee and meetings

One rule requires organisations to have a method of communicating and evaluating safety and health issues brought up by management or employees in their workplace. Larger employers must establish a safety committee. Smaller employers have the choice of either establishing a safety committee or holding safety meetings with a management representative present.

There is a difference between a safety committee and a safety meeting:

- A safety committee is an organisational structure where members represent a group. This gives everyone a voice but keeps the meeting size to an effective number of participants.
- A safety meeting includes all employees and a management person is there to ensure that issues are addressed. Typically, the safety committee is an effective safety management tool for a larger employer and safety meetings are more effective for a smaller employer.

Health and safety training

The Health and Safety at Work Act imposes a duty on employers to provide training to ensure a healthy and safe workplace. As well as being a way to obtain compliance with health and safety regulations, safety training enhances employees' knowledge, understanding and commitment.

Organisations implement safety training because it improves job knowledge and skills and ensures optimum employee performance at a specified level. In health and safety training, specified performance standards include attention to safety rules and regulations regarding safe work behaviour. All new staff under **induction** must receive training that ensures their safety both in normal working conditions and in cases of emergency.

Monitoring policy

Safety specialists argue that the safety policy should reflect the employer's commitment to develop safe systems of work and to pursue a healthy work environment.

There is a growing awareness that, in practice, many employers are turning a blind eye to health and safety requirements.

Furthermore, many safety policies are not that helpful in practice because of the failure to monitor their relevance to workplace arrangements, inadequate training, and supervisors and safety officers lacking authority to make decisions.

A proactive approach would involve Human Resources regularly checking to ensure that safety policies, management procedures and arrangements are working and are changed to suit new developments or work structures in the workplace.

Benefits of health and safety controls

- Employers' legal obligations for health and safety are being met.
- Cost savings – accidents and illness cost the employer money – legal damages and operating costs.
- Company image – company does not want to be associated with a poor health and safety record.
- To preserve the well-being of employees and others, improves employee morale, trust and motivation.

More detail on health and safety training

Health and safety training

- First, problems or training needs are identified by inspection, by accident reports and through discussion at the health and safety committee.
- Next, the planning, execution and evaluation of the training takes place.
- Because training programmes only have a short-term effect on employee's behaviour, regular refresher courses should be organised.
- Top management support is a key ingredient in the availability and success of health and safety courses.

Test your understanding 2

Required:

(a) Outline the main features of health and safety legislation.

(4 marks)

(b) Identify those responsible for ensuring that the organisation is a safe place in which to work.

(6 marks)

6 Discipline

The word discipline is used and understood in several different ways. It brings to mind the use of authority or force. To many, it primarily carries the disagreeable meaning of punishment. However, there is another way of thinking about discipline, based on the meaning of the original Latin distipulus – a learner or pupil. Discipline means learning, as in the discipline of management, along a set of rules.

Maintaining discipline (learning) among employees is an integral part of the functions of management. Discipline is present when the members of the enterprise follow goals or objectives sensibly without overt conflict and conduct themselves according to the standards of acceptable behaviour.

Discipline therefore can be considered as positive when employees willingly follow or go beyond the rules of the enterprise. Discipline is negative when employees follow the rules over-strictly, or disobey regulations and violate standards of acceptable behaviour.

The main purpose of taking disciplinary action is to achieve a change in behaviour of employees so that future action is unnecessary.

Disciplinary situations

There are several situations where work norms might not be adhered to and which would cause problems if there were no remedial action:

- leaving work early, lateness, absenteeism;
- defective and/or inadequate work performance;
- breaking safety or other rules, regulations and procedures;
- refusing to carry out a legitimate work assignment;
- poor attitudes which influence the work of others or which reflect on the public image of the firm, such as improper personal appearance.

The statutory procedures and the Code of Practice

Although organisations can be flexible about how formal or extensive their procedures need to be, there is a statutory procedure they must follow as a minimum if they are contemplating dismissing an employee – or imposing certain kinds of penalty short of dismissal such as suspension without pay or demotion. Unless employers follow the statutory procedure, employment tribunals will automatically find dismissals unfair.

The statutory procedure involves the following three steps:

- A statement in writing of what it is the employee is alleged to have done.
- A meeting to discuss the situation.
- The right of appeal.

The statutory procedure is the minimum standard. Employment tribunals expect employers to behave fairly and reasonably.

Disciplinary procedures are an aid to the effective management of people, and should not be viewed primarily as a means of imposing sanctions or as leading to dismissal. Where dismissal does occur, employees may make a complaint to an employment tribunal if they believe they have been unfairly dismissed, although ordinarily the employee must have one year's service.

It is for the employer to show the reason for the dismissal and that it was a fair reason.

The tribunal will determine whether the dismissal was fair or unfair and will take into account the size and administrative resources of the employer in deciding whether they acted reasonably or unreasonably. The tribunal consider how far the statutory procedures have been followed. Employment Tribunals expect employers to behave fairly and reasonably.

In the United Kingdom, there exists a set of advisory booklets about various employment practices published by the Advisory Conciliation and Arbitration Service (ACAS). These are often used as yardsticks against which internal disciplinary procedures are judged to be fair or reasonable. The disciplinary code of practice provides guidance on good practice in disciplinary and grievance matters in employment, and includes information on the right to be accompanied at a disciplinary or grievance hearing.

The stages involved in a disciplinary process

Employees need to be aware that certain actions will lead to disciplinary action.

Rules will normally cover issues such as absence, timekeeping and holiday arrangements, health and safety, use of the organisation's equipment and facilities, misconduct, sub-standard performance, discrimination, bullying and harassment.

Rules and procedures should be clear, and should preferably be put in writing. They should be known and understood by all employees.

Standards for handling disciplinary procedures:

- The informal talk.
- The oral warning.
- The written or official warning – first; second.
- Disciplinary layoffs or suspension.
- Demotion or transfer.

Standards need to be set for the right to appeal against these procedures.

In a well-managed organisation disciplinary procedures may not be needed very often. But if a problem does arise then they are vital. Good procedures can help organisations to resolve problems internally – and avoid employment tribunal claims.

ACAS code of practice

In the United Kingdom, there exists a set of advisory booklets about various employment practices published by the Advisory Conciliation and Arbitration Service (ACAS). These are often used as yardsticks against which internal disciplinary procedures are judged to be fair or reasonable. The disciplinary code of practice states that disciplinary procedures should:

- be in writing;
- specify to whom they apply;
- provide for matters to be dealt with quickly;
- indicate the disciplinary actions which may be taken;
- specify the levels of management which have the authority to take the various forms of disciplinary action;
- provide for individuals to be informed of the complaints against them and to be given an opportunity to reply;
- give individuals the right to be accompanied by a trade union representative or by a fellow employee;
- ensure that, except for gross misconduct, no employees are dismissed for a first breach of discipline;
- ensure that disciplinary action is not taken until the case has been carefully investigated;
- ensure that individuals are given an explanation for any penalty imposed;
- provide a right of appeal and specify the procedure to be followed.

Other recommended procedures:

- provide for individuals to be informed of the nature of their alleged misconduct;
- allow individuals to state their case, and to be accompanied by a fellow employee (or union representative);
- ensure that every case is properly investigated before any disciplinary action is taken;
- ensure that employees are informed of the reasons for any penalty they receive;
- state that no employee will be dismissed for a first offence, except in cases of gross misconduct;
- provide for a right of appeal against any disciplinary action, and specify the appeals procedure.

Handling discipline

Encourage improvement

The main purpose of operating a disciplinary procedure is to encourage improvement in an employee whose conduct or performance is below acceptable standards.

Act promptly

Problems dealt with early enough can be 'nipped in the bud', whereas delay can make things worse as the employee may not realise that they are below standard unless they are told. Arrange to speak to the employee as soon as possible – the matter may then be able to be dealt with in an informal manner and not as part of the disciplinary process.

Gather the facts

Whilst maintaining satisfactory standards and dealing with disciplinary issues requires firmness on the part of the manager, it also requires fairness. Be as objective as possible, keep an open mind, and do not prejudge the issues.

Having gathered all the facts, the manager or supervisor should decide whether to:

- drop the matter – there may be no case to answer or the matter may be regarded as trivial.
- arrange counselling/take informal action – this is an attempt to correct a situation and prevent it from getting worse without using the disciplinary procedure.
- arrange a disciplinary meeting – this will be necessary when the matter is considered serious enough to require disciplinary action.

Stay calm

Conduct enquiries, investigations and proceedings with thought and care.

Be consistent

The attitude and conduct of employees may be seriously affected if management fails to apply the same rules and considerations to each case.

Consider each case on its merits

While consistency is important, it is also essential to take account of the circumstances and people involved.

Follow the disciplinary procedure

The disciplinary procedure must be followed and the supervisor or manager should never exceed the limits of his or her authority.

If the employee is dismissed or suffers a disciplinary penalty short of dismissal – such as suspension without pay – the statutory minimum procedures must have been followed.

Suspension with pay

Where there appears to be serious misconduct, or risk to property or other people, a period of suspension with pay should be considered while the case is being investigated.

Self-discipline

Self-discipline is based upon socialisation, producing norms which follow reasonable standards of acceptable behaviour. Positive self-discipline is based upon the premise that most employees want to do the right thing. Most people accept the idea that following instructions and fair rules of conduct is part of the work ethic.

Once employees know what is expected of them and feel that the rules are reasonable, self-disciplined behaviour becomes a part of collective attitudes and group norms (i.e. the way in which employees behave as a work group), enabling 'responsible autonomy'. When new rules are introduced, the manager must try to convince employees of their purpose and reasonableness. If the work group as a whole accepts change, a strong sense of group cohesiveness on the employees' part will usually exert group pressure on possible dissenters, thus reducing the need for corrective action.

Douglas McGregor's 'hot stove rule'

This rule draws a comparison between touching a hot stove and experiencing discipline. When one touches a hot stove, the reaction is immediate, consistent, impersonal and with warning. The burn is immediate, with no questions of cause and effect. There is a warning, because everyone knows what happens if one touches a stove when the stove is red hot. The result is consistent; every time a person touches a hot stove, he is burned. The result is impersonal; whoever touches a hot stove is burned. One is burned because of what he or she does, because the stove is touched, not because of who the person is. The comparison between the 'hot stove rule' and disciplinary action is that discipline should be directed against the act and not against the person.

Immediacy means that after noticing the offence, the supervisor proceeds to take disciplinary action as speedily as possible, normally the preliminary informal investigation.

For example, emotional incidents such as arguments in public or insubordination often require immediate response.

Test your understanding 3

Three employees come back late from lunch. One just started work a few days ago, the second has been warned about this once before, the third employee has been late on numerous previous occasions.

Required:

Suggest appropriate measures which should be taken against each member of staff.

(3 marks)

7 Grievance procedures

Grievance procedures are not the same as disciplinary procedures. A grievance occurs when an employee feels superiors or colleagues are wrongly treating him or her; e.g. unfair appraisal, discrimination, prevented from advancing, being picked on, etc.

The grievance procedure often follows this sequence:

- The employee discusses the grievance with a colleague, staff or union representative.

- If the grievance is warranted, it is taken to the employee's immediate superior.
- If that superior cannot help, then it is referred to the superior's manager, at which stage the HR or Personnel department should be informed.
- Distinction should be made between an individual and a collective grievance.
- The colleague, staff or union representative should be permitted to be involved.
- Time-frames and deadlines should be stated to resolve the issue or submit an appeal.

Tribunals

A company may find that an employee is not happy with the outcome of a grievance procedure and that the individual wants to make a claim to an employment tribunal.

Employment tribunals are independent judicial bodies, less formal than a court, established to hear and determine claims to do with employment matters. Their aim is to resolve disputes between employers and employees over employment rights.

Examples include:

- unfair dismissal
- breach of contract
- discrimination
- equal pay.

Resolving disputes without a tribunal

In some cases it is possible to resolve disputes without the need for a tribunal. The following techniques may be used:

Arbitration

- used to decide cases of alleged unfair dismissal or claims under flexible working legislation.
- independent arbitrator hears the case and delivers a legally binding decision in favour of one party.

Benefits include:

- Speedy private informal hearing.
- No cross-examination.
- Limited grounds for review of the arbitrator's decision.

Conciliation

This can be used to settle a dispute before it gets to a tribunal hearing.

Benefits include:

- Confidentiality.
- Avoid time, stress and cost of attending a tribunal.
- Lessening damage to the employment relationship.
- Reaching an agreement that satisfies both parties.

Benefits of discipline and grievance procedure

- Employer's legal obligations are being met.
- Cost savings – legal damages and operating costs.
- Company image – company does not want to be associated with a discipline and grievance record.
- To preserve the well-being of employees and others, improves employee morale, trust and motivation.

Test your understanding 4

Peter Allan has worked in the customer services department of LMR company for two years. Last week he was sent to meet with Marcus Jones, a senior Human Resources manager.

At the meeting, which lasted less than ten minutes, Peter was told that the company were very unhappy with his performance and that his attitude was 'not as it should be'. He was informed that, in accordance with the company's discipline code, he was being demoted to a lower graded role in the credit control department and that this was with immediate effect.

Peter was shocked by this as he had never been informed of the company's unhappiness with him before and he was confused about the comment about his attitude. He had always enjoyed his job, and thought he got on well with his colleagues. He had also never heard of the company's discipline code.

Required:

Discuss what LMR have done wrong in the handling of this case and explain to Peter the actions which are available to him regarding this decision.

(10 marks)

8 Dismissal and redundancy

What is dismissal?

Under UK law, dismissal is described as *termination of employment* with or without notice by the employer, or in the case of *constructive dismissal*, resignation by the employee because the conduct of the employer was sufficient to be deemed to have terminated the contract by the employer's actions. Dismissal without notice is usually *wrongful dismissal*, that is breach of the contract of employment; it may or may not also be *unfair dismissal*.

Dismissal is normally fair only if the employer can show that it is for one of the following reasons:

- a reason related to the employee's **conduct**.
- a reason related to the employee's **capability** or qualifications for the job.
- because the employee was **redundant**.
- because a **statutory duty** or restriction prohibited the employment being continued.
- some **other substantial reason** of a kind which justifies the dismissal and that the employer acted reasonably in treating that reason as sufficient for dismissal.

> **Types of dismissal**
>
> - Constructive dismissal – resignation by the employee because the conduct of the employer was sufficient to be deemed to have terminated the contract by the employer's actions.
>
> - Wrongful (unfair) dismissal – dismissal without notice, a breach of the contract of employment.
>
>   For a dismissal to be fair, the employer must show that the reason for the dismissal is of a type acceptable under statute.

What is redundancy?

Redundancy is a dismissal. The grounds of redundancy may be justified on any of the following grounds:

- cessation of business;
- cessation of business in the place where the employee was employed;
- cessation of the type of work for which he or she was employed.

For the purposes of the right to be consulted, which applies when an employer proposes to make 20 or more employees redundant over 90 days or less, the law defines redundancy as: 'dismissal for a reason not related to the individual concerned or for a number of reasons all of which are not so related'. This definition might include, for example, a situation where dismissals are not related to the conduct or capability of the individuals but are part of a reorganisation.

> **Test your understanding 5**
>
> D Company, a national airline carrier, has made a net loss for the last five years. While its major competitors have pursued programmes of modernisation, D Company has been left behind and is reported to have administrative costs and average salary costs that are, respectively, 35% and 25% higher than those of its competitors. The use of outdated and fuel-inefficient aircraft, as well as a reluctance to make use of modern Internet systems for online reservation, have been among the factors that have contributed to D Company's decline.

> The board of D Company has produced a restructuring plan that includes 5,000 job cuts out of a workforce of 50,000; new, more demanding employment conditions; the sale of non-core assets; the establishment of twelve profit centres; a reduction in routes flown; replacement of its ageing fleet with fewer but more fuel-efficient aircraft and a complete overhaul of its reservation system.
>
> Fierce confrontation is expected with the fourteen airline unions, but the board of D Company is committed to the implementation of the restructuring plan.
>
> **Required:**
>
> Identify the key problems associated with making large-scale redundancies. With reference to the situation in D Company, discuss the ways in which redundancies can be managed to minimise these problems.

9 Fairness

Globalisation has changed the nature of companies in many ways. In terms of staff, it has meant:

- The end of the "job for life" ideal.
- A move from employee's effort due to loyalty to the company towards effort expecting appropriate rewards.
- Employees willing to look outside of the company for advancement opportunities.

Obtaining employee commitment is often seen as the key to competitive performance, but due to the above factors, commitment from employees is becoming more difficult for companies to obtain.

Rosseau and Greller looked into the relationship between what the employees believed was expected of them and what they expected in return from the employer. They called this the psychological contract. They defined three types of psychological contract:

- Coercive – employees feel forced to contribute and view rewards as inadequate.
- Calculative – employee acts voluntarily and works in exchange for an identifiable set of rewards.
- Cooperative – employees contribute more than would normally be expected from them. They actively seek to contribute further to the achievement of company goals.

In coercive contracts, motivation and commitment would be low, or even negative. In calculative contracts, motivation and commitment could be increased if the rewards were increased. In cooperative contracts motivation and commitment would be linked to achievement. Motivation was found to be highest when the contract was viewed in the same way by the organisation and the individual, that is where the employee perceived the practices of the company towards them to be fair.

Adam's equity theory

Employees judge fairness in two main ways:

- By comparing what they receive compared to what they contribute.
- By comparing their situation to that of others.

For example, suppose all employees in a company are given a bonus of $500, except one team which is given $600. All were probably happy with the $500 bonus, until they discovered that some got $600 and now they feel they are being treated unfairly.

Solomon

Solomon looked at the difficulty in achieving equity in relation to pay, there are many considerations:

- A living wage (compare employee needs and their income)
- Rate for the job (compare employees carrying out the same role)
- Output reward (compare the output of employees working in the same area)
- Responsibility (compare the responsibilities of employees at different levels of the organisation)
- Differentials (compare employees carrying out different roles within the organisation)
- Comparability (compare employees carrying out the same roles in different organisations)
- Status (compare employees carrying out different roles in different organisations)
- Contribution (compare the employee's pay to the profitability of the organisation)
- Supply and demand (compare the organisation's ability to pay and its need for labour)

Equality and Diversity

In the UK, **The Equality Act** (2010) is the most significant piece of equality legislation to be introduced for many years. It is there to strengthen protection, advance equality and simplify the law. The Equality Act brings together, and significantly adds to and strengthens, a number of previous existing pieces of legislation, including race and disability. One of the key changes is that it extends the protected characteristics to encompass:

- age
- disability
- gender reassignment
- marriage and civil partnership
- pregnancy and maternity
- race
- religion or belief
- sex
- sexual orientation.

Diversity

Every business wants the best person for the job. Unequal treatment, prejudice or harassment discredits businesses and can be very costly. The owner or manager of a business may also be held responsible for discriminatory action by its employees.

Under the new Equality Act (2010) it is unlawful to discriminate on the grounds of someone's sex, sexual orientation, status as a married person or a civil partner, race, colour, nationality, ethnic origin, religion, beliefs or because of a disability, pregnancy or childbirth, or subsequent maternity leave or because they are a member or non-member of a Trade Union. It is also unlawful to discriminate against part-time workers.

Equal opportunities

The object of providing equal opportunities on the workplace is to:

- ensure fair and non-discriminatory treatment is given by management to all job applicants and existing employees.

A positive approach to equal opportunities should:

- secure the best recruits from the widest available range of candidates.
- ensure the best use is made of the skills and abilities of all employees.
- reinforce the professionalism and image of the organisation itself.

The implementation of equal opportunities policies is important to all organisations. Unfair or unlawful discriminatory practices not only lead to resentment on the part of those who suffer from them: they also adversely affect public perceptions of the organisation and a career. A genuine belief in equal opportunities, couple with the knowledge that unfair or unlawful discriminatory practices will not be tolerated, should yield benefits within the organisation itself and lead to a more positive public belief in its fairness and professionalism and an improved relationship with its stakeholders.

The main points of a typical Equal Opportunities Policy should be as follows:

- Equal opportunities shall mean fairness for all; the recognition, development and use of everyone's talents.
- This fairness will run through recruitment, selection, training, promotion, specialisation and career development generally. It should also govern the relationship of all employees to each other.
- Equal opportunity does not just relate to sex or marital status, but the fact that people can be particularly disadvantaged for those reasons is reflected in legislation.
- No job applicant or employee shall receive unfavourable treatment directly or indirectly on the grounds of gender, sexual orientation, marital status, race, nationality, ethnic origin, religious beliefs and, where applicable, trade union membership, age or disability.
- Selection criteria and procedures will be frequently reviewed to ensure that individuals are selected, promoted and dealt with on the basis of merit, fitness and competence, subject only to the restrictions imposed by law.
- Training is an important part of the implementation of the Equal Opportunities Policy. Training programmes will be arranged to ensure that staff are fully aware of their roles and responsibilities and have the opportunity to develop and progress within the organisation.

Management control

The differences between equal opportunities and diversity:

Equal opportunities	Diversity
Removing discrimination	Maximising potential
Issue for disadvantaged groups	Relevant to all employees
A Human Resources role	A managerial role
Relies on proactive action	Does not rely on proactive action

Contracts of employment

HR or personnel department will also be responsible for the implementation of a system of **contracts of employment**.

A contract of employment places responsibilities on the employee and these form the basis of the control mechanism. The employee owes a duty of 'faithful service' to his or her employer, and this covers such matters as his or her competence, reasonable care and skill, obedience to instruction, accounting for money and property and the duty of personal service.

The board will decide whether the contract is written or oral. A contract can be oral and as informal as a chat. However, it can also be written and very formal giving the following details:

- name of employee, employer and job title
- date of commencement
- pay, holiday entitlement (pay) and hours of work
- sick leave (pay) and pension scheme
- notice period on both sides
- disciplinary procedures.

Working time directive

The **Working time directive** (2003) is a European Union Directive, which creates the right for EU workers to a minimum number of holidays each year, paid breaks, and rest of at least 11 hours in any 24 hours' work, while restricting excessive night work and, a default right to work no more than 48 hours per week.

Although the directive applies to all member states, in the United Kingdom it is possible to "opt out" of the 48 hour working week in order to work longer hours. Whilst it is possible to opt out of the 48 hour weekly limit it is not possible to opt out of the rest requirements.

This legislation lays down the minimum safety and health requirements for the organisation of working time with the aim of improving working conditions.

Provisions can include:

- A limit on hours in the working week
- A right to a number of hours rest per day
- A right to a number of days off per week
- A right to rest breaks after a specified number of hours worked
- A right to a minimum amount of annual leave.

This leads to:

- Increased productivity
- Increased motivation
- Good safety for workers
- Protection to workers.

Management choices on childcare provision

Child care

Employers have many choices when it comes to helping their employees balance work and child care responsibilities. The bottom line is when there are problems with child care a business is affected, lack of adequate child care support for working parents impacts on productivity and employee morale. The economic realities for employers are that child care benefits;

- Attract and retain good employees
- Result in reduced employee absenteeism and turnover, and an increase in productivity
- Enhance an employee's perception of their employer often leading to improved job performance
- Enhance an employer's public image in the community
- Can offer tax advantages for the employer and the employee

10 Summary diagram

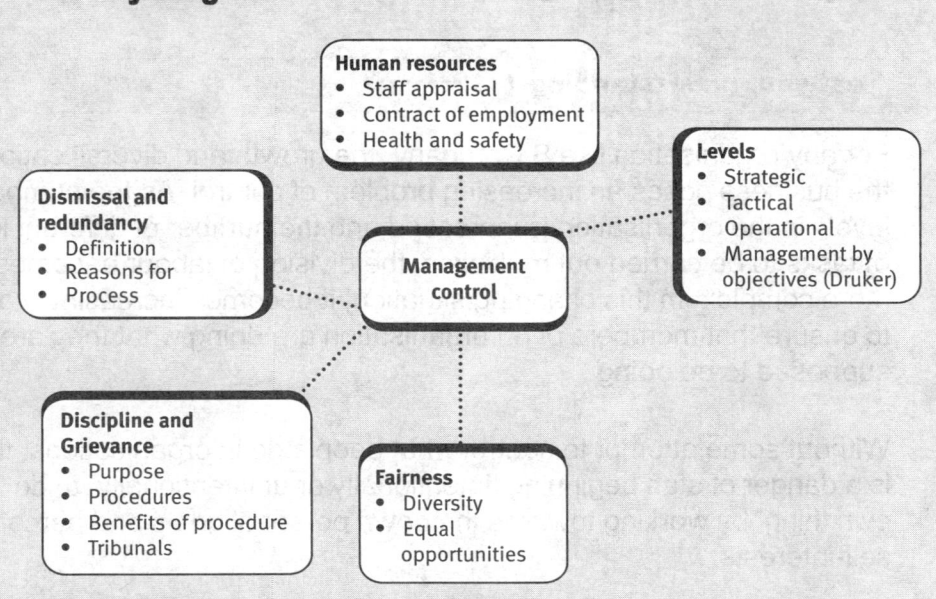

Management control

- **Human resources**
  - Staff appraisal
  - Contract of employment
  - Health and safety

- **Levels**
  - Strategic
  - Tactical
  - Operational
  - Management by objectives (Druker)

- **Dismissal and redundancy**
  - Definition
  - Reasons for
  - Process

- **Discipline and Grievance**
  - Purpose
  - Procedures
  - Benefits of procedure
  - Tribunals

- **Fairness**
  - Diversity
  - Equal opportunities

Test your understanding answers

Test your understanding 1

For any organisation like S Company, the growth and diversification of the business poses an increasing problem of control. As the number of levels in the organisation is increased and the number of different kinds of tasks to be carried out multiplies, the division of labour becomes more complex. In this changing situation, it becomes increasingly difficult to ensure that members of an organisation are doing what they are supposed to be doing.

Without some attempt to control what people do in organisations, there is a danger of staff beginning, intentionally or unintentionally, to do 'their own thing' by working towards their own personal goals and perceived self-interests.

To counteract the tendencies created by the processes of differentiation, and to ensure goal congruence, there is a need to create a 'common focus' in an organisation, which will control and integrate members' diverse activities. This is why organisations introduce a variety of formal controls.

In small, simple organisations it is possible for the owner manager or senior management to supervise subordinates' activities personally and systematically. Often, in such organisations, it is possible to achieve control in an informal way by setting employees tasks and then checking that they have been carried out. Any deviations from the accepted standard of performance can be communicated directly by the owner manager to particular employees and the necessary corrective action taken. In larger organisations, however, with a complex division of labour, and a taller hierarchy of responsibility, it is not physically possible to control people in such a simple manner. In such situations, formal policies, rules and procedures have to be put into place together with a system of rewards and punishments to ensure that the policies, rules and procedures are observed.

In such hierarchical organisations, policies and objectives are typically set, or at least confirmed, by occupants of higher-level positions and are then communicated to lower-level staff, who are then charged with the responsibility to carry out the necessary actions. It is up to the higher-level managers to determine whether or not the objectives have been met and, if not, to take the appropriate steps. This is the process of control.

It is important to note, however, that there are a number of different ways of exercising control in organisations and that the effectiveness of a particular type of control system depends on a number of factors including the organisation's strategy, culture, structure, environment and the type of goods or services produced.

In the case of S Company, it chose to use bureaucratic (administrative) forms of control, but as the CEO realised, such a form of control is not conducive to creativity and innovation.

Creativity, which can be defined as 'the generation of new ideas, and innovation, which is the transformation of creative ideas into tangible products or processes' varies considerably between one organisation and another. Some organisations have a reputation for creativity and innovation while other organisations hardly ever seem to generate new products or new ways of doing things.

The generation of new ideas and their translation into commercial use is a particularly important issue for an organisation like S Company because its future depends on a continuous supply of innovative software products. There are many factors influencing the rate of innovation in organisations, but research suggests that one reason has to do with how an organisation is structured and controlled.

Studies by Rosabeth Moss Kanter (1983) and others have found that excessive bureaucracy with its allegiance to central control and to rules and procedures discourages creativity and innovation. The focus on rules and procedures and the accompanying sanctions designed to ensure compliance means that employees 'play safe' by sticking to the rules rather than risk trying out new ideas. Rules can become 'ends in themselves'.

The division of labour that often accompanies the growth of an organisation also affects creativity and innovation because it restricts the sharing of ideas between individuals and between different units, departments or divisions. The case of S Company illustrates well the problems facing all large organisations at some time in their development – that of balancing the need to ensure adequate direction and control of staff and yet allowing sufficient freedom and discretion of middle managers and other employees to contribute their particular knowledge and expertise to the organisation. Too little direction and control can result in wasted effort and inefficiencies as the departments and divisions into which an organisation is subdivided pursue their own particular goals. Too much central control and lower level staff become frustrated by rules and procedures forced upon them from on high by those who are too far from the action to make informed decisions.

Test your understanding 2

(a)
- The **Health & Safety at Work Act (HASAWA)** was designed to have far-reaching consequences upon employers' premises and methods of work. The main provisions of the Act require an employer to provide a safe and healthy working environment in which to work. This includes the duty to provide training and appoint individuals responsible for maintaining safety at work, for example, safety representatives and trained safety officers.

- The **Health & Safety Executive (HSE).** The Commission, together with the Secretary of State makes appointments to the Health & Safety Executive whose duty it is to make adequate provision for the enforcement of the HASAWA. The main function of the HSE is providing workplace inspections to ensure compliance with the law and enforce the legal requirements, if necessary. The HSE also provides an advisory service to employers and unions.

(b)
- **Managerial responsibilities.** Health and safety at work is the responsibility of both employers and employees. Legislation can only provide the underpinning to safe working practices, ultimately, it is how the legislation is translated in practice that determines whether a workplace is safe, or not. There are a number of ways in which managerial responsibility can be discharged to make work safe. The management of an organisation carry the prime responsibility for implementing a policy they have laid down, and they also have responsibility under the Act for operating the plant and equipment in the premises safely and meeting all the Act's requirements whether these are specified in the policy statement, or not. Management has a duty to provide a safe and healthy working environment, which is hazard free, and to train others so that they are able to operate and maintain a safe and healthy working environment for themselves.

- **Employee responsibilities.** For the first time in health and safety legislation a duty is placed on employees while that are at work to take reasonable care for the safety of themselves and others. The employee is, therefore, legally bound to comply with the safety rules and instructions that the employer requires. Employers are also fully empowered to dismiss employees who refuse to obey safety rules on the grounds of misconduct, especially if the possibility of such a dismissal is explicit in the disciplinary procedure. Employees need to be enabled by management to carry out their duties and responsibilities. This might take the form of communicating policies and procedures about health and safety issues, appointing safety representatives, setting up committees and providing training.

- **Safety representatives.** To reinforce the employees' role in the care of their own health and safety, provision has been made for the appointment of safety representatives by trade unions. Safety representatives have a legal duty of consultation with employers and are entitled to paid time off for training to enable them to carry out their function. Under the HASAWA employers' are expected to set up safety committees and consult with safety representatives about the membership of that committee.

- **Safety committees.** Although the Act does not specifically instruct employers to set up safety committees, it comes very close. Safety representatives and training officers have to be consulted about the membership of the committee, and detailed advice on the function and conduct of safety committees is provided by the Health and Safety Commission. Since the Act there has been a great increase in the number of Safety Committees in operation. It has also been noted that the effectiveness of committees has been very much dependent on the employment of trained safety officers.

Test your understanding 3

A friendly, informal talk with the employee who just started work a few days ago. The second employee receives an oral warning, and the third employee might receive a written warning.

Test your understanding 4

LMR have acted against the statutory procedures laid down for companies in the way they have treated Peter.

Companies are expected to follow the ACAS code of practice in all disciplinary and grievance procedures.

The purpose of disciplinary procedures should be to improve the behaviour of the individual before action such as suspension, demotion or dismissal takes place. These actions should only occur in cases of gross misconduct or after a number of other courses of action have been taken first.

Management control

The stages which would normally be undertaken in this sort of case before a demotion would be:

- Informal chat
- Oral warning
- Written warning – first then second
- Suspension

It would appear that none of these stages had been undertaken as the meeting notifying Peter of his demotion was the first he knew of the company's unhappiness with his performance. He also does not appear to have been given any details, or shown any evidence about the source of their unhappiness and he has been given no opportunity to respond to their claims.

It is also significant that Peter was not aware of the company's discipline code. All employees should be made aware of this code when they join the company. The code should be clear about the expectations of the company and about actions which would be taken as a result of these expectations not being met.

Peter has obviously never had any sort of appraisal since joining the company or these matters would have been raised, and hopefully resolved, sooner.

In this case, Peter would have the right to appeal the decision at tribunal. As the company have not followed the statutory rules, it is likely that Peter would win his case.

Test your understanding 5

The key problems in any redundancy situation include that of deciding which personnel shall be made redundant, carrying out the redundancy process in a way that is fair and within the law, deciding what the redundancy package will consist of, and how to maintain the morale and motivation of the remaining workforce.

Selection for redundancy must be fair, carried out according to an agreed procedure laid down beforehand and consistently applied. This procedure does not have to be the 'last in first out' principle, although this is a popular method because of its ease of application.

In the United Kingdom, the ACAS Code of Practice provides a useful checklist that helps ensure that companies operate within the law and that individuals are treated fairly in the redundancy process. Other countries have similar codes of practice and these should be followed where available.

The ACAS code suggests that management should stop recruitment, reduce overtime, consider retraining or transfer of people to other jobs, retire those over normal retirement age and introduce short-time working. Where the redundancy is inevitable, as in the case of D Company, employers should give as much warning as possible, use voluntary redundancy and early retirement, and offer help in finding other work. Employers must also ensure that individuals are informed before any news leaks out, and should try to run down establishments slowly.

The redundancy package offered needs to be considered for a number of reasons. First, a basic legal minimum sum based on the number of years of employment can result in a substantial sum, and this has to be budgeted for. Second, D Company might consider paying over the legal minimum as a way of indicating to the remaining employees and the world more generally that it is a 'good' employer.

The needs of the remaining staff should also be considered. Their morale and confidence in the organisation will need to be boosted. In the case of a partial redundancy, those remaining at work may well have to change their work patterns by operating new machinery, coping with bigger jobs or changing their job location. This will need to be discussed with the trade union(s), the employees concerned and their supervisors.

The term 'outplacement' has come to be used to describe the efforts of management to place redundant employees in other economically active positions. Some consultants have become expert in revising curriculum vitae (CVs) of staff and 'selling' them to a network of contacts.

Management control

chapter 11

Corporate governance, ethics and social responsibility

Chapter learning objectives

- Analyse issues of business ethics and corporate governance.
- Discuss concepts in established and emergent thinking in strategic management.

Corporate governance, ethics and social responsibility

1 Session content diagram

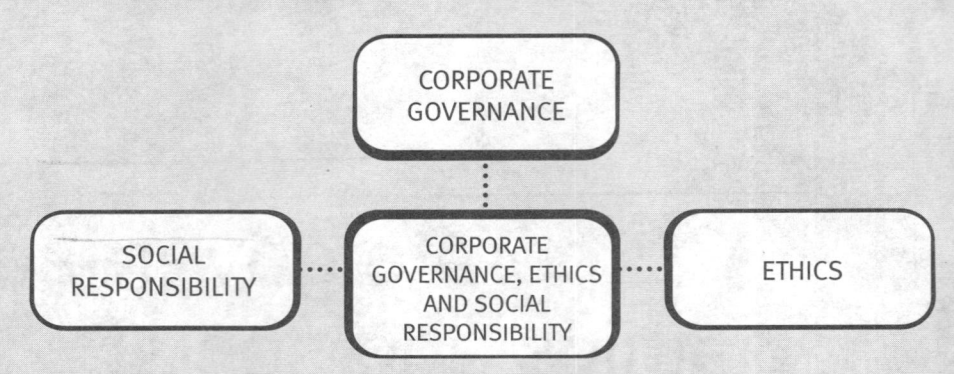

```
                    CORPORATE
                    GOVERNANCE
                        |
        ┌───────────────┼───────────────┐
        |               |               |
     SOCIAL        CORPORATE         ETHICS
  RESPONSIBILITY  GOVERNANCE, ETHICS
                   AND SOCIAL
                  RESPONSIBILITY
```

2 Corporate governance

Corporate governance can be described as 'the system by which companies are directed and controlled in the interests of shareholders and other stakeholders'.

Governance is an issue for all organisations, however the corporate governance rules covered in this chapter would principally be applied to large quoted companies. In large quoted companies the owners of the company (the shareholders) are often distinct from the people running the company (the directors). This creates what is known as the agency problem. The shareholders employ the directors to run the company on their behalf. In return the directors are accountable to the shareholders for their actions.

There has been an increased emphasis on governance regulations over the last 20 years as a result of a number of high profile scandals and corporate failures over that period.

Five principles of corporate governance

The OECD (Organisation of Economic Co-operation and Development) identifies five principles of corporate governance:

- the rights of shareholders.
- the equitable treatment of shareholders.
- the role of stakeholders.
- disclosure and transparency.
- the responsibility of the board.

The benefits of corporate governance

Good corporate governance should:

- **Reduce risk.** It helps to ensure that the personal objectives of the board and the company's strategic objectives are brought into line with those of stakeholders. It can help to reduce the risk of fraud.
- **Improve leadership.** It allows increased expertise to be brought to bear on strategic decision-making, through the influence of non-executive directors (NEDs), and because all board members are encouraged to examine board decisions critically.
- **Enhance performance.** It institutes clear accountability and effective links between performance and rewards which can encourage the organisation to improve its performance.
- **Improve access to capital markets.** It reduces the level of risk as perceived by outsiders, including investors.
- **Enhance stakeholder support** by showing transparency, accountability and social responsibility.
- **Enhance the marketability of goods and services.** It creates confidence among other stakeholders, including employees, customers, suppliers and partners in joint ventures.

Principles-based *versus* rules-based approaches to corporate governance

There are two different approaches to corporate governance; principles-based and rules-based. In the UK there is a principles-based approach (The UK Corporate Governance Code), while in the USA there is a rules-based approach (Sarbanes-Oxley). A rules based approach will provide a set of rules which must be followed in all circumstances. A rules-based legislation will also include punishment for non-compliance.

A principles-based approach is not a rigid set of rules, but consists of principles, which should be followed unless there is a justifiable explanation as to why not. The UK code adopts a 'comply or explain' approach – the main principles of the code should be adhered to, however some of the provisions to the code may not be followed exactly providing the departure can be justified and if it can be shown that good governance can still be achieved.

In this paper, it is the **UK Corporate Governance Code** which will be covered.

The UK Corporate Governance Code was published in June 2010 and supersedes the Combined Code.

The listing rules require each listed company to state in its annual report:

- How it has applied the principles of the Code.
- Whether or not it has complied with the provisions of the Code throughout the accounting period.

> ### The history of corporate governance in the UK
>
> #### History of corporate governance in the UK
>
> In the UK corporate governance has developed through a number of codes that have been endorsed by the stock exchange.
>
> *The Cadbury Report* (1992) in the UK recommended a Code of Best Practice:
>
> - *Openness* subject to commercial confidentiality.
> - *Integrity* – honest, balanced and complete financial reporting.
> - *Accountability* of directors to provide quality information and shareholders to exercise ownership powers responsibly.
>
> *The Greenbury Report* (early 1995) focused on directors' pay and its approach in this area was to:
>
> - Strengthen accountability.
> - Encourage improved performance through transparency.
> - Allocate responsibility appropriately for establishing directors' remuneration.
> - Ensure proper reporting to shareholders.
>
> Again, the London Stock Exchange required listed companies to state in their annual reports whether they had complied with the Code and to explain any non-compliance.
>
> The *Hampel Report* produced a *Combined Code of Principles of Good Governance* and a *Code of Best Practice (1998)* to pass to the Stock Exchange to sit alongside the listing requirements. The code embraced Cadbury, Greenbury and its own work, and companies are required to make a statement to show how they apply the principles, comply with the codes, and justify any major variations.

> *The Higgs Report* published in 2003 recommended changes to the Combined Code to require a greater proportion of independent, better-informed non-executives on the Board. Some proposals were controversial, for example that at least half of the Board should be independent non-executives, and that a chief executive should not be allowed to become chairman of the same company.
>
> It identified four main roles of non-executive directors:
>
> - Develop strategy.
> - Scrutinise performance of management.
> - Ensure risk management is robust.
> - Decide remuneration of executive board.
>
> It also incorporated the recommendation that the chairman should decide on a process of performance evaluation for the board and of individual directors.
>
> The *Smith Report* (2003) made recommendations with regards to audit committees. These were also incorporated into the Combined Code.

Principles of the UK Corporate Governance Code:

The code sets out five main principles:

(1) Leadership
(2) Effectiveness
(3) Accountability
(4) Remuneration
(5) Relations with shareholders

Leadership

- Every company should be headed by an effective board which is collectively responsible for the long-term success of the company.
- There should be a clear division of responsibilities at the head of the company between the running of the board (chairman) and the executive responsibility for the running of the company's business (CEO) so that no one individual should have unfettered powers of decision.

- The chairman is responsible for leadership of the board and ensuring its effectiveness on all aspects of its role.
- As part of their role, non-executive directors should constructively challenge and help develop proposals on strategy.

Effectiveness

- The board and its committees should have the appropriate balance of skills, experience, independence and knowledge of the company to enable them to discharge their respective duties and responsibilities effectively.
- There should be a formal, rigorous and transparent procedure for the appointment of new directors to the board.
- All directors should be able to allocate sufficient time to the company to discharge their responsibilities effectively.
- All directors should receive induction on joining the board and should regularly update and refresh their skills and knowledge.
- The board should be supplied in a timely manner with information in a form and of a quality appropriate to enable it to discharge its duties.
- The board should undertake a formal and rigorous annual evaluation of its own performance and that of its committees and individual directors.
- All directors should be submitted for re-election at regular intervals, subject to continued satisfactory performance.

Remuneration

- Levels of remuneration should be sufficient to attract, retain and motivate directors of the quality required to run the company successfully, but a company should avoid paying more than is necessary for this purpose. A significant proportion of executive directors' remuneration should be structured so as to link rewards to corporate and individual performance.
- There should be a formal and transparent procedure for developing policy on executive remuneration and for fixing the remuneration packages of individual directors. No director should be involved in deciding his or her own remuneration.

Accountability

- The board should present a balanced and understandable assessment of the company's position and prospects.
- The board is responsible for determining the nature and extent of the significant risks it is willing to take in achieving its strategic objectives.

- The board should maintain sound risk management and internal control systems.
- The board should establish formal and transparent arrangements for considering how they should apply the corporate reporting and risk management and internal control principles and for maintaining an appropriate relationship with the company's auditor.

Relations with Shareholders

- There should be a dialogue with shareholders based on the mutual understanding of objectives. The board as a whole has responsibility for ensuring that a satisfactory dialogue with shareholders takes place.
- The board should use the AGM to communicate with investors and to encourage their participation.

In carrying out the above principles, the company should set up a number of committees:

Remuneration committee

- Made up wholly of independent non-executive directors.
- Objectively determine executive remuneration and individual packages for each executive director.

Nomination committee

- Consists of a majority of non-executive directors with the aim of bringing an independent view to the selection and recruitment of both executive and non-executive directors.
- Meets when required. Should be high profile to demonstrate to stakeholders that a reasonable degree of objectivity exists in the selection process.

Audit committee

- Made up of non-executive directors.
- Have formal terms of reference.
- Meet at least three times per year.
- At least once a year, have a meeting with the external auditors without the presence of any executive directors; discuss any significant matters that arose on the audit.
- Recommend appointment and removal of external auditors and set audit fee after discussion with external auditors.

- Review internal audit programme and significant findings of internal auditors.
- Keep nature and extent of non-audit services of external auditors under review.
- Review arrangements by which staff of the company may, in confidence, raise concerns about possible improprieties in matters of financial reporting or other matters (whistleblowing).

Test your understanding 1

Sparks plc is an established company manufacturing small electrical goods. The company was founded by Sam Sparks over 60 years ago and has been run by the Sparks family since. The company became listed five years ago. The current CEO is Bob Sparks, Sam's grandson, and his brother Joe is the chairman.

Bob and Joe tend to make all the decisions in relation to the running of the company. They came up with the latest strategy while on holiday at Bob's Spanish villa. Joe then e-mailed the other four company directors, who are all employees of Sparks plc, and told them to start working on the new strategy straight away.

Bob and Joe spend approximately six months of the year at the villa. Most of the board communication is therefore via e-mail from Bob and Joe. The board rarely meet.

The last time the board met was six months ago. Bob called the directors together to celebrate his 60th birthday and at that meeting he set the remunerations for all the directors, including himself, for the forthcoming year.

After the meeting the other four directors discussed the fact that they felt that Bob's remuneration package was excessive, but none of them felt they could challenge him about it. The finance director was especially unhappy as she told the others that Bob had asked her to "hide" the level of his remuneration in the annual accounts.

Required:

Explain the corporate governance issues present in Sparks plc.

(10 marks)

3 Ethics

Ethics is primarily concerned with the distinction between what is considered 'right' and what is consider 'wrong' behaviour and with the way in which individuals arrive at such judgments in terms of moral duty and obligations that govern conduct.

Ethics refers to a code of conduct or behaviour that a society, a group or professional body, or an individual, considers correct. Ethical codes are belief based, not fact based; they therefore change between societies and over time, and it is possible to debate whether particular ethical codes are useful. Such a debate is likely to be influenced by the political views of those discussing the ethical codes.

Ethical issues and related behaviour may be considered at four levels:

- **Macro** level: Covers ethics in the international and national context.
- **Corporate** level: Those affecting the organisation.
- **Group** level: Those affecting particular professional groups and those affecting particular groups within an organisation.
- **Individual** level: The conduct and activities of individuals within an organisation.

Ethical issues

Managers face ethical issues all the time. Examples are:

- Dealing with direct and indirect demands for bribes and attempts at extortion.
- Situations of unfair competition.
- Expectations of social responsibility in relation to society and the environment.
- Demand for safety and compliance with legislative standards in relation to products and production.
- Honesty in advertising of jobs and products.
- Management of closures and redundancies.
- Non-exploitation of countries and people.
- Effects on customer of consuming products.
- Dealing with oppressive governments.
- Fairness in setting pay and work conditions.
- Implementing policies that imply social cost.
- The relations an organisation should have with political parties.

Blanchard and Peale suggest that individuals facing ethical dilemmas should ask themselves:

- Is it legal? Will you be breaking laws by engaging in the activity?
- Is it balanced? This means 'is it fair to all parties involved'?
- Is it right? How does this decision make you feel and would you like others to know about it?

The fact that there are so many possible approaches to the determination of what, in a given set of circumstances, would constitute 'right' behaviour shows how difficult is the translation of anything which could be regarded as an ethical principle into the world of business. Organisations may be judged by those with whom they come into contact, for example customers, regulators, suppliers or others, who expect them to exhibit 'right' behaviours, even though each group may have a different slant on what constitutes correctness.

The important messages to bear in mind with ethics are that:

- Not everyone makes the same ethical assumptions that you do. What may seem totally wrong to you is acceptable to them and vice versa. This can be a real problem for managers dealing with people:
    - from other social cultures (e.g. in foreign trading and business relations);
    - from other types of organisation (e.g. businesses dealing with the voluntary or caring services);
    - of different ages (i.e. morals change through time but not everyone changes with them).
- Different stakeholders may have different expectations of the firm's behaviour.
- Moral and ethical debates drive the actions of pressure groups and legislators.

Factors affecting ethical obligations

A number of factors will affect the ethical obligations of an organisation, for example: the law; extent of government regulation; industry and company ethical codes and social pressure. Carroll (1990) identifies eleven different ethical criteria which managers could use as a basis of judgment in relation to ethical business issues:

(1) The categorical imperative – whereby principles of action will be adopted only if they can be adopted, without inconsistency, by everyone else.

(2) The conventionalist ethic – whereby acting in your own self interest is permitted provided that the laws imposed by society are not thereby infringed.

(3) The golden rule – do unto others as you would have them do unto you.

(4) The hedonistic rule – if it feels OK, then it probably is OK.

(5) The disclosure rule – whereby the correctness of a particular action is judged by reference to how you would feel should it appear on the front page of a newspaper.

(6) The intuition rule – do whatever your emotions, as opposed to rational decision-making, tells you to do.

(7) The means to an end ethic – whereby it is permissible to act if the end result is defensible.

(8) The might equals right rule – where acting in accordance with the strength of your power base is permissible even though this runs contrary to social conventions.

(9) The organisational ethics in accordance with which loyalty to the organisation takes transcends all other considerations.

(10) The professional ethics under which adherence to the code of your profession transcends other considerations.

(11) The utilitarian principle under which the guiding principle is attaining 'the greatest good of the greatest number'.

Corporate governance, ethics and social responsibility

> **Illustration 1 – Example of an ethical issue**
>
> Imagine that a chain of shops decides to close down a branch situated in the centre of town in favour of an out-of-town location where profits will be higher. Elderly and poorer shoppers who lack private transport are now without a shop. Some will suffer reduced quality of life by having to make a bus journey to the new store. Disabled persons will need shopping done for them, so imposing a strain on social services or family members. Perhaps another local shop decides to exploit its monopoly position by raising prices, thereby forcing poorer families to forgo some of the things they need.
>
> It seems that pursuing the interests of the shareholder has harmed others.
>
> Is this an ethical decision?

Managerial ethics

The top management of an organisation formulate the strategic decisions and should behave ethically in addition to meeting the expectations of all stakeholders of being socially aware and socially responsible.

Many successful organisations proactively use an ethical and socially responsible stance as a means of strategically differentiating from competitors to achieve competitive advantage.

A committed top management may:

- establish corporate ethical codes;
- develop 'green' strategies and policies;
- establish environmental cost-reduction strategies;
- analyse and assess social effects of current activities;
- integrate social responsibility into the corporate strategy generation and planning system of the business.

4 Developing an ethical organisation

Having an ethical framework in place makes it easier for an organisation to choose the 'right' behaviour. There are two basic approaches to developing an ethical organisation:

Compliance based – this approach seeks not so much to promote ethical behaviour, but eradicate that which is unethical. It is designed to eliminate competitive disadvantage and to ensure that the organisation acts with regard to compliance.

Integrity based – aims to integrate ethics into the day-to-day activities and the organisation's culture and systems, guiding ethical values and patterns of behaviour. It emphasizes managerial responsibility for ethical behaviour.

The importance of communication channels which allow employees to voice their concerns, or whistle-blowing, cannot be overstated. Without this an employee may face a dilemma, on the one hand, they have doubts about the ethics of some aspect of work but on the other hand, they have to act ethically. Faced with this situation, the employee will either be forced to compromise his/her ethical principles or blow the whistle on his employer. The organisation's attitude to actual or potential whistle-blowers depends on the level of mutual trust which exists between employer and employee. In the past, it has frequently involved financial loss for the whistle-blower, since they often ended up losing their jobs

Ethics management involves creating an environment that will support ethically sound behaviour and instil a sense of shared accountability amongst members.

Statements of ethics

Some companies publish statements concerning their ethical beliefs. The following needs to be present if these statements are to be considered more than just a public relations exercise:

- Ethical guidelines are reasonably specific.
- Ethical performance is measured.
- Legal but unethical behaviour is punished.
- There is greater openness in business behaviour.
- Consumers are prepared to accept higher prices.

> **Illustration 2 – Example of an organisation's Code of Ethics**
>
> ### FirstGroup plc
>
> FirstGroup plc is the world's leading transport operator. It employs 125,000 staff throughout the UK and North America and transports 2.5 billion passengers a year.
>
> FirstGroup plc have a clear code of business ethics. This highlights the importance they place on business ethics, and also shows how wide ranging ethical policies must be. Their code of ethics covers the following areas:
>
> **Basic Standards of Conduct**
>
> **Employees**
>
> **Business Integrity**
>
> **National and International Trade**
>
> **Personal Conduct**
>
> **Bribery**
>
> **Gifts, Entertainment and Improper Payments**
>
> **Conflicts of Interest**
>
> **Confidentiality**
>
> **Political Activity**
>
> **Health and Safety**
>
> **The Environment**
>
> **Customers**
>
> **Shareholders**
>
> **Supply Chain**
>
> **Community Involvement**

> **More detail on FirstGroup plc's code of ethics**
>
> **This Code of Business Ethics sets out the standards we expect from our employees in their internal and external dealings with colleagues, customers, stakeholders and third parties.**
>
> **Basic Standards of Conduct**
>
> - We will conduct every aspect of our business with honesty, integrity and openness, respecting human rights and the interests of our employees, customers and third parties.
> - We will respect the legitimate interests of third parties with whom we have dealings in the course of our business.
> - We will maintain the highest standards of integrity for example, we will not promise more than we can reasonably deliver or make commitments we cannot or do not intend to keep.
>
> **Employees**
>
> We are committed to:
>
> - Developing a workforce where there is mutual trust and respect, free from bullying and harassment, where every person feels responsible for the performance and reputation of our company.
> - Respecting the rights of individuals their customs and traditions and their right to freedom of association and the right to decide whether or not to join a trade union. We will negotiate in good faith with properly elected representatives of our employees.
> - Recruiting, employing and promoting employees on the basis of objective criteria and the qualifications and abilities needed for the job to be performed in line with our Equal Opportunities Policy.
> - Maintaining good communications with employees through our information and consultation procedures.
> - Providing our employees with suitable training and assisting them in realising their potential.
> - Ensuring the privacy and confidentiality of our employees' personal information is respected.
> - Suitably rewarding our employees for their contribution to the success of the business.

Corporate governance, ethics and social responsibility

- Providing mechanisms whereby employees can raise legitimate concerns confidentially regarding malpractice and ensuring no one will be victimised for a report made in good faith.

- Providing employees with the appropriate information and training to comply with this Code and the associated policies

- Seeking to protect our employees from third party abuse that might be injurious to their safety, health or well-being.

Business Integrity

- We aim to develop strong relationships with our suppliers, stakeholders and others with whom we have dealings, based on mutual trust, understanding and respect. In those dealings, we expect those with whom we do business to adhere to business principles consistent with our own.

- We will conduct our operations in accordance with the principles of fair competition and applicable regulations.
FirstGroup's accounting and other records and supporting documents must accurately describe and reflect the nature of the underlying transactions.

- No unrecorded account, fund or asset will be established or maintained.

- We will comply with the laws and regulations applicable wherever we do business. We will obtain legal advice where felt necessary to comply with this commitment.

- We will review and track our business risks including social and environmental risks.

- FirstGroup will not facilitate, support, tolerate or condone any form of money laundering.

- To ensure that our business is run in an ethical and effective manner we will maintain internal controls in line with FirstGroup's Minimum Standards of Business Control.

National and International Trade

- We will seek to compete fairly and ethically within the framework of applicable competition and anti-trust laws and we will not prevent others from competing fairly with us.

- We will comply with all applicable export control laws and sanctions when conducting business around the world.

Personal Conduct

- All employees are expected to behave in accordance with the principles set out in this Code of Business Ethics.

- Employees are expected to protect and not misuse company assets such as buildings, vehicles, equipment, cash and procurement cards.

- Employees are expected to use e-mail, internet, IT and telephones in a manner appropriate for business purposes in line with the principles contained in this Code and any applicable IT policies.

Bribery

- No FirstGroup employee, or individual or business working on our behalf must accept or give a bribe, facilitation payment or other improper payment for any reason. This applies to transactions with government officials, any private company or person anywhere in the world. It also applies whether the payment is made or received directly or through a third party.

- FirstGroup shall ensure that adequate procedures are in place to prevent the risk of bribery and that these are effectively communicated and implemented across the Group in line with the requirements of the Bribery Act 2010.

Gifts, Entertainment and Improper Payments

- Accepting or giving any entertainment or gift that is designed to, or may be seen to influence business decisions, is not acceptable. No FirstGroup company or employee shall offer, give, seek or receive, either directly or indirectly, inducements or other improper advantages for business or financial gain. If an employee is in any doubt as to whether he or she may accept an offer, that employee should discuss the issue with his or her manager, Group Legal Director or General Counsel.

- Any gift or hospitality given or received by an employee should be reported for inclusion on the Group or Divisional Hospitality and Gift Registers. In the UK this applies to any gift or hospitality with an estimated or actual value of £50 or more. Similar arrangements are in place in relation to our North American operations.

Conflicts of Interest

- Whilst we respect the privacy of our employees, all FirstGroup employees are expected to avoid personal relations, activities and financial interests, which could conflict with their responsibilities to FirstGroup.

- FirstGroup employees and consultants must not seek gain for themselves or others through misuse of their positions or company property.

- All actual and potential conflicts (including those arising from the activities or interests of close relatives or partners) should be disclosed to and discussed with an employee's line manager.

- Employees who have access to price sensitive information are prohibited from being involved in dealings in FirstGroup securities unless given clearance by the Chief Executive or the Company Secretary. There should be no unauthorised disclosure of price sensitive information to third parties.

Confidentiality

- Information received by anyone in the course of his or her employment must not be used for personal gain or for any purpose other than that for which it was given. Where confidential information is obtained in the course of business that confidentiality must be respected.

Political Activity

- FirstGroup does not make any donations to political parties or take part in party politics. However, when dealing with Government we do make legitimate concerns known and will seek to influence Governments in relation to issues that could affect us, our shareholders, our customers or the local community. These relationships are conducted in accordance with this Code

Health and Safety

- We are committed to creating and maintaining a safe and healthy working environment for our employees, customers and the community. Our commitment to ensuring the safety and security of our employees is set out in our Injury Prevention and Security policies.

- We strive to avoid emergency situations but recognise the need to be prepared. We are committed to having effective emergency response procedures in place.

The Environment

- FirstGroup is committed to making continuous improvement in the management of its environmental impact as set out in our Environmental Policy.

- All employees are expected to adhere to the requirements of the local environmental management system and support the improvement in our environmental performance.

Customers

- FirstGroup is committed to providing safe, value for money, high quality, consistent, accessible and reliable services to its customers.

- All employees are expected to behave respectfully and honestly in all their dealings with customers and the general public in accordance with the principles set out in this Code.

- In particular we will safeguard and protect the welfare of vulnerable people who come into contact with our employees. Employees will be made aware that they hold a position of trust and that they must at all times maintain the highest standards of personal conduct that reflects this trust being placed with them.

Shareholders

- FirstGroup will conduct its operations in accordance with the principles of good corporate governance. We will provide timely, regular and reliable information on the business to all our shareholders.

Supply Chain

- We purchase a wide range of goods and services required in the operation of our business and we also rely heavily on a number of key suppliers for the delivery of our core services. Good working relationships with our suppliers are therefore central to the success of our business.

- Whilst we are committed to obtaining and retaining competitive goods and services we will at the same time seek to ensure they are from sources that have not jeopardised human rights, safety or the environment.

- We expect our suppliers to adhere to business principles consistent with our own. We expect them to adopt and implement acceptable safety, environmental, product quality, product stewardship, labour, human rights, social and legal standards in line with our Supplier Code of Conduct.

- We will seek to work with our suppliers to develop long-term meaningful relationships to benefit both parties with the aim of improving the quality, environmental performance and sustainability of goods and services.

Community Involvement

- Our operations touch members of the community daily, whether as customers, neighbours, employees, businesses or residents. We are committed to fostering good relationships with the communities in which we work and building community partnerships that deliver positive change.

Taken from the FirstGroup plc website May 2011

How businesses handle ethical issues

Firms will vary in the degree of their ethical behaviour. **Richard Daft** summarised the stances that different organisations adopt towards ethics as follows:

Business handling of social and ethical issues

Obstructive:	Defensive:	Accommodative:	Proactive:
Deny problems and responsibility, lose evidence, and fight all the way, for example, Enron and Arthur Andersen, tobacco companies during the 1970s and 1980s.	Admit some minor errors when defending its actions in order to try to deflect attention from major areas for concern, for example the actions of certain companies in the wake of major rail crashes within the UK over the past decade.	Accept responsibility under external pressure in the hope of avoiding further regulations being imposed. Most companies in the real world fall into this category most of the time.	Take the lead by initiating public interest programmes as a source of competitive advantage, for example Body Shop in the 1970s and 1980s, Co-operative Bank.

Test your understanding 2

You are the new divisional accountant of a company. You discover that the company is overcharging one of its customers. The previous divisional accountant seems to have misunderstood the cost calculation rules of the customer, and the customer has already approved and paid invoices.

Required:

Identify the factors you need to take into account in recommending a solution to this problem, and advise a course of action that the company should follow.

(10 marks)

Test your understanding 3

M is Chairman and Managing Director of Y Company which he started 15 years ago, specialising in the manufacture of hospital uniforms. The company has been very successful and through a series of acquisitions has diversified into the manufacture of a range of corporate and other uniforms, employing 3,500 people. M is a major force in the company. His management style is very autocratic and he is unwilling to involve others in decisions about the future strategic direction of the company. Recently, M announced to the Board that he is intending that Y Company becomes listed on the Stock Exchange.

D, the Finance Director of the company has become increasingly concerned about the decisions being made by M and the fact that he has put pressure on her to participate in some questionable accounting practices. She has had to cover up M's substantial remuneration package, which M has awarded to himself. D is also aware that M has accepted bribes from foreign suppliers and of insider dealing relating to a number of the acquisitions. There is a lack of appropriate control systems and accountability in the Company.

D has discussed her concerns with other members of the Board, all of whom work for Y Company, including the Marketing Director, Production Director and HR Director. However, they seem willing to overlook the wrongdoings of M and never challenge the decisions made by him. The opportunity to do so is limited since the Board meets on an irregular and infrequent basis.

Corporate governance, ethics and social responsibility

At the last Board meeting M set out his plans to close the existing factories and move operations to L country where he has been in secret negotiations with representatives of the government. The main objective is to benefit from low cost labour, since the county has very little in the way of employment legislation to protect workers and has a poor human rights record.

Required:

Explain the corporate governance and ethical issues facing Y Company.

Did these ethical companies sell out ?

There have been a number of cases where companies, which had reputations for being ethically responsible, were taken over by large conglomerates, which did not have the same ethical reputations. Did these ethical companies sell out?

Green & Black's – Cadbury Schweppes

Set up in 1991 by Craig Sams and his wife Josephine Fairley, the company produced organic, and in some cases, Fairtrade chocolate. In 2005 it was bought out by Cadbury Schweppes. Sams defended Cadbury's commitment to the brand's values saying: "Cadbury got its people to read the Fairtrade and organic regulations." Cadbury was bought by Kraft in 2010 and since then Green & Black have been keen to stress that the sourcing of the ingredients remain the same and the ethical, fair trade and organic principles of their business also remain untouched.

Ben and Jerry's – Unilever

All natural ice-cream company founded in 1978 by Jerry Greenfield and Ben Cohen. Bought by Unilever in 2000. The co-founders said: "We hope that, as part of Unilever, Ben & Jerry's will continue to expand its role in society." In February 2010, Ben & Jerry's announced its commitment to go fully Fairtrade across its entire global flavour portfolio. All of the flavours in all of the countries where Ben & Jerry's is sold will be converted to Fairtrade-certified ingredients by the end of 2013.

> **The Body Shop – L'Oréal**
>
> Founded on an ethical basis by Anita Roddick, the company was sold to L'Oréal in 2006. Dame Roddick said at the time, "Having L'Oréal come in and say, 'We like you, we like your ethics, we want to be part of you, we want you to teach us things,' it's a gift." The Body Shop is a leader in promoting greater corporate transparency, and have been a force for positive social and environmental change through campaigns around their five core Values: Support Community Fair Trade, Defend Human Rights, Against Animal Testing, Activate Self-Esteem, and Protect Our Planet.

5 Professional ethics

CIMA guidelines on professional ethics set standards of conduct for professional accountants and have sections applicable to all members and students, and also only to those in public practice.

In general, CIMA's professional ethical codes support accountants in resisting pressure that might distort their professional judgement, apply sanctions to those breaching the agreed code of conduct, and promote awareness of the code amongst members.

CIMA's ethical guidelines define a profession in the context of the mastery of skills by training, and the acceptance of duties to society as a whole, in addition to duties to clients or employers. The view is that a professional must have an objective outlook and render personal services to a high standard of conduct and performance.

The public interest is regarded as paramount as stakeholders require objectivity. The objectives for the accountancy profession that need to be achieved are credibility, professionalism, quality of services, and confidence, i.e. users should feel confident if accountants abide by a code of professional ethics.

Principles

The fundamental principles underlying the achievement of these objectives and the conduct of professional accountants are outlined from CIMA's guidelines as follows:

- *Confidentiality*: only disclosing confidential information if there is a legal or professional justification.
- *Objectivity*: being fair and not allowing prejudice or bias of others to influence judgement.

- *Professional competence and due care*: refraining from carrying out services for which no training is given; and carrying out services with due care, competence and diligence.
- *Professional behaviour*: acting in a manner consistent with the reputation of the profession and avoiding bringing the profession into disrepute.
- *Integrity*: being straightforward and honest; not falsifying records; not making misleading, false or deceptive statements; and not abusing privileged information to support a particular course of action.

Similar to the company codes of ethics covered earlier, CIMA has a published Code of Ethics (2010) which all members and students should be familiar with. Within this they have set out a conceptual framework approach to independence.

The conceptual framework

The conceptual framework requires a professional accountant to identify, evaluate and address threats to compliance with the fundamental principles, rather than merely comply with a set of specific rules. Compliance with the fundamental principles may potentially be threatened by a broad range of circumstances. Many threats fall into the following categories:

- Self-interest threats, which may occur as a result of the financial or other interests of a professional accountant or of an immediate or close family member.
- Self-review threats, which may occur when a previous judgement needs to be re-evaluated by the professional accountant responsible for that judgement.
- Advocacy threats, which may occur when a professional accountant promotes a position or opinion to the point that subsequent objectivity may be compromised.
- Familiarity threats, which may occur when, because of a close relationship, a professional accountant becomes too sympathetic to the interests of others.
- Intimidation threats, which may occur when a professional accountant may be deterred from acting objectively by threats, actual or perceived.

Safeguards to these threats include:

- Educational, training and experience requirements for entry into the profession.
- Continuing professional development requirements.

- Corporate governance regulations.
- Professional standards.
- Professional or regulatory monitoring and disciplinary procedures.
- External review by a legally empowered third party of the information produced by a professional accountant.
- Effective, well-publicised complaints systems operated by the employing organisation, the profession or a regulator, which enables colleagues, employers and members of the public to draw attention to unprofessional or unethical behaviour.
- An explicitly stated duty to report breaches of ethical requirements.

Cross-border activities

The default rule when engaged in cross-border activities is that the professional services should be carried out in accordance with the technical standards and ethical requirements of that country.

Exceptions to the default rule are:

- If the foreign country's ethical requirements are less stringent than CIMA's, use those of CIMA.
- If the foreign country's ethical requirements are more stringent than CIMA's, use those of the foreign country.
- If the home country's ethical requirements are more stringent than those of CIMA and the foreign country (and the home country's rules are imposed on subsidiaries), use those of the home country.

Principles-based *versus* rules-based approaches to professional ethics

As discussed earlier under corporate governance, there are rules-based and principles-based approaches. This is also the case with professional ethics.

CIMA use a principles-based approach. The CIMA fundamental principles offer a means by which students and members can be guided in their actions in all circumstances and in all situations. Broad-based principles guide action, rather than a slavish adherence to particular specified rules. Rule-based approaches to ethics suffer from the fact that no set of rules can ever cover every eventuality – loopholes exist for the unscrupulous to exploit.

For example, a rule-based approach to professional ethics could be expected to contain specific rules about following international- or UK-based GAAP, but would not be able to cope with situations not yet considered by the standards issuing boards. CIMA's fundamental principles to do with integrity and objectivity, however, can guide members in students in any situation, whether or not it has yet been the subject of a specific ruling or accounting standard.

The role of government and professional bodies in determining ethical standards

Governments recognise that services provided by professionals require high levels of ethical standards to be determined by the public interest as a professional's responsibility extends beyond the needs of individual clients and employers. The professional's norms, values, attitudes and behaviour when providing services have an impact on the whole economic and social environment.

As a result governments can enact legislation when they consider professional bodies to have failed in terms of self-regulation for its profession.

> **Test your understanding 4**
>
> A is employed by T Company as a management accountant. One of her duties is producing an analysis of the monthly sales figures. The finance director has asked her to omit the sales returns in the last period's report. He explained that if the figures were included, none of the directors would receive a bonus for the period and he was under pressure from the other directors to make sure that the bonuses were paid. He strongly hinted that if she did this, he would recommend her for promotion at her next annual appraisal. He explained that she could put the returns in the following period, so it was really just a timing issue.
>
> Both A and the finance director are members of CIMA.
>
> **Required:**
>
> Discuss how the fundamental principles of the CIMA Code of Ethics for Professional Accountants might be compromised if A complies with the finance director's request.
>
> **(10 marks)**

6 Social responsibility

Social responsibility is an ethical or ideological theory that an entity whether it is a government, corporation, organisation or individual has a responsibility to society. This responsibility can be "negative", meaning there is a responsibility to refrain from acting (resistance stance) or it can be "positive," meaning there is a responsibility to act (proactive stance).

From a business point of view, decisions on social responsibility are linked closely with strategic decision making.

> Social responsibility can be defined as 'taking more than just the immediate interests of the shareholders into account when making a business decision'.

Businesses embrace responsibility for the impact of their activities on the environment, consumers, employees, communities, stakeholders and all other members of the public sphere. Furthermore, they would proactively promote the public interest by encouraging community growth and development, and voluntarily eliminating practices that harm the public sphere, regardless of legality. Essentially, social responsibility is the deliberate inclusion of public interest into corporate decision making, and the honouring of a triple bottom line: **People**, **Planet**, **Profit**.

Issues associated with social responsibility include:

- Environmental pollution from production or consumption of products.
- Standards of factory safety.
- Non-discrimination in employment and marketing.
- Avoidance of the use of non-renewable resources.
- Non-production of socially undesirable goods.
- Production of non-degradable packaging and products.

In business decisions, a conflict may be encountered between what furthers the firm's interest and what satisfies society.

Illustration 3 – Tesco plc's corporate responsibility report

Tesco plc is committed to social responsibility (they use the term corporate responsibility). From their published corporate responsibility report, they state 'We understand that our success comes from behaving responsibly and earning the trust of our customers, suppliers and other stakeholders'.

They have highlighted 5 principle areas of corporate responsibility:

- Caring for the environment
- Actively supporting local communities
- Buying and selling our products responsibly
- Giving customers healthy choices
- Creating good jobs and careers

All staff from the shop floor to the boardroom are expected to consider these areas in everything they do from strategy-setting, to decision-making, to performance reviews.

Full details, which include targets and achievements under each of the headings, can be found on the Tesco plc website.

Kimberly-Clark – social responsibility

Kimberly-Clark, a well established global brand takes its social responsibility seriously. From their website they state:

We challenge ourselves to:

- Engage with people to build enduring relationships. We're committed to *social sustainability* through our practices and relationships with all our stakeholders and the communities we serve.

- Respect our planet and conserve its resources. We ensure our products provide *environmental sustainability* benefits and responsible business growth in a world with finite resources.

- Deliver quality products today and for generations to come. We offer products that deliver quality and performance at a good value. From raw materials, manufacturing processes and even our supply chain, we build *product sustainability* into every part of our business.

Social sustainability

We choose to continue to make more of our products with sustainable wood fibre, to help consumers find new ways to recycle our packaging, to channel our collecting thinking into making sustainability an integral part of everything we do. This isn't new. Throughout our history, we have woven our enduring values into the very fabric of our company. These values – authentic, accountable, innovative and caring – describe how we work with and will be judged by our consumers, business partners, investors and employees.

Environmental sustainability

We only have one planet; therefore, we strive to ensure our products provide sustainability benefits and responsible business growth in a world with finite resources. We work to find sustainable innovations that reduce the environmental impact of all our products today and for generations to come.

People around the world choose our products to improve their lives every day. Our products help people stay safe, prevent infection, increase comfort and allow for a healthy, active lifestyle.

As part of our strategy to grow responsibly, sustainable business practices are woven into the fabric of our Global Business Plan with clearly-articulated, ambitious metrics for all business units.

Our Consumer Tissue business has prioritised responsible fibre use; environmental improvements to packaging; sustainability partnerships with key customers; and reduced carbon emissions and water use.

Our Personal Care business focuses on building partnerships with environmentally progressive customers; developing environmentally sound products; manufacturing efficiency; and solid waste management.

Kimberly-Clark Professional aims to reduce waste and use of natural resources and be a leader in responsible fibre use.

Our Health Care business is aligning its sustainability efforts with those of its customers in the areas of waste management, health and safety, and infection prevention. We're also communicating our sustainability efforts so customers can make informed decisions about the products they buy and the partners with whom they do business.

Our Vision 2010 environmental program is designed to drive improvement toward energy, water and waste reduction targets.

> By taking this bold step, we're charting the course to a better future. We bring the best thinking of our global employees together to help treat our planet's resources more carefully. From raw materials, our manufacturing processes, even our supply chain, we're building sustainability into every facet of how we work.
>
> Customers can trust Kimberly-Clark to deliver innovative, high-quality products with environmental benefits.
>
> **Product sustainability**
>
> People around the world choose our essential products to make their lives better. Convenient and easy to use, our products help people stay safe (at work and elsewhere), they prevent infection, they reduce leakage and skin irritation and they increase comfort allowing for a healthy, active lifestyle.
>
> Our aim is to also ensure our products provide sustainable benefits and responsible business growth in a world of finite resources.
>
> We challenge ourselves every day to:
>
> - Incorporate into product development customer insights on how to make our products more sustainable
> - Systematically apply environmental principles when developing new products. We aim to consider the whole product life-cycle during product design.
>
> *Taken from the Kimberly-Clark website May 2011*

7 Social responsibility and shareholder wealth

The shareholder wealth view

There is a view that the management of a business has the responsibility of maximising its shareholders' wealth and that wider society will benefit from the economic activities of the business as the fruits of economic success will 'trickle down' from the rich to all members of society. This view is often referred to as a 'corporatist', 'libertarian', or 'Thatcherite' view.

The economist Milton Friedman (1963) supports the ethical argument in favour of shareholder supremacy with the dictum: **'The business of business is business.'**

The stakeholder view

There is an alternative view that business organisations are members of society, just as other stakeholders and members of the public are members of society. Social contract theory holds that all members of society are entitled to have their rights respected so long as they obey their responsibilities to other members of society. As such, organisations are afforded the right to exist and make profits from their trade so long as they observe the responsibility they have to other members of society by acting in a socially responsible way. This view is often referred to as a 'social-democratic', 'morally-grounded' view.

This social-democratic view argues that organisations have social responsibilities to others, particularly in the following areas:

- the environment, e.g. pollution.
- utilisation of public goods and services, e.g. roads, bridges, law and order, etc.
- consumers, e.g. monopoly situations in terms of control of markets.
- employment opportunities and working conditions.
- economies of specific regions and whole countries.

Social responsibility and business ethics may affect the mission and objectives of the organisation and may dilute the importance of shareholder wealth as a primary objective.

Must social responsibility conflict with benefiting shareholders?

Deciding to be socially responsible may conflict with shareholders' interests in several ways:

- *Firm may incur additional costs*. Examples of these extra costs include:
  - paying staff more than the minimum wage set by market forces or legislation to avoid accusations of exploitation;
  - treating emissions and waste to reduce environmental pollution;
  - increasing product and plant safety levels;
  - costs of monitoring compliance with social responsibility policies.

- *Firm may reduce revenues*. Examples include:
  - charging lower prices for products to avoid being accused of exploiting the consumer (e.g. pharmaceutical products);
  - refusing to supply particular governments;
  - not promoting a socially undesirable good to particular consumer groups (e.g. cigarettes or alcohol to the young).
- *Shareholder funds may be diverted to socially worthwhile projects*. This relates to charitable donations by firms to the arts, relief of social need or sponsorship of national projects. This money could otherwise be dividend.
- *Management and staff time may be wasted on social projects*. The management and staff are paid to run the business, not to indulge in social engineering.

Counter-arguments to suggest that social responsibility in business will improve shareholder returns:

- *Essential to being a sustainable enterprise*. A 'sustainable enterprise' is one whose competitive strategy does not fundamentally conflict with the long-term needs and values of society. Put simply, a non-sustainable enterprise is living on borrowed time and has no long-term future. It is in the interests of shareholders that firms become sustainable, if earnings are to continue into the future.

  For example, some writers question whether oil companies can be sustainable enterprises because their core business seems inevitably to lead to damage to the natural environment. These practices may be tolerated at present, the argument runs, but must eventually be brought to an end by legislation and financial penalties prompted by the rising tide of public concern about environmental degradation. Oil companies are aware of this criticism and have responded by developing processes to 'clean up their act'.

  Other industries which may need to address the issues of sustainability include the tobacco, brewing and car industries.

- *Attracts socially conscious investors*. Ethical investment funds will be attracted to firms with a good social responsibility score. This will cause their shares to trade at a premium price. This represents a direct rise in shareholder wealth.
- *Attracts socially conscious consumers*. The consumers will pay a premium price for products they regard as 'sound'. Examples include ethical cosmetics, organic foods, recycled paper products and 'fair trade' coffee.

- *Improves relations with governments and other regulatory bodies.* Many firms depend on the goodwill of governmental bodies for the granting of production licences, planning permission or convivial legislation. A good record in social responsibility may help convince the decision-maker to use discretion in the firm's favour.

- *Reduces stress on management and staff and permits improved morale.* This argument points to the fact that feelings of ethics and social responsibility are not solely external to the firm. The management and staff of the firm are members of society too and have similar values. If business decisions force managers and staff to contradict their private ethics on a daily basis, the impact will be to reduce morale and increase staff turnover. This will harm financial performance. A socially responsible firm, on the other hand, may be able to attract these staff.

Increasing shareholder wealth is the sole objective

Friedman: profit is the sole objective

The economist Milton Friedman (1963) supports the ethical argument in favour of shareholder supremacy with the dictum: **'The business of business is business.'** His argument can be presented as following a number of steps of reasoning:

- All economic systems are mechanisms to serve the needs of the population of the system.
- History has shown the market economy to be superior to other forms of systems, such as feudalism and socialism, in providing the greatest benefits to the greatest number of people.
- In a market economy, the needs of society are transmitted to firms by price signals emanating from the market.
- By following these signals, firms coordinate their activities to meet society's needs.
- The search for profit is what incentivises firms to respond to market needs.
- Therefore, by being profit motivated, firms will produce the best outcomes for society.
- If management ignore the profit motive or the state tries to intervene in the market mechanism, say by laws or taxation, they merely change the identity of the winners and losers. They do not actually remove the problem ('there's no such thing as a free lunch').

Elaine Sternberg: shareholder wealth is the natural purpose.

A different pro-shareholder argument is advanced by Elaine Sternberg (1994). Friedman stresses the ethical superiority of profit-seeking behaviour by reference to its consequences (i.e. higher standard of living for all). Sternberg, on the other hand, approaches from a perspective of natural justice, that is that to do other than maximise shareholder wealth takes business outside of its proper place in society. Sternberg's argument can be simplified as follows:

- Organisations are social institutions. We understand their nature and their place in society by considering what they do and how they are different from one another.

- Business organisations are distinguished from others by their pursuit of shareholder wealth. No other organisation, say governments, charities, trades unions or armies do this. The latter are different because they have other final purposes.

- If businesses start to become involved in social responsibility by considering other goals, they are changing their purposes and invading the domains of charities and government agencies. This would be a corruption of their essential nature and the natural order of things and would constitute the theft of assets or incomes from their rightful owners, the shareholders.

- Business cannot afford to ignore its impacts on customers and other stakeholders however, because in doing so it would forsake repeat business and alienate support. This would destroy its long-term value.

- The key principles of business ethics are therefore distributive justice (distributing organisational rewards among people according to the contribution they have made) and ordinary decency (building long-term trust by not resorting to dishonest or coercive means in the short run).

The egotistical view

Ayn Rand: the 'virtue of selfishness'

- The essence of human existence is the need for the individuals to assure their own survival.

- Therefore, the only rational (i.e. ethical) goal is the pursuit of individual survival through self-interest.

- If any person shows (or is compelled by law to show) consideration for the interests of others, this intrudes on achieving their own self-interest and they are effectively allowing themselves to become subordinate to other people's needs. Taken to extremes, this leads to slavery and oppression.

- Capitalism (stripped of any benevolent religious belief systems, which are themselves a form of oppression) is the only social and economic system which enables and rewards pursuit of unbridled self-interest.

- Owners of firms are therefore only ethical if they ruthlessly pursue economic self-interest.

In this approach there is no notion of social responsibility because it believes there is no such thing as society (other than as a concept invented by would-be oppressors). Rather, we are a collection of egoists. Objectivism would advocate leaving to their fate the people in the store example, on the basis that to compel the store (or the families and state) to help them would be to deny the self-interest of the helpers.

Test your understanding 5

Tomborough is a large region with a rugged, beautiful coastline where rare birds have recently settled on undisturbed cliffs. Since mining ceased 150 years ago, its main industries have been agriculture and fishing. However, today, many communities in Tomborough suffer high unemployment. Government initiatives for regeneration through tourism have met with little success as the area has poor road networks, unsightly derelict buildings and dirty beaches.

Digdown Explorations, a listed company, has a reputation for maximising shareholder returns and has discovered substantial tin reserves in Tomborough. With new technology, mining could be profitable, provide jobs and boost the economy. A number of interest and pressure groups have, however, been vocal in opposing the scheme.

Digdown Explorations, after much lobbying, has just received government permission to undertake mining. It could face difficulties in proceeding because of the likely activity of a group called the Tomborough Protection Alliance. This group includes wildlife protection representatives, villagers worried about the potential increase in traffic congestion and noise, environmentalists, and anti-capitalism groups.

Required:

(a) Discuss the ethical issues that should have been considered by the government when granting permission for mining to go ahead. Explain the conflicts between the main stakeholder groups.

(13 marks)

(b) By use of some (mapping) framework, analyse how the interest and power of pressure and stakeholder groups can be understood. Based on this analysis, identify how Digdown Explorations might respond to these groups.

(12 marks)

Test your understanding 6

Essentials is a retail company going through a period of rapid growth. It was able to increase its market share despite the general decline in the industry due to its competitive prices and ability to rapidly update clothing ranges in line with fashion changes.

To improve profitability and increase its appeal, the company decided to introduce new higher value items, such as organic cotton garments. As a way to reinforce the responsible retailer reputation, the company instructed its store managers to display an "ethical retailer" trademark in a prominent location within its outlets.

> Yesterday the company's CEO was contacted by the country's leading TV channel asking to comment on the result of undercover investigation of one of Essential's suppliers. It was established that the supplier breached the employment legislations by paying staff below minimum wage and not complying with the basic Health and Safety provisions. CEO has requested your help in preparing for the TV appearance aimed at restoring company's reputation.
>
> **Required:**
>
> Provide an outline of the ethical policy that would help Essentials to restore its reputation.
>
> **(10 marks)**

8 An ecological perspective

The ecological perspective of strategy is closely aligned with social responsibility. It is concerned with the relationship of the organisation with the natural environment in which it operates.

One approach suggested by Bennett and James (1996) lays down six areas in which this might be monitored:

(1) *Production*. This is primarily concerned with minimising the amount of materials and energy used to generate output.

(2) *Environmental auditing*. It focuses on improving relationship with the ecological environment and will cover such things as compliance with legislation, treatment of waste, product and process hazard and emissions.

(3) *Ecological approach*. This can be a lifecycle approach in which the product is traced from the extraction of the raw material through production and consumption of the product till disposal of the final exhausted product. At each point, the ecological impacts are noted and targets set for reducing them. Alternatively, a single site or project can be looked at and its impacts on its immediate locale considered.

(4) *Quality*. This anticipates a continuous improvement in the environmental performance of the business. Therefore targets are constantly amended to achieve better performance.

(5) *Accounting*. Dummy shadow prices are attached to the social costs of projects to create a separate set of accounts showing the environmental consequences of the firm's activities. These affect strategy through their inclusion in the investment appraisal and financial reporting process. Any strategies taken to reduce the impact of the firm on its environment will cause the ecoprofit to increase and also improve the ecobalance sheet.

(6) *Economic*. It charges environmental costs to any process, usually through budgets, to encourage management to avoid causing the environmental damage.

Implications for the management accountant

If an organisation is socially responsible, in order to achieve socially-desirable goals the management accountant should initiate activities which involve:

- Cost measurement of waste, efficiency etc.;
- Modelling of the impact of organisational plans upon the environment;
- Integrating environmental costs and benefits into investment appraisal decisions;
- Design of key environmental performance indicators (KEPIs) to measure progress;
- Analysis of performance against KEPIs.

The management accountant should take an active part in setting socially-desirable goals for the organisation and should provide financial and non-financial environmental information to allow management to make better decisions about the direction of the business and to allow them to better manage their overall environmental performance.

Test your understanding 7

An increasing number of companies have expressed their willingness to consider their wider social responsibilities. This often involves them in voluntarily undertaking extra responsibilities and costs, for example:

- In order to reduce pollution, they may decide to treat waste products to a higher standard than required by legislation.
- They may decline to trade with countries whose governments they find objectionable.
- They may pay wages above minimum levels.

Required:

(a) Discuss whether the pursuit of a policy of social responsibility necessarily involves a conflict with the objective of shareholder wealth-maximisation.

(6 marks)

(b) Discuss the extent to which the existence of a conflict between a company's objectives is acceptable.

(4 marks)

Test your understanding 8

C plc, a quoted chemical manufacturing company, has until recently achieved a steady increase in profitability over a number of years. It faces stern competition and the directors are concerned about the disquiet expressed by major shareholders regarding performance over the last two years. During this period it has consistently increased dividends, but its share price has not grown at the same rate as it did previously.

K plc, a direct competitor, is similarly experiencing a reduction in profitability. Its shareholders are diverse, with the majority being financial institutions. K plc has been criticised for under-investment and has achieved no product development over the last two years. Following a concerted media campaign, K plc is facing prosecution for discharging untreated pollutants into a river.

C plc is seriously considering making a bid to acquire K plc. The directors of C plc, however, are divided as to whether K plc should be closed down or permitted to continue production post-acquisition if a bid is made. In either situation, significant staff redundancies would follow.

Corporate governance, ethics and social responsibility

Required:

(a) Discuss the social and ethical implications for the managers and staff of both C plc and K plc if the acquisition goes ahead.

(10 marks)

(b) Discuss the environmental issues which would face the directors of C plc if it proceeds with the acquisition of K plc.

(8 marks)

(c) List the issues and prerequisites you would consider for an effective environmental audit.

(7 marks)

9 Summary diagram

CORPORATE GOVERNANCE
- Purpose
- History
- Benefits
- Rules

SOCIAL RESPONSIBILITY
- Corporate social responsibility
- Shareholders
- Ecological perspective
- Benefits

CORPORATE GOVERNANCE, ETHICS AND SOCIAL RESPONSIBILITY

ETHICS
- Definition
- Levels
- Ethical organisation
- Professional ethics

Corporate governance, ethics and social responsibility

Test your understanding answers

Test your understanding 1

There are a number of corporate governance issues in this company, including:

- The chairman is not independent – the chairman of the company should be an independent non-executive director (NED). In this case the chairman is the CEO's brother which means he lacks independence

- The chairman's job is to run the board, but this is not happening in Sparks. The CEO and chairman make all the decisions, the rest of the directors do not seem to get involved in any discussions about the running of the company.

- It is not clear if Joe considers himself a NED, but even if he does, he is not acting as one. Half the board should be NEDs. This is not the case here as all the other directors are employed by Sparks plc.

- One of the main roles of the NEDs is to scrutinise the decisions of the executive directors. There is no one challenging the CEO's decisions, shown by the fact that the strategy was emailed to the directors to start implementing, with no discussion.

- The board rarely meet. Boards should meet frequently and regularly.

- Bob was allowed to set his own remuneration. Remuneration of executive directors should be set by a remuneration committee made up of NEDs.

- Bob's remuneration is seen by the other directors as excessive. The remuneration of the directors should be set at a level which will allow the company recruit and retain good directors who will work in the best interests of shareholders. Excessive remuneration will rarely be in the best interests of the shareholders.

- Bob asked the finance director to hide the level of his remuneration. As part of good corporate governance, the remuneration of directors must be disclosed fully in the annual accounts.

Test your understanding 2

The following factors need to be considered in dealing with the problem:

- *Group*: non-quantifiable factors at group level, which include the company's reactions to the disclosure of error and reduced profits; the competence of the divisional management; and the advisability of future divisional investment.

- *Customer*: non-quantifiable factors in respect of the future relationships with the customer including the present and past honesty affecting future relationships; the need to lower costs and prices affecting margins and the volume of business; the embarrassment likely to be felt by those dealing directly with the customer; the possibility that disclosure will lead to the termination of the contract with the customer; and the possibility of the customer imposing penalties on the company.

- *Long-term and short-term considerations*: the probability of short-term profits being reduced and an adjustment needing to be made which will be significant and visible; the reduction of past profits; and the improvement of long-term profits after disclosure.

- *Risk*: including the chance of the customer discovering the error; the chance of a company employee informing the customer; and the potential legal problems which could ensue if fraud was suspected.

- *Moral and ethical judgements*: all the issues relating to the integrity of professionals and the trustworthiness of supplier companies.

- *Use of normal decision-making techniques*: dealing with economies and probabilities rather than the right or wrong of the issue.

Possible courses of action

There are three broad courses of action the company can take in dealing with the problem:

- Use the correct calculation for the contract and disclose past errors.

- Use the correct calculation for the contract but do not disclose the past errors.

- Use the incorrect calculation for future contracts and do not disclose the past errors.

The choice of action

Recommending a choice of action involves applying moral and ethical judgement, the corporate ethical code and CIMA Ethical Guidelines. Therefore the recommended action the company should take is to use the correct calculation for the contract and disclose the past errors.

Issues arising from implementing the recommendation

If the management suggests an unethical course of action:

- An explanation in terms of the need for compliance with professional ethics and the law of the country would be given as to why this is unacceptable.

- Discussion in confidence would be initiated with an objective third party.

- Established procedures including channels of communication would be followed.

- It would be important to establish that the issue is one of principle and not personality.

- There would be preparedness to take the issue to the board of directors or any audit committee of the board, as formalising the procedure makes the issue less susceptible to fraud.

- As a last resort, resignation making the reason clear is a possibility.

Disclosing the issue ('whistle-blowing') breaks the confidentiality guidelines.

Test your understanding 3

Corporate governance concerns the ownership and control of profit making organisations and the relationship between owners and manages. A number of reports have been produced to address the risk and problems resulting from poor corporate governance. In the UK the most significant reports include the Cadbury, Hempel and Greenbury reports. The recommendations are merged into a Combined Code which comprises the purpose and principles of good corporate governance for listed companies

There are a number of corporate governance issues facing Y Company:

- It is problematic for one person to hold both the role of Chairman and Managing Director since this can result in too much concentration of power being in the hands of one person, and the greater dangers of the misuse or abuse of power. As illustrated in the scenario, it is difficult for other directors to challenge M's decisions. M, through his dominance and associated behaviours, combining chairperson and chief executive roles contravenes much of the recent thinking on corporate governance. This advocates that the separation of the two roles is essential for good control.

- It is evident from the scenario that Board meetings are ineffective, they are held on an irregular and infrequent basis with M wielding his power over other directors. It would seem that he has forced through decisions that are in his own personal interest, and could be detrimental to the company. One of the core principles of the Combined Code is that listed companies should be led by effective Boards, which meet regularly and membership should be a balance of executive and non executive directors so that no individuals or small groups can dominate decision-making. It would be appropriate for non-executive directors to be appointed to the Board of Y Company to provide independent judgements on decisions.

- It seems that there is a lack of adequate control, accountability and audit in the company. The Board is responsible for presenting a balanced and understandable assessment of the company's financial position. It is responsible for maintaining a sound system for internal controls to safeguard the company's assets and shareholders investment. Y Company should establish through an audit committee formal and transparent arrangements for considering how to apply the principles of financial reporting and internal control. Non-executive directors should satisfy themselves on the integrity of financial information and that controls are robust.

- M has determined his own remuneration package, which he is keen to keep covered up. Good corporate governance practice states that no director should be involved in determining his/her own remuneration. Non-executive directors should be responsible for determining a policy on the remuneration of executive directors and specific remuneration packages for each director, a proportion of which should be linked to corporate and individual performance. It is good practice to include a report on the remuneration policy for directors to the annual accounts.

The above points would help support the Finance Director who has been placed in an awkward situation regarding the illegal accounting practices and M's remuneration.

Ethical issues arise when one person values conflict with those of others. M appears to be making decisions that are not within acceptable standards of honesty and integrity. In his position he should be setting the moral tone for Y Company, but in this case it seems that M is abusing his power. This is illustrated by M's lack of ethical behaviour regarding the acceptance of bribes, insider dealing, and the secret negotiations to move manufacturing to a country where there workers could be exploited. Other members of the Board may have different ethical values regarding the potential exploitation of labour and the loss of jobs but seem to be unwilling or unable to challenge M.

The Finance Director could be encouraged to 'whistle blow', a practice in which she could exposed the mis-deeds of M, preventing further wrongdoings and to preserve ethical standards. That said, because of the lack of legal protection, the Finance Director could risk losing her job. It is apparent from the scenario that she doesn't have the support of other colleagues on the Board.

Test your understanding 4

CIMA has a professional code of ethics which is designed to regulate the conduct of its members and, in doing so, protect the individual client or employer and the public interests more generally. A number of fundamental principles are in danger of being breached by the actions of the finance director and A, if she complies with the request to omit the sales returns figures in return for the promotion.

The finance director's request to omit sales returns figures breaches the principle of **professional behaviour**. Falsifying records in order to secure a personal bonus could bring the profession into disrepute. If the bonus has not been earned, then it should not be paid. To take the bonus in these circumstances is to show disregard to the shareholders who rely on the directors to run the company in their interests.

If A complies with the request, she is condoning this behaviour and is also acting against the principle of professional behaviour.

If A accepts the promotion in return for this omission, then the principle of **integrity** is compromised. A is not being honest in the reports she is producing. The finance director states that this is just a timing issue, but he is asking her to deliberately manipulate the figures for personal gain, which is fundamentally dishonest.

In addition, the principle of **professional competence and due care** is contravened since A is expected to deliver a competent behaviour towards her employer and act diligently in accordance with applicable technical and professional standards.

The principle of **objectivity** requires a professional accountant not to allow bias, conflict of interest or undue influence of others to override professional or business judgement. This could be compromised since A may feel she is under undue influence from the finance director. In accepting the promotion this could create a conflict of interest in that A may feel she needs to do whatever the finance director requests, because she may be worried that he might report her acceptance of the promotion at some point in the future.

In offering A a promotion, the Finance Director could be guilty of the charge of bribery and attempting to corrupt a fellow employee if no action is taken. This could have the effect of damaging the standing of CIMA as a professional body.

Test your understanding 5

(a) **Ethics**

Ethics are a code of moral principles that people follow with respect to what is right or wrong. General examples might include staying within the law, not engaging in bribery or theft, or endangering other people.

Also, a part of ethics is social responsibility: the duty towards the wider community or society in general which includes environmental issues, public safety, employment and exploitation of third world workers.

In this case ethical issues which the government should have considered when granting permission for mining include:

(1) **Employment in the local area**
The government has a duty toward people to provide them with jobs. In Tomborough there is significant unemployment so it is particularly important for the government to generate jobs in the area. The effect of the mining on employment levels should therefore be considered.

(2) **The local economy**
The government has an obligation to the people of Tomborough to improve the wealth of the people there. This largely depends on a successful economy. The local economy of Tomborough has been performing badly despite various initiatives based around tourism. The effect of mining on the local economy generally must be considered (i.e. jobs create income which is then spent in local shops, demand for property increases and prices rise for all in the area).

(3) **Environmental concerns**
Tomborough has a beautiful coastline with rare birds nesting there. The government has a responsibility towards society generally to preserve areas of natural beauty for all to appreciate and enjoy, and a moral obligation towards other species on the planet to protect them from extinction.

The effects of the mining operations on the rare birds, the beauty of the coastline and any pollution caused in the locality should therefore have been considered by the government.

(4) **Rights of local individuals**
Individuals have the right for their quality of life to remain high. While employment and an improved economy may improve the quality of life of many, there may also be negative effects for some local people such as increased noise and traffic congestion.

(5) **Right to free operation of business**
Many capitalist countries believe in free trade and removing barriers to trade. This may be seen as a right of the business, and it may be considered as part of the decision to allow Digdown to open the mining operation.

Conflicts between stakeholder groups

Stakeholders are people who are affected or interested in some way by the mining operations. In this case stakeholders include:

- national government
- local government
- local people
- wildlife protection groups
- environmental groups
- directors of Digdown
- employees of Digdown
- shareholders of Digdown.

The **conflicts** which may exist include the following:

(1) **National vs local government**
Local government will be interested in Tomborough and its interests. National government have to balance those needs with the needs of all people of the country. There may be a conflict over the amount of funding available to support local initiatives such as to help start up the mining operations.

(2) **Unemployed vs people based near mining operations/ working people**
Unemployed people of the area will notice a direct benefit from the mining operations through increased jobs and are likely to support it. Other local residents may simply view the operations as disrupting their existing life (noise/congestion) and oppose the idea.

(3) **Shareholders/directors of Digdown vs environmental/ wildlife protection groups**
Both shareholders and Directors of Digdown wish to make profits from Digdown's operations. The mining operations will enable them to make full use of an asset they own (tin reserves) and hence increase profit. They will wish it to go ahead, and may have very little interest in the broader impact.

Environmental groups aim to protect the environment and are likely to oppose any part of the mining operation which will effect the environment irrespective of profitability.

(b) **Stakeholder mapping**

A useful model that can be used to examine stakeholders and how an organisation should deal with them is Mendelow's Matrix.

Mendelow said that there are two key aspects of understanding stakeholders:

(1) **Power**
This is the degree to which the stakeholder group can exert influence over Digdown, its operations and likely profitability. The local government, for instance, have the power to grant or refuse planning applications and hence have a lot of power in the tin mining issue.

A local individual who feels strongly against the mining operations may have little power because whatever they do they are unlikely to be able to influence the decision. A large local group of people, on the other hand, have more power since they may be able to influence the local authority who must ensure the best interests of local people are met.

The greater the power a group has the more their views will be considered when decisions are being made. Digdown, for instance, will have ensured that all local government concerns are met in order to get permission to undertake mining.

(2) **Interest**

The level of interest which the stakeholder has in the company (or in this case the mining operations) is also important to the company. If a party is not interested then the company will not need to concern itself with communicating with them or adapting to meet their needs.

In this case for instance Central Government is likely to have little interest in the local issue even though they have significant power. As long as the issue is not seen to affect national issues they are likely to remain unconcerned.

The matrix

Stakeholders can be placed into Mendelow's matrix according to their interest and power. Depending on where they fall, a different response will be necessary from Digdown.

Mendelow's Matrix

	Level of Interest Low	Level of Interest High
Level of Power Low	**A** Lack of interest and power means they are likely to accept what they are told. **MINIMAL EFFORT** **[DIRECTION]**	**B** Present strategy as rational then may stop them joining forces with powerful dissenters. **KEEP INFORMED** **[EDUCATION/ COMMUNICATION]**
Level of Power High	**C** Keep them satisfied. Assure them of the likely outcomes of the strategy well in advance. **KEEP SATISFIED** **[INTERVENTION]**	**D** Can be major drivers or major opponents of change. Need to assure them that the change is necessary. **KEY PLAYERS** **[PARTICIPATION]**

The responses required are as follows:

Key player – keep close

Key players must be kept close to the company in all major issues relating to the mining operations. For example, close relationships should be built with the local government so that they are continually kept informed of new plans. This ensures the plans are acceptable and within regulation. Any new requirements are also quickly understood and can be dealt with promptly.

Keep satisfied

For example, the Central Government should be kept satisfied by ensuring that the issue does not affect their main concern, national issues as a whole. So long as this is the case they are unlikely to get involved in this local issue and exert their considerable power. If not 'kept satisfied' this group can move to the 'Key player' quadrant.

Keep informed

For example, Digdown employees will be very interested in the effect of the new operations on jobs. It may, for instance, create job security for them, or mean they have to relocate. It is therefore very important to ensure they understand the impact on them and expectations of them. Without formal notification, information will spread via rumour which may be inaccurate and cause undue concern. Although they have little power, the high interest displayed by members of this group can mean that they can have a strong influence on the key players.

Minimal effort

It is important to clarify which groups have little power or interest to avoid unnecessary effort being made. An example here is the general public outside Tomborough. They are likely to have little interest or power and so no effort needs to be made to keep them happy and there is little benefit from keeping them informed.

Test your understanding 6

Ethical policy of a company should outline what activities it deems to be acceptable and what behaviour, exhibited by employees, suppliers of third parties it views as reprehensible. In addition a range of measure to reinforce desirable behaviour and prevent or address violations needs to be included.

As consumers are becoming more aware and therefore concerned about social and environmental implications of companies' actions, their purchasing decisions are heavily influenced by the degree to which the conduct of an organisation is supported by good moral judgement.

Essentials plc needs to consider whether supplier's clearly illegal conduct is compatible with company's ethical retailer aspirations. If looked at from the compliance perspective, Essentials itself has not directly breached any legislation and therefore is not accountable. However the integrity viewpoint encourages the company to go above the minimum standard and ensure fair treatment of all stakeholders, such as taking responsibility for suppliers' actions.

Gap Inc, who has recently found itself in a similar situation, put forward a policy requiring a contractor found to use child labour to remove the child from the workplace, provide it with access to schooling and a wage, and guarantee the opportunity of work on reaching a legal working age. Thus collaboration with suppliers, encouraging them to adopt the right practices is seen as a better long term solution than immediately terminating the contract.

Essentials should require its suppliers to comply with following:

- All staff should receive training relevant to performance of their duties, there should be a designated officer with whom they could raise an issue if the facilities do not meet the basic standard expected.
- Staff wages should be set at a higher of minimum wage and industry standard, this should be sufficient to meet the living needs of staff and provide them with some discretionary income.
- Employment regulations should be made clear to all staff, they need to be familiar with their rights and be provided with a impartial channel for raising a grievance if treatment is seen as unfair.
- Working hours should not be excessive; the decision to work overtime should be made voluntarily with a premium rate offered as compensation. No discrimination is allowed on a basis of sex, gender or race in providing benefits to staff.

Essentials should initially assist the supplier in helping it to comply with the higher standards by providing advice on practical aspects of implementation. Regular inspection of supplier's facilities will help to ascertain whether a hygienic working environment is provided, the working processes are safe and all reasonable measures are taken to minimise hazards and the risk of accidents.

In the circumstances when a supplier is not willing to follow the given guidelines, Essentials would have to terminate the contract as associating with such contractor will further damage company's reputation.

Additional areas where ethical guidelines may be useful are:

- Reducing environmental impact by decreasing energy use, minimising transportation of stock to decrease harmful emissions, recycling packaging and using of biodegradable plastic.

- Essentials may considering donating part of its profits to charity or directly investing in community projects such as running educational programmes or building school and sanitation facilities in disadvantaged areas.

- Company need to create an inclusive working environment, where individual differences are valued and each employee is treated with dignity and respect. Being an equal opportunities employer, extending the benefits provision to include not only employees but the members of their family would raise the company's standing and employee's morale.

- Social responsibility reporting could be incorporated within company's financial statement to demonstrate the degree of commitment to the cause and provide a wide range of indicators responsible conduct should be measured against.

Test your understanding 7

(a) About 20 or so years ago, the idea that profitability was overwhelmingly the principal objective of a business would have been uncontroversial. Today's climate is different: increased public awareness of the social impact of large organisations has broadened the range of objectives which businesses must aim to achieve. New factors to be considered include pollution control, conservation of natural resources and avoidance of environmental damage.

In the short term, the measures described in the question would reduce profits; all of them involve profits or revenue forgone. And reduced profits imply reduced shareholders' wealth in the form of dividends and capital growth.

However, this analysis, though relatively straightforward in the short term, may not be so clear-cut in the long term. Many commentators argue that the reputation and image of corporations will suffer if they do not respond to heightened awareness of social responsibility amongst consumers. Given that many companies are already taking steps along this path, and making good public relations out of their efforts, there is pressure on other companies to follow suit. Failure to do so may lead to long-term decline.

(b) A conflict between company objectives implies a picture of managers pulling in opposite directions, some trying to meet criteria of social responsibility, others hell-bent on maximising profit. Given that all of the managers in a company are drawing on the same pool of resources this is a recipe for disaster.

However, this does not mean that companies are doomed to fail if they pursue more than one objective. The ideal is to agree on a balance between conflicting objectives, and to settle on a strategy which satisfies both sets of objectives, to the extent that they can be reconciled.

Test your understanding 8

(a) It is likely that fewer employees will be needed in the combined business. In particular, the providers of specialist expertise may be particularly vulnerable as duplication of this type of activity may not be required. It is likely, therefore, that a significant number of redundancies will occur. This will create a feeling of insecurity among staff. It is important that all staff are informed of the policy in respect of redundancies. This will be particularly important in the acquired company, especially if the bid is hostile. The rationalisation process will create uncertainty within both firms and it is important for the motivation of employees that the issue is handled with openness and honesty.

Changes in employees' working conditions within the combined firm is an important issue. If it is not handled well, it is likely that the overall synergy of the acquisition will be adversely affected. Uncertainty about employment will be a problem for the staff and a clear statement on the rationale for the acquisition and the employment policies to be adopted would appear essential. Remuneration, training programmes and assistance in finding alternative employment are topics which should be discussed to improve staff morale within the firm. It will demonstrate the attitude of the directors to the staff redundancies. It is important that employee motivation is retained if the acquisition is to reach its potential. Management must, therefore, handle the social and ethical implications of the acquisition sensitively, especially in respect of the staff redundancies which appear to be inevitable.

(b) After acquiring K plc, some environmental issues will need to be tackled by management. The pollution problem, in particular, will have to be addressed. It is clear that the matter of the untreated pollutants should be investigated immediately so that the level of pollution is brought under control. As a priority, the company should seek to establish acceptable levels of effluent pollution and the firm would be wise to participate in establishing these standards.

At the same time, steps will have to be taken to reduce the adverse publicity that may arise through the prosecution pending against K plc. It would seem to be necessary for the company to adopt and publicise an environmental policy within the community to ensure that the negative effects of the pollution problem are minimised.

It is likely that considerable expenditure will be needed to rectify the position. The continued success of the firm may depend on the way in which the pollution problem is handled. The projected success of the combined businesses will determine the amount of expenditure that might be incurred to reduce the pollution problems.

(c) The issues to be considered in respect of an environmental audit may be:

- The extent of compliance with legislation.
- Minimisation of potential liabilities.
- Minimisation of insurance costs.
- The need for baseline data.
- The need to emphasise environmental responsibility.
- The need for tailoring and flexibility.

The prerequisites for environmental audits to consider may be:

- Senior management commitment.
- The objectivity of the audit team.
- Competence in the technical and general aspects of environmental knowledge.
- Well-defined, systematic procedures.
- Written reports based on objective assessments.
- Quality assurance of auditing procedures.
- Follow-up by monitoring and review of implementation and the effect of the recommendations.

chapter 12

Principles of project management

Chapter learning objectives

- Identify a project, a programme and their attributes.
- Apply suitable structures and frameworks to projects to identify common project management issues.
- Construct an outline of the process of project management.
- Identify the characteristics of each phase in the project process.
- Produce a strategy for a project

Principles of project management

1 Session content diagram

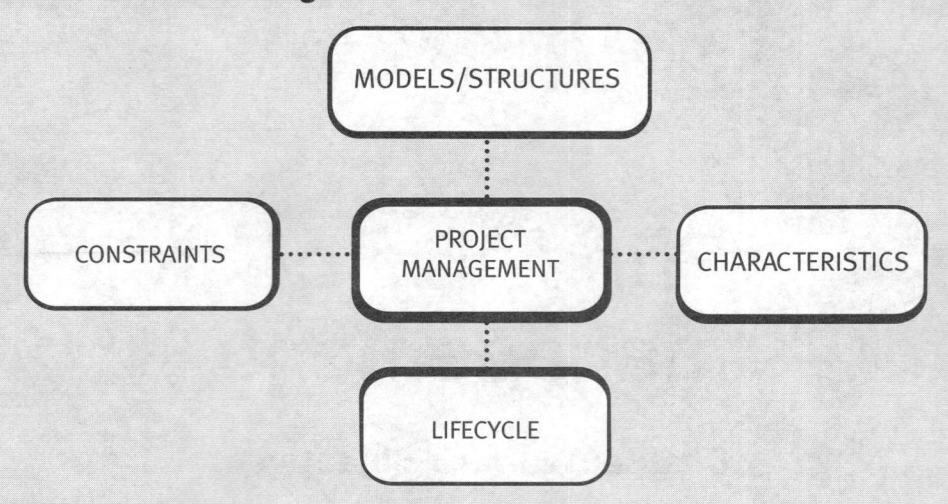

```
              ┌──────────────────┐
              │ MODELS/STRUCTURES│
              └────────┬─────────┘
                       ┊
┌───────────┐   ┌──────┴──────┐   ┌─────────────────┐
│CONSTRAINTS┊┈┈┈┤   PROJECT   ├┈┈┈┊ CHARACTERISTICS │
└───────────┘   │ MANAGEMENT  │   └─────────────────┘
                └──────┬──────┘
                       ┊
                ┌──────┴──────┐
                │  LIFECYCLE  │
                └─────────────┘
```

2 Defining a project, programme and project management

Project

A project is a **unique** undertaking to achieve a specific *objective*.

Once completed, it should then become integrated into the normal day-to-day activities of the business.

A project has a **defined beginning and end**.

A project has **resource**s, like staff and funding allocated specifically for the length of the project.

The project will also have **stakeholders**, i.e. all those who are interested in the progress and final outcome.

A project will inevitably have some degree of **uncertainty** as the uniqueness of it will lead to some degree of risk in the deliverables and the activities to achieve the deliverables.

The Association of Project Managers defines a project as: '*A human activity that achieves a clear objective against a time scale*.'

> *CIMA Official Terminology* defines project management as 'the integration of all aspects of a project, ensuring that the proper knowledge and resources are available when and where needed, and above all to ensure that the expected outcome is produced in a timely, cost-effective manner.

Programme

A Programme is a portfolio of related projects that, together, help to achieve a strategic objective. All of the individual projects will have their own individual timescales and budgets, but will also be part of the overall programme targets.

A programme is ongoing. It is part of what the organisation does both now and in the future. A programme is part of the organisation's mission and not something that might be considered an after-thought. A programme receives ongoing funding. It has people to attend to it ongoing basis.

Programme management

Programme management is the overall direction and control of this portfolio of projects. It includes the management of the inter-relationships between the various projects, where appropriate, including the management of shared resources, conflict resolution, high level reporting, etc. Thus, the key to programme management is co-ordination and ensuring that those involved in the individual projects understand the overall aim of the organisation. Programme management requires the same skills and capabilities as project management, with the added requirement of understanding the bigger picture. Also, it is likely that the Programme Manager will be dealing with people at Board level as well as other senior managers.

Is project management repetitive?

Project management is not a long line of repetitive or similar functions stretching ahead, such as you would find within operations areas such as manufacturing or sales.

Project management is about managing a specific group of specialists; the professional mix of this group is tailored specifically for the accomplishment of a project. This may be a year or less in some projects, and may run to five years and upward for long-range, high-budget projects.

3 Identifying a project and its attributes

Characteristics of a project:

- **Stakeholders** – all those who are interested in the progress or the final outcome of the project including the users, customers, shareholders, and those who provide the money for the project (sponsors);
- **Uniqueness** – it may never have been undertaken before and each project will differ from every other in some respect;

- **Objectives** – projects have to meet two sets of objectives: the one relating to accomplishing customer requirements of scope, quantity, quality and cost; and the other relating to the achievement of the organisation's objectives;
- **Resources** – including people, finance, information, materials, ideas, time and so on;
- **Schedules** – plans for events over time for resources and contingencies;
- **Quality** – measured in terms of customer satisfaction and the organisation's image;
- **Uncertainty** – inevitably, uniqueness leads to a context of risk in the deliverables, the activities, the contingencies associated with suppliers, subcontractors and with time/cost;
- **Finiteness** – a fixed time scale;
- **Change** – there is no practice or rehearsal and once the project is completed, the team will ideally move on to the next project.

A successful project requires:

- Consideration of stakeholders/ownership of project by key stakeholders.
- Setting of SMART objectives.
- Identification of the required resources and any limitations or constraints with resources.
- A time-scale agreed for completion.
- Quality requirements to be identified and measured.
- A financial plan.
- Risk assessment and scenario planning.
- A project manager with leadership and communication skills.
- A project team working as a team.

Threats to a project

Not all projects are successful and it is important to be aware of the various threats which projects face.

The following is a brief list of types of threats to a project, together with some suggestions as to how they may be avoided. Some of the suggested techniques for minimising the threats will be covered in more detail in the next few chapters.

Threat	Ways of minimising threat
Poor planning	Use of project management tools such as network analysis and Gantt charts
Few control mechanisms	Implement constant progress review, together with standardised reporting mechanisms
Specification changes	User requirements should be thoroughly examined at the systems analysis stage, using walk-throughs or prototyping
Unrealistic deadlines	The critical activities in the project should be highlighted to ensure that management's attentions are concentrated on achievement of these activities
Under-resourced budgets	Management should ensure that the budget (in terms of finance and manpower) is correctly balanced to ensure that the project can be successfully completed
Poor management	Training of project managers in management skills as well as technical skills

Remember it is important to make a list of the threats that may occur so that you can take the appropriate action.

> **Test your understanding 1**
>
> **Required:**
>
> Describe the characteristics that differentiate a project from other activities within an organisation.
>
> **(6 marks)**

4 Project strategy

In chapters 2 to 6 we looked at many aspects of strategic management. We focused on developing a strategy for an organisation. We saw that an organisation's strategy was determined at the corporate level, using either a planned (rational) approach, or a more reactive (emergent) approach. Projects are the way in which corporate strategy is implemented. It is essential that the projects implemented by the organisation tie on to the organisation's overall strategy.

Like the overall corporate strategy, we can also have a strategy for a project and it can be determined in a similar step-by-step way (you should recognise the similarities here with the rational model discussed in chapter 2):

- determine the reason for the project being carried out
- carry out analysis of the current situation and the desired situation
- consider the project stakeholders, as with the overall corporate strategy there may be conflict here which will require managing
- carry out a SWOT analysis
- consider the options – there may be a number of different projects which will help fulfil the identified need
- make a choice – select the project which is to be implemented
- agree the scope of the project
- manage the key project objectives of time, cost and quality
- implement the project, this will include setting up controls to monitor the progress of the project

All of these stages will be looked at in more detail throughout the next few chapters.

5 Project constraints

Every project has constraints. Constraints are anything which restricts, limits, prevents or regulates activities being carried out. When running a project it is critical that the constraints are known, so they can be taken account of throughout the project.

The primary constraints are time, cost and quality. These are often referred to as the "project triangle":

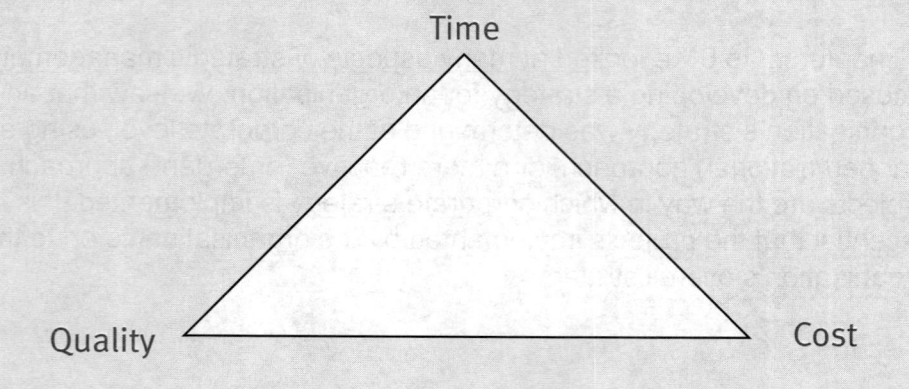

```
            Time
             /\
            /  \
           /    \
          /      \
         /        \
  Quality----------Cost
```

It is worth thinking about the conflicting nature of these constraints.

Time and cost tend to be positively correlated in projects (i.e. when time increases, so does cost), as taking longer to complete a project generally means that human resources are needed for longer. However, this is not always the case. If there is a degree of urgency in a project, it may be possible to reduce the timescale to completion by allocating additional resources, or by scheduling expensive overtime working. Both of these situations will increase cost while reducing time.

Project quality tends to be positively correlated with both cost and time, in that increasing the quality of the project will normally lead to an increase in both the cost of the project and its overall duration.

In additional to these three main constraints, there are a number of other constraints which will affect the project's delivery, such as legal, technological, political, environmental and ethical.

6 The project life cycle

Large-scale projects usually follow a life cycle made up of separate phases, which occur in sequence. There are a number of models which detail these phases. Regardless of which model is used, it is important to highlight the separate stages which the project goes through from beginning to end, and to understand what happens during each stage. A project life cycle is shown below:

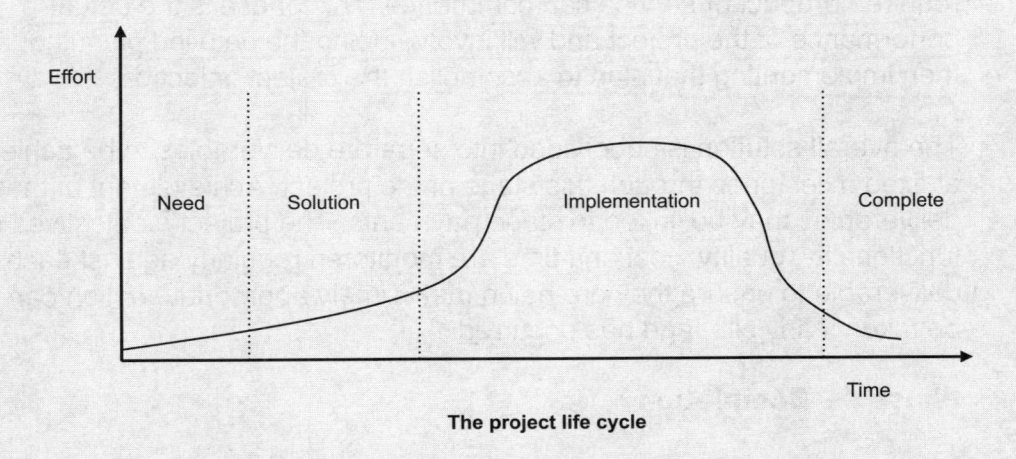

The project life cycle

Stages in the project life cycle

Gido and Clements identified four phases of large projects

Phase 1 – Identification of a need

The first phase of the project life cycle involves identification of a need, opportunity or problem. Initially, a feasibility study will be conducted to check the size of potential benefits and evaluate in broad outline potential alternative solutions and their lifetime costs. At the end of this phase, the company will decide whether to proceed with the project. If it does, then a project team is formed and a project initiation document (PID) is raised. This will include a vision and a business case for the project. The business case is an important guide to decision-making throughout the project, and the vision encourages motivation and congruent goals in the project team.

Phase 2 – Development of a proposed solution

The second stage of the project life cycle is the development of a proposed solution. All proposals for the solution will be submitted to the company, which then evaluates them and chooses the most appropriate solution to satisfy the need.

Phase 3 – Implementation

The third stage of the project life cycle is the implementation of the proposed solution. Once a proposed solution has been selected, the work to build the required product or service can commence. This phase is the actual performance of the project and will involve doing the detailed planning, and then implementing that plan to accomplish the project objective.

The overall solution is subdivided into separate deliverables to be achieved at fixed milestones through this stage of the project. Achievement of these deliverables may be linked to stage payments. The project's objectives of functionality, quality, cost and time are monitored regularly against each deliverable to ensure they are being met. Timely appropriate action can then be taken if any slippage has occurred.

Phase 4 – Completion

The fourth stage of the project life cycle is the completion or closure of the project. When a project closes, important tasks need to be carried out, such as confirmation that all deliverables have been provided and accepted, and all payments have been made and received. Project performance is evaluated and appraised in order to learn from the project for future reference. Obtaining customer feedback is important in improving the quality of future project provision. The business case is also revisited to check whether any subsequent actions are needed to ensure achievement of the anticipated benefits.

7 Five project management process areas

An alternative five stage project life cycle based on the Project Management Institute's 5 Project Management Process Areas identifies the stages as:

- Initiation
- Planning
- Execution (implementation)
- Controlling
- Completion

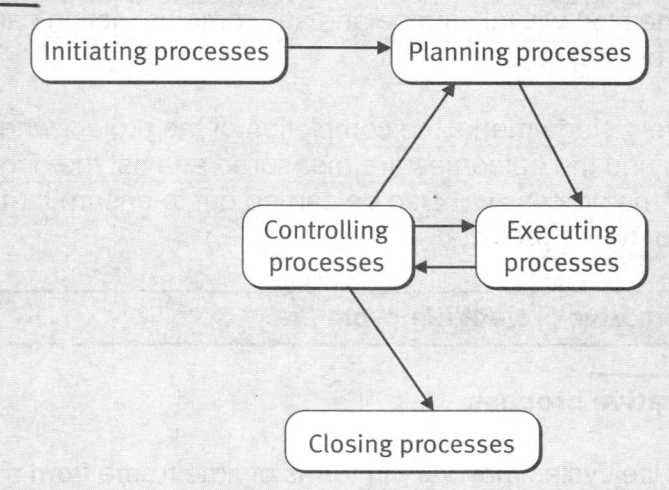

```
Initiating processes  →  Planning processes
                              ↑   ↓
                    Controlling ⇄ Executing
                     processes    processes
                              ↓
                      Closing processes
```

This model is very similar to the 'general' project life cycle above. However, it appears to place greater emphasis on the 'planning' and 'controlling' activities, as is to be expected from a professional project management institute.

This model will be the focus throughout this section of the syllabus. Chapter 13 deals with the initiation stage, Chapter 14, the planning stage and Chapter 15 deals with the remaining three stages; execution, controlling and completion.

8 The 4D project management model

Another project management model which links closely to the phases of the project lifestyle is the 4D model. This comprises of 4 steps:

- Define it
- Design it
- Develop it
- Deliver it

At the define it stage, the aims, objectives and outcomes of the project are set, along with high level timescales and cost estimates. This is similar to the initiation or need phase. This is seen as a critical stage in the project. The more time that can be spent on identifying expected outcomes, the more likely the project is to succeed.

The design it stage links in to the planning stage. At this stage the detailed planning for the project will take place. Time and cost estimates will be firmed up, activities will be detailed and constraints will be considered.

The development stage is where the work on the project is actually carried out, the execution stage. At this stage monitoring of progress of the project against the plan will take place and any remedial action can be taken to keep the project on track.

The delivery stage marks the completion of the project where the project is delivered and the outcomes are measured against the original objectives. A review of the process will also be carried out to ensure that lessons can be learned for future projects.

An alternative project life cycle

An iterative process

Project life cycles may vary in terms of time frame from a couple of weeks to several years, dependent on the complexity, size and content of the project. It is also important to recognise that not all projects will follow the exact phases of the project life cycle as presented above. Phases may be simultaneous or less structured and formal.

For smaller projects and for those where requirements are uncertain, the life cycle above may be too slow and involve customers too little during development. In these cases, the project life cycle may be repeated several times before a solution is agreed. Approximate requirements, the best ideas from competitors and the best parts of previous projects may be built with customers into a model or prototype. Key features of the proposed system are implemented in a simulated operational environment that can be used as a 'predictive model'. By trial use of the model, requirements are revised and the cycle is repeated until agreement is reached. This would reduce risk because team members can gain experience as this process evaluates complex processes, tests and validates design techniques and tools, designs test facilities, assesses aspects of system integration and can be used to persuade suppliers and users to accept the proposed solution.

The feedback from this iterative process can identify risky parts of project design or problems of integration and operation (Source: Field and Keller, 1998). In some cases, the model then becomes the final solution with no further implementation.

> **Test your understanding 2**
>
> **Required:**
>
> Use a personal example, such as a holiday, to describe the stages of the project life cycle.
>
> **(10 marks)**

9 Project approaches

A project may adopt a particular method or approach to identify all the requirements (and hence, project tasks) that will be needed to achieve the project objective. These methods effectively identify the starting point for the project, that is, what will be examined first. There are many different approaches that could be adopted. Here are some of the more well known:

- *Functional decomposition*. This involves determining a desired state and then determining all the components that would go into making that state possible. Then each of the components are analysed in turn to determine how to make those possible. This 'decomposition' continues until all the requirements are known. This approach is often used when a 'back to the drawing board' objective has been set.

- *Gap analysis*. By comparing the current system/process to the desired system/process, a set of 'gaps' can appear. The project can then be orientated to filling in those gaps and so 'moving from A to B'. This is fundamentally an incremental approach, building on what has gone before.

- *Reverse engineering*. This is essentially taking an existing object apart to see how it works in order to duplicate it or enhance it. In project terms, reverse engineering is going back to the basic design blocks to see how a thing works, to see where errors or weaknesses have occurred and to correct or improve them. It is especially useful in IT projects, where, for example, there is a constant need for updating and renovating business-critical software systems as business requirements change or technological infrastructure is modernised.

Principles of project management

10 Project structures

The McKinsey 7-S model

The McKinsey 7-S model was referred to in Chapter 7 when we looked at culture. It can also be used in project management. To recap, the model is shown below:

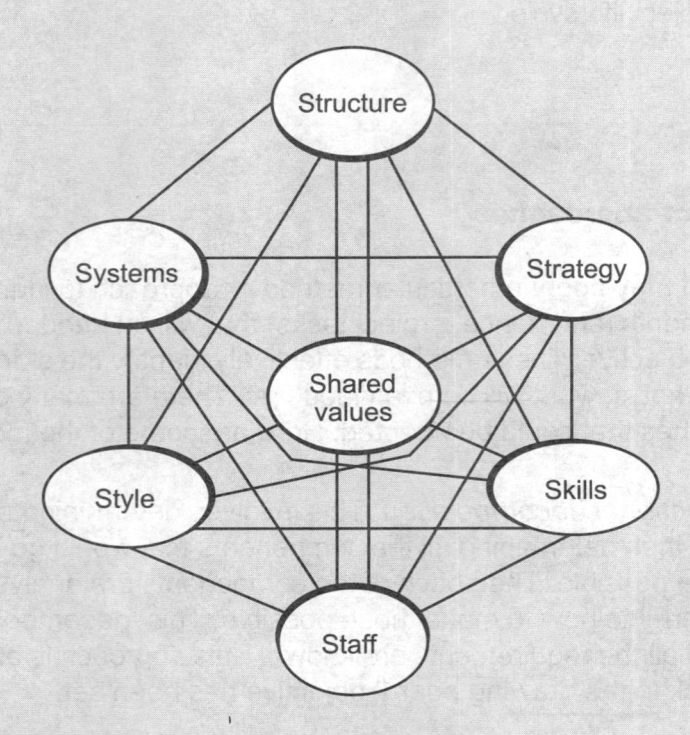

[Diagram: 7-S model showing Structure, Strategy, Systems, Shared values, Style, Skills, and Staff, all interconnected]

When used in project management, it provides a framework for the set of issues that need to be considered during the life of a project.

The model highlights how a change made in any one of the S factors will have an impact on all the others. Thus if a planned change is to be effective, then changes in one S must be accompanied by complementary changes in the others. This is helpful in project management to ensure that the impact of changes being considered are fully thought through for the whole organisation.

> **Using the 7-S model in project management**
>
> - Strategy. This will provide the high level requirements needed to fulfill the project objectives.
> - Structure. This reminds management that the nature of the appropriate structure for the project needs to be determined.
> - Systems. Systems are the methods for project work to be designed, monitored and controlled.

- **Staff.** This involves the selection of staff to work on the project, along with motivation, team management and staffing levels.
- **Style.** This refers to how the project manager leads the project and project team.
- **Skills.** These are the distinctive capabilities needed by staff working on the project.
- **Shared Values.** These refer to the guiding beliefs and the significant principles guiding the project.

The Systems Theory Approach to Project Management

The Systems Theory Approach to Project Management considers what inputs and processes are needed to achieve the required outputs.

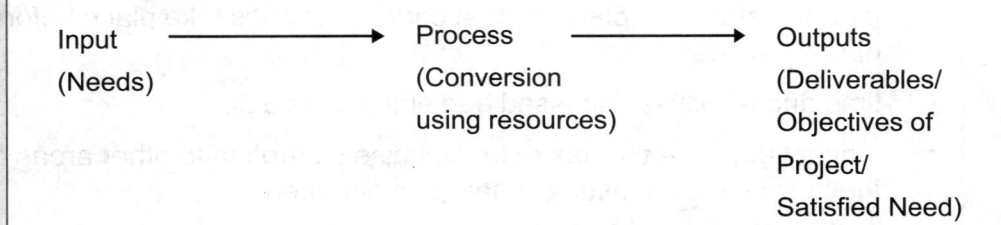

Input (Needs) → Process (Conversion using resources) → Outputs (Deliverables/ Objectives of Project/ Satisfied Need)

This offers a more flexible view of a project; that is, the project can be viewed as a conversion of some resources (input) into a final product or objective (output), as described by Maylor (2003). The project will take place under a number of constraints, often outside the project boundary, and the conversion process is carried out by a number of mechanisms that transform the resources during processing.

Inputs:

There will normally be a project brief, that is, a document that provides a statement of customer needs that is to be the foundation of the final project. There are likely to be explicit project requirements and also those that emerge during the course of the project as a result of the customer's changing needs or perceptions. The initial project brief is often open to interpretation and the expert opinions of the organisation carrying out the project, and is likely to be negotiated with the customer.

Constraints:

These may take any of the following forms:

- financial – the budget amount and timing of capital needed;
- legal – for example, planning permission requirements, health and safety regulations;
- ethical – behaving within ethical boundaries is becoming increasingly important as customers are becoming concerned about the ethical behaviour of organisations;
- quality – technical requirements specified and desired by the customer;
- environmental – organisations must consider environmental legislation and control;
- logic constraints – planning that certain activities take place before others can start;
- time and quality – discussed earlier in this chapter;
- indirect effects – the desire to minimise disruption to other areas of the business as a result of change in one area;
- politics – for example, crossing departmental boundaries may be beyond the scope of the project.

Outputs:

The output is the satisfied need – achievement of the deliverables required. An output may be tangible or intangible, but it must satisfy the current customer project objectives, for example, a new computer system plus effective training for the staff.

Mechanisms:

The mechanisms by which the output is achieved and processing carried out include the following:

- people – those involved directly and indirectly;
- knowledge and expertise – brought to the project by the people participating;
- capital – the money securing the resources;
- tools and techniques – methods of organising resources;
- technology – the physical assets performing the conversion process.

Project example L plc

The following scenario will be used throughout the project management section.

L plc, a manufacturer of small home electrical products, has enjoyed substantial growth over the last two years, mainly due to a large contract with the country's leading department store (B plc). Their profit in the last financial year topped $10m for the first time in their history. The contract with B plc now accounts for over 50% of their profit and meetings with B plc have indicated that they are looking to increase the size of their orders with L plc in 18 months time.

The finance director has calculated that the increased contract could be worth around $3m profit per year. L plc are keen to take on the larger order from B plc, but are concerned that at present, the capacity of their manufacturing plant would not allow them to increase production much beyond their current level. It has been estimated that L plc would require a 30% increase in capacity to deal with the larger order from B plc going forward.

This issue is scheduled to be discussed at next board meeting and J, the CEO has asked all the directors to consider how this may be resolved.

We can clearly see that L plc have identified a need, which is to increase their manufacturing capacity by at least 30%. This is a substantial challenge for L plc. In terms of constraints, there will be tight timescales given that the new capacity will have to be in place within 18 months to be able to deal with the additional order from B plc. There will also be cost constraints as the additional capacity will help to generate additional profits going forward, but L plc will have to carefully manage the cost of obtaining the additional capacity. Quality constraints will also have to be considered, as B plc will only continue their contract with L plc if the required quality of product is achieved.

There are a number of ways in which L plc may try to achieve this additional capacity. This will be looked at in the next chapter.

11 Summary diagram

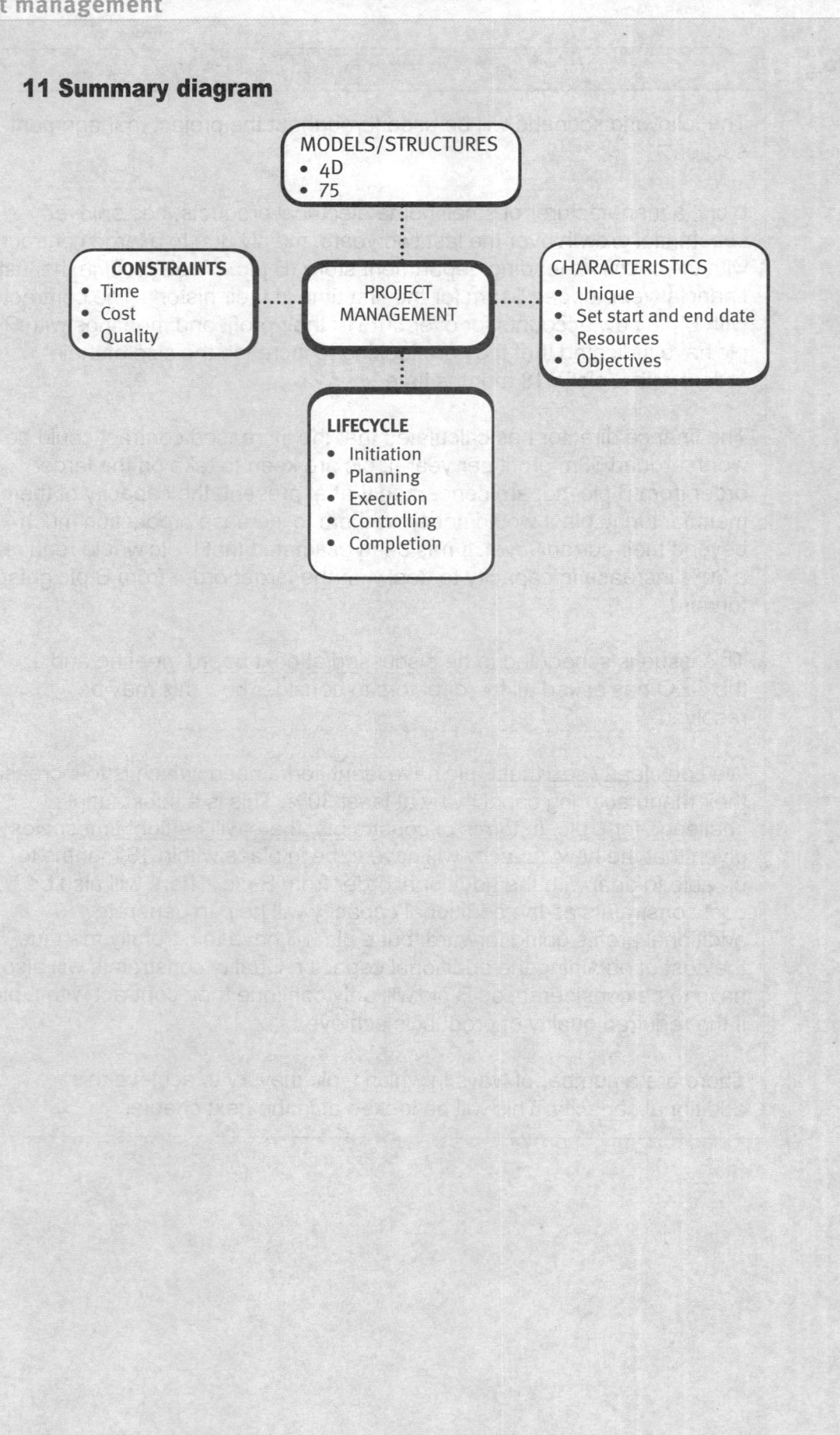

MODELS/STRUCTURES
- 4D
- 7S

CONSTRAINTS
- Time
- Cost
- Quality

PROJECT MANAGEMENT

CHARACTERISTICS
- Unique
- Set start and end date
- Resources
- Objectives

LIFECYCLE
- Initiation
- Planning
- Execution
- Controlling
- Completion

Test your understanding answers

Test your understanding 1

A project has several characteristics that distinguish it from other operations within an organisation:

A project usually has a number of different identifiable **stakeholders**. Stakeholders can be classified as either process stakeholders, who have an interest in how the project is performed, or completion stakeholders, who have an interesting the final outcome of the project. The stakeholders in a project might be different departments, external organisations (such as sub-contractors), suppliers and customers.

Each project should be **unique**, with its own objectives. Each project should be sufficiently different from preceding projects that there is no point in establishing a regular organisation structure for carrying out the work. The project managers should be responsible for ensuring that the objectives of the project are achieved.

A project should have allocations of **resources** (cost), schedules for completion and quality of achievement. Three key aspects of a project are usually cost, time scale and quality, and the project manager needs to maintain a satisfactory balance between the conflicting requirements of these three objectives.

A project should have an identifiable **beginning and end**, and a fixed time scale for completion, and there might also be schedules for completion of each phase of the project.

Since a project is a separately identifiable activity, it should have its own **identifiable risks**, and project risks should be suitably managed and controlled.

Finally, when a project is completed, everyone who has been involved in the project moves on to other work.

Consequently, a project is a **temporary** organisation structure and activity.

Principles of project management

> **Test your understanding 2**
>
> Using a holiday, we can describe the stages of the project life cycle:
>
> - Identify the need – you have been working hard and feel a holiday will make you feel better. A friend has suggested visiting a place that is very interesting archaeologically.
>
> - Develop a proposed solution – pick up brochures from the travel agents, look on sites on the internet to find a suitable venue. Check that the prices, times, modes of travel, health and political restrictions are all favourable. Buy a travel guide and note the places of interest. Check that the holiday chosen fulfils all the objectives and then book it at the best price available. Start planning the other aspects of the holiday – the clothes, passport, excursions and luggage.
>
> - Project performance (including the monitoring and control) – go on holiday and, while enjoying yourself, make sure that the travel arrangements and accommodation are as expected and all the planned trips can be achieved within budget.
>
> - Project closure – return home, evaluate and appraise the holiday and get back to work to pay for the next trip.

chapter 13

Project Stages – Initiation

Chapter learning objectives

- Identify the characteristics of each phase in the project process.
- Produce a basic project plan incorporating strategies for dealing with uncertainty, in the context of a simple project.

1 Session content diagram

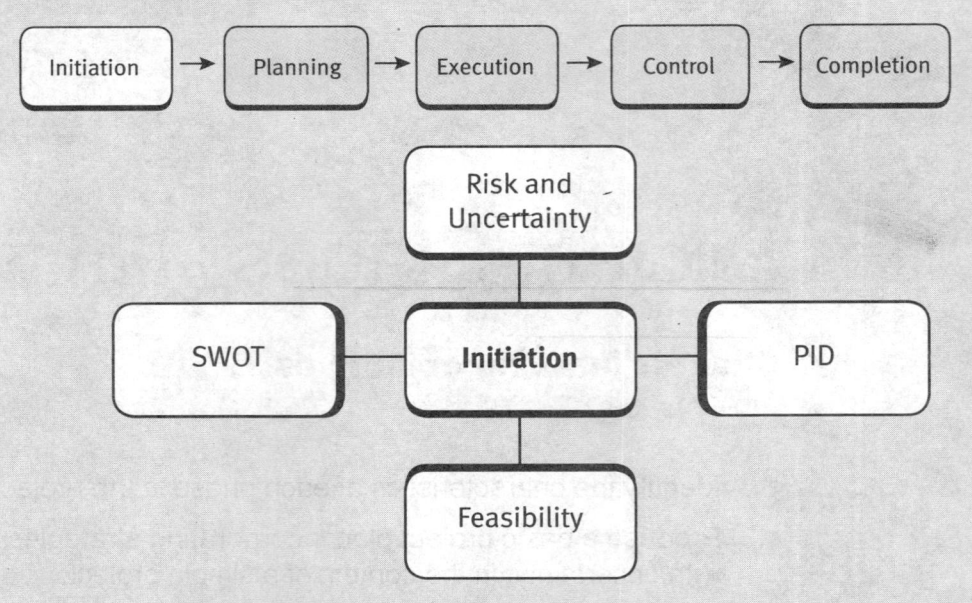

Initiation → Planning → Execution → Control → Completion

```
        Risk and
       Uncertainty
            |
SWOT ─── Initiation ─── PID
            |
        Feasibility
```

2 Initiating a project

Projects are initiated when a need or objective is defined.

Objectives are those things that the organisation wants to achieve. Typically, top-level objectives are profit-oriented, or in non-profit-making organisations objectives will be to improve the standard of living or education, and so on of members. It is usually a function of the board of directors to determine the high-level organisational objectives.

There are a number of reasons why a project would be initiated:

- To help meet the company's long term goals and objectives.
- Process/service enhancement.
- Solve problems identified internally or externally.
- To take advantage of new opportunities.
- Statutory/legal requirement.

Companies may have a number of potential projects they would like, or need to undertake, but they may not have the resources to carry them all out. They often have to go through a selection process to establish the most worthwhile projects.

Checklist for project proposal selection:

(1) List potential projects.
(2) Determine the need or opportunity for each project.
(3) Establish rough delivery dates.
(4) Establish preliminary costings and budget schedule.
(5) Establish the overall feasibility of each project.
(6) Establish the risk associated with each project.
(7) Review project list, objectives, feasibilities and risks with project team and senior management.
(8) Eliminate unfeasible or inappropriate projects (based on issues such as cost, lack of technology, skill, conflict with long-term organisational objectives, conflict with other projects).
(9) Prioritise the rest.
(10) Select the most important project.

Considerations in project selection:

There are a number of considerations which must be made at this stage of the project, we will cover each of the following in detail:

- Project requirements
- Feasibility
- SWOT
- Risk management

It is important that these considerations are looked at in detail at this stage of the project. The more detailed the analysis which is carried out at the initiation stage of the project, the more likely is the chance of success in the project. For many projects which fail, the failure can be traced back to failures at this stage of the project.

Project Stages – Initiation

> **Project example L plc**
>
> L plc example continued:
>
> At the board meeting, a number of proposals were put forward for ways in which the manufacturing capacity could be increased. A short list of three potential projects was drawn up:
>
> - Sell the existing manufacturing plant and relocate to larger premises
> - Attempt to buy the spare land adjacent to the current plant and extend the current facilities
> - Take over a smaller manufacturing company in the same sector
>
> J asked the directors to develop the details of each of these proposals, and to present the findings at the next meeting. At the next meeting, after much discussion, it became clear that the favoured approach would be to take over a smaller manufacturing company. It was agreed to take this proposal forward.

3 Project requirements

A **requirement** is a statement of what is expected of a project or product; it must be clearly defined and appropriate to meet the organisation's objectives. If a project requirement is set out clearly from the outset, the project has a greater chance of success, and less chance of escalation of costs due to rework, continual changes and customer dissatisfaction.

A requirement is different from a specification, in that the requirement is the statement of **the reason for what is being done** or developed, whereas a specification is the statement of the detailed characteristics of the project or product such as size or performance criteria. It is important that the customer and project team agree that the requirement is appropriate and meets the organisational needs and objectives (Field and Keller, 1998).

4 Feasibility

Purpose

The development of any new project requires careful consideration and planning. It will consume large volumes of resources, both financial and non-financial, and is likely to have a major effect on the way in which the organisation will operate.

In considering the development of a project, and in order to create benchmarks to evaluate its success, the following questions must be addressed.

- What is <u>required</u>?
- <u>What different ways are there to satisfy these requirements</u>?
- <u>Is it technically feasible?</u>
- <u>Does it make economic sense</u>?
- Will it <u>result in major changes in organisational structure or operation?</u>

Feasibility studies may be <u>carried out on a number of potential strategies</u> and the <u>aim of the study is to decide on which proposal to choose</u>.

Sometimes the potential project manager is involved in the feasibility study stage, but not always. However, it is <u>important for project managers to understand the process of feasibility assessment.</u>

Types of feasibility

There are a number of types of feasibility which could be considered, including the following:

- Technical feasibility
- Social (operational) feasibility
- Ecological (environmental) feasibility
- Economic (financial) feasibility

Example:

We will use the following example to explain the types of feasibility:

SMK plc, a manufacturer of car components, operates from a large industrial site in V town where it is the largest local employer. SMK is well respected in the town, and have always stated their commitment to the town and their employees. The current site is too small for the company's current needs and is in need of some upgrading. As such the board have been considering alternative courses of action to expand the current site.

Last week the board of SMK was approached with an offer to buy their current site for a substantial sum of money from a neighbouring mining company who have plans to develop the site as an open cast mine. As part of the deal, the mining company have offered to build SMK a new factory on land they own in H town, about 150 miles from SMK's current site. The board of SMK are considering the offer.

Technical feasibility – can it be done?

There are a number of key aspects regarding technology which must be considered, for example:

- Is the technology available?
- Is the technology tried and tested?
- What performance do we require of the technology?
- Is the technology suitable to satisfy the objective of the project effectively?

For SMK, this may involve considerations such as the ability to set up a fully functioning factory in H town. Given the nature of SMK's business, this may involve the moving and installation of large pieces of equipment. It will also have to be considered if all utilities required will be available at the new site, the ability to get planning permissions and so on. It seems likely that the project will be technically feasible.

Social (operational) feasibility – does it fit with current operations?

It is becoming increasingly necessary to assess operational/social factors affecting feasibility. These may include awareness of the social issues within a group or office (e.g. introducing a computerised system), or larger social awareness regarding the effect of projects or products on workers, employment or the environment. It is also important to ensure that the projects fits with business goals.

Social considerations include:

- Number of people required (during the project and after integration).
- Skills required – identify recruitment, training, redundancy.

Some of these issues can be directly costed (such as training costs). Others have less tangible effects that must be documented in the feasibility report.

For SMK, they may have difficulty with the social and operational feasibility of the project. It will mean moving from V town where they are a respected employer (and the largest local employer) and the move will result in many people losing their jobs. It is unclear how many jobs the mining operation would bring to the area, but it unlikely that the mining company would be able to take on all of those affected by the move. It would seem that the project would not be socially feasible.

Ecological (environmental) feasibility – how does it affect the environment?

Ecological considerations may be driven by the understanding that customers would prefer to purchase alternative products or services as they are more ecologically sound and less harmful to the environment.

Ecological considerations include:

- Affects on local community and what that might do to company image.
- What pollution could be caused by the project.

For SMK, there are some environmental implications of the proposal. Firstly for V Town, they would be losing a factory but gaining an open cast mine. This could have large adverse implications for the local environment. On the other hand, the new factory operated by SMK is likely to be more efficient and have less impact on the environment than the old factory, but the overall impact on the environment is likely to be adverse. How SMK's board feel about this will depend on their view of social responsibility. They have always stated their commitment to V town, but if the plan goes ahead they will cause unemployment and environmental damage to the area.

Economic (financial) feasibility – is it worth it?

The project (proposed system) must provide a benefit to the organisation. Economic feasibility will be assessed through a cost-benefit analysis. Cost-benefit analysis helps to identify and evaluate the costs of the proposal over its anticipated life. The other side to cost-benefit is the identification and evaluation of the benefits of the project over its life.

Benefits

- Tangible – those benefits that can be evaluated financially (reduction of employees when processes are automated).
- Intangible – those benefits that are not easy to evaluate financially (a new computer system may provide better information to managers for decision making and control).

Financial costs and benefits can be evaluated using investment appraisal techniques such as payback and discounted cash flow approaches. Although it is unlikely that you will be asked to carry out detailed calculations you may need to discuss their relevance to the project decision.

Remember that any intangible benefits will have been excluded in the financial evaluation process.

Remember, you would not rely on a single measure to determine the financial feasibility of a project.

The types of costs and benefits involved in a project will depend upon the precise nature and scope of that project and can vary greatly:

Costs

- *Capital Costs* – costs incurred in the acquisition of assets plus any additional costs of installation and maintenance.
- *Revenue Costs* – any costs other than for the purchase of assets. These costs are incurred on a regular basis and include repairs and consumables.
- *Finance Costs* – finance costs are usually incurred as interest charges. Sources of finance include banks, shareholders, retained profit from the business and grants or subsidies from the government.

For SMK, the cost of the project will include the cost of planning and building the new factory. The costs will also include kitting out the new factory and they will have to consider the employment costs. A number of current employees will not be able to move to work at the new site, therefore SMK may face redundancy costs and they will also incur costs in hiring and training a new workforce for the new factory. The costs will be high but a substantial sum of money will be received from the sale of their existing site.

Benefits should derive from the business case that identified the need to expand the current factory in the first place (e.g. capital growth, increased equity, increased capacity and income, profits). It seems likely that the project would be economically feasible.

The terms of reference for a feasibility study might contain:

- *Objectives* – what is expected at the end of the feasibility study, e.g. to produce a feasibility report, which recommends whether the project should proceed or not and, if progression is recommended, to produce a detailed timetable for the next phase.
- *Scope of the study* – the terms of reference should specify what is within the scope of the feasibility study.
- *Constraints that apply to the study* – the feasibility study may have to conform to company standards and its conduct and presentation has to take place in a prescribed way (perhaps to a certain quality standard). Other constraints may include time, e.g. the feasibility study must be concluded by 8 October.

- *Client of the study* – the feasibility study, and its eventual report, must be owned by someone within the organisation. The client or authority will agree the other aspects of the terms of reference as well as monitoring progress and signing-off the final product.

- *Resources available to undertake the feasibility study* – this defines the people, equipment and budget available for the study costs.

Test your understanding 1 – Project example L plc

L plc example continued.

It was agreed that a feasibility study would be carried out for this proposal. Further details on the proposal are as follows:

M Company has been selected as a potential take-over target. It is a medium sized, family run business, located 20 miles from L plc's manufacturing plant. M Company specialise in the manufacture of electrical components used in the car industry, but it is felt that their factory set up would be able to be adapted to manufacture L plc's products. Initial figures from the finance director suggest that the purchase price of M Company would be around $6m and he estimates the other costs (cost of refurbishing M Company's factory, new integrated computer systems, legal costs etc) would be around $3m.

L plc's operations director, H, will be appointed project manager and he will appoint a cross functional team from existing staff within L plc.

Required:

Assess the feasibility of L plc's proposal to take over M Company.

(10 marks)

Test your understanding 2

Required:

Make a brief list of technical, ecological and social questions you would need to ask to assess a proposal to collect and recycle household waste (such as bottles, cans, newspapers, etc.) within a local town by building a recycling plant.

(10 marks)

5 SWOT

We looked at SWOT analysis in chapter 3, where we applied it to the whole organisation. SWOT can also be used to assist in the selection of projects.

When using SWOT in project evaluation, it is important to evaluate whether the project helps in achieving the organisation's overall objectives.

SWOT analysis in project management

Assume that a company is part way through a project to renovate a house. The project's SWOT analysis might look as follows:

Strengths:

- relationships with key sub-contractors are good;
- the project is on schedule, and the current forecast is for completion on time.

Weaknesses:

- the project is over budget in the areas of plumbing, construction of the fireplace and rewiring the lounge.

Opportunities:

- the local furniture store is having a sale;
- a decorator has been identified, as a result of recommendation by a satisfied customer.

Threats:

- the builder is concerned that the cost and time estimates for the bathroom may be too low. He says he won't know for sure until he is part way through the work;
- the supplier says that the paint ordered is not in stock with the supplier – it may take six weeks to arrive.

Test your understanding 3

SWOT analysis is commonly used in project selection, as it helps the organisation focus upon projects that will facilitate the organisation's achievement of its strategic objectives.

Required:

(a) Explain the term SWOT analysis, and how a SWOT analysis is used in project selection.

(6 marks)

(b) When selecting a project, should the lowest price proposals always be selected? Give reasons for your answer.

(4 marks)

6 Risk and uncertainty

Risk

It is important to identify risks associated within projects, and to consider how these risks can be managed.

Classification of risk

Risk can be classified under three headings.

(1) **Quantitative risk** – This is risk that can be expressed as a financial amount. Estimation of risk is usually based on the probability of an event occurring, multiplied by the financial or non financial consequence of the event. It can be considered to be the product of three values:
   - the likelihood of an event occurring – p(E);
   - the likelihood the event will lead to a loss – p(L);
   - the monetary cost of the worst possible potential loss associated with that accident – M.

   The value of the quantitative risk is therefore p(E) x p(L) x M

(2) **Socially constructed risk** – this is when people believe some things to be a risk, even when statistics indicate they are not (and vice versa). This may often exceed quantitative risk. Companies must therefore also manage people's perceptions of risk.

(3) **Qualitative risk** – some risks cannot always be quantified accurately, but some way of categorising risks is useful. If we assess the impact and likelihood of risk, we can generate a table such as the following:

		Likelihood		
		Low	Medium	High
	High	C	B	A
Impact	Medium	D	C	B
	Low	E	D	C

Having done this, in our risk management programme we should address the category A risks first, then B's and so on. Do not worry too much about the E's.

Risk management process

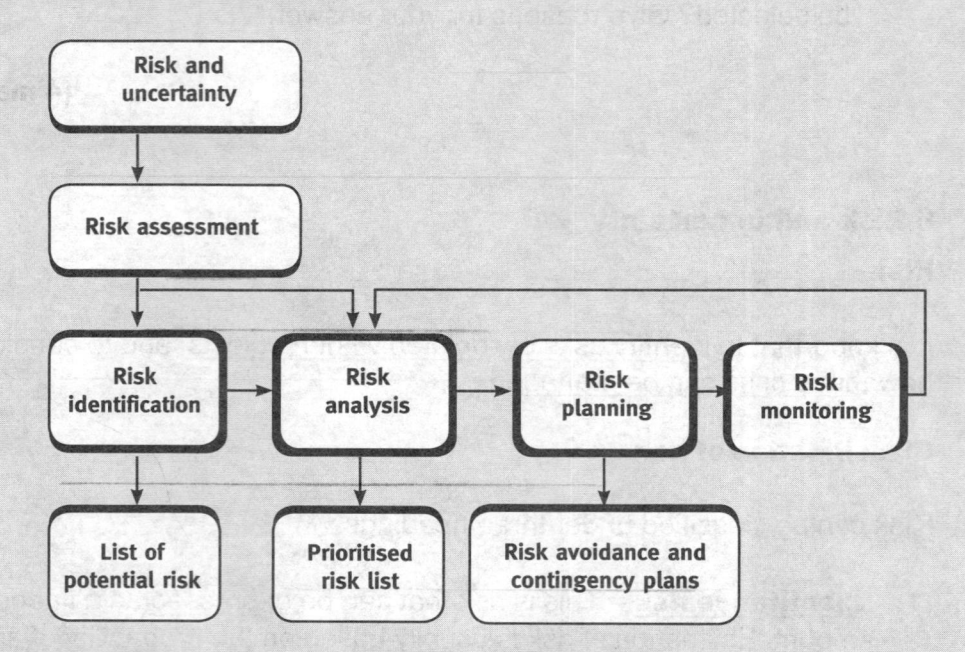

```
       Risk and
       uncertainty
           │
           ▼
       Risk assessment
           │
    ┌──────┼──────┬──────────┐
    ▼      ▼      ▼          │
  Risk → Risk → Risk → Risk monitoring
  identification  analysis  planning
    │      │      │
    ▼      ▼      ▼
  List of  Prioritised  Risk avoidance and
  potential risk list   contingency plans
  risk
```

- Identify risk – producing a list of risk items.
- Analyse risk – assess the loss probability and magnitude of each item.
- Prioritise – produce a ranked ordering of risk items.
- Management – decide how to address each risk item, perhaps by avoiding, transferring or reducing the risk.
- Resolution – produce a situation in which risk items are avoided or reduced.
- Monitoring – track progress towards resolving risk.

Managing risk

Once the risks have been listed they should be plotted on the following grid to determine whether the project should go ahead.

```
                    LIKELIHOOD
              Low              High
      L
      o    Accept            Reduce
      w
  I
  M
  P
  A
  C
  T   H
      i    Transfer           Avoid
      g
      h
```

A useful way to remember the risk management approaches is **TARA** (**Transfer, Avoid, Reduce, Accept**):

Transfer	• Subcontract the risk to those more able to handle it, such as a specialist supplier or insurer.
Avoid	• Abort the plan. • Escape the specific clause in the contract. • Leave the risk with the customer or supplier.
Reduce	• Take an alternative course of action with a lower risk exposure. • Invest in additional capital equipment or security devices to reduce risk or limit its consequences.
Accept	• Accept that some risks are an inevitable part of doing business. • Continue to monitor risks to ensure that their potential impact or likelihood have not increased.

Uncertainty

Unlike risk, uncertainty is impossible to evaluate because it is impossible to assign probability to an uncertain event. If the event is uncertain we cannot put in place management control to reduce the probability of its occurrence, simply because we do not know that probability. Instead we must use contingency planning.

Contingency planning

Contingency planning involves considering alternative actions should uncertain events occur.

Project Stages – Initiation

Contingency plans may include:

- contacting lenders to discuss possible additional finance.
- re-planning the remaining project with a longer duration.
- identifying if required materials are available from other possible suppliers.

The purpose of contingency planning is to speed up the planning process. The contingency plans may never be used, but we can do our contingency planning when it suits us. If we wait for the uncertain event before doing any planning, this may further delay the project.

Well known risk factors

Relative ranking of well know risk factors

(1) Lack of top management commitment.
(2) Misunderstanding of scope/objectives/requirements.
(3) Lack of client/end-user commitment/involvement.
(4) Changing scope/objectives.
(5) Poor planning/estimation.
(6) Inadequate project management.
(7) Failure to manage end-user expectations.
(8) Conflict among stakeholders.
(9) Change in senior management ownership.
(10) Lack of adequate change control.
(11) Shortage of knowledge/skills in the project team.
(12) Improper definition of roles and responsibilities.
(13) Artificial deadlines.
(14) Specifications not frozen.
(15) New or radically redesigned business process/task.
(16) Employment of new technology.
(17) Poor control against targets.
(18) Number of organisational units involved.
(19) Lack of effective methodologies.
(20) Staff turnover.
(21) Multiple vendors.

As taken from computerweekly.com

chapter 13

Test your understanding 4 – Project example L plc

L plc example continued.

Required:

Identify and explain four risks associated with the project.

(8 marks)

Test your understanding 5

The identification of risk involves an overview of the project to establish what could go wrong and the consequences.

Required:

Explain what sorts of questions need to be asked to accomplish this?

(5 marks)

Test your understanding 6

It is often claimed that all project management is risk management since risk is an inherent and inevitable characteristic of most projects. The aim of the project manager is to combat the various hazards to which a project may be exposed.

Required:

Explain the concept of risk and the ways in which risk can be managed in a project.

(12 marks)

7 Project initiation document (PID)

A project initiation document (PID) is a reference document produced at the outset of a project – at the end of the initiation stage. There are two primary reasons for having a PID:

(1) For authorisation by the project steering committee or project board;
(2) To act as a base document against which progress and changes can be assessed.

The PID can be used to ensure that the project team and project shareholders are in general agreement about the nature and parameters of the project.

This document therefore:

- Defines your project and its scope.
- Justifies your project.
- Secures funding for the project, if necessary.
- Defines the roles and responsibilities of project participants.
- Gives people the information they need to be productive and effective right from the start.

A project initiation document (PID) should contain at least the following sections:

- *Purpose statement* – explains why the project is being undertaken.
- *Scope statement* – puts boundaries to the project by outlining the major activities. This section is important in preventing 'scope creep', where additional activities are added making achievement of the cost and time objectives totally impossible.
- *Deliverables* – tend to be tangible elements of the project, such as reports, assets and other outputs.
- *Cost and time estimates* – it is a good idea for the project team to have some feel for the organisation's expectations in terms of the project budget. These estimates will be modified later in the project, but are necessary to give a starting point for planning.
- *Objectives* – a clear statement of the mission, CSFs and milestones of the project.
- *Stakeholders* – a list of the major stakeholders in the project and their interest in the project.
- *Chain of command* – a statement (and diagram) of the project organisation structure.

More on contents of a PID

In addition to the sections listed above, a PID could also contain:

- the approach to be taken to the project, for example whether it is primarily to be carried out in-house, or by external parties;
- any areas excluded from the project;
- any interfaces between this project and others, or with other organisations or parts of the organisation;
- any assumptions on which the PID is based;
- the project manager and team – roles and responsibilities;
- the communication plan (reports, meetings, etc.);
- the controls in place in the project.

Test your understanding 7 – Project example L plc

L plc example continued.

Required:

Produce a PID for the project.

(10 marks)

Test your understanding 8

The Board of the Solar organisation are about to authorise their first systems project to upgrade an old and failing computer system. Unfortunately, no member of the Board has any recent project management experience. The Board have recognised this as being an issue and asked the Finance Director to produce a list of requirements for the project. These requirements will be given to a systems analyst in preparation for a full feasibility study later in the year. The report from the Finance Director includes the following comments:

The project will update the current systems of the company.

The focus of the project is to provide the Board with the necessary information to run the organisation.

Project Stages – Initiation

We expect the project to take about 12 weeks. During this changeover phase we will use manual accounting to continue order processing and maintain the customer ledgers.

As we are a small company, the project is unlikely to be complex, so the work will be carried out by one systems analyst.

An initial budget of $24,000 has been set aside for the project.

As discussed, I will be in charge of the day-to-day running of the project.

Required:

(a) Evaluate the comments made the FD, showing any weaknesses in those comments.

(6 marks)

(b) At the start of many projects a document, sometimes called a project initiation document (PID), is produced. List and briefly describe the typical contents of such a document.

(4 marks)

8 Summary diagram

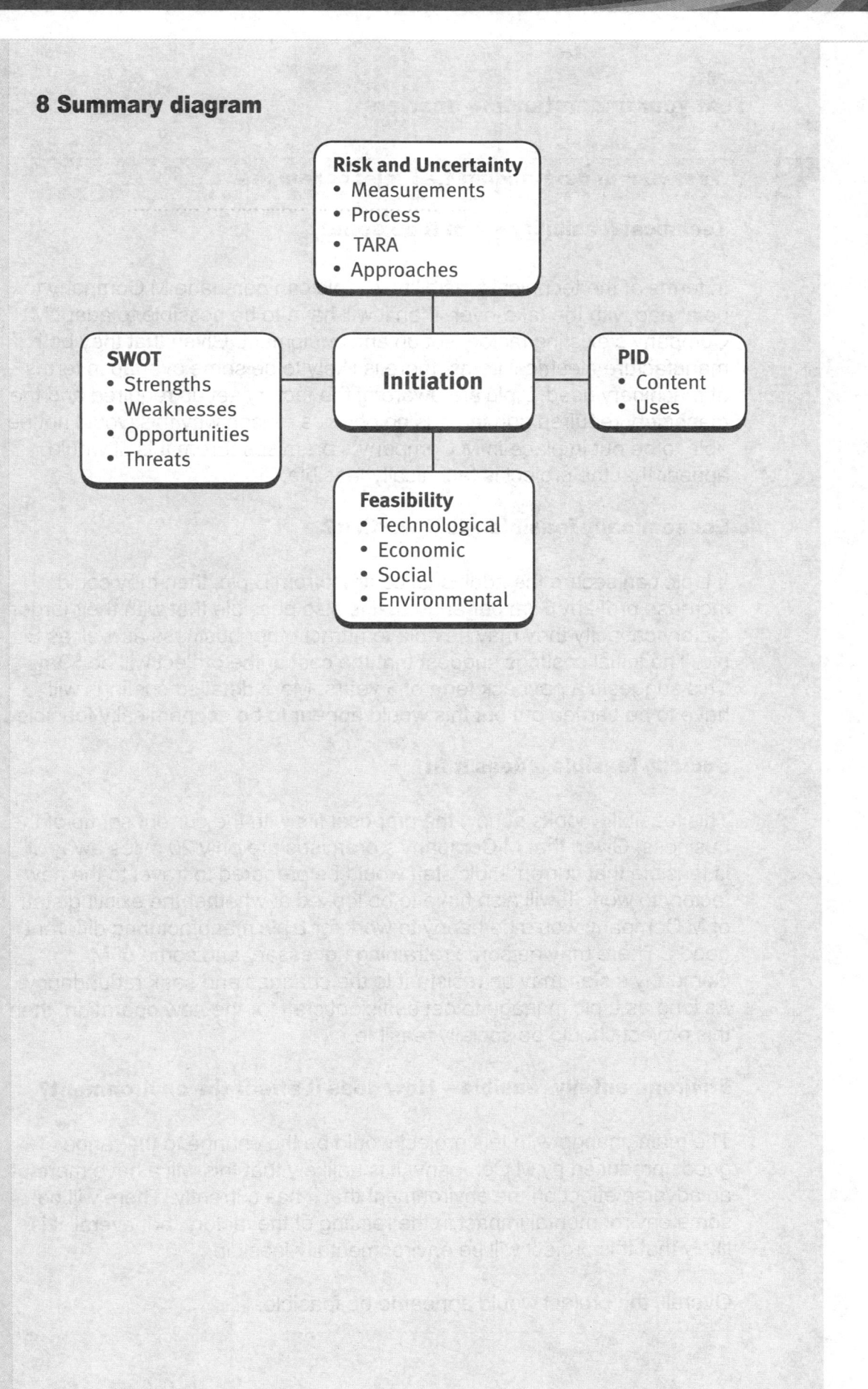

Risk and Uncertainty
- Measurements
- Process
- TARA
- Approaches

SWOT
- Strengths
- Weaknesses
- Opportunities
- Threats

Initiation

PID
- Content
- Uses

Feasibility
- Technological
- Economic
- Social
- Environmental

Test your understanding answers

Test your understanding 1 – Project example L plc

Technical feasibility – can it be done?

In terms of the technical feasibility, if L plc can persuade M Company to go ahead with the take-over, then it will have to be possible to adapt M Company's existing factory set up and equipment. Given that they both manufacture electrical items, there is likely to be some overlap in terms of machinery used. L plc are aware of the factory set up required and the machinery required and there is no obvious reason why this would not be able to be put in place in M Company's premises. From this, it would appear that the project is technically feasible.

Economically feasible – is it worth it?

If L plc can secure the additional contract from B plc, then they could increase profit by $3m per annum. It is also possible that with their larger factory capacity they may be able to attract other business as well as B plc. The initial costings suggest that the cost of the project will be $9m. This suggests a payback term of 3 years. More detailed costings will have to be carried out but this would appear to be economically feasible.

Socially feasible – does it fit?

This feasibility looks at how the proposal fits with the current set up of the business. Given that M Company's premises are only 20 miles away, it is feasible that current L plc staff would be prepared to travel to the new factory to work. It will also have to be looked at whether the existing staff of M Company would be happy to work for L plc manufacturing different goods. There may be some retraining necessary and some of M Company's staff may be resistant to the changes and seek redundancy. As long as L plc manage to get sufficient staff for the new operation, then this project should be socially feasible.

Environmentally feasible – How does it affect the environment?

The main change with this project would be the change to the range of goods produced by M Company, it is unlikely that this will a have more of an adverse effect on the environment that it has currently. There will be some environmental impact in the refitting of the factory, but overall it is likely that this project will be environmentally feasible.

Overall, the project would appear to be feasible.

Test your understanding 2

Technological factors

- Does the technology exist to carry out the recycling?
- How developed is the recycling process?

Ecological factors

- How much energy is consumed in the processing?
- Is the process clean or dirty?
- What waste products are produced, and how can they be utilised or disposed of?
- Is the location of the site likely to affect the local environment?
- Does the local road network have the ability to support the new site?

Social factors

- Are local people interested in recycling?
- Are there available locations to place recycle points, or should collections be made from homes?
- Will it affect local employment?
- How much disruption would there be in building a recycling plant in the town?
- Will the local community object to the plant?

Test your understanding 3

(a) A common analytical tool used in assessing project proposals and their feasibility is SWOT analysis (Strengths, Weaknesses, Opportunities and Threats). The strengths and weaknesses arise from the organisation's internal environment, whereas the opportunities and threats arise in the organisation's external environment.

When evaluating a project proposal, it is important to establish whether the proposal helps to achieve the organisation's long-term aims and objectives. Thus, for any project proposal, a SWOT analysis can establish whether a particular proposal has sufficient strengths that are compatible with the achievement of the organisation's objectives, or provides the organisation with sufficient opportunities to do so in the future. A SWOT analysis will also highlight the weaknesses and threats of particular proposals.

For example, consider a project proposal to implement a new marketing database. A SWOT analysis for this proposal may indicate a strength of improving customer relationships and an opportunity to increase market share. Increasing market share could be one of the organisation's long-term objectives, and, therefore, this would be an important factor in final project selection.

(b) The answer to this question is no. The lowest priced proposals should not necessarily be chosen. There are many other factors to consider when evaluating proposals, such as the reputation and experience of the project provider, the materials used, the timescales being offered, the level of quality and the level of technology being used. Cost is obviously an important factor in deciding who to choose to provide a project, but often other factors, such as quality, expertise, after-sales support and warranty terms are of more importance as deciding factors.

Test your understanding 4 – Project example L plc

In the take-over project the following risks can be identified:

Cost of the project overrunning. It is possible that the initial estimates are lower than the actual costs might be. This risk can be managed by ensuring a detailed budget is established at the beginning of the project and that the costs are closely monitored throughout the execution of the project.

Time delays in the project. The enhanced manufacturing capacity must be up and running within 18 months in order to meet the new order from B plc. If this deadline is not met and the contract is not enhanced, it may even be possible that L plc may lose their existing contract with B plc which would have a huge financial impact on them.

Insufficient human resources to run the enhanced operation. Skilled workers will be required to run both the existing facility in L plc and the new operation at M Company. There is a risk that the staff at M Company are unable, or unwilling to retrain and then L plc will have to spread their existing staff over the two operations while they attempt to recruit the required number of staff. This could delay the operation of the new factory, or could affect L plc's ability to produce goods of the required quality.

The project does not deliver what is required. There is a risk that the take-over of M Company and the refitting of its factory and retraining of its staff may not deliver the 30% increase in capacity required to meet the new level of demand.

Other risks could be identified in the project.

Test your understanding 5

The type of questions include.

- What are the sources of risk?
- What is the likelihood of the risk presenting itself?
- To what extent can the risk be controlled?
- What are the consequences of that risk presenting itself?
- To what extent can those consequences be controlled?

Test your understanding 6

Risk can be defined as the probability of an adverse or undesirable event occurring. Undertaking any project carries an element of risk and project management will be concerned with understanding what is risky about a particular project or activity within the project. Essentially this will involve identifying the different types of risk and then how to manage the risk. The first stage will require an assessment of the probability of risks occurring and their likely impact on the project. It will then require plans to be put in place to reduce or eliminate them. In other words, risk management which is what the project manager does to counteract or prepare for the risks.

The process of risk assessment involves obtaining a clear definition of the possible risks, for instance determining how important the risk is to the project, the likelihood of that risk occurring and what the severity of its occurrence would be, in other words its sensitivity. This can be achieved by some assessment of the likelihood and consequences of risks and then plotting the outcomes on a matrix which maps the potential impact of risk (low, medium, high) and the threat of likelihood (low, medium, high).

A number of stages are involved in the process of managing risk:

- Identification of risks, producing lists of risk items in a risk register.
- Analysis of the risks in terms of the impact of each risk item on project performance, schedule and quality.
- Estimate of the probability of the risk occurring during the execution of the project (project exposure).
- Prioritise the risk according to exposure, effect and problems associated with the risks (sensitivity).
- Carry out risk management strategies, deciding how to address each risk item.
- Review and monitor, tracking the success of resolving the risk and the risk management approach.

These steps will enable the project manager to monitor risk factors and take appropriate action during the execution of the project. In deciding what to do about the risk, in other words risk management, this should be determined in terms of the level of impact (e.g. either high or low) and the probability of the risk (high or low).

There are different strategies for dealing with risk, for example:

- Avoidance of risk – where the factors which give rise to the risk are removed totally from the work to be done.
- Reducing the risk – where the potential for the risk cannot be removed but analysis has enabled the identification of ways to reduce the incidence or consequences.
- Transference of the risk to others, which is where the risk is passed on to someone else, for example through insurance.
- Acceptance – this is when the potential risk is accepted in the hope or the expectation that the incidence and consequences can be coped with if necessary, perhaps having contingency plans should the risk occur.

Risk management is a continuous process through the life of the project. Procedures are necessary to regularly review and reassess the risks documented in the risk register.

Test your understanding 7 – Project example L plc

Project Initiation Document for L plc's proposed take-over of M Company

Purpose statement

The purpose of this project is to increase the manufacturing capacity of L plc in order that it may meet increased demand from its largest customer.

Scope

The project will involve the purchase of M Company and the refitting of its factory in order that L plc's existing product range can be manufactured at that facility. The project will also include the retraining of M Company staff in the new range of manufactured goods, and the development of a new integrated computer system.

There will be no upgrade to L plc's existing factory during this project.

Project Stages – Initiation

Deliverables

A fully operational factory facility housed at M Company's existing factory. The factory will have the facility to produce L plc's existing range of products.

A further deliverable is a new integrated computer system.

Cost and time estimates

The anticipated cost of the project is $9m.
The deadline for completion is 18 months.

Objectives

The main objective of the project is to increase the manufacturing capability of L plc by 30%.

Stakeholders

There are a number of interested parties in this project. These include the shareholders and directors of L plc, the owner and mangers of M Company, the staff of both L plc and M Company, the purchasing department of B plc and M Company's existing customers.

The shareholders of L plc and the owner of M Company will have financial interests in the project. The management of both companies and the staff of both companies will have interest in future employment security. B plc will be interested in L plc fulfilling the contracts they give them and the customers of M Company will be interested in whether the new company going forward will continue to manufacture and supply the goods they currently purchase.

Chain of Command

The sponsor of the project will be the L plc's finance director. The project owner is L plc's production manager. The project manager is H. The project team has yet to be appointed but will be taken from different functional areas within L plc.

Test your understanding 8

(a) A project normally has a **specific purpose** which can be readily defined. The statement from the FD is not specific concerning the systems to be updated or why they actually need updating. Providing this detail is essential to ensure that the project does meet the requirements and a post-implementation review can confirm that the requirements were, in fact, met.

The focus of the project on the Board may be inappropriate. Many projects are **focused on the customer** and customer expectations rather than internal requirements. As information systems are normally designed to provide some form of competitive advantage and provide appropriate customer service, the initial focus must be external. Additional sub-systems to provide Board information can be implemented later.

A project is made up of a **series of activities** that are linked together because they all contribute to the desired result. These activities range from an initial investigation into the existing systems through to implementing a new system. There is no need to stop using the existing system just because a project has started. The project manager will follow a recognised methodology which will allow for an appropriate changeover method, and it is only at this time that some processing ability may be temporarily lost.

Although the project will have clearly defined **time constraints** and a date when the results are required, these are normally suggested by the project manager and then agreed by the Board. To impose a time restriction before the project commences may severely limit the scope of the project as well as providing an information system that may not meet the organisation's needs.

Most projects are **complex** because the work involves people in different departments and even on different sites. Although there is no information about the processing systems within Solar, the systems change appears to be quite fundamental and so it will affect many different departments. A project team is likely to be required rather than a single systems analyst.

All projects have **cost constraints** which must be clearly defined and understood to ensure the project remains viable. The FD is therefore correct to start thinking about the cost of the project. However, agreeing a budget before the project is even started may cause some problems. There is no indication of whether the budget is for analyst costs or to cover replacement hardware/software etc. Setting a budget will normally wait until after a Feasibility Study; the FD may be wise to obtain a quote for this study first rather than try and constrain the whole project by an unrealistic cost estimate.

(b) There are no standard contents for a project initiation document (PID). However they will typically cover the terms of reference of the project and so include:

- Business objectives.
- Project objectives.
- Scope. What is to be considered by the project and what is not.
- Constraints. These may refer to standards, suppliers or time scales.
- Authority or client of the project. The ultimate customer of the project. This is the person who will resolve conflict between users and ultimately accept the project.
- Resources. These are the facilities made available to the project manager to achieve the project's objectives. These will include staff, technical and financial resources.
- Risks. A risk analysis of the project.
- Project plan.

Some PIDs also cover (as separate sections)

- Project organisation and management.
- Configuration and change control procedures.
- Purchasing and procurement policy.

chapter 14

Project Stages – Planning

Chapter learning objectives

- Identify the characteristics of each phase in the project process.
- Apply key tools and techniques, including the evaluation of proposals

Project Stages – Planning

1 Session content diagram

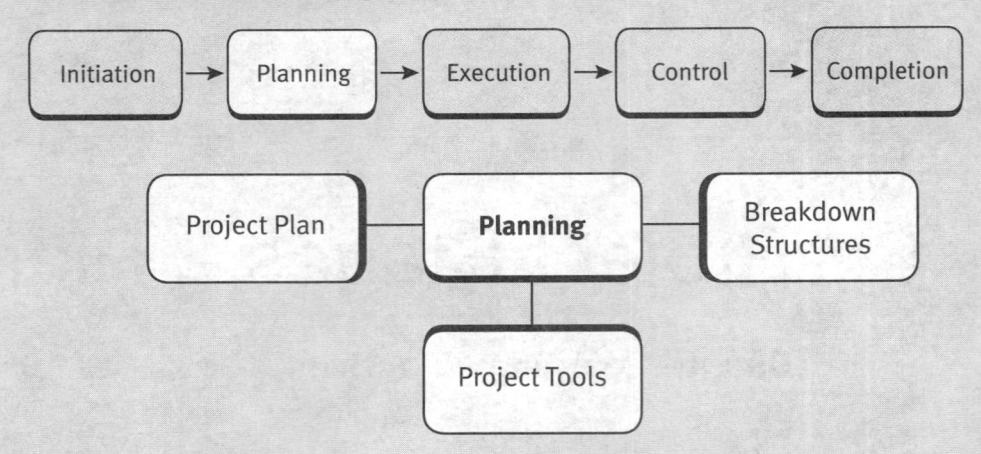

Initiation → Planning → Execution → Control → Completion

Project Plan — **Planning** — Breakdown Structures
                |
          Project Tools

2 Project planning

The planning stage of a project is essential – it helps to:

- Communicate what has to be done, when and by whom.
- Encourage forward thinking.
- Provide the measures of success for the project.
- Make clear the commitment of time, resources (people and equipment), and money required for the project.
- Determine if targets are achievable.
- Identify the activities the resources need to undertake.

In the planning stage, a number of separate detailed plans will be drawn up. For example, separate plans for:

- time
- cost
- quality
- resources
- contingency
- communication
- deliverables.

The broad content of each of these plans is as follows:

- The time plan lists all the activities, who will do what and how long each is planned to take. This includes the milestone finish dates of each stage of the project life cycle, and the estimated completion date of the whole project.

- The cost plan uses a rate per hour for each activity in the time plan, plus cost of purchases from the resource plan, plus contingency costs to create a budget for the project. This will be time phased to provide a cash flow forecast.

- The quality plan includes identification of the customers, the key outcomes each expects, acceptance criteria that has been agreed with them, a test plan for how each outcome will be tested, and responsibility for each test. This may include safety and security planning. It will also include an audit plan for the project management process.

- The resource plan checks peaks and troughs of workload to ensure the plan is feasible and lists purchases to be bought.

- Contingency planning includes assessment of risk and decides what additional activities and buffer of cost and time need to be added to the plan to ensure a reliable budget and completion date. A risk register will identify contingency plans for each of the key risks and allocates responsibility for monitoring each.

- The communication plan identifies the key people in the project, their likely concerns, message needed, planned method of communication and who will be responsible.

- The deliverables plan will detail exactly what has been agreed as the deliverables of the project. This must be agreed by the users and sponsors at the outset of the project.

The project manager and planning

It is important to understand the responsibilities of the project manager within the planning stage. The primary responsibility is to **define the project objective** clearly with the customer, then to **communicate** this objective to the rest of the project team, making it clear what constitutes a **successful project outcome**.

The project manager should involve the team members in the planning process, as this will encourage involvement, commitment and ownership of the project.

Project Stages – Planning

A project reporting information system should be set up to record and monitor the progress of the project against the plan. The comparisons between actual and plan should be communicated to team members on a regular basis. Responsibility structures may be used (i.e. ensuring that team members receive information on their own area of influence), but this must be carefully weighed against ensuring that project team members do not forget that their particular area of control is likely to affect other areas and will ultimately affect the overall achievement of the whole project objective.

Example of project planning

A project is to be undertaken to upgrade the computer system of Exam Company. Deadline for completion is 30 September 2011. Key personnel in the project are the project manager, Henry Smith and Jane Elliott, the Exam Company's IT manager. As the system will deal with examination results, security of the system will be critical.

The plan below would be issued to stakeholders such as corporate management, customers and the project team. There may be 'commercial-in-confidence' elements in it that would only be shown to the senior management. **There are no set layouts or contents of management plans**. Some illustrative examples have been used.

Section title	Contents
Overview or summary	Project objectives; organisation of the project team; schedule of work; especially the milestones; resources required including the budget and an assessment of significant risks.
Project name	For example, project for the upgrade of a computer system for the Exam Company.
Project players and responsibility	The project authorisation document will identify roles and responsibilities such as the project board, the project manager, and the project team. For example: Henry Smith, Project Manager. Responsible for: initiating the project; selecting the project team; preparing and implementing plans; managing the successful delivery of the project to time, cost and quality applications.
Project objectives	For example, to design and implement an upgraded examination system for the Exam Company, the customer, maintaining pre-existent standards but catering for an increase in candidate applications.

Project scope and contract	This is identified in the project authorisation document. Reasons for undertaking this project, what is to be achieved in terms of the deliverables (e.g. the completion of the contract with all user training by 30 September 2011 at a cost of £x).
Methodology	The project team will use project management techniques consistent with accepted UK standards.
Assumptions	These may refer to site access, costs of supplies, the cost of borrowing money, inflation, the availability of particular staff and so on. A major assumption for the Exam Company project is that the system is accessible in the quiet period between major application periods or examination dates.
Technical plan	The technical features of the project are identified. They will include requirements, specifications, system diagrams, site plans, tools, techniques, support functions, standards and any relevant document relating to the provision of the new exam administration system. In-house or subcontracted provision of modules will be specified.
Quality and management	The quality plan identifies our customer, the Exam Company, the key outcomes it expects, acceptance criteria agreed, a test plan of how each outcome is to be tested, and responsibility for each test. Safety and security planning will be essential, as this system must be 100 % secure. An audit plan will be included.
Communication plan	This will identify the key stakeholders in the project, what their interest in the project is and their concerns that will need to be addressed, what communication is planned and the responsible person. In our project, Henry Smith will be responsible for communicating with Jane Elliott, the Exam Company's IT manager on a weekly basis to update her on the progress and to tackle any concerns she has. Monthly status projects, monthly resource reports (financial – critical to this project – and human resource reports) will be issued and any milestones will be reported on in writing. Should any critical status reports be needed, they will be made outside the weekly meeting.

Project Stages – Planning

Organisation and personnel	The organisation plan describes the structure of the project team and each person's responsibilities. Included will be any sub-contract staff and staff from the Exam Company with any input to the project. Organisation charts will be drafted by position if staff need to be recruited. If so, recruitment methods, sources and training required will be identified with start times. In our project, we need to recruit one extra software engineer to bespoke the application.
Project schedule	This will describe the main phases of the project and highlight all key milestones. It is usually illustrated by a Gantt chart or with a network diagram.
Resources and facilities including budget breakdown	This includes checks on peaks and troughs of workload to ensure the plan is feasible and to ensure procurement is achieved by the provision of lists. The cost plan will give a rate per hour for all work and the costs of purchases. Contingency costs are included to give the project budget. Time phasing will give a cash flow forecast. The Exam Company has made it clear that no extra project money will be available, so Henry Smith must ensure as much as possible that his costings and time/resources management are accurately assessed. The contracting company will be bearing the risk of over-run and any other contingencies.
Risk assessment and risk management	The risks are identified and contingency plans made, including extra activities and cost and time buffers to be added to ensure reliable budget and completion date. The risk register identifies each contingency plan for each key risk and allocates responsibility for monitoring. In the Exam Company project, unauthorised access to candidate details or results is the greatest outcome risk. Security must be 100 %. This may mean that the best encryption software will be needed for online applications. There will be cost implications which Henry Smith has taken account of. He must also make contingency costing in line with his contingency plans.
Acceptance	The project manager will submit the final system for acceptance to the customer, in our example the Exam Company. It may sign off the project or return it with a specific statement of requirements that will make it acceptable. Acceptance will be in writing. The managing director of Exam Company will sign off the project with Jane Elliott.

Change management	Requests for change may be initiated by Henry Smith or the Exam Company represented by Jane Elliott. These will be reviewed and approved by the project board with decisions in writing.
Post-implementation audit	After the project, when all change requests have been reviewed to ensure completion, input should be sought from the project team, any subcontractors, suppliers and the customer. It will include a summary of performance reviewing all aspects of the project, including the way it was managed, the tools used, the time it took, the delivery of quality as required, the costs incurred against estimates, the performance of the team and its relationship with all other project members. The lessons learned to prevent recurrence of any problems should be identified. An action plan with recommendations for prevention should be drawn up. All documentation should be reviewed after filing.

Project constraints – time, cost and quality

Project constraints were discussed in Chapter 12. It was highlighted that the successful accomplishment of the project objective is usually constrained by three main factors: time, cost and quality. Recognising these, and the other constraints the project faces, is critical at the detailed planning stage as these constraints, and their interrelationships, will have to be taken into account of within each part of the project plan.

Project time

The schedule is the timetable for activities involved in achieving the project objective. The project will have a finite date for completion, either set by the customer or negotiated and agreed upon with the customer. For example, planning a wedding will require organisation of all activities to occur at a specific time and on a specific wedding date.

Project cost

The cost is the amount the customer agrees to pay for the final project or product. The project cost is based on the budget, which includes a cost estimate of the resources that will be used in the project. This will include salaries of the people working on the project, project materials, equipment purchase or hire, subcontractors' or consultants' costs and facilities costs.

Quality (customer satisfaction)

The objective of any project is to complete the project within the budget and by the agreed date to the customers' satisfaction and quality requirements. It is important to ensure that prior to the project planning the project team has a clear understanding of the customer specifications and requirements, that the customer is kept informed of project progress throughout the project life, and that the plan includes progressive testing to ensure that quality requirements are fully met. Quality in computer systems can be measured in the number and type of errors ('bugs') it still contains, response times, fitness for purpose (i.e. matches the business process it is intended to support) and so on.

Another important constraint is **scope/functionality.**

The scope of the project is all of the work that must be carried out to satisfy the project's objective. The customer will expect the work to be carried out to completion and that there is nothing expected which is missing. For example, when building a house the project scope will include clearing the land, building the house and landscaping, all within the agreed quality standards expected by the customer. Leaving windows or walls unfinished, a hole in the roof, or a garden full of rubble, will be unlikely to satisfy the customer! In computer systems, the scope is often defined by all the functions that the system is expected to fulfil.

Project scope tends to be positively correlated with both cost and time, in that increasing the number of tasks to be performed within the project will normally lead to an increase in both the cost of the project and its overall duration. Managing variations to scope is one of the most complex aspects of project management. The manager must ensure that every time the customer asks for a change or addition to the scope of the project, the customer is informed of (and 'signs off') the cost and time consequences of that change. Such changes should also be fully recorded and documented to avoid arguments about what changes were required and authorised.

Test your understanding 1

Project planning is considered to be one of the most important stages of the project management process.

Required:

(a) What is meant by project planning, and who should be involved in the process?

(5 marks)

(b) Explain why project planning is vital to project management.

(5 marks)

(c) Describe the steps involved in a detailed planning process.

(5 marks)

3 Tools and techniques

There are a number of tools, techniques and documents which are used throughout a project, particularly at the planning stage. These include:

- Breakdown Structures:
    - Work breakdown structures (WBS)
    - Work packages (WP)
    - Statements of work (SOWs)
    - Product breakdown structures (PBS)
    - Cost breakdown structures (CBS)
- Budget
- Project Quality Plan (PQP)
- Network Analysis/Critical path analysis (CPA)
- Project evaluation and review technique (PERT)
- Gantt charts
- Milestones and Gates
- Resource histograms
- Project Software

You need to be familiar with all of these; be able to discuss their purposes, strengths and weaknesses and in some cases, be prepared to produce them.

Detailed planning will involve the following steps:

(1) Dividing the project into work packages – WBS
(2) Estimation of resources and costs – WBS, Gantt charts & Resources histograms
(3) Define the activities graphically – CPA & PERT
(4) Determine the project schedule and budget – Budget
(5) Determine the quality requirements of the project – PQP

4 Breakdown structures

The following may be used.

(1) **Work Breakdown Structure (WBS)**

The WBS is an important starting point for planning. It contributes to planning in the following ways:

- Breaks complex tasks into manageable pieces.
- Sets out the logical sequence of project events.
- Provides a logical framework for making decisions.
- Provides an input into subsequent project processes, such as estimating time and resources.
- Provides a framework for continuous assessment of the project progression.
- Provides a communication tool.

An extract from a possible WBS appears below.

Note: it is unlikely that a drawing would be required by the examiner but it is often useful to give an example when describing any project management tool.

```
                        ┌─────────────────┐
                        │  Olympic Games  │
                        └─────────────────┘
        ┌──────────────┐  ┌──────────────┐  ┌──────────────┐
        │ 1. Events    │  │ 2. Facilities│  │ 3. Security  │
        └──────────────┘  └──────────────┘  └──────────────┘
```

1.1	Track & Field	2.1	Spectators	3.1	Spectators
1.1.1	Long Jump				
1.1.2	Javelin				
1.1.3	Hurdles				
1.2	Equestrian	2.2	Competitors	3.2	Competitors

(2) **Work Packages (WPs) and Statements Of Work (SOWs)**

- The work package <u>specifies the work to be done for each package described in the work breakdown structure</u>.
- The <u>statement of work describes the deliverables against which the project can be measured</u>.
- Both types of document <u>identify in detail work to be done and may state the standard to which the work is to be done</u>.
- The statement of work also <u>indicates who is responsible and when the work needs to be delivered</u>.

(3) **Product Breakdown Structure (PBS)**

- The <u>products required for each activity would then be listed</u>:
  - Long Jump
  - Sand pit
  - White board
  - Flag
- Describe the <u>complexes of machinery and equipment required</u> for the project.
- <u>Compare different suppliers.</u>
- <u>Estimate the costs of the entire complex.</u>

(4) **Cost Breakdown Structure (CBS)**

This will include <u>information gathered from</u>:

- <u>The WBS, WP and SOW.</u>
- <u>Product breakdown structures.</u>
- <u>Capital and revenue costs identified in the cost-benefit analysis and feasibility study documents.</u>

It describes the categories that require costing to ensure nothing is left out of the budget process.

Numbers and costs would be allocated to each product.

Long Jump

- Sand pit X no. x $s
- White board X no. x $s
- Flag X no. x $s

This creates the detailed **financial plan (budget)** for the project.

The benefits of using a WBS include:

- Summarising all the activities comprising the project, including support and other tasks;
- Displaying the interrelationships of the various jobs (work packages) to each other and the total project;
- Establishing the authority and responsibility for each part of the project;
- Estimating project cost;
- Performing risk analysis;
- Scheduling jobs (work in progress);
- Providing a basis for controlling the application of resources to the project.

5 Project Quality Plan (PQP)

This major document details the **standards** that must be adhered to in order to ensure a successful development process. It will provide a clear indication of procedures and policies that must be followed to maintain quality within the work carried out. It generally includes:

- *Risk assessment* – of the possible internal and external risks that are likely to affect the project and the alternative actions which are required to reduce the risks.
- *Project overview* – outline of the main activities to be carried out.
- *Project requirements* – details a description of the work to be carried out, timescales and deliverables and is cross referenced to the requirements specification.
- *Project organisation* – stating management roles and responsibilities, this will help to determine the allocation of resources to each of the project activities.

- *Monitoring and reporting procedures* – cross referenced to the project standards, this section identifies how the project will be monitored and what to do if slippage occurs. It also states the frequency and content of reports as well as key control processes, such as end of stage meetings, for example, when the steering meetings will take place and procedures for evaluating the final installed system.

- *Key development stages and processes* – the activities that will need to be completed during the life cycle.

- *Key standards to be used in the project (quality assurance)* – this will help to ensure quality outputs, standards that need to be evaluated and include hardware, software and development standards such as notation of modelling techniques.

- *Testing strategy* – this will identify the stages of development where testing is to be carried out, by whom and of what.

- *Procurement policy* – the procedures and standards for procurement will be stated and any variation from the normal procedure noted, with reasons.

- *Configuration management* – how this will be dealt with should be set out so that each version of the deliverables is identified.

6 Network analysis

Network analysis is a general term, referring to various techniques adopted to plan and control projects. It is used to analyse the inter-relationships between the tasks identified by the work breakdown structure and to define the dependencies of each task. Whilst laying out a network it is often possible to see that assumptions for the order of work are not logical or could be achieved more cost effectively by re-ordering them. This is particularly true whilst allocating resources; it may become self evident that two tasks cannot be completed at the same time by the same person due to lack of working hours or, conversely, that by adding an extra person to the project team, several tasks can be done in parallel thus shortening the length of the project.

Critical Path Analysis (CPA)

One of the component parts of network analysis is critical path analysis or CPA (this is often called network analysis). It is the most commonly used technique for managing projects.

The process of CPA.

(a) Analyse the project. The project is broken down into its constituent tasks or activities. The way in which these activities relate to each other is examined: which activities cannot be undertaken until some previous activity or activities are complete?

Project Stages – Planning

(b) **Draw the network.** The sequence of activities is shown in a diagrammatic form called the 'network diagram'.

(c) **Estimate the time and costs of each activity.** The amount of time that each activity will take is estimated, and where appropriate the associated costs are estimated.

(d) **Locate the critical path.** This is the chain of events that determines how long the overall project will take. Any delay to an activity on the critical path will delay the project as a whole; delays to other activities may not affect the overall timetable for completion. That is the distinction between critical and non-critical activities.

(e) **Schedule the project.** Determine the chain of events that leads to the most efficient and cost effective schedule.

(f) **Monitor and control the progress of the project.** This implies careful attention to the schedule and any other progress charts that have been drawn up, to monitor actual progress in the light of planned achievement.

(g) **Revise the plan.** The plan may need to be modified to take account of problems that occur during the progress of the project.

Let us now follow the steps to produce the diagram:

- First draw a dot-to-dot diagram – this can be completed quickly and allows the logic of the diagram to be tested before you begin to draw the final version.

- Each activity is represented by an arrow.

- Activities start and finish in circles known as nodes (O).

- The activity letter or description (or both) is written on the arrow.

- The activity duration is written below the arrow.

- Nodes are numbered so that each node has a unique identifier.

- The network diagram is written and read, from left to right.

- If two activities occur in parallel, dummy activities are inserted to allow only one activity arrow to join nodes together. Dummy activities do not consume any time or resources and are drawn in the diagram to make it clearer.

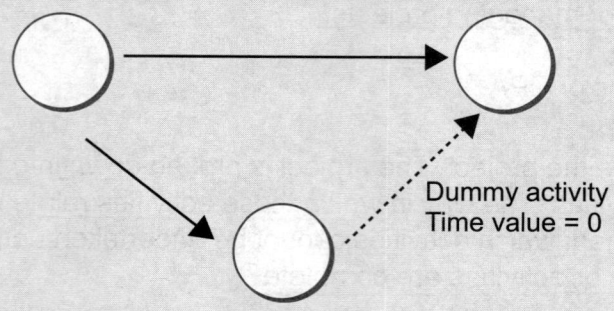

Dummy activity
Time value = 0

- Once the network has been drawn, we want to find the earliest time at which we could reach each node (event).
- A required completion date will be established and we will want to know the latest time by which each node must be reached.
- So each node will be associated with two times.

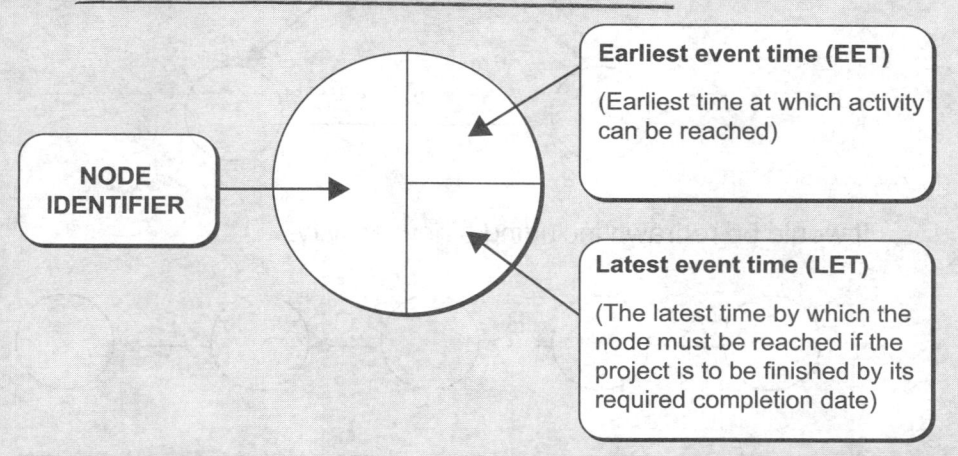

Earliest event time (EET)
(Earliest time at which activity can be reached)

Latest event time (LET)
(The latest time by which the node must be reached if the project is to be finished by its required completion date)

- Calculate the earliest event times (EET) – i.e. the earliest time the next event can start, that gives us the minimum project completion time.
- To calculate the EET, work left to right. Take the EET from the previous node and add this to the duration of the activity. **Where you have a choice of EETs, always select the highest.**
- Calculate the latest event times (LET) by considering the latest times that we can allow each event to occur if the project is to be completed by the target finish date.
- To calculate the LET, work right to left. Take the LET from the previous node and deduct the duration of the activity. **Where you have a choice of LETs, always select the lowest**.
- We can then identify the critical path, i.e. the activities where any delay will lead to a delay in the overall project. These are the activities for which EET = LET.
- The critical path is identified with //.
- Some activities could increase in duration and yet the project could still be completed by the required target date. Such activities are said to exhibit 'float'.
- Loops are not allowed because the network essentially shows a series of activities progressing through time. It focuses on the passage of time, not on the successful completion of activities. In other words, you cannot have a series of activities leading from one event that lead back to the same event.

For example, this diagram is not allowed.

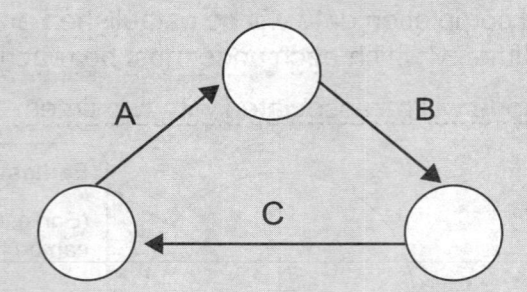

It would be redrawn including a new activity.

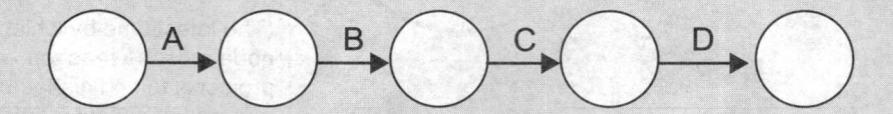

An activity can only occur once, so there cannot be two lines with the same activity.

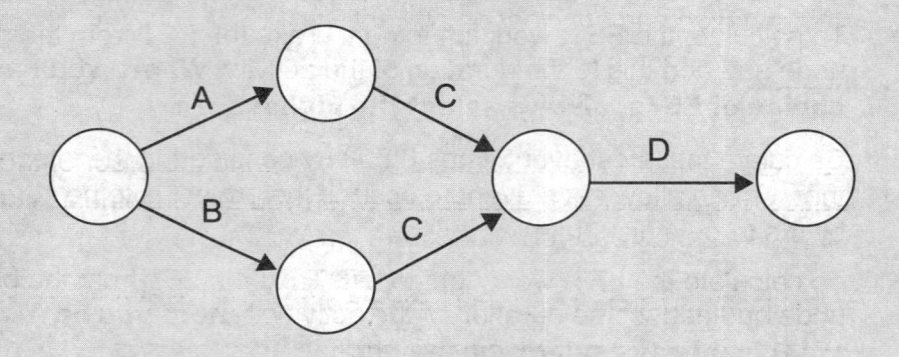

The diagram may need to be redrawn and/or a dummy activity used.

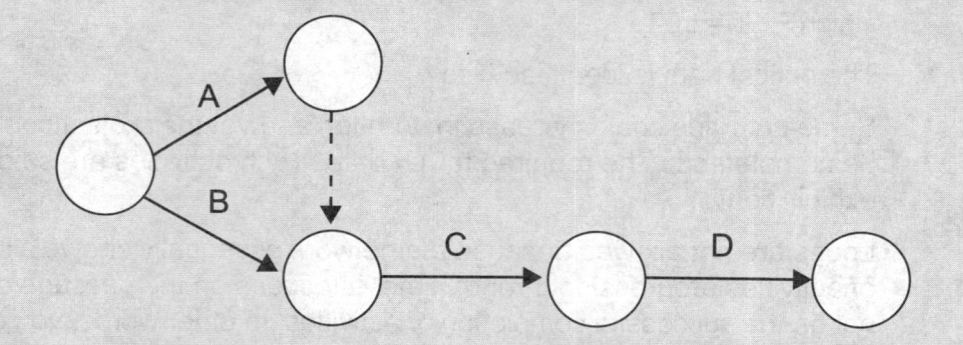

chapter 14

Illustration 1 – CPA worked example

Consider the follow details about a project. You are given the list of activities, their durations and the preceding activities. This last column tells you which order the activities must be drawn in.

Activity	Duration (weeks)	Preceding activity
A	8	–
B	10	A
C	6	–
D	4	C
E	8	B, D

Required:

Draw the network chart, and identify the critical path, the estimated project duration and any float on any activity.

Solution:

Step 1: draw the basic network diagram, showing the order of the activities. Remember the rules above when you are drawing it. You are aiming to move across your page from left to right.

Each activity must start and end with a node, so the first thing to do is to identify the activities which can start straight away – these are the ones with no preceding activity. In this case A and C can start straight away.

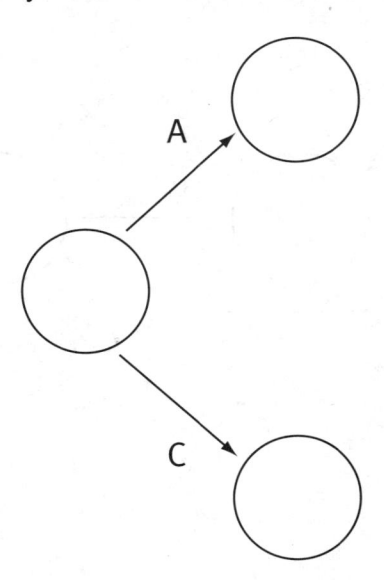

Now you can draw in the other activities. B follows A, and D follows C:

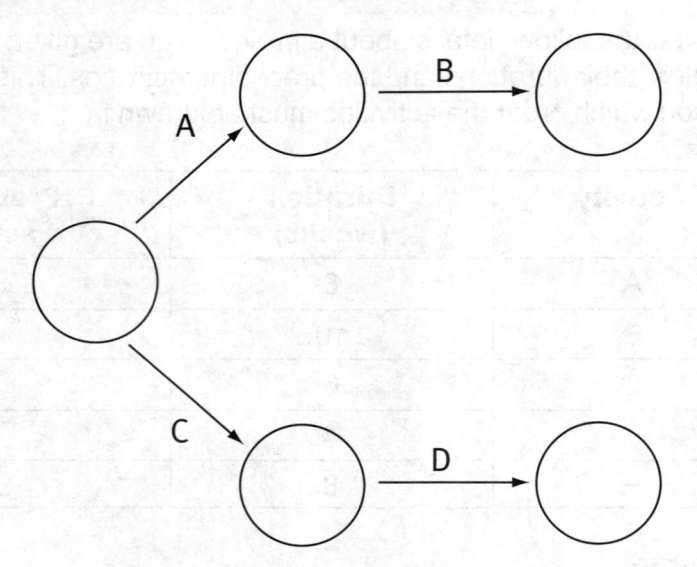

Activity E is a bit harder, because it follows B and D. This can be drawn using a dummy line. Connect the nodes at the end of B and D with a dummy line, and show E following that combined node:

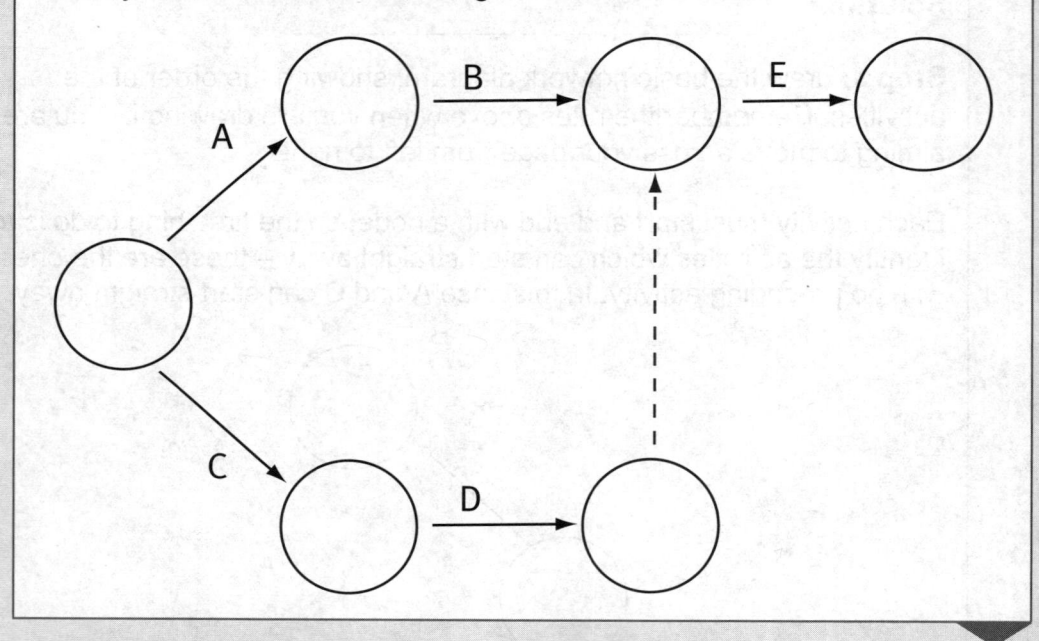

You could have drawn the diagram without the dummy line, as shown below. Both of the diagrams are acceptable and both show the correct flow of activities.

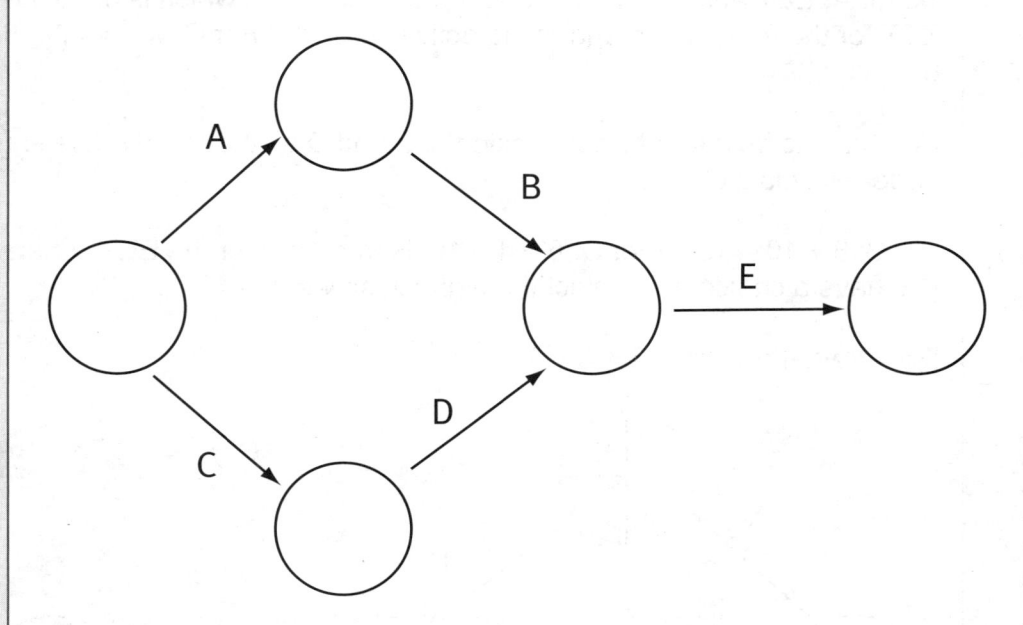

Step 2: Now the basic network diagram has been drawn, we can start to add in the details of the durations of each activity. These are shown on the activity lines. You can now draw in the node lines, ready for the calculations of EET and LET.

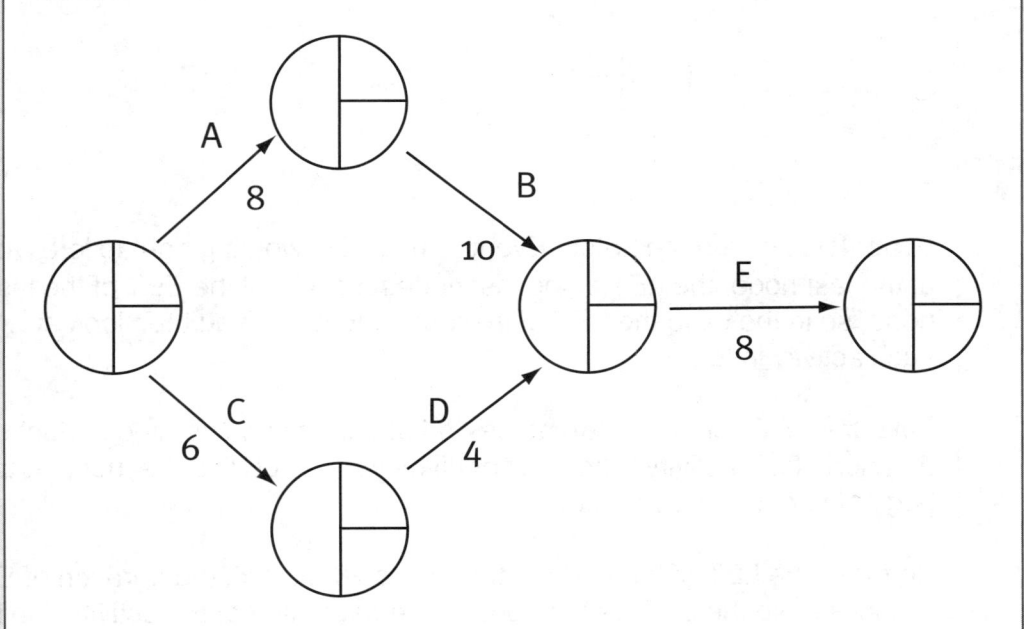

Step 3: Calculate the Earliest Event Time (EET) working left to right. Start at the first node: the EET of the first node must always be zero. You then look at each activity in turn.

Project Stages – Planning

Take the EET from the node at the beginning of the activity line, and add it to the duration of the activity, the answer gives you the EET for the node at the end of the activity line.

So for A, EET at the start is 0, add the duration of A, which is 8, so the EET for the node at the end of the activity line is 8. For C, we get 0 + 6 = 6.

You have to be careful when looking at B and D as they lead to the same node – this is a choice:

For B: 8 + 10 = 18, or for D: 6 + 4 = 10. Remember for the EET, when you have a choice, you select the highest, so we use 18.

E is straightforward: 18 + 8 = 26.

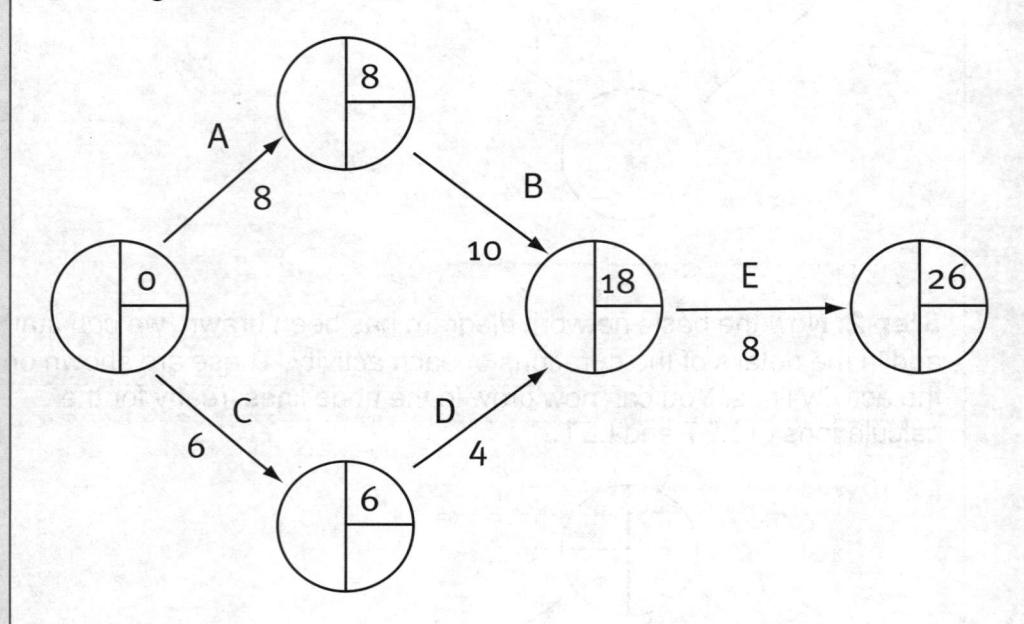

Step 4: Calculate the Latest Event Time (LET) working right to left. Start at the last node: the LET of the last node must equal the EET of the last node, so in the case the LET of the last node is 26. You then look at each activity in turn.

Take the LET from the node at the end of the activity line, and deduct the duration of the activity. The answer gives you the LET for the node at the beginning of the activity line.

So for E, the LET of the node at the end is 26, deduct the duration of E, which is 8, so the LET for the node at the beginning of E's activity line is 18. For D, we get 18 – 4 = 14, and for B we get 18 – 10 = 8.

For A and C you have a choice. Using A we get 8 – 8 = 0, or using C we get 14 – 6 = 8. When you have a choice for the LET, you always use the lowest, so we use 0.

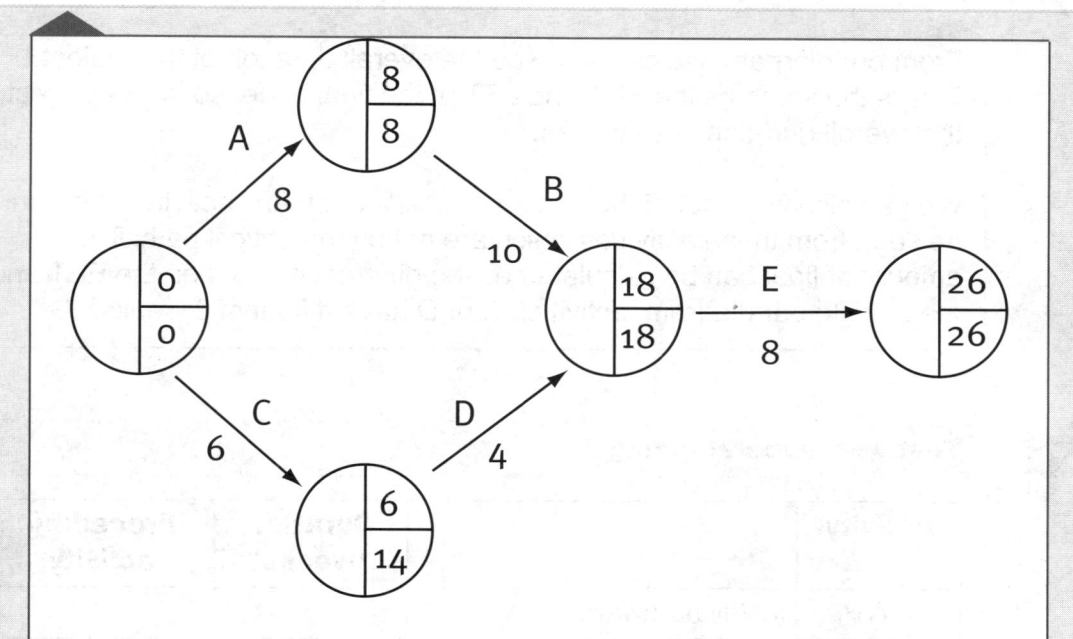

Our CPA is complete. We can now put in the reference numbers in each node (there are no rules here, just work left to right and number each node, it is just used for identification purposes).

We can now work out the critical path:

Look at your diagram. Where the nodes at the beginning and the end of an activity line have the same EET and LET, this tells you that the activity is critical. In our diagram we can see that activities A. B and E are critical. We note these on the diagram with double lines on the activity line. Always check that your critical path is a continuous path through the diagram from the first to the final node.

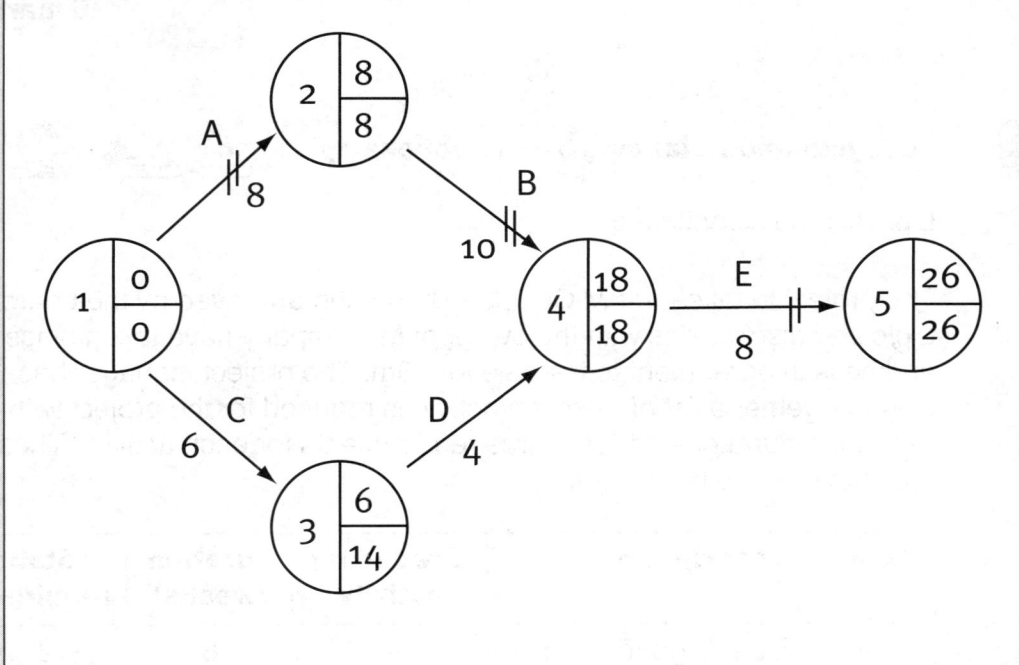

Project Stages – Planning

From our diagram, we can also see the overall duration of the project. This is the same as the EET and LET of the final node, so in this project, the overall duration is 26 weeks.

We can also work out of there is any slack/float on any activity. This can be seen from those activities which are not on the critical path. The amount of float can be calculated as the difference between the EET and the LET. In our diagram, activities C or D have a float of 8 weeks.

Test your understanding 2

Activity		Duration (weeks)	Preceding activity
A	Install hardware	3	–
B	Train staff	3	–
C	Load software	2	A
D	Transfer data	6	B, C
E	Run test data	14	D
F	Identify and correct errors	7	E

Required:

Draw the network chart, and identify the critical path, the estimated project duration and any float on any activity.

(6 marks)

Test your understanding 3 – Project example L plc

L plc example continued.

The project to take-over M Company has been approved by the board of L plc and discussions with the owner of M Company have taken place and he is in agreement to the sale for $6m. The project manager has drawn together a list of the main activities required for the project with estimated durations and resource requirements for each activity. These are shown in the table below:

Activity	Description	Preceding activity	Duration (weeks)	Staff required
A	Due diligence and drawing up of contracts	–	8	2

B	Planning of refit for M Company	A	4	3
C	Stocktaking and detailing of M Company factory operations	B	6	4
D	Purchase of equipment for refit of M Company factory	C	6	2
E	Clearing of M Company factory, surveys and planning permission for refit	B	28	10
F	Produce departmental structures and job description for the new venture	D	4	8
G	Staff selection and training	F	4	1
H	Refit of M Company factory	E	24	8

Required:

(a) Prepare a network diagram for the project. On the network diagram, the critical path should be highlighted.

(8 marks)

(b) Comment on the overall duration off the project shown on the network diagram, in light of the target deadline for the project of 18 months (78 weeks).

(2 marks)

Project Stages – Planning

Test your understanding 4

Activity		Duration (weeks)	Preceding activity
A	Problem definition	2	–
B	Prepare feasibility report	3	A
C	Studying existing system	2	A
D	Logical and physical design	4	C
E	Software and hardware development	4	B
F	Systems development report	8	D, E
G	Testing	4	F
H	File conversion	3	D, E
I	Changeover	6	G, H

Required:

Construct a network chart of the project's activities as detailed within the above table. Identify the critical path, overall project duration and any activities that have a float.

(8 marks)

Alternative method for network diagrams

An alternative method for constructing network diagrams is called activity on node.

Each activity is shown in a rectangular box or node. Activity flows from left to right as for the activity on arrow diagrams you have previously studied. Each node is subdivided in the following way:

	Task/activity	e.g. A, B, C etc
	Identity number of activity	Duration of the activity
	Earliest start time (EST)	Latest start time (LST)

To calculate the EST: EST (current activity) + DURATION (current activity) = ES (successor)

Proceed through the whole diagram from left to right, completing all the EST boxes. Should there be two preceding activities, take the **higher** figure.

To calculate the LST: LST (current activity) – DURATION (predecessor) = LST (predecessor)

Work through the diagram right to left. Should there be two previous activities (working backwards remember), take the **lower** figure.

Using the example from TYU 2:

Activity		Duration (weeks)	Preceding activity
A	Install hardware	3	–
B	Train staff	3	–
C	Load software	2	A
D	Transfer data	6	B, C
E	Run test data	14	D
F	Identify and correct errors	7	E

Required:

Using activity on node, draw the network chart, and identify the critical path, the estimated project duration and any float on any activity.

Solution:

First you need to work out the first logical precedence, then you can then calculate the ESTs working left to right and the LSTs working right to left. The completed network would look like this:

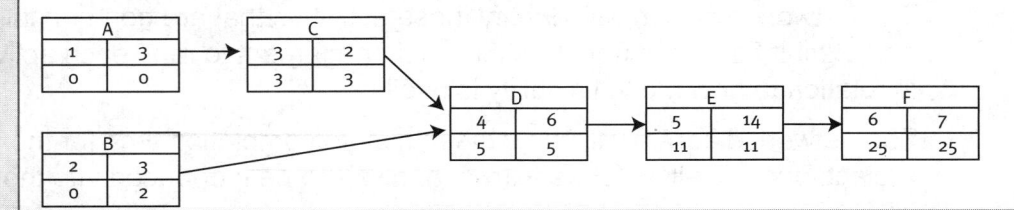

```
     A                C
  1  |  3          3  |  2
  0  |  0          3  |  3
                              D              E              F
                           4  |  6        5  |  14       6  |  7
                           5  |  5       11  |  11      25  |  25
     B
  2  |  3
  0  |  2
```

As with activity on arrow, from this we can see the critical path, the overall duration of the project and any slack in the project.

The critical path flows from the start to the end of the diagram and links the activities where the EST = LST. So, in our diagram the critical path will be ACDEF.

Be careful when looking for the overall duration of the project. Go to the last node: you can see that the LST for the activity is 25 weeks. Add this to the duration of the final activity, so the overall duration of the project is 25 + 7 = 32 weeks.

Slack in this diagram can be calculated as LST – EST. We have slack on activity B of 2 weeks.

Limitations of CPA

- It may be too time consuming to produce and monitor for large projects.
- Difficult to use for less routine projects with lots of uncertainty.
- Overly complex for some smaller short-term projects.

Benefits of CPA

- Assists in identifying all activities required for completing the project
- It will assist in identifying those activities that need to be completed before the next activity can start (dependent activities), and those that can happen at the same time (parallel activities)
- The network diagram will identify those activities that lie on the critical path. These activities cannot overrun, otherwise there would be delays in the overall project.
- The network diagram will identify those activities that are non-critical and exhibit float or buffer. This allows management to rank each activity in relation to how much flexibility is available.
- The network diagram will show the minimum completion time for the project, and will allow for sensitivity analysis to be introduced into the project.

7 Dealing with risk and uncertainty

Risk and uncertainty at the initiation stage of the project was covered in Chapter 14. At the detailed planning stage, risk and uncertainty must be considered again when the project manager is planning the time aspect of the project. There are a number of techniques which can assist with this:

- Project evaluation and review technique (PERT)
- Scenario planning
- Buffering.

Project evaluation and review technique (PERT)

This can be used to overcome uncertainties over times taken for individual activities in a network diagram.

Each task is assigned a time.

- An optimistic (best) time (o)
- A probable time (m)
- A pessimistic (worst) time (p)

It then uses a formula to calculate an expected time, and by calculating variances for each activity, estimates the likelihood that a set of activities will be completed within a certain time.

The expected time for each activity is then calculated as:

$$= \frac{o + 4m + p}{6}$$

These estimates are used to determine the average completion time.

Note: The examiner will not expect you to be able to calculate a detailed PERT analysis but you may be required to explain its function within the planning process.

Advantages:

- It gives an expected completion time.
- It gives a probability of completion before the specified date.
- It gives a Critical Path.
- It gives slack through earliest and latest start times.
- It allows calculation of contingency to be added to the plan.

Limitations:

- The activity times are very subjective.
- Assumes probability distribution of project completion time as the critical path.

Scenario planning

Although the use of PERT is one way to cope with risk in time planning there are ways of planning in a contingency for risk that are less complex. Wherever risk is identified as taking the form of alternative outcomes, a series of contingency or scenario plans may be constructed for each alternative.

Scenario planning involves considering one or more sets of circumstances that might occur, other than the 'most likely' or 'expected' set of circumstances used to prepare the budget or plan for a project. Each set of assumptions is then tested to establish what the outcome would be if those circumstances were actually to occur.

This would allow the project manager to switch to the appropriate plan for whichever contingency arose.

Buffering

A more simplistic way to incorporate risk by adding artificial slack into risky activities. It adds padding to the original estimates and allows for the fact that it can be very difficult to ensure that all stages and activities are carried out exactly as planned. This is known as 'buffering', but should not be encouraged because it leads to a build-up of slack in the programme and may lead to complacency.

chapter 14

Test your understanding 5

L is a project manager with K Company. He has been asked to manage a project to run a cycling race in the Highlands of Scotland. The race date has been set for 16 weeks from now. L has identified the various activities that need to be undertaken and has estimated the required timescales for each activity although he is unsure how realistic his estimates are as this is the first time he has tried to mange such an event. Activities and estimated timescales are shown below:

Activity	Weeks	Dependency
A – Design the course	2	–
B – Arrange sponsorship	4	A
C – Send out publicity and application forms	3	A
D – Recruit staff	2	A
E – Process application forms	2	B
F – Develop the course	6	C
G – Liaise with local authorities	1	D
H – Send out joining instructions	2	E,F,G

Required:

(a) Using the information in the scenario, prepare a network diagram for the cycle race, and identify the critical path, project duration and how much slack/float time there is in the project.

(6 marks)

(b) L is considering using a work breakdown structure to help plan the project. Discuss how a work breakdown structure (WBS) could help L in managing the project.

(4 marks)

(c) Explain to L what "buffering" is and how he could use it to make provision for the uncertainties within the project.

(4 marks)

8 Gantt chart

This is an alternative or complementary approach to network analysis. It also provides a graphical representation of project activities and can be used in both project planning and control.

A Gantt chart is a horizontal bar chart where the length of the bar represents the duration of the activity.

When a Gantt chart is used to help control a project it is usual to use two bars, one showing the planned duration and the second showing the actual duration.

To create a Gantt chart:

- Display a schedule of activities using bars.
- List the activities down the side of the page.
- Using a horizontal timescale, draw a bar for each activity to represent the period over which it is to be performed.
- Both budgeted and actual timescales can be shown on the same chart.

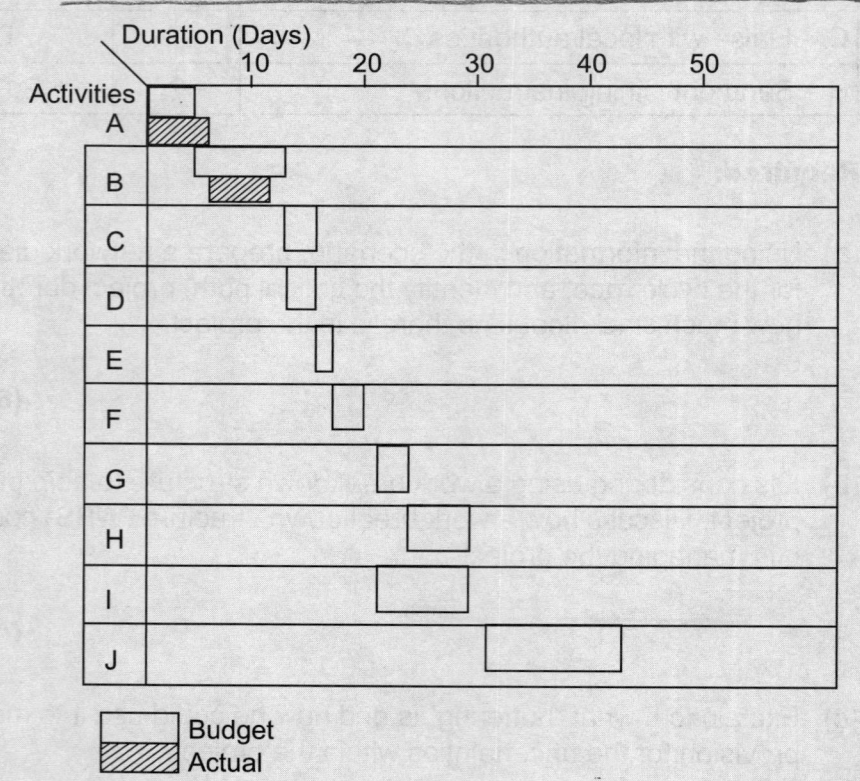

Gantt limitations:

The Gantt chart is a useful tool for tracking your project and anticipating delay problems before the final deadline is compromised. However, it will be of limited use when you have to deal with a relatively large project team. The more complex the team structure the higher the likelihood of schedule delays.

Remember, charting phases and monitoring progress is only a tool, not the solution itself.

For the more complex projects the Gantt chart has the following limitations:

- It does not identify potential weak links between phases.
- The chart does not reveal team problems due to unexpected delays.
- The chart does not coordinate resources and networking requirements needed at critical phases of the schedule.
- It does not show the degrees of completion for each phase.

Benefits of Gantt charts:

The Gantt chart shares some advantages with network analysis:

- Assists in identifying all activities required for completing the project
- It will assist in identifying those activities that need to be completed before the next activity can start (dependent activities), and those that can happen at the same time (parallel activities)
- The Gantt chart will show the minimum completion time for the project, and will allow for sensitivity analysis to be introduced into the project

In addition, the Gantt chart has further advantages over network analysis:

- Easier visualisation of relationships
- Unlike CPA, activities are drawn to scale so the most significant activities can be highlighted
- It is drawn in real time
- Actual durations can be shown alongside budget
- Aids resource allocation.

Project Stages – Planning

e.g Illustration 2 – Gantt chart example

An example of a project undertaken to examine the current procedures in the accounts payable department.

The project manager's first step is to break down the project into phases:

		Estimated time to complete
Phase 1	Document current procedures	4 days
Phase 2	Produce flowcharts	3 days
Phase 3	Summarise paper flow and methods for receiving, processing and sending information	5 days
Phase 4	List problem areas and develop initial recommendations	6 days
Phase 5	Develop improved processing procedures	3 days
Phase 6	Track sample transactions for one week under existing procedures	5 days
Phase 7	Track sample transactions for two weeks under proposed new procedures	10 days
Phase 8	Prepare and deliver a final report to the treasurer, including recommended changes in procedures and an estimate of savings	2 days

This could then be expressed in a Gantt chart using the most common method, the bar chart, the start of which is shown below. The budgets for the activities are shown, together with the actual durations underneath:

Days	1	2	3	4	5	6	7	8	9	10	11
Document current procedures											
Produce flowcharts											
Summarise paper flow and methods for receiving, processing and sending information											
List problem areas and develop initial recommendations											

Test your understanding 6 – Project example L plc

L plc example continued.

Required:

Using the information from test your understanding 3, produce a Gantt chart for the project.

(10 marks)

Test your understanding 7

A new on-line order entry system is currently being developed in your organisation. As part of the implementation procedures, users of the new system will require a number of training activities. The following table lists the activities, their duration, and the most appropriate sequence.

Activity	Preceding activity	Duration (weeks)
A	–	4
B	–	3
C	A	6
D	B	8
E	C, D	3

Required:

(a) Produce a network chart from this information, identifying the critical path through the network.

(5 marks)

(b) Explain how a Gantt chart might also be of use in this context, and identify any extra information which would then be required.

(5 marks)

Project Stages – Planning

Test your understanding 8

IDC has a contract with AZ Ltd for the supply of hardware and software to run a completely new stock control system and a website allowing access to the stock database. The design stage has been completed and the project is progressing through the implementation stage, but is falling behind schedule. An analyst of your team at IDC has prepared the following schedule of events for the 16-week implementation phase of the project.

Task	Planned start	Planned duration
Planned:		
Write programs	Start of week 1	8
Purchase and install hardware	Start of week 1	5
Create databases	Start of week 6	4.5
Convert existing files	Start of week 9	2.5
Test programs	Start of week 6	3
Test system	Middle of week 11	2.5
Select and train personnel	Start of week 8	5
Cutover	Start of week 14	3
Actual:		
Write programs	Start of week 1	9
Purchase and install hardware	Start of week 1	6
Create databases	Start of week 7	4
Convert existing files	Middle of week 10	1.5 (continuing)
Test programs	Start of week 7	5 (continuing)
Test system	Not started	
Select and train personnel	Start of week 8	4 (continuing)
Cutover	Not started	

Current date is start of week 12

Required:

(a) Prepare a Gantt chart for the AZ Ltd project.

(10 marks)

(b) Explain the purpose of a Gantt chart and interpret the information shown on the chart prepared for AZ Ltd.

(10 marks)

9 Milestones and control gates

One of the main reasons for constructing a network diagram is to improve the control of the project duration.

In order to facilitate this, a number of milestones can be identified in the network. They are not specifically shown on the diagram (except of course for the end activities), but they are shown on a Gantt chart as a small triangle or other symbol.

A **milestone**, as the name implies, is an event that is clearly identifiable as a measure of how far the project has progressed, and how far it has to run. This involves partitioning the project into identifiable and manageable phases that are well defined key events and unambiguous targets of what needs to be done and by when, and should be established during the project planning phase.

Milestones are important in assessing the status of the project and quality of the work. Monitoring the milestones enables the project manager to keep control over the projects progress, and allows any delays to be identified immediately.

Some milestones are key points in the project life cycle which give the project sponsor or steering committee an opportunity to review project progress, and make a decision whether to proceed further or to terminate the project. These milestones are called **'control gates'** and represent the significant completion of milestones. A gate can only be 'passed' if the process meets pre-defined performance standards. This could take the form of technical reviews or completion of documents.

'Gates' should be identified in the project plan and a gate review will be required to formally pass each gate. If at the gate review the criteria have not been met, the project should not continue. This may mean changes are needed to the overall project plan.

10 Resource histogram

This is a graphical aid for determining the total requirement for a specific resource during the project. The histogram identifies, in block graph form, the fluctuating need for finance, staff, technology resources or vendor services at any stage in the project. This can assist in planning. Reallocation of key tasks can reduce the excessive requirement at certain periods, providing a smooth flow of resources throughout the project.

This smooth flow is easier and cheaper to plan for. The histogram may also assist in control activities.

Project Stages – Planning

A resource histogram shows the amount and timing of the requirement for a resource or a range of resources using a stacked bar chart.

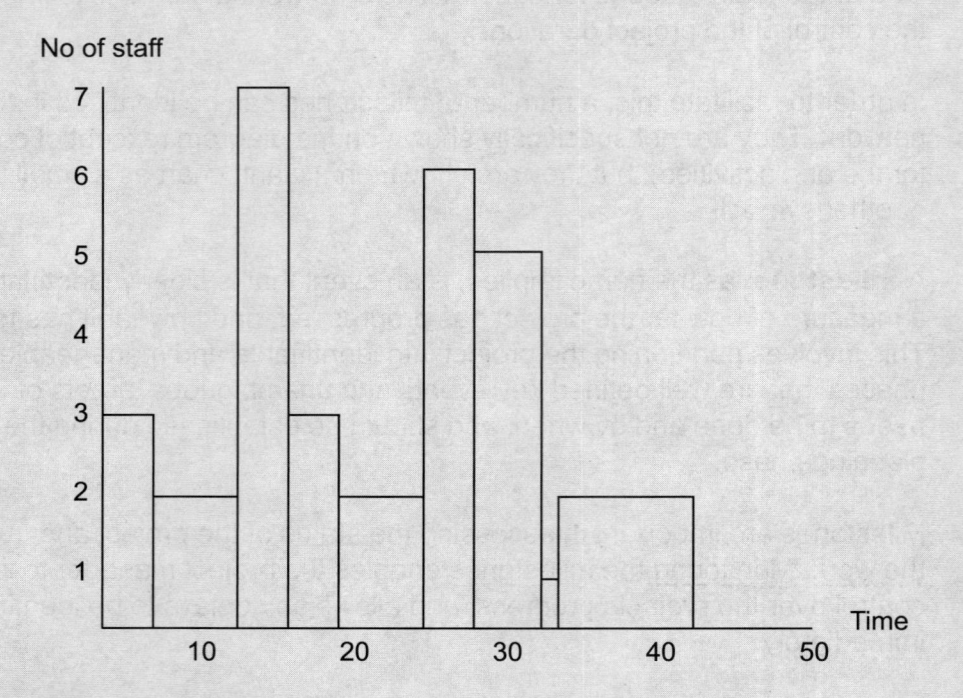

Benefits of resource histograms:

- It helps with capacity planning, resource scheduling and management
- Resource availability and allocations can be shown on a histogram, to highlight overloads and under-utilisation
- Easy visualisation of resource requirements
- It is drawn in real time

Illustration 3 – Resource histogram example

It is very common for a project budget to be constructed as shown below. Variance analysis and financial control are much easier when a spreadsheet package is used for project budgeting.

Month	1 $	2 $	3 $	4 $	5 $	6 $	7 $	8 $	9 $	10 $	11 $	Total $
Salaries	420	285	662	850	122	453	411	502	850	421	409	5385
Materials	0	125	0	0	1000	250	400	325	100	125	800	3125
Overheads	180	55	320	123	249	402	111	122	451	123	201	2337
Sub-con.	0	200	200	200	200	0	0	560	560	250	0	2170
Total	600	665	1182	1173	1571	1105	922	1509	1961	919	1410	13017

Such a budget can, of course, be shown as a histogram for immediate visual impact, as shown below:

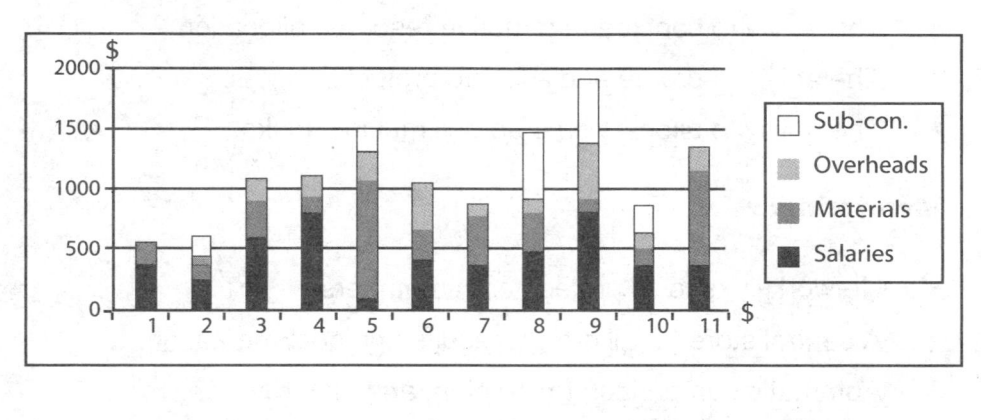

```
$
2000
1500                                                  ☐ Sub-con.
1000                                                  ▨ Overheads
 500                                                  ▨ Materials
   0                                                  ■ Salaries
     1  2  3  4  5  6  7  8  9  10  11  $
```

Test your understanding 9 – Project example L plc

L plc example continued.

Required:

Using the information from test your understanding 3, produce a resource histogram for the project.

(10 marks)

11 Project management software

While project management software can assist considerably at the planning stage, it is also useful at the other stages of the project.

The planning of the project will be assisted through the use of appropriate software. The type of output produced by the package will vary depending upon the package being used.

They may be used in a variety of ways.

Planning:

- The ability to create multiple network diagrams.
- The ability to create multiple Gantt charts.
- The ability to create Project Initiation Document (PID), Project Quality Plan (PQP) and Work Breakdown Structure (WBS).

Project Stages – Planning

Estimating:

- The ability to consider alternative resource allocation.
- The ability to create and allocate project budgets.
- The ability to allocate time across multiple tasks.

Monitoring:

- Network links to all project team members.
- A central store for all project results and documentation.
- Automatic comparison to the plan, and plan revision.

Reporting:

- Access to team members.
- Ability to create technical documents.
- Ability to create end of stage reports.

Advantages of using project management software

- Improved planning and control. Software includes various tools which can aid planning. All project data can be held centrally and this facilitates comparison between planned and actual data.
- Improved communication. Calendars, report generation and scheduling of activities can all aid communication during the project.
- Improved quality of systems developed.
- Accuracy. Particularly in large projects, manually drawing network diagrams can be prone to error.
- Ability to handle complexity. For large, complex projects, PM software is indispensable in managing and controlling large volumes of activities.
- What if analysis. The software allows the user to see the effect of different scenarios by altering elements of the project data. This enables the project manager to plan for contingencies and to assess consequences.
- Timesheet recording. In order to ease the project manager's burden of recording the actual effort and revised estimates to complete a task, a number of PM software packages allow this data to be captured from individual team member.
- Project management software recognises that there is a sequence in which activities need to be performed. The use of software can help to ensure that all necessary tasks are carried out as required.

When choosing project management software, or indeed any software package, it is important to:

- determine requirements of organisation including its current and future needs.
- document requirements including the essential functions/important/wish list.
- review all available packages to identify three/four products which meet the essential functions and fall within budget.
- have a demonstration of the packages on a trial basis if possible.
- select a package including 'roll out' strategy with installation, training, etc.

Despite the extensive use of project management software, projects can still go spectacularly wrong, over schedule and/or budget.

Here are some **common pitfalls:**

- *Emphasis on maintaining the plan rather than managing the project.* In a large project, maintaining the plan can be a full-time task. This can leave little time for dealing with important project issues. It is often better for project managers to delegate the input/maintenance responsibility to a project administrator and receive regular reports as a basis for managing the project.
- *Resources may not be managed realistically.* This especially applies when tasks are over-budget. Adding new people into a project at a late stage can make it later since the new team members will be slower at grasping what is required and actually divert the attention of other team members.
- *Estimates.* For planning purposes, the accuracy of estimates is vital to the identification of the critical path and the key milestones of the project. However, estimates are subjective and can vary wildly. Also, estimates have been made at a fixed point in time with a particular set of assumptions.
- *Skill levels.* Plans tend to talk about resources when actually they are referring to human beings with all the uncertainty that it brings. Where one individual may find a task within his/her skillset, another person may struggle. It matters which person does which task.
- *Work breakdown.* Some plans fail because the work breakdown into tasks does not match with how people work. Work breakdown assumes discrete units of work that someone will spend a fixed amount of time on a task before moving to the next task.

Project management software functions

The following is a list of functions that would commonly be found within a standard project management software package, such as Microsoft Project:

- *Budgeting and cost control*. At any time during the project, actual costs can be compared with budgeted costs for individual resources or activities, or for the whole project.
- *Calendars*. Calendars can be used for reporting purposes and to define working periods.
- *Graphics*. The ability to create and modify graphics, such as Gantt charts, is a useful feature of PM software. It will allow the tasks in Gantt charts to be linked so that preceding activities can be shown.
- *Multiple project handling*. Large projects often have to be broken down into smaller projects to make them more manageable. Alternatively, project managers may be responsible for more than one project at a time. Most PM software packages will store numerous projects quite easily.
- *Planning*. All PM software allows the user to define the activities that need to be performed. It will maintain detailed task lists and create critical path analyses. It will allow the project manager to plan several thousand activities, by allocating resources, setting start and completion dates and calculating expected time to complete.
- *Scheduling*. Most systems will build Gantt charts and network diagrams based on the task and resource list and all of their associated information. Any changes to those lists will automatically create a new schedule for the project. It is also possible to schedule recurring tasks, to set priorities for tasks, to schedule tasks to start as late as possible, and to specify 'must end by' and 'no later than' dates.
- *Resource planning*. A critical issue in project planning is resource management, that is ensuring the project has the correct level of manpower, equipment and material at the right place at the right time and in right quantities.

- *Resource histograms*. These provide the project manager with a visual display showing the usage and availability of resources over the project's life. This allows the project manager to see quickly and easily where there are either too few resources or where there are surplus resources to carry out a particular activity. The project manager then has the ability to reallocate resources or to obtain additional resources to ensure that critical activities are achieved on time and therefore the critical path is achieved. An example of a resource histogram is shown on top of next page.

- *Reporting*. The project manager has to report on the progress of the project to the stakeholders. PM software provides the facility to generate standard reports, such as progress to date, budget reports, allocation of resources reports, individual task or WBS reports and financial reports.

Test your understanding 10

The development of computer systems is a project-based activity. The development project has a start and, once it has met its objectives, an end.

Required:

Explain how computer software can be used to help in the planning, estimating, monitoring and reporting of project progress.

(10 marks)

Test your understanding 11

You are a trainee management accountant working for a firm of financial and management consultants (ZX Consultants) who have been contracted to assist in the management and control of a large international sporting event due to take place in four years' time.

A significant part of the project will be the provision of new buildings and facilities. Major new works associated with the project include the construction of a 30,000-seat indoor athletics stadium and a world press and media centre. A further consideration is the upgrade of the current transport network, with major development work required on the local rail system between the main stadium and the city centre, and an airport bus link.

Success will be measured in terms of trouble-free performance of the events, level of customer enthusiasm and satisfaction, and sustained economic activity generated in the region. Completion of the project on time is critical, even if cost or quality are adversely affected.

The main software development aspect of the project is the development of the communications software in the form of an information database. This will require development of a dedicated website to give public access to event information. The database will contain information about competitors and their events, time and location and availability of tickets.

The database will be designed to allow the general public to monitor the events, order tickets from the website for any event, and purchase merchandise. The website will also contain links to local hotels and restaurant facilities. The whole package of communications software and the telecommunications and IT hardware has been called the "Communications Infrastructure".

Project activities

The project can be broken down into the following areas of work:

Activity	Activity description	Preceding activity	Duration in weeks (after completion of preceding activities)
A	Obtain financing and sponsorship negotiation	–	22
B	Sporting facilities	–	52
C	Analysis and design of communications software	A	14
D	Construct media facilities	B, C	16
E	Program communications system	C	26
F	Install communications software and telecommunications hardware	D, E	6
G	Transport network update and construct athletes' accommodation	–	40
H	Security arrangements and checks	G, F	12
I	Public relations / advertising / marketing	F	10

J	Human resources and volunteers	I	12
K	Test games, trial events and media systems, and contingency	H, J	6
L	Events (including the opening and closing ceremonies)	K	2

Each of the above activities is carried out by individual specialist project teams, and is led by a project team manager. It is critical that these events are co-ordinated and planned effectively, as timing is critical to the success of this project.

One of the key tasks to undertake immediately is the determination of the critical path.

Required:

You have been asked by your management to prepare a report which includes:

(a) an explanation of the importance of undertaking critical path analysis for a project such as this.

(5 marks)

(b) a critical path analysis for the project, clearly identifying:

  (i) the critical path activities and the critical duration of the project;

  (ii) the Earliest Event Time for each activity (EET);

  (iii) the Latest Event Time for each activity (LET).
  Note: You are NOT required to prepare a Gantt chart as part of the report.

(8 marks)

(c) a calculation of the slack time on activity H and an explanation of how this information may assist decision making during this project.

(4 marks)

(d) an explanation of how using project management software may assist during this project.

(8 marks)

12 Summary diagram

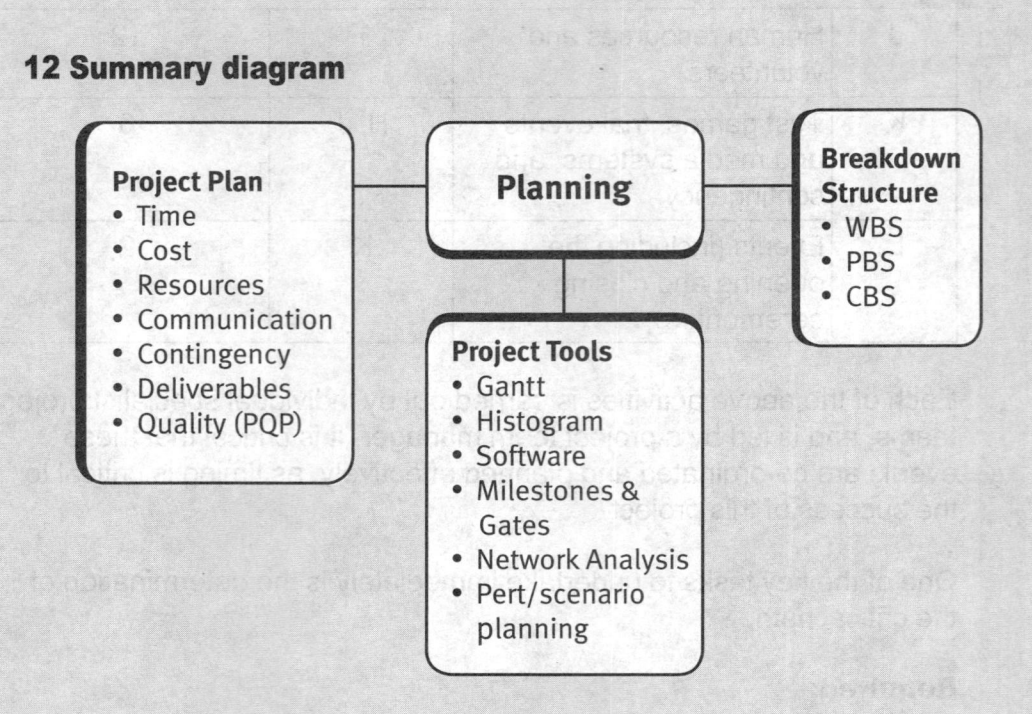

Project Plan
- Time
- Cost
- Resources
- Communication
- Contingency
- Deliverables
- Quality (PQP)

Planning

Breakdown Structure
- WBS
- PBS
- CBS

Project Tools
- Gantt
- Histogram
- Software
- Milestones & Gates
- Network Analysis
- Pert/scenario planning

Test your understanding answers

Test your understanding 1

(a) Project planning is the arrangement of the activities required to achieve the project objective. The first part of this stage is the establishment and agreement of the project objectives. This means determining exactly what the project aims to achieve. The next stage is to determine what activities or tasks need to be undertaken to achieve the objective.

The project plan articulates exactly what needs to be achieved, how it is to be achieved, by whom and at what time in the project's life. It is a benchmark against which actual project results can be compared and monitored. If the comparison of actual versus plan indicates a deviation, then corrective action needs to be taken.

It is important that the planning stage involves the members of staff who will be working on the project. These people will be in the best position to know what activities will be needed, how they will be performed and how long they will take. In addition, by encouraging team participation in planning, it is more likely that they will become committed to achieving their activity targets.

(b) Planning is a vital part of any project. It is important to lay out a 'road map' that clearly shows how the project activities and tasks will be accomplished, within budget and to schedule. Attempting to begin a project without a plan would be like trying to assemble a set of cabinets without first reading the instructions, or trying to drive from Glasgow to Southampton without first reading a map. Getting from A to B (the start of the project to final successful completion) is most likely to be achieved if all of the stages and tasks between A and B are broken down and planned carefully before beginning the project. The risk of project failure is much greater without project planning.

(c) Detailed planning involves the following stages:
- Obtaining project authorisation
- Time plan
- Resources plan including staffing
- Contingency plan
- Quality plan
- Cost plan
- Communication plan
- Audit plan.

Project Stages – Planning

From these can be developed:

- Work packages
- Estimates of time and cost
- Graphic illustrations of the schedule: Gantt charts, etc.
- Risk analysis and plans
- Project schedule and the budget
- Change management
- Acceptance process
- Post-project implementation audit.

Then the plan is issued to all major stakeholders, excluding any sensitive information that would only be given to senior management. In an exam question, you would be expected to give some detail for each category.

Test your understanding 2

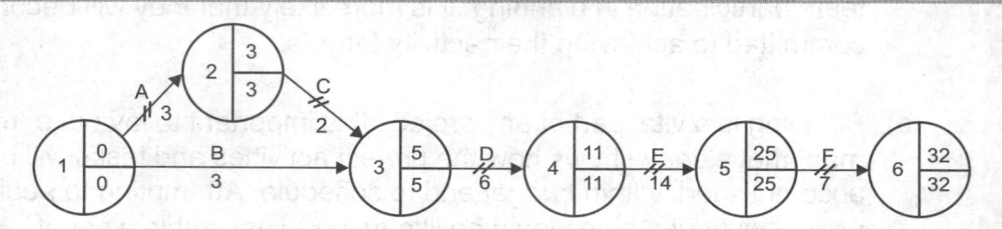

Node 1: 0/0 → A (3) → Node 2: 2/3, 3/3 → C (2) → Node 3: 3/5, 5/5 → D (6) → Node 4: 4/11, 11/11 → E (14) → Node 5: 5/25, 25/25 → F (7) → Node 6: 6/32, 32/32

B (3) from Node 1 to Node 3.

Critical path is   ACDEF

Project duration is   32 weeks

Float B   2 weeks

chapter 14

Test your understanding 3 – Project example L plc

(a) The critical path diagram is shown below:

Critical path A, B, E, H

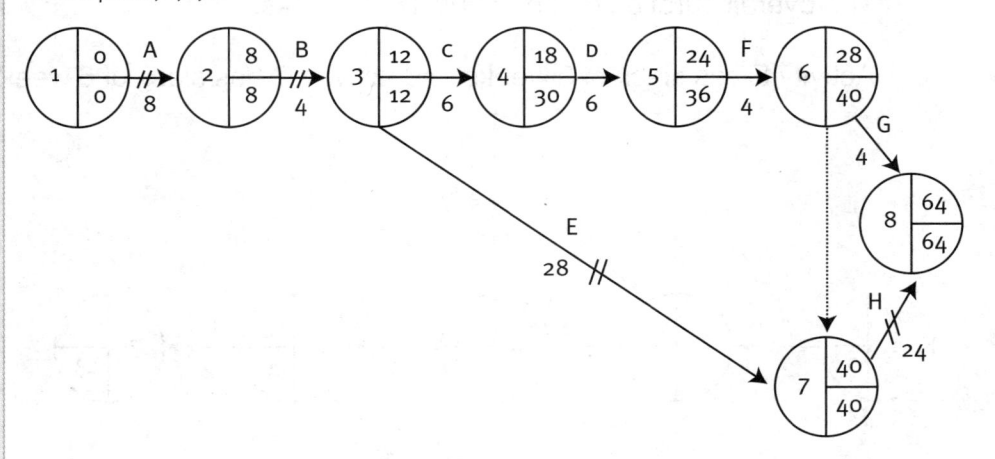

(b) The critical path diagram shows that the project has an overall duration of 64 weeks. The deadline for the project is 78 weeks, therefore the project has a contingency of 14 weeks.

Test your understanding 4

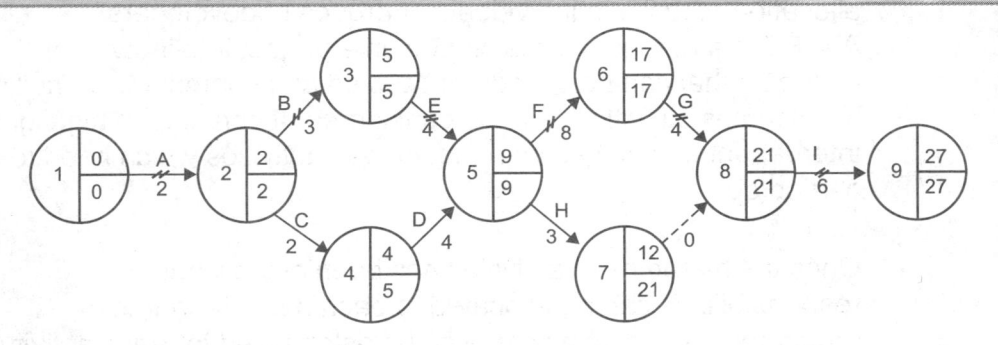

Critical path is	ABEFGI
Project duration is	27 weeks
Floats C, D	1 week
Float H	9 weeks

Project Stages – Planning

Test your understanding 5

(a) The critical path for the project is ACFH.

The overall duration of the project is 13 weeks.

Activity E has slack of 3 weeks and activity G has slack of 6 weeks.

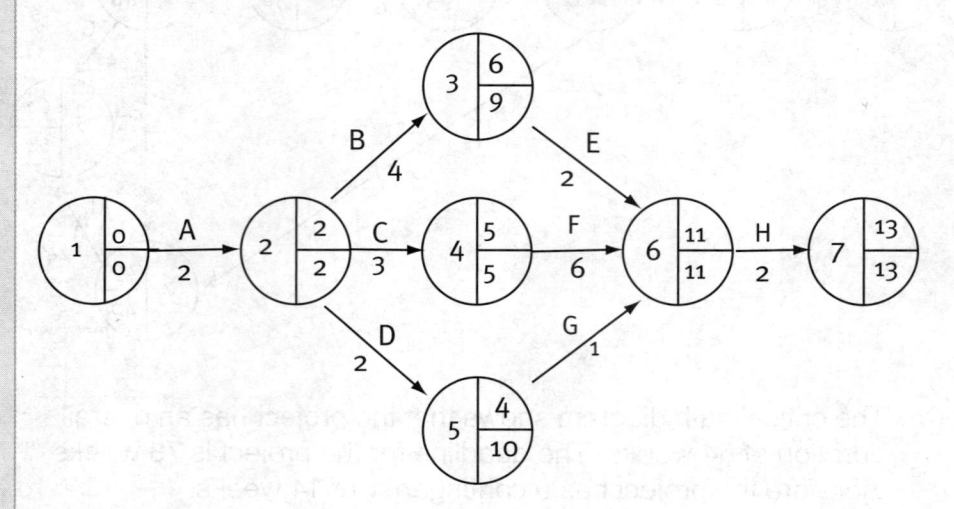

```
                    ┌─3─┬─6─┐
                    │   │ 9 │
                B          E
                4          2
┌1┬0┬0┐─A─┌2┬2┬2┐─C─┌4┬5┬5┐─F─┌6┬11┬11┐─H─┌7┬13┬13┐
           2                 3           5        6          2
                      D              G
                      2              1
                    ┌5┬4┬10┐
```

(b) A Work Breakdown Structure (WBS) is a set of documents identifying each stage and task to be performed during development. A hierarchy of work will be defined prior to the allocation of tasks to individuals or groups of developers.
A WBS is a means of breaking down a project into individual elements that can be scheduled, costed and controlled. Compiling a WBS forces all activities to be considered. It can help to highlight interdependencies between the various activities which need to be carried out.

Once the hierarchy of activities has been established, responsibilities can be allocated to each part. Resource requirements and costs can also be established for each activity and together these costs will form the budget for the project.

The details gathered from the WBS provide a basis for controlling the costs and resources of the project.

(c) Buffering is a technique which can be used with critical path analysis to deal with uncertainties and risk within the project. It involves adding extra durations to the estimates of the more risky or uncertain activities within the project. It is recognized that at the outset of the project it can be difficult to accurately assess the durations of the activities.

Care must be taken with buffering to ensure that too much slack is not added to the project which may encourage complacency. As it stands, L has slack added to activities E and G. The overall duration of the project is 13 weeks and the target date for completion is 16 weeks, so at the moment the project has a contingency of 3 weeks. L will have to consider if this, together with the slack in activities E and G give enough leeway so that unexpected events do not affect the successful outcome of the project.

Test your understanding 6 – Project example L plc

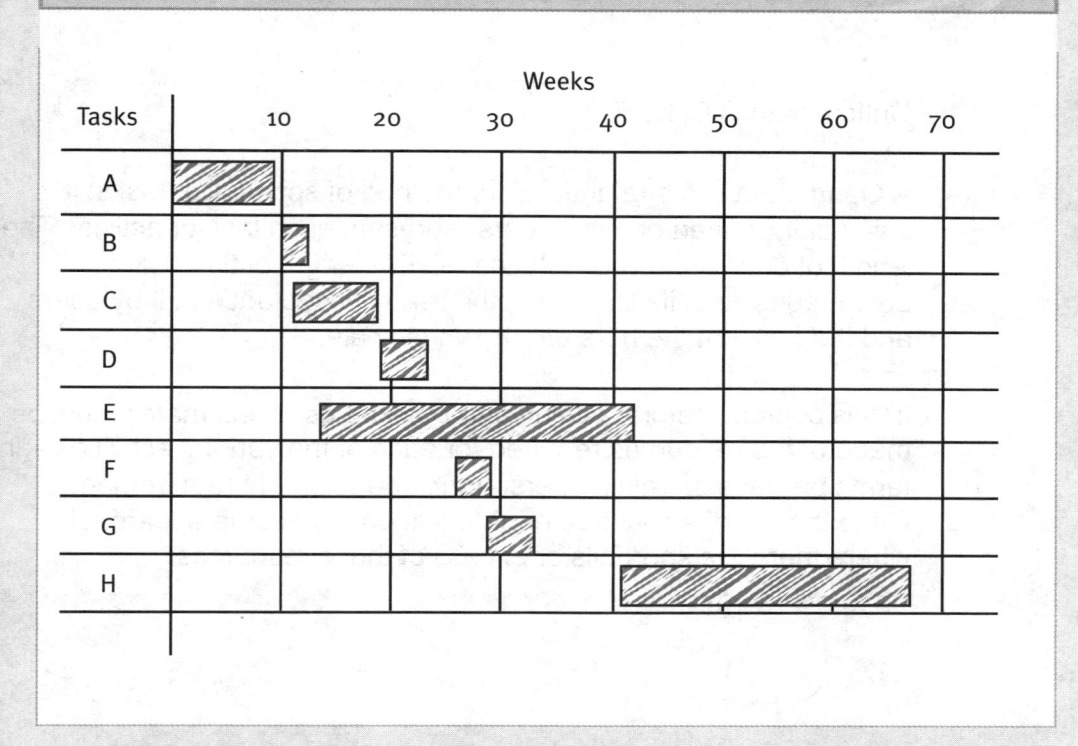

Test your understanding 7

(a) The network diagram is as follows.

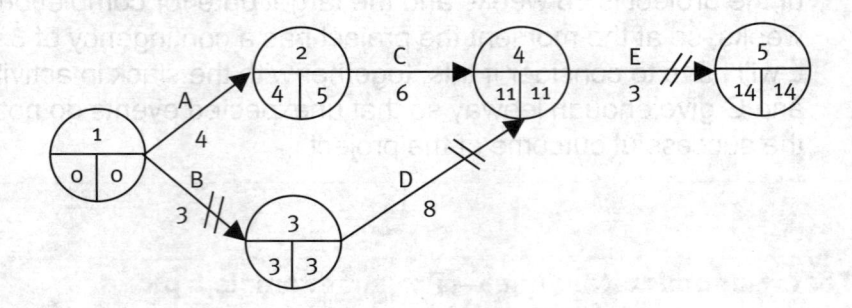

Critical path is B, D, E.

(b) A Gantt chart is a straightforward method of scheduling tasks; it is essentially a chart on which bars represent each task or activity. The length of each bar represents the relative length of the task. Its advantages lie in its simplicity, the ready acceptance of it by users, and the fact that the bars are drawn to scale.

In this context, before a Gantt chart can be used, estimates must be made of the resources required for each of the various activities – in terms perhaps of training personnel, or equipment requirements. Once the chart is constructed, it will at once become apparent where there are shortfalls or excess of those resources.

chapter 14

> **Test your understanding 8**
>
> | | Week | 1 | 2 | 3 | 4 | 5 | 6 | 7 | 8 | 9 | 10 | 11 | 12 | 13 | 14 | 15 | 16 |
> |---|---|---|---|---|---|---|---|---|---|---|---|---|---|---|---|---|---|
> | Write programmes | | ■ | ■ | ■ | ■ | ■ | ■ | ■ | | | | | | | | | |
> | | | ░ | ░ | ░ | ░ | ░ | ░ | ░ | ░ | | | | | | | | |
> | Purchase and install equipment | | ■ | ■ | ■ | ■ | | | | | | | | | | | | |
> | | | ░ | ░ | ░ | ░ | ░ | ░ | | | | | | | | | | |
> | Create databases | | | | | | | ■ | ■ | ■ | ■ | | | | | | | |
> | | | | | | | | | ░ | ░ | ░ | ░ | | | | | | |
> | Convert files | | | | | | | | | | ■ | ■ | | | | | | |
> | | | | | | | | | | | | ░ | ░ | | | | | |
> | Test programmes | | | | | | | ■ | ■ | | | | | | | | | |
> | | | | | | | | | | ░ | ░ | ░ | ░ | | | | | |
> | Test system | | | | | | | | | | | | ■ | ■ | ■ | | | |
> | Select and train personnel | | | | | | | ■ | ■ | ■ | ■ | ■ | | | | | | |
> | | | | | | | | | ░ | ░ | ░ | ░ | ░ | | | | | |
> | Cutover | | | | | | | | | | | | | | ■ | ■ | ■ | |
>
> planned time ■
>
> actual time ░
>
> (b) The Gantt chart's purpose is to help with project planning by showing the duration and sequence of activities in a project. The chart is also able to show actual progress alongside planned progress but does not show dependencies.
>
> The information shown on the attached Gantt chart for the stock control implementation shows the following:
>
> – The initial estimate for the time to write programs was 1 week less than the time needed. This 1 week delay meant that the file conversion could not start until Week 10; it actually started in the middle of Week 10, 1.5 weeks late, possibly due to the lack of available staff.
>
> – File conversion has not yet been completed, although it was meant to be finished in the middle of Week 11.

- The purchase and installation of equipment took 1 week longer than planned. This delay caused the creation of the database and test programs to be delayed by 1 week, starting in Week 7 instead of Week 6.

- The creation of the database went very well and the team completed the task in 4 weeks instead of 4.5 weeks.

- Testing programs started a week late due to the delay in purchasing equipment, but is still unfinished after 5 weeks; the original plan was for 3 weeks. This suggests problems are arising during testing, which could be related to the delays in writing the programs.

- Testing the system was meant to have started in the middle of Week 11, but has not started yet as it is dependent on the files being converted and the programs tested, neither of which is completed.

- The system cutover is likely to be delayed as file conversion and program testing are not yet finished and are holding up system testing. System testing is planned to take 2.5 weeks, so even if it started today the cutover will be delayed by half a week.

Test your understanding 9 – Project example L plc

To produce a resource histogram, you first have to have a gantt chart.

Go back to the gantt chart in test your understanding 6. Write the durations for each activity on each bar of the gantt chart. Underneath the gantt chart, using the same scale, add through all of the durations and draw a vertical bar showing these durations on the resource histogram.

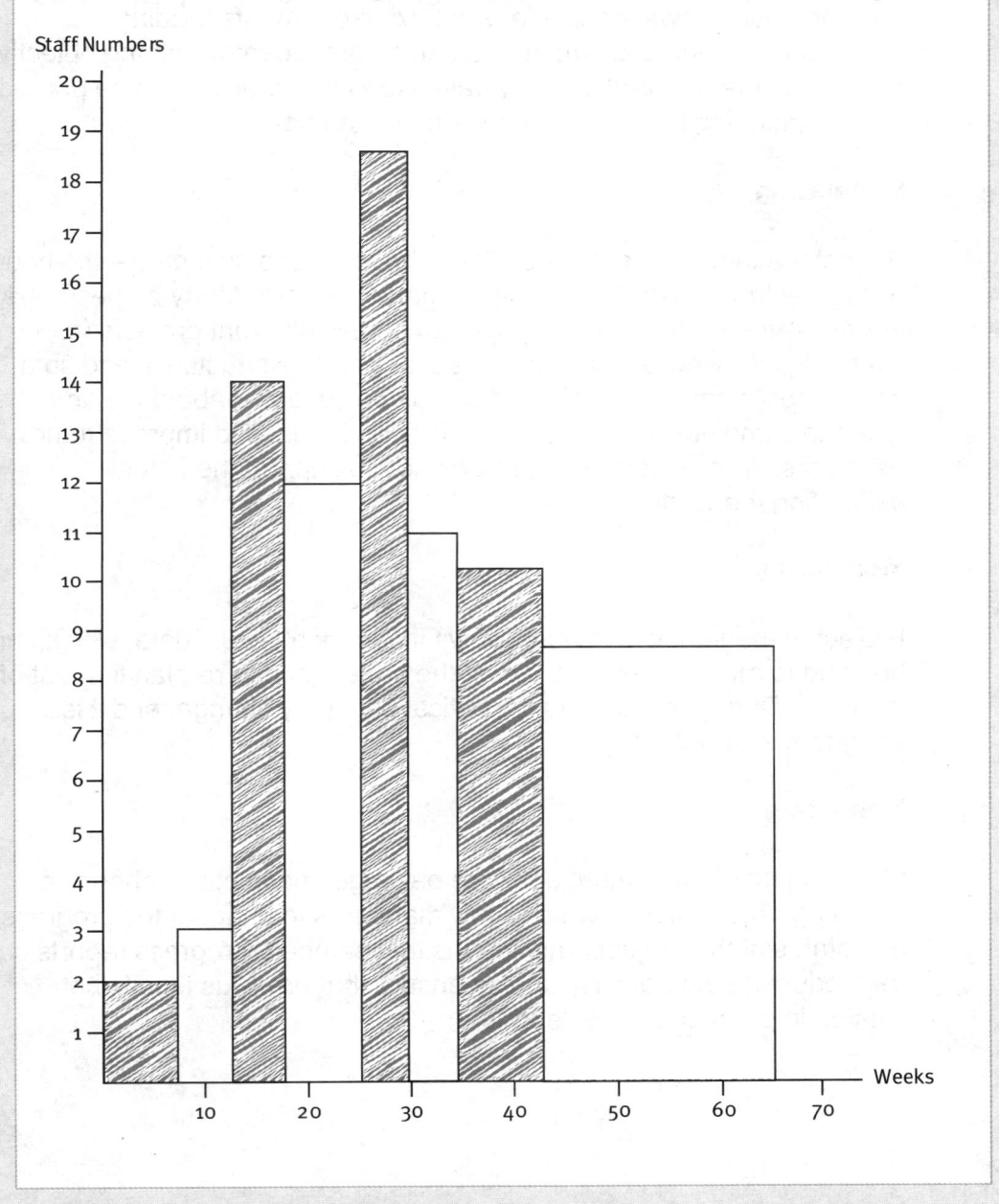

Test your understanding 10

Planning

Project management software can be used to enter activities, estimates, precedents and resources to automatically produce a network diagram (showing the critical path) and a Gantt chart (showing resource use). These diagrams are difficult to produce and maintain manually, and the software also allows for simple 'what if?' experiments (adding resources, changing estimates, re-setting precedents) with the objective of meeting the required delivery date. Resource profiles can be printed off as a planning tool for staff used on the project.

Estimating

Project management software allows the entry of actual data – the hours or days actually taken to complete a particular task. Many of these tasks are the same in systems development across different projects (for example, interview users, construct a logical data structure), and so a considerable amount of information can be collected about the time taken to complete common tasks. This can be used to improve future estimates. A computer may also be used to support the actual estimating model itself.

Monitoring

Project management software allows the entry of actual data, which can be used to monitor the progress of the project and to re-plan the rest of the work. During re-planning the critical path may change, and it is important to know this.

Reporting

Most project management software packages have comprehensive reporting requirements, which allow managers to print out the progress and status of the project. This means that standard progress reports can be produced automatically and so ensure that precious time is not wasted in producing such reports.

Test your understanding 11

(a)

Report

To: The SGCC
From: Management accountant, ZX
Date: XX/XX/XXXX

Critical path analysis

Critical path analysis is an important technique to assist with project management, when a project has to be completed within a given amount of time, or before a final target date. A CPA chart shows all the activities that must be carried out in order to complete the project, the sequence in which they must take place, the budgeted time for each activity, the minimum overall completion time for the project and the earliest times that each activity can start and must be finished to make sure that the target project completion date is achieved. The analysis therefore enables management to:

- decide whether the target date for completion is achievable
- if the target date is achievable, what is the latest time the project can begin
- identify which activities are critical to completion on time and must be started at the earliest possible time
- identify those activities that are non-critical, and how much 'slack' they have, so that they can be started late or might take longer than planned without affecting the overall project completion time
- identify which activities cannot start until another activity (or other activities) have finished, and which activities can be undertaken in parallel with each other.

Regular monitoring of actual progress against the CPA chart will provide management with valuable information to assist with efforts to ensure completion of the project on time.

(b) An activity-on-arrow CPA chart is shown.

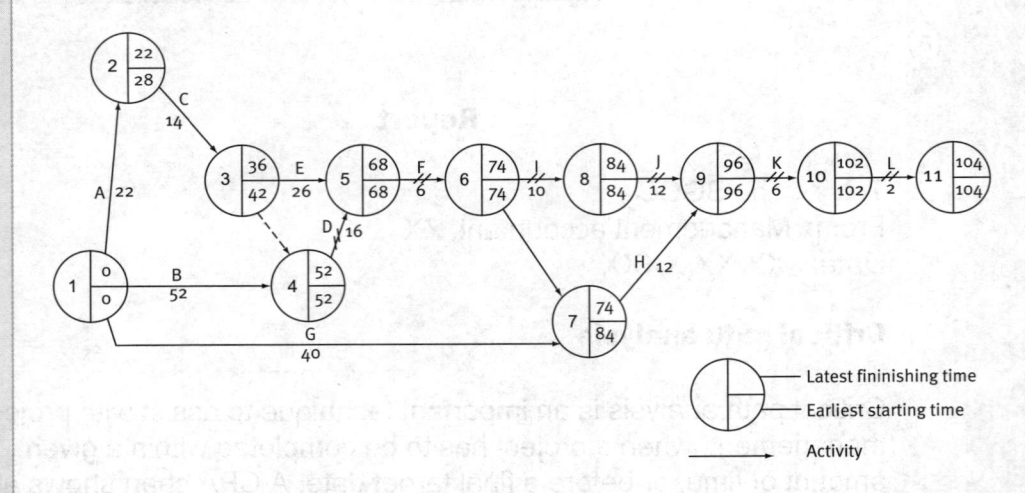

[Activity-on-arrow CPA chart with nodes 1 through 11, showing activities A(22), B(52), C(14), D(16), E(26), F(6), G(40), H(12), I(10), J(12), K(6), L(2). Each node shows earliest starting time (bottom) and latest finishing time (top). Key: Latest finishing time (top), Earliest starting time (bottom), Activity (arrow).]

The critical path is BDFIJKL

It indicates that the project will take at least 104 weeks, or two years exactly. To complete the project by the deadline it is essential to begin the project now.

(c) The slack time for activity H is 10 weeks.

This can be calculated as:

Latest finishing time − Earliest starting time − Activity duration
= (in weeks) 96 − 84 − 12 = 10 weeks.

This information could be valuable because it shows by how long the start of activity H could be deferred without affecting the overall project completion time. Similarly, it shows the amount of time by which completion of the activity could be delayed if it were to start at the earliest possible time.

This information can be useful in the following ways.

- If the start of Activity H is delayed by up to 10 weeks, there is no need to authorise overtime working or to bring in additional labour to 'catch up the lost time'.

- If another activity is running late, and threatens the overall completion time, it might be possible to divert resources from Activity H to the critical activity. This would not affect the project completion time if the delay to completion of Activity H is 10 weeks or less.

(d) **Planning**

Project management software can be used to enter activities, estimates, precedents and resources to automatically produce a network diagram (showing the critical path) and a Gantt chart (showing resource use). These diagrams can be difficult to produce.

Estimating

Project management software allows the entry of actual data – the hours or days actually taken to complete a particular task. Many of these tasks are the same in systems development across different projects and so a considerable amount of information can be collected about the time taken to complete common tasks.

Monitoring

Project management software allows the entry of actual data, which can be used to monitor the progress of the project and to re-plan the rest of the work.

Reporting

Most project management software packages have comprehensive reporting requirements, which allow managers to print out the progress and status of the project. This means that standard progress reports can be produced automatically.

ZX Consultants

Project Stages – Planning

536

chapter

15

Project Stages – Execution, control and completion

Chapter learning objectives

- Identify the characteristics of each phase in the project process.
- Compare and contrast project control systems
- Discuss the value of post-completion audit
- Apply a process of continuous improvement to projects

Project Stages – Execution, control and completion

1 Session content diagram

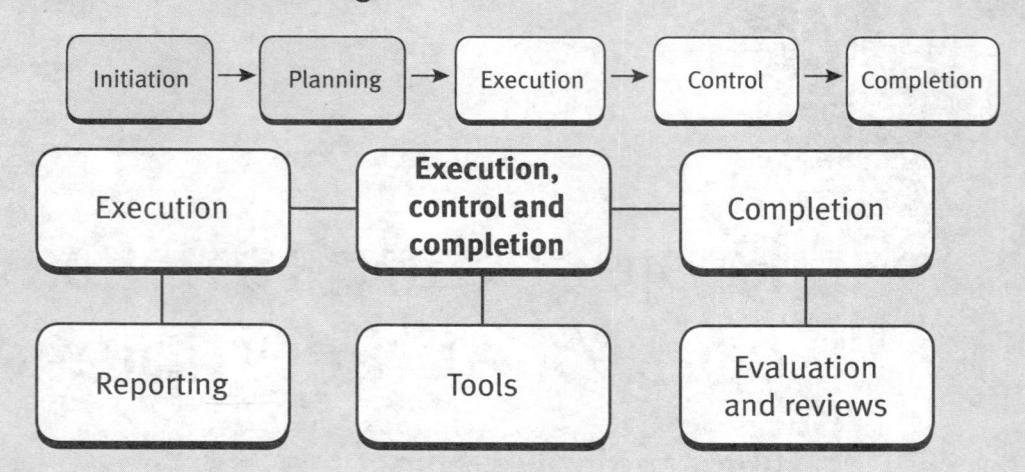

Initiation → Planning → Execution → Control → Completion

Execution — **Execution, control and completion** — Completion

Reporting — Tools — Evaluation and reviews

2 Execution

Once the project plan has been developed and agreed by the customer and project team, the project can commence. At this stage, the project manager must provide leadership and co-ordination to the project team members and other stakeholders with the aim of successfully delivering the project objectives. This is the stage where stakeholders need to be focused upon the project tasks and the project team will perform the tasks they are responsible for, as and when scheduled in the plan.

This stage can be weeks, months or years long.

An example of elements performed during this stage for **the development and installation of an organisational information system** could include (Gido and Clements, 1999):

- Undertaking **detailed design work**, including systems specifications, flow charts, programmes and a list of required hardware.
- Carrying out **design reviews** on a continual basis, which may result in modifications and design changes. This may result in a change in the project scope, price or schedule. It may also involve re-planning the original schedule.
- There will also be a plan prepared for **systems testing** once the system has been designed. This may involve the customers who may wish to participate in testing or at least review the test procedures.
- Carrying out the **writing and construction** of the software.
- **Testing the software**.
- Purchasing, assembling and **testing the hardware**, including detailed testing of sub-assemblies of hardware, and then a final test of the entire hardware system interface.
- Integrating hardware and software and **testing the whole system**.

- **Planning installation**, for example selecting the optimum changeover method and the time that is least disruptive to the organisation's operations.
- Preparation of **training materials** to enable users to understand, operate and maintain the system.
- Carrying out the **installation and changeover** procedure.
- Carrying out **training**.
- Conducting **final acceptance testing** of the new system to demonstrate that the system meets the original objectives.

The execution stage is closely linked with the control stage, we will look at the reporting carried out during execution under the control section.

3 Configuration management and change control

Change control

Change is an inevitable part of any project. This may arise from internal or external factors, and can often change the outcome of the project. It is therefore important to have an agreed change management process in place so that everyone involved in the project is aware of how change will be managed.

Change can be required at all stages of the project, very often during the execution phase as new factors emerge. It is important that the initial project documents, such as the PID and the detailed project plan, remain as "baselines" so that all changes can be carefully monitored and controlled.

A change control process is not to stop change happening, but to ensure that the changes, which will inevitably required during the project, are agreed and communicated to all parties before they are implemented. Failure to manage change adequately can result in a number of problems for the project:

- Team members may be working to the old plans which do not incorporate the changes. This can mean wasted time on aspects which may no longer be relevant.
- The project is unlikely to deliver the set objectives if change is not well managed.
- End users will be unhappy at the final product if their expectations have not been managed throughout the project and they have not been advised of changes.
- The project may end up costing more as costs may continue to be spent on aspects of the project which are no longer required, but that team members were unaware of.
- It can cause confusion and conflict for the project stakeholders.

Change process

At the outset of the project a change management process must be agreed. It should include the following:

- Method for prioritising changes requested. Changes requested will range from:
    - Must be done. Without these changes the project cannot succeed, to
    - Nice to have. These are changes requests suggesting enhancements to the current project plan. Not all changes of this nature are able to be incorporated into the final project.
- Authorisation for changes. It must be agreed who has the authority to agree to changes. This may be set as a sliding scale whereby the project manager is able to authorise small, low cost changes, but larger changes must be authorised at the highest level, for example the project committee or the project sponsor.
- Agreement of a change budget. It is likely that changes will result in additional cost to the project. A change budget may be set up for this purpose to avoid the project sponsor having to authorise every dollar of additional spend.
- Recording of changes. A set procedure should be agree for how all changes are to be recorded and who will manage this procedure.
- Communication of changes. The change management process must specify how changes to the project will be communicated to all interested parties.

Configuration management

PMBOK defines the configuration management plan as, "The configuration management plan defines those items that are configurable, those items that require formal change control, and the process for controlling changes to such items."

Configuration management is an important element within projects. It involves tracking and controlling all aspects of the projects and all documentation and deliverables from the project. The configuration management system for a project will specify how all aspects of the project are to be managed.

Included in configurations management will be:

- Version control for documentation

- Ownership and responsibility for documentation
- Authorisation and tracking procedures for any changes required to documentation
- Monitoring and control procedure to ensure only authorised documents and records are held
- Access control over project records

The change control process discussed above will be part of the configuration management system.

Without configuration management, several versions of documents or product may be being used and no one will be aware of which is the correct version. It also helps to ensure that the project runs smoothly, even when key personnel are unavailable.

4 Planning and control

Following the planning stage of the project, the project manager is responsible for monitoring and controlling its progress towards successful completion. Along with the project team members carrying out the particular tasks, the project manager will **collect actual project data on costs, schedule and progress** and **compare these against the project plan**. If a **deviation** is discovered (such as overspending or taking longer than anticipated), and the project manager considers that corrective action needs to be taken, the project manager must report the deviation and, following authorisation if necessary, take **corrective action** to get the project back on target. It is important that the project manager takes the advice of team members before deciding on a particular course of corrective action, because participation in the decision-making process will help to foster commitment of team members to the successful completion of the project objective.

Corrective action, when required, must be carried out as quickly as possible and communicated to all relevant stakeholders.

The most important aspect of project control is ensuring that monitoring progress is carried out on a regular basis. Effective project control will involve a system to regularly gather project data on actual project progress and performance, and carrying out corrective action where necessary as soon as possible. A regular project reporting period should be set up (e.g. daily, weekly or monthly), depending on the complexity or duration of the project. More complex projects are likely to require more frequent progress assessment.

Project planning and control methodology

Areas that need to be addressed by any project planning and control methodology are:

- Control begins at the inception of the project, not just before implementation. A clear and authorised brief is the foundation of any good control system; without it the whole project is destined to fail.
- When work is planned it will need to be controlled. The effective project manager considers, for each activity, what elements are critical to completion and defines control accordingly.
- A control system should be targeted at the agreed critical success factors not on the assumptions of the project manager.
- The milestone plan allows the project manager to define the go/no go control points in the project, and the enter and exit criteria for each activity.
- The responsibility matrix allows the project manager to communicate clearly the needs of the project and accountabilities for the completion of tasks.
- A control system needs to be balanced with the objectives of the project.

Project control systems

A project control system is simply a tool for the project manager. It enables **recognition of problems before they become too difficult to solve**.

The essence is that it integrates the actual work to be done with the cost of doing the work and the time needed to do it.

The purpose of a project control system is to develop a plan of the work that is to be accomplished and to develop a system that monitors that plan and the performance of the work.

This system must provide the information necessary so that the project team, company management, and the client can identify problem areas and initiate corrective action.

The decision to introduce a formal control system and the selection of a specific system should be based largely on two aspects of the project:

- **The risk involved** – high-risk situations, where the probability of undesired outcomes is significant due to the complexity of the project, justify the investment in a formal, well-designed control system.
- **The cost of the control system and its expected benefits** – the cost of control should never exceed the expected benefits (i.e. savings) due to the control system.

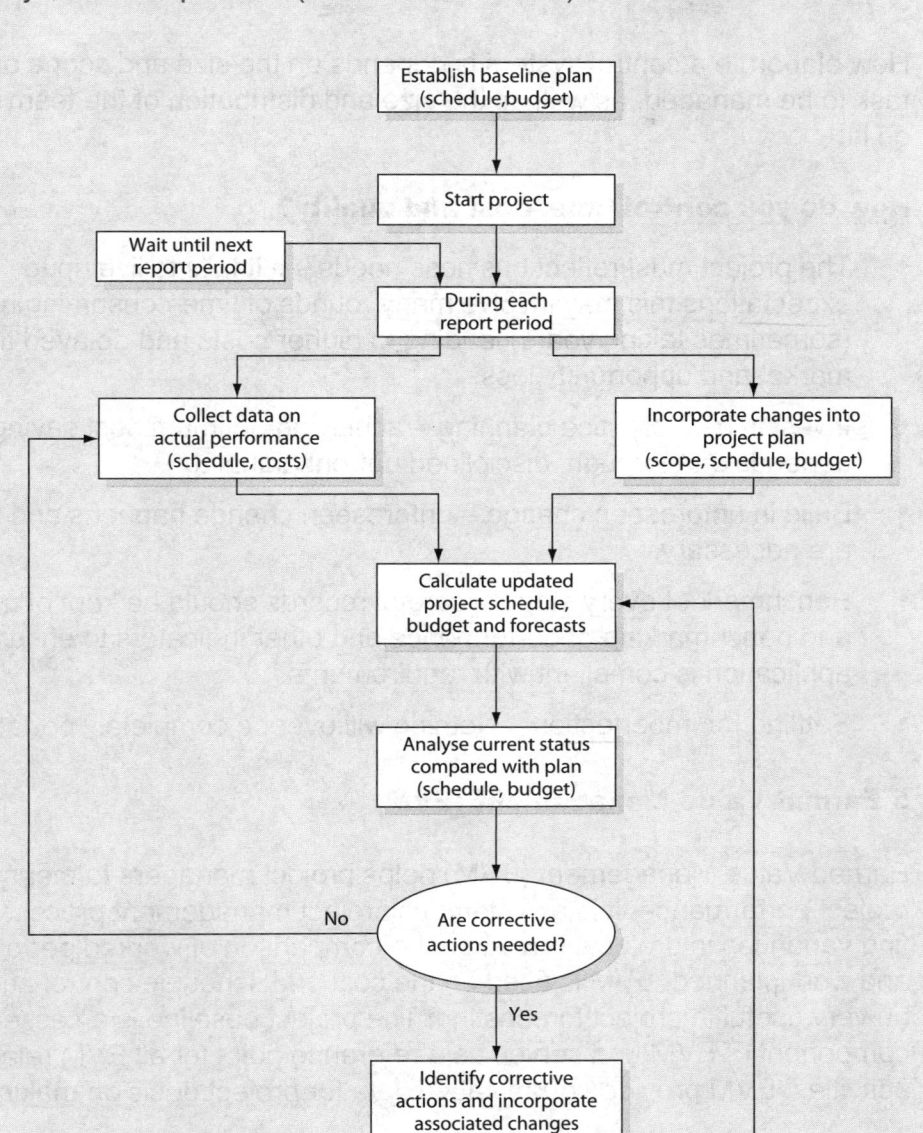

A project control process (Gido and Clements) is shown below:

```
                    ┌─────────────────────────┐
                    │ Establish baseline plan │
                    │   (schedule, budget)    │
                    └───────────┬─────────────┘
                                ▼
                    ┌─────────────────────────┐
                    │      Start project      │
                    └───────────┬─────────────┘
  ┌──────────────────┐          │
  │ Wait until next  │──────────┤
  │  report period   │          ▼
  └──────────────────┘ ┌─────────────────────────┐
                       │     During each         │
                       │     report period       │
                       └───────────┬─────────────┘
              ┌────────────────────┴────────────────────┐
              ▼                                         ▼
   ┌─────────────────────┐              ┌──────────────────────────┐
   │   Collect data on   │              │ Incorporate changes into │
   │  actual performance │              │      project plan        │
   │  (schedule, costs)  │              │ (scope, schedule, budget)│
   └──────────┬──────────┘              └─────────────┬────────────┘
              └────────────────┬────────────────────┘
                               ▼
                   ┌─────────────────────────┐
                   │   Calculate updated     │
                   │   project schedule,     │
                   │  budget and forecasts   │
                   └───────────┬─────────────┘
                               ▼
                   ┌─────────────────────────┐
                   │  Analyse current status │
                   │    compared with plan   │
                   │   (schedule, budget)    │
                   └───────────┬─────────────┘
                               ▼
                    ╱───────────────────╲
             No   ╱   Are corrective     ╲
        ◄───────┤    actions needed?      │
                  ╲                      ╱
                    ╲───────┬───────────╱
                            │ Yes
                            ▼
                   ┌─────────────────────────┐
                   │  Identify corrective    │
                   │ actions and incorporate │
                   │   associated changes    │
                   └─────────────────────────┘
```

What are the main controls?

- <u>Prevention of deviations</u>.
- <u>Correction of deviations</u>.
- <u>Prevention of any future deviations</u>, by revising plans, target, measures etc.
- <u>Implementation of conclusions</u> from monitoring, reviewing and evaluating the project.

What control system is best?

How elaborate a control system is depends on the size and scope of the task to be managed, as well as the size and distribution of the team working on it.

How do you control time, cost and quality?

- The project must reflect business needs – if it fails to live up to expectations this may involve many rounds of time-consuming reworks (sometimes taking years) leading to higher costs and delayed time-to-market and opportunity loss.

- Invest in best-practice planning – achieving optimum cost savings depends on thorough, disciplined upfront planning.

- Build in unforeseen change – unforeseen change happens and reworks are necessary.

- Benchmark at every stage – careful records should be kept of milestone and benchmarking of performance and other indicators to ensure the application is compliant with requirements.

- Settling for imperfection – Nothing will ever be completely perfect.

5 Earned Value Management (EVM)

Earned Value Management (EVM) helps project managers to measure project performance. It is a systematic project management process used to find variances in projects based on the comparison of worked performed and work planned. EVM is used on the cost and schedule control and can be very useful in project forecasting. The project baseline is an essential component of EVM and serves as a reference point for all EVM related activities. EVM provides quantitative data for project decision making.

It takes account not only what has been done to date but also what value has been added for that effort or expenditure. Hence it is a technique for monitoring progress as part of overall project monitoring and control.

It can be used to determine whether a project is meeting scope, time and cost goals by using information from the project and comparing it to the baseline plan.

EVA involves calculating three primary measurements for each activity from a project's work breakdown structure.

- Budgeted cost of work scheduled (BCWS)
- Actual cost of work performed (ACWP)
- Budgeted cost of work performed (BCWP)

From these three measurements, variances and indices can be calculated:

Schedule variance (SV) = BCWP − BCWS

If the absolute value of the difference is very small, then in terms of work content, the project is on schedule. A positive difference indicates that the project is ahead of schedule, and a negative difference implies that the project is late.

Cost variance (CV) = BCWP − ACWP

A positive CV indicates a lower actual cost than budgeted for the control period, while a negative CV indicates a cost overrun.

Schedule index (SI) = BCWP/BCWS

An SI value equal to 1 indicates that the associated activity is on schedule. Values larger than 1 suggest that the activity is ahead of schedule, and values smaller than 1 indicate a schedule overrun.

Cost index (CI) = BCWP/ACWP

A CI value equal to 1 indicates that the activity is on budget. CI values larger than 1 indicate better-than-planned cost performance, and values smaller than 1 indicate cost overruns.

These variances and indices help to measure the performance of the project to date and provide accurate prediction of the final cost and schedule, based on the current trends with respect to cost and schedule of planned and actual work.

EVM improves the chance of delivering a successful project by:

- *Preventing scope creep*: Scope creep would result in variances to cost and schedule, and deterioration of efficiencies, which will be highlighted by the EVM measurements.
- *Providing an objective measurement of the scope, schedule and cost*: EVM provides an integrated assessment of the performance of a project. Earned value focuses on how much value has been achieved so far based on the planned schedule and cost. This helps in measuring the efficiency of the project and in predicting whether the project will achieve the objectives with respect to its cost and schedule.

- *Improved effectiveness and accuracy of status reporting*: EVM is a technique used to accurately measure the project's planned value of the defined work against the earned value actually accomplished. This relationship between the Planned Value and Earned Value indicates precisely how much of the scheduled (planned) work has been accomplished as of the given point in time. It tells whether the project is on track, ahead, or behind schedule. Similarly, with the cost calculations, it is able to clearly tell whether the project is over budget, under budget, or within the estimated budget.

- *Improved communication with stakeholders*. The cost and schedule performance indicators help in providing a good estimation of the efficiency factor of the planned work and therefore providing a more accurate status of the project.

- *Reducing risk*: EVM measurements provide early indicators of potential risks with respect to cost and schedule. Project managers can take early proactive corrective actions to mitigate the risks.

- *Profitability analysis*: EVM measurements assist in performing profitability analysis, and enables project managers to take measures to improve profitability or cut losses. It helps management to make decisions, like whether to cancel the project, much earlier in the project lifecycle, before spending a huge amount of money and resources on the project.

- *Project forecasting*: EVM measurements enable project managers to forecast the project performance. A consistent variance in schedule and/or cost could also point to the fact that the project plan requires a revisit both in terms of cost and schedule. EVM can quickly highlight such issues, and bring to the attention of management the need to take corrective action.

Test your understanding 1

Required:

Explain the benefits EVM has over other methods of project evaluation.

(6 marks)

Performance measurement

Time and money, budgets and schedules are the most basic resources within which every project must operate.

Performance measurement is the integration of project work elements such as project schedules, project budgets, resource requirements and expenditures.

Control limits are set to assess the severity of deviations, and deviations that are larger than a predetermined value are used to trigger corrective action.

Measurement can include:

- Scope performance measures.
- Functional quality.
- Technical quality performance.
- Client satisfaction measures.

Quality management

Quality management is a systematic way of ensuring that the activities necessary to design, develop, and deliver products and services which are more likely to be fit for their intended purpose, take place as planned and are carried out efficiently and effectively.

There are three major aspects that require proactive management, namely:

- establishing what the business should be offering or doing;
- defining how it should be done;
- evaluating what can be done to improve the processes and service product offerings.

The third aspect helps to address the problem of implied needs, as customers' views should be solicited; areas of complaint or disappointment will often relate to implied needs.

There are two kinds of quality – perceived quality and conformance quality.

> Conformance quality depends upon compliance with technical specifications and relates to the use of superior operations management to reduce waste and costs, and increase uniformity.
>
> Perceived quality relates to the customers' expectations and experiences with the product. It is vitally important to ensure that the critical performance indicators set for quality match the two types together.
>
> **Conformance management systems** focus on:
>
> - inspection.
> - quality control.
> - quality assurance.

6 Reporting and meetings

Project reports

To enhance and facilitate the communication of control and progress throughout the life of the project, the following main reports are produced:

Project Initiation Document (PID)

This was looked at in detail in chapter 13. This report is utilised as the basis of general agreement within the project team and between the stakeholders about the nature of the project. It can be a useful starting point team members and normally contains the following details about the project:

- plans, budgets and timetables including deadlines.
- nature, background and scope.
- objectives and summary overview.
- organisation issues such as roles, responsibilities and signatories.

This document will be used for reference throughout the project life.

Exception reports

This is when everything is in accordance with the plan. Only exceptions are reported.

Effort reports

This is often handled on a 'completed/to go' basis. This has the effect of re-estimating the work content of an activity.

Progress reports

Both formal and regular, these note what has happened in the report period and the project status to date. It normally includes:

- Status against plan in terms of cost, timetable, and scope.
- Status and progress of resolving issues identified to date.
- New issues.
- Corrective action plan. (Corrective action requires consideration of alternatives before implementation. For instance, adding extra resources in order to get a project back on time will incur extra costs and may therefore overrun the project budget. The project manager needs to consider very carefully the implications of any corrective action upon the project scope, budget and schedule).
- Expected achievement of milestones before next report.
- Next report date.

Reports from the project manager to the project board should be made on a regular and frequent basis. In most projects, written reports are made monthly, with a major summary report quarterly (or on completion of a life cycle stage). These reports should have a standard format, both within and between projects, so the recipients become familiar with their content. Areas covered by the report would obviously focus on progress in terms of cost, scope, and time, with any anticipated variances from plan highlighted.

Illustration 1 – Example of a weekly progress report

Project Status Report	Client:	Global Business	Project Start Date:	
	Project:	New Accounting system	Project End Date:	
	Project Lead:	P. Manager	Week Ending:	

Project Stages – Execution, control and completion

Overall Status Summary	GREEN

Project status remains at Green; work on track:

- Requirements Documents produced as a result of CRP prepared & internally reviewed.
- Data Migration Strategy presented to business representatives.
- Technical Architecture documentation completed.
- New environment builds on new hardware progressing, continues next week.

Key Activities for past week

Management

- Functional, Development & Data Migration streams produced detailed plans.

Functional

- Requirements Documents produced as a result of CRP prepared & internally reviewed.

Technical

- Agreed Oracle environment configuration at project end/handover.
- Installed development environment.
- Technical Architecture document completed.

Data

- Draft Data Migration Strategy including approach presented to Process Owners.
- Continued production of Data Mapping and Functional specs for AR & AP Business Objects.

Testing

- No progress to report
- Change Management
- No progress to report

Transition

- Further review of Transition Plan undertaken.

Key Activities for next week

- Pull together Functional, Development & Data Migration detailed plans with overall project plan.
- Distribute Requirements Documents produced as a result of CRP for business review and sign off.

Risks & Issues for attention / escalation

High priority risks:

- Client sign-offs not completed in line with project timescales.

Example of a variance report

Variance report

Date: 31/9

Project: ERPS

Completion: 42%

	Budget	Actual	Variance	
Description	$	$	$	%
Labour	3,450	3,135	315	10
Variable expenses	525	615	(90)	(14.6)
Consulting	840	0	840	100
Total	4,815	3,750	1,065	28.4

The budget column is computed by multiplying the total budget by the indicated percentage completed (i.e. 42%). Actual are compared to the project to date budget.

A full explanation of the variances in each category would be given. For example the labour variances may be broken down by team or by individual and with an analysis of phase completion levels versus original assumptions.

The purpose of this report is to identify potential problems. The overall variance can be meaningless unless its components can be isolated and identified.

Labour variance (hours)

Team member	Hours for the Project-to-Date		
	Budget	Actual	Variance
Project manager	53	37	16
Processing unit	49	42	7
Systems development	70	61	9
Research	50	71	(21)
Documentation	10	8	2
Testing	1	1	0
Total Hours	233	220	13

The initial three phases required less time than anticipated and this was offset by higher than expected research time demands.

Project meetings

Regular project meetings are essential to enhance relationships and communicate objectives with the team. There are three main types of meetings.

Project status review meetings

These are regular meetings, involving the project manager, team members, and the customer.

In many projects, such a meeting might take place quarterly, and the project manager would present their summary report. This will allow those involved with the project to ask questions that are not covered by the written report. The purpose of the meeting is to provide an update on the project status, identify any issues and establish action plans from that point.

Project design review meetings

Where projects involve a design element, regular meetings are required to resolve design problems or to present new technical specifications.

Project problem solving meetings

These would be called as soon as a problem occurs to identify and resolve the issue.

Test your understanding 2 – Project example L plc

L plc example continued.

The first two months of the project went to plan. The purchase of M Company went ahead as scheduled, but as the work on the rest of the project got underway it became clear that H, the project manager was struggling to control the project. The project team complained to H that they were unsure about what they were supposed to be doing. They had only had one meeting with H since the commencement of the project, and they found him difficult to approach.

By month 3, J, L plc's CEO was concerned that he had received no information from H about the progress of the project. J called a meeting of interested parties to the project, and at that meeting H resigned from the project. He explained that the project was on a much larger scale to any projects he had been involved in before and he didn't think he could manage to deliver what was required. An experienced, external project manager, P, was quickly appointed to continue running the project. This delayed the project by four weeks while P got up to speed with what was required and added $200,000 to the cost of the project.

Required:

Explain what processes P should put in place in terms of project reporting and meetings and how these would benefit the project.

(10 marks)

Test your understanding 3

Required:

Explain the benefits of a well-defined project reporting system.

(6 marks)

Project Stages – Execution, control and completion

Test your understanding 4

Printplus Inc is a printing company that has recently begun implementing a new computerised job costing system. The project manager who had started the project is now no longer with the company. You have been asked to step into the role of the project manager and complete the task of implementing the new system.

Required:

(a) Briefly describe the key factors that you will need to review in order to get to grips with the current status of the project.

(5 marks)

(b) Identify possible threats to timely completion of the project, and state briefly how they can be minimised.

(5 marks)

7 Completion

The final stage of the project life cycle is the closure of the project once the project work is finished. A number of activities must be undertaken at this stage:

- Project is delivered to users
- End of project meeting
- Formal sign off of project
- Project review meetings
- Final report issued
- Project team disbanded

An end of project meeting confirms closure of the project by a formal sign-off. At this meeting or another shortly afterwards, a review evaluates how well the project was managed: if deadlines were met, quality standards maintained and budgets adhered to. Lessons learned from the review are used in future projects.

Project review meetings should be carried out both internally with project team members and externally with the customer.

End of project review meetings

The internal review (team)

This is:

- an opportunity to review the planning, management, reporting and control
- an opportunity to discuss the success and failures of the project process
- establish what can be learned in future for the benefit of other projects
- an opportunity for the project manager to discuss with individual team members their role in the project and the means by which they could improve their own performance on future projects.

The external review (customer)

This is:

- a crucial aspect of project closure
- an important part of establishing whether the project has satisfied the customer's requirements
- to obtain feedback to help improve future projects
- when customers can voice any concerns regarding how the project was carried out.

Business review

An evaluation from the business perspective is also essential.

Are the benefits from the feasibility study likely to be realised? If not, what ongoing actions need to be taken?

The final report

The contents of the final project report will include:

- Brief overview of project.
- Customer original requirements and original project deliverables.
- List of deliverables which the customer received.
- Actual achievements re costs, schedules and scope.
- Degree to which the original objective was achieved.
- Future considerations.

To produce this report reference will be made to the following documentation:

- feasibility study & report
- PID
- project planning reports
- milestones & gates.

The purpose of this stage of the process is:

- To ensure that the project is finally completed and conforms to the latest definition of what was to be achieved.
- Formal comparison between PID and project outcomes.
- To evaluate performance of project against agreed levels of performance.
- Cost of the system in comparison with budgeted cost with an explanation of variances.
- Comparison of time taken with the budgeted time anticipated.
- Effectiveness of the management process.
- Significance of any problems encountered.
- To complete project termination activities:
    - Organising and filing all project documentation.
    - Receiving and making final payments to suppliers of resources.
    - Agreeing formally with the customer that all agreed deliverables have been provided successfully.
    - Meeting with project team and customers to report on project successes and failures.
    - Disbanding the project team.
- To provide continuous improvement and feedback – any improvement, even a small one, is important.
- To learn from the experience.

chapter 15

> **Test your understanding 5 – Project example L plc**
>
> L plc example continued.
>
> P's project management experience showed and the progress of the project continued well until month 9, where a survey revealed a problem in the foundations of M Company's factory building. This delayed the refit of M Company's factory by 8 weeks.
>
> During month 12, it was agreed that no further work would be carried out on the integrated computer system, so this would not be delivered as part of this project. Work was underway with this part of the project and the full budget for the computer system included in the project had already been spent, but due to technical issues encountered it was agreed that the completion of this system would be looked at as part of a separate project at a later date.
>
> In the final months of the project, the selected supplier of the machinery for the refit went out of business. Because of the previous delays in the project, P needed to obtain delivery of the machinery within 2 weeks, or the project deadline would not be met. P managed to source the machinery from two suppliers:
>
> A could deliver the machinery for the agreed cost, but would take 4 months to deliver.
>
> B could deliver the machinery within 2 weeks, but would have to treat this as a special order and therefore their cost was $700,000 higher than the original estimate for the machinery.
>
> After consultation with the project status committee, it was decided that the deadline for the project must be met, so supplier B was selected.
>
> The rest of the project was delivered on time and the new operation in M Company's factory commenced operation in time to take on the order from B plc.
>
> **Required:**
>
> Discuss what activities would be carried out at the end of the project, including what would be included in the final report for the L plc project.
>
> **(10 marks)**

8 Post Completion Audit (PCA)

A meeting of managers, users and developers, held a few months after the project has been completed.

- Designed to review the success of the project as a whole as well as to receive the user's feedback on it.
- It may also highlight specific issues with the project and the review meeting may organise a set of actions to deal with these issues.
- It should also establish whether the project has helped the business to deliver the benefits defined in the original business case.

Key areas to consider:

- Technical performance review (was scope of project achieved?).
- Extent to which the quality has been achieved.
- Whether benefits have been achieved.
- Cost/budget performance.
- Schedule performance.
- Project planning and control.
- Team relationships.
- Problem identification.
- Customer relationships.
- Communication.
- Risk evaluation and assessment of risk management policies.
- Outstanding issues.
- Recommendations for future management of projects.

Test your understanding 6 – Project example L plc

L plc example continued.

Three months later, a review has been carried out on the efficiency of the new operation. The new factory operation has increased capacity by 35% and the management of B plc are delighted with how L plc is managing the new contract. In addition, some of the existing contracts help by M Company have been able to be continued which has provided L Plc with an additional income stream which they are looking to grow in the future.

Required:

Discuss the issues which would be considered during a post completion review of the L plc project.

(10 marks)

Test your understanding 7

Required:

(a) Explain the process of a post-completion audit.

(5 marks)

(b) Demonstrate its importance in the management of a project.

(5 marks)

Test your understanding 8

T has just returned to his job in the finance department of Z Company, having spent the last six months as a member of a project team working on the development of an educational visitors centre for the company.

Reflecting on his experiences whilst working on the project, he feels that most of his time was spent in meetings that did not achieve anything, but rather wasted his time. He also feels that the final stages of the project were not dealt with effectively, with the project members going back to their functional jobs without any discussion or feedback on the project performance and outcomes.

He has now been asked to take on the role as project manager for a new project and is determined that he will improve the experience for his project team.

Required:

Evaluate the contribution of the various activities that should be carried out as part of project closure, the post completion review and audit of the project.

(10 marks)

9 Continuous improvement

Many organisations view project management as a strategic competence, from which they can gain a competitive advantage. This is particularly true of organisations in project-based industries, such as engineering and consultancy.

Such organisations have begun to see that using project management without continuous improvement to the methodology allows for the repetition of mistakes and poor practices. Excellence in project management requires the development of a methodology, a culture that believes in the methodology, and continues improvements to the methodology.

Elements of continuous improvement can be seen in the activities carried out during the completion and post-completion stages of the project. As part of the internal review at the end of the project, an aspect of learning takes place whereby the project team review how well the project was carried out and considers lessons learned which could be taken forward to benefit future projects.

All members of the team, and the project manager, are encouraged to consider their performance in the project and to take forward ideas of how performance could be enhanced in future projects. Likewise the external review by customers will also give feedback on how well the project was carried out so that mistakes or inefficiencies in the project management are not carried forward to future projects.

Similar reviews are carried out during the post-completion audit where any issues with the project and the management of the project can be raised with the intention of learning lessons for the benefit of future projects.

This is one of the main ways of justifying the cost of the post-completion audit.

The primary benefit derived from the post-completion audit is to augment the organisations experience and knowledge. This may be difficult to quantify, it may be necessary to justify the cost of the post-completion audit by carrying out a cost benefit analysis. In this case, the expected savings to future projects should be offset against the cost of the audit.

Other benefits of PCAs include more realistic forecasting of a project's costs and revenues, enhanced understanding of project failures, and improved future decision making and project management performance.

The Project Management Maturity Model (PMMM)

One approach which encourages continuous improvement in project management is the PMMM proposed by Kerzner in 2001.

The program management maturity model (PMMM) is an industry standard benchmarking process. It allows an organisation to evaluate a single program, multiple programs, a single division or multiple divisions in comparable terms.

Level 1 – Common knowledge

In this level, the organisation recognises the importance of project management and the need for a good understanding of the basic knowledge of project management, along with the accompanying language/terminology. The emphasis here is on training and education.

Level 2 – Common processes

In this level, the organisation recognises that common processes need to be defined and developed such that successes on one project can be repeated on other projects. Also included in this level is the recognition that project management principles can be applied to and support other methodologies employed by the company, such as total quality management and time-to-market.

Level 3 – Singular methodology

In this level, the organisation recognises the synergistic effect of combining all corporate methodologies into a singular methodology, the centre of which is project management. The synergistic effects also make process control easier with a single methodology than with multiple methodologies. However, in some firms the information systems personnel may still have a separate methodology.

Level 4 – Benchmarking

This level contains the recognition that process improvement is necessary to maintain a competitive advantage. Benchmarking must be performed on a continuous basis. The company must decide whom to benchmark and what to benchmark.

Level 5 – Continuous improvement

In this level, the organisation evaluates the information obtained through benchmarking, and must then decide whether or not this information will enhance the singular methodology.

When the levels of maturity (and even life cycle phases) are discussed, there exists a common belief that all work must be accomplished sequentially (i.e. in series). This is not necessarily true. Certain levels can and do overlap. The magnitude of the overlap is based upon the amount of risk the organisation is willing to tolerate. For example, the company can create a centre for excellence in project management before benchmarking is undertaken.

Project management maturity models allow companies to more easily identify corporate-wide training initiatives for each level, as well as the establishment of a professional development career path for project managers. As companies begin recognising the importance of strategic planning for excellence in project management, the marketplace may see several more maturity models similar to the one described above. Like strategic planning, these models should be generic such that they can be applied and custom-designed to individual companies.

> **e.g** **Illustration 2 – Example of the PMMM**
>
> In 2003 the Telecom Systems Department of Vodafone UK Technology (TS) took part in the trials of the Office of Government Commerce (OGC), Project Management Maturity Model (PMMM). It saw this as an opportunity to benchmark itself against an emerging standard.
>
> As a result of the feedback from the trial and internal business pressures, TS decided in 2004 that they would achieve 'Level 3' accreditation using the OGC PMMM as a key step towards improving their project delivery capability.
>
> Vodafone already had as a policy the use of PRINCE2 as the preferred method to manage projects and decided to obtain "Level 3" in the PRINCE2 Maturity Model (P2MM) in order ensure its use was pragmatic and fit for purpose.

The "improving capability" project was initiated in April 2004 using PRINCE2 and was completed in December 2004. It was broken down into five main management stages:

- Initiation – base line current capability.
- Investigation – determine the solution and create standards.
- Training – in the new standards for different stakeholder groups.
- Roll out – convert all existing work to meet the new standards.
- Assessment – formal assessment against PMMM and P2MM.

Vodafone was the first organisation to be awarded level 3 by the APM Group in both PMMM and P2MM.

By the end of the project a £1.2M saving was already directly attributable to the project, with projected benefits £16M capex.

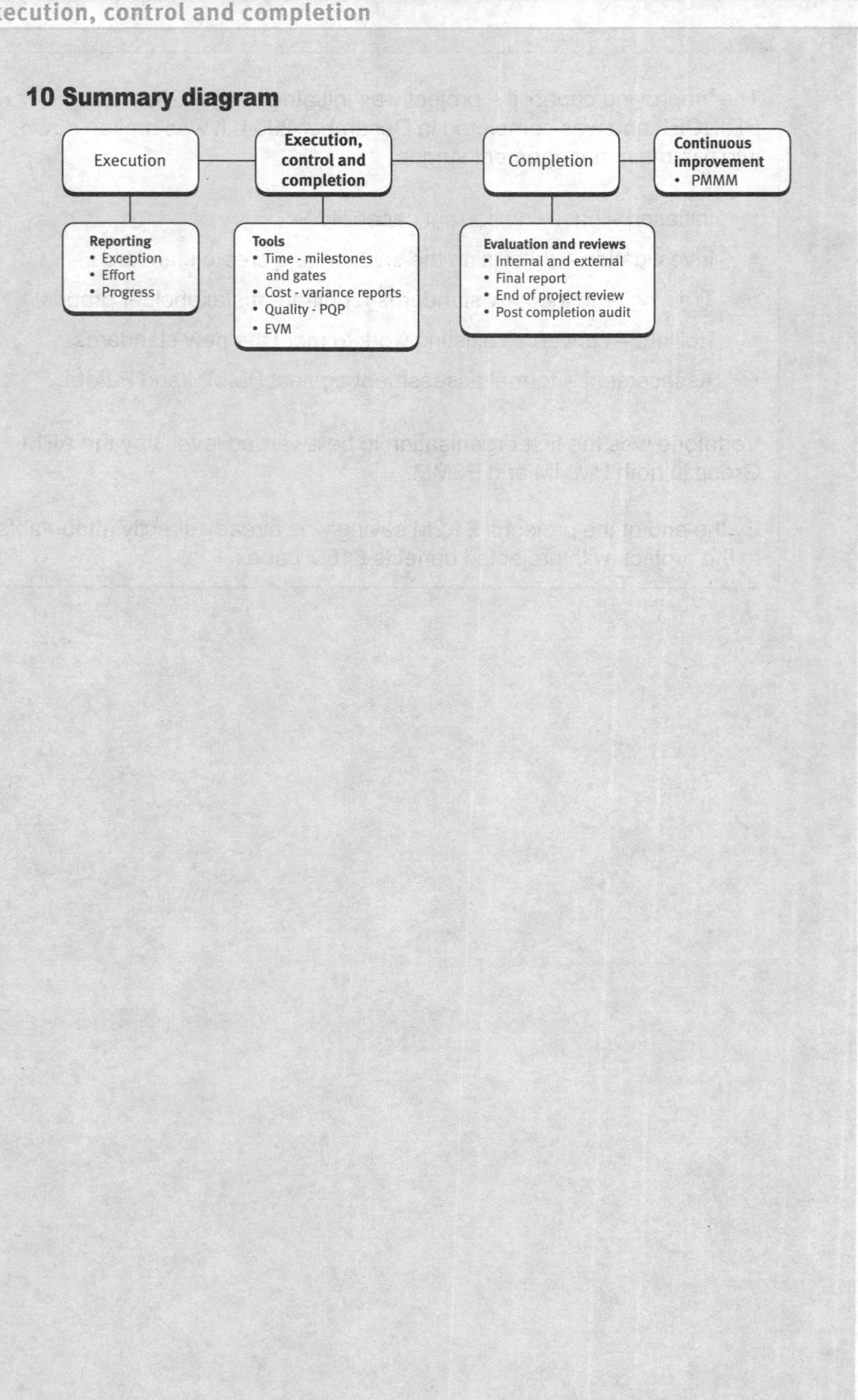

Project Stages – Execution, control and completion

10 Summary diagram

- **Execution**
  - **Reporting**
    - Exception
    - Effort
    - Progress

- **Execution, control and completion**
  - **Tools**
    - Time - milestones and gates
    - Cost - variance reports
    - Quality - PQP
    - EVM

- **Completion**
  - **Evaluation and reviews**
    - Internal and external
    - Final report
    - End of project review
    - Post completion audit

- **Continuous improvement**
  - PMMM

Test your understanding answers

Test your understanding 1

EVM is an integrated method for measuring the performance of a project in terms of work completed, cost and time factors. Other performance tools may measure only one of these aspects at a time, making it more difficult to gauge the overall performance of the project.

EVM makes it easier for project managers to predict the outcome of the project. By analysing the trends shown by the EVM measures, it can be easier to estimate whether the project will come in on time or under budget. Where problems are highlighted with the project, EVM will allow these problems to be highlighted at an earlier stage which can allow remedial action to be taken sooner to get the project back on track.

Using EVM indices will also help to highlight the scale of any problem discovered and can help project managers discover the root cause of any problems.

EVM is a commonly used tool in project management, therefore many people involved in the running of the project will be familiar with it and how to use it.

Overall using EVM will increase the chances of bringing the project in on time, under budget and generally will increase the chance of successful delivery of the project objectives.

Test your understanding 2 – Project example L plc

P should set up several types of meetings and reports for the project:

Project status meetings: Regular meetings should be held by the project manager to inform interested parties of the progress of the project. These meetings should include the CEO and other directors of L plc who are interested in the project. It would be useful to include representatives from different areas of the business. It may also be useful to include some senior members of M Company. Project team members may be asked to attend the meetings where they can update the meeting on specific areas of the project.

Decisions affecting the project can be made at these meetings and progress can be discussed. This helps all interested parties to be aware of the status of the project and all can contribute to finding solutions for any problems encountered.

Given the timescales of this project, these meetings should be held monthly for the duration of the project.

Progress reports: P should set up a system of regular progress reporting for the project. This would involve producing a progress report on a monthly basis. This report should be presented at each project status meeting. The progress report should detail how the project is performing against the project plan, in terms of time, cost and scope.

Any issues encountered in the project should be highlighted on the report so that these issues can be discussed at the status meeting and resolutions can be sought.

The project reports should be presented in a standard style each month so that the recipients can become familiar with the layout and contents.

Team meetings: the project manager should be holding regular team meetings. These meetings are designed to ensure that all team members are aware of their roles and responsibilities and it allows the project manger to ensure that all team members are performing as they should be. These meetings will give the team members and the project manager opportunities to discuss any issues with the project and how these issues could be resolved.

Given the lack of management by H, P may have to hold initial one-to-one meetings with each team member to ensure that they are clear about their role and to try encourage their participation in the project. Communication with the project team should help to increase the morale of the members of the team which should lead to an improvement in productivity.

Test your understanding 3

A well defined project reporting system will have the following benefits:

- It will enhance the communication throughout the project.

- It ensures that all team members are aware of the importance of regular monitoring and control. Everyone involved in the project will know that their progress will be monitored and reported on which will encourage hard work within the team.

- It ensures that all stakeholders can be kept informed of the progress of the project, which means that issues affecting the project are advised to the relevant parties on a timely basis.

- Corrective action can then be undertaken sooner to ensure that the project stays on track.

- It is necessary to compare with planned performance, although it must be done regularly to ensure progress is maintained. Reporting can be daily, weekly or monthly, depending on the complexity and timescales involved.

- Standard reports will make it easier for all parties to follow the progress of the project, and to compare the progress of projects against each other.

Test your understanding 4

(a) The following key factors should be considered in reviewing the current status of the project.

- **Time.** The progress reports on the project should be reviewed, to determine whether or not the project is currently on target for completion within the expected time. An assessment should be made as to whether the remaining tasks can be completed by the original deadline.

- **Resources.** I shall also need to identify the resources that have been allocated to the project. Resources include both human resources and computer equipment/time. Having established what resources have been made available, I should then make an assessment of how sufficient or effective these are for achieving the project goals.

- **Cost.** I should look at the original budget for the project and review this in the context of the actual costs incurred to date. I should then try to make a sensible estimate of the further costs that will be incurred in completing the project.

- **Quality.** The project plan should be reviewed to find out whether or not any quality standards were agreed for the intermediary stages of the project. If they were, I need to establish whether or not these standards are being met.

Project Stages – Execution, control and completion

(b) The following may be identified as key threats to completion of the project on time.

Possible threat	Minimise by
Poor management of time	• Discuss stage and completion deadline with the project team • Stress the importance of completion targets • Regular progress reports and progress meetings
Poor planning	• Using planning tools such as Gantt charts or CPA
Lack of control mechanisms	• Set milestones • Ensure progress reporting throughout the project
Unrealistic deadlines	• Identify critical activities and the critical path • Negotiate deadlines with stakeholders
Insufficient budget	• Focus cost compromises on least critical areas • Negotiate injection of resources to complete on time

Test your understanding 5 – Project example L plc

At the end of the project:

- Project is delivered to users. The new facility in M Company's old factory should become operational.

- End of project meeting. This formal meeting should be help to formally draw the project to a close and for the project to be formally signed off as delivered. After the project meeting, the project team can be formally disbanded.

- End of project review meetings. Meeting should be held with:
  - the project team – to assess how well the project was run
  - the customer – to assess that the deliverables are as they required and to assess their opinion as to how well the project was run

- Final report issued. A final report will be issued at the end of the project.

Final report

Brief overview of project

The purpose of this project is to increase the manufacturing capacity of L plc in order that it may meet increased demand from its largest customer

Customer original requirements and original project deliverables

A fully operational factory facility housed at M Company's existing factory with the facility to produce L plc's existing range of products.

A further deliverable is a new integrated computer system.

List of deliverables which the customer received

The fully operational factory facility housed at M Company's existing factory with the facility to produce L plc's existing range of products was delivered, but the integrated computer system was not.

Actual achievements re costs, schedules and scope

The budgeted cost of the project was $9m. The actual cost was $9.9m. This overspend was due to the recruitment of a new project manager during the project (additional cost $200,000) and the use of a new supplier for the machinery required at short notice (additional cost $700,000).

The deadline for completion was 18 months and this deadline was achieved.

Future considerations

The integrated computer system was not delivered as part of the project. A separate project will be looked at in the future to deliver this.

Issues with the management of the project initially could have been avoided by the recruitment of a suitably experienced project manager at the outset of the project.

Test your understanding 6 – Project example L plc

Technical performance review (was scope of project achieved?)

The initial project required the delivery of a new factory operation and an integrated computer system.

The factory operation was delivered, but it was agreed during the project to postpone the delivery of the integrated computer system.

Extent to which the quality has been achieved

The new factory is now fully operational and no problems with quality have been reported. The main customer is delighted with the products and service being provided, so it would appear that the required quality has been met.

Whether benefits have been achieved

The initial objective was to increase capacity by 30%. It has been measured that the increase in capacity achieved is 35%, therefore the project has delivered the benefits required by the users.

In addition, the new operation will be able to supply to some of M Company's existing customers which will provide a further benefit going forward.

Cost/budget performance

The project was over budget by $900,000 (10%). The reasons for this have been looked in to and it was found that most of the additional cost was unavoidable given the circumstances. The additional capacity delivered should help to offset this additional cost over a short period of time.

Schedule performance

The project was delivered on schedule. The delivery date for this project was fixed due to the B plc contract which amounted for the extent of the overspend, but meeting the deadline was deemed priority.

Project management/Team relationships

There were initial problems in the project with the first project manager being inexperienced, but these were overcome with the appointment of P who managed the project well. The project team also suffered under the management of H, but these problems were addressed and overcome with the appointment of P.

Communication

The initial communication in the project was very poor. No team meeting or project status meetings were being held, and no progress reports were being produced. These elements should be present as a matter of course in a well run project. All of these element were introduced by P during the remainder of the project.

Outstanding issues

The integrated computer system will be looked at at a later date.

Recommendations for future management of projects

The importance of a strong project manager has been highlighted on this project and in future projects, the appointment of the project manager will be considered more carefully.

The tendering procedure for suppliers will also be tightened up. It must be ensured that proper analysis is carried out when vetting suppliers, in particular their financial health and ability to deliver. In this case, the choice of the wrong supplier cost the project $700,000.

Test your understanding 7

(a) The process of a post-completion audit

When the project solution has been delivered, the final phase – an audit of the entire project – is conducted.

Assessment of the following should take place:

- The extent to which the required quality has been achieved.
- The efficiency of the solution during operation compared with the agreed performance standards.
- The cost of the project compared with the budgeted expenditure and the reasons for over- or under-expenditure identified.
- The time taken to develop the solution compared with the targeted date for completion, and reasons for a variance identified.
- The effectiveness of the management process and structures in managing the project.
- The significance of any problems encountered, and the effectiveness of the solutions generated to deal with them.

The primary benefit derived from the post-audit analysis is to augment the organisation's experience and knowledge.

(b) Post-completion audit is of particular importance for the following reasons:

- When a project appears to have been badly planned, an investigation into project planning must be carried out, and recommendations for improvement to future projects must be produced.
- When the objectives (particularly the critical success factors) of the project have become confused, the project manager will need to ascertain what the organisation's original objectives for the project were, and how these have changed during the life of the project.
- When there have been a large number of failures in the management and control of the project, the project manager may be wise to use the project as a case study on which to base a 'project management manual' for future reference. This would hopefully improve the management of future projects.
- It may be proving particularly difficult to identify the costs and benefits of the project.

Test your understanding 8

Project closure is the final stage of the project life cycle and occurs once the project work has finished. The purpose is to ensure benefits are gained in the final stages. It is important to maintain commitment of the team until all the work is completed since people tend to be more motivated to move on to new projects rather than tying up the loose ends. It is also important to evaluate the conduct of the project in order to learn from experiences which will help the company improve on its performance in future projects. The questions that could be asked include:

- Was the project completed to quality, on time and within budget?
- Did the project deliver according to the objectives set?
- Are there lessons to be learnt?
- Are there any follow up action on this project needed?

Project closure activities would involve practical tasks such as organising and filing all project documentation and ensuring that members of the project team have jobs to return to. It should also involve formally agreeing with the 'client' that all the agreed deliverables have been achieved. The business case should be reviewed to check that intended benefits are likely to be realised. In other words, examining project performance by comparing achievement with the original project plan to show that the project has delivered the outputs.

In addition, there should be a review of the project organisation and methods to recommend future improvements. This can be achieved through the **post completion review and audit**. The main purpose of the post completion review is to evaluate the overall project and to learn from the experiences gained before the project team is disbanded. This might involve debriefing meetings which enable all parties involved in the project to assess their own performance.

It provides a forum to discuss with individual team members their role in the project and how they could improve their own performance for the future. An evaluation from the client's perspective will establish if the project was successful in satisfying their requirements and has given them the opportunity to voice any concerns.

The review will provide an opportunity to discuss the successes and failures of the project process. The feedback should provide reinforcement of good skills and behaviours and the identification of areas for improvement or change in practice for the smooth running of future projects.

The **post completion audit** is the final stage and involves conducting a formal audit of the entire project against a checklist. This will include an assessment of the extent to which:

- the required quality of the project has been achieved; the efficiency of the solution compared with the agreed performance standards;
- the actual cost of the project compared with budgets and reasons for over/under expenditure;
- the time taken to develop the solution compared with target dates and reasons for any variances;
- the effectiveness of project management methodologies.

Together, the review and audit can provide a case history of the project, providing a repository for the knowledge captured. The project manager should issue a report summarising project performance and advising on how it could be improved in the future. The reason that post project activities are not always undertaken is that it is often difficult to quantify in a tangible way the benefits derived, given the associated costs of review and audit.

chapter 16

Project management methodologies

Chapter learning objectives

- Apply suitable structures and frameworks to projects to identify common project management issues.

1 Session content diagram

Methodologies → **Project management methodologies** → Why projects fail

2 PRINCE2 methodology

PRINCE is a project management methodology, capable of supporting complex projects. The UK Government as an open standard method for managing Information Technology projects originally launched PRINCE in 1989. Since then it has been adopted by many organisations both within government and in outside industry for projects.

PRINCE2 (PRojects IN Controlled Environments, version 2) is a process-based approach for project management providing an easily tailored and scaleable method for the management of all types of projects. Each process is defined with its key inputs and outputs in addition to the specific objectives to be achieved and activities to be undertaken.

The main purpose of PRINCE2 is to deliver a successful project, which is defined as:

- delivery of the agreed outcomes
- on time
- within budget
- conforming to the required quality standards.

To do this it contains a large number of control elements which can be applied to all sorts of projects, small and large.

The *main control features* are:

- It enforces a clear structure of authority and responsibility.
- It ensures the production of key products – PID, project budget, plan & progress reports.
- It gives a clear understanding of the tasks to be completed.
- It contains several quality controls, such as clearly defined procedures.

PRINCE2 structure

The major component parts of the PRINCE2 methodology address the issues of:

- **Organisation** – PRINCE2 suggests using an organisation chart for the project so that there is a clear structure of authority and responsibility. Everyone on the project should understand their role and responsibility for the delivery of objectives.

    Within PRINCE, responsibilities are defined in terms of roles, rather than individuals. The basic PRINCE project organisational structure is illustrated below (arrows indicate accountability):

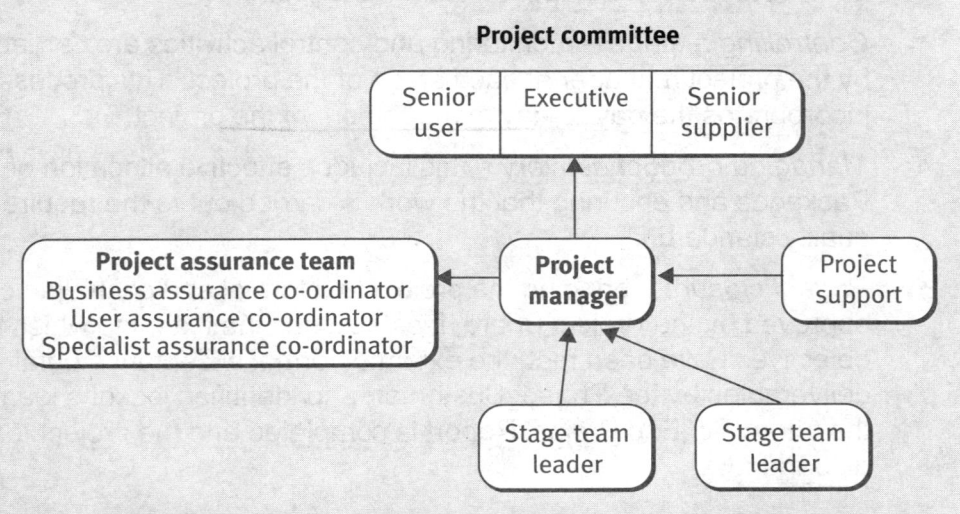

    Project committee

    - Senior user
    - Executive
    - Senior supplier

    - Project assurance team
      - Business assurance co-ordinator
      - User assurance co-ordinator
      - Specialist assurance co-ordinator
    - Project manager
    - Project support
    - Stage team leader
    - Stage team leader

- **Plans** – successful control includes setting plans/standards for everything that needs to be delivered (time, quality, responsibility, communication).

- **Controls** – (TARA) regular and formal monitoring of actual progress against plan is essential to ensure the timeliness, cost control and quality of the project.

- **Products** – includes a number of tools associated with the control of projects (initiation document, budget, progress reports).

- **Quality** – quality should be defined and controlled on the project (zero defects). Quality plans should set the standards required (e.g. using recognised methodologies such as PRINCE2).

- **Risk management** – identifying different types of risk will allow us to plan to reduce them or avoid them.

- **Control of change management** and **configuration management** – any change to the project should only be after the appropriate approval has been authorised. The management of these changes means knowing which versions are the current ones.

PRINCE2 process areas

- *Starting up a project* – a pre-project process, this stage involves designing and appointing the project management team, creating the initial stage plan and ensuring that information required by the project team is available.

- *Initiation* – akin to a feasibility study, this stage establishes whether or not there is the justification to proceed with the project. The Project Board take ownership of the project at this stage.

- *Managing stage boundaries* – the primary objective at this stage is to ensure that all planned deliverables are completed as required. The Project Board is provided with information to approve completion of the current stage and authorise the start of the next. Lessons learned in the earlier stages can be applied at later stages.

- *Controlling a stage* – monitoring and control activities are carried out by the project manager at each stage of the project. This process incorporates the day-to-day management of the project.

- *Managing product delivery* – this includes effective allocation of Work Packages and ensuring that the work is carried out to the required quality standard.

- *Project closure* – bringing the project to a formal and controlled close approved by the Project Board, it establishes the extent to which the objectives have been met, the extent of formal acceptance obtained of deliverables by the Project Customer, and identifies lessons learned for the future. An End Project Report is completed and the project team disbanded.

Whilst these could all be considered to be elements of any good project management, the difference with PRINCE2 is the level of structure and documentation that is required. This helps in providing controls on the planning and execution of projects and forces the identification of potential problems.

Note: students are advised to read the article on PRINCE2 from the Cimaglobal website. It can be found using the following link: http://www.cimaglobal.com/Documents/ImportedDocuments/PRINCE2_P5_article.pdf

PRINCE2 (2009 version)

PRINCE2, the UK's most widely used project management framework has been refreshed following consultations between some 160 organisations and the OGC.

The name remains the same, i.e. it will not be called PRINCE3, but there will be some fundamental enhancements. PRINCE2 had already gone through two major updates since its launch in 1996, in 2002 and 2005. These updates were mainly corrections to the manual with a few incremental improvements, whilst the method remained largely unchanged.

However, the pace of change today and the level of communication meant that projects now faced challenges that didn't exist when PRINCE2 was introduced in 1996.

The OGC launched the updated PRINCE2 method in June 2009. So, what has changed in the updated version?

There are now two guides:

- One for those who manage and work on projects
- One for those who direct and sponsor projects

Another change is that the new method has seven basic principles which did not exist in the current version. These seven principles are universal and self-validating, in that they have been shown in the past to be true, i.e. empirical evidence suggests these do contribute to successful projects. In other words, principles can be thought of as a guide to good project management best practices, such as business justification and management of risk. The principles are universal in that they can be applied in any language, culture or geography and are designed to empower those people who direct and manage projects to exercise control over what happens on the project.

The process model which currently describes the activities to be performed throughout the project has been simplified with activities describing what needs to be done, when and by whom. The complex sub-process diagrams of the current method found particularly confusing have been removed.

In summary, the updated PRINCE2 is a simpler method, more easily customisable to different project contexts. The new method should provide those managing and directing projects with a better set of tools with which to deliver projects on time, within budget and within the quality constraints required.

Project management methodologies

Test your understanding 1

Trend plc is a large fashion retail chain. It currently has 48 stores throughout the country, mostly in prime high street locations. These are coordinated by head office through six regional general managers who take full responsibility for the performance of the stores in their region.

You are currently employed by Trend as project finance manager on a major capital investment – the full refurbishment of a newly acquired city centre store. This project, with a total budget in excess of $8 million, has been in progress for nine months and is nearing completion. All the major structural work has been completed to schedule, and the services (gas, electricity, water, etc.) installed on time. The building is now undergoing its 'fit-out' stage, where the interior is installed.

On arriving at work this morning, you received a message from Jane Bell (the regional general manager responsible for the new store) informing you that the project manager of the refurbishment project has resigned. Jane asked you to deputise as project manager until a replacement could be recruited. This situation obviously provides you with a challenging opportunity, and you expect to gain valuable experience from it.

Talking to colleagues, you have managed to establish the circumstances leading to the unexpected departure of the project manager. Apparently, there was a very heated meeting between the project manager, Jane, and the subcontract supplier of the goods elevator which is being installed to carry stock from the basement stockroom to the retail floors. At the meeting, the site manager of the elevator supplier apparently mentioned that the installation was running late by three weeks. Jane pointed out that this situation would delay the opening of the store, with disastrous cash flow impact.

At some point during the meeting, Jane appears to have become angry with the subcontractor and the project manager. Jane feels that she should have been informed about the possible delay at the earliest opportunity, and that the project manager and subcontractor were trying to hide the delay from her. The project manager apparently claimed (rather forcefully) that it was his responsibility to manage the project, not Jane's. The project manager also suggested that the delay was 'a minor detail', and that opening would not be delayed. Jane apparently disagreed. Shortly afterwards the project manager resigned and left the site. The subcontractor has refused to do further work until Jane apologises.

Jane says she has been 'left in the dark' by the project manager and 'doesn't like surprises'. Apparently, Jane had always experienced problems in persuading the project manager to discuss progress, and has received only three written progress reports during the last nine months. Other than occasional conversations when she visited the site, this has been her only contact with the project manager. Jane has called a 'crisis meeting' for tomorrow with the managing director and finance director of Trend, which she wants you to attend.

You then call Anne Martensen, the head of quality assurance at Trend's head office. She tells you that there are no standard procedures for the control of capital projects, as all her department's time is taken up with designing and implementing control procedures for the retail activities of the organisation. Anne is surprised to hear about the problem with your project, but is unable to offer any help as she and her staff have little experience of managing major projects.

Anne says that she is sure that other project managers would appreciate a set of procedures to improve the project management process.

Required:

(a) Describe the main controls used in formal approaches to project management (e.g. PRINCE2).

(b) Explain how such controls could be used in this and future projects.

The Project Management Body of Knowledge (PMBOK)

The Project Management Body of Knowledge (PMBOK) developed by the Project Management Institute (PMI) is a collection of processes and knowledge areas generally accepted as best practice within the project management discipline.

The PMBOK describes nine Project Management Knowledge Areas:

(1) *Project **Integration** Management* – processes for ensuring that the various elements of the project are properly co-ordinated.

(2) *Project **Scope** Management* – processes for ensuring that the project includes all the work required and only the work required to complete the project successfully.

(3) *Project **Time** Management* – processes for ensuring timely completion of the project. All projects are finite, and time ranks as one of the main limits.

(4) *Project **Cost** Management* – processes for ensuring that the project is completed within the approved budget. All projects must have a budget.

(5) *Project **Quality** Management* – processes for ensuring that the project will satisfy the needs for which it was undertaken.

(6) *Project **Human Resource** Management* – processes required to make the most effective use of the people involved in the project.

(7) *Project **Communications** Management* – processes required to ensure timely and appropriate generation, collection, dissemination, storage, and ultimate distribution of project information.

(8) *Project **Risk** Management* – processes concerned with identifying, analysing and responding to project risk.

(9) *Project **Procurement** Management* – processes for acquiring goods and services from outside the performing organisation.

PMBOK is not intended as an alternative to the project life cycle, but rather as a view of the knowledge and skills required in order to carry out each of the stages of the life cycle. It can be viewed as a toolbox. So, for example, at the 'initiating' stage, the project manager would need to consider integration management activities, scope management activities, and so on.

Test your understanding 2

A hospital has just received funding to build a new X-ray unit. An internal project team of hospital managers and technicians will be established to assist and advise the external contractors for the project. The project team members will be drawn from various departments of the hospital that will have close involvement with the new X-ray unit when it is established.

The hospital regularly establishes project teams to support new developments, and assigns individuals from different departments to these teams.

The chief executive of the hospital has appointed an individual to head the project team who has no previous experience on project work. This individual has asked for some guidance. He is particularly concerned about the fact that two of the project team members will be more senior in the hospital management hierarchy than himself. He is also keen to learn more about some of the project management techniques and methods that he might use.

> **Required:**
>
> (a) Explain the nature of a project and project management, and describe the main differences between project management and traditional line management in organisations.
>
> **(6 marks)**
>
> (b) Explain the Project Management Institute nine key process areas (PMBOK), and suggest how these might help the project manager to carry out his tasks more effectively.
>
> **(6 marks)**

3 Other project management methodologies

A number of other methodologies have emerged in the project management marketplace. Whereas PRINCE2 is largely in the public domain (due to sponsorship by the UK Government), other methodologies have been developed which are increasing in popularity in various industry sectors. It is worth being aware of these alternatives:

- IDEAL/INTRo – IDEAL is a process-improvement and defect-reduction methodology from the Carnegie Mellon Software Engineering Institute (SEI). INTRo is a particular application of the methodology for rolling out technology, for example a new computer system. The institute has a reputation for researching and improving the project management process (particularly in the software development and deployment arena).

- PMBoK (Project Management Body of Knowledge) – While not strictly a methodology, the US-based Project Management Institute (PMI) has defined best-practice project management principles and processes into a volume entitled PMBoK. It describes nine key areas in terms of inputs, outputs, tools, techniques and how they fit together.

- SixSigma – It is another process-improvement and defect methodology that has its roots in improving manufacturing and product development processes.

Which structure or framework is best?

Since every organisation is unique, and undertakes unique projects, there is no 'one-size fits all' answer.

There are five important but difficult questions:

- What is the relationship in our organisation between projects and processes?
- What groups of project-related management processes are important to our organisation?
- What areas of expertise do we have?
- What kinds of model should we consider?
- What kind of benefits can we expect, and will it be worth the effort?

The development of the standard processes is obviously helpful as these, together with standard templates for the documents used, help many project issues to be anticipated and worked around.

A popular choice – PMBOK v PRINCE2

PMBOK provides a knowledge base and roadmap for effective project management while PRINCE2 provides a more pragmatic 'How To' approach. Both approaches are customisable which is beneficial as it allows for better integration into the level of project management maturity the organisation is currently at and aspires to be at in the future.

Benefits and limitations of having a single methodology for all projects

Benefits of a single methodology:

- Provides a structured step-by-step approach to managing projects
- Stages in the methodology become familiar which speed up the completion of the project.
- Helps to keep the project on track and to identify any deviations at an early stage.
- Users become familiar with the tools and reports used, so can compare different projects.
- Team members and project managers become familiar with the approach used and this improves the overall management of projects.
- The methodology can be developed over time and can result in a best practice approach.

Limitations of a single methodology:

- If the methodology selected is unsuitable, it may make managing projects more difficult.
- No one methodology can be suitable for all projects.
- All projects are different, so the methodology may need modifying for each project, but this may be difficult.
- Some methodologies will be too detailed for smaller projects.
- Strictly adopting a methodology may become too bureaucratic.
- All features of the methodology may not be required for all projects.

Test your understanding 3

R Company, a manufacturer and retailer of fashion clothes, has invested in a new technology system to improve the logistics of the movement of clothes between its warehouses and chain of 250 retail outlets. Ensuring that the outlets have the right supply of clothes is a critical success factor for the company.

However, the warehousing stock control and logistics project set up to develop and deliver the new system has experienced numerous problems. The project ended up being well over budget and was also late in delivering the system. Now, only three months after the new system has been installed, it is apparent that the project has not delivered its objective. Instead, the company is facing a crisis with many store managers complaining that they are not receiving the correct stock. Even worse, some stores are out of stock of key ranges, whereas the warehouses are full of clothing.

A meeting between the project team and project sponsor has ended up with everyone blaming each other, saying it was not their responsibility. It is clear that they did not use a project management methodology and did not have adequate control systems in place so that the problems that have now transpired could have been identified and rectified earlier in the project life cycle.

Required:

Recommend to R Company a project management methodology/ approach, explaining how it could have helped to prevent the failures of the warehousing, stock control and logistics project.

(10 marks)

4 Why is it that some projects fail?

Projects fail when they do not meet the following criteria for success:

(1) Delivered on time.
(2) On or under budget.
(3) Delivered the benefits required.

Only few projects achieve all three. Many more are delivered which fail on one or more of these criteria, and a substantial number are cancelled having failed badly. Some of the main reasons for failure are:

Lack of user involvement

Lack of user involvement has proved fatal for many projects. Without user involvement nobody in the business feels committed to a system, and can even be hostile to it.

Long timescales

Long timescales for a project have led to systems being delivered for products and services no longer in use by an organisation. The key recommendation is that project timescales should be short, which means that larger systems should be split into separate projects.

Vague requirements

Many projects have high level, vague, and generally unhelpful requirements. This has led to cases where the developers, having no input from the users, build what they believe is needed, without having any real knowledge of the business. Inevitably when the system is delivered business users say it does not do what they need it to. This is closely linked to lack of user involvement, but goes beyond it.

Scope creep

Scope is the overall view of what a system will deliver. Scope creep is the insidious growth in the scale of a system during the life of a project. This is a management issue closely related to change control. Management must be realistic about what is it they want and when, and stick to it.

Business change

Despite everything businesses change, and change is happening at a faster rate than ever before. So it is not realistic to expect no change in requirements while a system is being built. However uncontrolled changes play havoc with a system under development and have caused many project failures.

Lack of testing

The developers will do a great deal of testing during development, but eventually the users must run acceptance tests to see if the system meets the business requirements. However acceptance testing often fails to catch many faults before a system goes live because:

- Poor requirements which cannot be tested.
- Poorly, or non planned tests meaning that the system is not methodically checked.
- Inadequately trained users who do not know what the purpose of testing is.
- Inadequate time to perform tests as the project is late.

How do you avoid project failure?

Throughout the last few chapters we have looked at how to run a successful project, the undernoted are elements which should help avoid project failure:

- Greater top management support.
- More commitment from users.
- More power and decision-making authority.
- Greater financial control and flexibility.
- Greater control over staff resources.
- Commitment to requirements and scope once specified.
- More project management training. Commitment to a stable project management method.
- Alignment of IT project initiatives to business strategy.
- Greater understanding of project management on the part of top management, project boards and clients.
- Greater realism in setting targets. Several respondents railed against imposed rather than planned targets and deadlines.
- Establishment of a supportive Project Programme/Office.

Illustration 1 – Example of project failure

The C-Nomis project

In 2004 the Home Office launched the £234m National Offender Management Information System project called C-Nomis. The aim was to provide a single database of offenders to replace a range of legacy systems, which would enable prison and probation staff to:

- share information in real time
- manage risk
- manage sentencing and rehabilitation
- increase efficiency.

The system required new ways of working, an improved information technology infrastructure and the training of around 80,000 staff. Its introduction throughout the prison estate and 42 separate probation service areas was planned to take a little over two years.

So why did it fail?

Overview:

- The costs soon escalated to a forecasted £690m.
- The main C-NOMIS base release, encompassing full prison and probation functionality, was supposed to be available no later than July 2008.
- This deadline was not achieved.

Detailed reasons:

- First, the project board met once every two months but did not manage the project because it accepted the programme team's assurances that the scheme was delivering on time and to budget.
- Second, accurate reports to ministers on the problems were non-existent. People had asked questions but they were told that actually the programme was all going well.
- Third, C-Nomis was managed as an IT project, not an IT-enabled change programme. The result was that the scale of change was underestimated. The committee was told that the management capacity needed to drive a complex project and deliver the changing way of working 'simply was not put in at that early stage'.

- Fourth, the senior responsible owner of the project had never run an IT project before. MPs on the committee were unable to ascertain why she had been appointed SRO. She later left the civil service.
- Fifth, the original budgeted cost was a gross underestimate.

Other causes of the failure were that there was:

- A lack of control over changes to the system. There were 800 change requests in 2005 and 2006.
- Over-enthusiasm for what looked like a good solution. Hence complexity was underestimated, as was the extent of changes needed to customise the software.
- Not enough heavyweight programme management grinding away at the detail.
- A failure to manage EDS the main contractor. Difficultly establishing how much EDS has been paid.
- A failure to act quickly or decisively enough on gateway reviews which highlighted weaknesses in the project's management.
- A failure to realise that most of benefits of the original system could be gained with a less ambitious, simpler design using three databases instead of one.

Detail on why so many government IT projects fail

Watmore tells MPs why so many UK Government IT projects fail – June 2009 Computer Weekly 10/06/09

One of the highest paid IT experts in government, Ian Watmore, justified every penny of his £190,000 salary at a single hearing of the Public Accounts Committee.

A man who has made mistakes and is not afraid to admit it, Watmore gave MPs the most credible account – from within government – of what's wrong with public sector IT, what needs to be done, and how innovation can be stimulated.

He put the differences between private and public IT in simple terms: that the government has 'too many initiatives', for example.

Project management methodologies

And his comments bordered on the politically incorrect when he said that Gateway reviews should be published. Gateway reviews are independent internal assessments of risky IT projects, such as the ID cards scheme, the NHS IT programme and technology to support the Olympics.

Watmore also confirmed the long-held suspicion of MPs and others that departments are wasting money hiring consultants to say things civil servants do not want to say.

And he said the government keeps alive some failing projects too long. They could be stopped earlier and 'cheaply'.

Test your understanding 4

The business of the N organisation involves tendering for individual projects.

Originally, this required input from a number of design departments, which often needed further information from the client. There were also co-ordination difficulties. Orders were lost due to the time taken to produce tenders, and losses were incurred due to design and tendering faults.

Improving the situation became urgent. A Project Section was therefore quickly set up. This was, in effect an autonomous work group, responsible for design and estimating, and for liaising with clients. It consisted of twelve people. Some of these were clerks providing support for the majority, who were experts in various fields. One of the group was a management accountant who collected the data determined by these specialists, evaluated it, and presented the information to the management of N.

There was no formal organisation or control of the group, but their proposals were prompt and proved correct. The costs of running the Section were low compared to the estimating departments of comparable organisations. There was no formal section manager and leadership passed from one expert to another as the situation demanded. Members of the section appeared to enjoy their work, and there was no pressure for improved rewards.

After three years the situation changed. Reports were delayed and often proved faulty. Friction developed among the group members and there were demands for transfers or promotion.

Required:

Suggest reasons for the deterioration in the effectiveness of the Project Section.

(10 marks)

5 Summary diagram

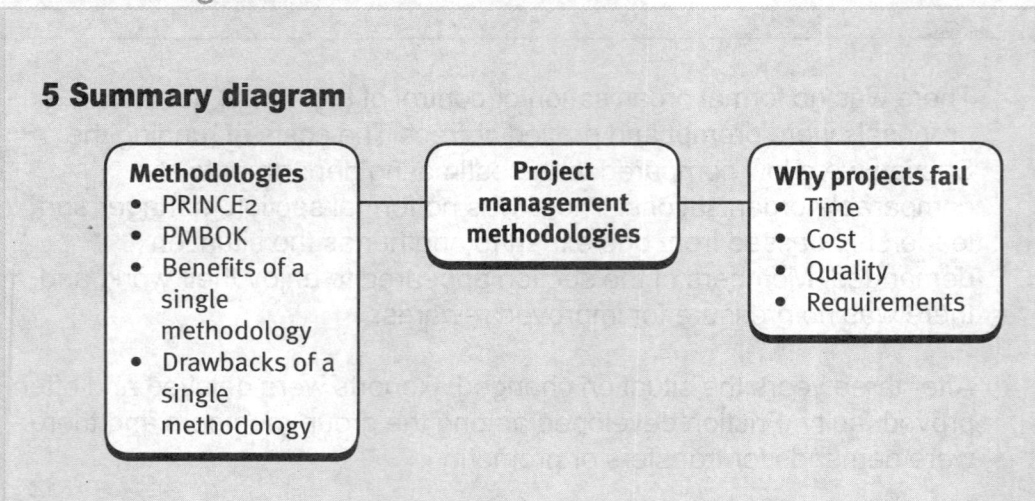

Methodologies
- PRINCE2
- PMBOK
- Benefits of a single methodology
- Drawbacks of a single methodology

→ **Project management methodologies** →

Why projects fail
- Time
- Cost
- Quality
- Requirements

Test your understanding answers

Test your understanding 1

(a) Types of control. If we take as our basis for discussion that a control is any mechanism designed to ensure that a project achieves its objectives, then the PRINCE2 methodology (as do others) contains a wide number of control elements.

- The organisation structure of the project team under PRINCE2 enforces a clear structure of authority and responsibility on the participants. The structure of supervision and reporting (see below) seeks to ensure that each party has clear objectives and that they are supported from both above and below in achieving those objectives.
- In PRINCE2, there are a series of 'management products' associated with the management and control of the project. These include, for example, the project initiation document, the project budget, the project plan, the quality plan and various checkpoint and progress reports.
- The PRINCE2 methodology includes various different types of plans. These ensure that all the participants in the project have a clear understanding of the tasks to be completed and the relationships between them.
- PRINCE2 contains many quality controls such as clearly defined technical and management procedures. These ensure that work is completed not just on time but also at an appropriate level of quality.

(b) Control framework. We can take some of the most appropriate control elements from the PRINCE2 methodology and use them to improve the management of major projects within Trend. I would suggest that, as a minimum, the following aspects of project management should be covered by control procedures.

- Each project should have a formal organisation structure. The control responsibilities of the various parties are outlined below.
- The Trend organisation (in the form of its directors) is responsible for project selection and the overall approval of the project plan and budget. This approval would be in overview only, as the detailed breakdown of both plan and budget are operational issues. The organisation should provide a clear set of objectives and constraints to the project.

- The project sponsor (or, in a complex project, the steering committee) is responsible for ensuring that project objectives are achieved. The sponsor also reports progress and issues on a periodic basis (perhaps quarterly) to the organisation. The project sponsor agrees the detailed plan and budget with the project manager, and provides advice and support downwards

- The project manager is responsible for the day-to-day management of the project team and subcontractors. He/she will communicate objectives and monitor performance against the plan and budget. Any variations to the project must be recorded and agreed with the sponsor, and any issues or slippages reported upwards. A series of review meetings (weekly) will take place between the project manager and sponsor, and these will be supported by periodic progress reports (monthly), including a project overview using SWOT analysis and a report of progress against plan using a Gantt chart.

- The members of the project team, and the representatives of subcontractors, will report to the project manager on a frequent basis. This will take the form of daily briefings, supported by weekly or monthly written progress reports.

- Copies of all project documentation and reports will be kept in a well referenced filing system. This will allow any of the project participants to check what has been agreed.

- At the end of the project, an independent quality assurance inspector will carry out a full post-completion audit of the project. All participants will be briefed on the findings of the audit and encouraged to discuss the issues that arise. Their suggestions for the improvement of future projects will be recorded and circulated widely throughout the organisation. This will allow the participants in other projects to learn and improve.

Test your understanding 2

(a) A project is an organised task with a specific aim or goal. A project team is brought together to accomplish the goal by working together, and each individual remains in the team only as long as he or she has further contributions to make to the effort. When the goal of the project has been achieved, the project team is disbanded since it no longer has any purpose.

The role of the project manager is to lead the team, and ensure that the project activities are planned, implemented, monitored and controlled.

The members of a project team should have differing skills, each individual bringing particular skills to the collective effort. In large projects, it might be necessary to take on several individuals all with the same skills, such as a number of bricklayers and electricians for a large building project.

Project management differs from traditional line management because it is temporary, whereas line management is 'permanent'. Individuals who are recruited to a project team might even hold a line position within the organisation, and continue to fulfil some line management responsibilities whilst also contributing to the project team.

(b) The PMBOK has developed standards in nine areas of 'knowledge', and each of these nine areas must be managed if the project as a whole is to deliver the desired results. The nine areas of project management that are critical to success are project integration, identifying and controlling the scope of the project, time management cost management, quality management, human resources management, communications management, risk management and the management of procurement.

A project manager should consider each of these nine management areas for each phase of the project, and should apply standards or management guidelines in each area. The PMBOK standards provide a framework which managers can use to ensure that none of the areas are overlooked.

Test your understanding 3

A project management methodology that could have been used by R Company is PRINCE2. This is an acronym for PRojects IN Controlled Environments and is a structured approach to project management, used by the UK government and private sector organisations. It includes bureaucratic controls on the planning and execution of projects, identifies some of the potential problems that may arise and early resolution. Whilst it could be argued that aspects of PRINCE2 could be considered to be just good project management, the difference is in the level of structure and documentation required.

The key processes of PRINCE2 methodology offer a number of features that would have benefited R Company including:

- A defined management structure
- A system of plans
- A set of control procedures
- A focus on product based planning.

The main purpose is to deliver a successful project, which can be defined as:

- Delivery of agreed outcomes
- On time
- Within budget
- Conforming to the required quality standards.

PRINCE2 has a set of progressive documents for a project and control is achieved through the authorisation of work packages. These include controls on quality, time and costs and identify reports and handover requirements, all of which are problems that have led to the failure of the project in R Company. The methodology includes a series of 'management products', for example project initiation documents, project budget, quality plan and various checkpoint and progress reports, which would have improved controls for R's project.

The key processes and documentation of PRINCE2 would have enforced the project team in R Company to have a clear structure of authority and responsibility between members in the project team, so that each party has clear objectives. As part of this, the control responsibilities of the various members of the project team would have been determined. This should mean that the different participants in the warehousing stock control and logistics project would have had a clearer understanding of the various tasks and the relationships between them and should have prevented the problems R Company is now facing.

The exception plan concept in PRINCE2 would mean that if R's project was going to exceed its tolerance, for example variances in time, cost or quality, this would have been reported to the project board. The implications on the whole project deliverables should have been discussed and plans amended to reflect any changes needed to ensure the project delivered its objectives.

Test your understanding 4

The project team of N organisation is an autonomous work group submitting analysed information to management. The team was highly motivated with informal leadership. Deterioration has taken place over three years. There are several possible causes for this.

The team may have lost the clarity of its original reason for existence. In the beginning, each project had to be tackled afresh and the results evaluated for a management that had previously suffered from a system of faulty design and tendering. Now that time has passed, some projects may have a large repeat element of work and management expectations have changed. It may be that individuals within the project team feel that they have lost sight of the needs of N's operating departments. This could be accentuated if management now expects a continuous high performance standard but does not involve the project team in the operating decisions of the company.

Initially, the team would be highly task centred and individuals would relish the freedom and leadership demands of their new work. Individuals would be developing their team roles. Now after three years, some individuals may feel the need to move on from the project team; for example, the management accountant may feel that his/her professional development is being hindered by absence from the main accounting function. Similarly, some of the clerical support staff in the team may feel that they are now capable of a wider job and there may not be any promotion prospects within the team because the higher level work demands expertise and qualifications.

Although the project team may not have changed substantially, it may be that external factors have altered. For example, company reorganisation, change of senior management personnel, change of emphasis in the nature of projects undertaken, trading conditions. Any of these structural changes could have emerged during the three year period and affected the way in which the team sees its current and future standing.

For example, a change in the nature of projects would emphasise demands for different skills in team members. Some individuals could then find that their skills, previously highly regarded, are now being seen as less important.

Time and work pressures will probably have changed over three years. The project team may feel that they have not been consulted about changes that have taken place but are expected to operate under increased time and work pressures. There may also be a shift in work content so causing some members of the project team to be overwhelmed within their expertise, whilst other skills are under utilised. In addition, the team's success will have raised management's expectations and this will increase pressures on the project team.

There may be signs of staleness within the project team. In the beginning members were keen to participate in this new venture and establish a new team. They would have enjoyed the freedom and informality of operating. Established team members may now feel stale and may have lost the edge of curiosity and excitement that distinguishes an effective team. New members may lack the motivation of the team founders and so block the effectiveness of performance.

Staleness may also express itself through a role culture superseding a task culture as time passes. Individuals see themselves fulfilling terms of reference rather than achieving an excellent end result.

The Project Section was quickly set up in a time of poor performance and proved effective. The section members would have been in the spotlight of attention and felt their contribution was central to the company's success. As time progresses, the focus of attention will have changed and some of the experts in the team may feel that they are losing professional experience in comparison with colleagues employed in other functions. There may be a lack of personnel transfer from project staff to management positions in operating departments. Section members may develop a feeling of being in a career backwater, away from the mainstream of the company's efforts.

A further factor could be changes in roles as the project team progresses. Certainly new entrants would amend the roles they inherit. Initially, the high enthusiasm of team members would have meant a willingness to fill the gaps by assisting others to fulfil their role. As staff change, so established working relationships are broken and team roles will change. For example, a willing deputy manager may adopt a cynical role if passed over for the promotion that he believes he deserves. Team co-operativeness will suffer and friction would develop.

Some role change is inevitable and will be affected by the stages of the team development. So rapid turnover of personnel following a period of relative stability can cause severe role stress and low motivation.

Project management methodologies

chapter 17

People and projects

Chapter learning objectives

- Recommend strategies for the management of stakeholder perceptions and expectations.
- Explain the roles of key players in a project organisation.
- Identify structural and leadership issues that will be faced in managing a project team.

People and projects

1 Session content diagram

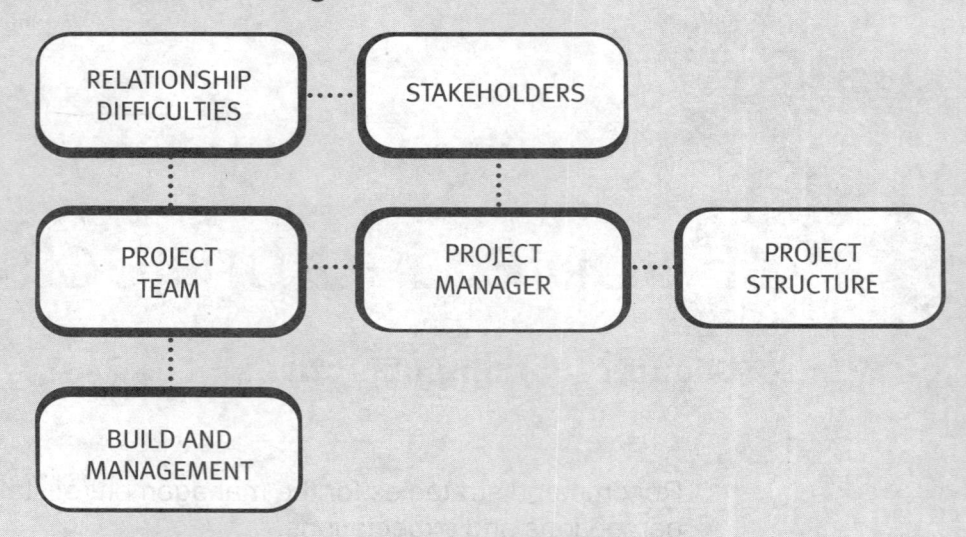

```
RELATIONSHIP ······ STAKEHOLDERS
DIFFICULTIES
     :                    :
     :                    :
PROJECT ······ PROJECT ······ PROJECT
TEAM           MANAGER        STRUCTURE
     :
     :
BUILD AND
MANAGEMENT
```

2 Who is involved in the project?

Note: A lot of the material in this chapter will be familiar to students from the earlier chapters on relationship management. Much of the material in the relationship management part of the syllabus will be equally applicable in the context of a project.

A key aspect in ensuring the success of a project is having the right people involved in the project. Decisions need to be made about the people involved in the project after the need for the project has been identified and the methodology has been selected.

Having the right people, with the right knowledge and skills, involved in the project will significantly enhance its chance of success.

There are various interested parties who are involved in or may be affected by the project activities. They are known as its '**stakeholders**', as they have a 'stake' or interest in the effective completion of the project. Obviously, the number of people involved will depend on the size of the project.

A project is much like an organisation in that it has a hierarchical set of relationships. This hierarchy is put in place for two main reasons:

- to create a structure of authority so everyone knows who can make decisions, and
- to create a series of superior-subordinate relationships so each individual or group has only one 'boss'.

Project stakeholders should all be committed to achieving a common goal – the successful completion of the project.

Stakeholder hierarchy

Based on the principles of 'one person – one boss' and a decision-making authority, the hierarchy shown below is adapted from the one shown in *Successful Project Management*, **Gido J and Clements J**, 1999.

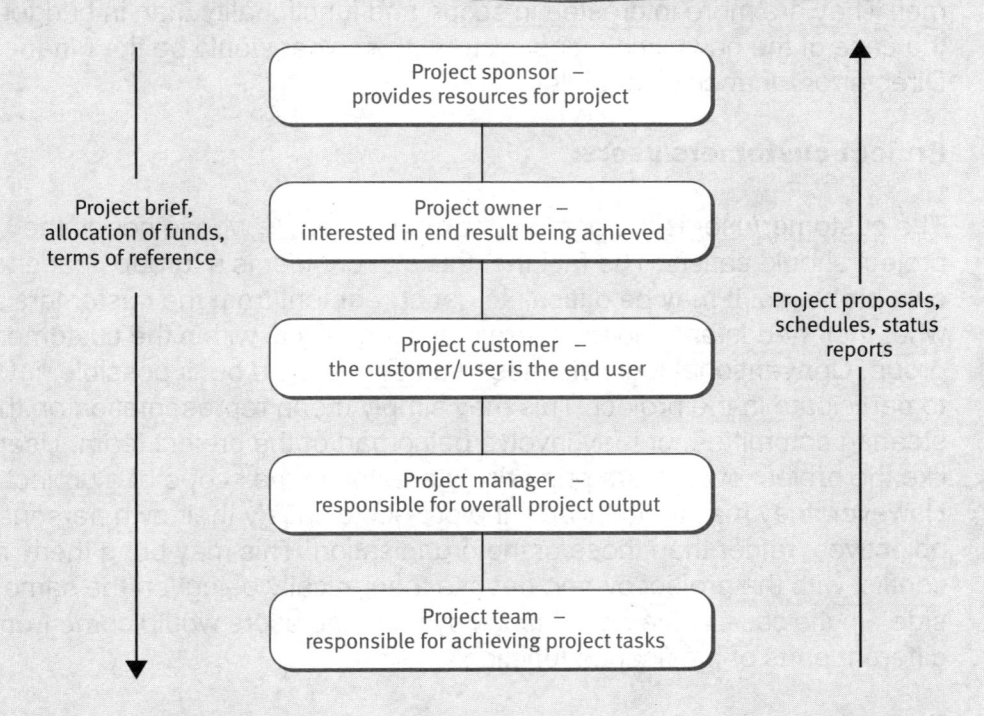

```
                    ┌─────────────────────────────────┐
                    │ Project sponsor –               │
                    │ provides resources for project  │
                    └─────────────────────────────────┘
                                    │
   Project brief,       ┌─────────────────────────────────────────┐
   allocation of funds, │ Project owner –                         │       Project proposals,
   terms of reference   │ interested in end result being achieved │       schedules, status
                        └─────────────────────────────────────────┘       reports
                                    │
                    ┌─────────────────────────────────────┐
                    │ Project customer –                  │
                    │ the customer/user is the end user   │
                    └─────────────────────────────────────┘
                                    │
                    ┌─────────────────────────────────────┐
                    │ Project manager –                   │
                    │ responsible for overall project output │
                    └─────────────────────────────────────┘
                                    │
                    ┌─────────────────────────────────────┐
                    │ Project team –                      │
                    │ responsible for achieving project tasks │
                    └─────────────────────────────────────┘
```

The roles of the various stakeholders:

Project sponsor:

The project sponsor makes yes/no decisions about the project.

The role of the sponsor:

- Initiates the project. They must be satisfied that a business case exists to justify the project.
- Appoints the project manager.
- Makes yes/no decision regarding the project. The sponsor is responsible for approving the project plan.
- Provides the resources for the project and are responsible for its budget.
- Monitors the progress of the project from the information provided by the project manager.
- Provides support and senior management commitment to the project.

Project owner:

The project owner is the person for whom the project is being carried out. They are interested in the end result being achieved and their needs being met. They are more interested in scope and functionality than in budget. In the case of the new accounting system, the owner would be the Finance Director or Financial Controller.

Project customers/users:

The customer/user is the person or group of people whose needs the project should satisfy. The fact that this stakeholder is a 'group' leads to its own problems. It may be difficult to get agreement from the customers as to what their needs are; indeed there may be conflicts within the customer group. Conventional logic dictates that users should be, if possible, invited to participate in the project. This may simply mean representation on the steering committee, or may involve being part of the project team. Users, like the project owner, are primarily interested in the scope of a project. However, they may try to 'hijack' the project to satisfy their own personal objectives, rather than those of the organisation. This may bring them into conflict with the project owner, despite theoretically being 'on the same side'. In the case of the new finance system, the users would come from the different parts of the finance function.

Project manager:

The project manager is responsible for the successful delivery of project objectives to the satisfaction of the final customer. As projects are interdisciplinary and cross organisational reporting lines, the project manager has a complex task in managing, coordinating, controlling and communicating project tasks.

The role of project manager involves:

- Ensuring project objectives are achieved.
- Making decisions relating to system resources.
- Planning, monitoring and controlling the project.
- Selecting, building and motivating the project team.
- Serving as a point of contact with management hierarchy.
- Communicating with the chain of command.
- Selecting and managing subcontractors.
- Recommending termination where necessary.

In essence, the project manager takes responsibility for providing leadership to the project team who carry out the project tasks in order to achieve the project objectives. The project manager will lead and coordinate the activities of the project team to ensure that activities are performed on time, within cost and to the quality standards set by the customer. An important aspect of project management is to ensure that the team members are organised, coordinated and working together.

Project team – The members of the project team will be given individual responsibility for parts of the project. Projects are often interdisciplinary and cross organisational reporting lines. The project team is likely to be made up of members drawn from a variety of different functions or divisions: each individual then has a dual role, as he or she maintains functional/divisional responsibilities as well as membership of the project team.

In addition to the above, suppliers, subcontractors and specialists are also important stakeholders. The project will often require inputs from other parties, such as material suppliers or possibly specialist labour, such as consultants. Each of them will have their own objectives, some of which conflict with those of the project. For example, suppliers will seek to maximise the price of the supply, and reduce its scope and quality, in order to reduce cost. This conflicts directly with the objectives of the sponsor and customers. In the case of the new finance system, suppliers may provide hardware and software, and specialists might include members of the organisation's IT, purchasing or internal audit departments.

Other stakeholders that we can include are the organisation, customers, steering committee and users.

Project steering committee/project board

Overseeing the project and making all high level decision regarding the project will be a steering committee or project board. In smaller projects there will be either a steering committee or a project board, but larger scale projects will have both. Where a project has both, the project board sits above the steering committee in the hierarchy and is in charge of the overall management of the project. All high level decisions regarding the project will be made by the board.

While the steering committee may meet monthly, the board will meet less frequently, maybe only several times a year. They will require progress reports about the project, but these will be high level reports, focusing on the main aspects of the project. A strong project board can make the difference between success and failure of a large, complex project.

The steering committee/board will normally be chaired by the project sponsor and the members should represent all major areas of interest in the project, for example the project owner would sit on the committee/board. The representatives of each area should be at a sufficient level of seniority so that they have the authority to take decisions on behalf of their areas. The project manager will report all progress to the steering committee/project board.

Project Champion

Some high profile projects may have a project champion, or supporter. This is an informal role within the project, with no decision making or reporting responsibility. The role of the project champion is simply that, to campaign on behalf of the project at the highest levels of the organisation. They will show their support of the project by marketing it at every opportunity, even though they have no formal role in the project.

3 Managing stakeholder relationships

At the beginning of a project potential stakeholders need to be identified and their interests in the project assessed. This is a vital project management activity to enable the relationships within the groups to be managed. A plan can be drawn up to secure and maintain their support and to foresee and react to any problems. The project manager can concentrate on the critical stakeholder relationships, assess the risks associated with certain groups, indicate where attention needs to be focused and thus reduce the vulnerability of the project.

The project manager has to balance a number of values, beliefs and assumptions in attempting to navigate a project to a successful conclusion. These values, beliefs and assumptions relate to the stakeholders in the project, who may be defined as any party with a vested interest. The ability to be able to discern stakeholder values, beliefs, assumptions and expectations is a positive tool in the project manager's 'competence toolbox', not least because they often conflict and may not always be benevolent to the project.

Once stakeholders are identified they can be mapped in relation to:

- The likelihood of each stakeholder group attempting to impress their expectations on others.
- The power and means available for them to do so.
- The impact of stakeholder expectations on the project.

Mendelow's matrix, which was covered in chapter 3, could be used to aid the project manager in managing the project stakeholders.

Stakeholder conflict

Most conflict within projects arises from the interaction of individuals, and a good project manager must have the interpersonal skills to be able to manage conflict.

Within a project, there will be a number of stakeholders and they may not share the same objectives, which may cause conflict. Among the most common reasons for conflict within projects are the following:

- Unclear objectives for the project.
- Role ambiguity within the project team.
- Unclear schedules and performance targets.
- A low level of authority given to the project manager.
- Remote functional groups within the project, working almost independently.
- Interference from local or functional management.
- Personality clashes, or differing styles of working.

The project manager should establish a framework to predict the potential for disputes.

This involves:

- risk management – since an unforeseen event (a risk) has the potential to create conflict; and
- dispute management – matching dispute procedures with minimum impact on costs, progress and goodwill.

Risk management is covered in the next chapter.

The techniques used for dispute management are:

- Negotiation – involving the parties discussing the problem. This may or may not resolve the problem.
- Mediation or 'assisted negotiation' – involves a neutral third party (the mediator) intervening to reach a mutually agreeable solution. In practice, disputes are often resolved by accepting the view of the stakeholder that has financial responsibility for the project. In such a situation, mediation and negotiation may only deliver an outcome that is a reflection of the original power imbalance.

- **Partnering** – focuses on creating communication links between project participants with the intention of directing them towards a common goal – ahead of their own self-interest.

- **Compromise** – is the most obvious approach to conflict management, although it does imply that both parties in the conflict must sacrifice something.

> **Test your understanding 1**
>
> Ash Felt is a major construction company that has just won a major contract for a large road-widening scheme through an area of countryside that has been officially designated as an 'area of outstanding natural beauty'. The work will be carried out to some extent by direct employees of Ash Felt, but most of the work will be undertaken by sub-contractors.
>
> The scheme has already attracted a considerable amount of publicity and the Preserve the Countryside Movement, a large national pressure group, has already announced its intention to organise demonstrations and protests against the construction work. More extreme and radical protest groups have threatened disruptive action.
>
> The project is being financed by the transport department of the central government, and the managers of Ash Felt who are responsible for the project have already spoken to the police authorities about the preservation of public order. A security firm will be employed to provide physical protection to employees and assets.
>
> Ash Felt is also aware, however, that some local government authorities of areas through which the road passes oppose the plans of the central government transport department for the road widening. These local authorities believe that the damage to the environment will be unacceptably heavy.
>
> A traffic survey conducted for the central government has suggested that, during the time that the road widening is taking place, there will be severe disruption to normal road traffic and severe delays for drivers on their journeys will be inevitable.
>
> **Required:**
>
> Identify the stakeholders in this project, how their relative strengths might be assessed and how an understanding of the project stakeholders and their concerns can assist with project management.
>
> **(15 marks)**

Test your understanding 2

GPConnect (GPC) is the name given to a project being undertaken by the Southern Regional Health Authority (SRHA) to connect all medical centres and hospitals within the region to a national information network, called the 'Healthweb'.

You are a senior management accountant working for one of the southern region hospitals, and, as part of the project team, it is your responsibility to communicate with all SRHA medical centres and hospitals on the progress of the project.

The SRHA is one of four regional government-controlled authorities, responsible to the central government Department of Health. Each regional health authority manages and controls the provision of medical care to the public within its local area. The SRHA is responsible for fifty medical centres and ten hospitals within the region, all of which are publicly funded (i.e., the SRHA is not responsible for private medical centres and hospitals).

The SRHA has been set a target by the central government to have 80 % of all medical centers and 90 % of all hospitals within the region connected to the Healthweb by July 2014. Prior to the project commencement, most information within the hospitals and medical centres was kept by a manual, paper-based system, and all data exchange was done by means of telephone or by post. The senior management team of the SRHA set up a project board to oversee the progress of the project and to specify the project objectives.

Required:

You have been asked by the executives of your own hospital to prepare a memorandum to the other senior managers in the hospital which should discuss the relationship of the project manager to:

(a) the project sponsor (i.e., the central government);

(b) the project board;

(c) the medical and administrative users (in medical centres and hospitals).

Include in your answer a discussion of the potential conflicting project objectives of the above stakeholders.

(15 marks)

4 Project manager

The skills required by a project manager

The skills that the project manager brings to the project are critical to its success. To help remember some of the skills required we can use the following:

Not **P**reparing **T**he **P**roject's **F**inancial **P**lan **C**ould **C**ause **D**isastrous **L**osses

N – Negotiation

P – Planning & control

T – Technical awareness

P – People skills (motivation)

F – Financial awareness

P – Problem solving (conflict)

C – Communication

C – Change management and configuration management

D – Delegation

L – Leadership

> **Main project management skills**
>
> **Leadership**
>
> Leadership is the ability to obtain results from others through personal direction and influence. Leadership in projects involves influencing others through the personality or actions of the project manager. The project manager cannot achieve the project objectives alone; results are achieved by the whole project team. The project manager must have the ability to motivate the project team in order to create a team objective that they want to be part of.

Communication

Project managers must be effective communicators. They must communicate regularly with a variety of people, including the customer, suppliers, subcontractors, project team and senior management. Communication is vital for the progression of the project, identification of potential problems, generation of solutions and keeping up to date with the customer's requirements and the perceptions of the team.

Project managers should communicate by using a variety of methods:

- regular team meetings
- regular meetings face-to-face with the customer
- informal meetings with individual team members
- written reports to senior management and the customer
- listening to all the stakeholders involved in the project.

Negotiation

Project managers will have to negotiate on a variety of project issues, such as availability and level of resources, schedules, priorities, standards, procedures, costs, quality and people issues. The project manager may have to negotiate with someone over whom he or she has no direct authority (e.g. consultants), or who has no direct authority over him or her (e.g. the customer).

Delegate

A further key skill required for a project manager is that of delegation. A project manager will communicate and clarify the overall project objective to the team members, and will then further clarify the individual team member's role in achieving that objective by a process of delegation. Delegation is about empowering the project team and each team member to accomplish the expected tasks for his or her area of responsibility. The project manager has neither the time nor the skills to carry out all the project tasks, so he or she must delegate responsibility to those who do have the skills.

Problem solving

Project managers will inevitably face numerous problems throughout the project's life. It is important that the project manager gathers information about the problem in order to understand the issues as clearly as possible. The project manager should encourage team members to identify problems within their own tasks and try to solve them on their own, initially. However, where tasks are large or critical to the overall achievement of the project, it is important that team members communicate with the project manager as soon as possible so that they can lead the problem-solving effort.

Change-management skills

One thing is certain in projects, and that is change. Changes may be:

- requested by the customer
- requested by the project team
- caused by unexpected events during the project performance
- required by the users of the final project outcome.

Therefore, it is important that the project manager has the skills to manage and control change. The impact that change has on accomplishing the project objective must be kept to a minimum and may be affected by the time in the project's life cycle when the change is identified. Generally, the later the change is identified in the project life cycle, the greater its likely impact on achieving the overall project objective successfully. Most likely to be affected by change is the project budget and its timescale.

The project manager and negotiation

One of the required skills of a project manager is negotiation. While running a complex project, the project manager may get involved in a number of negotiations.

Project managers will have to negotiate on a variety of project issues, such as availability and level of resources, schedules, priorities, standards, procedures, costs, quality and people issues. The project manager may have to negotiate with someone over whom he or she has no direct authority (e.g. consultants), or who has no direct authority over him or her (e.g. the customer).

The following table gives examples of the types of issues for which the project manager may get involved in negotiation.

Negotiation point	Possible issues	Negotiate with
Resources	Funding	Senior management
	Staff	Line managers
	Equipment	Purchasing
	Time scale	Customer/senior management
Schedules	Order of activities	Customer/teams
	Duration of activities	Line managers/team members
	Timing of activities	Line managers/team members
	Deadlines	Customer/line managers
Priorities	Over other projects or work	Senior management
	Between cost, quality and time	Customer/team members
	Of team members' activities	Team members
Procedures	Methods	Team members
	Roles and responsibilities	Team members/customer
	Reporting	Senior management/customer
	Relationships	Team members
Quality	Assurance checks	Customer/teams
	Performance measures	Customer/teams
	Fitness for purpose	Customer/team members
Costs	Estimates	Accountants/team members
	Budgets	Customer/senior management
	Expenditure	Customer/accountants
People	Getting team to work together	Team members
	Getting required skills	Team members/line managers
	Work allocations	Team members/line managers
	Effort needed	Team members/line managers

People and projects

Test your understanding 3

Required:

List the activities that the project manager must do in order in respect of organising, planning and controlling the project.

(10 marks)

Test your understanding 4

The new Operations Director of DAK transport is the project manager of the team set up to recommend the future direction and development of the order processing system. The Operations Director has asked for a brief description of the responsibilities of the project manager so that he understands his role before he takes on the project manager's job.

Required:

Describe five responsibilities of a project manager.

(10 marks)

Test your understanding 5

Explain the skills required of a project manager.

(8 marks)

5 Building and managing the project team

The basic project team consists of the project manager (and possible team leaders), and a group of specialists assigned or recruited for the project.

The project team should include everyone who will significantly contribute to the project, both managerial and non-managerial people, whether they are full-time or part-time.

The project team will obviously include all of the technical people responsible for the project's efforts toward research, design, development, procurement, production and testing. Team members are expected to attend all project meetings, and to participate in project decision-making. Therefore, care should be taken in making sure that the team does not have any non-performing members. The project team is likely to be made up of a range of staff with different skills and experience. Effective team working is essential for the success of a project and it is important to foster this through regular meetings to establish team cohesion, helping to develop a team which is integrated, has common objectives and positive group dynamics.

The ideal project team will achieve project completion on time, within budget and to the required specifications. They will do all this with the minimum amount of direct supervision from the project manager.

The project manager must get the individual team members to view the project from the 'big-picture' perspective, and to concentrate on overall project goals.

Building the team

Tuckman's model of team development was covered in Chapter 9. It applies equally to projects as it does to business as usual. Likewise the other models of team working, such as Belbin, can also be applied to project teams.

Managing project teams

In the management of project teams we must pay attention to two particular characteristics of each team:

- Each project is a complete entity, and unique in terms of experiences, problems, constraints and objectives.
- The members of the team concerned may well have not worked together as a group on any previous occasion.

The **style of management** for the team must be the relevant approach aimed at the creation of the appropriate internal team environment or, in other words, team climate. Some large organisations provide the team with initial status by providing it with all the necessary support and resources, such as office accommodation, a budget, support secretarial staff, and so on. Other organisations simply appoint a leader, authorised by the board to appoint team members and acquire resources at his or her own discretion.

People and projects

The **planning and controlling of the team** activities are vital aspects of management in that a major project cost lies in the fact that team members are not undertaking their own tasks but have been taken from these temporarily. It is essential that there should be an unambiguous statement of:

- the project objective(s) – what is to be achieved?
- the project approach, methods – how is it to be achieved?
- the location of activities – where is it to be achieved?
- the allocation of responsibilities – what is to be done by whom?
- the project budget – at what cost?

Test your understanding 6

The project manager does not and cannot complete a project on his or her own. It requires effective teamwork and team motivation.

Required:

Explain what the project manager can do to help foster a motivated project team environment.

(10 marks)

Test your understanding 7

Using the Ash Felt scenario from test your understanding 1:

Required:

A task of the project manager and his management team should be to give leadership to the project and to get the best possible performance out of employees. Suggest what leadership style is most likely to be successful for a project such as this road-widening scheme. Give your reasons and make reference to any theories of leadership style with which you are familiar.

(10 marks)

6 Project structure and support

Structure

Establishing an effective project management structure is crucial for its success. Every project has a need for direction, management, control and communication, using a structure that differs from line management. As a project is normally cross functional and involves partnership, its structure needs to be more flexible, and is likely to require a broad base of skills for a specific period of time. The project manager needs a clear structure, consisting of roles and responsibilities that bring together the various interests and skills involved in, and required by, the project.

In conventional (functional or divisional) structures, there is often a lack of clarity as to how authority is divided between line managers and project managers. If a project is relatively small or short term, for example an information system redevelopment, this may not be a major issue. However, if the project forms a major part of the business of the organisation, such as in a construction company, this may necessitate an organisation structure such as a matrix, where lines of authority are clearer.

Matrix and project structure

Definition: A matrix structure aims to combine the benefits of decentralisation (motivation of identifiable management teams, closeness to the market, speedy decision making) with those of co-ordination (achieving economies and synergies across all business units, territories and products).

The matrix structure seeks to add flexibility and lateral coordination. One way is to create project teams made up of members drawn from a variety of different functions or divisions. Each individual has a dual role as he/she maintains their functional/divisional responsibilities as well as membership of the project team.

Both vertical and horizontal relationships are emphasised, and employees have dual reporting to managers. The diagram below shows a mix of product and functional structures.

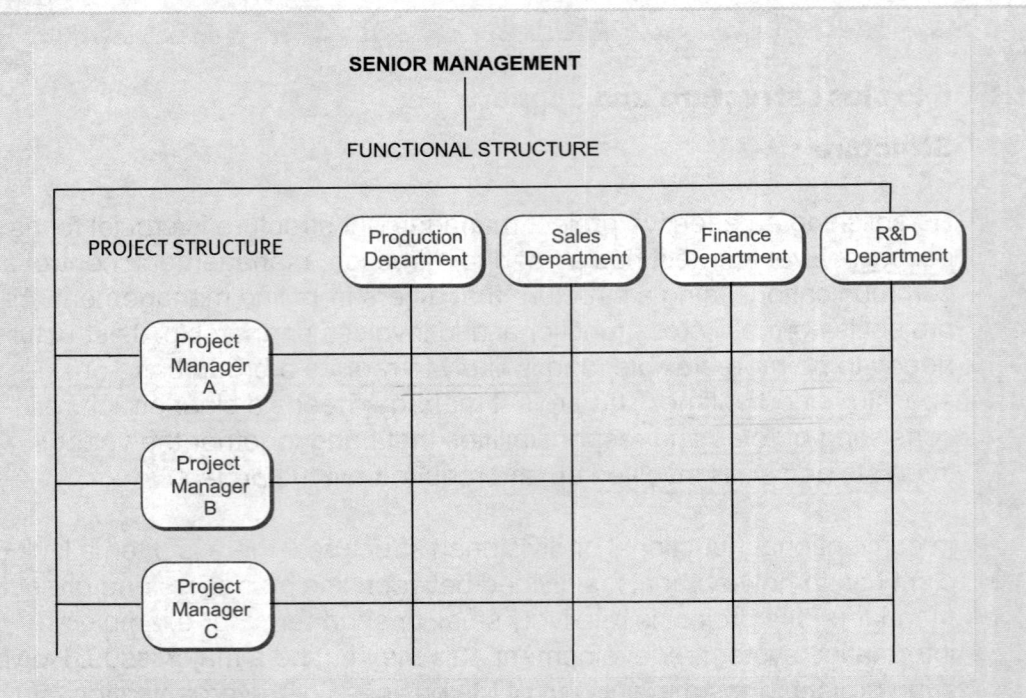

```
                          SENIOR MANAGEMENT
                                  |
                          FUNCTIONAL STRUCTURE

                    ┌─────────┬─────────┬─────────┬─────────┐
                    │Production│  Sales  │ Finance │   R&D   │
PROJECT STRUCTURE   │Department│Department│Department│Department│
                    └─────────┴─────────┴─────────┴─────────┘
     ┌─ Project
     │  Manager A
     │
     ├─ Project
     │  Manager B
     │
     └─ Project
        Manager C
```

The matrix organisation structure has been widely criticised, but is still used by many organisations in industries such as engineering, construction, consultancy, audit and even education. The characteristics of the organisation that lead to *a matrix being the most suitable organisation structure* are as follows:

- The business of the organisation consists of a series of projects, each requiring staff and resources from a number of technical functions.
- The projects have different start and end dates, so the organisation is continually reassigning resources from project to project.
- The projects are complex, so staff benefit from also being assigned to a technical function (such as finance of logistics) where they can share knowledge with colleagues.
- The projects are expensive, so having resources controlled by functional heads should lead to improved utilisation and reduced duplication across projects.
- The projects are customer-facing, so the customer requires a single point of contact (the project manager) to deal with their needs and problems.

If implemented successfully matrix structure can:

- improve decision-making by bringing a wide range of expertise to problems that cut across departmental or divisional boundaries;
- replace formal control by direct contact;
- assist in the development of managers by exposing them to company-wide problems and decisions;
- improve lateral communication and cooperation between specialists.

There are, however, disadvantages with a matrix structure:

- a lack of clear responsibility;
- clashes of priority between product and function;
- functions lose control of the psychological contract;
- career development can often be stymied;
- difficult for one specialist to appraise performance of another discipline in multi-skilled teams;
- project managers are reluctant to impose authority as they may be subordinates in a later project;
- employees may be confused by reporting to two bosses;
- managers will need to be able to resolve interpersonal frictions and may need training in human relations skills;
- managers spend a great deal of time in meetings to prioritise tasks.

Project support

Project office

The effective management of any project requires a lot of administration work to keep the project in order. In a *small project*, the project manager will probably take care of the administration with the support of an administrator or secretary.

For *large complex projects* they may need project support teams. In organisations where there is a significant number of large scale projects there will often be a large *project office/project support office*. The function of this office is to assist in all aspects of the management of project work and provide administrative support to an ongoing programme of projects.

The project office provides a central function comprising of staff that have specialist skills and knowledge of how to run the project process.

Tasks that may be undertaken by a project office, such as:

- Scheduling
- Network analysis
- Servicing progress meetings
- Managing project files
- Preparing contracts
- Monitoring progress
- Management and control of project software.

Benefits of a project office:

- Consistent approach to projects
- Staff can transfer easily from projects
- Central repository of knowledge
- Learn from experiences.

In summary the project office can provide administrative support, but in some organisations it is central to the overall control of projects.

Test your understanding 8

H Company designs and manufactures sports equipment and is currently positioned as the market leader in the industry. However, whilst operating in a growth market, there are new competitors entering the market with innovative new product offerings. The Marketing Director is aware that to retain market leader position, the company must improve its practices involved with new product development (NPD), and the time taken to get from the product idea to launch needs to be much quicker.

The company has a functional structure with the Marketing Director heading up the marketing function, and the R&D Director heading up the function responsible for research and product development; in addition, there are separate functions for Production, Human Resources, Finance, Sales and IT.

The Marketing Director feels that the functional structure is impeding the NPD process. Having recently read an article on organising for NPD, he is proposing that the best way to manage the process would be through introducing a matrix structure and the use of cross functional teams. However, at a recent meeting of the functional heads, the Research and Development Director said that, in his experience, the potential difficulties in using a matrix structure offset the benefits.

Required:

Describe the advantages and disadvantages of H Company using a matrix structure in project management work for NPD.

(10 marks)

7 Summary diagram

RELATIONSHIP DIFFICULTIES
- Blocks to effectiveness of project teams
- Conflict and use of Mendelow

STAKEHOLDERS
- Identification
- Objectives

PROJECT TEAM
- Selection
- Tuckman
- Belbin
- Leadership theories

PROJECT MANAGER
- Roles and responsibilities
- Skills

PROJECT STRUCTURE
- Matrix

BUILD AND MANAGEMENT
- Tuckman

Test your understanding answers

Test your understanding 1

Stakeholders are the groups or individuals who have an interest in the project and its outcome.

The stakeholders include the shareholders of Ash Felt, who have an interest in the successful and profitable completion of the project. Similarly, the sub-contractors and their shareholders have a stakeholder interest for the same reason.

- The senior management and directors of Ash Felt might have an interest in the project process, because successful completion of the project could affect their future prospects for career advancement and rewards (for example, bonus payments).

- Individuals working on the project are stakeholders. They are paid for their involvement in the project work, and could also be affected by the security aspects and the threat of action by demonstrators and protestors.

- In view of the threats of demonstrations and disruption, the police force which has to maintain law and order, and the security firms involved in providing protection, have a stake in the project. They will want to ensure that, as far as possible, order is maintained and individuals and assets are protected.

- Central government, local governments and the protest groups are both stakeholders. Central government (the transport department) are sponsoring and financing the scheme, and so are concerned that the scheme should be completed on time and within budget. The central government will also have a concern that the completed scheme should meet its intended objectives for the improvement of road transport.

- Local government, and presumably the protest groups, are also concerned with the process of the road-widening. Local governments will want to ensure that excessive environmental damage is not caused in their area. Protestors will be involved in demonstrating, and perhaps trying to disrupt, the project work. All of them also have a concern about the outcome from the project, which is likely to be a deterioration in the environment. The outcome will therefore affect the general public as a whole, not just the members of the protest groups.

The strength of the various stakeholder groups can be assessed with reference to their ability to ensure that their interests are protected or promoted.

- Clearly, two of the most influential stakeholders in this project are the central government, which is financing the work and can decide what should be done by the contract: if it is influenced by political pressure against the project, it also has the power to bring the project to an end.

- The management of Ash Felt are also major stakeholders, because they will decide how the work should be planned and implemented and they have control over day-to-day project operations.

- However, the protest groups and the police authorities might also be significant stakeholders in this project. The strength of the protestors depends on their ability to arouse sympathetic publicity and political support, or to disrupt construction work. If a serious disturbance to the peace is threatened, the police force might use its power either to control the demonstrators or possibly to restrict the progress of the construction work.

- The strength of the local governments is likely to be fairly limited, since local government is usually required to comply with the wishes of central government.

- The strength of the protestors and the police cannot be properly assessed until the project work begins. However, the management of Ash Felt as well as central government will need to monitor the views and activities of these groups.

Trying to understand the concerns and interests of stakeholder groups – and the strength of each group – could be valuable for the management of Ash Felt.

- Instead of assuming that confrontation with protestors and demonstrators is inevitable, the management of Ash Felt might consider ways of restricting the impact of some of the work and consult with representatives of the protest groups.

- Similarly, Ash Felt management could consider the concerns of the police authorities, and take suitable measures to reduce the likelihood of police intervention to halt or slow down the construction work, in order to preserve public order.

- Even if Ash Felt's management cannot reach any meaningful agreement with the protestors, trying to understand their views, and what they might do to enforce their views, could be necessary simply in order to ensure the successful completion of the project work.
- For central government, the issue is somewhat different. Central government should try to understand the concerns of the protest groups and the local government authorities, because losing the 'publicity war' with these groups could be damaging politically to the government.

Test your understanding 2

Project management relationships and conflicts

(a) **Project manager and project sponsor**

T, as the company responsible for carrying out the GPC project, is contracted directly by the central government (the project sponsor). Therefore, the project manager will need to work through the project sponsor for any contractual dealings with T.

The project sponsor is usually the party responsible for payment of projects, but in this case the amount of funding from the central government is not clear, neither in the initial funding nor the on-going running costs. Therefore, the project manager will need to work with the sponsor to resolve potential conflict over project costs. The role of the central government in this project as a fund provider may cause conflict between central government and the SRHA.

The project manager has little direct reporting/communication with the central government, as responsibility for the project progress is mainly to the project board.

However, the ultimate achievement of long-term project objectives is to the central government, who, as the project sponsor, will be evaluating strategic level objectives and who will be concerned with ensuring that the whole project is not seen to waste public resources.

(b) **Project manager and the project board**

The project manager is responsible for achieving the objectives set by the project board. The project board is responsible for the overall running of the project, and their objectives are to delegate the achievement of the sponsors' targets without disrupting the achievement of their own business objectives.

Direct communication between the project manager and the project board is necessary, with on-going regular reporting of project milestone review meetings.

The project board will be concerned with the achievement of management/business level objectives, in particular that the project improves business efficiency and effectiveness.

(c) **Project manager to medical and administrative users**

The project manager is responsible for the overall delivery of the final working system to the end users. The objectives of the users are to care for their patients, while minimising their workload. The first role of the project manager is to 'sell' the benefits of the new system to the users, as without their backing the project is unlikely to succeed. Good communication between the project manager and the end users is essential to the implementation of a successful project. The project manager is responsible for reviewing the needs of each group of users to ensure that systems design meets the needs of the users as far as possible within the project constraints, and ensuring that training is effective. In addition, the project manager will need to manage both medical and administrative staff expectations of the system as the project progresses.

The administrative and medical staff will be evaluating the operational day-to-day objectives of the project.

Possibility of conflicting objectives

The sponsor's objectives are the achievement of improved service to patients. This may conflict with the objectives of the staff, who will seek to minimise their workload while providing good care for their patients. Staff are likely to have concerns about the implementation workload, the on-going costs and workloads and the patient record security.

There is also likely to be conflict between the sponsor and the project board over funding. Although a technology fund has been set up by the central government, it is evident that this funding has not been easy to obtain, causing a financial burden upon the SRHA and the individual hospitals and medical centres. A number of doctors have already expressed concern over resources being spent on the new system rather than on direct patient care, but the central government has made it quite clear that this project is not discretionary. However, the central government are sending out rather mixed signals by allowing individual hospitals and medical centres to decide upon their individual method of operation.

In addition, the central government and project board may be concerned with funding and cost minimisation, whereas the end users may see this as cost-cutting, thus reducing the value of the end product.

As a public sector project, financial objectives should not be primary ones. Quality and customer perspective should be of more importance to all of the stakeholders. However, public funds must not be seen to be wasted.

Test your understanding 3

In respect of organising the project, the project manager must:

- secure project resources
- assign tasks to internal/external providers
- assign responsibility
- organise the project team.

In respect of planning the project, the project manager must:

- define the project objective
- agree the objective with the customer
- communicate the objective to the team
- set up a system to compare actual results with the plan.

In respect of controlling the project, the project manager must:

- implement and monitor the project information system
- take action if variations occur
- communicate with the team and the sponsor on the progress of the project.

> **Test your understanding 4**
>
> Six illustrative responsibilities are:
>
> **Agree the terms of reference of the project.** Every project should start with Terms of Reference describing the objectives, scope, constraints, resources and project sponsor or client. It is the responsibility of the project manager to compile and agree these Terms of Reference. In particular he or she must be confident that the project can meet its objectives within the time agreed (a constraint) with the resources available. The Terms of Reference may be expanded into a Project Quality Plan which will describe such issues as quality procedures, standards and a risk assessment. Producing the Project Quality Plan will also be the project manager's responsibility.
>
> **Plan the project**
>
> **The agreed project will have to be broken down into lower level tasks** and activities, each of which will be given a time estimate. Precedences (which tasks must be completed before others can start) will also be agreed. The project task breakdown, the precedences of tasks, and task estimates will form the basis of the project plan. This will allow the project manager to determine the critical path and hence the elapsed time of the project. The project manager will also be able to see more clearly the resource requirements of the project. The project manager usually has the responsibility to produce and interpret the project plan, often using a computerised tool.
>
> **Monitor the project**
>
> **During the project the project manager must ensure that the overall project remains on target.** Hence he or she will monitor the progress of tasks and record their completion on the project plan. Some of these tasks will over-run their original estimates and the consequences of this have to be carefully monitored and managed. The project will also be affected by new user requirements, staff illness and holidays and other external factors that cannot be predicted at the start of the project. The project manager has to reflect all these in the project plan and produce revised versions showing the effect of these changes.

Report on project progress

It is usually the responsibility of the project manager to report project progress both upwards (to the project sponsor or client) and downwards (to the rest of the project team). Progress reports usually specify what tasks have been completed in the last period, what tasks have been started but not completed (with perhaps an estimate to completion) and what tasks are scheduled to start in the next period. Reports should also highlight problems and changes, showing the effect of these on the project plan and suggesting a course of action. The project sponsor can then decide whether such changes are implemented in the project or left until a later phase of the development. Project reports may also contain important cost and time information showing the overall cost of the project to date.

A post-project review usually takes place at the end of the project and it will be the responsibility of the project manager to organise and chair this review and report on its conclusions and recommendations. The post-project reviews will consider both the products of the project (such as the robustness of the software, the satisfaction of users etc.) and the organisation of the project itself. It may review the estimates of project cost and duration and compare these with actual costs and duration. Large variances will be discussed and analysed and any lessons learnt recorded and fed back into the project management method.

Most projects are undertaken by a multi-disciplinary team brought together for the purpose of undertaking the project. Once the project is complete the team will probably be disbanded. **During the project it is the responsibility of the project manager to motivate team members** so that the tasks they are assigned are completed on time and to the required quality. Project managers have direct influence over the work that is assigned to the team members, the amount of responsibility individual team members are given and the recognition they are accorded on completion of their work. How the project manager goes about these management tasks will critically affect the morale and motivation of the team members.

Test your understanding 5

Project managers should:

- be able to stimulate action, progress and change.
- have an accurate perception of the technical requirements of the project so that business needs are addressed and satisfied. Experience in IT projects would be essential, either as project manager or as a participant.
- have the ability to evaluate alternatives and to make informed decisions.
- be able to motivate and enthuse their teams and have a constant personal drive towards achieving the project's goals.
- be able to demonstrate their individual competence and have a complete working knowledge of the internal administration of their project.
- be constantly monitoring progress against the plan and taking any necessary corrective action using modern planning and monitoring methods.
- be proficient in risk management and have a broad financial knowledge. Controlling the escalating budget of this project will be a major task.
- understand the basics of procurement and be able to develop the procurement strategy for their project.
- be able to express themselves clearly and unambiguously in speaking and writing and be able to do this in a wide range of situations and with a wide range of people.
- be skilful in managing their clients and should be able to plan and carry out a negotiation strategy.
- be able to understand the contract that defines their project and should be able to manage subcontractors to ensure that the contractual terms are met.
- have an awareness of any legal issues that could affect their project, such as the Data Protection Act

Test your understanding 6

The project manager needs to understand his or her team members first in order to understand what motivates them. The project manager should attempt to create a project environment that is supportive and where team members feel enthusiastic and want to work towards the overall project goal.

How does the project manager create such an environment?

- Ensuring that the team is made up of the correct people. The project manager should be aware of Belbin's model and ensure that all required roles in the team are met. This will avoid conflict and foster good working relationships.

- Adequate knowledge and experience in team. The project manager must ensure that all team members are able to participate fully in their role and that they possess the required knowledge and skills

- Adopting a participative style of management.

- By encouraging participation in project decision-making

- By delegating decisions to the team members, thus encouraging involvement and ownership.

- Holding regular project meetings whereby team members can participate and air their views and put forward their experience.

- Holding regular one-to one meetings with individual team members, encouraging them to put forward their own ideas and suggestions for project improvement.

- Ensuring that conflict is minimised by ensuring that all team members are clear about their role and what is required of them.

The project manager needs to demonstrate that he/she values the contribution made by team members and that their contribution is important to the overall project.

> **Test your understanding 7**
>
> The most effective leadership style within an organisation will depend on the circumstances, and might well differ for different types of employee and different types of task.
>
> According to Adair, the most appropriate leadership style depends on the relative significance of three factors – task needs, group needs and individual needs. Task needs refer to the tasks that the leader must carry out, such as setting objectives, planning tasks, allocating responsibilities, setting performance standards and giving instructions for work to be done. Group needs refer to the management responsibilities for communication, team-building, motivation and discipline. Individual needs relate to the manager's responsibilities for coaching, counselling and motivating individual employees. The relative significance of task needs, group needs and individual needs will vary from one situation to another, and the most appropriate leadership style will depend on the relative significance of each of these three factors in the given circumstances.
>
> In managing a road widening project, it seems likely that the task needs will be the most significant and individual needs the least. If this is the case, a task-orientated leadership style – in other words an authoritarian style of leadership – might be most appropriate.
>
> Fiedler, another contingency theorist, argued that the most appropriate leadership style in a given situation depended on the extent to which the task is highly structured, the leader's position power and the nature of the leader's existing relationship with the work group. If the task is highly structured and the leader's position power is high, and if the relationship between the leader and the work group is already good, Fiedler suggested that the most appropriate leadership style would be a task-orientated leader. These circumstances probably apply to the management of construction projects such as a road-widening scheme.
>
> A similar conclusion might also be made if Hersey and Blanchard's situational theory is considered. They argued that the most appropriate leadership style in a given situation depends on the maturity of the individuals who are being led. The greater the maturity of the employees, the more a leader should rely on relationship behaviour rather than task behaviour. With construction work, the maturity of many employees might be considered fairly low, however, and a task-orientated leadership style would therefore be more appropriate.

People and projects

Test your understanding 8

As the Marketing Director in H Company has noted, the ability to develop new products and get them to market quickly requires the cooperation of a range of individuals from various functions. H could fundamentally reorganise to form a matrix structure. This type of structure is based on a dual chain of command and is often used as a structure in project management. In the case of H Company it would involve establishing a cross functional team to design and develop new sports equipment products. Each individual would have a dual role in terms of their functional responsibility as well as membership of a project team. For instance, an individual could belong both to the marketing function and to the NPD project. Employees would report both to a functional manager and a project manager.

As the Marketing Director suggests, this structure does bring a number of benefits to NPD project work. The matrix structure is particularly suited to a rapidly changing environment, such as that facing H Company, creating flexibility across the project, with the aim of speedy implementation. It can improve the decision-making process by bringing together a wide range of expertise to the new product development process, cutting across boundaries which can be stifled by normal hierarchical structures. Lateral communication and cooperation should be improved. From an employee's perspective it can facilitate the development of new skills and adaptation to unexpected problems, broadening a specialist's outlook.

Whilst there are benefits, the Research and Development Director is also correct in his view that there are downsides to the matrix structure. One of the main problems is associated with the lack of clear responsibilities and potential clashes and tensions between the different priorities of the project tasks and the specialist function. Employees may end up being confused by having to report to two bosses and deciding whose work should take precedence. There is also the question of who should do the appraisal of their performance?

The complexity of the matrix structure can often make it difficult to implement. Inevitably, conflicts will arise due to the differences in the backgrounds and interests of staff from different functional areas.

CIMA 2010 Chartered Management Accounting Qualification – Specimen Examination Paper E2
Published November 2009

CIMA

Pillar E

E2 – Enterprise Management

Specimen Examination Paper

Instructions to candidates

You are allowed three hours to answer this question paper.

You are allowed 20 minutes reading time **before the examination begins** during which you should read the question paper and, if you wish, highlight and/or make notes on the question paper. However, you are **not** allowed, **under any circumstances**, to open the answer book and start writing or use your calculator during this reading time.

You are strongly advised to carefully read all the question requirements before attempting the question concerned (that is, all parts and/or sub-questions). The requirements for all questions are contained in a dotted box.

ALL answers must be written in the answer book. Answers or notes written on the question paper will **not** be submitted for marking.

Answer the FIVE compulsory questions in Section A on pages 2 to 4.

Answer the TWO compulsory questions in Section B on pages 5 and 6.

The list of verbs as published in the syllabus is given for reference on the inside back cover of this question paper.

Write your candidate number, the paper number and the examination subject title in the spaces provided on the front of the examination answer book. Also write your contact ID and name in the space provided in the right hand margin and seal to close.

Tick the appropriate boxes on the front of the answer book to indicate the questions you have answered.

E2 – Enterprise Management

TURN OVER

© The Chartered Institute of Management Accountants 2009

SECTION A – 50 MARKS

[the indicative time for answering this section is 90 minutes]

ANSWER *ALL* FIVE QUESTIONS IN THIS SECTION – 10 MARKS EACH

Question One

CN Company is a manufacturer of confectionary products with a well established position and brand recognition in Country P. The potential for future growth in Country P is, however, limited, with the market reaching saturation. A proposal put forward is that to achieve growth CN Company should move into new markets in other countries, offering its existing product range. One possible method of achieving market entry that has been identified is through a joint venture with a company that is already established in Country K.

The business development team are undertaking a feasibility study to explore the viability of the proposed strategy to sell CN Company's confectionary product range in Country K. As part of the feasibility study there will need to be some assessment of industry competition and the attractiveness of the market in Country K.

Required

Explain how Porter's Five Forces model could be used by the business management team to assess the confectionery industry competition in Country K.

(Total for Question One = 10 marks)

Question Two

Required:

Explain how the work breakdown structure (WBS) technique and Gantt charts can assist in the project management process.

(Total for Question Two = 10 marks)

Section A continues on the opposite page

Question Three

OD Company is in the business of designing, manufacturing and retailing outdoor equipment including hiking boots, rucksacks, tents and other associated products. The company's headquarters, including its manufacturing function, is in LM town where it is one of the major employers. It also has a chain of 25 retail shops in Country A.

The company is still owned by its founder J, who has been hugely successful in building up the OD brand, which now has global recognition. J has recently received a takeover bid from ZZ Company, which is based in another country. ZZ Company is particularly interested in buying the brand and design capability of OD Company. If the bid was accepted, then ZZ Company would close down the manufacturing activity in LM town and would outsource this to other parts of the world where production and labour costs are significantly lower. This would mean the loss of over 800 jobs in LM town, and the trade union has already stated it will fight any job cuts.

J is contemplating whether or not he should accept the bid.

Required:

Discuss the power and interests of the different stakeholder groups who are likely to be affected by the takeover bid.

(Total for Question Three = 10 marks)

Question Four

MT is the entrepreneurial owner of S Software Development Company which he set up five years ago with his business partner ZF, who provided the financial backing. Since that time the company has grown. Despite MT not having any clear view on what should happen, strategies have tended to emerge without any formal approach. ZF feels that, whilst still a small business, the company has come to a point in its lifecycle where perhaps a more formal approach to establishing its future strategic direction would be beneficial. However, MT has a different view and argues that the company has been a success to date. He feels that ZF's suggestion to adopt a formal rational approach to strategy development would have more disadvantages than advantages.

Required:

Describe the potential advantages and disadvantages of the formal rational approach to strategy development for S Software Development Company.

(Total for Question Four = 10 marks)

Section A continues over the page

TURN OVER

Question Five

E is Chairman and Managing Director of SP Company which he started 10 years ago, specialising in the manufacture of kitchen cabinets. The company has been very successful and through a series of acquisitions has diversified into the manufacturing of a range of household furniture and currently employs around 2,000 people. SP is now a public quoted listed company, and whilst E is no longer the majority shareholder, he remains a major force in the company. He still acts as if he is the owner manager and his management style is very autocratic, illustrated by his unwillingness to involve other Board members in decisions concerning the future strategic direction of the company.

F, the Finance Director, has become increasingly concerned about the decisions being made by E and the fact that he has put pressure on her to participate in some illegal accounting practices. This included covering up the substantial remuneration package which E has awarded to himself. F is also aware that E has accepted bribes from foreign suppliers and of insider dealing relating to a number of the acquisitions.

F has discussed her concerns with other members of the Board including the Marketing Director, Production Director and HR Director. However, they seem willing to overlook the wrongdoings of E and never challenge the decisions made by him. The opportunity to do so is limited since the Board meets on an irregular and infrequent basis with no external representatives.

Required:

Discuss the corporate governance issues facing SP Company.

(Total for Question Five = 10 marks)

Total for Section A = 50 marks

Section B starts on the opposite page

SECTION B – 50 MARKS

[the indicative time for answering this section is 90 minutes]

ANSWER *BOTH* QUESTIONS IN THIS SECTION – 25 MARKS EACH

Question Six

P is the project manager responsible for the implementation of a new customer information database in G Company. This is the first time he has taken on the role of project manager and was selected for the position on the basis of his strong technical skills. His project team is made up of representatives from different parts of the company, including the Customer Services Department, Finance Department and IT Department.

The project represents an important development and financial investment for G Company. A number of different business areas in the company have strong interests in the success of the project and are dependent on the new customer information database going live. It is business critical that the project is delivered on time, which is in six months time.

Unfortunately, the project is not going well. P feels that he lacks the support of his project team, who keep complaining that they do not know what they are supposed to be doing. It would appear that some members of the project team are not completing tasks on time and are not providing the information needed to progress with the database development. However, members of the project team feel that P is the cause of the problems. They have criticised P for getting too involved in the detailed technical aspects of the design of the customer information database and, as a result, is ignoring his wider responsibilities as project manager.

Required:

(a) Distinguish the attributes of the project work in G Company from 'business as usual' work.

(8 marks)

(b) Explain to P what his role and responsibilities should be as project manager for the customer information database project.

(17 marks)

(Total for Question Six = 25 marks)

Section B continues on the opposite page

Question Seven

F is the Chief Executive of RM Company, a manufacturer of ready made meals. The company is facing difficult business conditions as a result of strong competition from supermarket own brand products and consumer demand for variety and new products.

F appreciates that the company needs to improve its performance in bringing new products to market. However, she is aware of the problems the company currently faces in its approach to new product development (NPD). Whilst collaboration is essential to successful NPD, in the past the NPD process in the company has resulted in disagreements and arguments between the various departments.

The marketers complain that the Research and Development (R&D) Department is very slow in responding to their proposals for new recipes and the whole process of R&D takes too long. The Production Department complains that R&D does not consider the implications for the production process when coming up with new recipes and product packaging. The sales team is frustrated with the length of time the whole NPD process takes. It says that the lack of new products puts it at a disadvantage when negotiating with retailers to sell RM Company's products.

The Finance Department is concerned that the investment in NPD does not provide adequate returns, and both the Marketing and R&D Departments are always over budget. However, the other departments see Finance as controlling and sanctioning spend rather than supporting new product development.

F knows that to remain competitive NPD is essential but that changes need to be made to the NPD process in the company. She has decided to establish a cross functional team to work on a new range of luxury ready made meals designed to appeal to the sophisticated end of the market. She has appointed T as head of NPD and given him the particular remit of leading and managing the NPD team.

Required:

(a) Identify the nature and sources of conflict between the different departments in RM Company.

(10 marks)

(b) Discuss what T should do to be effective in leading and managing the NPD team.

(15 marks)

(Total for Question Seven = 25 marks)

(Total for Section B = 50 marks)

End of Question Paper

LIST OF VERBS USED IN THE QUESTION REQUIREMENTS

A list of the learning objectives and verbs that appear in the syllabus and in the question requirements for each question in this paper.

It is important that you answer the question according to the definition of the verb.

LEARNING OBJECTIVE	VERBS USED	DEFINITION
Level 1 - KNOWLEDGE What you are expected to know.	List State Define	Make a list of Express, fully or clearly, the details/facts of Give the exact meaning of
Level 2 - COMPREHENSION What you are expected to understand.	Describe Distinguish Explain Identify Illustrate	Communicate the key features Highlight the differences between Make clear or intelligible/State the meaning or Purpose of Recognise, establish or select after consideration Use an example to describe or explain something
Level 3 - APPLICATION How you are expected to apply your knowledge.	Apply Calculate Demonstrate Prepare Reconcile Solve Tabulate	Put to practical use Ascertain or reckon mathematically Prove with certainty or to exhibit by practical means Make or get ready for use Make or prove consistent/compatible Find an answer to Arrange in a table
Level 4 - ANALYSIS How you are expected to analyse the detail of what you have learned.	Analyse Categorise Compare and contrast Construct Discuss Interpret Prioritise Produce	Examine in detail the structure of Place into a defined class or division Show the similarities and/or differences between Build up or compile Examine in detail by argument Translate into intelligible or familiar terms Place in order of priority or sequence for action Create or bring into existence
Level 5 - EVALUATION How you are expected to use your learning to evaluate, make decisions or recommendations.	Advise Evaluate Recommend	Counsel, inform or notify Appraise or assess the value of Propose a course of action

Enterprise Pillar

Management Level Paper

E2 – Enterprise Management

Specimen Paper

Tuesday Afternoon Session

The Examiner's Answers - Specimen Paper
E2 - Enterprise Management

SECTION A

Note: Some of the answers that follow in Sections A and B are fuller and more comprehensive than would be expected from a well-prepared candidate. They have been written in this way to aid teaching, study and revision for tutors and candidates alike.

Answer to Question One

Porter's five forces model is a useful framework that the business development team of CN Company could use to help it assess the competitive forces at work in the confectionary industry in Country K. It can be used to help management of CN decide whether the industry is an attractive one to enter.

Porter's model brings together the following five competitive forces:

- Threat of new entrants/barriers to entry
- Bargaining power of suppliers
- Bargaining power of buyers
- Threat of substitute products/services
- Competitive rivalry

It is the collective strength of these forces that will determine the profit potential of the confectionary industry in Country K. Essentially, it would only be a sensible strategic decision for CN Company to enter Country K if the forces are relatively weak and the potential returns are high. The information from the analysis would also help in identifying the factors driving profitability and inform the competitive strategy needed.

Taking each force in turn:

CN Company will be a new entrant so it needs to assess the potential barriers to entering the confectionary industry in Country K. These might include issues associated with gaining access to appropriate distribution channels for its confectionary. However, the fact that it is seeking to enter the market in a joint venture with a company already established in K Country could help minimise this barrier.

Another possible barrier to entry is product differentiation. If there are already established firms in Country K with strong brands in the confectionary market it may be hard for a new entrant to rival these. CN Company will also have to assess government policy in Country K to determine whether there are any legal or bureaucratic factors to deter foreign businesses entering the marketplace. From this information, the business development team should be able to assess whether entry barriers are high, moderate or low.

Bargaining power of suppliers is primarily related to the power of suppliers to raise their prices to the industry. Power will increase where the supply is dominated by a few firms, or suppliers have propriety product differences. It is unlikely that the supply of raw materials and resources needed for the production of confectionary will be concentrated in the hands of a few suppliers; therefore supplier power is likely to be moderate to low.

The bargaining power of buyers is gained through their ability to either gain products/services at lower prices or get improved product quality. It also depends on the size and number of buyers. Power will be greater when buyer power is concentrated in a few hands and when products are undifferentiated. CN Company will need to determine who its buyers are but assuming these are the end consumers, as individual buyers they will have relatively little bargaining power. Buyer power is increased when there are low switching costs, in other words where moving to a different supplier involves little risk. This would be the case in terms of buying confectionary products, from the perspective of the end consumer, because they are relatively low value purchases.

The buyer could, however, be the distribution channels in which case buyer power may be high if there is a concentration of these buyers.

Pressure from substitutes is where there are other products that satisfy the same need. In the case of confectionary products, it is probable that there will be a high threat of substitutes in the industry since there are many alternatives such as light food snacks, savoury snacks, fruit and other healthier product options available in most markets.

In the confectionary industry, the rivalry amongst existing competitors will be influenced by the number of firms operating in the industry, and industry growth rates. If there are numerous organisations, particularly with strong brand images already operating in Country K, and there is low industry growth then this will not be an attractive market for CN Company. If however, in contrast, the rivals are relatively small domestic producers with a poor brand image, the market could prove to be attractive.

Answer to Question Two

WBS is an abbreviation for work breakdown structure and is a systematic approach to ensure that all activities required to complete a project are included and carried out. It helps in setting out the logical sequence of project events through breaking down of the project work into smaller parts which are known as work packages. These work packages can be put into the project plan as a comprehensive list of tasks and activities that need to be undertaken during the lifecycle of the project. This provides a hierarchical tree of the way a project is structured and identifies the manageable work elements that need to be undertaken by the project team in order to deliver the project. It also helps in the sequencing of tasks and priorities.

WBS can be used to help calculate the total cost of the project by asking those responsible for each work package to estimate the time and resources needed to deliver the project objectives. Each work package will have defined deliverables which can then be allocated to the appropriate person in the project team so aiding communication of responsibilities amongst the project team and providing a framework for monitoring and control.

Gantt charts can use information from the WBS process to construct a graphical illustration of the activities of a project shown as a bar chart with start and finishing times clearly identified. They can provide a simple representation of a project in terms of presenting the planned time that each activity will take. This helps in showing the resources required for each activity at a point in time.

Gantt charts can be used as a reporting tool in the monitoring of actual progress of the project, for example on a week-by-week basis, or indeed a day-by-day basis. As part of project control they could be used to illustrate both the planned duration of an activity and the actual duration, so any variances are clearly identified. Gantt charts can assist in project co-ordination and are useful as a communication tool since they are easy to understand and provide an overview of responsibilities and the progress of the project. For instance a Gantt chart could be produced for each member of the project team to show their total workload.

Answer to Question Three

In making his decision J will need to consider the potential influence of different stakeholder groups. Mendelow's matrix can be used to plot the power of interest of different stakeholder groups, which would help T in understanding the effect of his decision of those groups. The stakeholder groups who will be impacted by the takeover bid will include:

T, as owner of the OD Company will have significant power in deciding whether or not to accept the bid. His interest may be in terms of the money he will make from the takeover. However, assuming T is a good employer with an awareness of the social responsibilities of his company, he should also have an interest in how the takeover bid would impact on his employees and wider stakeholder groups.

Employees who work in the manufacturing function of OD Company will have a high level of interest in whether or not the takeover bid is accepted, since they will be most affected in terms of potentially losing their jobs. Whist as individuals they may have relatively little power, they could collectively lobby the local government of T town in order to gain support, have demonstrations and take industrial action gaining media attention. These actions could damage the reputation and brand of OD Company.

Linked to the above point, the trade union will have high level of interest in how the takeover bid will impact on its members, and could use its power to coordinate industrial action and support its workers.

Employees in design function and retail stores will have a high level of interest in the takeover bid since, whilst they would hope to keep their jobs if the takeover bid is accepted, they would have a new owner, who may have a different style of management, and may want to make changes to the way they work. They would have relatively little power, although if any changes to their working conditions were proposed, the trade union could act on their behalf. They may feel that they are in a difficult position in terms of how they support their fellow workers in the manufacturing function.

The Board of ZZ Company making the takeover bid will have a high level of interest since it will want T to accept the bid to gain access to the brand and design capability. The power they have is linked to financial resources, for example, in terms of how much they are prepared to offer for OD Company.

Other stakeholders who will have an interest in the takeover, but perhaps have relatively little power are the existing domestic suppliers to OD Company. If OD Company is one of their major customers, the proposal to outsource manufacturing could result in them losing business. This could impact on their future viability, unless they can find new customers.

The community in T town and families of those losing their jobs are also stakeholder groups who will have an interest in the takeover bid and T's response. They could support the workers through industrial action and lobbying of local government and politicians regarding the potential impact on the community and economy of T town, particularly since OD Company is a major employer in the town.

Answer to Question Four

The formal rational approach to strategic planning being proposed by ZF usually results in a consciously thought out or deliberately intended strategy. It assumes that strategy making is a rational process with strategies based on careful analysis of the opportunities and threats posed by the external environment, and consideration of the organisation's strengths and weaknesses, relative to other players in the industry. MT says that he prefers to let his strategy emerge. This approach arises from ad-hoc, unanticipated or uncontrollable circumstances. It is often referred to as developing from patterns of behaviour in response to unexpected events rather than a consciously thought out or a deliberately intended strategy.

Whilst there are a number of disadvantages to the formal rational approach, ZF's view is that there are a number of potential benefits / advantages. These might include:

The process could help S Software Development Company take a longer term view than a short term reactive approach to strategy development. It should help encourage both MT and ZF to actively monitor the business environment and conduct formal analysis of the company's strengths, weaknesses, opportunities and threats to help them in understanding how they can best stay ahead of the game. The outcomes should inform plans and decisions, helping identify future strategic issues and promote a more proactive approach.

A rational approach could also help the company in assessing the optimum way to allocate its resources more effectively. It can also assist in establishing standards against which the performance of the organisation is measured and controlled. This would provide a basis for strategic control so that there are targets and reports enabling review of the success of the strategy.

As an entrepreneur, it is possible that MT may get frustrated with the bureaucracies that often accompany organisational growth, and he may decide to move on and sell his stake in the business. A rational approach can avoid succession problems, since the strategy of the company should be articulated and understood by other employees.

However, the formal rational process may also have disadvantages for S Software Development Company, as suggested by MT.

The potential disadvantages include the following:

The rational approach can be very expensive, time consuming and complicated for a small business. The opportunity cost needs to be considered, in terms of the time MT would need to spend on planning, taking him away from his main interest in software design which has been the basis for the company's success in the past.

Rational planning may also be considered too static and a process that tends to be undertaken on an annual basis. In a rapidly changing environment, it could be argued that the outcomes on which formally planned strategies are based often become quickly outdated, with the result that the intended strategy fails.

MT may be concerned that such an approach will just end up as a bureaucratic process with systems and targets unhelpful to a small business. The rational approach could also get in the way of MT's interest and talent in software design, since it could be conceived as a rigid approach bound up in processes, undermining MT's core competencies.

One of the aims of formal strategic planning is to achieve goal congruence between different business areas and stakeholders. However, in the case of S Software Development Company the goals are likely to be inseparable from the goals of MT and ZF as the owners. In a small business it could be argued that the rational approach is not appropriate because the success is more dependent of the ideas of MT. Indeed MT may not have aspirations for growth.

As an entrepreneur MT may have a desire to maintain absolute control and may well be unwilling to share or delegate control to others, that may be required as a result of formal strategic planning.

Answer to Question Five

Corporate governance concerns the ownership and control of profit making organisations and the relationship between owners and managers. A number of reports have been produced to address the risk and problems resulting from poor corporate governance. In the UK the most significant reports include the Cadbury, Hempel and Greenbury reports. The recommendations are merged into a Combined Code which comprises the purpose and principles of good corporate governance for listed companies.

There are a number of corporate governance issues facing SP Company.

Firstly, it is problematic for one person to hold both the role of Chairman and Managing Director since this can result in too much concentration of power being in the hands of one person, and the greater dangers of the misuse or abuse of power. E, through his dominance and associated behaviours, combining chairperson and chief executive roles contravenes much of the recent thinking on corporate governance. This advocates that the separation of the two roles is essential for good control. As illustrated in the scenario, the current arrangement makes it difficult for other directors to challenge E's decisions.

One of the core principles of the Combined Code is that listed companies should be led by effective Boards which meet regularly. Membership should be a balance of executive and non executive directors so that no individuals or small groups can dominate decision making. It is evident from the scenario that Board meetings of SP Company are ineffective; it would seem that they are held on an irregular and infrequent basis with E wielding his power over other directors. It would appear that E has forced through decisions that are in his own personal interest, and could be detrimental to the company. If SP Company does not have non executive directors on the Board, then it would be appropriate to make some appointments to provide independent judgements on decisions.

It also seems that there is a lack of adequate control, accountability and audit in SP Company. The Board should be responsible for presenting a balanced and understandable assessment of the company's financial position. It is responsible for maintaining a sound system for internal controls to safeguard the company's assets and shareholders' investment. To meet corporate governance recommendations, SR Company should establish an audit committee and introduce formal and transparent arrangements for considering how to apply the principles of financial reporting and internal control. The non executive directors appointed to the Board should satisfy themselves on the integrity of financial information and that controls are robust.

The scenario suggests that E has determined his own remuneration package, which he is keen to keep covered up. However, good corporate governance practice states that no director should be involved in determining his/her own remuneration. Non executive directors should be responsible for determining a policy on the remuneration of executive directors and specific remuneration packages for each director, a proportion of which should be linked to corporate and individual performance. It is good practice to include a report on the remuneration policy for directors in the annual accounts. The above points would help support the Finance Director who has been placed in an awkward situation regarding the illegal accounting practices and E's remuneration.

The Finance Director could be encouraged to 'whistle blow', a practice in which she could expose the misdeeds of E, preventing further wrongdoings. That said, because of the lack of legal protection, the Finance Director could risk losing her job. It is apparent from the scenario that she doesn't have the support of other colleagues on the Board.

Note: Answers which reflect the form of corporate governance in the candidates' own country will be rewarded appropriately.

SECTION B

Answer to Question Six

Requirement (a)

The customer information database project will have a number of characteristics or attributes that differentiate it from 'business as usual' work. The project can be characterised as having a lifecycle, since it will tend to pass through a number of phases, starting with the identification of need, followed by the development of a solution, implementation and completion.

A project is usually undertaken for a specific purpose to accomplish an objective or goal through a set of interrelated tasks and as such is a temporary process. It will have a clearly defined start and end time and will usually be determined in terms of the scope, schedule and cost. In this case the objective of the project is to develop a new customer information database. The project will be focussed on the tasks needed to design and implement the new database which needs to be completed in the six month period. All tasks must be scheduled to meet this pre-determined end date.

The customer information database project will have a budget allocated to deliver its objectives. The project manager must plan the project activities within this budget for costs and resources needed.

It will also have stakeholders, i.e. all those who are interested in the progress and final outcome of the customer information database project. For example, the project will have a project sponsor, that is the individual or group who will provide the funds for the project and who may also chair the project steering committee (sometimes called project board) to whom the project manager reports. Other project stakeholders will be the project customer/end users and project owner.

A key feature of a project is that it is unique, in other words it is a non-repetitive activity and does not usually involve routine work. Development of the new customer information database will be a one off activity.

A project will often cut across organisational and functional lines, in this case it includes representatives from the customer services department, finance department and the IT department.

Requirement (b)

P, as the project manager, should play a key role in determining the overall success or failure of the customer information database project. He is the person who will ultimately be responsible for ensuring that the desired result of the project is achieved on time and within budget to the satisfaction of the various project stakeholders. Since the project is interdisciplinary and crosses organisational reporting lines, he will have a complex task in managing, coordinating, controlling and communicating project tasks. The scenario suggests that he is not fulfilling these tasks very well. The role of project manager involves managing people, so P must take responsibility for the whole project team who are carrying out the various project tasks in order to achieve the project objectives. It also involves carrying out the process, i.e. the project work and tasks and producing the final deliverables, in this case the customer information database, on time.

P will be responsible for coordinating the project from initiation to completion, making use of project management tools and techniques so that activities are performed on time within budget and to the quality standards set out in the project plan. He is, therefore, responsible for planning, teambuilding, communication and coordinating the various project activities, monitoring and controlling, problem resolution and quality controlling.

In the early stages of the project P should work with the project sponsor and project customer to clearly define the project objectives, and then communicate these to the project team so that everyone is clear on what constitutes a successful project outcome.

P also has the responsibility for taking the lead in the planning and organisation of work for the project team throughout the project lifecycle. He is responsible for ensuring that the necessary resources required for performing the project tasks are available and for assigning particular project members to carry out the work. In addition, he should delegate responsibility for performing certain project tasks to team members, who will then be accountable to him for the accomplishment of those tasks. From the information in the scenario it would appear that P is not doing this, since project members have said they are uncertain about what they should be doing. He should make sure they know what is going on and that all the members of the project team are properly briefed.

P is not only responsible for building a cohesive project team but also for supervising the activities of individual team members. He must provide advice or make appropriate decisions in case of technical difficulties, taking action to keep the project on target for successful completion.

As project manager, P has responsibilities to the project sponsor in that he must ensure resources are used efficiently and should keep the project steering committee informed with timely and accurate communication. P must coordinate the intercommunications between the various project stakeholders, and linked to this must attempt to satisfy the objectives of both outcome and process stakeholders.

P should be responsible for monitoring and controlling the progress of the project towards its successful completion. He must take corrective action and solve any problems as they arise in the project and communicate the implications of any changes to planned activities.

From the above, it is clear that in view of the various responsibilities of the project manager role, P cannot rely solely on his technical skills but needs a range of skills. For example, P needs strong leadership and teambuilding skills, communication, negotiation, good inter-personal skills, and also problem solving skills.

Answer to Question Seven

Requirement (a)

Organisational conflict can occur on a number of different levels and can have a detrimental impact on the business, as in the case of RM Company. The problems mean that management time and effort is being wasted on addressing conflicts rather than concentrating on NPD. Collaboration between the different departments is not occurring. The conflict in RM Company is best characterised as horizontal conflict. This is where conflict occurs between groups or departments at the same level in the hierarchy.

A number of sources creating conflict can be discerned:

Goal incompatibility is often the main cause, where the goals of one area block the achievement of other areas. In RM Company the functional structure of the organisation could encourage employee loyalty to particular departments with employees wanting to concentrate on their own goals. The goals of different departments are often seen as mutually exclusive and it is this that is potentially resulting in conflict and lack of cooperation between the different departments in RM Company.

Goals of innovation can often cause more conflict than other goals since the NPD process requires departments to co-operate. However, as task interdependence between different departments increases, the potential for conflict is also likely to increase. The greater task interdependence means that some departments may exert pressure for fast response since their work has to wait or is reliant on the completion of work by other departments. Employees will need to spend time to share information and communicate across departments, but this can lead to differences in goals and attitudes resulting in conflict.

In RM Company there appears to be a lack of understanding and appreciation of the pressures and needs of other departments during the NPD process. For example, whilst the R&D Department will want to come up with the best possible menus for the new range of luxury ready made meals from a technical perspective, in doing so they may not take account of the cost aspect, nor of the implications for the mass production of a product, which will be an issue for the Production Department.

The sales staff focus will be on achieving their sales targets and they want the new product ready for market as quickly as possible. They are disinterested in the various activities involved in the NPD process, they just want results. The Finance Department is viewed very much as a controller and an obstacle to the NPD process. The marketers and R&D staff may see finance staff as only taking a short term view rather than investing for the future of the Company.

Another source that can lead to horizontal conflict is the differences in the cognitive and emotional orientations of managers in different functional departments. This is often apparent in the values of individuals, for example, it is probable that those working in marketing will have different values from R&D food scientists. This stems from the different skills, attitudes and time horizons of the people working in these areas.

Requirement (b)

There are a number of things that T must do if he is going to be effective in leading and managing the NPD team.

Firstly, when forming the NPD team, T should consider the team members in terms of their personalities and characteristics and their personal goals, since the NPD team will bring together individuals from different specialisms and functional departments to contribute to the process of NPD.

In establishing the NPD team, T should consider the suitability of members by assessing how members are likely to fit with the rest of the team and whether or not the team has a balanced portfolio of characteristics relative to the task, in this case the NPD process. To help him T could draw on the research by Belbin who suggests that an effective group should have a balance of team roles. Belbin provided managers with a tool to help guide the nature or mixture of people who will be required to undertake the NPD project. The classification of roles identified by Belbin included: the coordinator; the shaper; the monitor-evaluator; the resource investigator, the implementer; the team worker; the finisher; the specialist.

In addition, when first establishing the NPD team, T should consider the stages of team development and maturity which can affect the effectiveness of the team. Tuckman identifies four successive stages of group development: **forming** where the group come together and starts to establish the purpose of the group, structure and leadership; **storming**, where members get to know each other better. At this stage disagreements can occur over roles and behavioural expectations; this can lead to conflict and hostility; **norming** where the group will establish agreed guidelines and standards and develop their own norms of acceptable behaviour and performance; **performing** which occurs when the group has progressed through the earlier stages of development and created the structure to work effectively as a team.

T will need to ensure that team members understand their roles, responsibilities in the NPD process and the activities that the other team members are contributing. Therefore, it important that T establishes clear communication procedures holds regular team meetings and status reviews. If T can help individuals to understand each other's roles, rather than for which functional department individual comes from, this should have a positive impact on the interactions between team members.

As well as encouraging members to communicate and interact regularly it is important that T establishes a common task/goal that all team members are working towards. T should set out the objectives for NPD and set targets so that all members of the team are clear on what they need to work towards, and provide feedback on progress. He should encourage all members to participate in team meetings. It is important that T motivates all members of the team so that they are committed to achieving the NPD objectives, and feel accountable for their individual activities.

T should also think about the environment such as the physical surroundings at work and where team members are situated. If they are in close proximity then this is probably more conducive to encouraging team work and effective communication than where members are geographically separated from each other.

T also needs to consider the form of leadership style he adopts since this can influence the relationship between members of the team, and can have a major impact on team effectiveness. The team will be affected by the way in which the manager gives guidance and encouragement to the team, provides opportunities for participation and deals with any conflicts. Usually a participative or democratic style of leadership is most appropriate to encouraging high team performance.

© The Chartered Institute of Management Accountants 2009

Index

3 Es, 34
4-D model, 441-442
5 project management process areas, 441
7-S model, 178-180, 444-445
9 project management knowledge areas, 581-582

A

Abilene paradox, 278
ACAS see Advisory Conciliation and Arbitration Service (ACAS)
Accountability, 217
Action centred leadership, 249-250
Adair, John, 249-250
Adam's equity theory, 363
Additive model, 285
Administrative school, 224-225
Advisory Conciliation and Arbitration Service (ACAS), 354
Alternative approaches, strategic management, 130-134
Amazon.com, 159, 164
Appraisal:
    performance, 344-346
Arbitration, 358-359
Asset specificity, 162-165, 168-169, 172-175
Authoritarian style, 240
Authority, 215-216
Autocratic style, 240

B

Bargaining power:
    buyers, 77, 77-93, 98
    suppliers, 77, 79, 81
Barney, J., 136
Belbin, Meredith, 282-283
Benchmarking, 119
Benevolent authoritative style, 244
Blake, Robert, 245-247
Blanchard, H.H., 251, 386
Boston Consulting Group (BCG), 109-111
Bounded rationality, 162
Boyd, 252-253
BPO see Business Process Outsourcing (BPO)
Brand competitors, 112
Brand name capital specificity, 163-164, 168, 172, 175
Breakdown structures see Work breakdown structures
British Airways mission statement, 24
Budgeting:
    projects, 487

Buffering, 506
Bureaucracy management, 225-226
Burns, T., 232
Business Process Outsourcing (BPO), 312-313
Business strategy, 15-17, 22, 30
Buyers bargaining power, 77, 79-83, 98

C

Cadbury Report, 380
Channel Tunnel (Eurotunnel) example, 163, 165
Charismatic authority, 216
Child care, 368
Classical theories of management, 222-226
Clements, 440, 543
Coase, 160
Coercive power, 214-215
Collectivism, 198
Committee of Sponsoring Organisations (COSO), 339-340
Communication, 300-302
    barriers, 301-302
    process, 300-301
Competences:
    threshold, 64, 66, 92
    core, 64, 66, 92, 136-138, 142, 148
Competing objectives, 58-59
Competition:
    five forces model, 62, 71, 76-79, 83, 100
    differentiation, 37
    rivalry, 78, 80-81
    substitute products, 37, 77-78, 80-81, 99
Competitive advantage, 16, 21, 36-37, 43, 61, 64, 67, 92, 99, 104, 107, 118, 121, 135, 138, 144, 148
    national competitive advantage, 152, 155, 159, 168
Competitive environment, 71, 76-77, 104, 110
Competitive rivalry, 78, 80-81
Competitor analysis:
    Boston Consulting Group (BCG), 109-111
    gathering competitor intelligence, 113, 116
    Grant's 4 stage framework, 107
    Information sources, 115
    levels, 112
    qualitative research, 116-118
    quantitative research, 118
Complementary model, 285
Complex organisation forms, 156-157
Conflict,
    causes, 287
    constructive, 290

I.1

Index

destructive, 290
horizontal, 288-289
industrial relations, 298
intergroup, 293
management, 292-283
stakeholder, 57-60
symptoms, 287
types, 288-290
vertical, 289
Conjunctive model, 285
Consultative style, 244
Contingency planning, 463
Contingency theory, 232-234, 249
Continuous improvement, 560-562
Contracts of employment, 366
Controls,
internal systems, 339
levels, 340-341
organisations, 338-339
reporting structure, 342
Core competence, 64, 66, 92, 136-138, 142, 148
Corporate appraisal, 61-62
Corporate governance,
benefits, 379
history, 380
principles, 378
principles based v rules based, 379
UK Corporate Governance Code, 379
Corporate strategy, 15-18, 36, 43
COSO see Committee of Sponsoring Organisations (COSO)
Country club style, 246
CPA see Critical path analysis (CPA)
Critical path analysis (CPA), 487, 491-504
Critical success factors (CSFs), 29-30, 32-33
Culture:
cultural web, 178, 193-196
Handy/Harrison, 188-189
importance, 184
influences, 182-183
levels, 181-182
Ouchi, 192-193

D

Daft, R., 290, 396
Deal and Kennedy, 183, 190
Dedicated asset specificity, 163-165, 168, 172, 175
DEEPLIST, 73
Delegation, 218-220
benefits, 219-220

methods, 219
Delegative style, 240
Democratic style, 240
Differentiation, 37
Digital Equipment Corporation, 286
Discipline, 351
disciplinary situations, 352
procedures, 352-353
Disjunctive model, 285
Dismissal, 360
Diversity, equal opportunities, 364
Drucker, Peter, 346-348

E

Earliest event time, 493, 497-498
Earned value management, 544-546
Ecological feasibility, 457
Ecological perspective, 413
Economic feasibility, 457
Emergent strategies, 127, 129-131
Environmental analysis,
data, 84
information sources for, 85
macro-environmental analysis, 71, 76
micro- /industry environment analysis, 72
uncertainty, 128-130
Equality, 364
Equality Act, 364
Ethics,
chartered management accountants, 399-401
examples, 390
levels, 385
managerial, 388
professional, 399
statement of, 389
Eurotunnel plc, 163, 165
Expert power, 214-215
Exploitive authoritative style, 244
External analysis, 61, 71, 76

F

Fairness, workplace, 362
Fayol, 224-225
Feasibility studies, 454-459
Feminine/masculine cultures, 198
Fiedler, F.E., 250-251
Finance function:
Business Process Outsourcing (BPO), 312-313
external stakeholders, 316

Index

importance of, 311-312
shared service centres (SSC), 312-314
Five forces model, 62, 71, 76-81, 100
Float, 500, 504, 506
Formal groups, 277
Formation, groups, 281-282
Free reign, 240
Freewheeling opportunism, 130-134
French, 214-215
Friedman, M., 409
Functional strategies, 15-16, 18, 43

G
Gantt charts, 487, 508-509
Gap analysis, 443
Gido, 440, 543
Globalisation, 150
   impact on strategy, 151
Goals structure, 29
Governance see Corporate governance
Greenbury Committee, 380
Greller, 362
Grievance procedures, 357-359
Groups:
   benefits, 277-278
   definition, 276-277
   development, 281
   formal, 277
   Koontz and O'Donnell, 218
   problems, 278-279
   roles, 282-284
   Steiner models, 285
   Types, 276-277
see also Teams
Groupthink, 278

H
Hamel, 136
Hampel Committee, 380
Handy, C., 188-189, 296
Harrison, Roger, 188-189
HASAWA (Health and Safety at Work Act 1974), 248-349
Health and safety, 348-351
   training, 350
Helicopter factor, 239
Hersey, P., 251
Herzberg, Frederick, 227-231
Hierarchy of needs, 231
Hierarchy of project stakeholders, 603
Hierarchy solutions, 160-162

Histograms see Resource histograms
Hofstede, 197-199
Horizontal conflict, 288-289
Hot stove rule, 357
Human asset specificity, 163-164, 168, 172, 175
Human relations school, 226-231
Hygiene factors, 228-230

I
Incremental approach to strategy, 130, 132-133, 145
Impoverished style, 247
Individualism, 198
Industrial relations, 298
see also Conflict
Industry/micro-environment analysis, 72
Information sources, for environmental analysis, 85
Interest assessment, stakeholders, 50-52
Internal analysis, 61, 63, 66
Investment and resource strategies, 18-19

J
Johnson, G., 193-194
Joint ventures, 157

K
Key performance indicators (KPIs), 29-31
KPIs see Key performance indicators (KPIs)

L
Laissez-faire style, 242-243
Latest event time, 493, 497-498
Leadership, 236-239
   personality traits, 239
   situational styles, 251
   style theories, 240-247
   transformational leaders, 252-253
   types, 237
see also Management
Legitimate power, 214-215
Levels of strategy, 15, 17-18, 43
Lewin, Kurt, 242-243
Life cycles, projects, 439-442
Likert, Rensis, 243-245
Logical incrementalism, 133
LoNGPEST, 73

Index

M

Macro-environmental analysis, 71, 76
Mainwaring, 287, 297-298
Management by objectives (MBO), 346-348
Managerial grid, 245-247
Market solutions, 160-162
Masculine/feminine cultures, 198
Maslow, 231
Matrix structure, 617-619
Mayo, Elton, 226-227
MBO see Management by objectives (MBO)
McGregor, Douglas, 241-242, 357
McKinsey 7S model, 178-180, 444-445
Mechanistic organisation, 232-233
Meetings:
    problem avoidance, 304-305
    team members, 304
Mendelow matrix, 50, 56
Mentoring, 308-310
    Benefits, 309-310
Mergers and acquisitions, 156
Methodologies:
    projects, 576-585
    benefits of single, 584
Micro- /industry environment analysis, 72
Middle road style, 247
Milestones and gates, 487, 513
Mintzberg, H., 11
Mission, 20, 23
    statements, 24-25
Morgan, Gareth, 235-236
Motivation factors, 228-230
Mouton, Jane, 245-247

N

National competitive advantages, 152, 155, 159, 168
    demand conditions, 152-153, 155
    factor conditions, 152, 154-155
    firm structure, strategy and rivalry, 152, 154-155
    government, role of, 154
    related and supporting industries, 152-153
Negotiation, 306-308
    process, 307-308
    skills, 307, 610-613
Network analysis see Critical path analysis
Network organisations, 157-159
    transactions cost theory, 160-162
New ventures, 156
Not for profit organisations, 34-35

O

Objectives, 20, 23-29
    competing, 58-60
    not for profit organisation, 34-35
    PRIME, 28
    SMART, 28
OECD, 378
Operational strategies see Functional strategies
Opportunism, 130, 134
Opportunities see SWOT analysis
Organic organisation, 232-233
Ouchi – Theory A, J and Z, 192-193
Organisational iceberg, 180-181

P

Participative style, 240-244
Performance,
    appraisal, 344-346
Person culture, 188-189
PERT see Project evaluation and review techniques (PERT)
PEST(LE), 71-74, 76
Physical asset specificity, 163-164, 168, 466-467
PID see Project initiation documents (PID)
Planning, 480-521
    example, 482-485
PMBoK® methodology, 581-582
PMMM see Project Management Maturity Model
Porter's five forces model, 62, 71, 76-81
Porter's diamond, 152-156
Porter's generic strategies, 37
Porter's value chain, 62-63, 66-70, 93
Positioning view, 135, 140
Post-completion audits, 558
Power:
    culture, 188
    distance, 197
    types, 214-215
Prahalad, C.K., 136
PRINCE2 methodology, 576-579
Product breakdown structure (PBS) see Work breakdown structure (WBS)
Professional advisors, 316-318
Professional ethics, 399-401
    conceptual framework, 400-401
    fundamental principles, 399-400
Project evaluation and review techniques (PERT), 487, 505
Project initiation, 452-468
Project initiation documents (PID), 466-467
Project life cycles, 439-442

Index

Project management:
    approach, 443
    board, 605
    champion, 606
    change management, 539-540
    characteristics, 435
    completion, 440, 554-558
    configuration management, 539-541
    constraints, 438-439, 485-486
    continuous improvement, 560-562
    control, 541-544
    definition, 434
    development, 440
    ecological feasibility, 457
    economic feasibility, 457
    execution, 538-539
    failures, 586-587
    feasibility studies, 454-459
    identifying a need, 440
    implementation (execution), 440
    initiation, 452-468
    life cycles, 439-442
    meetings, 548-552
    methodologies, 576-585
    planning, 480-521
    PMBoK® methodology, 581-582
    post-completion audits, 558
    programme, 435
    project manager, 604-613
    project office, 619-620
    reporting, 548-552
    risk management, 461-464
    social feasibility, 456
    software, 487, 515-519
    steering committee, 605
    strategy, 437-438
    structures, 444, 617
    support, 617
    systems theory approach, 445-446
    teams, 605
    technical feasibility, 456
    tools, 487-521
    uncertainty, 463, 505
Project Management Maturity Model (PMMM), 561-563
Project managers, 604-613
    change-management skills, 610, 612
    communication skills, 610-611
    delegation skills, 610-611
    leadership skills, 610
    negotiation skills, 610-613
    problem-solving skills, 610, 612
    skills needed, 610
    team building skills, 610, 614-616
Project office, 619-620
Project owner, 604
Project planning, 480-521
Project quality plan (PQP), 487, 490-491
Project sponsor, 603
Project stakeholders, 603-606

Q

Qualitative risk, 462
Quantitative risk, 461

R

Rand, A., 411
Rational strategy process, 20-23
    corporate appraisal, 35, 61-63
    criticism, 124-127
    evaluation and choice, 36, 38, 40
    external analysis, 20, 71-81
    implementation, 39-40
    internal analysis, 20, 63-71
    mission, objectives and goals, 20, 23-29
    review and control, 39
Rational-legal authority, 216
Raven, 214-215
RBT see Resource-based theory (RBT)
Redundancy, 361
Referent power, 214-215
Resource-based view, 135-140
Resource histogram, 487, 513-515
Resources:
    audit, 64
    basic, 64
    unique, 64
Responsibility, 217
Reward power, 214-215
Risk management, 461-464
Role cultures, 188
Role definition teams, 281-284
Rosseau, 362

S

Satisficing, 58
SBU see Strategic business unit (SBU)
Scenario planning, 506
Schein, Edgar, 181, 276
Schmidt, 245
Scientific management, 223
Shared service centres (SSC), 312-314

Index

Shareholder wealth and ethics, 406
Sherif and Sherif, 294
Situational leadership, 251
Slack, 500, 504, 506
Small businesses, 128
SMART objectives, 28
Social feasibility, projects, 456
Social responsibility, 403
    ecological perspective, 413
    examples, 404-406
    shareholder wealth and ethics, 406
    stakeholders, 407
Software, 487, 515-519
Solomon, 363
SSC see Shared service centres (SSC)
Stakeholders, 48-60
    analysis, 48-49
    conflicts, 57-60
    interest assessment, 51-52
    Mendelow, 50-53
    power, 51-52
    projects, 603-606
Stalker, 232
Statements see Mission, statements
Steiner group models, 285
Sternberg, 210
Strategic alliances, 157-158
Strategic business unit (SBU), 16-17
Strategic management, 12-14
    elements, 18-19
    emergent strategies, 130-131
    incremental approaches, 130, 132-133, 145
    levels, 18
    opportunism, 130, 134
    positioning view, 62-63, 66-70, 90, 135, 140
    rational model criticism, 124-127
    resource-based view, 135-140
    small businesses, 128
Substitute products, 77-78, 80
Suppliers, bargaining power, 77, 79, 81
SWOT analysis, 61-62, 460
Synergy, 278
Systems theory, 231-232

T

Tannenbaum, A.S., 245
TARA, 337-338, 463
Task cultures, 188-189
Task-oriented style, 246
Taylor, F.W., 223

Teams:
    definition, 276-277
    member roles, 282-284
    performance, 282
see also Groups
Team style, 247
Technical feasibility, projects, 456
Temporal specificity, 163-165
Theory A, J and Z, 192-193
Theory X and Theory Y, 241-242
Thomas Kilmann Conflict Mode Instrument (TKI), 292-293
Threat of entry, 77, 79
Threats, see SWOT analysis
Time orientation, 198
Top-down strategy process, 20-23
Traditional authority, 216
Transaction cost theory, 160-162
Transformational leaders, 252-253
Tribunals, 358
Trist and Bamforth, 231-232
Tuckman, 281-282

U

UK Corporate Governance Code, 379
Uncertainty, 463
Uncertainty avoidance, 197

V

Vaill, 285-286
Vertical conflict, 289

W

Weber, 216, 225-226
Woodward, 233
Work breakdown structures (WBS), 487-490
    cost breakdown structure (CBS), 487
    product breakdown structure (PBS), 489
    statement of works (SOWs), 489
    work packages (WPs), 489
Working time directive, 367